THE ROUTLEDGE HANDBOOK OF EUROPEAN SECURITY LAW AND POLICY

The Routledge Handbook of European Security Law and Policy offers a holistic discussion of the contemporary challenges to the security of the European Union and emphasizes the complexity of dealing with these through legislation and policy.

Considering security from a human perspective, the book opens with a general introduction to the key issues in European Security Law and Policy before delving into three main areas. Institutions, policies and mechanisms used by Security, Defence Policy and Internal Affairs form the conceptual framework of the book; at the same time, an extensive analysis of the risks and challenges facing the EU, including threats to human rights and sustainability, as well as the European Union's legal and political response to these challenges, is provided.

This Handbook is essential reading for scholars and students of European law, security law, EU law and interdisciplinary legal and political studies.

E. Conde is Professor of Public International Law in the Faculty of Law of the Complutense University of Madrid, Spain; coordinator of the Jean Monnet Project "*European Union and Security: Defense of Common Interests and Spaces*" (reference number: 565277-EPP-1-2015-1-ES-EPPJMO-PROJECT); main investigator on the project "*The Arctic Race: Issues of International Law Arising in the Light of Climate Change*" (reference number: DER2012–36026, 2013–2016); and a member of the project "*International Drug Control: Problems and Solutions*" (reference number: DER2016–74872-R, 2017–2019). She is also associate researcher at the Complutense Institute of International Relations (since 2015) and the Stefansson Arctic Institute (since 2016); Spanish delegate at the Human and Social Sciences Group of the International Arctic Scientific Committee (since 2012) and member of the International Arctic Social Sciences Association (since 2012); board member of the Canada Foundation (since 2013); and a member of the Club of Rome (since 2013).

Zhaklin V. Yaneva received her PhD in Political Science and Administration and International Relations from the Complutense University of Madrid, Spain. She completed her Master's Degree in International Law in 2014, specializing in Public International Law, at the Faculty of Law of the Complutense University of Madrid, Spain, and obtained her Bachelor's Degree in International Relations in 2013 from the Faculty of Law of the University of Sofia "San Clemente de Ojrid," Bulgaria. Her main research interests are related to the Arctic region; the Law of the Sea; the peaceful settlement of conflicts; and the history of international relations, among others.

Marzia Scopelliti is a PhD candidate in Law at the Complutense University of Madrid. She received her MSc Degree in International Relations from the University of Milan. She has held research positions at the Complutense University of Madrid, the University of Fribourg, Switzerland, and the Kobe University, Japan. In 2019, she was a Blue Book trainee at the Directorate General for Maritime Affairs and Fisheries of the European Commission. She has contributed to collective works and academic journals with publications related to her research interests: International Environmental Law, Arctic Governance and Climate Change Law.

THE ROUTLEDGE HANDBOOK OF EUROPEAN SECURITY LAW AND POLICY

Edited by E. Conde (editor in chief),
with
Zhaklin V. Yaneva and Marzia Scopelliti (co-editors)

Routledge
Taylor & Francis Group
LONDON AND NEW YORK

First published 2020
by Routledge
2 Park Square, Milton Park, Abingdon, Oxon OX14 4RN

and by Routledge
605 Third Avenue, New York, NY 10017

First issued in paperback 2021

Routledge is an imprint of the Taylor & Francis Group, an informa business

Publisher's Note
The publisher has gone to great lengths to ensure the quality of this reprint but points out that some imperfections in the original copies may be apparent.

British Library Cataloguing-in-Publication Data
A catalogue record for this book is available from the British Library

Library of Congress Cataloging-in-Publication Data
A catalog record has been requested for this book

Typeset in Bembo
by Wearset Ltd, Boldon, Tyne and Wear

ISBN 13: 978-1-03-224005-3 (pbk)
ISBN 13: 978-1-138-60999-0 (hbk)

CONTENTS

CONTRIBUTORS

E. Conde is Professor of Public International Law in the Faculty of Law of the Complutense University of Madrid, Spain; coordinator of the Jean Monnet Project "*European Union and Security: Defense of Common Interests and Spaces*" (reference number: 565277-EPP-1–2015-1-ES-EPPJMO-PROJECT); main investigator on the project "*The Arctic Race: Issues of International Law Arising in the Light of Climate Change*" (reference number: DER2012–36026, 2013–2016); and a member of the project "*International Drug Control: Problems and Solutions*" (reference number: DER2016-74872-R, 2017–2019). She is also associate researcher at the Complutense Institute of International Relations (since 2015) and the Stefansson Arctic Institute (since 2016); Spanish delegate at the Human and Social Sciences Group of the International Arctic Scientific Committee (since 2012) and member of the International Arctic Social Sciences Association (since 2012); board member of the Canada Foundation (since 2013); and a Member of the Club of Rome (since 2013).

Zhaklin V. Yaneva received her PhD in Political Science and Administration and International Relations from the Complutense University of Madrid, Spain. She completed her Master's Degree in International Law in 2014, specializing in Public International Law, at the Faculty of Law of the Complutense University of Madrid, Spain, and obtained her Bachelor's Degree in International Relations in 2013 from the Faculty of Law of the University of Sofia "San Clemente de Ojrid," Bulgaria. Her main research interests are related to the Arctic region; the Law of the Sea; the peaceful settlement of conflicts; and the history of international relations, among others.

Marzia Scopelliti is a PhD candidate in Law at the Complutense University of Madrid. She received her MSc Degree in International Relations from the University of Milan. She has held research positions at the Complutense University of Madrid, the University of Fribourg, Switzerland, and the Kobe University, Japan. In 2019, she was a Blue Book trainee at the Directorate General for Maritime Affairs and Fisheries of the European Commission. She has contributed to collective works and academic journals with publications related to her research interests: International Environmental Law, Arctic Governance and Climate Change Law.

Kåre Dahl Martinsen (PhD, M.Litt) is Professor of European security studies at the Norwegian Institute for Security Studies of the Norwegian Defence University College, Oslo, Norway. He has published extensively on German, French and British security politics. His recent works have focused on the parliamentary war powers, the political role played by the soldiers killed in Afghanistan, and the demise of the Transatlantic Trade and Investment Partnership.

Gorazd Meško is Professor of criminology and Head of the Institute of Criminal Justice and Security Research at the Faculty of Criminal Justice and Security, University of Maribor, Slovenia. His recent research is related to policing and crime prevention in Europe, and security in local communities.

Rajko Kozmelj is a PhD student at the Faculty of Criminal Justice and Security, University of Maribor, Slovenia. He is an expert in policing, EU security and prevention of radicalisation. Until recently, he was a project leader at the Geneva Centre for the Democratic Control of Armed Forces' office in Ljubljana, Slovenia.

Branko Lobnikar is Associate Professor of security studies and Vice-Dean for research in the Faculty of Criminal Justice and Security, University of Maribor, Slovenia. His recent research includes policing, management of security organisations, prevention of radicalisation and domestic violence.

Akasemi Newsome is Associate Director of the Institute of European Studies and Executive Director of the Center for German and European Studies at the University of California, Berkeley. She received her PhD in Political Science from the University of California, Berkeley, an MA in Political Science from the University of North Carolina at Chapel Hill and a BA in History from Columbia University. Her research on Europe examines the politics of labor, immigration and comparative racialization, and addresses topics at the forefront of international and comparative political economy, including rights and global governance, institutions, capitalist development and social movements. Her publications include co-edited special issues and articles in the *Journal of European Integration, Comparative Labor Law and Policy Journal, Perspectives on Europe* and *PS: Political Science and Politics* and a forthcoming co-edited *Handbook on EU Crisis* with Palgrave Macmillan.

Marianne Riddervold is Professor in Political Science at the Inland School of Business and Social Sciences and the Norwegian Institute of Foreign Affairs. She is also Senior Fellow at the Institute of European Studies, University of California, Berkeley.

David García Cantalapiedra (PhD in Political Sciences) is Associate Professor in the Department of International Relations and Global History at the Complutense University of Madrid and Director of the Research Group on Security and Cooperation. He also teaches US Foreign Policy and Transatlantic Relations at the Spanish Foreign Service School and is Lecturer in the Joint Staff Course at the Spanish Armed Forces School. He worked for NATO in Afghanistan and as a member of the Working Group on NATO Nuclear Posture during 2008–2011. His latest book is *The Greater Maghreb. Hybrid Threats, Security and Europe* with Lexington Books (forthcoming, 2019).

Rafael García Pérez is Professor of International Relations at the University of Santiago de Compostela; Professor at the Gutierrez Mellado University Institute (Ministry of Defense – UNED); and holder of the Jean Monnet module on Foreign Policy of the European Union. He holds a PhD in History from the Complutense University of Madrid, a Diploma in

Constitutional Law and Political Science from the Center for Political and Constitutional Studies (Madrid) and is a Graduate in National Defense Studies from the Center for the Study of National Defense (CESEDEN – Ministry of Defense).

Fernando Serrano Antón is Full Professor at the Complutense University of Madrid; Tax Governance and Fiscal Transparency Jean Monnet Chair; Member of the Permanent Scientific Committee of the International Fiscal Association; Researcher at the Complutense Institute of International Studies; and Principal Researcher on the project "*Taxation and Robotics*" at the Spanish Ministry of Economy, Industry and Competitiveness (reference number: DER2017–87238-R).

Marta Gómez-Puig is Professor in the Department of Economics of the University of Barcelona. She has carried out research stays at the Massachusetts Institute of Technology, the European Central Bank and Cass Business School. She has worked in the Barcelona Stock Exchange and in Analistas Financieros Internacionales (Madrid, Spain). Her most important field of research is International Macroeconomics and Finance, mainly focused in the euro area.

Simón Sosvilla-Rivero has an MSc in Economics (Autonomous University of Barcelona, Spain and London School of Economics, UK) and a PhD in Economics (University of Birmingham, UK). His current research interests are in the inter-disciplines of international economics and applied econometrics. He has published articles in international journals in this field. He is currently Professor of Economics at the Complutense University of Madrid (Spain).

Bruce Morley is an Economics Lecturer in the Economics Department at the University of Bath (UK) and his main research and teaching interests are in international macroeconomics and finance, environmental economics and cricket, using largely empirical approaches. He has researched the economics of the European housing markets and convergence in the Eurozone. Since 2017 he has been Fellow of the Higher Education Academy.

Briseida Sofía Jiménez-Gómez was awarded her Ph.D. (*cum laude*, Doctor International Mention) in Law from Complutense University of Madrid. She holds an LL.M. in European Law from the College of Europe (Bruges) and two Bachelors in Law and Business Administration from the University of Murcia. Her research fields are Private International Law, Arbitration, EU Competition Law, Comparative Procedural Law, Internet Law and New Technologies.

Xesús Pérez López is Assistant Professor at the Rey Juan Carlos University (Madrid, Spain). Author of three books and about 20 papers and book chapters, he has conducted long research stays in academic institutions in Rome, Munich and Montpellier. He has taken part in several European, French and Spanish research projects coping with diverse aspects of IT Law, such as geolocation, "privacy by design," cybercrime and online money laundering.

Concepción Anguita Olmedo is Accredited Professor of International Relations at the Complutense University of Madrid; Researcher at the Complutense Institute of International Studies; Member of the RIS XXI research team; and Researcher at the Center for Studies on Transnational Organized Crime of the Institute for International Relations of the University of La Plata. She has a Diploma in Higher Defense Studies.

Irene Rodríguez Ortega is a researcher in the PhD program in Political Science and International Relations and Administration, in co-tutorship with the Faculty of Law, at the Complutense University of Madrid. Her research is framed within the studies of international security and defense, specifically on the use of robots with artificial intelligence in armed conflicts. She specializes in international terrorism, organized crime and cybersecurity studies. She works simultaneously as an analyst and researcher in cybersecurity in a multinational company in the area of training and awareness-raising.

Marco Pedrazzi is Full Professor of International Law at the Department of International, Legal, Historical and Political Studies of the University of Milan; President of the Ethics Committee at the University of Milan; Member of the International Law Association, Space Law Committee, European Centre for Space Law, International Institute of Humanitarian Law, and Italian Society of International Law; and author of various publications in international space law, international human rights law, international law of armed conflict, arms control law and other areas of international law and EU law. He has also been lecturer in various Italian and foreign universities.

Carlos Teijo García is Lecturer in Public International Law and European Union Law at the University of Santiago de Compostela. He has written books on the legal status of international NGOs (2005) and development cooperation (2009), as well as more than fifty journal articles and book chapters. His research fields are international civil society, international human rights law, EU law and the law of the sea. His recent research focuses on the external dimension of the EU's Common Fisheries Policy and its connection with maritime security within the framework of the research project "Spain in the face of the new challenges of maritime security: Instruments and strategies in the international, European and Iberian framework", DER2016-78272-R, financed by the Spanish Ministry of Economy, Industry and Competitiveness.

Lara Lázaro Touza holds a PhD from the London School of Economics, an MSc in Environmental Assessment and Evaluation from the LSE and a BSc in Economics from the Autonomous University of Madrid. She is Senior Analyst in the Energy and Climate Change Programme at Real Instituto Elcano in Madrid and Lecturer in Economic Theory at Cardenal Cisneros University College (attached to the Complutense University of Madrid). She is currently working on an EU-funded H2020 research project titled "*Market Uptake of Solar Thermal Electricity through Cooperation*" and on a project funded by the Spanish Ministry of Economy and Business analysing the impact of China's Belt and Road Initiative on global governance.

Ángel Gómez de Ágreda is Colonel of the Spanish Air Force. He holds a Master's Degree in Terrorism and Counter-Terrorism and is currently a PhD candidate at the Technical University of Madrid in Industrial Engineering. In his current position at the Ministry of Defense, he is the head of the Geopolitical Analysis Area working for the Secretary General for Defense Policy. A former Professor of the Higher Defense School of the Spanish Armed Forces, he has published extensively in both English and Spanish.

Miriam Solera Ureña is a freelance researcher and consultant. She holds a BSc in Telecommunication Engineering from the Polytechnic University of Madrid (Spain) and a PhD in Political Sciences from the National Distance Education University of Madrid. Her areas of research comprise energy, climate and foreign policies, low-carbon technologies, sustainable transitions, international relations and system theory. She was Lecturer in the Department of Political Sciences at the Heidelberg University. She has broad experience as an expert engineer and technology development consultant in the telecommunication sector.

Ramses A. Wessel is Professor of International and European Law and Governance and Co-Director of the Centre for European Studies at the University of Twente, The Netherlands. He also teaches at the University of Leiden. His additional functions include: Chair of the standing Advisory Committee on Issues of Public International Law of the Netherlands' Government; Member of the Governing Board of the Centre for the Law of EU External Relations in The Hague; Editor-in-Chief and founder of the *International Organizations Law Review*, the *Netherlands Yearbook of International Law* and *ESIL Reflections*; Editor of *European Papers* and of Nijhoff Studies in European Union Law; and member of the Editorial Board of the CLEER Papers series and of *Europe and the World*.

Milena Costas Trascasas is an independent human rights adviser. She works as a consultant for the UN Human Rights Council's Advisory Committee and the Center for Studies of International Humanitarian Law (IHL) of the Spanish Red Cross. Previously, she worked as Research Fellow at the Geneva Academy of International Humanitarian Law and Human Rights; the University of Castellón; and the University of Milan. She has been involved as Researcher in several projects dealing with the impact of counter-terrorism measures and policies on human rights and IHL. In 2018, she was Visiting Professor at the University of Sassari where she gave a course on the "Fight against terrorism and human rights: EU's policy and practice." She studied at the University Complutense of Madrid and has a PhD in international law. Since May 2016 she has been a member of the OSCE/ODIHR Panel of Experts on the Freedom of Assembly and Association.

Carmen Pérez González (JD and PhD, University Carlos III of Madrid) is Associate Professor of Public International Law at Carlos III University of Madrid, Spain. Between 2004 and 2008 she served as Adviser for International Affairs in the Cabinet of the Spanish Secretary of State for Migration and between 2009 and 2010 as alternate member of the Management Board of the Fundamental Rights Agency of the European Union. She has been the Project Leader of a Spanish national project on the legal protection of vulnerable migrant women, and a member of the team project entitled "*The Fight against Trafficking in Human Beings in EU: Promoting Legal Cooperation and Victim's Protection*," founded by the European Commission in 2012. She has been Visiting Fellow at the European University Institute (Florence), the Max Planck Institute for Comparative Public Law and International Law (Heidelberg) and the Refugee Studies Centre (Oxford). She has written extensively in the area of international and EU migration and asylum law, protection of human rights of migrants, trafficking in human beings and obligations imposed on states under the *non-refoulement* principle.

Professor **Alexander Proelss** is the Chair of the International Law of the Sea and International Environmental Law, Public International Law and Public Law in the Faculty of Law of the University of Hamburg. International environmental law and the international law of the sea, together with selected aspects of EU law and domestic constitutional law, constitute the focal points of his research. He obtained his doctoral degree in 2003 and was awarded the postdoctoral lecture qualification (*Habilitation*) by the Faculty of Law at the University of Tübingen in 2010.

Araceli Manjón-Cabeza Olmeda is Professor of Criminal Law and Director of the Extraordinary Chair "*Drugs XXIst Century*" of the Complutense University of Madrid. She is a former General Director of the Spanish National Plan on Drugs and Magistrate of the Criminal Chamber of the Spanish High Court. She has acted as Spanish expert on the topic at the meetings of the United Nations General Assembly on Drugs and the Commission on Narcotic Drugs. She is special advisor for the assessment of the Law of Legalization of Marijuana of Uruguay and for several international committees. She advises political groups on the regulation of recreational and medicinal cannabis in Spain. She is currently main researcher on the project "*International Drug Control: problems and solutions*" (reference number: DER2016-74872-R).

Víctor Carlos Pascual Planchuelo is Lecturer in International Law and Human Rights at the Faculty of Political Sciences, Complutense University of Madrid. He is Legal Advisor and International Consultant for international organizations (such as UNDP or OSCE) and non-governmental organizations in the field of human rights and elections. He is also an electoral observer for the European Union, OSCE and OAS in some countries such as Senegal, Ukraine or México. He has a PhD in International Law.

José Antonio Sanahuja is Full Professor of International Relations at Complutense University of Madrid, Fellow at the Complutense Institute of International Studies, and Professor at the Spanish Diplomatic Academy. He holds a PhD. in Political Science from Complutense University, and an M.A. from the United Nations University for Peace. He has been a researcher and consultant for the European Commission and the European Parliament, the UNDP, the Ibero-American General Secretariat and the Spanish Ministry of Foreign Affairs and its Agency for International Cooperation and Development. He has been also Robert Schuman Fellow at the European University Institute (Florence).

ACKNOWLEDGEMENTS

The editors of this Handbook want to thank Routledge publishing house for its receptivity to our ideas and its patience and comprehension, as collective works are not so easy to complete.

We also want to thank Complutense Institute of International Studies, all its staff and research members and, particularly, its Director, Professor Isabel Álvarez González, for welcoming and hosting all our initiatives and workshops with true interest and a warm reception.

This publication is the fruit of the deliberations and discussions during three workshops and a final conference that were possible through the funding of the Jean Monnet Project "*European Union and Security: Defense of Common Interests and Spaces*" (reference number: 565277-EPP-1-2015-1-ES-EPPJMO-PROJECT) of which I was the coordinator. I thank Ana Peyró Llopis who was the main person responsible for the original proposal to the EU. Many of the contributors to this Handbook participated at these events and gave their very interesting insights on the topics addressed.

That said, the *Routledge Handbook on European Security Law and Policy* would not have been possible without the generosity of our contributors. We thank all of them for sharing with us their analysis and expertise on so many different aspects of EU security, for their patience, for accepting our very meticulous reviews and for suffering the dictatorship of the rules of style with resignation.

Finally, as chief editor of this collection of essays, I want to thank my two co-editors, Dr. Zhaklin V. Yaneva and PhD candidate Marzia Scopelliti, who have always worked loyally under my supervision. In collecting and reviewing thoroughly the works submitted by our contributors they have made an important effort: without their continuous support the Jean Monnet Project and, afterwards, this Handbook would not have been possible. I also thank them and Johan Vibe for their "English reviews" of my Introduction. Irene Rodríguez, PhD candidate at Complutense University, also under my co-supervision, has helped us with some of the reviews. Additionally, José Erick Chávez Marín, a visiting researcher from Pontificia Universidad Católica de Chile who worked under my supervision during the first semester of 2019, helped me with some bibliographical research.

E. Conde

INTRODUCTION

E. Conde

Background

The origin of this Handbook can be found in the Jean Monnet Project entitled "European Union and Security: Defense of Common Interests and Spaces" (reference number: 565277-EPP-1-2015-1-ES-EPPJMO-PROJECT) of which I was the coordinator and whose main aims were to establish a social and academic dialogue in relation to contemporary challenges to European security. Security threats such as terrorism in its contemporary forms, the use of and competition for common goods, cyberattacks and core European values nowadays at risk were amongst the many topics addressed by experts, public servants and citizens. As a matter of fact, these subjects were discussed with the audience during several workshops and a final conference was organized under the framework of this Jean Monnet Project, with the idea of identifying and proposing possible contributions of the European Union (EU) to tackling them. As both the threats themselves and the measures that can be adopted to cope with them may challenge some of the EU's core principles and values, the academic team involved in this project – among them the co-editors of this work – thought that it could be important to point out the limits of EU actions, especially with regard to the protection of human rights at stake; thus, these constraints were also considered by the experts, public servants and citizens invited to give their insights to the workshops.

Objectives

Since the inception of the project, we have approached EU security from a holistic point of view. This implies taking into account the risks to European citizens, states, societies and values. This perspective has inspired this Handbook as well. With these ideas in mind, *The Routledge Handbook of European Security Law and Policy* intends to deal with challenges to both inland and foreign European security as we firmly believe that EU internal security and global security are mutually dependent and interlinked. The EU response must, therefore, be comprehensive and based on a coherent set of actions combining the internal and external dimensions of the EU, to further reinforce links and coherence between Justice and Home Affairs and Common Security and Defense Policy (CSDP).

In this sense, the spirit that is behind the *rationale* of this publication is a comprehensive conception of European security, one that considers as paramount the protection of European citizens, their common and shared values, particularly in respect of our idea of what human rights must be. For all these reasons we have stressed this aspect of EU security, taking the idea of French president Macron in favor of a Europe that protects:[1] European citizens need to feel confident that, wherever they move within Europe, their freedoms and their security are well protected, in full compliance with the Union's values, including the rule of law and fundamental rights. Further on this aspect, a true European vision of freedom and human rights advocates for their respect not only in favor of European citizens but also in favor of aliens, as we think that the most dangerous threat that Europe confronts nowadays is that of "nothing to fear but fear itself."[2]

> A new ghost goes through Europe: it is called populism, although it should be called by its true name, nationalism. It is not the people against the oligarchy, but the nation against the other, the foreigner, the emigrant, or against the traitor to the unique and true nation. This resurgence of nationalism, which seeks to build walls or raise borders, comes full of populism, as usual, since there is no nation to be built without a people to mythologize.[3]

Structure of the book

The editors of the Handbook invited authors from different academic backgrounds – law, political science, economic science – to contribute from their expertise and knowledge to this very comprehensive idea of EU security. As such, *The Routledge Handbook of European Security Law and Policy* has been divided into three main Parts.

Part I offers a set of different academic studies that deal with institutions, policies or mechanisms used both by security and defense policy and by home and interior affairs. With the aim of offering a critical and prospective review of the existing EU security policies and tools, these contributions mark the conceptual framework around which the rest of the book revolves.

Accordingly, this part opens with a chapter written by **Professor Dahl Martinsen** on the European agenda on security. The author has taken the title of his contribution from the EU Commission document[4] that has served as a general inspiration to this Handbook, to analyze critically the international agendas of the main EU rivals, namely, Russia, China and the United States of President D. Trump. Professor Dahl Martinsen, in his insight, considers that Russia and China threaten Europe, as both countries try to exploit internal tensions in Europe to weaken Europe's ability to mount a unified answer. In this sense, even if the Russian war against Ukraine was met with European and United States' sanctions, this did not prevent the signing of a lucrative gas export deal between Germany and Russia, a deal that, in his opinion, will have a detrimental impact on regional stability. Additionally, close links between Russia and European nationalist and anti-EU parties might impair the EU's continued assistance to the countries on the Union's eastern border. Professor Dahl Martinsen considers that China is primarily a threat to European industrial prowess and economic competitiveness. Takeovers of European enterprises, industrial espionage and targeted investments in poorer EU countries have given China a troubling foothold inside the European Union. Although the problems posed by China are largely similar in Europe and the USA, no efforts have been made to agree on a common response. The Trump administration's coupling of trans-Atlantic trade with security has so far made this impossible.

The apparatus of EU internal security is extensively analyzed by **Gorazd Meško, Rajko Kozmelj** and **Branko Lobnikar** in Chapter 2 on police cooperation in the EU in response to serious transnational crime, where they offer their expertise on the topic, mainly considered from an internal concept of EU security. In their appraisal, they rely on the European Union's serious and organized crime threat assessment that emphasizes the importance of dealing with organized crime, terrorism and violent extremism, among other things. Having in mind all these important challenges, the chapter presents the institutional and procedural efforts made by the EU in ensuring a high level of security through measures that prevent and combat crime and through policies for active coordination and cooperation between police and judicial authorities and other competent authorities in the EU.

The tools and mechanisms developed by EU institutions in the design of EU foreign and security policies are the object of the contribution of **Professors Newsome** and **Riddervold** (Chapter 3). In their valuable introduction, they recall that Member States are the formal initiators and decision-makers in the EU Common Foreign and Security Policy (CFSP). The European External Action Service (EEAS) and the Commission prepare and implement decisions, while the European Parliament has the right to be informed and can give opinions and advice. Yet a growing number of studies suggest that the de facto role and influence of the EU institutions in policy-making processes falling under the CFSP procedures differ substantially from this formal description. They also discuss the institutions' various forms of interaction with the High Representative/Vice-President (HR/VP) and the EEAS, focusing particularly on if and how such interactions have been used as avenues to influence CFSP developments or affect their institutional powers. The chapter thus assembles evidence that the Member States' veto powers in the domain have clearly become limited owing to the de facto powers of the Commission – powers that it to a large degree has taken on itself, over time – as well as the cooperation between the EEAS and the Commission. Although the Parliament has significantly fewer formal competences in CFSP than the Commission, this institution has generously interpreted its statutory formal powers, for example, in budgeting and treaty assent, to extend its role in CFSP.

The reader will find in this Handbook two analyses of the European Security Strategy 2016 (Chapter 4 and Chapter 23), as the policy document that tackles both the risks the EU faces and will face in the near future and the political strategy designed and chosen to confront them. In spite of the fact that both contributions come from two colleagues in the International Relations Department of the Political Science Faculty of the Complutense University of Madrid and both are pessimistic about the international environment in which the EU Strategy will be deployed, they contemplate the EU Global Strategy from very different points of view, which explains the different places they occupy in the rationale of this book. Indeed, the contribution of **Professor García Cantalapiedra** (Chapter 4), entitled "Realism, international order and security: time to move beyond the 2016 European Union Global Strategy," analyses the process of creation of that document since June 2016, when the European Council received, from the HR/VP Federica Mogherini, a new strategic vision, "A Global Strategy for the European Union's Foreign and Security Policy," presenting a CSDP with a more defined role, and opening a process for enhancing the effectiveness and strengthening of military capabilities and the European defense industry through an "Implementation Package." No doubt, the process and creation of such a document represented a remarkable achievement in the European integration process. However, this was happening in a less than favorable context: first, the EU was still in the wake of the 2008 Great Recession and in the midst of a refugee/immigration crisis never seen before, at least since the end of World War II; second, Europe was engulfed in one of the bloodiest periods of terrorism on European soil in ten years; third, the Ukraine crisis had marked European security with a dangerous conflicting dynamic since 2014, with a worsening of relations with Russia and the United States turning toward other more pressing interests in the Indo-Pacific and, under the Trump administration, unconcerned with the defense of the liberal international order; and, finally, affecting the deepest core of the European integration process and its own reputation, the decision by the United Kingdom to leave the EU. In the author's analyses, this environment has created a discouraging scenario for European integration, European security, and for the future EU's global role. However, in the author's opinion, the most serious long-term strategic problem that the European Union is likely to face goes right to the core of the EU's mission and vision: a declining ability to sustain an already embattled multilateral liberal international order. According to this background, and paradoxically, the process towards a more realist strategic review appears as a demanding necessity for the EU, as Professor García Cantalapiedra points out.

The widely used and much coveted, but barely known concept of the strategic autonomy of the European Union, is considered by **Professor García Pérez** (Chapter 5). In recent years, significant steps have driven the Common Foreign and Security Policy in a direction that seeks to bring the Union closer to the undefined notion of *strategic autonomy*. The measures adopted underpin a common objective: the improvement of the EU's operational capacity so that Member States can carry out military missions outside their borders. Given the fact that none of these initiatives clarifies what strategic autonomy is, and what it consists of, the concept remains mired in doctrinal ambiguity that contrasts with its growing use. As such, this contribution explores the different interpretations of this concept that are under current academic and practical discussion and exposes the basic grounds of the incipient debate on the future of European defense, a debate in which *strategic autonomy* plays a substantive role.

Closing Part I, **Professor Serrano Antón** deals with a very practical issue, that of budget and EU security (Chapter 6), as without financial support there is no security at all. Every seven years, the Union decides on its future long-term budget: the Multiannual Financial Framework. This is an opportunity for Member States and European institutions to design the European vision for the coming future. A new seven-year EU budget always consists of a crucial financial element to implement the EU agenda, in this case to foster the EU Defense Budget for the very first time. Negotiations on the next Multiannual Financial Framework will have an important impact on how to deal with the challenges ahead. Choices taken will shape the Union for the decades to come. In particular, new security threats require new responses. The refugee crisis suffered, the regional powers' re-arming, the terrorist strikes in Europe and the escalation of cyberattacks – all these causes force the EU to tackle the threats with some harder responses. Geopolitical instability is increasing and the values and democratic principles on which the European Union is founded are being tested. Surrounded by this unfavorable environment, the Commission proposes a European Defence Fund to promote cooperation and cost savings among Member States in producing state-of-the-art and interoperable defense technology and equipment. Offering support for the research and development parts of the lifecycle will make sure that the results of research are not lost due to lack of funding for developing and testing the technology. It will also avoid duplication, allowing for economies of scale and resulting in a more efficient use of taxpayers' money, the author concludes.

In selecting the topics that compose Part II, we have had in mind both the relevance and the true impact of these issues in the daily lives of European citizens and, going further, the consequences of at least some of these subjects for the sustainability of the whole planet or the management of the so-called "global commons."

Starting with the challenges that the EU and its citizens will face in the near future, **Professors Gómez-Puig** and **Sosvilla-Rivero**, in their chapter on EU monetary and economic integration (Chapter 7), give a general overview of the economic integration process in the European Union, putting special emphasis on the Economic and Monetary Union and the sovereign debt crisis, exploring as well the different scenarios about its future evolution. To that end, the authors present several analytical tools to provide a framework for the interpretation of this process and offer a survey of empirical research in this area to illustrate the academic results regarding the evaluation of the European experience. The chapter also analyses the challenge of reinvigoration of the completion of the integration process to achieve the Lisbon Agenda's goal of becoming the world's most competitive economy, while re-orienting the regulatory framework to monitor the financial system and identify potential risks and vulnerabilities. Despite the remarkable progress, the authors contend that a structural rethinking of the European project is needed in accordance with the principles of subsidiarity and of sustainable and shared development enshrined in the Treaties.

In his essay, **Bruce Morley** offers a very interesting approach to *Brexit*, analysing the economic consequences of this complex process not yet culminated (Chapter 8). The author contends that following the vote to leave the European Union in 2016, there has been a great deal of debate on how the relationship between the United Kingdom (UK) and the EU should develop and the economic consequences of leaving. The analysis of the potential impact of *Brexit* on the UK and EU economy and its security has taken many forms, with an emphasis on simulations and the effects on trade, in particular based on gravity model type approaches. Along with this macroeconomic approach, some studies have assessed the effects on individual industries, such as the financial sector, especially the regulatory framework after *Brexit*. The results of the analysis tend to be mixed, although mostly they indicate an overall negative effect on trade and output. However, the author concludes with the difficulty of saying with certainty what the repercussions of the decision to leave will be, as there is no precedent to base the analysis on.

The legal aspect of financing business in the digital economy (Chapter 9) is the topic addressed by **Briseida Sofía Jiménez-Gómez** in her contribution, in which she reveals the transcendental consequences of this matter for the real lives of companies. In her chapter, she provides an interesting insight into some of the challenges that enterprises face in the digital economy when trying to access credit. The author highlights that despite the increasing ratio of intangible assets in companies, there are still obstacles for businesses of which the value is more frequently based on intangible assets. She reviews the main shortcomings of the under-use of intangible assets as resources and presents the existing valuation risks and the territorial limitations in order to gain understanding of the current situation. In this landscape, the author advocates for an improvement of the European regulatory framework. The disharmony of national laws considering secured transactions on intangibles is an issue of legal uncertainty. The action taken in conflict of laws on securities in the field of financial collateral arrangement illustrates a critical step for certainty at the European level. In her contribution, she argues that further legal developments concerning substantive laws of security interests plus conflict of law rules would be beneficial to improve legal certainty and predictability of use of intangible assets in financing transactions in Europe. The outcome of this analysis offers some recommendations to outweigh the legal risks associated with intangible property.

Professor Pérez López tackles the very timely topic of virtual currencies and the EU's options for their regulation (Chapter 10). The path cryptocurrencies have followed to this moment has led to the clarification of some of their more controversial aspects, such as their relation to fiat money. However, some major questions remain open, such as that of their regulatory perspectives in the EU. Even if some minor steps have been taken as to the fiscal framing of cryptocurrency-related activities such as mining or exchanging – mostly by courts (both the Court of Justice of the EU and national courts) and Member States' administrations – the reform of the Anti-Money Laundering Directive of May 2018 conveys the first EU major regulatory reaction to the phenomenon. Its dispositions including key actors of cryptocurrency economy (exchangers, wallet custodians) in its list of "obliged entities," comprising a long-awaited legal definition of "virtual currencies," have drawn up a starting point for further statutory developments. However, and beyond the limits laid down by the focus on the reforms themselves, the specific extent of its effects will not be fully clear until its transposition to national law.

The very relevant question of organized crime in the European Union is the topic into which **Professor Anguita Olmedo** delves (Chapter 11). The challenges to international security have evolved since the attacks of 2001. While terrorism and armed conflicts are among the major concerns of international society, other threats such as organized crime in all its manifestations have been incorporated into the international security agendas. The process of globalization has conditioned the evolution of criminal organizations, the current characteristics of which are determined by technological adaptation, the execution of operations that are increasingly complex and the formation of flexible structures that make their detection difficult. Similarly, the criminal manifestations, such as drug trafficking, cybercrime, trafficking in human beings or the trafficking of arms, have evolved to adapt themselves to the environment in which they are developed. In this sense, organized crime in the European Union does not respond to a single typology, but traditional gangs are joined by others that incorporate new technologies and act in a network, giving them greater invisibility and the ability to overcome geographical limits. To address these threats, the European Union has adopted certain prevention measures, but it has also focused on increasing response and reaction capabilities, in which the cooperative instruments and tools of solidarity, the involvement of all EU institutions and the interdependence between internal and external security are fundamental pillars for the adoption of a European security model capable of facing the risks and threats of the new century.

Related to this topic, that of the challenges of extremism and terrorism are considered by **Irene Rodríguez Ortega** (Chapter 12). In her approach to this theme, she takes for granted that religious extremism and terrorism are not recent phenomena in the EU. Anyway, in recent years, terrorism has emerged as a serious threat both to the security and stability of the values of our democratic societies and to the rights and freedoms of European citizens. Since 2015, religiously inspired terrorist attacks in the EU have increased, making the fight against terrorism a top priority for the EU and every state in the Union.

The rest of the contributions in Part II assess the balance between EU security and the management of several global commons. Of the different senses in which the notion of global commons could be considered, we have relied on the one that is contained in studies of geopolitics and security, a genuinely American notion even though it has its roots in the Anglo-Saxon tradition.[5] On that appraisal, the so-called global commons would be physical or intangible spaces on which the free traffic of goods, resources, people and ideas depends, that is, all oceanic spaces, air space, outer space and cyberspace. This conception is the mirror of the strategic interests of the United States of America (USA), as, since the end of World War II, they have been the main guarantor but also the main beneficiary of these essential goods. For the last century up to now, the hegemony of the USA has been based not only on its broad economic and military power, but also, and especially, on the export of these powers to the whole world and its chief role in the process of globalization, which has consisted, above all, in the mass dissemination of liberal and capitalist values by using freely accessible global commons. From a soft perspective, the EU has been an advocate and supporter of this vision that needs to be revisited in order to tackle the most urgent dangers that humankind faces in the near future. However, this idyllic scenario, in which the control of global commons has been supported on these eminently liberal foundations, has begun to be challenged by the emergence of new non-Western powers – especially in the case of China or that of Russia – or even non-state actors, who do not act in accordance with the customary rules of conduct in state subjects. In our eminently interconnected world, any limitation in access to global commons has consequences for the global geopolitical balance, a feature that the new state powers or other non-state agents try to exploit to their advantage and to the detriment of the powers already consolidated.

In this vein, **Professor Pedrazzi**'s contribution on EU space security policy (Chapter 13) considers that, given the rising strategic and military interests in space, the security and safety of space assets are becoming a major concern. The EU, nowadays a major user of security-related space assets, especially through its Galileo and Copernicus programs, has become an active promoter of the development of a global normative framework to guarantee space security. To this end, it proposed to the international community in 2008 a draft Code of Conduct for Space Activities. A revised version of the Code, intended as a non-binding instrument, was issued in 2014. Besides the interest shown by many States, including the USA, others, such as China and Russia, have opposed the project, leading to its de facto rejection. The EU is therefore currently trying to find alternative ways to pursue, in the relevant international fora and in cooperation with other actors, the goal of a safer and more secure outer space environment.

The very demanding and urgent question for humankind of the sustainable management of fisheries is considered by **Professor Teijo García** (Chapter 14), who offers his remarkable expertise on the subject. Illegal, Unreported and Unregulated (IUU) fishing is one of the maritime risks identified by the 2014 European Union Maritime Security Strategy. However, European institutions have not taken specific actions in order to tackle this problem by increasing control of fishing activities, not only on the high seas managed by Regional Fisheries Management Organizations but also in the Exclusive Economic Zones of third coastal States that do not have the capacity to monitor extractive practices by their own means. The approach taken by the EU to combat illegal fishing, defined by Council Regulation (EC) 1005/2008, has preferred to prioritize monitoring carried out by port and flag States, building up a complex system of administrative and commercial sanctions against individual, private companies and third States involved in illegal fishing practices. This chapter defends the view that this approach should be complemented with larger participation of EU military forces in surveillance activities to be carried out on the high seas or in the jurisdictional waters of third States.

Climate change has been described as an emerging threat to national security, human security and ecological security. In areas with pre-existing socioeconomic and environmental tensions it can put development gains at risk, and it can help fuel instability, migration and conflict. Unabated climate change can also affect military infrastructures and operations. Europe and neighboring countries could be severely affected by the impacts of climate change if globally concerted climate action fails to meet the goals of the Paris Agreement. Questions remain, however, regarding the precise nature, timing and severity of climate impacts, whose security is at stake and how to address climate change. Despite the need to achieve conceptual clarity regarding the climate–security nexus, policy makers in the EU (and elsewhere) have begun to integrate climate change in their security strategies, although further definition of targets, timetables and benchmarks would help ground climate action in the implementation of the European Union Global Strategy. By dealing with these demanding aspects, Chapter 15 by **Lara Lázaro Touza** and **Ángel Gómez de Ágreda** explores the climate–security binomial from a European foreign policy and security perspective.

Miriam Solera Ureña goes into energy security in the EU (Chapter 16), considering that since the Treaty on the Functioning of the European Union conferred in 2009 shared competence between the Union and the Member States, energy and environmental policies have become an essential remit for the EU. With an overall EU energy import volume that accounts for more than half of its total energy consumption, energy security is at the core of the European Union policy. Currently, the EU is confronted with a wide range of complex and contentious issues that pose a challenge to energy security. Some of these issues fall beyond the realm of geopolitics and economics. The uncertainty and the various risks arising from both current and future changes in the energy markets should be managed appropriately. However, remarkable structural differences in national energy markets and differing (pragmatic) interests among Member States may cause reluctance to let energy national interests converge in order to achieve common European aims. This chapter provides a comprehensive understanding of relevant current issues, which the EU will have to tackle in the coming years. The chapter concludes with brief remarks on a desirable future landscape in which progress towards convergence within the EU and the avoidance of any mistrust should facilitate reliable interdependence relations with energy suppliers and further third countries.

"Cybersecurity in the European Union: resilience through regulation?" This is the very evocative title of the contribution written by **Professor Wessel** (Chapter 17). He assumes that cybersecurity is high on the policy agenda of the European Union and can be seen as an emerging field of research, both in policy and in legal studies. The recent adoption of new directives on information and network security and on cybercrime reveals the possibilities for the EU to use existing competences in other policy fields to regulate aspects of cybersecurity. "Resilience" of existing structures as well as of EU values is at the core of the Union's approach to cybersecurity. Yet a comprehensive approach is missing, leading to a risk of fragmentation and incoherence. So far, measures related to the Single Digital Market and to cooperation on criminal law have been more elaborate than measures related to cyber-defense.

Finally, Part III of the Handbook goes to the response that the EU offers to critical challenges, analysing them from the human side, that is, considering whether they remain respectful of the inspiring values and principles of the EU project or, on the contrary, reflect the most dangerous trends of our days – xenophobia, ultra-nationalism, rise of extreme right-wing parties, populisms – which are also taking form in the EU.

Going further on this idea, **Milena Costas Trascasas** offers her critical vision on the way in which the EU tackles terrorism in her contribution entitled "EU counterterrorism policy and human rights: are we on the right track?" (Chapter 18). This contribution seeks to demonstrate that in the name of counter-terrorism policies, important structural systemic reforms at the international level have been introduced, and that the EU is a major actor in the implementation of the global strategy in the fight against terrorism. With a view to strengthening a concerted response among its Member States, it has undertaken a very proactive role in proposing legislation and identifying new areas where increased cooperation would enhance the Union's security. As a result, today, the EU counts on an enormous and complex arsenal of restrictive measures directly impacting on the individual's rights and freedoms. The efficiency in the passing and implementation of counter-terrorism policies contrasts with the lack of practical measures aimed at enhancing respect of human rights in their implementation. The number of legal provisions that have been challenged and annulled by the EU Court of Justice shows a failure in the assessment of the human rights impact of EU legislative proposals and policies on counter-terrorism in both its internal and its external dimensions. There is also an evident democratic deficit in the oversight of restrictive measures and lack of accountability for possible violations committed by Member States in this context. The sum of all these issues raises the question of whether the EU is giving proper weight to human rights concerns. The EU formally acknowledges the importance of human rights compliance, but what research shows is that few steps have been taken in that direction, at least at the policy level. Without an adequate assessment of the threat posed by terrorism and due consideration of fundamental rights, the capacity of EU policy and legislative proposals to attain its objectives is under question. The trend to major "securitization" of Europe through a "pre-emptive" approach may bring in the long-term irreparable damage to the European project. An analysis of the different role played by the various EU institutions and actors in the designing and implementation of counter-terrorism policy reveals a failure in the EU's checks and balances. Against what stems from official declarations, the EU decision-makers seem not to have intimately adhered to the conviction that an enhanced Union's security cannot be made at the cost of reducing the area of freedom and justice.

In this same vein, **Professor Pérez González** delves into the very timely issue of the protection of migrant and refugee children against trafficking and exploitation, assessing how the EU responses have been consequent to the international human rights perspective (Chapter 19). It is evident that migrant and refugee children constitute a vulnerable group facing severe risks. The Council of Europe Group of Experts on Action against Trafficking in Human Beings has recently affirmed that, on average, children represent a quarter of identified victims of human trafficking in Europe for sexual exploitation, labor exploitation, forced marriage and, increasingly, forced criminality. The aim of the author's work is twofold. First, she examines the main aspects of the EU law and policy normative framework on the protection of migrant and refugee children against trafficking and exploitation. International obligations imposed upon the EU and its Member States by International Human Rights Law have inspired the analysis. Second, the study reflects on the weaknesses of that framework and proposes adequate reforms in the light of the upcoming Global Compact for Safe, Orderly and Regular Migration.

Closely related to the above mentioned essay, **Professor Proelss** offers his expertise on maritime border control in the European Union (Chapter 20). In his legal and political analysis, he demonstrates that while the pertinent legal measures taken by the EU have become more diverse and sophisticated over time, the EU has not established, and arguably could not establish, a truly supranational external border policy due to its limited legislative powers in the field concerned. The chapter takes the view that the main legal challenges to the EU maritime border control regime continue to arise in the context of ensuring that the European measures, in particular the FRONTEX Regulation and the External Sea Borders Regulation, are enacted and implemented in such a way that they respect the pertinent standards of the international law of the sea as well as human and fundamental rights law. Following a detailed assessment of how the EU has reacted to these challenges, the author submits that the Union has clearly enhanced the relevant standard of protection over the years by amending the legal measures applicable to maritime border control. That said, he considers that there is still ample need for improvements in relation to whether the regulations concerned are also implemented accordingly in legal practice, and that the uncertainties relating to whether maritime border control activities ought to be attributed to the EU or to the Member States – or even to both of them – continue to have a negative effect on the conditions under which legal remedies may be invoked against these activities.

EU drug policy and its shortfalls from the perspective of new international trends in the regulation of some substances – particularly cannabis – and that of their consumers, is considered by Criminal Law **Professor Manjón-Cabeza Olmeda** in Chapter 21. In her appraisal of the subject, the author reviews the current focus of the Union's policy on drugs, with particular reference to Council Framework Decision 2004/757/JHA of October 25, 2004, which sets down minimum provisions on the constituent elements of criminal acts and penalties in the field of illicit drug trafficking. This review takes into account the international context, the existence of regimes regulating the entire lifecycle of cannabis products, the position of the United Nations, which continues to be based on the drug control conventions of 1961, 1971 and 1988, and the movements in recent years calling for a paradigm shift in drugs policy. It focuses on the significance of the claim that drugs pose a threat to individual and collective interests in Europe, with particular reference to security-based approaches to the issue.

Focused on a wide perspective of the *soft power* of the EU, **Professor Pascual Planchuelo** considers that electoral observation can be a powerful tool in order to establish and implement the values of EU security in third States (Chapter 22). He points out that with the approval of its 2016 Security Strategy, the European Union adopted a broad perspective that acknowledges the fact that its internal and external security is connected to the protection of human rights, democracy and the rule of law in the international community and in neighboring countries. Under this approach, the EU will roll out several political and diplomatic tools with the aim of contributing to the reinforcement of international security. Equally, the author considers that Election Observation Missions (EOMs) should be included within these tools, given the essential function that these EOMs are performing in the prevention and resolution of the numerous conflicts arising in the context of electoral processes.

Closing Part III and the whole contents of this Handbook, is the contribution of **Professor Sanahuja,** the second evaluation of the 2016 EU Global Strategy for Foreign and Security Policy. The subtitle of this chapter – "Security narratives, legitimacy, and identity of an actor in crisis" – and the contents made it advisable for it be included as a final and critical chapter (Chapter 23). Departing from the idea that the 2016 Global Strategy intends to adapt the EU's external action to a more complex and uncertain global scenario, a visible "pragmatic turn" and a marked focus on societal resilience and in its neighborhood, this chapter provides a description as well as an interpretation of the strategy itself. In order to do that, it takes into account its institutional foundations, its material content and its nature as a security narrative – that is, as a discursive device that shapes the identity and values of the EU, as well as the internal–external axis of European security and its external action – thus entailing noticeable normative dilemmas. The chapter concludes that the 2016 Global Strategy contributes to shaping a new security legitimation for an EU that suffers a deep existential crisis.

Notes

1 Emmanuel Macron, "Pour une Renaissance Europeénne," L'Élysée official website, March 4, 2019, accessed April 24, 2019, www.elysee.fr/emmanuel-macron/2019/03/04/pour-une-renaissance-europeenne.

2 We have taken the inspiring sentence from the title of the Demos report *Nothing to Fear but Fear Itself.* The Foreword of the report expresses very accurately what we intend to convey to the reader:

> *Nothing to Fear but Fear Itself* was conceived on the idea that Europe – which at the time (in 2015) was thoroughly bogged down with the migrant crisis, economic crisis and a counter-terror crisis – was also experiencing a new type of crisis. One less visible, but with the potential to become just as important. In the declining level of political engagement and trust, the growth of populist parties and anti-immigrant sentiment, we saw a common thread of fear weaving its way through European societies, with the potential to foster a divisive new political culture, to destabilise democratic governance, and to challenge the "liberal consensus" of modern times.

The report is accessible on the following website: https://demosuk.wpengine.com/wp-content/uploads/2017/04/DEMJ5104_nothing_to_fear_report_140217_WEBv2.pdf.

3 Santos Juliá, "Sobre el futuro de nuestra democracia," *El País*, April 28, 2019, accessed May 1, 2019, https://elpais.com/elpais/2019/04/26/opinion/1556288551_432586.html.

4 European Commission, Communication from the Commission to the European Parliament, the Council, the European Economic and Social Committee and the Committee of the Regions: The European Agenda on Security, COM(2015) 185 final (Strasbourg: European Union, April 28, 2015).

5 This vision has its roots in the classic work of Alfred Thayer Mahan, *The Influence of Sea Power upon History 1660–1783*, which emphasized the economic and military benefits derived from the use of the seas as major channels of communication and commercial exchange, granting the greatest power to whoever manages to master these routes. These ideas would be re-considered in Barry Posen's study, *Command of the Commons: The Military Foundation of U.S. Hegemony*, to support the US leadership in the current international system through the control of such assets. It is also necessary to take into account the authoritative doctrine of the USA.

PART I

EU Security

Interplay between the foreign security policy and the internal security policy

1
THE EUROPEAN AGENDA ON SECURITY

Kåre Dahl Martinsen

Introduction

Different analyses of European security draw different conclusions depending on their focus. If attention is given to the EU, the communiques issued, institutional innovations agreed and money spent, the conclusion has tended to be optimistic. This applies to many security scholars writing around the turn of the millennium. Some concluded that EU members had now reached a level of integration where national interests yielded to a common European security identity.[1] Common to these analyses was the claim that the foundations for a united response to the security threats confronting the Union were close to becoming a reality. Yet there was no real sense of urgency since the threats were few. None of them required a co-ordinated military response involving several countries or large numbers of troops on the ground. At regular intervals, the EU made plans for military capacities capable of prolonged battle deployments, only to be delayed, watered down or shelved.[2] This rarely caused much concern since diplomacy and soft power were seen as having the future on their side.[3] NATO's emphasis on military deterrence was regarded as a remnant from the Cold War.[4] US complaints about European burden shedding were nothing new and, perhaps for that reason, were not perceived as pressing; besides, allied participation in US-led wars in Afghanistan and (for some) in Iraq softened the pressure coming from Washington. Only the Baltic countries and Poland pointed to Russia as a threat; in the eyes of many Western security scholars this seemed more based on history than reality. Besides, whatever real threat there may have been diminished as Russia was being integrated with the West; EU exports quadrupled from 2000 to 2008.[5] Much in the same vein, China was primarily framed as a lucrative market. Few doubted that the country was on a Westernizing trajectory; joining the World Trade Organization in 2001 was taken as a clear sign that the rulers in Beijing had opted for a Western capitalist model.[6]

Today that optimism is gone. Russia has changed international borders by force and is engaged in active warfare against Ukraine. Its armed forces are a key vehicle for exerting Russian influence not only in Europe, but also in Africa and the Middle East. Russia's state-sponsored hacking and disinformation have scored notable victories on both sides of the Atlantic. China is no longer just an economic opportunity, but a political opponent. Investments, take-overs, and trade agreements are tools used to gain influence and dilute any criticism of Chinese infringements of human rights or international law. Like Russia, China openly frames itself as a superior alternative to the Western political and economic model, and both nations work to weaken Western cohesion.[7]

Co-ordination on how to respond to Russia – both across the Atlantic and within the EU – has largely been successful. Finding a common policy on China is more difficult. One reason is certainly President Trump's lack of enthusiasm for any multilateral solution combined with his disdain for the EU. The US decision to pull out of the Intermediate-Range Nuclear Forces Treaty (INF) has strained trans-Atlantic relations further. Before discussing the potential repercussions of that move, the threats posed by Russia and China will be surveyed. My focus will be restricted to the EU and NATO; they are the only organizations with the capacities and resources to counter Russia and China. The Organization for Security and Co-operation in Europe (OSCE) and the European Council do not, and will not be included. Key topics like cybersecurity, energy supplies, or the development of EU defense policy are dealt with in detail by other authors; here they are included only to illustrate their impact on European security autonomy. Finally, of all the European countries, France and Germany will be referred to repeatedly over the next pages. The reason is not their much acclaimed joint role as the EU's political and economic locomotive. As will be shown, on security issues there is little coordination and even less harmony.

Russia and the new Cold War

Russia emerges on the European security agenda under three different headings: the Nord Stream gas pipeline, the war in Ukraine, and political disruption. These all inter-relate, but since the war is the event that led the EU to revise its relationship with Russia, this is where I will start.

In late 2013 the Ukrainian president Viktor Yanukovych unexpectedly announced his rejection of an EU association agreement awaiting his signature, and preferred instead a lucrative Russian offer made at the last minute. His decision would have cemented the country into the Eurasian Economic Union, a Russian dominated block. The democratically motivated economic reforms agreed with the EU would have been halted. His decision triggered mass protests in the larger cities with calls for a continued rapprochement with the West. The President and his entourage fled to Russia in late February 2014. Russian forces occupied Crimea a few days later. Then in July the same year, Russian forces invaded the Donbass region in Eastern Ukraine. Russian reasons for intervening militarily are complex and many, but a few are worth mentioning: without Ukraine, the Eurasian Economic Union would not only lack a geographical bridge to the EU but economic links would be severed.[8] No less important was the unwelcome contrast a democratic Ukraine made to Putin's model of autocracy.[9]

EU's response to Russia's actions was sanctions. The start was somewhat wavering. The snapshot of a civil servant leaving Downing Street with a memo stressing the need to shield the City of London from any economic punishment placed on Russia expressed a mood not exclusively British.[10] Gradually EU members closed ranks around a set of sanctions that were subsequently expanded and prolonged. This was done in tandem with the US sending a strong message of Western cohesion. Nevertheless, there were some significant differences: the US measures lacked the European specificity. Intended or not, without clear dos and don'ts, foreign investors shied away from the Russian market fearing they could be subject to US punitive measures.[11]

The question of whether the sanctions have been successful is difficult to answer. Russia has not withdrawn from Eastern Ukraine and Crimea. However, the sanctions have probably played a role in deterring Russia from taking the war further into Ukraine; the rhetoric used by Putin in 2014 when he referred to the Ukrainian Black Sea Coast as part of Novorossiya and ipso facto Russia, has been abandoned.[12] The economic impact of the sanctions is difficult to measure because the downturn in Russian economic growth started the year before the sanctions were imposed. An analysis published by the Bank of Finland's research institute concludes that the impact has been 'relatively limited on the aggregate level,' but grave for companies and individuals directly targeted.[13] The EU has not issued an assessment of the sanctions' impact; the closest it has come is a 2018 briefing on the use of sanctions as a foreign and security instrument. It is admitted that sanctions rarely achieve their goals; yet it is asserted that an absence of change is not tantamount to failure.[14] According to the report, sanctions are the expression of a joint EU commitment to uphold a set of values: remaining silent would have been 'morally unacceptable.'[15] That is laudable, yet this seems to imply that the need to convince EU citizens of a determination to act may have played a stronger role than hitherto acknowledged. The report contains nothing on what more the Union could do to force Russia to commit to a cease-fire.

European willingness to uphold the sanctions has so far remained intact. That has not prevented some politicians from arguing for their removal. Populist parties such as the German AfD (Alternative für Deutschland) or Marine le Pen's Front National/Rassemblement nationale have pointed to the lack of result, arguing that they affect their countries unduly hard.[16] It should be added that whenever these politicians are elected into office, their objections tend to be muted. Examples are the Austrian vice-chancellor Heinz-Christian Strache from the right-wing FPÖ (Freiheitliche Partei Österreichs) and the Italian prime minister Matteo Salvini who pleaded in favor of ending the sanctions, but who refrained from opposing the EU after making the transition from parliament to government.[17]

The sanctions regime was combined with negotiations to end the war. Convening in early 2015, the leaders of Ukraine and Russia met with the French president and the German chancellor in the Belarusian capital Minsk to agree on a cease-fire. The negotiations were undertaken at Chancellor Merkel's initiative and she soon assumed a leading role. It is notable that the EU was not one of the parties, possibly reflecting Russian opposition against including the organization identified by the Kremlin as the main instigator of Ukraine's westward turn. The parties agreed on a set of measures, including a cease-fire and the removal of heavy weaponry from the war zone. Fighting has abated in some parts of Eastern Ukraine only to reignite in others; the war has been transformed into a low-intensity, frozen conflict with the number of victims exceeding 10,000.[18] Apart from the provision made in the agreement that the parties are to convene regularly, none of the other agreed targets have been fully met.[19] Monitoring compliance, or the lack of it to be more precise, has been delegated to the OSCE. This is similar to what was done in Georgia from 1992 to 2008. This means that the EU is not directly involved in the peace efforts. Nikolaus von Twickel, a former member of OSCE's monitoring team, has concluded that the agreements 'all suffer from a lack of clarity and lack of political will to implement them.'[20] Despite OSCE's dismal record and Russian sabotaging of the organization's monitoring work in Eastern Ukraine, Germany proposed sending OSCE to monitor the conflict in the Sea of Azov only to be rebutted by Russia.[21]

Soon after the outbreak of hostilities in 2014, US politicians started questioning whether Ukraine should be permitted to buy US weapons. A bi-partisan Congress passed the Ukraine Freedom Support Act in 2014, allocating $350 million in security assistance. The sum was intended to include US-made weapons. If carried through, Moscow would certainly have taken it as proof that the West was behind the war. To avert escalating tensions, President Obama vetoed including weapons. Three years later, the restrictions were lifted when the Trump administration permitted the export of anti-tank missiles to Ukraine.[22] Since then, Western military experts have traveled to Ukraine to assist the country's armed forces to resist Russian pressure.

This pressure is set to increase in the coming years as the result of Nord Stream 2, the new Russo-German pipeline crossing the Baltic Sea. It comes in addition to the already operating Nord Stream 1. The new pipeline will reduce the need for Russia to transit gas across Ukraine. Without the gas, the Ukrainian state will lose approximately EUR 3 billion in transit fees. This is roughly the same amount provided by the EU in economic assistance to soften the social impact of economic reforms. Without the fees, domestic tensions are likely to increase, making the country more susceptible to Russian divisionary tactics. If so, regional stability will be further impaired. This was the reason for the repeated protests against the pipeline from the Danish, Swedish, Polish, and Baltic governments. Out of security concerns, the Swedish government refused the construction company access to a Swedish harbor.[23] The German government line, as expressed by Chancellor Merkel at the 2019 Security Conference in Munich, is that Nord Stream is a purely commercial enterprise.[24] She did not refer to the concerns voiced by the country's neighbors; as far as can be ascertained, they have not been mentioned the few times the issue has been discussed in the Bundestag. This contrasts with European Parliament's report on the state of EU–Russia relations, where the detrimental impact of the gas deal was referred to in no uncertain terms.[25]

In the wake of Nord Stream 2, Russian influence in German politics is set to grow.[26] Its predecessor Nord Stream 1 shows how. Chancellor Gerhard Schröder gave the go-ahead to the construction in 2005. This was just before he lost the parliamentary elections and had to resign; shortly after, he was made chairman of the Nord Stream shareholders' committee. In September 2017, he was given the same position but this time in the Russian state-controlled oil company Rosneft. After leaving the chancellorship, he has been one of Putin's most vocal supporters in Germany.[27] What is noticeable here is the German leadership's refusal to accept the implications of the deal for Ukraine, but also that the increased dependency on Russian gas goes against the EU's strategy in which Russian energy is regarded as a source of vulnerability.[28] The price has been a growing isolation of Germany within the EU.[29] France, with whom Germany had just renewed the 1963 Elysée Treaty pledging renewed bilateral co-operation, voiced its concerns over the security implications of the pipeline.[30] Also Poland's pro-US line in foreign and security politics should be seen as a lack of confidence in German willingness to include others in a multilateral solution.

Another part of Europe where Russia has played a disruptive role is the Balkans. In early 2019 President Putin visited Serbia. Thanks to Russian refusal to recognize Kosovo's independence, his popularity in the country is vast. He stated during his visit that Serbia was being forced to make 'an artificial choice' between Russia and the EU.[31] President Aleksandar Vučić countered that the country is on track to becoming an EU member. Despite the rapturous welcome Putin received, Russian power in the Balkans is on the decline. This is also the case for the Republic of North Macedonia, which is expected to enter accessions negotiations with the EU in 2019. The country joined NATO in February 2019. Seen together with Montenegro's membership in the alliance dating back to 2017, Russian ambitions have suffered a setback. As seen from Russia, the loss of Montenegro means the loss of access to an Adriatic port. In 2018 Russia supported nationalists in Greece and North Macedonia in opposing the Prespa Agreement paving the way for the latter's NATO membership. The Russian security expert Maxim Samorukov pointed out that Russian resistance has suddenly made a confined dispute into a geo-political issue enabling everybody to blame Russia for whatever hiccups arise.[32] This is indeed what happened: the EU's report on the relationship with Russia specifically condemns Russian efforts to undermine the Agreement.[33]

China as the 'systemic rival'[34]

China's disruptive undertakings differ from Russia's in that they are subtler, and more successful. China has the economic resources Russia lacks to support a wide range of activities. Among these are the creation of expert groups or think tanks – or membership in regional or specialist forums and networks – that focus on such topics as maritime issues, green energy, and regional development. This is a smart way for China to gain influence as small-scale initiatives rarely attract much political attention. Gaining a complete picture of the Chinese from Europe is difficult and for that reason, the EU has so far failed to come up with a concerted policy. China has singled out countries like Greece, Italy, and Spain to take part in different co-operative forums, all of them countries where the need for foreign investments is pronounced. France, whose official line has been critical of China's industrial espionage and violations of human rights and international law, is not included in any of these forums.[35]

China, like Russia, has been particularly keen on investing in the Balkans where democratic institutions are comparatively new and political corruption rife.[36] The lion's share of the investments have gone toward developing rail connections (Serbia and Hungary) and port facilities.[37] The need to maintain the stream of investments certainly played a key role in the Greek government's decision in 2017 to stop the EU from criticizing China's human rights violations at the UN.[38] In the more developed European countries, Chinese investors have systematically targeted the high-tech sector, in particular enterprises at the forefront in their field.[39] This comes in addition to mounting industrial espionage.[40] When Germany warned that it would bar a Chinese take-over of a German toolmaker for security reasons, it marked a change in Chinese–European relations.[41] At the EU level, plans were made for a screening mechanism on foreign investments that would have revealed the scope of Chinese activities. However, enough countries resisted making it compulsory, settling instead for a voluntary scheme.[42] Still, within the EU, awareness of the threat posed by China to the Union's industrial prowess is growing. A clear sign was a report launched in March 2019 by the European Commission.[43] It was issued soon after news broke that Italy had given the green light for a Chinese take-over of an Italian harbor; and in Prague the anti-EU Czech president Miloš Zeman declared that he welcomed Chinese investments.[44] Without them, Czech exports to China might be threatened, he added. These events contrast with the report's conclusion that 'Neither the EU nor any of its Member States can effectively achieve their aims with China without *full unity*.'[45]

The question of a joint trans-Atlantic China policy has surfaced in relation to the export of dual-use technology, i.e., technology that has a military value in addition to civilian use. After the 1989 Tiananmen massacre, the EU Parliament managed to push through an arms embargo, much to the chagrin of the French president and German chancellor at the time. This embargo did not prevent the export of technology that could be and indeed was used for the modernization of the Chinese armed forces.[46] This prompted Theresa Fallon, an expert on EU–Asia relations to conclude that the

> EU does not invest adequately in defense to secure its own neighborhood nor does it usefully support the United States in Asia. Loosely defined, dual-use technology sales by European companies to the PRC [People's Republic of China] have accelerated the PLA's [People's Liberation Army] development of military might.[47]

Fallon was an exception; for many years, Chinese rearmament was an issue few Europeans regarded as affecting them, China was too far away and was tied up in conflicts with surrounding countries. In 2016, Gunnar Wiegand, the Union's managing director for the Asia-Pacific for the European External Actions Service, gave a keynote speech at the Center for Strategic and International Studies in Washington outlining not so much the EU's approach to China as the limitations to it, by declaring that the 'European Union does not do geopolitics.'[48] The reluctance to do so has also meant that the EU, with the notable exception of the EU Parliament, for years refrained from protesting against China's imperialism at sea, the persecution of the Uighurs, oppression of Christians, and incarceration of human rights activists. It is worth recalling that parliamentary protests are not the same as the EU's policy on China. Only after Chinese takeovers led to political worries did the EU start to draw up a policy aimed at protecting European competitiveness. This is the key message in the 2019 Commission report on China, an unexpected addition being the attention given to the Chinese military as a threat to European security.[49] Increasing Chinese naval presence in European waters in recent years has served as a reminder that Chinese ambitions are not restricted to Asia. In 2017, Chinese vessels participated in a joint exercise with the Russian navy in the Baltic Sea. The Chinese navy has been growing in the Mediterranean in recent years. China has also shown a strong interest in the Arctic, eager to exploit Greenland's need for investments.[50]

Different degrees of dependence on China have also impeded a joint EU response to Chinese state-sponsored hacking of EU institutions and members. In January 2019, Britain offered evidence that the country had been the target of Chinese state-sponsored cyberattacks.[51] British hopes for a joint EU response in the form of a protest, let alone sanctions, turned out to be futile. The Chinese response when British authorities announced what had been uncovered was that any measures would endanger bilateral co-operation with China.[52] The usual explanation given is China's growing economic importance for the Union. Yet, at the same time, China's very direct retaliation against countries certainly has a deterring impact. Britain and France have deviated from the EU's silence on China: both countries have naval vessels patrolling the international waters in the China Sea claimed by Beijing. Doing that, they express a will to uphold international law against Chinese maritime annexation. The EU lacks the military means to do the same.[53] The report issued by the European Parliament may signal a change, yet it remains to be seen whether member countries will implement it. The possibility that some will quietly overlook it should not be excluded.

European cohesion

The populist parties on the rise in the EU want to reduce Brussels' say over the members' foreign policy.[54] Some larger parties are already adopting parts of their policies to attract voters. Growing EU skepticism plays a key role here, most recently seen in the negative response given to President Macron's attempts to start a debate on the future of the Union.[55] His emphasis on a common foreign and security policy was singled out for particular scorn. Among the first victims of this growing skepticism will be costly EU foreign and security projects. So far, EU cohesion on sanctions and support for Ukraine has been maintained, not least because members with the strongest pro-Russian sympathies are all net receivers of EU funding. If funding is cut, they may well demand reductions in the economic transfers to Ukraine or Moldova, which are not even members. That the EU is already now suffering from what has been labeled 'Eastern Partnership fatigue' means that these countries have fewer advocates now than when the partnership projects were launched in 1994.[56]

Cohesion is also challenged by the EU's re-launched defense plans. Populist parties and external pressure play a minor role here when compared with the considerable differences in strategic cultures and national interests. In the past, this was less evident because the plans never reached the stage where they could be implemented due to British opposition. London's line was that NATO was the prime security alliance and EU plans were a waste of scarce resources and a threat to trans-Atlantic relations. US administrations would echo this, most poignantly through Secretary of State Madeleine Albright, who in 1998 warned against the 'Three Ds': duplication, decoupling from the US, and discrimination against non-EU NATO members.[57] Without Britain playing the role of the perpetual block, plans can now be made. A larger trigger has been President Trump's questioning of continued US protection of allies that do not live up to spending pledges.[58]

In 2017, the European Commission published a survey of the members' defense spending, concluding that more co-operation would make the sums go much further.[59] Soon after, a cluster of initiatives were undertaken, aimed at increasing the Union's defense capabilities by ensuring better priorities for what to develop and by facilitating and funding joint projects.[60] Notable among these initiatives was PESCO – Permanent Structured Cooperation – which covers a catalog of projects aimed at boosting co-operation between members in order to develop capabilities that can be used in future EU military operations.[61] The initial enthusiasm has now been dampened; the projects seem more aimed at catering to national preferences than furthering European military autonomy.[62] A further obstacle to joint defense industry projects is that there are different export rules in France and Germany, the Union's largest arms producers.[63] The size of the European markets makes sales to foreign countries a necessity to lower costs. The French approach is that export deals open the way for political contacts and influence. In Germany, human rights records will often play a key role in vetoing a deal. The two nations have clashed over the sale of arms to Saudi Arabia. Germany voted no, making it impossible for France to sell arms with a German component.[64] Merkel admitted at the Munich Conference in February 2019 that the rules had to be harmonized, an uphill struggle since only the two conservative parties are in favor of such a harmonization and neither of them are in a majority. Most likely, the current practice for European arms producers of avoiding German parts so as not to be affected by German export restrictions will continue.[65]

When launching his plans for greater European military autonomy in 2017, Macron had wanted a 'common intervention force, a common defense budget, and a common doctrine for action.'[66] Significantly, Macron left the EU-linkage unmentioned, thus being free to assemble a military unit of countries with relevant military capacities and, no less important, the willingness to use them. This would open the way for a post-Brexit Britain to join, which is difficult to harmonize with Merkel's insistence that any armed force must be under EU control.[67] Moreover, the underlying differences between Germany and France in strategic outlook and use of military means remain unresolved, and these differences are particularly pronounced when the two countries are contrasted. Both have a long record of military co-operation. The visible expression of this co-operation is the Franco-German Brigade established in 1989.[68] When units from the Brigade are deployed, strict German rules of engagement mean that German soldiers leave the front line to the French.[69]

France's willingness to act as leader on European defense stops short of extending the role played by the country's nuclear weapons to other countries. Trump's disparaging NATO views cast doubts on continued US nuclear protection of the continent. Without it, could France or possibly Britain fill the need? The 2010 Lancaster House Treaty on military and security co-operation between the two countries underlines in the preamble that a threat to the 'vital interests' of one is shared by the other, giving each other a de facto mutual nuclear guarantee. Neither is willing to extend the protection to other countries; in a statement made in February 2019, Paris ruled out a pan-European role for French nuclear weapons.[70] Although French strategic thinking opens the way for a greater degree of concerted action with the country's

European allies, this is not the same as moving towards a European co-determination. There is no real substitute for the US nuclear umbrella.

Trans-Atlantic tensions

Whereas trans-Atlantic cohesion on how to respond to Russian aggression against Ukraine and the violations of the INF Treaty has so far been quite successful, China has caused the opposite response. It need not have been so: the economic importance of China is considerable to both the EU and the US. Like the US, the EU continues to record a significant trade deficit with China.[71] European firms experience exactly the same problems as their US counterparts concerning enforced technology transfer.[72] Still, instead of moving toward a joint approach, the US conflict with China has added to an already tenuous trans-Atlantic relationship. The Chinese telecommunications company Huawei is currently at the center of attention; US Secretary of State Mike Pompeo stated that, if NATO members chose the Chinese Huawei to supply the next generation of communication network, the US would have to be more careful sharing information.[73] The Secretary made the statement in Hungary, the country where Huawei has established a base for its activities in the region and invested more than $1.2 billion. How receptive the European audience is to US pressure depends largely on the perception of threat and the corresponding dependence on the US for protection. In Poland, the response has been very different from the one expressed in Germany where the response to the US position has been vehemently negative.[74]

The US is not without responsibility for the lack of European unity. Signs of EU division have been welcomed by President Trump, his open encouragement of Brexit being perhaps the most glaring illustration. His administration has attempted to exploit cracks in European unity on sensitive issues like the nuclear treaty with Iran, which the EU supports but Trump opposes. The decision to hold a US-sponsored Middle East Summit in Warsaw in early 2019 sought to divide the European countries and garner support for the US line on Iran. European initiatives seen as going against US interests provoke immediate and loud condemnations; the continued European support for the nuclear deal with Iran is an apt example.[75] Likewise, when Macron launched the idea of a European army, Trump's response was negative in the extreme.[76] However, it might be pertinent to recall that although Trump's tweets are new, trans-Atlantic distancing is not. President Obama was known for his disenchantment over the EU bureaucracy, where things took too long and what came out in the end was irrelevant.[77] He only paid a courtesy call to the EU headquarters just before his second term was up; his assistant Secretary of State Victoria Nuland and her use of expletives when referring to EU passivity during the Ukraine crisis in 2014 prove that the current administration's scant regard for the EU is long-standing.[78] Trump's coupling of security with trade, threatening the EU with punitive tariffs to avoid what his administration regards as unfair competition, is a new and worrisome signal.[79] Again, to balance the prevailing perception of Trump as an all-round wrecker, it is worth recalling that the Transatlantic Trade and Investment Pact agreed during Obama's administration was cancelled in 2016 well before Trump was elected: the US did not withdraw but the German government did. Officially, this was due to a lack of negotiations transparency; contradicting this, German observers saw the main reason as a distinct German lack of interest in consolidating the relationship with the US.[80]

Trump's harsh words and disparaging comments are not always reflected in the politics implemented. US troop presence in Central Europe has grown, new defense plans for the Northern flank have been launched, and command structures have been geared toward high intensity conflicts. The US has also decided to relaunch the Second Fleet responsible for the US

East Coast and the North Atlantic. In case of an attack, reinforcements for Europe would be transported across this area; without a US fleet presence it is questionable whether this would be possible. In addition, NATO established a Joint Force Command in Norfolk to sustain possible combat operations in the Atlantic. Trump has stated that the US will increase the sums allocated to the European Defence Initiative from $4.8 billion in 2018 to $6.5 billion in 2019.[81] The US deploys three brigades to Europe on a rotational basis. Ammunition and equipment storage in Europe is growing, not decreasing. The stationing of multinational units with US soldiers in the Baltic republics is a strong signal of Alliance unity; pressure has been growing that NATO should do the same in the Black Sea region in response to increased Russian military activity there.[82] Air and naval patrols in both the Baltic and the Norwegian Seas have grown. This is hardly the expression of US policy withdrawal. It is also very different from the Obama administration's belief in a 'reset' of relations with Russia.

A recent challenge to trans-Atlantic unity emerged when the US decided to withdraw from the Intermediate-Range Nuclear Forces Treaty signed in 1987. In 2013, Washington publicly alleged that Moscow had violated the pact by testing and had been deploying a prohibited cruise missile system since 2017.[83] Russia rejected calls for inspection. The general deterioration in NATO–Russia relations following the annexation of Crimea and the war in Ukraine are hardly conducive. Within NATO, and especially among the European members, concerns were expressed that the US withdrawal might potentially achieve what Russia, and before that, the Soviet Union had always aspired to: a division of trans-Atlantic security. The Russian intermediate missiles targeting Europe cannot reach the US mainland. Moreover, due to their mobility and thus difficulty of detection, they make allied reinforcements of flank countries (Norway, the Baltic republics, the Balkans) vulnerable. The missiles can be used to intimidate governments and people from retaliating against an attack due to the danger of being hit with nuclear war heads.[84] If so, the willingness to support a common response might be in jeopardy. NATO's immediate response demonstrated unity with all European members supporting the American position.[85] NATO has so far declared it will not respond with the deployment of new nuclear missiles. Popular opinion would have made that difficult.

Conclusion

Implicit in much of the survey given above is European impotence. Faced with hard security threats, the EU has no credible response. As referred to above, new initiatives have been undertaken and funding earmarked to facilitate closer military integration. Whether it will increase the military power of the Union is too early to say. Institutional innovations and the sums allocated cannot hide the fact that member countries have different priorities. Germany is the main brake, despite Chancellor Merkel's comments that Europe can no longer rely entirely on the US for its security needs.[86] She is not alone in this diagnosis, but her solution is very different from that proffered by her closest ally, France. To Germany, strengthening European security is primarily a tool to further European integration; to France it is about military strength.

Running the danger of committing exactly the same error I warned against in the introduction, i.e., mistaking written reports and resolutions for actual policy, there is clearly a will to address European security deficiencies more openly than in the past. Still, there is no European lead nation here. Kissinger's famous question that he did not know whom to phone when he wanted to talk to Europe remains valid. On all important security issues – Russia, China, the US – the initiative still seems to be largely state-by-state. The EU discusses the issues, makes resolutions, but it is up to each country to decide how far it will go. This is most evident in the case of China, where it is beyond the authority of the EU to block a Chinese take-over or investment. As implied above, Germany carries a large share of responsibility for this state of affairs. Whereas German politicians have often complained over the lack of a European approach or solutions to important issues, Nord Stream shows that the government in Berlin differs little from its EU colleagues when a lucrative business agreement is at stake. The unwillingness to forego national interest undermines all attempts to formulate a working European security strategy.

Notes

1 Paul Cornish and Geoffrey Edwards, "Beyond the EU/NATO Dichotomy: The Beginnings of a European Strategic Culture," *International Affairs* 77, no. 3 (2001): 587–603; Jolyon Howorth, "The CESDP and the Forging of a European Security Culture," *Politique européenne* 4, no. 8 (2002): 88–109; Victor Mauer, "Eine Sicherheits- und Verteidigungspolitik für Europa," *Aus Politik und Zeitgeschichte* 47 (2002): 22–30.

2 EU battlegroups may fit all of the three, agreed at the 1999 Helsinki Summit, declared to have reached operational capacity in 2007, though they have yet to be used.

3 European Union, *A Secure Europe in a Better World. European Security Strategy* (Brussels: General Affairs and External Relations Council, 2003). For an analysis of the security strategy: Asle Toje, "The 2003 European Union Security Strategy – a Critical Appraisal," *European Foreign Affairs Review* 9, no. 1 (2005): 117–34.

4 For a summary of this debate, see Helga Haftendorn, "NATO and the Arctic: Is the Atlantic Alliance a Cold War Relic in a Peaceful Region Now Faced with Non-Military Challenges?" *European Security* 20, no. 3 (2011): 337–61.

5 Eurostat, "File: EU-27 and Russia, trade in goods, 2000 to 2010 (EUR millions)" (Luxembourg: European Union, 2012), accessed April 4, 2019, https://ec.europa.eu/eurostat/statistics-explained/index.php?title=File:EU-27_and_Russia,_trade_in_goods,_2000_to_2010_(EUR_millions).PNG.

6 Paul Haenle and Erik Brattberg, "Shifting European Perceptions of China," *China in the World* podcast, episode 103 (Carnegie–Tsinghua Center for Global Policy, 2018).

7 "Chinese Democracy Proves Itself a Viable Alternative to West," *China Daily*, March 21, 2018; Benjamin Bidder, *Vereint gegen liberale Werte: Wie Russland den rechten Rand in Europa inspiriert und fördert* (Bonn: Bundeszentrale für politische Bildung, 2017).

8 Tor Bukkvoll, "Why Putin Went to War: Ideology, Interests and Decision-Making in the Russian Use of Force in Crimea and Donbas," *Contemporary Politics* 22, no. 3 (2016): 267–82; Rilka Drageva and Kataryna Wolczuk, *The Eurasian Economic Union. Deals, Rules and the Exercise of Power* (London: Chatham House, 2017), 11–12.

9 Dominique Moïsi, "L'Ukraine et la grande peur de la Russie face à la démocratie," *Les Echos*, February 3, 2014; Andrew Wilson, "The Ukraine Crisis Brings the Threat of Democracy to Russia's Doorstep," *European View* 13 (2014): 67–72.

10 Nicholas Watt, "UK Seeking to Ensure Russia Sanctions Do Not Harm City of London," *Guardian*, March 3, 2014.

11 "Russian Central Bank: Certain Chinese Credit Entities Treat Sanctions 'Broadly,'" *Sputnik News*, November 21, 2018.

12 Vladimir Putin, "Transcript: Vladimir Putin's April 17 Q&A," *Washington Post*, April 17, 2014; Andrei Kolesnikov, *Why the Kremlin Is Shutting Down the Novorossiya Project* (Moscow: Carnegie Moscow Center, 2015).

13 Iikka Korhonen, Heli Simola, and Laura Solanko, *Sanctions, Counter-Sanctions and Russia – Effects on Economy, Trade and Finance*, BOFIT Policy Brief 4 (BOFIT, 2018).

14 Martin Russell, "EU Sanctions: A Key Foreign and Security Policy Instrument," Briefing (Brussels: European Parliament, 2018), 7, 9.

15 Ibid., 9.

16 Philippe Loiseau, Louis Aliot, and Mylène Troszczynski, "Sanctions contre la Russie: Les Républicains seraient-ils schizophrènes?" Front National – Communiqués, 2016; Jörg Meuthen, "Dialog und Kooperation mit Russland statt Konfrontation und sinnlose Sanktionen," Alternative für Deutschland – Beiträge (2018).

17 "Italiens Innenminister Salvini droht mit Veto," *Frankfurter Allgemeine Zeitung*, July 16, 2018; "Strache fordert Ende von Russland-Sanktionen," *Die Presse*, June 2, 2018.

18 European Parliament, *Report on the State of EU-Russia Political Relations* (Brussels: Committee on Foreign Affairs, 2019), 5.
19 Tim B. Peters and Anastasiia Shapkina, *The Grand Stalemate of the Minsk Agreements* (Kharkiv: Konrad-Adenauer-Stiftung, 2019); United States Mission to the OSCE, *Ongoing Violations of International Law and Defiance of OSCE Principles and Commitments by the Russian Federation in Ukraine* (Washington, DC: Department of State, 2017).
20 Nikolaus von Twickel, *The State of the Donbass. A Study of Ukraine's Separatist-Held Areas* (Brussels: 3dcftas, 2019), 41.
21 Vladimir Socor, "Some Lessons from Germany's Failed Proposal on the Azov Sea and Kerch Strait," *Eurasia Daily Monitor* 15, no. 176 (2018).
22 Peter J. Marzalik and Aric Toler, "Lethal Weapons to Ukraine: A Primer," Atlantic Council (2018).
23 Randi Häussler, "Wie Gotland sich plötzlich von Nord Stream 2 abwendete," *Deutschlandfunk*, December 22, 2016.
24 Angela Merkel, "Rede von Bundeskanzlerin Merkel zur 55. Münchner Sicherheitskonferenz am 16. Februar 2019 in München," Die Bundeskanzlerin/Presse- und Informationsamt der Bundesregierung (2019). For an analysis of the economics behind Nord Stream: Mikhail Krutikhin, "Dorogo i serdito. Potsjemu 'Severnyj potok – 2' budet postrojen," *Republic*, May 3, 2018.
25 European Parliament, *Report on the State of EU-Russia Political Relations*, 10.
26 Stefan Meister, "Die Sackgasse der deutschen Ostpolitik: Wie die Bundesregierung ihre eigene Russland- und Ukrainepolitik torpediert," DGAPstandpunkt (2019).
27 "Schröder: Putin weiter 'lupenreiner Demokrat,'" *Frankfurter Allgemeine Zeitung*, March 7, 2012. Another politician-cum-lobbyist is the conservative Norbert Pflüger, see Ulrich Müller, "Friedbert Pflüger, Gas-Lobbyist mit Doppelrolle," LobbyControl (2018).
28 Pasquale de Micco, *A Cold Winter to Come? The EU Seeks Alternatives to Russian Gas* (Brussels: Directorate-General for External Policies Policy Department, European Parliament, 2014).
29 Philipp Fritz, "Deutschland schwimmt gegen den Strom," *Die Welt*, February 13, 2019.
30 Stefan Ulrich, "Deutschland muss mehr Rücksicht auf seine Partner nehmen," *Süddeutsche Zeitung*, February 8, 2019; Johanna Luyssen, "Le projet de gazoduc Nord Stream 2, signe de l'étiolement de la relation franco-allemande?," *Libération*, February 8, 2019.
31 Shaun Walker, "Putin Gets Puppy and Hero's Welcome on Serbia Trip," *Guardian*, January 17, 2019.
32 Maxim Samorukov, "Macedonia Joining NATO Is Self-Inflicted Defeat for Russia" Carnegie Moscow Center, 2019.
33 European Parliament, *Report on the State of EU-Russia Political Relations*, 7.
34 European Commission, *EU-China – A Strategic Outlook* (Brussels: High Representative of the Union for Foreign Affairs and Security Policy, 2019), 1.
35 Alice Ekman, "La Chine en Méditerranée: une presence émergente," Notes de l'Ifri (OCP/Ifri, 2018).
36 "Corruption Perceptions Index 2017," Transparency International, www.transparency.org/news/feature/corruption_perceptions_index_2017.
37 Joanna Kakissis, "Chinese Firms Now Hold Stakes in over a Dozen European Ports," *NPR*, November 9, 2018. The only known case where security concerns prevented a Chinese take-over of a port occurred in Sweden in 2018 "Kineser säger nej till djuphamn i Lysekil," *SVT Nyheter*, January 30, 2018.
38 Helena Smith, "Greece Blocks EU's Criticism at UN of China's Human Rights Record," *Guardian*, June 18, 2017.
39 Frédéric Lemaître, "L'Europe est incapable de se protéger face à la Chine," *Le Monde*, September 8, 2018; Valérie Nicquet, *Chinese Objectives in High Technology Acquisitions and Integration of Military and Civilian Capabilities: A Global Challenge* (Paris: Fondation pour la Recherche Stratégique, 2018).
40 Christophe Cornevin and Jean Chichizola, "Les techniques d'espionnage utilisées par la Chine pour piller le savoir-faire français," *Le Figaro*, September 23, 2018.
41 Kerstin Schwenn, "Chinesische Übernahme von westfälischem Maschinenbauer geplatzt," *Frankfurter Allgemeine Zeitung*, August 1, 2018. The Chinese company withdrew its offer immediately afterwards.
42 European Parliament, "EU Framework for FDI Screening," Briefing/EU Legislation in Progress (European Parliament, 2019).
43 European Commission, *EU-China – A Strategic Outlook.*
44 Tobias Piller, "Italien als Teil von Chinas neuer Seidenstraße," *Frankfurter Allgemeine Zeitung*, March 15, 2019; Jaroslav Spurný, "Miloš Zeman firmu Huawei neochrání," *Respekt*, January 29, 2019.

45 European Commission, *EU–China – A Strategic Outlook*, 2. Emphasis in the original.
46 Oliver Bräuner, "Beyond the Arms Embargo: EU Transfers of Defense and Dual-Use Technologies to China," *Journal of East Asian Studies* 13 (2013): 457–82.
47 Theresa Fallon, "Is the EU on the Same Page as the United States on China?," *The Asan Forum*, June 30, 2016.
48 Gunnar Wiegand, "Strengthening EU-U.S. Cooperation in the Asia-Pacific Region – Keynote & Panel 1," CSIS' EU-US Dialogue for the Asia-Pacific region initiative, accessed February 22, 2018. www.youtube.com/watch?v=YkRSrJGXpx0.
49 European Commission, *EU-China – A Strategic Outlook*, 7.
50 Kenneth Elkjær, "Efterretningstjeneste: Grønland skal passe på Kina," Kalaallit Nunaata Radioa/ Greenlandic Broadcasting Corporation, June 27, 2018.
51 Natalia Drozdiak, Nikos Chrysoloras, and Kitty Donaldson, "EU Considers Response to China Hacking after U.K. Evidence, Sources Say," Bloomberg, February 11, 2019.
52 Ibid.
53 The German CDU leader Annegret Kramp-Karrenbauer has proposed the building of an EU aircraft carrier to project the image of the EU as a 'peaceful power.' If ever to touch water, the peace emphasis would most likely preclude a deployment to the China Sea. Annegret Kramp-Karrenbauer, "Europa richtig machen," *Welt am Sonntag*, March 10, 2019.
54 For a survey of anti-EU parties in the Union, see Catherine De Vries, *Euroscepticism and the Future of European Integration* (Oxford: Oxford University Press, 2018), 129–52.
55 Matthew Karnitschnig, "The rise and fall of Macron's European revolution," *Politico*, December 5, 2018.
56 Jana Kobzova, "Easing the EU's Eastern Partnership Fatigue," Wider Europe Forum/European Council on Foreign Relations, 2017.
57 Madeleine Albright, "Statement to the North Atlantic Council Brussels, Belgium, December 8, 1998. As released by the Office of the Spokesman U.S. Department of State." U.S. Department of State Archive, 1998.
58 Robin Emmott and Steve Holland, "Trump Directly Scolds NATO Allies, Says They Owe 'Massive' Sums," Reuters, May 25, 2017.
59 European Commission, *Reflection Paper on the Future of the European Defence* (Brussels: European Union, 2017).
60 See Chapter 8.
61 European External Action Service, "Permanent Structured Cooperation – PESCO. Deepening Defence Cooperation among EU Member States," factsheet on EEAS website, #EUDefence (EEAS, 2018).
62 Joshua Beer, "Machen 34 Projekte die EU verteidigungsfähig?," *Frankfurter Allgemeine Zeitung*, March 26, 2019.
63 "Seven European Countries Make the Top 10 of World's Major Arms Exporters," *Euronews*, March 11, 2019.
64 German components produced on license in third countries are not subject to the same rules; see Johanna Luyssen, "Berlin bloque Riyad et désarme ses partenaires," *Libération*, February 28, 2018.
65 Anne-Marie Descôtes, "Vom 'German-free' zum gegenseitigen Vertrauen," Arbeitspapier Sicherheitspolitik, no. 7 (Bundesakademie für Sicherheitspolitik, 2019).
66 Emmanuel Macron, "Initiative pour l'Europe – Discours d'Emmanuel Macron pour une Europe souveraine, unie, démocratique," *L'Élysée*, September 26, 2017, 1.
67 Ottfried Nassauer, "Gastkommentar EU-Verteidigungspolitik. Der kleine, aber feine Unterschied," *taz*, November 19, 2018; Jacopo Barigazzi, "Door Opens to Keep Britain in EU (Security)," *Politico*, September 5, 2018.
68 Thomas Hanke, "The French-German Brigade That Could Be the Basis of an EU Army," *Handelsblatt*, November 2, 2018. The brigade has been deployed to Mali; for a French view of its role see Hannah Peters and Mathieu Boch, "Mali: la France combat, l'Allemagne critique," *Info et société: Décryptages* (www.arte.tv, 2019).
69 Florian Flade and Torsten Jungholt, "Frankreichs Krieg und Deutschlands Beitrag," *Die Welt*, September 16, 2018; Harald Kujat, "Europäische Armee oder Nato – Was will die Bundesregierung denn nun?," *Die Welt*, November 18, 2018.
70 Michaela Wiegel, "Frankreich will Deutschland keinen nuklearen Schutz garantieren," *Frankfurter Allgemeine Zeitung*, February 14, 2019.

71 Anna Saarela, *A New Era in EU-China Relations: More Wide-Ranging Strategic Cooperation?* (Brussels: Policy Department for External Relations, European Parliament, 2018), 12.
72 World Trade Organisation, "DS549: China – Certain Measures on the Transfer of Technology," dispute settlement, January 21, 2019.
73 Nick Wadhams and Zoltan Simon, "Pompeo Hints at Huawei Ultimatum to Countries Buying Equipment," Bloomberg, February 12, 2019.
74 Bojan Pancevski and Sara Germano, "Drop Huawei or See Intelligence Sharing Pared Back, U.S. Tells Germany," *Wall Street Journal*, March 18, 2019; Krzysztof Ziemiec, "Brudziński o wykluczeniu Huawei z polskiego rynku: Coraz częściej tego typu argumenty padają," *rmf24*, January 12, 2019; Johannes Leithäuser, "Amerika droht Deutschland mit Einschränkung der Geheimdienstkooperation," *Frankfurter Allgemeine Zeitung*, March 11, 2019.
75 Nicole Gaouette, Allie Maloy, and Kylie Atwood, "Trump Admin Pushes for Tougher Action on Iran, Swipes at Europe," *CNN Politics*, February 14, 2019.
76 "Armée européenne: Trump juge les propos de Macron 'très insultants,'" *Le Figaro*, November 9, 2018.
77 Kristian L. Nielsen, "Continued Drift, but without the Acrimony: US European Relations under Barack Obama," *Journal of Transatlantic Studies* 11, no. 1 (2013): 83–108.
78 Jonathan Marcus, "Ukraine Crisis: Transcript of Leaked Nuland-Pyatt Call," BBC News, February 7, 2014.
79 David J. Lynch, Josh Dawsey, and Damian Paletta, "Trump Imposes Steel and Aluminum Tariffs on the E.U., Canada and Mexico," *Washington Post*, August 31, 2018.
80 Matthias Bauer, "Pferd(e) und Reiter in den Protest-Kampagnen um TTIP in Deutschland und Europa," ECIPE Policy Brief (ECIPE, 2016); Ludvig Greven, "Lechts und Rinks kann man verwechseln," *Die Zeit*, October 2, 2016.
81 Piotr Buras and Josef Janning, *Divided at the Centre: Germany, Poland and the Troubles of the Trump Era*, Policy Brief (European Council of Foreign Relations/Konrad-Adenauer-Stiftung, 2018), 10–11.
82 "Russland hat dramatisch aufgerüstet," *Die Welt*, February 15, 2019.
83 U.S. Department of State, "Russia's Violation of the Intermediate-Range Nuclear Forces (INF) Treaty," fact sheet (U.S. Department of State, 2018).
84 There is nothing new in this, as in 2015 the Russian ambassador to Denmark threatened his host country with a nuclear attack should Denmark join NATO's anti-missile defense system; see Adam Whitnall, "Russia Threatens Denmark with Nuclear Weapons if it Tries to Join Nato Defence Shield," *Independent*, March 22, 2015.
85 Quentin Lopinot, *American Withdrawal from the INF Treaty: What Consequences for Europe's Defense?* (Paris: Institut Montaigne, 2018).
86 James Kirchick, "Die neue Distanz der Angela Merkel," *Frankfurter Allgemeine Zeitung*, May 31, 2017.

Bibliography

Albright, Madeleine. "Statement to the North Atlantic Council Brussels, Belgium, December 8, 1998. As released by the Office of the Spokesman U.S. Department of State." U.S. Department of State Archive, 1998.
"Armée européenne: Trump juge les propos de Macron 'très insultants.'" *Le Figaro*, November 9, 2018.
Barigazzi, Jacopo. "Door Opens to Keep Britain in EU (Security)." *Politico*, September 5, 2018.
Bauer, Matthias. "Pferd(e) und Reiter in den Protest-Kampagnen um TTIP in Deutschland und Europa." ECIPE Policy Brief. ECIPE, 2016.
Beer, Joshua. "Machen 34 Projekte die EU verteidigungsfähig?" *Frankfurter Allgemeine Zeitung*, March 26, 2019.
Bidder, Benjamin. *Vereint gegen liberale Werte: Wie Russland den rechten Rand in Europa inspiriert und fördert.* Bonn: Bundeszentrale für politische Bildung, 2017.
Bräuner, Oliver. "Beyond the Arms Embargo: EU Transfers of Defense and Dual-Use Technologies to China." *Journal of East Asian Studies* 13 (2013): 457–82.
Bukkvoll, Tor. "Why Putin Went to War: Ideology, Interests and Decision-Making in the Russian Use of Force in Crimea and Donbas." *Contemporary Politics* 22, no. 3 (2016): 267–82.
Buras, Piotr, and Josef Janning. *Divided at the Centre: Germany, Poland and the Troubles of the Trump Era.* Policy Brief. European Council of Foreign Relations/Konrad-Adenauer-Stiftung, 2018.
"Chinese Democracy Proves Itself a Viable Alternative to West." *China Daily*, March 21, 2018.

Cornevin, Christophe, and Jean Chichizola. "Les techniques d'espionnage utilisées par la Chine pour piller le savoir-faire français." *Le Figaro*, September 23, 2018.
Cornish, Paul, and Geoffrey Edwards. "Beyond the EU/NATO Dichotomy: The Beginnings of a European Strategic Culture." *International Affairs* 77, no. 3 (2001): 587–603.
"Corruption Perceptions Index 2017." Transparency International. Published electronically February 21, 2018. www.transparency.org/news/feature/corruption_perceptions_index_2017.
De Micco, Pasquale. *A Cold Winter to Come? The EU Seeks Alternatives to Russian Gas*. Brussels: Directorate-General for External Policies Policy Department, European Parliament, 2014.
Descôtes, Anne-Marie. "Vom 'German-free' zum gegenseitigen Vertrauen." Arbeitspapier Sicherheitspolitik, no. 7. Bundesakademie für Sicherheitspolitik, 2019.
De Vries, Catherine. *Euroscepticism and the Future of European Integration*. Oxford: Oxford University Press, 2018.
Drageva, Rilka, and Kataryna Wolczuk. *The Eurasian Economic Union. Deals, Rules and the Exercise of Power*. London: Chatham House, 2017.
Drozdiak, Natalia, Nikos Chrysoloras, and Kitty Donaldson. "EU Considers Response to China Hacking after U.K. Evidence, Sources Say." Bloomberg, February 11, 2019.
Ekman, Alice. "La Chine en Méditerranée: une presence émergente." Notes de l'Ifri. OCP/Ifri, 2018.
Elkjær, Kenneth. "Efterretningstjeneste: Grønland skal passe på Kina." Kalaallit Nunaata Radioa/Greenlandic Broadcasting Corporation, June 27, 2018.
Emmott, Robin, and Steve Holland. "Trump Directly Scolds NATO Allies, Says They Owe 'Massive' Sums." Reuters, May 25, 2017.
European Commission. *EU-China – A Strategic Outlook*. Brussels: High Representative of the Union for Foreign Affairs and Security Policy, 2019.
European Commission. *European Economic Forecast. Winter 2019*. Luxemburg: Publications Office of the European Union, 2019.
European Commission. *Reflection Paper on the Future of the European Defence*. Brussels: European Union, 2017.
European External Action Service. "Permanent Structured Cooperation – PESCO. Deepening Defence Cooperation among EU Member States." Factsheet on EEAS website, #EUDefence (2018).
European Parliament. "EU Framework for FDI Screening." Briefing/EU Legislation in Progress. European Parliament, 2019.
European Parliament. *Report on the State of EU-Russia Political Relations*. Brussels: Committee on Foreign Affairs, 2019.
European Union. *A Secure Europe in a Better World. European Security Strategy*. Brussels: General Affairs and External Relations Council, 2003.
Eurostat, "File: EU-27 and Russia, trade in goods, 2000 to 2010 (EUR millions)." Luxembourg: European Union, 2012. Published electronically January 25, 2012. https://ec.europa.eu/eurostat/statistics-explained/index.php?title=File:EU-27_and_Russia,_trade_in_goods,_2000_to_2010_(EUR_millions).PNG.
Fallon, Theresa. "Is the EU on the Same Page as the United States on China?" *The Asan Forum*, June 30, 2016.
Flade, Florian, and Torsten Jungholt. "Frankreichs Krieg und Deutschlands Beitrag." *Die Welt*, September 16, 2018.
Fritz, Philipp. "Deutschland schwimmt gegen den Strom." *Die Welt*, February 13, 2019.
Gaouette, Nicole, Allie Maloy, and Kylie Atwood. "Trump Admin Pushes for Tougher Action on Iran, Swipes at Europe." *CNN Politics*, February 14, 2019.
Greven, Ludvig. "Lechts und Rinks kann man verwechseln." *Die Zeit*, October 2, 2016.
Haenle, Paul, and Erik Brattberg. "Shifting European Perceptions of China." *China in the World*, episode 103. Podcast. Carnegie–Tsinghua Center for Global Policy, 2018.
Haftendorn, Helga. "NATO and the Arctic: Is the Atlantic Alliance a Cold War Relic in a Peaceful Region Now Faced with Non-Military Challenges?" *European Security* 20, no. 3 (2011): 337–61.
Hanke, Thomas. "The French-German Brigade That Could Be the Basis of an EU Army." *Handelsblatt*, November 2, 2018.
Häussler, Randi. "Wie Gotland sich plötzlich von Nord Stream 2 abwendete." *Deutschlandfunk*, December 22, 2016.
Howorth, Jolyon. "The CESDP and the Forging of a European Security Culture." *Politique européenne* 4, no. 8 (2002): 88–109.

"Italiens Innenminister Salvini droht mit Veto." *Frankfurter Allgemeine Zeitung*, July 16, 2018.
Kakissis, Joanna. "Chinese Firms Now Hold Stakes in over a Dozen European Ports." *NPR*, November 9, 2018.
Karnitschnig, Matthew. "The rise and fall of Macron's European revolution." *Politico*, December 5, 2018.
"Kineser säger nej till djuphamn i Lysekil." *SVT Nyheter*, January 30, 2018.
Kirchick, James. "Die neue Distanz der Angela Merkel." *Frankfurter Allgemeine Zeitung*, May 31, 2017.
Kobzova, Jana. "Easing the EU's Eastern Partnership Fatigue." Wider Europe Forum/European Council on Foreign Relations, 2017.
Kolesnikov, Andrei. *Why the Kremlin Is Shutting Down the Novorossiya Project*. Moscow: Carnegie Moscow Center, 2015.
Korhonen, Iikka, Heli Simola, and Laura Solanko. *Sanctions, Counter-Sanctions and Russia – Effects on Economy, Trade and Finance*. BOFIT Policy Brief 4. BOFIT, 2018.
Kramp-Karrenbauer, Annegret. "Europa richtig machen." *Welt am Sonntag*, March 10, 2019.
Krutikhin, Mikhail. "Dorogo i serdito. Potsjemu 'Severnyj potok – 2' budet postrojen." *Republic*, May 3, 2018.
Kujat, Harald. "Europäische Armee oder Nato – Was will die Bundesregierung denn nun?" *Die Welt*, November 18, 2018.
Leithäuser, Johannes. "Amerika droht Deutschland mit Einschränkung der Geheimdienstkooperation." *Frankfurter Allgemeine Zeitung*, March 11, 2019.
Lemaître, Frédéric. "L'Europe est incapable de se protéger face à la Chine." *Le Monde*, September 8, 2018.
Loiseau, Philippe, Louis Aliot, and Mylène Troszczynski. "Sanctions contre la Russie: Les Républicains seraient-ils schizophrènes?" Front National – Communiqués, 2016.
Lopinot, Quentin. *American Withdrawal from the INF Treaty: What Consequences for Europe's Defense?* Paris: Institut Montaigne, 2018.
Luyssen, Johanna. "Berlin bloque Riyad et désarme ses partenaires." *Libération*, February 28, 2018.
Luyssen, Johanna. "Le projet de gazoduc Nord Stream 2, signe de l'étiolement de la relation franco-allemande?" *Libération*, February 8, 2019.
Lynch, David J., Josh Dawsey, and Damian Paletta. "Trump Imposes Steel and Aluminum Tariffs on the E.U., Canada and Mexico." *Washington Post*, August 31, 2018.
Macron, Emmanuel. "Initiative pour l'Europe – Discours d'Emmanuel Macron pour une Europe souveraine, unie, démocratique." *L'Élysée*, September 26, 2017.
Marcus, Jonathan. "Ukraine Crisis: Transcript of Leaked Nuland-Pyatt Call." BBC News, February 7, 2014.
Marzalik, Peter J., and Aric Toler. "Lethal Weapons to Ukraine: A Primer." Atlantic Council, 2018.
Mauer, Victor. "Eine Sicherheits- und Verteidigungspolitik für Europa." *Aus Politik und Zeitgeschichte* 47 (2002): 22–30.
Meister, Stefan. "Die Sackgasse der deutschen Ostpolitik: Wie die Bundesregierung ihre eigene Russland- und Ukrainepolitik torpediert." DGAPstandpunkt, 2019.
Merkel, Angela. "Rede von Bundeskanzlerin Merkel zur 55. Münchner Sicherheitskonferenz am 16. Februar 2019 in München." Die Bundeskanzlerin/Presse- und Informationsamt der Bundesregierung, 2019.
Meuthen, Jörg. "Dialog und Kooperation mit Russland statt Konfrontation und sinnlose Sanktionen." Alternative für Deutschland – Beiträge, 2018.
Moïsi, Dominique. "L'Ukraine et la grande peur de la Russie face à la démocratie." *Les Echos*, February 3, 2014.
Müller, Ulrich. "Friedbert Pflüger, Gas-Lobbyist mit Doppelrolle." LobbyControl, 2018.
Nassauer, Ottfried. "Gastkommentar EU-Verteidigungspolitik. Der kleine, aber feine Unterschied." *taz*, November 19, 2018.
Nicquet, Valérie. *Chinese Objectives in High Technology Acquisitions and Integration of Military and Civilian Capabilities: A Global Challenge*. Paris: Fondation pour la Recherche Stratégique, 2018.
Nielsen, Kristian L. "Continued Drift, but without the Acrimony: US European Relations under Barack Obama." *Journal of Transatlantic Studies* 11, no. 1 (2013): 83–108.
Pancevski, Bojan, and Sara Germano. "Drop Huawei or See Intelligence Sharing Pared Back, U.S. Tells Germany." *Wall Street Journal*, March 18, 2019.
Peters, Hannah, and Mathieu Boch. "Mali: la France combat, l'Allemagne critique." In *Info et société: Décryptages*. www.arte.tv, 2019.

Peters, Tim B., and Anastasiia Shapkina. *The Grand Stalemate of the Minsk Agreements*. Kharkiv: Konrad-Adenauer-Stiftung, 2019.
Piller, Tobias. "Italien als Teil von Chinas neuer Seidenstraße." *Frankfurter Allgemeine Zeitung*, March 13, 2019.
Putin, Vladimir. "Transcript: Vladimir Putin's April 17 Q&A." *Washington Post*, April 17, 2014.
Russell, Martin. "EU Sanctions: A Key Foreign and Security Policy Instrument." Briefing. Brussels: European Parliament, 2018.
"Russian Central Bank: Certain Chinese Credit Entities Treat Sanctions 'Broadly.'" *Sputnik News*, November 21, 2018.
"Russland hat dramatisch aufgerüstet." *Die Welt*, February 15, 2019.
Saarela, Anna. *A New Era in EU-China Relations: More Wide-Ranging Strategic Cooperation?* Brussels: Policy Department for External Relations, European Parliament, 2018.
Samorukov, Maxim. "Macedonia Joining NATO Is Self-Inflicted Defeat for Russia." Carnegie Moscow Center, 2019.
"Schröder: Putin weiter 'lupenreiner Demokrat.'" *Frankfurter Allgemeine Zeitung*, March 7, 2012.
Schwenn, Kerstin. "Chinesische Übernahme von westfälischem Maschinenbauer geplatzt." *Frankfurter Allgemeine Zeitung*, August 1, 2018.
"Seven European Countries Make the Top 10 of World's Major Arms Exporters." *Euronews*, March 11, 2019.
Smith, Helena. "Greece Blocks EU's Criticism at UN of China's Human Rights Record." *Guardian*, June 18, 2017.
Socor, Vladimir. "Some Lessons from Germany's Failed Proposal on the Azov Sea and Kerch Strait." *Eurasia Daily Monitor* 15, no. 176 (2018).
Spurný, Jaroslav. "Miloš Zeman firmu Huawei neochrání." *Respekt*, January 29, 2019.
"Strache fordert Ende von Russland-Sanktionen." *Die Presse*, June 2, 2018.
Toje, Asle. "The 2003 European Union Security Strategy – a Critical Appraisal." *European Foreign Affairs Review* 9, no. 1 (2005): 117–34.
Ulrich, Stefan. "Deutschland muss mehr Rücksicht auf seine Partner nehmen." *Süddeutsche Zeitung*, February 8, 2019.
United States Mission to the OSCE. *Ongoing Violations of International Law and Defiance of OSCE Principles and Commitments by the Russian Federation in Ukraine*. Washington, DC: Department of State, 2017.
U.S. Department of State. "Russia's Violation of the Intermediate-Range Nuclear Forces (INF) Treaty." Fact sheet. U.S. Department of State, 2018.
Von Twickel, Nikolaus. *The State of the Donbass. A Study of Ukraine's Separatist-Held Areas*. Brussels: 3dcftas, 2019.
Wadhams, Nick, and Zoltan Simon. "Pompeo Hints at Huawei Ultimatum to Countries Buying Equipment." Bloomberg, February 12, 2019.
Walker, Shaun. "Putin Gets Puppy and Hero's Welcome on Serbia Trip." *Guardian*, January 17, 2019.
Watt, Nicholas. "UK Seeking to Ensure Russia Sanctions Do Not Harm City of London." *Guardian*, March 3, 2014.
Whitnall, Adam. "Russia Threatens Denmark with Nuclear Weapons if It Tries to Join Nato Defence Shield." *Independent*, March 22, 2015.
Wiegand, Gunnar. "Strengthening EU–U.S. Cooperation in the Asia-Pacific Region – Keynote & Panel 1." CSIS' EU-US Dialogue for the Asia-Pacific region initiative. Published electronically February 18, 2016. www.youtube.com/watch?v=YkRSrJGXpx0.
Wiegel, Michaela. "Frankreich will Deutschland keinen nuklearen Schutz garantieren." *Frankfurter Allgemeine Zeitung*, February 14, 2019.
Wilson, Andrew. "The Ukraine Crisis Brings the Threat of Democracy to Russia's Doorstep." *European View* 13 (2014): 67–72.
World Trade Organisation. "DS549: China – Certain Measures on the Transfer of Technology." Dispute settlement, January 21, 2019.
Ziemiec, Krzysztof. "Brudziński o wykluczeniu Huawei z polskiego rynku: Coraz częściej tego typu argumenty padają." *rmf24*, January 12, 2019.

2

POLICE AND PROSECUTORIAL COOPERATION IN EUROPE IN RESPONSE TO SERIOUS TRANSNATIONAL CRIME[1]

Gorazd Meško, Rajko Kozmelj and Branko Lobnikar

Introduction: a historical perspective on police and prosecutorial cooperation in the EU

Police and prosecutorial cooperation in the EU is an ongoing process that develops in response to changes in the European social and business environment, both in the EU Member States and in the world beyond the continent. From the time when the so-called *Maastricht Treaty* or the Treaty on European Union was signed in Maastricht on February 7, 1992 and entered into force on November 1, 1993, until now, we have witnessed the continuous strengthening of cooperation in Justice and Home Affairs among the Member States and within the institutions of the EU. In the meantime, however, EU Member States agreed to only limited amounts of formal police cooperation, an area which has been left largely to higher level international negotiations on enhanced cooperation. In the Treaty of Amsterdam, which was signed on October 2, 1997 and came into force on May 1, 1999, specific policies were established with regard to three core aspects: *freedom, security* and *justice*. The Treaty of Amsterdam introduced the concepts of "area of freedom, security, and justice" in place of the conventional concepts of "justice and home affairs." The concept of freedom indicates a common policy of free movement, an asylum system and legal immigration in the EU; the concept of justice pertains to EU policies on justice matters; and the concept of security denotes common policies on crime and terrorism. As pointed out by the European Council in Tampere on October 15–16, 1999, the aim was to combine the freedom of movement within the EU with a high level of security and legal guarantees for all Member States.

With the Treaty of Lisbon, which was signed on December 13, 2007 and came into force on December 1, 2009, the EU took a noteworthy step forward to further strengthen police cooperation within the EU. Up to this point, police and prosecutorial cooperation had undergone a number of key foundational changes in legislative procedures and to a lesser extent in operational cooperation as the legislative initiatives of the European Commission grew more robust over time. The implementation processes of the Treaty[2] reinforced the role of Justice and Home Affairs agencies within the Member States, and further promoted operational police cooperation between and among EU Member States within the EU policy cycle.[3]

The Commission continued to work with all Member States on the full implementation and application of existing information systems, notably with those Member States that are still at an insufficiently advanced stage of implementation of the EU Passenger Name Record (PNR) Directive;[4] this directive had to be to be fully implemented by May 25, 2018. The Commission will also be taking action to step up the support provided to Member States for countering radicalisation, in both off-line and on-line forms, in particular by following up on the preliminary findings and recommendations of the High-Level Expert Group on Radicalisation[5] and by stepping up work with Internet platforms against terrorist content posted on-line. Preventing and countering radicalisation remains a key challenge for Member States that requires a collective approach between national governments and local level stakeholders. The Expert Group, established in July 2017 to elaborate recommendations for future work, identified a number of priority topics that require further action.

In Europe, institutions with the mandate for prevention, detection, investigation and prosecution of crime are subject to rapid changes and new security challenges associated with those changes. Improved and more accessible transport infrastructure and the development of the Internet further facilitated the nefarious activities of organised crime. The European Parliament resolution on organised crime in the EU[6] points out that organised crime has a substantial social cost, in that it violates human rights, undermines democratic principles, and diverts and wastes financial, human and other scarce resources, distorting the free internal market, contaminating businesses and legitimate economic activities, encouraging corruption and often polluting and destroying the environment.

One of the primary objectives of the European Union is to create an area of freedom, security and justice without internal borders, one in which crime is effectively prevented and combated. Another objective is to ensure a high level of security through measures that prevent and combat crime and measures for active coordination and cooperation between police and judicial authorities and other competent authorities. Likewise, through the mutual recognition of judgements in criminal matters and, if necessary, through the approximation of criminal laws it is intended that police and prosecutorial cooperation will lead to a safer, more just and secure EU community.

The purpose of this chapter is to present recent instruments of the European Union that are governing the field of police and prosecutorial cooperation at the level of the European Union. What follows is a presentation of the legal frameworks and organisational forms of police and prosecutorial cooperation in the contemporary EU.

Contemporary main challenges to security and EU response to them

At the beginning of the decade, in both the Special Eurobarometer[7] and Standard Eurobarometer,[8] EU citizens accorded a very high level of importance to internal security. According to respondents from EU countries, the most important security risk is that of economic and financial crisis (34 per cent); in second place is terrorism (33 per cent); and in third, organised crime (21 per cent). The Eurobarometer results (2018) also indicate that four out of ten EU citizens believe that the EU needs better instruments in the ongoing fight against organised crime, terrorism and violent extremism.

The ten EU security priorities formally identified are based on the recommendations made in the European Union Serious and Organised Crime Threat Assessment (SOCTA)[9] prepared by the European Police Office (Europol) in 2017. The priorities are as follows:

1 At the top of the list, we can find *cybercrime*. Every year, €400 billion is lost globally due to cyberattacks. The EU intends to boost its fight against cybercrime, focusing on three areas:

countering attacks against information technology systems; tackling non-cash payment fraud; and improving the safety of children on-line, including by combating the production and distribution of child abuse content.

2 *Drug trafficking* and drug production remain among the most profitable activities for criminal organisations in the EU. For the next five years, the EU would like to reduce the production and traffic of synthetic drugs, such as ecstasy and LSD, and to disrupt the criminal activities of organisations smuggling cannabis, heroin and cocaine into the EU.
3 Facilitation of *illegal immigration* into the EU is a very recent security challenge. Migrant smuggling to Europe has been largely driven by criminal traffickers. Today, 90 per cent of migrants pay traffickers to reach Europe. So, the goal in this area is to tackle the criminal networks which exploit vulnerable migrants, especially those which use methods that endanger people's lives, offer their services on-line and use document fraud as part of their business model.
4 *Organised theft and burglary* are issues of concern in Europe. The EU seeks to disrupt international criminal groups that currently exploit the lack of interoperability between cross-border surveillance tools to perpetrate domestic burglaries, steal cars or target businesses.
5 Not only in connection with the illegal migrations, *trafficking in human beings* remains an important area for relocating security resources. The EU aims to target trafficking in people in the EU, especially sexual and labour exploitation and all forms of child trafficking. The identification of victims and their protection is the main goal.
6 Dealing with excise (e.g. alcohol, tobacco and energy duties)[10] and *missing trader intra community* (MTIC) fraud is also an important challenge. Every year, €60 billion is stolen by crime groups that exploit the way VAT is treated in cross-border transactions.
7 Experience gained in the previous policy cycle will be used to target criminal groups. The EU is committed to disrupting the criminal organisations that *traffic in firearms, distribute firearms and use firearms.*
8 *Environmental crime* has become one of the world's most profitable organised criminal activities. It has an impact not only on the environment, but also on society and the economy as a whole. The EU will focus its activities on disruption of criminal organisations involved in wildlife trafficking and combating those involved in illegal waste trafficking.
9 Profit is the ultimate goal of criminals and innovations in financial services – such as virtual currencies and anonymous pre-paid cards – have created new opportunities for *money laundering and financial crime*. The EU aims to confiscate the profits criminal networks generate by money laundering, target businesses offering money-laundering services, and target criminal organisations which use new payment methods to launder money earned as profit of crime.
10 In connection with the main security challenges described above, combating *document fraud* is important. Travel document security is important in the fight against terrorism and organised crime, and likewise contributes to border protection and migration management. The EU aims to target criminal organisations involved in the production of false documents and their provision to other criminals.[11]

The Member States and Europol adopted an upgraded system to detect threats of certain types of serious and organised crime, and to determine priorities for the suppression of organised crime and serious international crime. During the sessions of November 8 and 9, 2010, the Justice and Home Affairs Council decided that in the field of serious international and organised crime a multi-annual cycle must be developed and implemented. The *EU policy cycle for serious international and organised crime*[12] aims to improve the detection, identification, and decision making on the priority tasks of the EU as a response to threats to internal security. The purpose of this policy cycle is to establish a coordinated and methodically arranged manner of data collection in collaboration with the competent services of Member States, EU institutions, EU agencies, third countries and other relevant stakeholder organisations. The EU policy cycle on serious international and organised crime for 2018–2021 consists of taking four specific steps.

- *Assessment of criminal threats impacting the EU.*
  The European Union Serious and Organised Crime Threat Assessment provides a complete picture of major criminal threats.
- *Adoption of the EU crime priorities for 2018–2021.*
  On the basis of the recommendations identified in the EU SOCTA, but also taking into account other assessments and policies, the Council adopted ten EU crime priorities. For each of these priorities, a four-year multi-annual strategic plan (MASP) was developed. The MASPs were then translated into one-year operational action plans (OAP) which detail the actions and activities required to achieve the strategic goals set out in the MASP. Both the MASP and the OAP are adopted by the Standing Committee on Operational Cooperation on Internal Security (COSI) of the Council of the European Union.
- *Implementation and monitoring.*
  The implementation of an OAP is led by a Member State, the so-called driver, and is monitored by COSI every six months.
- *Evaluation.*
  An independent assessment of the policy cycle will be carried out at the end. The results will be transmitted to the Council, and will feed into the next EU policy cycle.

Police and prosecutorial cooperation in the EU: recent institutional and legal developments

At the end of 2009, the new Treaty on European Union[13] (TEU) and the Treaty on the Functioning of the European Union[14] (TFEU), together known as the Treaty of Lisbon,[15] created an important new legal framework for cooperation between Member States in the prevention, detection, investigation and prosecution of crime. EU Member States have set a goal that the EU shall set up measures for internal security and thus be more able to act proactively in the areas of freedom, security and justice, concrete measures which will directly increase the effectiveness of the fight against serious crime, including terrorism. In regard to the European legal system, the most noteworthy enhancements of the Treaty of Lisbon are key changes in the law-making and decision-making process of the EU. Police cooperation has previously been subject to a consensus-seeking process within the Council of the EU, a process which has now been turned into a qualified majority voting decision-making process under the provisions of the Treaty of Lisbon.[16] The changes also affect the role of the European Parliament since, until the Treaty of Lisbon entered into force, any legislative acts in the field of police and judicial cooperation were adopted only in consultation with the European Parliament. It is now established that police cooperation will be viewed as a feature of the regular legislative process; the European Parliament is now directly involved in the ongoing coordination and legislative decision-making process pertaining to police cooperation. Furthermore, another important change in the EU legal system has been introduced providing that EU measures and national measures adopted in these areas are subject to judicial review by the EU Court of Justice after a five-year transition period, or after the adoption of a new act within that period. All of these institutional changes noted will serve to the development of a more coherent common framework for police cooperation for the EU.

Another key new feature introduced by the Treaty of Lisbon was a mechanism for the coordination of crime prevention measures in the EU. Within the framework of the Council of the EU, the *Standing Committee on Operational Co-operation on Internal Security* (COSI) – mentioned above – was established. It started operating by a special decision of the EU Council[17] and had its first meeting in March 2010. The COSI[18] looks at deepening the cooperation between Justice and Home Affairs (JHA) agencies, as well as looking at ways to improve Member States' data supply to the JHA agencies and enhanced cooperation between and among Member States. When the COSI started operating, the formal role of the working group of the European police chiefs – the European Police Chiefs Task Force – was abolished.

It is also important to point out the so-called solidarity clause with respect to EU legal system changes recently made. With Article 222, the Treaty of Lisbon established a mechanism for mutual assistance in case one of the Member States is affected by a terrorist attack, natural disaster or human-induced disaster. The purpose of this mechanism is that the EU becomes better equipped, better organised and more successful in the event of major disasters affecting the internal security of the community of nations.

From the perspective of some other institutional advances that have taken place at EU level recently in the field of police and prosecutorial cooperation, the following agencies should be borne in mind.

- **The European Police Office**[19] (Europol), which in 2010 became an EU agency, has won a key role in providing support to the competent national authorities to manage crime. The Treaty of Lisbon has defined the tasks of Europol as that of supporting and strengthening action by the Member States' police authorities and other law enforcement services and facilitating their mutual cooperation in preventing and combating serious crime affecting two or more Member States, terrorism and forms of crime which affect a common interest covered by a Union policy (Article 88). In 2016, within the implementation process of the Treaty of Lisbon (so-called "*lisbonisation*" of EU agencies), the EU adopted a new founding act for Europol – Regulation (EU) 2016/794. In accordance with Article 6 of the Regulation on Europol regarding a request by Europol for the initiation of a criminal investigation, this may take place in specific cases where it considers that a criminal investigation should be initiated into a crime falling within the scope of its objectives. Europol is empowered to request the competent authorities of the Member States concerned via the national units to initiate, conduct or coordinate such a criminal investigation. Europol national units are required to inform Europol without delay of the decision of the competent authorities of the Member States. Europol adapted its internal structure to better respond to the new security challenges at stake and established the Internet Referral Unit (IRU), the European Cybercrime Centre (EC3), the European Migrant Smuggling Centre (EMSC), the European Counter Terrorism Centre (ECTC), and the Intellectual Property Crime Coordinated Coalition (IPC3). Europol also incorporated Financial Intelligence Units (FIU.net) within its structure in January 2016, and in 2017 Europol initiated the development of a Situation Report on Counterfeiting and Piracy in the European Union.
- Council Decision 2002/187/JHA of February 28, 2002 resulted in setting up **Eurojust**[20] with a view to reinforcing the fight against serious crime. This decision was amended by Council Decision 2003/659/JHA and by Council Decision 2009/426/JHA of December 16, 2008 on the strengthening of Eurojust. The "lisbonisation" of Eurojust has not yet been completed. In its meeting in December 2014, the Council reached an agreement on a partial general approach on a regulation on Eurojust (16139/14). Eurojust stimulates and

improves the coordination of investigations and prosecutions between the competent authorities in the Member States, in particular by facilitating the execution of international mutual legal assistance and the implementation of extradition requests. Eurojust supports in any way possible the competent authorities of the Member States to render their investigations and prosecutions more effective when dealing with matters of cross-border crime. Eurojust's competence covers the same types of crime and offences for which Europol has competence. For other types of offences, Eurojust may assist in investigations and prosecutions at the request of a Member State. Eurojust also provides assistance to the Secretariat of the European Judicial Network (EJN), the Genocide Network and the joint investigation teams (JITs), develops JIT Evaluation Reports, and provides timely freezing and confiscation tools to police and prosecutors in Member States.

- **The European Public Prosecutor's Office** was established with the adoption of Council Regulation (EU) 2017/1939 of October 12, 2017, implementing the plan for enhanced police and prosecutorial cooperation on the establishment of the European Public Prosecutor's Office ("the EPPO"). The EPPO, based in Luxembourg, will investigate, prosecute and bring to judgement by national courts the perpetrators of "PIF" (protection of the Union's financial interests) offences (crimes affecting the financial interests of the EU, especially those having a cross-border dimension)[21] and "ancillary offences" inextricably linked to them, such as i) cases involving two or more Member States participating in the EPPO, including cases where the criminal activity is carried out in a single country, but the suspect has a habitual residence in, or is a national of, another Member State; ii) cases involving two or more Member States, one of which is not part of enhanced cooperation; or iii) cases involving at least one third country. In line with the Parliament's request, its scope of action will cover cross-border VAT fraud with a total damage of at least €10 million. The European Commission, at an informal meeting of justice ministers in Bulgaria held in January 2018, confirmed the Commission's intention to have the EPPO fully up and running by the end of 2020.
- The "lisbonisation" of the **European Union Agency for Law Enforcement Training** (CEPOL) was completed by the adoption of Regulation (EU) 2015/2219 of November 25, 2015,[22] replacing and repealing Council Decision 2005/681/JHA. CEPOL (Budapest, Hungary) is tasked with developing, implementing and coordinating training for EU law enforcement officials. It brings together a network of training institutes located in the several EU Member States for planning and curriculum development, and supports them in providing targeted training on issues related to EU priorities in the security field.
- The former European Agency for the Management of Operational Cooperation at the External Borders of the Member States of the European Union was established by Council Regulation (EC) 2007/2004. Widely known as **Frontex**, it has been converted during the "lisbonisation" process into the **European Border and Coast Guard Agency**[23] by Regulation (EU) 2016/1624. The seat of this agency is Warsaw, Poland. Frontex promotes, coordinates and develops European border management policy and practices. The agency analyses data to help identify migratory patterns, as well as documenting trends in cross-border criminal activities at and beyond EU's external borders. The agency coordinates and organises joint operations and rapid border interventions, and deploys European Border and Coast Guard teams, including a pool of 1,500 border guards at the ready. Frontex may carry out operations on the territory of non-EU countries neighbouring at least one Member State (in case of heavy migratory pressure). The agency assists EU Member States in forced returns, and supports ongoing cooperation between law enforcement authorities, EU agencies and customs at EU sea borders. It also runs the European Border Surveillance System (known as Eurosur). Frontex shares any relevant intelligence

gathered during its operations in a timely manner with relevant national authorities and Europol.

- Another EU agency – the "**eu-LISA**" European Union Agency for the Operational Management of Large-Scale IT Systems in the Area of Freedom, Security and Justice)[24] – was established in 2011 via Establishing Regulation (EU) No 1077/2011 and started its activities on December 1, 2012. The administrative headquarters of eu-LISA are in Tallinn, Estonia, whilst its operational centre is in Strasbourg, France. There is also a business continuity site for the systems under its management based in Sankt Johann in Pongau, Austria, and a Liaison Office in Brussels, Belgium. The agency's primary aim is to provide a long-term solution for the operational management of large-scale IT systems, which are today essential instruments in the implementation of the asylum, border management and migration policies of the EU. The agency is currently managing Eurodac, the second generation Schengen Information System (SIS II) and the Visa Information System.
- In the context of the presentation of the key agencies working in the field of Justice and Home Affairs, it is necessary to point out the **European Anti-Fraud Office**[25] (Office européen de lutte anti-fraude – OLAF). OLAF is the EU's administrative investigation service, designed to combat fraud and corruption affecting the EU, and to protect the EU budget. It acts in the interests of European taxpayers as an office of fiscal accountability. The Office was established in 1999 by Commission Decision No. 1999/352/EC and Council Regulation (2003) No 58/2003. Its headquarters are in Brussels, Belgium. The powers and mandated tasks of OLAF cover three main areas: investigation and coordination, data collection and the development of policies to combat fraud. OLAF is empowered to carry out administrative investigations, but may also assist the authorities of the Member States in their internal administrative or criminal investigations related to the tasks of the agency. Reports prepared by the end of the investigation contain only recommendations. If there is sufficient evidence of a possible criminal offence, the report is sent to the national law enforcement authorities for their disposition.
- Regulation (EU) 2017/2101 amending Regulation (EC) No 1920/2006 as regards information exchange on, and an early warning system and risk assessment procedure for, new psychoactive substances, "lisbonised" the EU agency **European Monitoring Centre for Drugs and Drug Addiction**[26] (EMCDDA). EMCDDA was duly established in 1993. Inaugurated in Lisbon in 1995, it is one of the EU's various decentralised agencies. The EMCDDA exists to provide the EU and its Member States with a factual overview of European drug problems, and to provide a solid evidence base to support the debate on drug policy. Today it offers policymakers the data and scientific interpretations they need for drawing up informed drug laws and strategies. It also helps professionals and practitioners working in the field pinpoint best practices and new areas of research being done to enhance our collective knowledge. Europol is a key EMCDDA partner within the European Union Early Warning System on new psychoactive substances (EU EWS), and involvement in organised crime is an integral part of the scientific risk assessment of all new substances of abuse. The scaling up of the monitoring of illicit drug supply in Europe is manifested through its development of key indicators in three domains: drug markets, drug-related crime and drug supply reduction. Work with Europol has focused on the development of systematic data collection on synthetic drug production sites, cannabis production sites, and secondary cocaine extraction laboratories where cocaine is chemically removed from carrier materials such as plastics.
- Regulation (EU) No 526/2013 of the European Parliament and of the Council of May 21, 2013 "lisbonised" the **European Union Agency for Network and Information**

> **Security**[27] (ENISA) and repealed Regulation (EC) No 460/2004. ENISA is a centre of expertise for cybersecurity in Europe. The agency is located in Greece, with its seat in Heraklion, Crete, and an operational office in Athens. The mission of ENISA is to contribute to securing Europe's information society by raising "awareness of network and information security and to develop and promote a culture of network and information security in society for the benefit of citizens, consumers, enterprises and public sector organizations in the EU."

The Regulation of the European Parliament and of the Council on the European Union Agency for Asylum, repealing Regulation (EU) No 439/2010, is going to turn the existing European Asylum Support Office into a fully fledged **European Union Agency for Asylum**. EASO acts as a centre of expertise in matters of asylum, providing scientific and technical support to Member States, particularly to those whose asylum and reception systems are under particular pressure. Through its support function, EASO assists EU Member States in fulfilling their European and international obligations in the field of asylum.

Judicial cooperation

Even though this chapter is mainly restricted to police cooperation in developing measures to combat crime, the various instruments of cooperation devised cannot avoid the area of judicial cooperation. An important part of the EU's programme for the suppression of crime is represented by the European Convention on Mutual Assistance in Criminal Matters[28] of 2000, and the Protocol to the Convention[29] of 2001. These two legal instruments provide for some important forms of cooperation among EU law enforcement agencies. The connection of police and judicial cooperation can be seen in the fact that in the first stages of a Member State's request for legal assistance, the requests may fall within the framework of international legal assistance, and in the implementation phase, also in the field of police cooperation. Examples are the actions of joint investigation teams between Member States in the areas of Article 13, controlled deliveries in criminal investigations of Article 12–related investigations, and covert investigations flowing from Article 14 of the Convention on Mutual Assistance in Criminal Matters since 2000. In the field of information exchange, Article 6 of the Convention stipulates that the mutual legal assistance contemplated takes place through direct contact between competent judicial authorities, and only in exceptional cases with the participation of the central authority for legal assistance.

The Schengen acquis

In the European countries, special attention was already paid to police cooperation by the Schengen Agreement[30] and the Schengen Convention.[31] With the implementation of the Treaty of Amsterdam in 1999, the so-called *Schengen acquis* also became EU law, and thus binding for EU Member States. The Schengen acquis fundamentally defines conditions and measures for the abolition of border controls at internal borders of Member States.[32] Unavoidably, free movement of persons and goods across national borders, where there are no longer border passport and other controls, establishes advantageous conditions for cross-border crime. To compensate for the potential security deficit, the Schengen acquis also provides for measures of police cooperation and measures that must be introduced by EU Member States before they can become members of the Schengen area. Above all, such measures include the timely exchange of information and data, and the establishment of forms of active and ongoing police cooperation, cooperative arrangements which are established on either a bilateral or a multilateral basis between Member States or on the basis of EU-wide measures. The Schengen Information System acts as both a search system and an arrest warrant system, on the basis of which the competent authorities carry out direct actions (such as a request for refusal of entry of third-country nationals, or the arrest of a person for whom an European arrest warrant is issued; or countries may for other reasons require information on wanted persons and seizure of property). On the basis of bilateral and multilateral treaties, EU countries have entered into legal frameworks for various types of police activities in the field of cross-border law enforcement cooperation. This set of bilateral and multilateral legal frameworks includes mainly the areas of cross-border pursuit, cross-border tracking, joint police patrols, joint police operations, and joint investigation teams.

The mass influx and subsequent secondary migratory movements coming via the Eastern Mediterranean route since 2015 witnessed unprecedented movements of migrants arriving in the European Union. This situation led several of the most highly exposed Member States to reintroduce temporary border controls at their internal borders, in line with the existing Schengen rules. The persistence of the threats to public policy or internal security in several Member States resulting from the continuing movements of irregular migrants led the Commission to trigger for the very first time the specific procedure of Article 29 of the Schengen Borders Code. This was one of the steps foreseen by the Commission in its roadmap back to a normally functioning Schengen area in its Communication of March 4, 2016.[33] The procedure in Article 29 may be used in exceptional circumstances where the deficiencies in the management of the external borders, detected during a Schengen evaluation, put the functioning of the entire Schengen area at risk.

On May 12, 2016, the Council recommended,[34] on the basis of a Commission proposal,[35] that the five Member States most affected by the secondary movements coming from Greece reintroduce border controls at specific sections of their internal borders. Despite the gradual improvements in the overall situation, the pressure on the five Member States concerned continued and justified subsequent prolongations of the emergency internal border controls.[36] On May 11, 2017, the Council authorised these five Member States for the third time under this procedure to extend these controls until November 11, 2017.

As part of the Commission's efforts to maximise the potential of existing EU information systems, the Commission adopted three legislative proposals in December 2016 intended to strengthen the Schengen Information System (SIS).[37] These proposals include key measures to step up the fight against terrorism, such as introducing an obligation on Member States to create an alert in SIS if a person is sought in relation to a terrorist offence. Discussions in the European Parliament and the Council have also included the need to share information on terrorist offences in SIS with Europol, with amendments being proposed to make it possible for Europol and Member States to exchange supplementary information on SIS hits related to terrorism, and for Europol to cross-check information on newly created alerts and hits on such alerts against its databases and analytical work files.[38] Negotiations between the European Parliament and the Council on these proposals began in November 2017, and due to the great importance of these proposals the Commission urged the co-legislators to reach an agreement on the proposals by early 2018. In parallel, as has been planned since 2016, work continues to strengthen the SIS by introducing an automated fingerprint identification system (AFIS) within the system. This addition will allow end users of SIS to search the SIS on the basis of fingerprint data, allowing for reliable identification of people, including those who are travelling under false identities.

External dimension for internal security of the EU

The EU's Global Strategy for European Foreign and Security Policy (2016) offers reassurances that the European Union will promote peace and guarantee the security of its citizens and territory and notes that internal and external security are ever more intertwined, with our security at home entailing a parallel interest in peace in our neighbouring and surrounding regions. The Council conclusions on the development of the renewed Internal Security Strategy of December 2014 and the Council conclusions on the renewed European Union Internal Security Strategy 2015–2020 acknowledge the growing links between the European Union's internal and external security and stress the importance of an integrative, complementary and coherent approach towards key third countries and partners on security aspects of mutual interest. In this vein, good practice has been developed through the EU-initiated **Western Balkan Integrative Internal Security Governance (IISG)**. In September 2017, the several ministers of the interior/security from Western Balkan countries, in close cooperation with the EU and supported by other IISG Partners (United Nations representatives, interested EU Member States, EU agencies and institutions, other international actors, donors and representatives of the international community), convened at the Kick-Off Meeting of the IISG Board (Brdo, Slovenia). At that meeting the Member States involved reiterated that regional cooperation in the area of internal security remains a priority concern for the Western Balkan countries. They each expressed their respective commitments to devoting their best efforts toward the achievement of greater long-term sustainability of the solutions in this area of policy brought by the contributions of the international community as a whole. They articulated a desire to achieve a higher level of regional responsibility and to adopt an efficient and holistic approach to the challenges in the area of internal security faced simultaneously by the region and the EU.

The IISG should not be viewed as merely a project/initiative – it should instead best be seen as a policy process integrating all forms of external assistance (including projects and initiatives) to the Western Balkan beneficiaries – namely, Albania, Bosnia and Herzegovina, Kosovo,[39] the Former Yugoslav Republic of Macedonia, Montenegro and Serbia. The IISG is EU-initiated, but this does not limit ownership to the EU. Its primary responsibility is to its beneficiaries, who are in charge of monitoring and participating in the articulation of their needs in all crucial phases of planning. It is also a process owned by all international and regional state and non-state actors/donors (including the United Nations agencies, the Organization for Security and Cooperation in Europe, the Council of Europe, and all country donors) who support the process in order to maximise the effectiveness and long-term sustainability of their efforts.

Effective police and prosecutorial cooperation and information sharing – *conditio sine qua non* for EU internal security goals achievement

Effective and secure cross-border cooperation and exchange of information is a precondition for achieving the goals of internal security in the European Union. The need for a coherent and effective cross-border approach is heightened by the growing mobility of citizens, the increasing complexity of crime phenomena and, therefore, the EU policies to counter them, as well as by the necessity for the EU and the Member States to maximise their available resources and optimise their use through enhanced cooperation. In spite of the need, citizens of the EU require that protection of their privacy is appropriately balanced against their expectations of security, and that cross-border law enforcement information exchange has to strike a balance between business needs and the safeguarding of citizens' fundamental rights where data protection, data security and data quality have always to be respected.

In November 2009, the Council responded to the need for better coherence and consolidation in developing information management and exchange, and approved Conclusions on an **Information Management Strategy**[40] (IMS) for EU internal security. The IMS aims at supporting, streamlining and facilitating the management of information necessary for carrying out expedient cross-border information exchanges between local law enforcement authorities, authorities responsible for border management, and judicial authorities dealing with criminal matters. Regulation (EU) 2017/2226 of the European Parliament and of the Council of November 30, 2017 established an Entry/Exit System (EES) to register entry and exit data and refusal of entry data of third-country nationals crossing the external borders of the Member States. That regulation likewise determined the conditions for access to the EES for law enforcement purposes, and amended the Convention implementing the Schengen Agreement and Regulations (EC) No 767/2008 and (EU) No 1077/2011. The purpose of this Regulation is to contribute to the modernisation of the external border management process by improving the quality and efficiency of the external border controls of the Schengen area. This was done in order to help Member States deal with ever-increasing number of travellers to the EU without having to increase the number of border guards, to reinforce internal security, strengthen the fight against terrorism and serious crime, and systematically identify over-stayers (individuals remaining in the Schengen area after the end of their authorised stay). The **European Travel Information and Authorisation System** (ETIAS) proposal (Proposal for a Regulation of the European Parliament and of the Council establishing a European Travel Information and Authorisation System (ETIAS) and amending Regulations (EU) No 515/2014, (EU) 2016/399, (EU) 2016/794 and (EU) 2016/1624) will be an EU system for visa-exempt third-country nationals when crossing the external EU borders. The system would enable immigration officials to determine whether the presence of such persons on the territory of the Member States would pose an irregular migration, security or public health risk. For this purpose a travel authorisation would be introduced as a new condition for entering the Schengen area, and the absence of a valid ETIAS travel authorisation would result in a refusal of entry into the Schengen area. Moreover, where applicable, carriers would have to check that their passengers have a valid ETIAS travel authorisation before allowing them to board their transportation means when bound for a Schengen country. A valid travel authorisation would be a reliable indication to the visitor that the risk assessments performed in advance of arrival at a Schengen border crossing point made him/her, a priori, an eligible person for entering into the Schengen area. The border guard would still conduct the border control checks as provided under the Schengen Border Code and would make the final decision for granting or refusing entry. An ETIAS will also facilitate the crossing of the Schengen external border by visa-exempt third-country nationals. An ETIAS authorisation would be obtained through an application process, which would be simple, cheap, fast and would in the vast majority of cases not require any further steps. According to the experience of other countries with similar systems for travel authorisations (US, Canada, Australia), an estimated 95 per cent or more would result in a positive reply, one which would be communicated to applicants within minutes via a dedicated and secure website. Fingerprints and other biometric data would not be collected in the process. The authorisation would be valid for five years, and would be good for multiple trips. The authorisation prior to travel would offer clarity to visa-exempt third-country nationals bound for the Schengen area. Once the applicants received their individual travel authorisation, they would have a reliable early indication of admissibility into the Schengen area.

The **European Criminal Records Information System** is going to be set up through the adoption of the Proposal for a Regulation of the European Parliament and of the Council establishing a centralised system for the identification of Member States holding conviction information on both third-country nationals and stateless persons (TCN) to supplement and support the European Criminal Records Information System (ECRIS-TCN system) and amending Regulation (EU) No 1077/2011. The European Criminal Records Information System (ECRIS) established by Framework Decision 2009/315/JHA and by Council Decision 2009/316/JHA provides for an electronic exchange of criminal record information on a decentralised basis between EU Member States. The ECRIS system has been operational since April 2012, and it allows Member States' criminal records authorities to obtain complete information on previous convictions of an EU national from the Member State of that person's nationality. Although it is possible to exchange information on convictions concerning third-country nationals and stateless persons (TCN) through ECRIS today, there is no procedure or mechanism in place to do so efficiently and in a timely manner. The proposal supplements the Commission's 2016 proposal for a Directive to amend the ECRIS Framework Decision and to repeal the ECRIS Council Decision. The supplementary proposal focuses on establishing and regulating a central ECRIS-TCN system, whilst the 2016 proposal regulates the decentralised exchanges of conviction information on TCN that should take place after it is established which particular Member State has conviction information via the ECRIS-TCN system. Once both proposals have been adopted by EU legislators, there will be two separate legal instruments regulating both the ECRIS and the ECRIS-TCN systems: the ECRIS Framework Decision 2009/315/JHA and Council Decision 2009/316/JHA, as amended by the Directive, and the ECRIS-TCN Regulation establishing the centralised ECRIS-TCN system. Improving ECRIS with regard to TCN is an important part of the European Agenda on Security.

Conclusion

The development of police and prosecutorial cooperation in the past 20 years went in the direction of continuous development of greater cooperation and enhanced mutual trust, improvement of the exchange of police information and data collected in pre-trial criminal proceedings, but definitely not in the direction of transferring investigative and police powers to the authorities of other Member States or any of the EU institutions/agencies. In any limited bilateral relations, Member States authorise only a limited implementation of investigative or police powers. The established trend of EU police cooperation will continue further in the direction of simplifying the rules and using a bottom-up approach to prioritise needs, thereby achieving better quality instruments of cooperation on the basis of genuine needs. The key enhancement of the EU's internal security policy is the creation of COSI, whose task it is to coordinate the actions of the competent authorities of EU Member States, including in the field of police cooperation. Because of this challenging task, the eyes of the Member States and EU institutions and agencies are most focused on the work of this committee.

Whether police cooperation can continue to develop successfully at the EU level will depend largely on the performance of this committee. The measures they adopt must ensure greater protection for EU citizens, catalysed by the needs shared among a majority of Member States. How many powers and permitted actions taken for ensuring better EU internal security will Member States continue to transfer to the EU in response to the new security challenges, with their great complexity? How much emphasis will the new Commission put on security at the beginning of the new decade? At this time, there is no complete answer to these important questions. Thus far, active and ongoing police and judicial cooperation among Member States provides an excellent example of effective regional collaboration among sovereign states combating substantial transnational crime. Moreover, such cooperation can develop further even in the absence of a political agreement and a mandate for EU institutions and agencies to take the lead on behalf of and for the benefit of all EU Member States.

Notes

1 This chapter is based on a national research project "*Safety and Security in Local Communities*" (Project No. 5-0397, 2015–2018; 2019–2024, financed by the Slovenian Research Agency), focusing on the cross-border security issues in Europe and responding to crime in municipalities bordering the Schengen border of the EU.

2 Council of the European Union, Treaty of Amsterdam Amending the Treaty of the European Union, the Treaties Establishing the European Communities and Certain Related Acts, OJ C 340, November 10, 1997.

3 The EU policy cycle is a robust action intended to target the most pressing criminal threats. In 2010, the EU set up a four-year policy cycle in order to create a greater measure of continuity for the fight against serious international and organised crime. In 2017, the Council decided to continue the EU policy cycle for organised and serious international crime for the period 2018–2021. "EU Policy Cycle – EMPACT," accessed November 25, 2018, www.europol.europa.eu/crime-areas-and-trends/eu-policy-cycle-empact.

4 European Parliament and Council of the European Union, Directive (EU) 2016/681 of the European Parliament and of the Council of 27 April 2016 on the Use of Passenger Name Record (PNR) Data for the Prevention, Detection, Investigation and Prosecution of Terrorist Offences and Serious Crime, OJ L 119, May 4, 2016.

5 European Commission, Commission Decision of 27 July 2017 Setting-up the High-Level Commission Expert Group on Radicalisation, C(2017) 5149, OJ C 252, August 3, 2017.

6 European Parliament, European Parliament Resolution of 23 October 2013 on Organised Crime, Corruption and Money Laundering: Recommendations on Action and Initiatives to Be Taken (Final Report) (2013/2107(INI)), accessed February 3, 2019, https://oeil.secure.europarl.europa.eu/oeil/popups/ficheprocedure.do?lang=en&reference=2013/2107(INI).

7 "Special Eurobarometer 371: Internal security," accessed October 13, 2018, https://data.europa.eu/euodp/en/data/dataset/S998_75_4_EBS371.

8 "Standard Eurobarometer 75: Public opinion in the European Union," accessed October 13, 2018, http://ec.europa.eu/public_opinion/archives/eb/eb75/eb75_en.htm.

9 "Serious and Organised Crime Threat Assessment (SOCTA) 2017," accessed November 2, 2018, www.europol.europa.eu/activities-services/main-reports/european-union-serious-and-organised-crime-threat-assessment-2017.

10 "Excise Duties on Alcohol, Tobacco and Energy," accessed February 3, 2019, https://ec.europa.eu/taxation_customs/business/excise-duties-alcohol-tobacco-energy_en.

11 "Serious and Organised Crime Threat Assessment (SOCTA) 2017."

12 Council of the European Union, Council Conclusions on the Creation and Implementation of an EU Policy Cycle for Organised and Serious International Crime, Council document 15358/10.

13 European Union, Consolidated Version of the Treaty on European Union, OJ C 326, October 26, 2012, 13–390.

14 European Union, Consolidated Version of the Treaty on the Functioning of the European Union. OJ C 326, October 26, 2012, 47–390.

15 European Union, Treaty of Lisbon Amending the Treaty on European Union and the Treaty Establishing the European Community, Signed at Lisbon, 13 December 2007, OJ C 306, December 17, 2007, 1–271.

16 European Union, Treaty of Lisbon (OJ C 115, May 9, 2008), OJ EU 2007/C 306/01, accessed February 2, 2019, http://europa.eu/lisbon_treaty/full_text/index_en.htm.

17 Council of the European Union, Council Decision of 25 February 2010 on Setting up the Standing Committee on Operational Co-operation on Internal Security, 2010/131/EU, OJ L 52, March 3, 2010, 50.

18 COSI's objective is to facilitate, promote and strengthen the coordination of operational cooperation of EU countries in the field of internal security. In this capacity, it acts in a number of different areas, including police and customs cooperation, the protection of external borders and judicial cooperation in criminal matters. It must submit a regular report on its activities to the Council, which then informs the European Parliament and the national parliaments.

19 European Parliament and Council of the European Union, Regulation (EU) 2016/794 of the European Parliament and of the Council of 11 May 2016 on the European Union Agency for Law Enforcement Cooperation (Europol) and Replacing and Repealing Council Decisions 2009/371/JHA, 2009/934/JHA, 2009/935/JHA, 2009/936/JHA and 2009/968/JHA, OJ L 135, May 24, 2016, 53–114.

20 Council of the European Union, Council Decision of 28 February 2002 Setting up Eurojust with a View to Reinforcing the Fight against Serious Crime (2002/187/JHA), OJ L 63, March 6, 2002, 1–13.

21 "Legislative train schedule – area of Justice and Fundamental Rights; protection of the Union's financial interests (PIF directive)," retrieved from www.europarl.europa.eu/legislative-train/theme-area-of-justice-and-fundamental-rights/file-protection-of-the-union-s-financial-interests-(pif-directive).

22 European Parliament and Council of the European Union, Regulation (EU) 2015/2219 of the European Parliament and of the Council of 25 November 2015 on the European Union Agency for Law Enforcement Training (CEPOL) and Replacing and Repealing Council Decision 2005/681/JHA, OJ L 319, December 4, 2015, 1–20.

23 European Parliament and Council of the European Union, Regulation (EU) 2016/1624 of the European Parliament and of the Council of 14 September 2016 on the European Border and Coast Guard and Amending Regulation (EU) 2016/399 of the European Parliament and of the Council and Repealing Regulation (EC) No 863/2007 of the European Parliament and of the Council, Council Regulation (EC) No 2007/2004 and Council Decision 2005/267/EC, OJ L 251, September 16, 2016, 1–76.

24 European Parliament and Council of the European Union, Regulation (EU) No 1077/2011 of the European Parliament and of the Council of 25 October 2011 Establishing a European Agency for the Operational Management of Large-Scale IT Systems in the Area of Freedom, Security and Justice, OJ L 286, November 1, 2011, 1–17.

25 Council of the European Union, Council Regulation (EC) No 58/2003 of 19 December 2002 Laying Down the Statute for Executive Agencies to Be Entrusted with Certain Tasks in the Management of Community Programmes, OJ L 11, January 16, 2003, 1–8.

26 European Parliament and Council of the European Union, Regulation (EC) No 1920/2006 of the European Parliament and of the Council of 12 December 2006 on the European Monitoring Centre for Drugs and Drug Addiction (Recast), OJ L 376, December 27, 2006, 1–13.

27 European Parliament and Council of the European Union, Regulation (EU) No 526/2013 of the European Parliament and of the Council of 21 May 2013 Concerning the European Union Agency for Network and Information Security (ENISA) and Repealing Regulation (EC) No 460/2004 Text with EEA Relevance, OJ L 165, June 18, 2013, 41–58.

28 Council of the European Union, Council Act of 29 May 2000 Establishing in Accordance with Article 34 of the Treaty on European Union the Convention on Mutual Assistance in Criminal Matters between the Member States of the European Union, 2000/C 197/01, OJ C 197, July 12, 2000, 1.

29 Council of the European Union, Protocol to the Convention by the Council under Article 34 of the Treaty on European Union, on Mutual Assistance in Criminal Matters between the Member States of the European Union, OJ C 326, November 21, 2001, 2–8.

30 European Union, Agreement between the Governments of the States of the Benelux Economic Union, the Federal Republic of Germany and the French Republic on the Gradual Abolition of Checks at their Common Borders, OJ L 239, September 22, 2000, 13.

31 European Union, Convention Implementing the Schengen Agreement of 14 June 1985 between the Governments of the States of the Benelux Economic Union, the Federal Republic of Germany and the French Republic on the Gradual Abolition of Checks at Their Common Borders, OJ L 239, September 22, 2000, 19.

32 Countries that fully implement the Schengen acquis are Austria, Belgium, Czech Republic, Denmark, Estonia, Finland, France, Greece, Italy, Iceland, Latvia, Liechtenstein, Lithuania, Luxembourg, Hungary, Malta, Germany, Netherlands, Norway, Poland, Portugal, Slovakia, Slovenia, Spain, Sweden and Switzerland.

33 European Commission, Communication from the Commission to the European Parliament, the European Council and the Council: Back to Schengen – A Roadmap, COM(2016) 120 final (Brussels: European Union, March 4, 2016).

34 Council of the European Union, Council Implementing Decision (EU) 2016/894 of 12 May 2016 Setting Out a Recommendation for Temporary Internal Border Control in Exceptional Circumstances Putting the Overall Functioning of the Schengen Area at Risk, OJ L 151, June 8, 2016, 8.

35 European Commission, Commission Proposal of 4 May 2016 for a Council Implementing Decision Setting Out a Recommendation for Temporary Internal Border Control in Exceptional Circumstances Putting the Overall Functioning of the Schengen Area at Risk, COM(2016) 275 final (Brussels: European Union, May 4, 2016).
36 Council of the European Union, Council Recommendations (EU) 2016/1989 of 11 November 2016 and (EU) 2017/246 of 7 February 2017 for Prolonging Temporary Internal Border Control in Exceptional Circumstances Putting the Overall Functioning of the Schengen Area at Risk.
37 The Schengen Information System (SIS) assists competent authorities in Europe regarding border control and cooperation, law enforcement cooperation and cooperation on vehicle registration. The future developments of the SIS are related to biometrics, counter-terrorism, vulnerable persons, irregular migration and enhanced access to EU agencies. See: "Schengen Information System," accessed February 3, 2019, https://ec.europa.eu/home-affairs/what-we-do/policies/borders-and-visas/schengen-information-system_en.
38 European Commission, Communication from the Commission to the European Parliament, the European Council and the Council: Twelfth Progress Report towards an Effective and Genuine Security Union, COM(2017) 779 final (Strasbourg: European Union, December 12, 2017).
39 This designation is without prejudice to the position on status, and is in line with United Nations Security Council Resolution 1244/99 and the International Court of Justice (ICJ) opinion on the Kosovo Declaration of Independence.
40 Council of the European Union, Council Conclusions on an Information Management Strategy for EU Internal Security, Council of the European Union (16637/09 JAI 873 CATS 131 ASIM 137 JUSTCIV 249 JURINFO 145), October 30, 2009.

References

Council of the European Union. Council Act of 29 May 2000 Establishing in Accordance with Article 34 of the Treaty on European Union the Convention on Mutual Assistance in Criminal Matters between the Member States of the European Union. 2000/C 197/01. *Official Journal of the European Union* C 197, July 12, 2000.

Council of the European Union. Council Conclusions on an Information Management Strategy for EU Internal Security. 16637/09, JAI 873, CATS 131, ASIM 137, JUSTCIV 249, JURINFO 145. November 25, 2009.

Council of the European Union. Council Conclusions on the Creation and Implementation of an EU Policy Cycle for Organised and Serious International crime. Council document 15358/10.

Council of the European Union. Council Decision of 25 February 2010 On Setting Up the Standing Committee on Operational Co-operation on Internal Security. 2010/131/EU. *Official Journal of the European Union* L 52, March 3, 2010, 50.

Council of the European Union. Council Decision of 28 February 2002 Setting Up Eurojust with a View to Reinforcing the Fight against Serious Crime. 2002/187/JHA. *Official Journal of the European Union* L 63, March 6, 2002.

Council of the European Union. Council Implementing Decision (EU) 2016/894 of 12 May 2016 Setting Out a Recommendation for Temporary Internal Border Control in Exceptional Circumstances Putting the Overall Functioning of the Schengen Area at Risk. *Official Journal of the European Union* L 151, June 8, 2016, 8.

Council of the European Union. Council Recommendation (EU) 2016/1989 of 11 November 2016 for Prolonging Temporary Internal Border Control in Exceptional Circumstances Putting the Overall Functioning of the Schengen Area at Risk. *Official Journal of the European Union* L 306, November 15, 2016, 13–15.

Council of the European Union. Council Recommendation (EU) 2017/246 of 7 February 2017 for Prolonging Temporary Internal Border Control in Exceptional Circumstances Putting the Overall Functioning of the Schengen Area at Risk. *Official Journal of the European Union* L 36, February 11, 2017, 59–61.

Council of the European Union. Council Regulation (EC) No 58/2003 of 19 December 2002 Laying Down the Statute for Executive Agencies to Be Entrusted with Certain Tasks in the Management of Community Programmes. *Official Journal of the European Union* L 11, January 16, 2003.

Council of the European Union. Protocol to the Convention by the Council under Article 34 of the Treaty on European Union, on Mutual Assistance in Criminal Matters between the Member States of the European Union. *Official Journal of the European Union* C 326, November 21, 2001.

Council of the European Union. Treaty of Amsterdam Amending the Treaty of the European Union, the Treaties Establishing the European Communities and Certain Related Acts. *Official Journal of the European Union* C 340, November 10, 1997.

European Commission. Commission Decision of 27 July 2017 Setting-up the High-Level Commission Expert Group on Radicalisation. C/2017/5149. *Official Journal of the European Union* C 252, August 3, 2017.

European Commission. Commission Proposal of 4 May 2016 for a Council Implementing Decision Setting Out a Recommendation for Temporary Internal Border Control in Exceptional Circumstances Putting the Overall Functioning of the Schengen Area at Risk. COM(2016) 275 final. Brussels: European Union, May 4, 2016.

European Commission. Communication from the Commission to the European Parliament, the European Council and the Council: Back to Schengen – A Roadmap. COM(2016) 120 final. Brussels: European Union, March 4, 2016.

European Commission. Communication from the Commission to the European Parliament, the European Council and the Council: Twelfth Progress Report towards an Effective and Genuine Security Union. COM(2017) 779 final. Strasbourg: European Union, December 12, 2017.

European Parliament. European Parliament Resolution of 23 October 2013 on Organised Crime, Corruption and Money Laundering: Recommendations on Action and Initiatives to Be Taken (Final Report) (2013/2107(INI)).

European Parliament and Council of the European Union. Directive (EU) 2016/681 of the European Parliament and of the Council of 27 April 2016 on the Use of Passenger Name Record (PNR) Data for the Prevention, Detection, Investigation and Prosecution of Terrorist Offences and Serious Crime. *Official Journal of the European Union* L 119, May 4, 2016.

European Parliament and Council of the European Union. Regulation (EC) No 1920/2006 of the European Parliament and of the Council of 12 December 2006 on the European Monitoring Centre for Drugs and Drug Addiction (Recast). *Official Journal of the European Union* L 376, December 27, 2006.

European Parliament and Council of the European Union. Regulation (EU) No 1077/2011 of the European Parliament and of the Council of 25 October 2011 Establishing a European Agency for the Operational Management of Large-Scale IT Systems in the Area of Freedom, Security and Justice. *Official Journal of the European Union* L 286, November 1, 2011.

European Parliament and Council of the European Union. Regulation (EU) 2015/2219 of the European Parliament and of the Council of 25 November 2015 on the European Union Agency for Law Enforcement Training (CEPOL) and Replacing and Repealing Council Decision 2005/681/JHA. *Official Journal of the European Union* L 319, December 4, 2015.

European Parliament and Council of the European Union. Regulation (EU) 2016/1624 of the European Parliament and of the Council of 14 September 2016 on the European Border and Coast Guard and Amending Regulation (EU) 2016/399 of the European Parliament and of the Council and Repealing Regulation (EC) No 863/2007 of the European Parliament and of the Council, Council Regulation (EC) No 2007/2004 and Council Decision 2005/267/EC. *Official Journal of the European Union* L 251, September 16, 2016.

European Parliament and Council of the European Union. Regulation (EU) 2016/794 of the European Parliament and of the Council of 11 May 2016 on the European Union Agency for Law Enforcement Cooperation (Europol) and Replacing and Repealing Council Decisions 2009/371/JHA, 2009/934/JHA, 2009/935/JHA, 2009/936/JHA and 2009/968/JHA. *Official Journal of the European Union* L 135, May 24, 2016.

European Parliament and Council of the European Union. Regulation (EU) No 526/2013 of the European Parliament and of the Council of 21 May 2013 Concerning the European Union Agency for Network and Information Security (ENISA) and Repealing Regulation (EC) No 460/2004 Text with EEA Relevance. *Official Journal of the European Union* L 165, June 18, 2013.

European Union. Agreement between the Governments of the States of the Benelux Economic Union, the Federal Republic of Germany and the French Republic on the Gradual Abolition of Checks at Their Common Borders. *Official Journal of the European Union* L 239, September 22, 2000.

European Union. Consolidated Version of the Treaty on European Union. *Official Journal of the European Union* C 326, October 26, 2012.

European Union. Consolidated Version of the Treaty on the Functioning of the European Union. *Official Journal of the European Union* C 326, October 26, 2012.

European Union. Convention Implementing the Schengen Agreement of 14 June 1985 between the Governments of the States of the Benelux Economic Union, the Federal Republic of Germany and the French Republic on the Gradual Abolition of Checks at Their Common Borders. *Official Journal of the European Union* L 239, September 22, 2000.

European Union. Treaty of Lisbon Amending the Treaty on European Union and the Treaty Establishing the European Community, Signed at Lisbon, 13 December 2007. *Official Journal of the European Union* C 306, December 17, 2007.

"Europol. Main Reports." Accessed October 25, 2018. www.europol.europa.eu/activities-services/main-reports.

"Excise Duties on Alcohol, Tobacco and Energy." Accessed February 3, 2019. https://ec.europa.eu/taxation_customs/business/excise-duties-alcohol-tobacco-energy_en.

"Legislative train schedule – area of justice and fundamental rights; Protection of the Union's financial interests (PIF directive)." Accessed February 3, 2012. www.europarl.europa.eu/legislative-train/theme-area-of-justice-and-fundamental-rights/file-protection-of-the-union-s-financial-interests-(pif-directive).

"Schengen Information System." Accessed February 3, 2019. https://ec.europa.eu/home-affairs/what-we-do/policies/borders-and-visas/schengen-information-system_en.

"Serious and Organised Crime Threat Assessment (SOCTA) 2017." Accessed November 2, 2018. www.europol.europa.eu/activities-services/main-reports/european-union-serious-and-organised-crime-threat-assessment-2017.

"Special Eurobarometer 371: Internal security." Accessed October 13, 2018. https://data.europa.eu/euodp/en/data/dataset/S998_75_4_EBS371.

"Standard Eurobarometer 75: Public opinion in the European Union." Accessed October 13, 2018. http://ec.europa.eu/public_opinion/archives/eb/eb75/eb75_en.htm.

3

THE ROLE OF EU INSTITUTIONS IN THE DESIGN OF EU FOREIGN AND SECURITY POLICIES

Akasemi Newsome and Marianne Riddervold

Introduction

The member states of the EU have transferred authority to common institutions in an unprecedented manner. Under the "ordinary legislative procedure," decision-making is based on qualified majority voting, legislative powers are shared between the member states and the European Parliament, policy initiatives come from the Commission, while the Court of Justice of the European Union (CJEU) oversees the application of EU law and settles legal disputes. The Commission also has extensive management roles and is the guardian of the treaties, including the right to take cases of noncompliance to the Court. The only exemption to this "ordinary" legislative procedure is the Common Foreign and Security Policy (CFSP). In this domain, member states have decided not to delegate authority to the supranational institutions, instead keeping it as an intergovernmental instrument run by special procedures. The CFSP is the only EU policy area where the European Parliament does not have co-decision powers, but instead has the right to be informed and can give opinion and advice. The Commission does not have the right to initiate new policies, nor is it the guardian of the treaties. Neither does the Commission have management functions within the CFSP. Instead, the administrative work in the CFSP lies mainly with the new "EU foreign service," the EU External Action Service (EEAS), which is responsible for implementing the Union's external action and maintaining diplomatic relations with the rest of the world. The formal principal-agent relationship in the Common Foreign and Security Policy is in other words clear: Member states are initiators and decision-makers, and the EEAS and the Commission prepare and implement their decisions.

A growing number of studies suggest, however, that the de facto role and influence of the EU institutions in policy-making processes falling under the CFSP procedures differ substantially from this formal description. The de facto role and influence of the EU institutions are key to this development. Rather than simply advising or implementing the member states' decisions, the EU institutions – the High Representative of the Union for Foreign Affairs and Security Policy (HR/VP) and her foreign service, the EEAS, the Commission, and the Parliament – are important drivers of the policies agreed in the CFSP, influencing agenda setting, decision-making, and implementation of CFSP policies and decisions.

The aim of this chapter is to shed light on this phenomenon, systematically describing these institutions' influence on the CFSP. What de facto influence do these institutions have on CFSP, beyond their delegated powers? The answers to this question have important consequences for our understanding of the day-to-day working of EU foreign and security policies and indeed of the EU more broadly, and are hence of great importance to the citizens of the EU. Empirically, the influence of these institutions is puzzling as one would not expect this within an intergovernmental policy area. In the CFSP, the member states remain the sole decision-makers and can in principle at will veto any decisions on common EU positions or actions. It follows that democratic control of the CFSP is supposed to be indirect: Member states' executives decide on common policies and actions through unanimity and are again held accountable at the national level. The fact that institutional actors such as the Commission and the EEAS influence the policies they agree to conduct, therefore, challenges not only the way we conventionally perceive foreign and security policy as the prerogative of the states, but also the idea that citizens can hold their elected governments accountable in this domain.

To systematically explore the influence of the EU institutions on the CFSP, the chapter proceeds as follows. In the next part, we first discuss the formal organization of the CFSP, including the Common Security and Defence Policy (CSDP), as described in the EU treaties and as interpreted by legal scholars. The subsequent section contains the analysis, discussing, first, how the Parliament's and then the Commission's influence differs from this formal description. In this section, we also discuss their various forms of formal and informal interactions with the HR/VP and the EEAS in the domain, focusing particularly on if and how such interactions have been used as avenues to influence CFSP developments or affect their institutional powers. Analytically, and as further elaborated below, we here draw on Cross' concept of *agency*[1] to illustrate how the institutions not only have influence over policy developments but also have increased their powers beyond the member states' control or in spite of the member states' attempt to keep the CFSP a member state prerogative. Empirically, we discuss findings from our own studies of EU maritime foreign and security policies[2] and of the Parliament's role in human rights protection[3] as well as other studies exploring the institutions' influence in the CFSP. Part IV contains the conclusion, summing up our findings and discussing some of their implications for our understanding of the functioning and democratic legitimacy of the CFSP and indeed the EU more broadly.

The CFSP legal structure: the formal role of the institutions in the CFSP

The EU's Common Foreign and Security Policy is a formal decision-making structure covering all foreign policy decisions that are not part of the EU's external relations. Most importantly, the CFSP includes the Common Security and Defence Policy, i.e. the EU's civilian and military operations and common security strategies, EU sanctions, EU diplomacy, as well as common EU policies and positions in a variety of intergovernmental organizations. As discussed in the introduction, formally, and despite the removal of the pillar structure following the adoption of the Lisbon Treaty in 2009, EU foreign and security policies continue to be "subject to specific rules and procedures."[4] General principles and overall aims are set by the European Council. Building on these overall strategic goals, the Council decides on common policies in the form of joint actions (specifying common actions, including CSDP mission) or common positions (defining guidelines to which member states' policies must conform regarding a particular situation or in an international organization). All decisions are taken by unanimity, following special procedures within special CFSP institutions.[5] Accordingly, the competences of the EU institutions are limited.

The European Parliament

The role of the European Parliament (EP) in Common Foreign and Security Policy was formally circumscribed in the 1993 Treaty of European Union which designated CFSP as belonging to the intergovernmental second pillar. Only member states could propose policies for the EU in CFSP and policies could only be adopted through unanimous votes taken by member states.[6] Although the Treaty of Lisbon did not formalize parliamentary decision-making in the CFSP and maintained the primacy of member states, the creation of new actors in the CFSP other than member states in the Council opened new possibilities for participation for the EP, in that individuals occupying these positions could choose to take a neutral or positive view towards the input of the EP in CFSP.[7] The fused position of the High Representative of the Union for Foreign Affairs and Security Policy and Vice-President of the Commission and the European External Action Service took effect in 2009 with the Treaty of Lisbon. As the EP had consistently pushed for a transformation of the High Representative into an EU foreign minister, as well as the introduction of an EU diplomatic corps, the emergence of these two actors represents a fulfillment of parliamentary demands separate from potential pathways of influence for the EP on CFSP. According to Article 21(TEU) Parliament has the right to be updated and the right to be solicited for input on CFSP matters. In practice, the EP regularly responds to CFSP updates in parliamentary proceedings and offers suggested policy changes to the Council, High Representative/Vice-President of the Commission and the EEAS. In 2010 HR/VP Catherine Ashton issued a declaration that bolstered the EP's rights to information on the CFSP by institutionalizing Joint Consultation Meetings between MEPs, the Council, and the Commission on Common Security and Defence Policy, by supporting the 2002 Inter-Institutional Agreement (IIA) allowing the EP to view confidential information on CFSP missions, and by institutionalizing EP hearings where the HR/VP updates the EP on CFSP and CSDP.

In addition to its right to information about CFSP, the EP has significant veto powers over spending allocations for the CFSP. The Parliament can veto the CFSP budget and has a key role in funding decisions for programs overlapping in content with CFSP such as the European Instrument for Democracy and Human Rights. The EP is also broadly involved in EEAS administration and provides recommendations and input the placement procedures and mission focus of different EEAS delegations. The EP is a key broker of international agreements including those of association as the Council cannot become a party to an agreement if Parliament opposes it. The EP's formal power to approve international agreements does not include a formal spot at the table to define the terms of such agreements. In practice, however, the EP exercises informal power to define the terms of international agreements by potentially blocking an international agreement which the Commission has an interest in concluding.[8] In order to more effectively acquire information and provide policy input, the Parliament has also institutionalized committees with foreign and security policy expertise: the Committee on Foreign Affairs (AFET) and its two subcommittees on Security and Defence (SEDE) and Human Rights (DROI); the Committee on International Trade (INTA); and the Committee on Development (DEVE). Given Parliament's role in budgetary oversight, committees such as the Budgetary Control Committee (CONT) and the Budgets Committee (BUDG) also provide avenues for the EP to influence CFSP.[9]

The European Commission

The Commission's formal role and influence in EU foreign policy-making depends on its treaty-based competences, which vary across policy areas. Within what is often termed "EU external relations" it plays a leading role. In international organizations, the Commission must, for example, be involved in the member states' coordination processes when issues link to or overlap with community policies, which is often the case. Competences are, for instance, shared between the member states and supranational institutions within enlargement, environmental, and anti-terrorism policies.[10] Unlike governments in national systems, the competences the Commission holds in community policy areas do not, however, travel automatically to the international level. In most international organizations, the EU states remain members and signatories to conventions, also in cases where the EU itself is a signatory. The Commission is, for instance, not a signatory to all international treaties dealing with issues falling under its competences and needs a mandate from the member states to negotiate on their behalf, for example, during trade negotiations.[11]

In the CFSP, where the member states as discussed above have maintained exclusive competence, the Commission's formal competences are much more limited. In contrast to all other policy areas, the administrative work in the CFSP lies with the new "EU foreign service," the EU External Action Service. The Commission does not control the intergovernmental external action units in the EEAS.[12] Due to the establishment of the EEAS, scholars have even argued that the latest EU treaty, the Lisbon Treaty, *reduced* the Commission's formal influence within the CFSP. After all, with the Lisbon Treaty, the Commission's previous "full association" in the CFSP has been "replaced by the HR's [i.e. High Representative of the Union for Foreign Affairs and Security Policy and her foreign service, the EEAS] involvement who in CFSP does act outside the Commission's ambit control."[13] The fact that the HR/VP is also vice-president of the Commission and chairs the Foreign Policy Council meetings does not change this. The HR/VP and the Commission can jointly suggest policies and actions, but it is up to member states to decide on any common policies or actions through unanimity. Instead, the Commission's role in the CFSP is linked mainly to the treaty requirement that all EU policies should be coordinated and consistent. Due to the EU Treaty's overall aim of "consistency between the different areas of its external action and between these and its other policies"[14] the Commission and the High Representative, i.e. the EEAS, "shall cooperate" to ensure consistency between the CFSP and other EU policies.[15] The Treaty also states that the two should cooperate with the Council for this purpose, which in practice often means cooperating with the Council secretariat and the country holding the Presidency.[16] The Commission and the HR/EEAS may thus also "submit joint proposals to the Council."[17] These requirements do not, however, apply to the Common Security and Defence Policy. In the area of security and defense, the Treaty explicitly states that the EEAS and the Commission are not to cooperate, and they cannot submit any common proposals.

The European External Action Service was established following the Lisbon Treaty, as an EU foreign service led by the High Representative of the European Union for Foreign Affairs and Security Policy. It is the EU's foreign and security policy apparatus, and is responsible for implementing the Union's foreign policies and maintaining diplomatic relations with the rest of the world. It does not have a role in any other EU policy areas. In its own words, "the EEAS is the European Union's diplomatic service. It helps the EU's foreign affairs chief carry out the Union's Common Foreign and Security Policy."[18] As already mentioned, the Commission and the EEAS have to cooperate to the extent needed to ensure coherence between foreign and security and other policy fields, but they are formally two distinct administrative entities, and the Commission does not control the administrative units of the EEAS in any way. Formally, the member states' control over the EEAS hence remains strong: The EEAS is part of the special CFSP organization structure, under the control of the HR/VP who, when chairing the EU Foreign Affairs Council, "receives her instructions from the Council in CFSP," tasked to implement the decisions that are taken by the member states.[19]

The HR/VP has three distinct functions, often referred to as "triple-hatted."[20] S/he has to conduct the Union's common foreign and security policy; preside over the Foreign Affairs Council (FAC); and be one of the vice-presidents of the Commission.

According to Keukeleire and Delreux[21] the HR/VP's task can be broken down into four interrelated elements: decision-making; implementation; external representation; and consistency.

Regarding decision-making, the HR/VP chairs the Foreign Affairs Council and can make proposals with the EU member states and with the Commission (Articles 18 (2), 27 (1), 30 (1), and 42 (4)). Following Articles 26 (3) and 27 (1) of the Treaty of Lisbon (ToL), the HR/VP is also responsible for implementing the CFSP decisions adopted by the Council. Following a decision, the HR/VP and the ministers for foreign affairs "shall coordinate their activities within the Council."[22] The HR/VP moreover coordinates CSDP missions together with the Political and Security Committee (PSC) (Article 38 of the ToL). Externally, the HR/VP represents the Union on CFSP connected issues in relation to third parties or in international organizations. Lastly, and as mentioned above, the HR/VP, the Council and the Commission have to ensure consistency within the EU's external actions (Articles 18 (4), 21 (3), 24 (3) and 26 (2) of the ToL).

The institutions' de facto influence in the CFSP: drivers of integration?

As mentioned in the introduction, in reality, there is an increasing amount of supporting evidence that the CFSP may not be as different from other policy areas as this formal description suggests. Despite the CFSP's formally intergovernmental structure, there are a number of studies which suggest that processes of socialization, institutionalization, and the development of informal decision-making norms have led to a de facto "move beyond intergovernmentalism" in the CFSP.[23] The role of the EU institutions is key to this description. This section of the chapter moves on to discuss this development, exploring the de facto influence of the EP, the Commission and the HR/VP and the EEAS in the CFSP. Since the member states are formally the sole decision-makers in the CFSP, when seeking to explore the institutions' influence on this process, it is their impact on the member states' decisions on policy and actions that we ultimately want to illustrate. We also start from the assumption that the institutions have a vested interest in trying to increase their own powers or influence particular in policy development.[24] Consequently, an actor's "influence" is here defined as the impact it has on the member states' common policies: It has influence if its behavior and actions cause the member states to conduct a different EU foreign and security policy or give the institutions more powers than they would otherwise have had. This narrow definition builds on Dahl's classic definition, being that actor A has power if s/he makes another actor, B, do something s/he would otherwise not have done.[25] We use this definition of influence because it is the type of influence one would least expect to find in a policy area that formally lies exclusively with the member states. More precisely, to operationalize this, we build on Cross' concept of *agency*.[26] Initially developed to study the role of international diplomats, Cross' argument[27] is that diplomats have agency when they act beyond their delegated authority "in ways that statesmen do not anticipate" (ibid.), that is, beyond their delegated powers. There are three empirical indicators of institutional agency within intergovernmental organizations such as the CFSP.[28] The first two are linked to the member states' control of the institutions' involvement, while the third is linked to the member states' veto powers. Within an intergovernmental setting such as the CFSP, non-state actors have delegated powers only, foremost to solve practical questions or to secure the member states' commitments.[29] If the member states' ability to control is undermined due to an EU institution's actions or behavior, this would thus imply that it has the ability to act beyond its delegated authority in ways that are not anticipated by the member states. More precisely, evidence of institutional agency includes: (1) at least some of the member states having unsuccessfully tried to limit some or all of the EU institutions' participation in particular cases; and/or (2) the institutions having influenced EU policies by circumventing the member states' intergovernmental decision-making structures, cooperating with each other to achieve particular goals behind the member states' representatives' backs; and/or (3) an institution's actions and behavior having resulted in a different outcome than the one initially decided by the member states. So, then, to what extent do the EU institutions have agency in the CFSP, as suggested by this definition and these indicators?

The European Parliament's agency in the CFSP

There are several empirical findings to suggest that the EP indeed exercises some agency in the CFSP. As a first example, the EP successfully secured a change in the maritime security intervention, ATLANTA, although member states initially opposed the EP's policy recommendations. The Parliament wanted ATLANTA to provide cover to European commercial fishing ships in addition to the focus on containers and tankers. For example, Member of Parliament (MEP) de Grandes Pasqual noted in a plenary discussion in November 2009 that "Operation ATLANTA is inadequate ... It has to become possible to protect not only the routes along which humanitarian aid moves, but also community fishing and merchant vessels."[30] The Council responded to this EP demand initially with an assertation of territoriality and member state sovereignty, yet by 2012 the Council had implemented this EP demand to include commercial fishing within the scope of the mission. Notwithstanding this important policy change, the EP has not been successful in regularizing and transforming its informal role in developing the European Maritime Security Strategy to a formal one.[31] In another example, the EP took advantage of an impasse among member states on how to deal with Ukraine by proposing an increased role for a parliamentary envoy to the Ukraine. Nitoiu and Sus point out that despite the unwillingness expressed by members of the Council and the Commission that the EP should get involved,[32] the EP organized a mission to Ukraine led by past president of Poland Aleksander Kwasniewski and past president of the EP Pat Cox. Kwasniewski and Cox traveled to Ukraine to witness the legal proceedings against Ukraine's previous prime minister, Julia Tymoshenko. In so doing, the EP created the space for a new parliamentary role in EU foreign policy towards Ukraine.[33] One of the key achievements of the mission by Cox and Kwasniewski was to push the Ukrainian government to improve the treatment of political dissidents including the release of some. As an incentive, the EP representatives reaffirmed the EU's interest in closer relations with the Ukraine with the goal of motivating the Ukrainian government to hew more closely to international humanitarian standards. Still, the mission fell short of the progress needed by the EU association agreement.[34]

The EP has also expended some efforts in widening the substantive scope of CFSP to include human rights, democracy, and the rule of law.[35] Starting in the early 1980s, the EP has provided summary assessments of the state of human rights globally and succeeded in modifying the criteria for both EU trade agreements and development funding to incorporate human rights scoring and measures for potential partners and recipients.[36] Given its pivotal position in budgetary proceedings, the EP established the European Instrument for Democracy and Human Rights (EIDHR) as part of CFSP and has renewed financial support for EIDHR annually since the mid 1990s.[37] For example, the EP strongly criticized the terms of international treaties owing to insufficient attention to the poor human rights track record of Central Asian governments.[38] In the area of democracy and rule of law, the EP went as far as to refuse consent to international treaties with Morocco and the US as well as agreements with more than two parties such as the "ACTA treaty on intellectual property rights enforcement and anti-counterfeit."[39]

Although the EP lacked a formal role to shape policies addressing terrorist acts committed within the EU's territory, by creatively relying on "issue linkage" the EP expressed its objections to potential privacy violations included in the "American Terrorist Finance Tracking Programme (TFTP)."[40] Counter to the wishes of the member states, particularly the UK which was interested in remaining in good standing with the Obama administration, the EP went as far as to openly reject cooperation with the US counter-terrorism agencies in order to facilitate information sharing on monetary transactions in Europe linked to terrorist networks and organizations. This step taken by the EP also clashed with the views of the Commission's, which was also willing to share information on monetary transactions with the US. The grounds for the rejection of the "Interim Agreement" were the lack of privacy safeguards for EU citizens, the lack of a mandated oversight role for the courts and minimal general oversight provisions. The EP did capitulate in that it received only some of the privacy controls that it desired, as well as an independent monitor of the data being transferred to ensure those privacy controls were followed, before consenting to the revised agreement with the US.[41]

Not only are there formal institutions, there are also many informal ways allowing the EP to engage in CFSP. For example, as "mandated by the EP's Conference of Presidents," parliamentarians may go overseas to solicit or share expertise with legislative bodies around the world as an "ad-hoc delegation." Given that political parties represented in the European Parliament have established European networks beyond national borders, as do NGOs and lobbying groups aligned on common issues, Members of Parliament regularly exchange information, receive policy input and travel overseas to share expertise on issues directly involving or linked with foreign and security policy.[42]

Another example in which the EP exercised agency in CFSP beyond its formal powers can be seen in the recognition of Kosovo as a sovereign state. Initially, EU member states did not all support the 2008 decision of national authorities in Kosovo to declare themselves a sovereign nation. In fact, at the time of writing, certain EU member states continue to reject Kosovo's aspiration to statehood: Cyprus, Greece, Romania, Slovakia, and Spain. Supranational bodies also have been reluctant to validate Kosovo's status as a sovereign nation and Redei notes that "neither the European Council nor the Council of Ministers … has an official position on Kosovo's independence."[43] Notwithstanding these objections by individual member states and the Council, the EP continued to issue statements to Kosovo and replicate parliamentary practices that it reserved for other sovereign nations with it, effectively legitimating and buttressing its aspirations to independence. In so doing, the EP effectively shaped the EU's approach to Kosovo such that most recently, HR/VP Mogherini met with the heads of state of Kosovo and Serbia to discuss the contentious issue of redrawing territorial boundaries, thus validating Kosovo's independence claims further in line with the EP's original goal of full state recognition for Kosovo.[44]

The European Parliament and the EEAS: the EP increases its own role

The EP has also influenced the role and functions of the HR/VP and the EEAS, in particular contributing to defining and expanding its own powers and responsibilities vis-à-vis this newly established institution. The Treaty of Amsterdam created the position of High Representative for Common Foreign and Security Policy and Secretary General of the Council of the European Union and Javier Solana served in this role for two five-year terms from 1999–2009. For most of Solana's term, the EP struggled to expand its role in CFSP to include areas other than access to information about the policy process. In this, member states retained CFSP firmly within their purview.[45] However, the EP did succeed in broadening the scope of the types of information it received access to, namely by convincing member states to institutionalize the sharing of "sensitive information" on CFSP by the Council with the EP.[46] This institutionalization occurred with the implementation of the Inter-Institutional Agreement of November 20, 2002, which specified a deadline by which the Parliament had to receive access to CFSP decisions made by Council and defined missions and policies impacting security and defense that could thus not be publicly communicated as within the domain of parliamentary access. Here, "five working days" were delimited as the maximum amount of time that the Council could wait before sharing decisions with the EP.[47]

An expanded role for the High Representative of the Union for Foreign Affairs and Security Policy to also include that of Vice-President of the European Commission came into being with the Lisbon Treaty. By 2009, the HR/VP would also lead the newly launched EU diplomatic corps – the European External Action Service. In this "triple-hatted position," Catherine Ashton served a single five-year term from 2009–2014. It is important to contrast the duties of the HR/VP during the tenure of Javier Solano in which the HR was seen to be "representative of the collective power of the member states" in comparison with Ashton who faced the obligation of "tak[ing]up the tasks of the former external relations Commissioner and the rotating presidency in matters of CFSP."[48] At the start, the EP and Ashton had very different views of the legislative role in CFSP and the High Representative's office. The EP wanted "oversight of the [External Action] service's budget, personnel, aid policy and ratification procedure" and "public parliamentary hearings for top positions." Ashton, on the other hand, thought a more effective EEAS should take the shape of "an autonomous agency reporting directly to the HR-VP ... equally answerable to the Council, Commission and the member states ... with a pyramidal hierarchy headed by a powerful Secretary General."[49] Notably absent from her vision for the EEAS was a consequential role for the European Parliament. Although the EP did not succeed in molding the EEAS in its desired image and appointments to the Service incorporated "closed-door hearings with no [legislative] veto,"[50] the EP did shape some features of the EEAS by interpreting its already existing powers of "staff regulation" and "financial regulation" to extend to the EEAS.[51] The EP made the case that as the EU's representative body, the EP has a vested interest in ensuring that the EU institutions account for the principles of gender parity as well as the regional location within EU territory for individual EU member states in staffing the EEAS. In an effort to carve out influence for itself in CFSP, the EP thus proposed that the EU's new diplomatic service should reflect these balances when filling appointments and thereby created a way for the EP to review EEAS appointments through "issue linkages."[52] Ashton eventually acquiesced to some of the EP demands by agreeing to regular updates of the EP and prioritizing a substantive focus on "human rights and democracy promotion within the EEAS."[53]

Between the second and third HR/VP, the EP exerted considerable energies in shaping the modes of interaction between the HR/VP and the EEAS on the one hand and the EP on the other hand. The EP pushed for Ashton to consult with the EP on a scheduled basis and sought to codify the type and rank of officials who could substitute for the HR/VP *in absentia* in the text of the "Declaration on Political Accountability" (DCA). The DCA also detailed a mechanism by which diplomatic envoys dispatched by the HR/VP first had to brief the EP prior to traveling overseas. In this way, the EP expanded its own role in CFSP by broadly interpreting and formalizing its ability to "scrutinize" in a way that "deviates from the original intention."[54] The EP continued the practice of exercising its agency and influence in CFPS as expansively as possible under the third HR/VP, Federica Mogherini, who took office in 2014 and is expected to remain in office through 2019. Where Ashton chafed under the scheduled briefings with the EP, Mogherini accepted as settled her informal mandate to brief the EP on a scheduled basis. The EP also succeeded in informally inserting its views into the 2016 EU Global Strategy. Shortly after taking office, Mogherini announced her intention of developing a new EU Global Security Strategy by 2016. In an effort to informally shape the new Global Security Strategy, the EP released a report addressing key issues in CFSP taking care to link CFSP to "instruments over which the EP has legislative powers."[55] For example, the EP flagged the expansion of investment in research to include defense given that the EP "exercises legislative budgetary functions as well as political control and consultation functions."[56]

The European Commission's agency in the CFSP

Next we turn to the de facto influence of the Commission in the CFSP. The fact that the Commission is present in different CFSP decision-making forums is well established. Dijkstra[57] has, for example, studied the involvement of the Commission in the CFSP over time, while Joachim and Dembinski[58] argue that "the Commission has moved from being an observer to an active participant in the CFSP." Similarly, both Smith[59] and Kostadinova[60] show that the Commission is present in forums where foreign and security policies are discussed. More importantly, there is also evidence to suggest that the Commission has agency in the CFSP – that it has influence beyond the member states' control. Suggesting that the Commission has been able to increase its own powers in spite of the member states' traditional strong resistance to supranational elements in the CFSP, Blauberger and Weiss[61] found that the strategic use of a combination of threats and promises accounts for the Commission's success in increasing its competence in the defense sector, in particular "the Commission's strategic use of Court jurisprudence in overcoming member states' resistance to European secondary legislation."[62] The directives are particularly important in understanding the Commission's increasing of its own powers, as they are the very first supranational directives in the domain, and hence represent a departure from the understanding that the CFSP is intergovernmental only (ibid). Strikwerda[63] adds important knowledge to our understanding of the Commission's role in this process, highlighting how the Commission "was able to accomplish policy change in (at least) three member states by publishing a non-legally binding Guidance Note on offsets during the implementation process of the Defence and Security Procurement Directive."[64]

Also in the domain of EU maritime foreign and security policies, there is evidence to suggest that the Commission has *agency*, i.e. that it influences policies beyond the control of the member states.[65] The Commission influences EU maritime foreign and security policy-making first and foremost in two ways: first, through its expertise in interlinked policy areas and, second, by indirectly influencing policy developments through actions outside of the formal CFSP arenas, to some extent circumventing the formal CFSP procedures, in particular by cooperating with the EEAS. In the cases explored in Riddervold's 2018 book on EU maritime foreign and security policy (EU Arctic policies, the EU's naval missions and the EU's maritime security strategy), the Commission has been most influential when linking EU maritime foreign and security polices to community policy areas, when cooperating with presidencies with particular interests in furthering EU maritime security integration, and when developing policy proposals together with the EEAS, independently of the member states. For example, in the formally intergovernmental process of developing and adopting an EU Maritime Security Strategy, the Commission took on a much bigger role in the process than it should on the basis of its formal competences. And, more importantly, it did so contrary to several member states' explicit attempts to limit the Commission's role in this process, and it exerted much of its influence behind many of the member states' backs. In the making of the Maritime Labour Convention (MLC) in the International Labour Organization (ILO) maritime sessions, the conflict between the Commission and some of the member states was particularly clear. Negotiations on the MLC took place at a time when the role of the Commission in international organizations was unsettled and the EEAS had not yet been established, and the Commission very explicitly used this international process to increase its own competences in the domain. As a result, the conflict between the member states on the one hand and the Commission on the other was clear: The Commission spoke in the ILO meetings despite member states claiming it had no such role, it presented opinions specifying linkages to community policy areas that reduced the member states' ability to act individually and that strongly influenced the common positions reached. Due to the clear opposing views on what role the Commission should play, the member states even met outside of the regular coordination meetings to discuss how they could better control the Commission and reduce its influence on the MLC. In the end, however, the Commission got its way, eventually playing a bigger role in the MLC than in any other previous international processes falling under the CFSP procedures.[66] These are only a few of many examples, but, in sum, the Commission has gradually increased its own competences significantly. Due to these and other processes, maritime foreign and security policy has gradually developed to become an area in which the Commission has a stronger role than was initially anticipated or even wanted by many of the member states. Over time, the Commission has built an increasingly strong and more accepted role for itself in all phases of policy-making, where it is now not merely an agent of the member states but more importantly an important agenda setter and de facto co-decision taker. On the one hand, one may argue that this is only natural. After all, the Commission's increased involvement in EU maritime foreign and security policies is also linked to the fact that maritime security is a cross-sectoral policy field, covering not only foreign and security, including Common Security and Defence (CSDP) issues, but also community policy issues. There are also several formal reasons why the Commission is becoming more involved in the CFSP after Lisbon, in particular the "triple hattedness" of the HR/VP and the treaty-based duty to coordinate CFSP issues with all other policy areas. This duty to coordinate CFSP with other policy areas and the focus of developing a comprehensive approach to external issues will necessarily lead to more cooperation between the Commission and the EEAS and the member states, including the Presidency.[67] One may even argue that this is particularly so in a per definition cross-sectoral policy field such as maritime security. On the other hand, however, there is a difference between having access to or being involved in decision-making and actually influencing outcomes in a policy area that member states explicitly have sought to keep under their control.[68] More importantly, studies of EU maritime foreign and security policy processes reveal how the Commission has contributed to increase its own role and influence during these policy processes. Put differently, the influence the Commission has in EU foreign and security policy has not been delegated by the member states as one would expect in an intergovernmental system but has to a large degree been taken by the Commission itself.

The EEAS and the de facto functioning of the CFSP administration – EEAS and Commission circumvention

Lastly, we move on to explore how the Commission influences the CFSP through its interactions with the EEAS. Riddervold and Trondal suggest[69] that the EEAS is also much more independent of the member states than its formal role entails, to a large degree cooperating informally with the Commission outside of the formal, intergovernmental CFSP special structure and procedures. It is also much more integrated into the structures of the Commission in its daily functioning than the treaty-based distinction between the intergovernmental pillar, the CFSP, on the one hand and the community pillar on the other hand would suggest. Again, the making of the EU Maritime Security Strategy is a revealing example. During the first, defining stages of this process, the Commission and the EEAS acted independently of the member states: They wrote the Joint Communication and they to a large extent controlled the member states' involvement. The findings moreover suggest that the EEAS and the Commission while cooperating on maritime security issues have institutionalized a new system on how to work together on a day-to-day basis. How the EEAS and the Commission were to cooperate in the domain remained rather unspecified in the Lisbon Treaty, allowing the two to develop a system of their own, to a large degree adopting the Commission's procedures. And most importantly, they did so beyond the control of the member states, without consulting their formal principles. In the system that has been established, the Commission has a bigger role than what has been formally delegated by the member states, and the two to a large degree also influence policy outcomes beyond the member states' control. From other studies we know that this mainly informal cooperation between the EEAS and the Commission is important for understanding not only the European Union Maritime Security Strategy (EUMSS) but also the development of the EU's Arctic policies and the launch of the naval mission "Sophia" in response to the migrant crisis.[70] In the latter case, the member states' agreement to act in response to the migrant crisis was to a large degree driven by humanitarian concerns linked to the so-called Lampedusa accident, where more than 800 people drowned in the waters off the Italian island. However, the EEAS and the Commission's actions were important for understanding the choice of a military mission: When the member states decided to take action to help migrants in despair at sea, the way in which they should respond was suggested and pushed by the EEAS and the Commission, who largely copied what was successfully done the last time the EU faced a crisis at sea (anti-piracy mission ATLANTA).[71] The strong cooperation developed between the EEAS and the Commission on the EUMSS also laid much of the basis for the EU's Arctic policy. According to Østhagen,[72] the very initiation of an EU Arctic policy can be traced back to the Commission: "The EU begun to develop an Arctic Policy as a result of the European Commission acting as a policy entrepreneur to secure its own competence and relevance in the domains of foreign policy." And this work was taken further by the EEAS and the Commission in parallel with their work on the EU Maritime Security Strategy. As with the maritime strategy, the 2012 Joint Communication on an EU Arctic policy was not only developed in parallel with the maritime strategy – it was to a large degree written and coordinated by the same persons from the two institutions, without much member state involvement.[73] And as was the case with the maritime strategy, this work has later laid the ground for much of the EU's Arctic policies.[74]

Findings and implications

This chapter set out to systematically explore the influence of the EU institutions on the CFSP by focusing on how the EP and the Commission have agency in the domain, i.e. whether they influence CFSP policy-making processes and outcomes beyond the member states' initial wishes and interests. Discussing evidence across a number of cases, we have shown how the two have both influenced policies and increased their own competences in the domain. In this way, we also explored how the two institutions have affected the functioning of the EEAS and indeed the de facto functioning of this domain more widely.

The fact that the Commission and the EP so clearly have influence beyond their delegated powers in the CFSP challenges the way we conventionally perceive foreign and security policy as the prerogative of the member states. Contrary to the assumption that policy-making processes and outcomes within the CFSP reflect the member states' material interests and relative strength, we have shown that the supranational institutions have far more influence than the member states have agreed to delegate. Indeed, the CFSP is a policy area where the member states explicitly have tried to avoid delegating authority to these institutions, and still we see that in particular the Commission increasingly exercises influence in that domain. Although this might vary somewhat from case to case, the member states' veto powers in the domain have clearly become limited due to the de facto powers of the Commission – powers that it to a large degree has taken on itself, over time – and the cooperation between the EEAS and the Commission. The Parliament has significantly fewer formal competences in CFSP than the Commission. Yet, the EP has generously interpreted its statutory formal powers, for example, in budgeting and treaty assent as well as substantively through "issue linkage" to extend its role in CFSP beyond what the member states prefer. The HR/VP and EEAS also bear the stamp of the EP in that not only did the EP insert itself into the supranational information flow on CFSP previously limited to the Commission and Council in the change of administration between Ashton and Mogherini, the EP succeeded in institutionalizing its access to information. Undoubtedly, the member states are still key actors and decision-makers in the CFSP. The member states set the political priorities and they still have to give their final consent for policies to be adopted. But as our discussion has illustrated, there is much more to CFSP decision-making processes than member state bargaining, and much of this development takes place informally at lower levels and outside of the formal CFSP setting, often in incremental steps.

These findings have important implications not only for our understanding of the functioning of EU foreign and security policy but also for our understanding of the democratic legitimacy of this domain. This chapter hence contributes to the debate about the EU's democratic deficit, in particular in the CFSP.[75] However, it takes this argument forward by identifying several of the informal mechanisms that increase the democratic challenges in this domain. Conventionally being perceived as an intergovernmental policy area where decisions are taken by unanimity and all states have veto powers over common outcomes, the argument has been that the CFSP's democratic legitimacy can be secured indirectly. As long as it is the national executives who decide on common policies and actions and they all have the right to say no, these executives can be held accountable at the national level, through their various national procedures. However, if the premise for this argument does not hold, the argument of indirect democracy does not hold either. And as we have shown, the executives do not fully control CFSP decisions, and they do not have veto powers over all developments in the domain. Instead, evidence that so much of the Commission's influence, often together with the EEAS, remains informal and takes place at least partly without the member states' control or even knowledge suggests that the democratic deficit in the CFSP is bigger than we have anticipated. The fact that we also find that the EP is increasing its influence in the CFSP does not really solve this challenge either. Indeed, as the EP grows in influence in a de facto more supranational CFSP, this might also decrease the CFSP's legitimacy. In this way, the democratic challenges linked not only to the national but also to the supranational executives' powers in the domain remain.

Notes

1 Mai'a K. Davis Cross. *The European Diplomatic Corps: Diplomats and International Cooperation from Westphalia to Maastricht* (Basingstoke, UK: Palgrave Macmillan, 2007).

2 Marianne Riddervold, *The Maritime Turn in EU Foreign and Security Policies: Aims, Actors and Mechanisms of Integration* (London: Palgrave Macmillan, 2018); Marianne Riddervold, "(Not) in the Hands of the

Member States. How the Commission Influences EU Foreign and Security Policies," *Journal of Common Market Studies* 54, no. 20 (2016): 353–69; Marianne Riddervold and Guri Rosén, "Trick or Treat: How the Commission and the European Parliament Exert Influence in EU Foreign and Security Policies," *Journal of European Integration* 38, no. 6 (2016): 687–702; Marianne Riddervold and Jarle Trondal, "Integrating Nascent Organizations. On the Settlement of the European External Action Service," *Journal of European Integration* 39, no. 1 (2017): 33–47.

3 Akasemi Newsome, "Credible Champions: Transatlantic Relations and Human Rights in Refugee Crises," *Journal of European Integration* 40, no. 5 (2018): 587–604.

4 European Union, Consolidated Version of the Treaty on European Union, OJ C 326, October 26, 2012, art. 24.1(2).

5 Hans Merket, "The European External Action Service and the Nexus between CFSP/CSDP and Development Cooperation," *European Foreign Affairs Review* 17, no. 4 (2012): 625–52; Daniel Thym, "The Intergovernmental Constitution of the EU's Foreign, Security and Defence Executive," *European Constitutional Law Review* 7 (2011): 453–80; Riddervold and Rosén, "Trick or Treat."

6 Stephan Keukeleire and Tom Delreux (eds.), *The Foreign Policy of the European Union* (Basingstoke, UK: Palgrave Macmillan, 2014), 63.

7 Anna Herranz-Surralés, "The EU's Multilevel Parliamentary (Battle) Field: Inter-parliamentary Cooperation and Conflict in Foreign and Security Policy," *West European Politics* 37, no. 5 (2014), 966.

8 Kolja Raube, "Parliamentarization Approaches: Parliamentary Control in EU Foreign Policy," in *New Approaches to EU Foreign Policy*, eds. Maciej Wilga and Ireneusz Pawel Karolewski (London: Routledge, 2014), 132–33.

9 Keukeleire and Delreux, *The Foreign Policy of the European Union*; Ben Crum, "Parliamentarization of the CFSP through Informal Institution-Making? The Fifth European Parliament and the EU High Representative," *Journal of European Public Policy* 13, no. 3 (2006): 383–401.

10 Daniel C. Thomas, "Explaining EU Foreign Policy: Normative Institutionalism and Alternative Approaches," in *Making EU Foreign Policy: National Preferences, European Norms and Common Policies*, ed. Daniel C. Thomas (Houndmills: Palgrave Macmillan, 2011), 10.

11 Riddervold, *The Maritime Turn in EU Foreign and Security Policies.*

12 Thym, "The Intergovernmental Constitution of the EU's Foreign, Security and Defence Executive," 469.

13 Ibid., 468.

14 European Union, Consolidated Version of the Treaty on European Union, art. 21.3.

15 Ibid.

16 Riddervold, *The Maritime Turn in EU Foreign and Security Policies*; Riddervold and Rosén, "Trick or Treat."; Riddervold and Trondal, "Integrating Nascent Organizations. On the Settlement of the European External Action Service."

17 European Union, Consolidated Version of the Treaty on European Union, art. 22.

18 European External Action Service, *2017 Annual Activity Report* (Brussels: European External Action Service, 2018).

19 Thym, "The Intergovernmental Constitution of the EU's Foreign, Security and Defence Executive," 467.

20 Rosa Balfour, David Spence and Jozef Bátora (eds.), *The European External Action Service: European Diplomacy Post-Westphalia* (London. Palgrave Macmillan, 2015), 35.

21 Keukeleire and Delreux, *The Foreign Policy of the European Union*, 78.

22 European Union, Treaty of Lisbon Amending the Treaty on European Union and the Treaty Establishing the European Community, Signed at Lisbon, 13 December, 2007, OJ C 306, December 17, 2007, art. 32.

23 Helene Sjursen, "Not So Intergovernmental After All? On Democracy and Integration in European Foreign and Security Policy," *Journal of European Public Policy* 18, no. 8 (2011): 1078–95. Also: David Allen, "Who Speaks for Europe? The Search for an Effective and Coherent External Policy," in *A Common Foreign Policy for Europe? Competing Visions of the CFSP*, eds. John Peterson and Helene Sjursen (London: Routledge, 1998), 41–58; Cross, *The European Diplomatic Corps: Diplomats and International Cooperation from Westphalia to Maastricht*; Deirdre Curtin and Morten Egeberg, "Tradition and Innovation: Europe's Accumulated Executive Order," *West European Politics* 31, no. 4 (2008): 639–61; Jolyon Howorth, "Decision Making in Security and Defense Policy: Towards Supranational Intergovernmentalism?" *Cooperation and Conflict* 47, no. 4 (2012): 433–53; Ana E. Juncos and Karolina Pomorska, "In

the Face of Adversity: Explaining the Attitudes of EEAS Officials vis-à-vis the New Service," *Journal of European Public Policy* 20, no. 9 (2013): 1332–49; Valentina Kostadinova, "The European Commission and the Configuration of Internal European Union Borders: Direct and Indirect Contribution," *Journal of Common Market Studies*, 51, no. 2 (2013): 264–80; Per M. Norheim-Martinsen, "Beyond Intergovernmentalism: European Security and Defence Policy and the Governance Approach," *Journal of Common Market Studies* 48, no. 5 (2010): 1351–65; Michael E. Smith, *Europe's Foreign and Security Policy. The Institutionalization of Cooperation* (Cambridge: Cambridge University Press, 2004); Jakob C. Øhrgaard, " 'Less Than Supranational, More Than Intergovernmental': European Political Cooperation and the Dynamics of Intergovernmental Integration," *Millennium* 26, no. 1 (1997): 1–29.

24 Laura Cram, "The European Commission as a Multi-organization: Social Policy and IT Policy in the EU," *Journal of European Public Policy* 1, no. 2 (1994): 195–217; Meng-Hsuan Chou and Marianne Riddervold, "The Unexpected Negotiator at the Table: How the European Commission's Expertise Informs Intergovernmental EU Policies," *Politics and Governance* 3, no. 1 (2015): 61–72.

25 Robert A. Dahl, "The Concept of Power," *Behavioral Science* 2, no. 3 (2007): 201–15.

26 Cross, *The European Diplomatic Corps: Diplomats and International Cooperation from Westphalia to Maastricht*.

27 Ibid., 3.

28 Riddervold, *The Maritime Turn in EU Foreign and Security Policies*, 109–10.

29 Sjursen, "Not So Intergovernmental After All? On Democracy and Integration in European Foreign and Security Policy."

30 Riddervold and Rosén, "Trick or Treat," 694.

31 Ibid., 695.

32 Cristian Nitoiu and Monika Sus, "The European Parliament's Diplomacy – a Tool for Projecting EU Power in Times of Crisis? The Case of the Cox-Kwasniewski Mission," *Journal of Common Market Studies* 55, no. 1 (2017): 79.

33 Ibid., 78–79.

34 Ibid., 73.

35 Newsome, "Credible Champions: Transatlantic Relations and Human Rights in Refugee Crises," 587–604.

36 Stelios Stavridis and Daniela Irrera (eds.), *The European Parliament and Its International Relations* (New York: Routledge, 2015), 22.

37 Keukeleire and Delreux, *The Foreign Policy of the European Union*, 88.

38 Francis Jacobs, Richard Corbett, and Michael Shackleton, *The European Parliament* (London: John Harper, 2005), 152, 227–28.

39 Ricardo Passos, "The European Union's External Relations a Year after Lisbon: a First Evaluation from the European Parliament," in *The European Union's External Relations: A Year after Lisbon*, ed. Panos Koutrakos, CLEER Working Paper 2011/3 (The Hague: CLEER, 2011), 52–55.

40 Joerg Monar, "The EU as an International Counter-Terrorism Actor: Progress and Constraints," *Intelligence and National Security* 30, no. 2–3 (2015): 345.

41 Monar, "The EU as an International Counter-Terrorism Actor: Progress and Constraints," 345.

42 Daan Fonck, "Parliamentary Diplomacy and Legislative-Executive Relations in EU Foreign Policy: Studying the European Parliament's Mediation of the Macedonian Political Crisis (2015–17)," *JCMS: Journal of Common Market Studies* 56, no. 6 (2018): 1308.

43 Lorinc Redei, "The European Parliament as a Diplomatic Precedent Setter: The Case of Parliamentary Relations with Kosovo," in *The European Parliament and Its International Relations*, eds. Stelios Stavridis and Daniela Irrera (New York: Routledge, 2015).

44 Ibid., 273; Shaun Walker and Andrew MacDowall, "US-backed Kosovo Land-Swap Border Plan under Fire from All Sides," *Guardian*, September 3, 2018.

45 Crum, "Parliamentarization of the CFSP through Informal Institution-Making? The Fifth European Parliament and the EU High Representative."

46 Anna Herranz-Surralés, "The EU's Multilevel Parliamentary (Battle) Field," 964.

47 Guri Rosén, "EU Confidential: The European Parliament's Involvement in EU Security and Defence Policy," *Journal of Common Market Studies* 53.2 (2015): 383–98.

48 Niklas Helwig and Carolin Rueger, "In Search of a Role for the High Representative: The Legacy of Catherine Ashton" *The International Spectator* 49, no. 4 (2014): 3.

49 Jolyon Howorth, "Catherine Ashton's Five Year Term: A Difficult Assessment," *Les Caheirs europeens de Sciences Po*, 3 (2014): 8.

50 Ibid., 9; Elmar Brok and Roberto Galtieri, *Draft Report for a European Parliament Recommendation […] on the 2013 Review of the Organization and the Functioning of the EEAS* (2012/2253 INI) (Brussels: European Parliament, March 25, 2013).

51 European Parliament and the Council of the European Union, Regulation (EU, EURATOM) No 1080/2010 of the European Parliament and of the Council of 24 November 2010 Amending the Staff Regulations of Officials of the European Communities and the Conditions of Employment of Other Servants of Those Communities, OJ L311/1, November 26, 2010; European Parliament and the Council of the European Union, Regulation (EU, EURATOM) No 1081/2010 of 24 November 2010 Amending Council Regulation (EC, EURATOM) No 1605/2002 on the Financial Regulation Applicable to the General Budget of the European Communities, as Regards the European External Action Service, OJ L 311/9, November 26, 2010; Elisabeth Wisniewski, "The Influence of the European Parliament on the European External Action Service," *European Foreign Affairs Review* 18, no. 1 (2013): 81–102.

52 Raube, "Parliamentarization Approaches: Parliamentary Control in EU Foreign Policy," 134.

53 Keukeleire and Delreux, *The Foreign Policy of the European Union*, 86.

54 Guri Rosén and Kolja Raube, "Influence beyond Formal Powers: The Parliamentarization of European Union Security Policy," *British Journal of Politics and International Relations* 20, no. 1 (2018): 75.

55 Ibid., 77.

56 European Parliament, European Parliament Resolution of 16 March 2017 on Constitutional, Legal and Institutional Implications of a Common Security and Defence Policy: Possibilities Offered by the Lisbon Treaty (2015/2343(INI)).

57 Hylke Dijkstra, "Approaches to Delegation in EU Foreign Policy: The Case of the Commission," in *New Approaches to EU Foreign Policy*, ed. Ireneusz Pawel Karolewski and Maciej Wilga (London: Routledge, 2014).

58 Jutta Joachim and Matthias Dembinski, "A Contradiction in Terms? NGOs, Democracy and European Foreign and Security Policy," *Journal of European Public Policy* 18, no. 8 (2011): 1155.

59 Smith, *Europe's Foreign and Security Policy*.

60 Kostadinova, "The European Commission and the Configuration of Internal European Union Borders."

61 Michael Blauberger and Moritz Weiss, "'If You Can't Beat Me, Join Me!' How the Commission Pushed and Pulled Member States into Legislating Defence Procurement," *Journal of European Public Policy* 20, no. 8 (2013).

62 Ibid., 2.

63 Johanna Strikwerda, "Sovereignty at Stake? The European Commission's Proposal for a Defence and Security Procurement Directive," *European Security* 26, no. 1 (2017): 19–36.

64 Ibid., 12.

65 Riddervold, "(Not) in the Hands of the Member States."; Riddervold, *The Maritime Turn in EU Foreign and Security Policies*.

66 Ibid., Ch. 5.

67 Riddervold and Rosén, "Trick or Treat."

68 Riddervold, *The Maritime Turn in EU Foreign and Security Policies*.

69 Riddervold and Trondal, "Integrating Nascent Organizations. On the Settlement of the European External Action Service."

70 Riddervold, *The Maritime Turn in EU Foreign and Security Policies*, Ch. 6.

71 Ibid., Ch. 9. Also: Ruxandra-Laura Bosilca, "An EU Maritime Security Policy in the Making: The Case of Military CSDP Operations at Sea," PhD dissertation, Bucharest/Oslo: National University of Political Studies and Public Administration, 2017.

72 Andreas Østhagen, "Utenrikspolitisk Entreprenørskap. EU og Utviklingen av en Arktis-Politikk," *Internasjonal Politikk* 69, no. 1 (2011): 7.

73 Riddervold, *The Maritime Turn in EU Foreign and Security Policies*, Ch. 9.

74 Ibid.

75 For example, Sjursen, "Not So Intergovernmental After All? On Democracy and Integration in European Foreign and Security Policy."

References

Allen, David. "Who Speaks for Europe?: The Search for an Effective and Coherent External Policy." In *A Common Foreign Policy for Europe? Competing Visions of the CFSP*, edited by John Peterson and Helene Sjursen, 41–58. London: Routledge, 1998.

Balfour, Rosa, David Spence, and Jozef Bátora. *The European External Action Service: European Diplomacy Post-Westphalia*. London: Palgrave Macmillan, 2015.
Blauberger, Michael, and Moritz Weiss. "'If You Can't Beat Me, Join Me!' How the Commission Pushed and Pulled Member States into Legislating Defence Procurement." *Journal of European Public Policy* 20, no. 8 (2013): 1120–38.
Bosilca, Ruxandra-Laura. "An EU Maritime Security Policy in the Making: The Case of Military CSDP Operations at Sea." PhD dissertation, Bucharest/Oslo: National University of Political Studies and Public Administration, 2017.
Brok, Elmar, and Roberto Galtieri. *Draft Report for a European Parliament Recommendation [...] on the 2013 Review of the Organization and the Functioning of the EEAS* (2012/2253 INI). Brussels: European Parliament, March 25, 2013.
Chou, Meng-Hsuan, and Marianne Riddervold. "The Unexpected Negotiator at the Table: How the European Commission's Expertise Informs Intergovernmental EU Policies." *Politics and Governance* 3, no. 1 (2015): 61–72.
Cram, Laura. "The European Commission as a Multi-organization: Social Policy and IT Policy in the EU." *Journal of European Public Policy* 1, no. 2 (1994): 195–217.
Cross, Mai'a K. Davis. *The European Diplomatic Corps: Diplomats and International Cooperation from Westphalia to Maastricht*. Basingstoke, UK: Palgrave Macmillan, 2007.
Crum, Ben. "Parliamentarization of the CFSP through Informal Institution-Making? The Fifth European Parliament and the EU High Representative." *Journal of European Public Policy* 13, no. 3 (2006): 383–401.
Curtin, Deirdre, and Morten Egeberg. "Tradition and Innovation: Europe's Accumulated Executive Order." *West European Politics* 31, no. 4 (2008): 639–61.
Dahl, Robert A. "The Concept of Power." *Behavioral Science* 2, no. 3 (2007): 201–15.
Dijkstra, Hylke. "Approaches to Delegation in EU Foreign Policy: The Case of the Commission." In *New Approaches to EU Foreign Policy*, edited by Ireneusz Pawel Karolewski and Maciej Wilga, 38–55. London: Routledge, 2014.
European External Action Service. *2017 Annual Activity Report*. Brussels: European External Action Service, 2018.
European Parliament. European Parliament Resolution of 16 March 2017 on Constitutional, Legal and Institutional Implications of a Common Security and Defence Policy: Possibilities Offered by the Lisbon Treaty (2015/2343(INI)).
European Parliament and Council of the European Union. Regulation (EU, EURATOM) No 1080/2010 of the European Parliament and of the Council of 24 November 2010 Amending the Staff Regulations of Officials of the European Communities and the Conditions of Employment of Other Servants of Those Communities. *Official Journal of the European Union* L311, November 26, 2010, 1.
European Parliament and Council of the European Union. Regulation (EU, EURATOM) No 1081/2010 of the European Parliament and of the Council of 24 November 2010 Amending Council Regulation (EC, EURATOM) No 1605/2002 on the Financial Regulation Applicable to the General Budget of the European Communities, as Regards the European External Action Service. *Official Journal of the European Union* L 311, November 26, 2010, 9.
European Union. Consolidated Version of the Treaty on European Union. *Official Journal of the European Union* C 326, October 26, 2012.
European Union. Treaty of Lisbon Amending the Treaty on European Union and the Treaty Establishing the European Community, Signed at Lisbon, December 13, 2007. *Official Journal of the European Union* C 306, December 17, 2007.
Fonck, Daan. "Parliamentary Diplomacy and Legislative-Executive Relations in EU Foreign Policy: Studying the European Parliament's Mediation of the Macedonian Political Crisis (2015–17)." *JCMS: Journal of Common Market Studies* 56, no. 6 (2018): 1305–22.
Helwig, Niklas, and Carolin Rueger. "In Search of a Role for the High Representative: The Legacy of Catherine Ashton." *The International Spectator* 49, no. 4 (2014): 1–17.
Herranz-Surrallés, Anna. "The EU's Multilevel Parliamentary (Battle) Field: Inter-parliamentary Cooperation and Conflict in Foreign and Security Policy." *West European Politics* 37, no. 5 (2014): 957–75.
Howorth, Jolyon. "Catherine Ashton's Five Year Term: A Difficult Assessment." *Les Caheirs europeens de Sciences Po*, 3 (2014): 2–21.
Howorth, Jolyon. "Decision Making in Security and Defense Policy: Towards Supranational Intergovernmentalism?" *Cooperation and Conflict* 47, no. 4 (2012): 433–53.

Jacobs, Francis, Richard Corbett, and Michael Shackleton. *The European Parliament*. London: John Harper, 2005.

Joachim, Jutta, and Matthias Dembinski. "A Contradiction in Terms? NGOs, Democracy and European Foreign and Security Policy." *Journal of European Public Policy* 18, no. 8 (2011): 1151–68.

Juncos, Ana E., and Karolina Pomorska. "In the Face of Adversity: Explaining the Attitudes of EEAS Officials vis-à-vis the New Service." *Journal of European Public Policy* 20, no. 9 (2013): 1332–49.

Keukeleire, Stephan, and Tom Delreux. *The Foreign Policy of the European Union*. Basingstoke, UK: Palgrave Macmillan, 2014.

Kostadinova, Valentina. "The European Commission and the Configuration of Internal European Union Borders: Direct and Indirect Contribution." *Journal of Common Market Studies* 51, no. 2 (2013): 264–80.

Merket, Hans. "The European External Action Service and the Nexus between CFSP/CSDP and Development Cooperation." *European Foreign Affairs Review* 17, no. 4 (2012): 625–52.

Monar, Joerg. "The EU as an International Counter-Terrorism Actor: Progress and Constraints." *Intelligence and National Security* 30, no. 2–3 (2015): 333–56.

Newsome, Akasemi. "Credible Champions: Transatlantic Relations and Human Rights in Refugee Crises." *Journal of European Integration* 40, no. 5 (2018): 587–604.

Nitoiu, Cristian, and Monika Sus. "The European Parliament's Diplomacy – a Tool for Projecting EU Power in Times of Crisis? The Case of the Cox-Kwasniewski Mission." *Journal of Common Market Studies* 55, no. 1 (2017): 71–86.

Norheim-Martinsen, Per M. "Beyond Intergovernmentalism: European Security and Defence Policy and the Governance Approach." *Journal of Common Market Studies* 48, no. 5 (2010): 1351–65.

Øhrgaard, Jakob C. "'Less Than Supranational, More Than Intergovernmental': European Political Cooperation and the Dynamics of Intergovernmental Integration." *Millennium* 26, no. 1 (1997): 1–29.

Østhagen, Andreas. "Utenrikspolitisk Entreprenørskap. EU og Utviklingen av en Arktis-Politikk." *Internasjonal Politikk* 69, no. 1 (2011): 7–35.

Passos, Ricardo. "The European Union's External Relations a Year after Lisbon: a First Evaluation from the European Parliament." In *The European Union's External Relations: A Year after Lisbon*, edited by Panos Koutrakos, 49–56. CLEER Working Paper 2011/3. The Hague: CLEER, 2011.

Raube, Kolja. "Parliamentarization Approaches: Parliamentary Control in EU Foreign Policy." In *New Approaches to EU Foreign Policy*, edited by Maciej Wilga and Ireneusz Pawel Karolewski, 125–42. London: Routledge, 2014.

Redei, Lorinc. "The European Parliament as a Diplomatic Precedent Setter: The Case of Parliamentary Relations with Kosovo." In *The European Parliament and Its International Relations*, edited by Stelios Stavridis and Daniela Irrera, 272–85. New York: Routledge, 2015.

Riddervold, Marianne. "(Not) in the Hands of the Member States. How the Commission Influences EU Foreign and Security Policies." *Journal of Common Market Studies* 54, no. 20 (2016): 353–69.

Riddervold, Marianne. *The Maritime Turn in EU Foreign and Security Policies: Aims, Actors and Mechanisms of Integration*. London: Palgrave Macmillan, 2018.

Riddervold, Marianne, and Guri Rosén. "Trick or Treat: How the Commission and the European Parliament Exert Influence in EU Foreign and Security Policies." *Journal of European Integration* 38, no. 6 (2016): 687–702.

Riddervold, Marianne, and Jarle Trondal. "Integrating Nascent Organizations. On the Settlement of the European External Action Service." *Journal of European Integration* 39, no. 1 (2017): 33–47.

Rosén, Guri. "EU Confidential: The European Parliament's Involvement in EU Security and Defence Policy." *Journal of Common Market Studies* 53, no. 2 (2015): 383–98.

Rosén, Guri, and Kolja Raube. "Influence beyond Formal Powers: The Parliamentarization of European Union Security Policy." *British Journal of Politics and International Relations* 20, no. 1 (2018): 69–83.

Sjursen, Helene. "Not So Intergovernmental After All? On Democracy and Integration in European Foreign and Security Policy." *Journal of European Public Policy* 18, no. 8 (2011): 1078–95.

Smith, Michael E. *Europe's Foreign and Security Policy. The Institutionalization of Cooperation*. Cambridge: Cambridge University Press, 2004.

Stavridis, Stelios, and Daniela Irrera. *The European Parliament and Its International Relations*. New York: Routledge, 2015.

Strikwerda, Johanna. "Sovereignty at Stake? The European Commission's Proposal for a Defence and Security Procurement Directive." *European Security* 26, no. 1 (2017): 19–36.

Thomas, Daniel C. "Explaining EU Foreign Policy: Normative Institutionalism and Alternative Approaches." In *Making EU Foreign Policy: National Preferences, European Norms and Common Policies*, edited by Daniel C. Thomas, 10–28. Houndmills: Palgrave Macmillan, 2011.

Thym, Daniel. "The Intergovernmental Constitution of the EU's Foreign, Security and Defence Executive." *European Constitutional Law Review* 7 (2011): 453–80.

Walker, Shaun, and Andrew MacDowall. "US-backed Kosovo Land-Swap Border Plan under Fire from All Sides." *Guardian*, September 3, 2018.

Wisniewski, Elisabeth. "The Influence of the European Parliament on the European External Action Service." *European Foreign Affairs Review* 18, no. 1 (2013): 81–102.

4

REALISM, INTERNATIONAL ORDER AND SECURITY

Time to move beyond the 2016 European Union Global Strategy

David García Cantalapiedra

EU identity and the International Multilateral Liberal Order

According to Pr. John Ikenberry, the International Liberal Order would be an "open and rule-based international order ... enshrined in institutions such as the United Nations and norms such as multilateralism."[1] This order is composed of a set of inchoate but often powerful shared norms in which any security order established by the states system would be an order in which what states can and cannot do is not simply determined by power. This belief lies at the core of the EU's identity[2] and it has been sustaining a proactive agenda to support that system in setting an economic, institutionalized and secure order. Paradoxically, what is problematic for the EU identity is the problem of a changing international environment: the EU built itself as a result of the European integration process, as a reconciliation project, but also was a product of the Cold War power competition. However, some structural factors have had a decisive impact on the general framework of the International System during the last decade and will probably remain influential for the coming years: the 2008 Great Recession, the rise of Asia as the center of world affairs and the Fourth Industrial and Tech Revolution.[3] Probably there has not been a strategic shock of such magnitude since the end of the Cold War, severely affecting the strategic position of the transatlantic-led international order. No doubt the security and defense realm was one of the most affected by this state of affairs, which impacted severely on an already embattled sector, including a reduction on deterrence, crisis management, and political influence. Former US secretary of defense Robert Gates had already issued a stern warning to European governments in 2010, not only about defense budget limitations but about the dangers of going "too far in the other direction." For him, large parts of the general public and political class were so averse to military force and the risks that go with it that they have become an impediment to achieving real security:

> These budget limitations relate to a larger cultural and political trend affecting the alliance.... I believe we have reached an inflection point, where much of the continent has gone too far in the other direction.... The demilitarization of Europe – where

> large swaths of the general public and political class are averse to military force and the risks that go with it – has gone from a blessing in the 20th century to an impediment to achieving real security and lasting peace in the 21st … Not only can real or perceived weakness be a temptation to miscalculation and aggression, but, on a more basic level, the resulting funding and capability shortfalls make it difficult to operate and fight together to confront shared threats.[4]

This situation has had a dangerous impact on the EU political and strategic position, not only in the short term but, and this is more important, for the long term. It could present an image of declining ability to allies and partners in Asia and the Americas – ability to manage security cooperation over common security problems – and could reduce the perception of strategic assurance at a time of rapid global change. Moreover, an absence of a global vision, instruments and political will would reduce the EU's credibility for present and future commitments and cooperation. Such perceptions and images tend to offer this kind of conclusion to a large array of competitors and other unfriendly actors and adversaries.[5] The EU's commitment to and defense of an international rules-based order still seems clear, but the changing dynamics in the global security environment could represent a different challenge for the EU, which would probably mean a major game change in the EU strategic vision and mission. The new structure of the International System could mean that the EU should rethink its project or even the basis of its "identity": the European integration project was mainly a reconciliation project, not the creation of a world power. Maybe the EU should reconsider this option again. If not, the trip to strategic irrelevance will be faster and more difficult than the elites and the general population think.

The European Union and the structure of the International System: narratives and realities

Some structural factors have had a decisive impact on the general framework of the International System during the last decade and will probably continue to do so for the coming years: the 2008 Great Recession, the rise of Asia as the center of world affairs and the Fourth Industrial and Tech Revolution.[6] Narratives and official positions in many security strategies and policies[7] assume multipolarity as the structure of the International System, which is mainly seen as being the result of these developments. These analyses are based on a series of convergent factors: certain developments related to US policies; the decline of some Western and Asian allies (in Europe and Asia); and the (re)rise of other great powers (especially the People's Republic of China).[8] Some factors, such as the redistribution of capacities or deconcentration of power (for some, diffusion of power), have tended to produce a greater perception of anarchy and uncertainty in the International System, as well as a series of realignments at different levels, be they large, medium or small powers, although in other cases there has been reaffirmation of existing alignments and alliances. Actually, in structural terms, the number of poles selects and "socializes" the actors towards a certain form of behavior. These behaviors depend on structural variables and perceptions of position, capabilities and threats.[9] The structure of the system (anarchy and distribution of capacities-polarity) impacts on the interactions of the actors; that is, there is a systemic impact of indetermination. Thus, there is an indetermination in behavior, which is why it is necessary to use perceptions about strategic incentives according to the vision of the different capacities of the actors. Is multipolarity actually the structure of the system?[10] Will it be the structure in the near future? Even carrying out an analysis using Susan Strange's structural powers theory,[11] the future of the structure of the system could lead to bipolarity between the United States and the People's Republic of China, or, probably, a system with a superpower, a potential emerging superpower and a number of great powers.[12] Meanwhile, the campaign of attrition toward the US leadership during the Bush Administration, changes in policies during the Obama Administration, the uncertainty produced by the Great Recession and the arrival of the Trump Administration, has been accompanied by a campaign to delegitimize the International Liberal Order, which has been sustained by the United States and its allies since the end of the Second World War. However, this would be but a phase in a process towards the end of that unipolarity.[13] Paradoxically, the United States itself has carried out a series of strategic, political and even narrative reviews during the Obama Administration that have favored the image of decline and a multipolar situation, even recognizing the existence of other centers of power as, for example, in its 2010 National Security Strategy. This process should, however, be related to how the actors respond to the structure of the International System, and to the capacity to impact on that structure.[14] For the EU, in a situation of relative decline, the lack of strategic clarity is really dangerous. Certainly, some positions come from a very specific situation in EU Member States' domestic policy and in the EU institutions. Although the 2016 EUGS (EU Global Strategy) makes basic reference to the uncertainty in the International System, paradoxically it will not make reference to the specific policies to be implemented in this context. The EU considers the world today as a place of controversy. In this sense, the International System today has many more actors, less and worse leadership, and a more complex agenda than in the past. It is also important to note that despite the correct identification of the state of affairs, the new strategy offers perhaps a little over-optimism insofar as it considers that it has a series of capacities that it does not have in real terms.[15] It is clear that the EU does not have the precise mechanisms to deal with the threats it has previously identified, and that one of the clearest options was to reinforce its alliances and partnerships. In this sense, the EU started launching an initiative to sign a joint declaration with NATO at the Warsaw Summit in July 2016.[16] Options for alliances and the behavior of states in terms of policies are impacted by the structure of the International System, as well as by the perceptions of strategic incentives and the creation of security dilemmas. Errors of perception and misidentification of the structure of the system can lead to strategic errors or undesirable effects. For instance, multipolarity, as a structural factor that impacts the actors, would increase the indeterminacy by: including more actors, calculations of strategic incentives, and perceptions;[17] considering multipolar or bipolar scenarios when they are tripolar;[18] or producing erroneous perceptions about the advantage of the offensive or defense as in the First and Second World Wars.[19] The situation of unipolarity has created a contestation to US policies[20] but the relative decline of the West (probably greater in Europe than in North America) and the change of US strategic priorities have also impacted on the global status quo regarding the relative position of Europe. The European Union has attempted, sometimes in a difficult and tortuous way, the definition of itself and its role in an international environment in transformation which will hardly respond to the international framework integrated by Western countries since the end of the Second World War and after the end of the Cold War.

The European Union does not seem to intend to rely mainly, or to a large extent, on its capacity for the projection of power. Instead, the EU prides itself on being a model for prosperity and a mechanism for the peaceful resolution of problems and reconciliation. Europe leads this model as an example for the rest of the world, and there is a powerful logic behind this notion. The problem is that the farther away the geographical area, the less the influence of European leadership and the greater the reduction of the EU's influence. Still, the whole periphery presents first-class strategic problems, which can no longer be solved with normative power, such as the Middle East–Persian Gulf situation or that of Eastern Europe–Caucasus–Central Asia. The reduced capacity to influence developments, as demonstrated during the Arab

Spring, the civil war in Syria, and the Crimean crisis and Ukraine with Russia,[21] would point out a lack of correlation between the EU's vital interests, its strategic neighborhood and its military, economic and technological capabilities and instruments.[22] This could bring the EU into a hard security dilemma, not perhaps in the short or medium term, but in the long term. This dynamic clearly responds to the fact that states suffer a security dilemma in international politics:[23] uncertainty regarding the current and future motivations of other actors in a situation who are under the influence of anarchy in the structure of the International System makes the levels and trends in relative power into fundamental causal variables, that is, giving strategic uncertainty. This fuels the security dilemma and becomes apparent as states take measures to increase their security that others perceive as reductions in theirs. This problem is exacerbated by the incentives that actors have to deceive one another.[24] States have sought different ways to face the security dilemma, suffering the problems of uncertainty, the processes of perception and, finally, the self-destructive process of the search for security in an anarchic international system. Thus, accordingly, this dilemma will be more severe in multipolar systems than in bipolar or unipolar systems: this would be due to the fact that multipolar systems are less stable.[25] Given the situation of the EU and the dynamic of the structure of the International System, strategic uncertainty, that is, uncertainty about the present and, especially, the future intentions of others that makes the levels and trends in relative power fundamental causal variables,[26] is the key problem for the EU's future security.

The "resilience trap": uncertainty, deterrence and other unanswered questions

In any case for the European Union, a narrative of relative decline should not necessarily establish the strategic options available. Indeed, the tremendous impact of the Great Recession created in the domestic politics of the Member States and the EU an economic and social crisis but also a deep crisis of values and goals. Nevertheless, it is vital that an analysis of the International System takes place, based on an understanding of its structure as one of the essential factors when developing the necessary policies and strategies. It would be a key mechanism to rewrite significant interests, policies and strategies, not only in the Member States but in the European Union itself. Despite the fact that the 2016 EUGS makes constant reference to the uncertainty in the International System, paradoxically it did not explicitly refer to the specific policies to be implemented in this context:

> Our world today is more connected, contested and complex. This makes our global environment more unpredictable, creating instability and ambiguity, but also leads to new opportunities. In the European Union's neighborhood, a set of concurrent and heightened crises create an arc of instability. This will have implications for the Union and the wider world for many years to come. The European Union needs to take a fresh look at this uncertain environment, in which opportunities and challenges coexist. An EU Global Strategy on Foreign and Security Policy will enable the Union to identify a clear set of objectives and priorities for now and the future.[27]

The decline of such an International Liberal Order, in which the EU was comfortable and dominant in practical and theoretical terms, imposing and spreading its normative view, fuels the weaknesses in the EU's current approach: the unsolved problem of uncertainty, and the end of the Western dominance over the structure of this International Order. Probably, the EU does not trust in its ability to face uncertainty, not only for material (in term of resources) and political (lack of consensus) reasons, but also because of a loss of confidence in terms of rational approach and capability. John Stuart Mill's warning words about predictions of "a certain order of possible progress" could be dangerous regarding linear ideas of progress,[28] which appeared after the heralded Fukuyama's "End of History"[29] and were enthusiastically adopted by the EU: the expansion and adoption of a liberal agenda internationally offered a wishful thinking scenario to Brussels and other capitals in Europe. After the Great Recession, the EU lost direction and lost its main axis, provoking a crisis of identity and interests. Uncertainty appeared at the very front line of the EU's strategic thinking, not the promotion of a liberal agenda, and, to a certain point, it was a kind of concept somehow strange for the EU's strategic community culture due to the conceptual background, mostly based on constructivist approaches to international relations. From this background, uncertainty is mainly indetermination. Thus, information is ambiguous because it lacks meaning in the absence of norms and identity. Notions appropriate to particular conceptions are necessary for interpretation. The malleability of norms and identity makes international relations indeterminate and permanently subject to change on the part of the implied agents.[30] The implication of uncertainty as indeterminacy is that states and statesmen in international relations have somewhat of a tabula rasa. They are not predisposed toward conflict or cooperation. States have no inherent interests. States are uncertain about what to do primarily because action is impossible without norms, which prescribe appropriate action given a set of identities. International relations are uncertain in that they are indeterminate given the tabula rasa of state identities and norms. Information has no intrinsic meaning absent these social constructions. Learning is not the simple accumulation of information, but rather the definition of new identities as information is interpreted through and wedded to normative understandings.[31] Thus, the crisis in the international organizations, which form the vertebrae of the structure of the International Liberal Order and are primary actors in constituting international norms and identities, given their moral authority as representatives of the international community's interest, means a growing uncertainty in terms of indeterminacy for the EU identity and its role in the world. As uncertainty poses major practical and theoretical problems to the EU's security approach, the response has been found in a concept which really has behind it the same ideas of human security and sustainable development adopted after the end of the Cold War: resilience as the ability of states and societies to reform, thus withstanding and recovering from internal and external crisis. Thus, the main features of a resilient state and society, according to HR/VP Mogherini, would be "featuring democracy, trust in institutions, and sustainable development."[32] However, the decline of the Liberal Order would mean a shift toward other systems, in which multilateralism, democracy and trust in institutions will not be main features anymore. And, unfortunately, these would be systems in which sustainable development could also be provided by non-democratic states. Some critics establish this concept as the 2016 EUGS's leitmotif, turning over responsibility mainly to local communities and individuals, since the rejection of a structural pressure from power competition, the focus on the security concept (human security and development) and the acceptance of a certain inability to foresee the intentions of actors due to this uncertain international system together create a perfect middle ground between over-ambitious liberal peacebuilding and the under-ambitious objective of stability.[33] Responsibility for security is redistributed from government to municipalities, from the national to the local, and from security authorities to citizens, stimulating self-organization and control. As some positions warn, "resilience governance decentralizes power and responsibility to the locale, inverting traditional security logics based on state level control."[34] The resilient subject is one that "must permanently struggle to accommodate itself to the world: not a subject that can conceive of changing the world."[35] This conception follows the constructivist idea of co-constitution between actor and structure, and drives it in a process in which structures constitute actors in terms of their interests and identities, but structures are also produced, reproduced and altered by the discursive practices of agents.[36] Nevertheless, states are uncertain not only about others' intentions, but also about how to understand the information they find in front of them. This makes them less certain about how to respond, and, in this context, society and other sub-state actors will be even worse prepared to face this environment. This dynamic could dangerously shift responsibility for security toward private hands, losing the state its control over monopoly of force, for instance, through the use of private military/security companies, or allowing companies to hack back in cases of cyber-attacks. In the case of certain societies or groups, this responsibility could easily be in the hands of clans or tribes, and when a situation of a fragile state exists, the population could accept this situation even from insurgents or cartels if there is no other source of security available from the state. At the same time, and paradoxically, the EU relinquishes a main feature of resilience as sustainable development in non-democratic governments and other organizations and initiatives promoted by them, who do not share the EU's core vision and values. Really, the concept of security central to the EUGS is far from clear and well defined. Attempting to place resilience as a de facto security concept, the document nominally still uses human security. It is problematic, since there is no single definition of human security and the EUGS does not itself define human security, although it is supposed that it refers to EU conceptions enclosed in "A Human Security Doctrine for Europe"[37] and "From Hybrid Peace to Human Security: Rethinking EU Strategy towards Conflict."[38] Yet, it establishes an excessively broad definition of security, placing human rights issues at the center of the agenda. Human security defenders establish causal relations between socio-economic issues and political issues, or between the safety of the individual and the maintenance of international peace, relation which are not completely clear or accepted. In the same vein, a remarkable number of experts consider that, at best, "resilience" is an "abstract and malleable" concept (this may also have contributed to its acceptability to policymakers), while others consider it nothing more than an empty catch-phrase, and, at worst, as little as an ontological fact.[39] In fact, a key EU document about resilience – the EU report "Resilience in Practice"[40] – establishes multiple possible definitions of resilience, repeating the problem observed with the definition of human security: the report itself admits this situation in its executive summary, stating "Both the definition and the approach are specific to each organization."

Nuclear weapons renaissance, deterrence and the EU

The 2016 EUGS does not lay out a clear definition and prioritization of terrorism, hybrid threats, cyber- and energy security, organized crime and external border management. Since all these concepts are defined as challenges, none is considered to be a risk or a threat to security. At the same time, there is no reference to cyber-attacks, cyber-warfare or weapons of mass destruction (WMD), a nuclear arms race or military competition. WMD proliferation is not treated as a security threat, but as a global governance problem; hybrid threats are not defined either, and there is not even a clear idea of how to approach and face them. Here rests an important part of the resilience trap: resilience changes the perception of threats, risks and crises, and this has profound implications for our understanding of human agency. Thus, the document really does not face the problematic of how to deter complex threats in a context of asymmetry–interdependence–multipolarity/multi-order complex. Moreover, as it is not really a security strategy, threats and challenges are scattered here and there, sometimes creating confusion. The strategy, in this way, is not clear and is somewhat chaotic. The exposure of threats and challenges, something essential in this type of document, leaves its centrality to the exposition of the values and principles that must guide the external action. At the end, it seems that the EU thinks that security is a development problem and that it can be solved with an integrated approach:

"The EU will foster human security through an integrated approach."[41] Unfortunately, first, this approach does not work properly, as Iraq, Afghanistan and other experiences have shown; second, there are power competition and security dilemmas that cannot be solved only through governance mechanisms (one of the effects of this is the resurgence of nuclear weapons as a valuable tool in international politics). How are we to face an arms race of autonomous weapons, cyber-weapons, space weapons and nuclear weapons using resilience and human security? For instance, the WMD proliferation is seen as a governance problem, as it is located in the part of the EUGS dedicated to governance.[42] Probably the example and the success of achieving the Iran agreement (Joint Comprehensive Plan of Action) allows that way of thinking. That framework paradoxically created a key role for the EU in Middle East affairs, something the EU and some European countries have been looking for for decades, above all after the US invasion of Iraq. But this approach is intrinsically problematic, because it does not solve security dilemmas among powers in the Middle East; on the contrary, it seems to exacerbate them. The reference to the WMD proliferation is reduced to this point and it is not regarded as a challenge, risk or threat. Certainly, the EUGS neglects a trend in the International System to nuclear multipolarity, its impact on strategic stability and the dangerous relationship with cyber-war.[43] This is also understandable, due to the lack of an EU nuclear capability (with the exception of France), the 2003 EU WMD strategy and the existing institutional structure to manage the issue within the EU.[44] After Brexit, UK nuclear forces will remain in NATO but not in the EU. European states have been under the US nuclear umbrella through NATO but, meanwhile, the United States, France, the UK and NATO have been disarming and changing their strategies and doctrines on nuclear weapons, reducing their reliance on nuclear forces. At the same time, nuclear rearmament and modernization programs have been growing during the last ten years in spite of policies such as the zero global, the reinforcement of the non-proliferation regime, and agreements such as the 2010 New START treaty.[45] China, India, Pakistan, North Korea and Russia have been developing new nuclear weapons, some of them with first-use doctrines as Pakistan's.[46] The United States and other countries have been denouncing the 1987 Intermediate Nuclear Forces Treaty (INF) violation by Russia at least since 2007[47] at the same time as withdrawing from the 1990 Conventional Armed Forces in Europe Treaty (CFE).[48] Still other non-declared nuclear powers (Israel), latent nuclear powers (Iran) and NNWS (non-nuclear weapons states) with other countries' nuclear deployed weapons exist. Even taking into account this context, the 2016 EUGS does not contemplate deterrence as a meaningful tool or strategy, naming it once in the document as part of conflict prevention and resolution.[49] It seems as if there was an idea about deterrence in practice that is shifting because of expanded normative constraints on using force, leaving the concept old-fashioned and inadequate for contemporary security challenges. This is a somewhat flawed perspective.[50] There is insufficient agreement on how to get a suitable consensus for strengthening the non-proliferation regime, which has some deterrence capabilities but hardly makes using them a high priority. Less attention has been given to how to apply deterrence more effectively, particularly by using force. Deterrence is about "threatening enough harm to prevent an attack, being ready to inflict it and being credible."[51] In fact, deterrence has never been about just threatening and inflicting only enough harm to the attacker. Revisionist states could challenge the status quo even if the military prospects are bleak and the possibilities of destruction considerable. Not only can rational calculation lead such states to challenge the status quo, but there may be strong psychological pressures to conclude that a situation that is believed to be intolerable can be changed. WMD proliferation in highly dissatisfied states will not necessarily repeat the pattern of Soviet–American stability. Now, the United States has denounced the Joint Comprehensive Plan of Action (JCPA) with Iran,[52] is embarked on the most ambitious program of modernization of its nuclear forces, including a turn in its policy and strategy through the 2017 Nuclear Posture Review and the 2018 National Defense Strategy,[53] and is tracking toward the denunciation of the 1987 Intermediate Nuclear Forces Treaty. From this point of view, the last process is also related to China's growing nuclear-capable and conventional missile inventory mostly composed of systems in the INF Treaty–prohibited range of 500 to 5,500 kilometers, including cruise missiles.[54] This situation has left the EU in a problematic situation for the future management of a growing nuclear arms race, with poor options: on the one hand, improbable non-proliferation treaty (NPT) regimes reinforcement, disarmament agreements and nuclear ban treaties, and, on the other hand, trying to develop an *indigenous* nuclear force.[55]

War, levels of order and a new multi-domain security space

Coming from a time and place in which it was easy to establish the difference between peace and war, and between interior security and external security, it was also easy to face a comprehensive security concept and an idea of a security complex in which the security of states and individuals was intrinsically linked.[56] But these notions originate in a certain idea of order(s) and were based mainly in a Westphalian model. For instance, Hedley Bull already established in his seminal work *The Anarchic Society* the changes that could take place in the structure of the International System when the States, that Westphalian system, begin to lose their dominance: a progressive loss of sovereignty in favor of non-state actors, which would provoke the emergence of private violence and the loss of a monopoly in the use of force, including the influence of transnational actors and technology that could progressively make borders disappear. Bull argued that if these dynamics occurred, the International System could return to a pre-Westphalian situation and that there would be a whole series of non-state actors that would not only compete with the state as main entities of the International System, but they could even replace it.[57] Paradoxically, an institution that Bull considered inseparable from that system of States was the War: "War is organized violence carried out by political units against each other. Violence is not war unless it is carried out in the name of a political unit." He also considered the development of the modern concept of war as organized violence among sovereign states as the result of a process of limiting or confining violence. Thus, in any real hostility to which we can give the name of "war," norms or rules, whether legal or otherwise, invariably play a role. However, if the system of States would evolve to that pre-Westphalian situation that Bull posed, is it only the organized violence of political units carried against each other that we would consider War, or would this concept be extended? What would happen if there were non-state political units, or even non-political units, from the point of view of the definition of War; would War between them and the States be possible? Moreover, would War, as Bull understood it, be possible in a pre-Westphalian system? Really, in that system, politics was not only the patrimony of the State nor of its exclusivity. Bull articulated his concept of War through the difference between war in the material sense, that is, real hostilities, and war in the legal or normative sense, a theoretical state created by the satisfaction of certain legal or normative criteria: "If we talk about war in the legal sense, the distinction between war and peace is absolute. On the other hand, war in the material sense is sometimes difficult to distinguish from peace." But Bull recognized the impossibility of separating the two since the dynamics of hostilities sometimes play against that separation. Volatile, uncertain, complex and highly ambiguous conflicts have been the norm, while conventional warfare basically emerged after the World Wars. Many seem unaware of this fact, which explains in part why "hybrid threats" or "gray zones" seem to be new. This lack of historical awareness also contributes to our lack of conceptual preparation.[58] As the cases of (conventional) war between states become increasingly rare, this variation of the war will become the predominant method in the near future. Hybrid threats are defined as "any adversary that simultaneously and adaptively employs a tailored mix of conventional, irregular, terrorism and criminal means or activities in the operational battlespace," and a hybrid threat or challenger may be comprised of a combination of state and non-state actors.[59] The US Military also define them as a "diverse and dynamic combination of regular forces, irregular forces, criminal elements, or a combination of these forces and elements all unified to achieve mutually benefitting effects."[60] It is remarkable that there is no longer a clear distinction between what is and is not a battlefield, with the complex phenomenon of criminal insurgency.[61] Physical spaces (Global Commons) are all potential battlefields, but social spaces such as political, economic and cultural spheres, cyberspace and even the psyche are also at risk. Some authors, such as Frank Hoffman, Peter Singer, Colin S. Gray, Max Boot or John Arquilla, have debated about the nature and impact of these threats. However, there is neither a debate about the impact of these categories in the different schools of security studies nor a real attempt at delivering new approaches and definitions of the concept of Security. This concept is undergoing a perceptible change insofar as it has become transversal, transnational and globalized. Hybrid threats have created a new scenario that exceeds the traditional separation between internal and external security. Current security concepts do not exhaustively explain certain phenomena. Therefore, this question is leading to a more exhaustive explanation and analysis of phenomena of which the procedures and objectives do not comply with the parameters known up to now and that encompass multiple spaces and dimensions. Security is a phenomenon essentially polyhedral and transversal, that affects the different levels, domains and "Global Commons." The dynamics present mixed and multi-level threats: there is self-synchronization, unpredictability and non-linear actions by different groups and/or organizations. In the field of Defense this situation leads to the "Multi-domain Battlefield."[62] However, this dynamic is moving to the security realm: the hybridization of threats is pushing to establish new policing approaches in a multi-domain/trans-domain security space. For instance, as Rosa Brooks establishes: "Similarly, we struggle to tell the difference between 'civilians' and 'combatants.' What counts as a protected civilian object in cyberspace? When can a hacker, a financier, or a propagandist be considered a combatant?"[63] Not only do we face "new" threats and "Gray Zones"; we face a new concept of security. Again, resilience is a bleak solution for hybrid threats as human security and development will not solve this dynamic, and the EUGS does not even include any definition of hybrid threats. These dynamics converge, leading to a "militarization" of Security, and a "policing" of Defense, blurring the division and differences between interior security and external security:

> Internal and external security are ever more intertwined: our security at home entails a parallel interest in peace in our neighboring and surrounding regions. It implies a broader interest in preventing conflict, promoting human security, addressing the root causes of instability and working towards a safer world.[64]

In fact, as internal and external security are more and more intertwined, so will be security and defense: this is a convergence dynamic militarizing security and policing defense. Preventing conflict for the EU will need more forward conflict prevention – that is, not only in time but also in space, including sometimes the use or threat of use of force. But this is not only for promoting democracy, institutions and sustainable development: The rise of hybrid threats and the gray zones is creating a multi-domain security space that has nothing to do with the environment the EUGS describes. In this new multi-domain security space, the goal does not seem to be mainly to secure state, societies and human beings: first, since the meaning of state is not clear, societies and human beings are receptors of this protection; and second, all the domains are not equal in importance – nor are some of them domains at all, because it is far from clear that there exists a clear "dominance" of every domain.[65] However, the goal seems to be to control the domains of conflict: Physical (land, sea, air, space), Information/Cyber, Cognitive, Moral and Social.[66] The continued shift of political and social loyalties to causes rather than nations, and the increasing power of smaller and smaller entities and networks, their divergence in goals but similarities in procedures, create permanent competition with States. The dismay of the latter at new interpretations of once-fixed legal concepts can push them to take a middle ground, quietly questioning "gray zones" or "new" interpretations about the problem of militarization and policing while trying to strengthen their previous interpretations. However, this expansion of the domains of conflict makes possible the exponential expansion of the concept of the battlefield beyond the physical domain by removing its geographical and political constraints and allowing it to become omnipresent. In response to the question, "Where is the battlefield?" two PLA (People's Liberation Army) colonels Qiao Liang and Wang Xiangsui, in their 1999 book *Unrestricted Warfare* answer simply "everywhere": "Using all means, including armed force or non-armed force, military and nonmilitary, and lethal and non-lethal means to compel an enemy to accept one's interests."[67]

Conclusion: great powers' competition, deterrence and power projection

The International Liberal Order was probably never what we thought. It has been and will be more, in Stephen Walt's words, a "lopsided Multipolarity," maintaining great powers competition as a main feature.[68] For the EU it is vital, and strategically relevant, to correctly analyze the International System, based on an understanding of the structure of the system as one of the fundamental factors when developing the necessary policies and strategies. The 2016 EUGS is not a security strategy because is undoubtedly weak in content, the hierarchy of threats and challenges, and means to face them, although it sees the challenge of sophisticated threats as the effects of asymmetry, interdependence and multipolarity, including the regional crisis in the Eastern and Southern Neighbourhoods.[69] It faces a security dilemma mainly created by the reduction in the allocation of resources in the security and defense realm (above all during the Great Recession, but also before that) and the perception of a partial abandonment of the transatlantic alliance by the United States. It is not a Grand Strategy either, as it is far from attaining that status devised by the major powers. It cannot reach such a level because the EU is not yet such a strategic, unitary or autonomous player. Nevertheless, it seems more like a foreign policy project: the EUGS frames security and defense aspects within the context of the EU's external action, setting out the main principles, values and operational patterns of its international conduct. The Lisbon Treaty and the 2016 EU Global Strategy draw a new structure and vision for the future of EU integration regarding the European Union's global role which it should urgently review. Given the current rapid evolution to a non-liberal international order, the EU should rethink its international role, policies and strategies, and the capabilities necessary to face these changes. The EU was thought up as a reconciliation project, not as the creation of a world power, but probably for defending this project and promoting its values, a change to effective mechanisms and means will be needed in order to play this new game. The EU capability for reinforcing collective security, deterrence and power projection has been reduced due to Brexit: the UK probably represents 25 percent of the EU's military capability and is a solid actor regarding intelligence capabilities and power projection. Future security arrangements between the UK and the EU will be extraordinarily difficult to resolve. However, the European Union does not seem to present itself as relying mainly or to a large extent on its capacity for the projection of power. Instead, the EU prides itself on being a model for prosperity and a mechanism for the peaceful resolution of problems and reconciliation. Europe leads this model as an example for the rest of the world and this idea has a compelling logic behind it. Unfortunately, this position also maintains a series of postulates that are either outdated or have not responded to the dynamics of the International System. The influence of European leadership decreases rapidly with an increase in geographical distance and the reduction of the EU's economic capacity. Paradoxically, the states on its borders present a whole series of strategic problems, which cannot anymore be faced with normative power alone. The EU's behavior, as demonstrated during the Arab Spring, the civil war in Syria, and the Crimea/Ukraine crisis has shown a worrying correlation between the EU's vital interests and the necessary military, economic and technological capabilities and instruments. The slow decoupling of the US–EU partnership and a role in the Indo-Pacific limited to trade and economic agreements focused only on defending a rules-based Liberal Order, does not display a realistic understanding of the nature, rules and consequences of a new and alternative International System-in-the-making. Failing to change, the EU could face a security dilemma, not perhaps in the short or medium term, but in the longer term, strongly affecting its position and role in world affairs and the defense of the future of the Multilateral Liberal International Order.

Notes

1 John Ikenberry, "The Future of the Liberal World Order," *Foreign Affairs* (May/June 2011): 56.
2 Manuel Castells, *The Construction of European Identity: Statement Prepared for the European Presidency of the European Union*, 2000.
3 Henry Kissinger, "The Three Revolutions," *Washington Post*, April 7, 2008.
4 US Secretary Robert Gates, NATO Strategic Concept Seminar, National Defense University, Washington, DC, February 23, 2010.
5 Robert Jervis, *The Logic of Images in International Relations* (Princeton: Princeton University Press, 1970), 5; Robert Jervis, *Perceptions and Misperceptions in International Politics* (Princeton: Princeton University Press, 1976), 15.
6 Henry Kissinger, "The Three Revolutions."
7 Among others, the 2010 US National Security Strategy; 2017 French Strategic Review of Defence and National Security; the 2016 Foreign Policy Concept of the Russian Federation; 2013 and 2017 Spanish National Security Strategy (https://www.dsn.gob.es/es/2017-spanish-national-security-strategy); US National Intelligence Council, *Global Trends 2030: Paradox of Progress* (US National Intelligence Council, 2017), https://www.dni.gov/files/documents/nic/GT-Full-Report.pdf.

Of these, the Spanish National Security Strategy is the framework of reference for National Security Policy, a State Policy with a comprehensive understanding of security, at the service of the citizens and the State. The current Strategy, which was approved by the National Security Council on the 1st of December 2017, delves into the concepts and lines of action defined in 2013, and adapts said Policy and the instruments and state resources that support it to a security environment in constant change.

With reference to the Global Trends reports, every four years since 1997, the National Intelligence Council has published an unclassified strategic assessment of how key trends and uncertainties might shape the world over the next 20 years to help senior US leaders think and plan for the longer term. The report is timed to be especially relevant for the administration of a newly elected US president, but Global Trends increasingly has served to foster discussions about the future with people around the world. We believe these global consultations, both in preparing the paper and sharing the results, help the NIC and broader US Government learn from perspectives beyond the United States and are useful in sparking discussions about key assumptions, priorities, and choices.

8 Andrew Mitcha, "The Deconstruction of the West." *The American Interest*, April 12, 2017.
9 Robert Jervis, *Perceptions and Misperceptions in International Politics.*
10 There are also non-polarity system arguments, "Unipolarity-Multipolarity complex," Smart Power categorizations or even multi-order models. See Richard Hass, "The Age of Non-polarity," *Foreign Affairs* (May/June 2008); Samuel Huntington, "The Lonely Superpower," *Foreign Affairs* (March/April

1999); Joseph S. Nye, "Get Smart: Combining Hard and Soft Power," *Foreign Affairs* (July/August 2009): 160–63: Theresa Flockhart, "The Coming Multi-order World," *Contemporary Security Policy* 37, no. 1 (2016): 3–30.

11 Susan Strange, *States and Markets* (London: Pinter Publishers, 1988); Susan Strange, *The Retreat of the State – The Diffusion of Power in the World Economy* (Cambridge: Cambridge University Press, 1996); David García Cantalapiedra, "EE.UU y la construcción de un Nuevo Orden Mundial: la Administración Bush, las Relaciones Transatlánticas y la Seguridad Europea (1989–1992)," PhD Dissertation, Complutense University of Madrid, 2001.

12 Stephen F. Brooks and William Wohlforth, "The Rise and Fall of the Great Powers in the Twenty-First Century," *International Security* 40, no. 3 (Winter 2015/16): 7–53; Nuno Monteiro, "Unrest Assured. Why Unipolarity Is Not Peaceful," *International Security* 36, no. 3 (Winter 2011–12): 9–40.

13 Randall Schweller and Xiaoyu Pu, "After Unipolarity: China's Visions of International Order in an Era of U.S. Decline," *International Security* 36, no. 1 (Summer 2011): 41–72.

14 Kenneth Waltz, "Structural Realism after the Cold War," *International Security* 25, no. 1 (Summer 2000): 27.

15 European External Action Service. *Shared Vision, Common Action: A Stronger Europe. A Global Strategy for the European Union's Foreign and Security Policy* (Brussels: European External Action Service, 2016), 16.

16 European Union, *Joint Declaration by the President of the European Council, the President of the European Commission, and the Secretary General of the North Atlantic Treaty Organizations* (Brussels: European Union, 2016).

17 Thomas Christiansen and Jack Snyder, "Chain Gangs and Passed Bucks: Predicting Alliance Patterns in Multipolarity," *International Organization* 44, no. 2 (1990): 137–68.

18 Randall Schweller and Xiaoyu Pu, *Deadly Imbalances: Tripolarity and Hitler's Strategy of World Conquest* (New York: Columbia University, 1998).

19 Robert Jervis, "Cooperation under the Security Dilemma," *World Politics* 30, no. 2 (1978): 168–214.

20 Nuno Monteiro, "Unrest Assured. Why Unipolarity Is Not Peaceful."

21 Henrik Boesen Lindbo Larsen, *Great Power Politics and the Ukrainian Crisis: NATO, EU and Russia after 2014*, Danish Institute for International Studies, 2014.

22 Stephen F. Brooks and William Wohlforth, "The Rise and fall of the Great Powers in the Twenty-First Century."

23 Robert Jervis, "Cooperation under the Security Dilemma."

24 Dale Copeland, "The Constructivist Challenge to Structural Realism: A Review Essay," *International Security* 25, no. 2 (2000).

25 Kenneth Waltz, *Theory of International Politics* (Reading: Addison-Westley, 1979), 172.

26 John Mearsheimer, *The Tragedy of Great Power Politics* (New York: Norton, 2001).

27 EUGS Introduction at the web page. European External Action Service, *Shared Vision, Common Action*, https://eeas.europa.eu/headquarters/headquarters-homepage/search/site/shared-vision-common-action-stronger-europe_en.

28 Adam Roberts, "International Relations after the Cold War," *International Affairs* 84, no. 2 (2008): 2.

29 Francis Fukuyama, "The End of History?," *The National Interest* 16 (1989): 3–18.

30 Brian C. Rathbun, "Uncertain about Uncertainty: Understanding the Multiple Meanings of a Crucial Concept in International Relations Theory," *International Studies Quarterly* 51 (2007): 534.

31 Ibid., 550–3.

32 European External Action Service, *Shared Vision, Common Action*, 24.

33 Wolfgang Wagner and Rosanne Anholt "Resilience as the EU Global Strategy's New Leitmotif: Pragmatic, Problematic or Promising?," *Contemporary Security Policy* 37, no. 3 (2016): 414–30.

34 Jon Coaffee and Pete Fussey, "Constructing Resilience through Security and Surveillance: The Politics, Practices and Tensions of Security-Driven Resilience," *Security Dialogue* 46, no. 1 (2015): 87.

35 David Chandler and Julian Reid, *The Neoliberal Subject: Resilience, Adaptation and Vulnerability* (London: Rowman & Littlefield International, 2016), 53.

36 Dale Copeland, "The Constructivist Challenge to Structural Realism: A Review Essay," 190.

37 Study Group on Europe's Security Capabilities, *A Human Security Doctrine for Europe: The Barcelona Report of the Study Group on Europe's Security Capabilities* (Study Group on Europe's Security Capabilities, 2004); Human Security Study Group, *A European Way of Security: The Madrid Report of the Human Security Study Group* (Human Security Study Group, 2007), http://eprints.lse.ac.uk/40207/1/A_European_Way_of_Security%28author%29.pdf.

38 Mary Kaldor, Iavor Rangelov, Vesna Bojicic-Dzelilovic, Alex de Waal, Sabine Selchow, Mary Martin and Rim Turkmani, *From Hybrid Peace to Human Security: Rethinking EU Strategy towards Conflict. The Berlin Report of the Human Security Study Group*, London: Security in Transition (SIT), European Research Council, Friedrich-Ebert-Stiftung (FES), 2016.
39 Wolfgang Wagner and Rosanne Anholt, "Resilience as the EU Global Strategy's New Leitmotif: Pragmatic, Problematic or Promising?," 10.
40 European Commission, *Resilience in Practice: Saving Lives and Improving Livelihoods* (Brussels: European Commission, October 2015), 9.
41 European External Action Service, *Shared Vision, Common Action*, 29.
42 Ibid., 41–42.
43 Beyza Unal and Patricia Lewis, "Cybersecurity of Nuclear Weapons. International Security Department," Research Papers (Chatham House, Royal Institute of International Affairs, 2018); David Gompert and Mick Libicki, "Cyber Warfare and Sino-American Crisis Instability," *Survival* 56, no. 4 (2014): 7–22; Stephen J. Cimbala, "Nuclear Deterrence and Cyber. The Quest for Concept," *Air & Space Power Journal* 87 (2014); Rebecca Slayton, "What Is the Cyber Offense-Defense Balance? Conceptions, Causes, and Assessment," *International Security* 41, no. 3 (2016/17).
44 Larks-Erik Lundin, "The European Union and Weapons of Mass Destruction: A Follow-On to the Global Strategy?," Non-Proliferation Papers 58 (May 2017). EU Non-Proliferation Consortium, 2017.
45 The New Strategic Arms Reduction Treaty (New START) was signed April 8, 2010 in Prague by Russia and the United States and entered into force on February 5, 2011. New START replaced the 1991 START I treaty, which expired December 2009, and superseded the 2002 Strategic Offensive Reductions Treaty (SORT), which terminated when New START entered into force. See Arms Control, "New START at a Glance," Fact Sheet, March 2018, www.armscontrol.org/factsheets/NewSTART.
46 Jaganath Sankaran, "Pakistan's Battlefield Nuclear Policy: A Risky Solution to an Exaggerated Threat," *International Security* 39, no. 3 (2015): 118–51.
47 Congressional Research Service, "Russian Compliance with the Intermediate Range Nuclear Forces (INF) Treaty: Background and Issues for Congress," Congressional Research Service, April 13, 2016, www.fas.org/sgp/crs/nuke/R43832.pdf; Ankit Panda, "The Uncertain Future of the INF Treaty," Council on Foreign Relations, February 21, 2018, www.cfr.org/backgrounder/uncertain-future-inf-treaty.
48 "Russia Suspends Participation in CFE Treaty," Radio Free Europe, December 12, 2007, www.rferl.org/a/1079256.html.
49 European External Action Service, *Shared Vision, Common Action*, 32.
50 Patrick M. Morgan, "The State of Deterrence in International Politics Today," *Contemporary Security Policy* 33, no. 1 (2012): 89.
51 Ibid., 97.
52 The White House, "President Donald J. Trump Is Ending United States Participation in an Unacceptable Iran Deal," *Foreign Policy*, May 8, 2018.
53 Congressional Budget Office, *Approaches for Managing the Costs of U.S. Nuclear Forces, 2017 to 2046*, October 31, 2017, www.cbo.gov/publication/53211; Office of the Secretary of Defense, Nuclear Posture Review, February 2018, https://media.defense.gov/2018/Feb/02/2001872886/-1/-1/1/2018-NUCLEAR-POSTURE-REVIEW-FINAL-REPORT.PDF; Summary of the 2018 National Defense Strategy of the United States of America, https://dod.defense.gov/Portals/1/Documents/pubs/2018-National-Defense-Strategy-Summary.pdf.
54 Debalina Ghospal, "China and the INF Treaty," *Comparative Strategy* 35, no. 5 (2016), www.tandfonline.com/doi/full/10.1080/01495933.2016.1240982.
55 Oliver Thränert, "No Shortcut to a European Deterrent," *Policy Perspectives* 5, no. 2 (2017).
56 Barry Buzan, Ole Waever and Jans de Wilders, *Security: A New Framework for Analysis* (Boulder: Lynne Rienner Publishers, 1998).
57 Hedley Bull, *The Anarchical Society: A Study of Order in World Politic* (New York: Columbia University Press, 1977); Susan Strange, *The Retreat of the State.*
58 Henry Kissinger, "Military Policy and Defense of the 'Grey Areas,'" *Foreign Affairs* 33, no. 3 (1955); Antulio Echeverria, *Operating in the Gray Zone: An Alternative Paradigm for U.S. Military Strategy* (Pennsylvania: United States Army War College Press, 2016).
59 Frank Hoffmann, "Hybrid Warfare and Challenges," *Joint Forces Quarterly* 52 (2009), http://smallwarsjournal.com/documents/jfqhoffman.pdf; Frank Hoffmann, "Conflicts in the 21st Century: The Rise

of Hybrid Wars," (Potomac Institute for Policy Studies, 2007). www.potomacinstitute.org/images/stories/publications/potomac_hybridwar_0108.pdf; Frank Hoffmann, "Hybrid vs. Compound War: The Janus Choice of Modern War: Defining Today's Multifaceted Conflict," *Armed Forces Journal* (2009), www.armedforcesjournal.com/hybrid-vs-compound-war/.

60 ADRP 3–0. *Army Doctrine Reference Publication. No. 3–0.* Headquarters Department of the Army. Washington, DC, 6 October 2017, 1–3.

61 John Sullivan, "From Drug Wars to Criminal Insurgency: Mexican Cartels, Criminal Enclaves and Criminal Insurgency in Mexico and Central America. Implications for Global Security," *Fondation Maison des sciences de l'homme* (2012). https://halshs.archives-ouvertes.fr/halshs-00694083; David García Cantalapiedra and Julia Pulido, "El nuevo espacio de seguridad trans/multi-dominio. Las amenazas híbridas y la insurgencia criminal: la evolución del concepto de sociedad anárquica de Hedley Bull," in *Cambios en la naturaleza de la Diplomacia y de la Guerra en los cuarenta años de la Sociedad Anárquica de Hedley Bull*, ed. Rafael Grasa and Caterina Garcia (Valencia: Tirant lo Blanch, 2019).

62 Shmuel Shmuel, "Multi-Domain Battle: AirLand Battle, Once More, with Feeling," *War on the Rocks*, June 20, 2017. https://warontherocks.com/2017/06/multi-domain-battle-airland-battle-once-more-with-feeling/.

63 Rosa Brooks, "Rule of Law in the Grey Zone," *Modern War Institute*, July 2, 2018; Rosa Brooks, *How Everything Became War and the Military Became Everything* (New York: Simon and Schuster, 2016).

64 European External Action Service, *Shared Vision, Common Action*, 10.

65 Erik Heftye, "Multidomain Confusion: All Domains Are Not Created Equal." *The Strategic Bridge*. May 26, 2017.

66 Donald Reed, "Beyond the War on Terror: Into the Fifth Generation of War and Conflict," *Studies in Conflict & Terrorism* 31, no. 8 (2008): 684–722.

67 Qiao Liang and Wang Xiangsui, *Unrestricted Warfare* (Beijing: PLA Literature and Arts Publishing House, 1999).

68 Stephen Walt, "What Sort of World Are We Headed For? The Liberal World Order Never Really Existed. Great-Power Politics Are Here to Stay," *Foreign Policy*, October 2, 2018, https://foreignpolicy.com/2018/10/02/what-sort-of-world-are-we-headed-for/.

69 Raquel Barras and David García Cantalapiedra. "Hacia un nuevo y diferente Flanco Sur en el Gran Magreb-Sahel," *Revista UNISC/UNISCI Journal* 39 (2015): 11–46; David García Cantalapiedra and Raquel Barras, "El Norte de África y el Sahel en la Estrategia Global de Seguridad Europea de 2016," *Revista UNISCI/UNISCI Journal* 42 (2016): 173–96.

Bibliography

ADRP 3–0. *Army Doctrine Reference Publication. No. 3–0.* Headquarters Department of the Army. Washington, DC, 6 October 2017.

Arms Control. "New START at a Glance." Fact Sheet, March 2018. www.armscontrol.org/factsheets/NewSTART.

Barras, Raquel, and David García Cantalapiedra. "Hacia un nuevo y diferente Flanco Sur en el Gran Magreb-Sahel." *Revista UNISCI/UNISCI Journal* 39 (2015): 11–46.

Brooks, Rosa. *How Everything Became War and the Military Became Everything*. New York: Simon and Schuster, 2016.

Brooks, Rosa. "Rule of Law in the Grey Zone." *Modern War Institute*, July 2, 2018. https://mwi.usma.edu/rule-law-gray-zone/.

Brooks, Stephen F., and William Wohlforth, "The Rise and Fall of the Great Powers in the Twenty-First Century." *International Security* 40, no. 3 (2015/16): 7–53.

Bull, Hedley. *The Anarchical Society: A Study of Order in World Politic.* New York: Columbia University Press, 1977.

Buzan, Barry, Ole Waever and Jans de Wilders. *Security: A New Framework for Analysis.* Boulder: Lynne Rienner Publishers, 1998.

Castells, Manuel. *The Construction of European Identity. Statement Prepared for the European Presidency of the European Union*, 2000.

Chandler, David, and Julian Reid. *The Neoliberal Subject: Resilience, Adaptation and Vulnerability.* London: Rowman & Littlefield International, 2016.

Christiansen, Thomas, and Jack Snyder. "Chain Gangs and Passed Bucks: Predicting Alliance Patterns in Multipolarity." *International Organization* 44, no. 2 (1990): 137–68.

Cimbala, Stephen J. "Nuclear Deterrence and Cyber. The Quest for Concept." *Air & Space Power Journal* 87 (2014): 87–107.

Coaffee, Jon, and Pete Fussey. "Constructing Resilience through Security and Surveillance: The Politics, Practices and Tensions of Security-Driven Resilience." *Security Dialogue* 46, no. 1 (2015): 86–105.

Congressional Budget Office. *Approaches for Managing the Costs of U.S. Nuclear Forces, 2017 to 2046*. October 31, 2017. www.cbo.gov/publication/53211.

Congressional Research Service. "Russian Compliance with the Intermediate Range Nuclear Forces (INF) Treaty: Background and Issues for Congress," Congressional Research Service, April 13, 2016. www.fas.org/sgp/crs/nuke/R43832.pdf.

Copeland, Dale. "The Constructivist Challenge to Structural Realism: A Review Essay." *International Security* 25, no. 2 (2000): 187–212.

Echeverria, Antulio. *Operating in the Gray Zone: An Alternative Paradigm for U.S. Military Strategy*. Pennsylvania: United States Army War College Press, 2016.

European Commission. *Resilience in Practice: Saving Lives and Improving Livelihoods*. Brussels: European Commission, October 2015.

European External Action Service. *Shared Vision, Common Action: A Stronger Europe. A Global Strategy for the European Union's Foreign and Security Policy*. Brussels: European External Actions Service, 2016.

European Union. *Joint Declaration by the President of the European Council, the President of the European Commission, and the Secretary General of the North Atlantic Treaty Organizations*. Brussels: European Union, 2016.

Flockhart, Theresa. "The Coming Multi-order World." *Contemporary Security Policy* 37, no. 1 (2016): 3–30.

Fukuyama, Francis. "The End of History?" *The National Interest* 16 (1989): 3–18.

García Cantalapiedra, David. "EE.UU y la construcción de un Nuevo Orden Mundial: la Administración Bush, las Relaciones Transatlánticas y la Seguridad Europea (1989–1992)." PhD Dissertation. Complutense University of Madrid, 2001.

García Cantalapiedra, David, and Julia Pulido. "El nuevo espacio de seguridad trans/multi-dominio. Las amenazas híbridas y la insurgencia criminal: la evolución del concepto de sociedad anárquica de Hedley Bull." In *Cambios en la naturaleza de la Diplomacia y de la Guerra en los cuarenta años de la Sociedad Anárquica de Hedley Bull*, edited by Rafael Grasa and Caterina Garcia, 211–20. Valencia: Tirant lo Blanch, 2019.

García Cantalapiedra, David, and Raquel Barras. "El Norte de África y el Sahel en la Estrategia Global de Seguridad Europea de 2016." *Revista UNISCI/UNISCI Journal* 42 (2016): 173–96.

Gates, Robert (US Secretary). NATO Strategic Concept Seminar, National Defense University, Washington, DC, February 23, 2010.

Ghospal, Debalina. "China and the INF Treaty, *Comparative Strategy* 35, no. 5 (2016): 363–70.

Gompert, David, and Mick Libicki. "Cyber Warfare and Sino-American Crisis Instability." *Survival* 56, no. 4 (2014): 7–22.

Hass, Richard. "The Age of Non-polarity." *Foreign Affairs* (May/June 2008).

Heftye, Erik. "*Conflicts in the 21st Century: The Rise of Hybrid Wars*." Potomac Institute for Policy Studies (2007). www.potomacinstitute.org/images/stories/publications/potomac_hybridwar_0108.pdf.

Heftye, Erik. "Hybrid vs. Compound War: The Janus Choice of Modern War: Defining Today's Multifaceted Conflict." *Armed Forces Journal* (October 2009). www.armedforcesjournal.com/hybrid-vs-compound-war/.

Heftye, Erik. "Hybrid Warfare and Challenges." *Joint Forces Quarterly* 52 (2009): 34–9.

Heftye, Erik. "Multidomain Confusion: All Domains Are Not Created Equal." *The Strategic Bridge*, May 26, 2017. www.realcleardefense.com/articles/2017/05/26/multi-domain_confusion_all_domains_are_not_created_equal_111463.html.

Hoffmann, Frank. "Conflicts in the 21st Century: The Rise of Hybrid Wars." Potomac Institute for Policy Studies, 2007. www.potomacinstitute.org/images/stories/publications/potomac_hybridwar_0108.pdf.

Hoffmann, Frank. "Hybrid vs. Compound War: The Janus Choice of Modern War: Defining Today's Multifaceted Conflict." *Armed Forces Journal* (2009). www.armedforcesjournal.com/hybrid-vs-compound-war/.

Hoffmann, Frank. "Hybrid Warfare and Challenges." *Joint Forces Quarterly* 52 (2009). http://smallwarsjournal.com/documents/jfqhoffman.pdf.

Human Security Study Group. *A European Way of Security: The Madrid Report of the Human Security Study Group*. Human Security Study Group, 2007. http://eprints.lse.ac.uk/40207/1/A_European_Way_of_Security%28author%29.pdf.

Huntington, Samuel. "The Lonely Superpower." *Foreign Affairs* (March/April 1999).
Ikenberry, John. "The Future of the Liberal World Order." *Foreign Affairs* (May/June 2011).
Jervis, Robert. "Cooperation under the Security Dilemma." *World Politics* 30, no. 2 (1978): 168–214.
Jervis, Robert. *Perceptions and Misperceptions in International Politics*. Princeton: Princeton University Press, 1976.
Jervis, Robert. *The Logic of Images in International Relations*. Princeton: Princeton University Press, 1970.
Kaldor, Mary, Iavor Rangelov, Vesna Bojicic-Dzelilovic, Alex de Waal, Sabine Selchow, Mary Martin and Rim Turkmani. *From Hybrid Peace to Human Security: Rethinking EU Strategy towards Conflict. The Berlin Report of the Human Security Study Group*. London: Security in Transition (SIT), European Research Council, Friedrich-Ebert-Stiftung (FES), 2016.
Kissinger, Henry. "Military Policy and Defense of the 'Grey Areas.'" *Foreign Affairs* 33, no. 3 (1955).
Kissinger, Henry. "The Three Revolutions." *Washington Post*, April 7, 2008.
Larsen, Henrik Boesen Lindbo. *Great Power Politics and the Ukrainian Crisis: NATO, EU and Russia after 2014*. Danish Institute for International Studies, 2014.
Lundin, Lars-Erik. "The European Union and Weapons of Mass Destruction: A Follow-On to the Global Strategy?" Non-Proliferation Papers 58 (May 2017). EU Non-Proliferation Consortium, 2017.
Mearsheimer, John. *The Tragedy of Great Power Politics*. New York: Norton, 2001.
Mitcha, Andrew. "The Deconstruction of the West." *The American Interest*, April 12, 2017.
Monteiro, Nuno. "Unrest Assured. Why Unipolarity Is Not Peaceful." *International Security* 36, no. 3 (2011–12): 9–40.
Morgan, Patrick M. "The State of Deterrence in International Politics Today." *Contemporary Security Policy* 33, no. 1 (2012): 85–107.
Nye, Joseph S. "Get Smart: Combining Hard and Soft Power." *Foreign Affairs* (July/August 2009): 160–63.
Office of the Secretary of Defense. *Nuclear Posture Review*. February 2018. https://media.defense.gov/2018/Feb/02/2001872886/-1/-1/1/2018-NUCLEAR-POSTURE-REVIEW-FINAL-REPORT.PDF;.
Panda, Ankit. "The Uncertain Future of the INF Treaty." Council on Foreign Relations, February 21, 2018. www.cfr.org/backgrounder/uncertain-future-inf-treaty.
Qiao, Liang and Wang Xiangsui. *Unrestricted Warfare*. Beijing: PLA Literature and Arts Publishing House, 1999.
Rathbun, Brian C. "Uncertain about Uncertainty: Understanding the Multiple Meanings of a Crucial Concept in International Relations Theory." *International Studies Quarterly* 51 (2007): 533–57.
Reed, Donald. "Beyond the War on Terror: Into the Fifth Generation of War and Conflict." *Studies in Conflict & Terrorism* 31, no. 8 (2008): 684–722.
Roberts, Adam. "International Relations after the Cold War." *International Affairs* 84, no. 2 (2008): 335–50.
"Russia Suspends Participation in CFE Treaty." Radio Free Europe, December 12, 2007. www.rferl.org/a/1079256.html.
Sankaran, Janath. "Pakistan's Battlefield Nuclear Policy: A Risky Solution to an Exaggerated Threat." *International Security* 39, no. 3 (2015): 118–51.
Schweller, Randall, and Xiaoyu Pu. "After Unipolarity: China's Visions of International Order in an Era of U.S. Decline." *International Security* 36, no. 1 (Summer 2011): 41–72.
Schweller, Randall, and Xiaoyu Pu. *Deadly Imbalances: Tripolarity and Hitler's Strategy of World Conquest*. New York: Columbia University, 1998.
Shmuel, Shmuel. "Multi-Domain Battle: AirLand Battle, Once More, with Feeling." *War on the Rocks*, June 20, 2017. https://warontherocks.com/2017/06/multi-domain-battle-airland-battle-once-more-with-feeling/.
Slayton, Rebecca. "What Is the Cyber Offense-Defense Balance? Conceptions, Causes, and Assessment." *International Security* 41, no. 3 (2016/17): 72–109.
Strange, Susan. *States and Markets*. London: Pinter Publishers, 1988.
Strange, Susan. *The Retreat of the State – The Diffusion of Power in the World Economy*. Cambridge: Cambridge University Press, 1996.
Study Group on Europe's Security Capabilities. *A Human Security Doctrine for Europe: The Barcelona Report of the Study Group on Europe's Security Capabilities*. Study Group on Europe's Security Capabilities, 2004.
Sullivan, John. "From Drug Wars to Criminal Insurgency: Mexican Cartels, Criminal Enclaves and Criminal Insurgency in Mexico and Central America. Implications for Global Security." Fondation Maison des sciences de l'homme, 2012. https://halshs.archives-ouvertes.fr/halshs-00694083.

Thränert, Oliver. "No Shortcut to a European Deterrent." *Policy Perspectives* 5, no. 2 (2017).
Unal, Beyza, and Patricia Lewis. "Cybersecurity of Nuclear Weapons: Threats, Vulnerabilities and Consequences." Research Papers. Chatham House, Royal Institute of International Affairs, 2018.
US Department of Defense. Summary of the 2018 National Defense Strategy of the United States of America. https://dod.defense.gov/Portals/1/Documents/pubs/2018-National-Defense-Strategy-Summary.pdf
US National Intelligence Council. *Global Trends 2030: Paradox of Progress* (US NIC,. 2017). https://www.dni.gov/files/documents/nic/GT-Full-Report.pdf.
Wagner, Wolfgang, and Rosanne Anholt. "Resilience as the EU Global Strategy's New Leitmotif: Pragmatic, Problematic or Promising?" *Contemporary Security Policy* 37, no. 3 (2016): 414–30.
Walt, Stephen. "What Sort of World Are We Headed For? The Liberal World Order Never Really Existed. Great-Power Politics Are Here to Stay." *Foreign Policy*, October 2, 2018. https://foreignpolicy.com/2018/10/02/what-sort-of-world-are-we-headed-for/.
Waltz, Kenneth. "Structural Realism after the Cold War." *International Security* 25, no. 1 (2000): 5–41.
Waltz, Kenneth. *Theory of International Politics*. Reading: Addison-Westley, 1979.
The White House. "President Donald J. Trump Is Ending United States Participation in an Unacceptable Iran Deal." *Foreign Policy*, May 8, 2018.

5

STRATEGIC AUTONOMY OF THE EUROPEAN UNION

A perspective

Rafael García Pérez

Introduction

Since the adoption of the EU Global Strategy (EUGS)[1] in June 2016, the Union has entered a stage of great activism, and some confusion, regarding its defense policy. Activism refers to the multiple means adopted to contrast with a dormancy that has permeated European defense for years. Confusion refers to the fact that long-blocked decisions are being made without addressing a structured debate among the Member States about what the diffuse concept of *strategic autonomy*, introduced by the EUGS, signifies and involves. It is a concept that remains formally undefined, giving rise to each European State, perhaps with each change of government, interpreting it in a different way and adapting it to its own interests.

"The Strategy nurtures the ambition of strategic autonomy for the European Union."[2] In pursuit of this ambition, in the last two years, transcendent steps have been taken in the Common Foreign and Security Policy (CFSP) in a direction that tries to bring the Union closer to the undefined notion of *strategic autonomy*. This deployment of measures has taken place in an environment of increasing geopolitical deterioration of the interests of the Union. With a reorientation of the US foreign policy driven by the current Trump Administration, and a deep internal crisis fueled by *Brexit*, the European governments have been forced to adopt greater commitments in the area of defense dedicated to reaffirming the validity of the integration project. All these measures share a common goal: to improve the EU's operational capacity so that Member States can carry out military missions outside their borders. Given that none of these measures makes it possible to clarify what *strategic autonomy* is, and what it consists of, the concept remains mired in doctrinal ambiguity that contrasts with its growing rhetorical use by politicians and experts, albeit with very different meaning.

What is understood by *strategic autonomy*?

In formal terms, *strategic autonomy* can be understood as the capacity of an international actor to pursue its own interests without the restriction of other actors, but within the current political context of the EU; the scope of this expression has not been defined. While the Global Strategy does not define it, several clues are offered. This is a misleading way to proceed, similarly used with other key concepts addressed in the text, such as with the concept of resilience.[3]

The EUGS qualifies strategic autonomy as a "necessity" to promote European interests, reinforcing cooperation with NATO partners and "*new players*" with whom they will be linked through "new formats." The transatlantic link, therefore, is not threatened. On the contrary, the "deepening" of these relationships should be kept,[4] as it is considered an "important" way of improving the EU's military capacity "inside and outside" its borders.[5] Therefore, its capabilities must be strengthened in the following areas: "defence, cyber, counterterrorism, energy and strategic communications."[6] It must also count on a "sustainable, innovative and competitive" European industrial base.[7]

Strategic autonomy, as it is defined, does not compromise the sovereignty of Member States in terms of defense, nor does it weaken existing alliances. Basically, it would strengthen the capacities in certain critical areas to improve the operational availability of the Member States' own industrial base, improving cooperation between them. At the operational level, it would allow European States to act with the United States whenever possible, and autonomously when necessary, through either the EU itself, NATO or the United Nations.

The EUGS foresaw the development of a sector-specific strategy on this issue by the European Council. Its objective was to define "the civil-military level of ambition, tasks, requirements and capability priorities."[8] Unfortunately, this was not the strategy that was developed. The European Defence Action Plan was approved in its place, identifying critical deficiencies that must be overcome by the Member States through an industrial effort.[9]

This way of proceeding – evading strategic definition while focusing on material, organizational or industrial actions – is not new to the EU. Consequently, the EU has never expressly defined what it understands as *strategic autonomy*, and this necessary strategic debate has always been diluted through armaments programs of industrial development. Rather than strategically defining its interests and objectives as an international actor through a shared discourse among the Member States, this debate has been systematically avoided. The EU instead concentrates on the development of material and operational capacities, with disappointing results achieved by the successive initiatives developed in the last two decades.[10] Nevertheless, the current international environment makes it increasingly inappropriate to continue acting in this way.

Since its inception, the EU's initiatives in the field of defense have prioritized the operational dimension above its strategic conception. In fact, in the 2003 European Security Strategy, the expression "strategic autonomy" was not used[11] and the political responsibility for developing its content was transferred to the then newly created European Defence Agency, responsible for defining the necessary resources to improve the operational capacity of the Member States. This way of proceeding has been reiterated in all decisions adopted by the European Council on this matter,[12] and has been consecrated with the development of a European Defence Technological and Industrial Base (EDTIB).[13]

Understood by the Union in these terms, the content of these initiatives has been associated with the concept of "*security of supply*," the objective of which is to favor national control of military resources. It is a concept deeply rooted in the doctrines and policies of some Member States under different terms: *industrial and operational sovereignty* for the British, or *autonomie stratégique* for the French.

According to an exhaustive analysis carried out by F. Mauro,[14] the first appearance of the concept of *strategic autonomy* in an official EU document was in a European Parliament report from 2010.[15] However, its use by the institutions was not generalized until 2013, and of course, during the development of the EUGS.[16]

Subsequently, its use has been erratic. The European Commission's Defence Action Plan from November 30, 2016 hardly mentions it,[17] and it was completely ignored by the *White Paper on the Future of Europe*,[18] as well as the *Reflection Paper on the Future of European Defence*.[19] It did gain prominence, however, in the documents related to the creation of the European Defence Fund,[20] converting it into a primary objective.

Only as a result of *Brexit* and the election of Donald Trump in the US presidential elections has the Union incorporated *strategic autonomy* into its program documents, thus making it a strategic objective. After the approval of the EUGS, it has become a fashionable term used in diverse contexts and without precise meaning. In reality, it is a notion with French roots, absent in the Western strategic tradition. According to F. Mauro,[21] the term *autonomie stratégique* was mentioned for the first time in the 1994 document, *White Paper of the French Defense* (henceforth LBDN 1994).[22] Until then, and since the time of General De Gaulle, the concept of "*indépendance nationale*" was used in the sense of freedom of political action as it relates to nuclear power. After the end of the Cold War, the defense policy of the Western armies went from being oriented towards threats, to focusing on capabilities. In this way, *autonomie stratégique* came to mean (in France) "having a military structure that would permit acting outside national borders, since nuclear deterrence could not ensure its role in the face of new types of conflicts that were beginning to take place." They had to prepare themselves to carry out "*missions extérieures de prévention de règlement des crises, sans risque direct d'escalade nucléaire ni perspective de guerre totale.*"[23]

The former Treaties of the European Union[24] inaccurately reflected this aspiration, and its practical realization was blocked by disagreements between France and the United Kingdom, fearing a weakening of the transatlantic relationship. Evidence of the EU's inability to act militarily in the Gulf War and the Yugoslav crisis led to the 1998 Saint-Malo Declaration,[25] by which the French and the British agreed on the foundation on which the European defense policy had been based in the last two decades: to achieve a capacity for crisis management beyond the borders of the Union without needing to rely on US participation. This excludes the command and control resources provided by NATO, an organization that considers its function of guaranteeing the territorial defense of the allies sacred.

Since the beginning of the current century, all French doctrinal documents on defense[26] have used the concept of *strategic autonomy* repeatedly, with an increasingly expanding demarcation by providing a political, and not only military, dimension. This includes both diplomatic means and development cooperation to fulfill its purposes.[27]

President Emmanuel Macron has also used the concept in his main political program speeches. In his speech at the Sorbonne in 2017,[28] he avoided the specific use of the term, setting his ambition to achieve "*la capacité d'action autonome de l'Europe, en complément de l'OTAN,*" and reaffirming once again the operational dimension, as opposed to the other facets involved. In 2018, in his speech at the annual meeting with the ambassadors of France,[29] the literal references to the term were numerous, converting *autonomie stratégique* into a kind of universal response to all the threats that France and Europe, not necessarily the EU territorial space,[30] face.

Surprisingly, *strategic autonomy* is absent from the doctrinal defense approaches of the main EU Member States, and their interpretations of the concept are not uniform.[31] This significant difference allows for consideration of the possibility that the practice, unanimously achieved by the main initiatives recently adopted, like the Permanent Structured Cooperation (PESCO), coexists with a diverse perception of risks and strategic culture among the Member States. This is the main reason why the notion of strategic autonomy lacks a precise definition: for fear of opening a disaggregating debate within the Union.

Strategic autonomy within the current debate on security in the European Union

Although the debate on the future of security in Europe is not formally raised at the intergovernmental level, it is indisputable that it is taking place at different levels.

On the part of the Member States, each of them has a specific perception of what *strategic autonomy* should mean, but only the largest states of the EU have their own criteria to define their position.[32] As discussed, France is its main driver. Within the French doctrine exists a necessary and positive complementarity between European strategic autonomy and national strategic autonomy in a country that possesses nuclear capabilities. While Italy has not yet defined its concept of *strategic autonomy*, the 2015 *Libro Bianco*[33] established a primacy of industrial interests over strategic ones. Spain maintains a similar position, associating *strategic autonomy* with the industrial capacity necessary to meet the interests defined in the 2017 *Estrategia de Seguridad Nacional*.[34] Significantly, Germany does not mention *strategic autonomy* in its most recent doctrinal documents: the 2016 *Weißbuch zur Sicherheitspolitik*,[35] and the 2018 *Konzeption der Bundeswehr*.[36] However, some main elements are identified in the industrial field, such as the preservation of national technologies and development through European cooperation.

In general terms, all Member States distinguish between their own technological capabilities, which they intend to defend and expand on, and those that can be generated through cooperation within the European framework. They share a perception of complementarity between national and European efforts to protect their industrial, operational and strategic interests. This shared approach requires each Member State to exert influence so that the construction of the EU's *strategic autonomy* meets its own individual priorities, in the functions of perceived threats and industrial capacities. All of this will end up testing European capacity for cooperation in this sphere.

The European deployment of defense initiatives following the *Brexit* referendum has been the result of proposals launched by France and Germany, with bilateral, multilateral and EU-wide scope. The Member States have mostly joined these initiatives, but perceptions of these efforts are far from unanimous. In some cases, there is a familiar desire for a revitalized Franco-German axis to take up the initiative and ensure the Union's response to the challenges it faces. At the same time, there is a feeling of fear at the imposition of a Franco-German leadership if US withdrawal is finally confirmed. In general, the differences that arise in the application of industrial cooperation programs are difficult to resolve, although they are tempered by the fear of paralyzing the initiatives underway.

If these discrepancies are recognizable among all Member States, the structural differences in terms of defense between France and Germany have not disappeared either. They remain in the same conditions that, traditionally, have been attributed to the different strategic cultures of each country. R. Kempin and B. Kunz[37] highlight the fact that the main discrepancy lies in an unequal perception that each country has about its defensive needs, despite there being a remarkable coincidence in the perception of threat.[38] For France, having the capacity for autonomous defense is of essential urgency, while it does not represent a priority for Germany. These differences also manifest themselves within the European context, but rarely develop into disagreements or competitive visions. Although direct oppositions do not occur, a transactional relationship between both parties is noticeable.

For example, the implementation of the PESCO showed the difficulties in reconciling their respective approaches. France sought to improve the operational efficiency of the EU through organizing cooperation efforts among a small number of countries with political resolve and military capacity. The German perspective won, however, opting for an inclusive approach focused on capabilities.[39] Something similar happened with the Military Mobility Program promoted by Germany, where France participated only as an observer.[40] Although the Franco-German impetus is evident, the EU is still far from exercising a shared leadership in matters of defense.

At the academic level, there is an open debate about the meaning and composition of the concept of *strategic autonomy* developed after the approval of the Global Strategy in 2016. Without the aim of being exhaustive,[41] all studies focus on the military dimension of the concept and, in particular, three main levels: operational, industrial and future relationships between the EU and NATO.

With regard to the operational dimension, *strategic autonomy* has often been associated with so-called "*Entry Operations*,"[42] that is, with having the autonomous capacity to launch expeditionary operations designed to reduce the threat posed by an adversary, and to exercise force (terrestrial, naval or air) over a distant scenario.

G. Varga[43] takes up a similar position and argues that, although the widespread opinion is that *strategic autonomy* primarily refers to industrial autonomy, it should be mainly understood as the EU's capacity to carry out operations in its closest regional environment.

In relation to the industrial dimension, an Armament Industry European Research Group (ARES) study[44] analyzed the concept's perception by eight Member States, asking what level of strategic autonomy would be appropriate for each of them.

The implications of *strategic autonomy* in future relations with NATO and, ultimately, with the United States have garnered great attention, largely due to the reluctance expressed by the Trump Administration to the project. On this issue, all opinions consulted seem unanimous: their objective is not to go against the United States or to weaken NATO. On the contrary, there is intent to sustain and strengthen the transatlantic link.

If the EU were to persevere in achieving strategic autonomy, J. Howorth considers various scenarios for cooperation with NATO and argues that the Union should accept the challenge repeatedly put forth by Washington to progressively assume the management of the security of its regional environment.[45] The United States should offer its decisive political support and provide the necessary material support in critical areas until Europe can count on its own capabilities. This scenario would meet the best expectations for US interests: "*to have a competent, mature and self-reliant partner with which to face the global challenges of the 21st century*."[46]

R. Kempin and B. Kunz also defend the US interest in the EU achieving *strategic autonomy*.[47] They blame Washington's reticence on the lack of definition of the concept by Brussels and the absence of a structured debate on its scope. They convincingly affirm that the "*emancipation from the United States is clearly no longer on the agenda for anyone*," and that the United States has nothing to worry about. Once the process is completed, it will be time to address "*the future of Euro-Atlantic security, fair burden-sharing, defense acquisition, market access, and potential geographical and functional divisions of labor*."[48]

S. Biscop argues along the same lines, defending the idea that the implementation of PESCO, if successful, will improve Euro-Atlantic security. The main objection from Washington is that it will affect its weapons exports, "*but if Washington truly wants the Europeans to step up, it cannot expect them to simply spend more money on American military equipment*."[49]

British analysts A. Billon-Galland and A. Thomson, also insist on this point, contending: "*It is politically unrealistic to suppose that Europe would become increasingly able to look after its own security while at the same time becoming increasingly dependent on US R&D and US defence equipment*."[50] They maintain that strategic autonomy would strengthen, without threatening, the defense association with the US, allowing for a reinforced alignment with NATO and the post-*Brexit* United Kingdom.

To conclude this brief analysis, it is necessary to mention the contribution of researchers R. Kempin and B. Kunz[51] that, by developing the idea put forth by F. Arteaga,[52] offer a comprehensive understanding of the elements that make up the concept of *strategic autonomy*:

- Political autonomy is "*the capacity to take security policy decisions and act upon them*."
- Operational autonomy is understood as "*the capacity, based on the necessary institutional framework and the required capabilities, to independently plan for and conduct civilian and/or military operations*."

- Industrial autonomy encompasses "*the capacity to develop and build the capabilities required to attain operational autonomy.*"

In his study noted for its breadth and depth, F. Mauro[53] highlights the substantive difference between the terms in which this debate between academics and experts is based, and the opinions that all European leaders convey when they talk about *strategic autonomy*. France is the notable exception. For most of these leaders, however, it is a concept only applicable to its industrial dimension and, to the extent that the operational dimension is addressed, specifying the necessary measures to be able to launch autonomous missions is deliberately avoided. There is also a significant lack of questioning on the decision-making processes currently in force:[54] neither the creation of a common budget nor the elimination of the unanimity rule is on the agenda. In this way, *strategic autonomy* manifests itself as another example of the doctrinal ambiguity that permeates the 2016 Global Strategy. It is possible that this way of proceeding has previously produced positive results in the integration process, but it is doubtful that maintaining this inertia will allow the EU to address the defense challenges nowadays at stake.

Integrating *strategic autonomy* into a general debate on European defense

It is increasingly inappropriate to continue avoiding a strategic definition of the interests and needs of European security in the near future, taking into account the gap between the possible challenges faced, and available capacities.

In an unstructured, but increasingly recognizable way, a substantive debate on security is beginning to take place in Europe, in which political leaders are beginning to participate. In October 2017 a manifesto was published by the German Marshall Fund,[55] drafted by leading German foreign policy analysts, asking if Germany, and by extension Europe, should preserve the transatlantic link or seek an autonomous defense policy that they qualified as "*post-atlanticist.*" The position they defended was explicitly "*atlantist*" but the manifesto gave rise to the publication of various positions, initiating a debate in which the German minister of foreign affairs,[56] Sigmar Gabriel, ended up participating, expounding his opinion as "*post-atlanticist.*"[57]

The first change introduced by this trend that must be highlighted is that, since the end of the Cold War, the proposed terms of the security debate in Europe have varied. If two poles were traditionally identified as the defenders of "*l'Europe de la défense*" and the "*atlanticists,*" these categories no longer serve to reflect the divergences in the security perceptions and interests that Member States currently maintain with respect to defense, offering a much more complex scenario. B. Kunz[58] defends the existence of a three-dimensional quality to this debate, where *strategic autonomy* would be just one of the poles, along with two other key issues. First, it is necessary to define the strategic priorities: territorial defense capacity or to project force? This dilemma is exemplified by the author through the different perspectives maintained by the Eastern and Southern countries of the continent regarding their security. The third dimension of the debate is about the future role that the US will play in the defense of Europe and, consequently, the redefinition of the transatlantic link. It is impossible to isolate the three components of this debate as their elements are inextricably linked.

The unequal perception of threats between the East and the South is one of the conditioning factors of the Union's difficulties in defining a collective project on defense issues. Obviously, the solution to this false disconnect is not to choose between the two options, but to integrate them within the same defense strategy. This is a difficult step for governments to take, however, due to the multiple implications that it would entail. Among other transcendent issues, taking on the security needs of their fellow states would eventually dilute the remnants of sovereignty retained by the Member States.

In any case, this East vs. South dimension of the debate goes beyond the hierarchy of some threats (Russia) over others (jihadist terrorism). The East tries to preserve the European security regime while the South aims to stabilize the Mediterranean region and the Middle East. The first requires a collective defense of the territory while the second involves having the operational capacity to launch expeditionary operations in close regional environments, and having the necessary political conditions to send and direct them. To a large extent, France and Germany embody each of these two options. Germany considers the challenges of jihadist terrorism, but prefers political action and development cooperation to neutralize it. Its priority is territorial defense, as highlighted by the 2018 *Konzeption der Bundeswehr*, which will be amplified if the strategic reorientation of the United States is confirmed. In practice this will translate into the fact that German defense efforts will focus on strengthening NATO while advances in European defense will fulfill the complementary function of moving forward on the path of integration. For France, the projection of force and military intervention are essential and urgent to neutralize jihadist threats and other problems spurring from an increasingly destabilized region that may be plunged into chaos. Although territorial defense is not underestimated, it is not prioritized when one considers the assurance of nuclear arsenal.

A second dimension to the debate on European security has to do with the future role that the US would play in the defense of the continent. The uncertainties regarding the survival of the transatlantic link cannot be reduced to the erratic statements of President Donald Trump regarding the European allies of NATO.[59] On the contrary, they respond to substantive reasons that drive a long-term change in the orientation of US foreign policy, as the "*rebalancing*" towards Asia promoted by the Obama Administration has already shown, despite the difficulties encountered in making it happen.[60] Although the NATO summit held in Brussels in July 2018[61] presumed a reaffirmation of Article 5 of the Washington Treaty, divergences with the allies were strongly evidenced by Trump's speech accusing Germany of being "*captive to Russia*."[62] Both Berlin and Paris are aware that even if the alliance is maintained, it should not be put to the test. Chancellor Merkel has expressed emphatically on several occasions: "*Wir Europäer müssen unser Schicksal wirklich in unsere eigene Hand nehmen*."[63]

Once again, the possible American disaffection has different effects on distinct European countries. For France, the US is a key ally, but it is not the ultimate guarantor of its national security, as is the case with Germany and the rest of the eastern Member States. The shared response to the current situation has been to boost Europe's *strategic autonomy* without defining its strategy and aims, and assuming an implicit contradiction: the more progress is made in achieving the desired and necessary autonomy, the greater the incentive is for the US to consider a disengagement, which is not desired by the Europeans. One of the main challenges facing European defense policy is whether Washington contemplates EU *strategic autonomy* as a reinforcement of the transatlantic link.

Conclusion

Strategic autonomy may be an undefined concept, a fashionable term with an ephemeral life expectancy, but its inclusion in the EUGS has opened a debate on European defense that had been dormant for years. This is a discussion that cannot be postponed because the regional and global strategic circumstances present a degree of uncertainty about the security of the continent that require political responses that may need several decades to be implemented, and the operational capabilities to be developed could be available now. The EU needs to generate a political consensus that allows the adoption of a common idea regarding how its defense will be in 2050. This goal, aimed at rebalancing and reaffirming the transatlantic link, can be achieved through the leadership of the Member States, the close involvement of the EU, and the diplomatic and material support of the United States.

In the words of H. Kudnani,[64] the momentum of the defense initiatives adopted in recent years presents a "*necessary and impossible*" objective. It is necessary in that the Union's lack of capacity to act militarily compromises its defense, which depends entirely on the United States. At the same time, it is impossible because even if the current developments come to fruition, the security of European countries would continue to depend on the US in the next decades.

Through the evolution of the debate spurred by *strategic autonomy*, the EU must assume that the gap that exists between political aspirations and the military reality obliges us to maintain, in the short and medium term, dependence on the United States. If *strategic autonomy* is adopted as a long-term political project, with a gradual and pragmatic approach, it can contribute to the construction of a more integrated EU, with more capacity for international action and less dependence on Washington. If, on the other hand, the approach of strategic autonomy is circumscribed to its industrial dimension, there is a reasonable risk that the divergent interests among the Member States will reproduce meager results, similar to those of the initiatives adopted in the last two decades.

Adopting a long-term political project may not mean explicitly defining the concept of *strategic autonomy* from the onset. Perhaps it can be understood that the persistence of the differing perceptions on the part of France and Germany have conditioned the adoption of this path to define its meaning by means of material advances achieved. But a move towards a closer strategic convergence that includes the whole of the Member States with their own "eastern" and "southern" vision of defense, and also that of the post-*Brexit* United Kingdom, cannot be postponed. Unfortunately, the Franco-German treaty signed in Aachen in 2019 still does not address this need.[65]

The European States must urgently address critical deficiencies in military capabilities and the organization of their armies, and should work with particular determination to achieve a confluence in strategic visions and possession of adequate political decision-making structures, as well as the command to be able to use them. European societies must also embrace and participate in the debate on the security of the continent, overcoming the inertia and stereotypes forged in a historical era that has already disappeared. It is necessary that the European integration project takes responsibility for its own defense. The momentum of this open-ended debate on *strategic autonomy* should move the EU forward in this way.

Notes

1 European External Action Service, *Shared Vision, Common Action: A Stronger Europe. A Global Strategy for the European Union's Foreign and Security Policy* (European External Action Service, 2016), accessed February 22, 2019, https://eeas.europa.eu/top_stories/pdf/eugs_review_web.pdf.
2 Ibid. 4.
3 Wolfgang Wagner and Rosanne Anholt, "Resilience as the EU Global Strategy's New Leitmotif: Pragmatic, Problematic, or Promising?," *Contemporary Security Policy* 37 (2016): 414–30.
4 European External Action Service, *Shared Vision, Common Action*, 4.
5 Ibid., 9 and 19.
6 Ibid., 9.
7 Ibid., 46.
8 Ibid., 45.
9 David Christopher Jaklin, "The EU's Steps towards More Strategic Autonomy: The European Defence Action Plan," *AIES Fokus* 2 (2018).

10 Félix Arteaga, "Strategic Autonomy and European Defence," Real Instituto Elcano, 2017.
11 Although in the Declaration adopted in the Cologne Council the expression "capacity for autonomous action" was used, there was more precision when establishing the pursued objectives: "[The] Union must have the capacity for autonomous action, backed up by credible military forces, the means to decide to use them, and a readiness to do so, in order to respond to international crises without prejudice to actions by NATO." Annex III – European Council Declaration on Strengthening the Common European Policy on Security and Defence, European Council, Conclusions of the European Council 150/99 REV 1, Cologne, June 3 and 4, 1999, accessed June 4, 2018 www.consilium.europa.eu/media/21070/57886.pdf.
12 European Council, Conclusions of the European Council EUCO 217/13 (Brussels: European Union, December 20, 2013) accessed June 4, 2018, http://data.consilium.europa.eu/doc/document/ST-217-2013-INIT/en/pdf.
13 Directorate-General for External Policies of the Union (European Parliament), *The Development of a European Defence Technological and Industrial Base (EDTIB)*, EXPO/B/SEDE/2012/20 (Brussels: European Parliament, June 10, 2013), accessed July 4, 2018, www.europarl.europa.eu/RegData/etudes/etudes/join/2013/433838/EXPO-SEDE_ET%282013%29433838_EN.pdf.
14 Frédéric Mauro, "Strategic Autonomy under the Spotlight: The New Holy Grail of European Defence," *GRIP Report* (2018): 11.
15 European Parliament, *Annual Report on the Implementation of the European Security Strategy and the Common Security and Defence Policy* (2009/2198(INI)) (Brussels: European Union, March 10, 2010), accessed July 4, 2018, https://eur-lex.europa.eu/LexUriServ/LexUriServ.do?uri=OJ:C:2010:349E:00; Mauro, "Strategic Autonomy under the Spotlight," 11.
16 Mauro, "Strategic Autonomy under the Spotlight," 11–13.
17 European Commission, *European Defence Action Plan*, COM(2016) 950 final (Brussels: European Union, November 11, 2016), accessed June 6, 2018, https://eeas.europa.eu/sites/eeas/files/com_2016_950_f1_communication_from_commission_to_inst_en_v5_p1_869631.pdf, 3.
18 European Commission, *White Paper on the Future of Europe. Reflections and Scenarios for the EU27 up to 2025* (Brussels: European Union, March, 1, 2017), accessed June 6, 2018, https://ec.europa.eu/commission/sites/beta-political/files/white_paper_on_the_future_of_europe_en.pdf.
19 European Commission, *Reflection Paper on the Future of European Defence* (Brussels: European Union, June 7, 2017), accessed June 6, 2018, https://ec.europa.eu/commission/sites/beta-political/files/reflection-paper-defence_en.pdf.
20 European Commission, Communication on Launching the European Defence Fund, COM(2017) 295 final (Brussels: European Union, June 7, 2017), accessed June 6, 2018, https://eeas.europa.eu/sites/eeas/files/launching_the_european_defence_fund.pdf, 2.
21 Mauro, "Strategic Autonomy under the Spotlight," 3.
22 Ministère de la Défense, *Livre Blanc sur la Défence 1994*, accessed June 6, 2018, www.ladocumentationfrancaise.fr/var/storage/rapports-publics/944048700.pdf.
23 Ibid., 52.
24 Treaty of Maastricht, art. J.4.1.; Treaty of Amsterdam, art. J.7.
25 *Joint Declaration on European Defence* (Saint-Malo: British-French Summit, December 4, 1998), accessed June 6, 2018, www.cvce.eu/content/publication/2008/3/31/f3cd16fb-fc37-4d52-936f-c8e9b-c80f24f/publishable_en.pdf.
26 *Défense et Sécurité Nationale: Le Livre Blanc* (2008); *Livre Blanc sur la Défense et la Sécurité* (2013); *Revue stratégique de défense et de sécurité nationale* (2017); Mauro, "Strategic Autonomy under the Spotlight," 8–12.
27 Mauro, "Strategic Autonomy under the Spotlight," 11.
28 Emmanuel Macron, *Initiative pour l'Europe – Discours d'Emmanuel Macron pour une Europe souveraine, unie, démocratique* (Paris: University of Sorbonne, 2017), September 26, 2017, accessed June 6, 2018, www.elysee.fr/declarations/article/initiative-pour-l-europe-discours-d-emmanuel-macron-pour-une-europe-souveraine-unie-democratique/, 4.
29 Emmanuel Macron, *Discours du Président de la République lors de la Conférence des Ambassadeurs*, August 27, 2018, accessed August 28, 2018, www.elysee.fr/videos/discours-du-president-de-la-republique-emmanuel-macron-lors-de-la-conference-des-ambassadeurs-et-des-ambassadrices/.
30 Nick Whitney, "Macron and the European Intervention Initiative: Erasmus for soldiers?," *ECFR Commentary* (2018), accessed July 6, 2018, www.ecfr.eu/article/commentary_macron_and_the_european_intervention_initiative_erasmus_for_sold; Nicole Koenig, "The European Intervention

Initiative: A look behind the Scenes," Jacques Delors Institut–Berlin (2018), accessed July 6, 2018, www.delorsinstitut.de/en/all-publications/the-european-intervention-initiative-a-look-behind-the-scenes/.

31 Hans-Peter Bartels, Anna Maria Kellner and Uwe Optenhögel, *Strategic Autonomy and European Defense. On the Way to a European Army?* (Bonn: Dietz, 2017).

32 Félix Arteaga, et al., *Appropriate Level of European Strategic Autonomy*, ARES Report 8 (ARES, 2016).

33 Ministero della Difesa, *Libro Bianco per la Sicurezza Internazionale e la Difesa* (2015), accessed June 15, 2018, www.difesa.it/Primo_Piano/Documents/2015/04_Aprile/LB_2015.pdf.

34 Departamento de Seguridad Nacional, *Estrategia de Seguridad Nacional* (2017), www.dsn.gob.es/es/estrategias-publicaciones/estrategias/estrategia-seguridad-nacional-2017; Arteaga, "Strategic Autonomy and European Defence."

35 Bundesregierung, *Weißbuch 2016 zur Sicherheitspolitik und zur Zukunft der Bundeswehr* (2016), accessed January 14, 2017, https://m.bundesregierung.de/Content/Infomaterial/BMVg/Weissbuch_zur_Sicherheitspolitik_2016.pdf;jsessionid=F19A4B313E2F99D32B0FFD92D205F944.s7t1?__blob=publicationFile&v=4.

36 Bundesministerium der Verteidigung, *Die Konzeption der Bundeswehr. Ausgewählte Grundlinien der Gesamtkonzeption* (2018), accessed August 25, 2018, www.bmvg.de/resource/blob/26546/befaf450b146faa515e19328e659fa1e/20180731-broschuere-konzeption-der-bundeswehr-data.pdf.

37 Ronja Kempin and Barbara Kunz, "France, Germany and the Quest for European Strategic Autonomy: Franco-German Defence Cooperation in a New Era," Notes de l'IFRI/Notes du CERFA 141 (2017), accessed June 11, 2018, www.ifri.org/sites/default/files/atoms/files/ndc_141_kempin_kunz_france_germany_european_strategic_autonomy_dec_2017.pdf.

38 The biggest difference lies in the perception of the global economy: 45 percent risk for France, compared to only 22 percent in Germany. Jacob Poushter and Dorothy Manevich, "Globally, People Point to ISIS and Climate Change as Leading Security Threats: Concern about Cyberattacks, World Economy Also Widespread" (Pew Research Center, 2017), accessed July 10, 2018, www.pewglobal.org/2017/08/01/globally-people-point-to-isis-and-climate-change-as-leading-security-threats/.

39 Alice Billon-Galland and Martin Quencez, "Can France and Germany Make PESCO Work as a Process toward EU Defense?," GMF Policy Brief 33 (German Marshall Fund, 2017), accessed June 13, 2018, www.gmfus.org/publications/can-france-and-germany-make-pesco-work-process-toward-eu-defense.

40 European Commission, "Action Plan on Military Mobility: EU Takes Steps towards a Defence Union," March 28, 2018, accessed June 15, 2018, http://europa.eu/rapid/press-release_IP-18-2521_en.htm.

41 Mauro, "Strategic Autonomy under the Spotlight," 17–21.

42 Corentin Brustlein, "L'entrée en Premier et L'avenir de L'autonomie Stratégique," Études de l'IFRI / Focus stratégique 70 (2016), accessed June 15, 2018, www.ifri.org/fr/publications/etudes-de-lifri/focus-strategique/lentree-premier-lavenir-de-lautonomie-strategique.

43 Gergely Varga, "Towards European Strategic Autonomy: Evaluating the New CSDP Initiatives," KKI Studies-Institute for Foreign Affairs and Trade, 2017, accessed June 6, 2018, http://kki.hu/assets/upload/07_KKI-Studies_CSDP_VargaG_20171003.pdf, 3.

44 Félix Arteaga, et al., "Appropriate Level of European Strategic Autonomy."

45 Jolyon Howorth, "Strategic Autonomy and EU-NATO Cooperation: Squaring the Circle," Security Policy Brief 85 (Egmont, 2017), accessed June 20, 2018, www.egmontinstitute.be/content/uploads/2017/05/SPB85.pdf?type=pdf.

46 Ibid., 4.

47 Ronja Kempin and Barbara Kunz, "Washington Should Help Europe Achieve 'Strategic Autonomy', Not Fight It," *War on the Rocks* (2018), accessed July 20, 2018, https://warontherocks.com/2018/04/washington-should-help-europe-achieve-strategic-autonomy-not-fight-it/.

48 Ibid.

49 Sven Biscop, "Letting Europe Go Its Own Way. The Case for Strategic Autonomy," *Foreign Affairs* (2018), accessed July 24, 2018, www.foreignaffairs.com/articles/2018-07-06/letting-europe-go-its-own-way.

50 Alice Billon-Galland and Adam Thomson, "European Strategic Autonomy: Stop Talking, Start Planning," European Defence Policy Brief (European Leadership Network, 2018), accessed July 20, 2018, www.europeanleadershipnetwork.org/wp-content/uploads/2018/05/ELN-Policy-Brief-European-Strategic-Autonomy-Stop-Talking-Start-Planning.pdf.

51 Kempin and Kunz, "France, Germany and the Quest for European Strategic Autonomy," 10.

52 Arteaga, "Strategic Autonomy and European Defence."
53 Mauro, "Strategic Autonomy under the Spotlight."
54 Jochen Rehrl, *Handbook for Decision Makers. The Common Security and Defence Policy of the European Union* (Wien: Federal Ministry of Defence and Sports of the Republic of Austria, 2014).
55 Thomas Kleine-Brockhoff et al., "In Spite of It All, America," *New York Times*, October 11, 2017, accessed July 10, 2018, www.nytimes.com/2017/10/11/world/europe/germany-united-states-trump-manifesto.html.
56 Melissa Eddy, "In Era of Trump, Germany Seeks a Stronger Role Abroad," *New York Times*, December 5, 2017, accessed July 10, 2018, www.nytimes.com/2017/12/05/world/europe/germany-trump-sigmar-gabriel.html.
57 Hans Kundnani and Jana Puglierin, "Atlanticist and 'Post-Atlanticist' Wishful Thinking," GMF Policy Essay 1 (The German Marshall Fund of the United States, 2018), accessed July 10, 2018, www.gmfus.org/publications/atlanticist-and-post-atlanticist-wishful-thinking.
58 Barbara Kunz, "The Three Dimensions of Europe's Defense Debate," GMF Policy Brief 24 (The German Marshall Fund of the United States, 2018), accessed August 22, 2018, www.gmfus.org/publications/three-dimensions-europes-defense-debate.
59 Martin Kettle, "Trump Is Hellbent on Destroying the NATO Alliance," *Guardian*, June 27, 2018, accessed July 15, 2018, www.theguardian.com/commentisfree/2018/jun/27/donald-trump-nato-europe-ally.
60 David E. Sanger and Mark Landler, "Obama's Strategic Shift to Asia Is Hobbled by Pressure at Home and Crises Abroad," *New York Times*, April 21, 2014, accessed August 22, 2018, www.nytimes.com/2014/04/22/world/asia/obamas-strategic-shift-to-asia-is-hobbled-by-pressure-at-home-and-crises-abroad.html.
61 "Brussels Declaration on Transatlantic Security and Solidarity," NATO website, July 11, 2018, accessed July 12, 2018, www.nato.int/cps/en/natohq/official_texts_156620.htm.
62 "Trump vs. Merkel: Blistering Salvo Meets Quiet Rejoinder," *New York Times*, July 11, 2018, accessed July 12, 2018, www.nytimes.com/2018/07/11/world/europe/germany-merkel-russia-trump-nato.html.
63 "We Europeans really have to take our fate into our own hands" and "Merkel hält USA für nicht mehr verlässlich," *Süddeutsche Zeitung*, May 28, 2017, accessed September 10, 2017, www.sueddeutsche.de/politik/g-gipfel-merkel-haelt-usa-fuer-nicht-mehr-verlaesslich-1.3524283.
64 Hans Kundnani, "The Necessity and Impossibility of 'Strategic Autonomy,'" The German Marshall Fund of the United States, January 10, 2018, accessed July 24, 2018, www.gmfus.org/blog/2018/01/10/necessity-and-impossibility-strategic-autonomy.
65 Barbara Kunz and Ronja Kempin, "The Treaty of Aachen. New Impetus for Franco-German Defense Cooperation?," Éditoriaux de l'Ifri, January 2019, accessed January 31, 2019, www.ifri.org/en/publications/editoriaux-de-lifri/treaty-aachen-new-impetus-franco-german-defense-cooperation.

References

Arteaga, Félix. "Strategic Autonomy and European Defence." Real Instituto Elcano (2017). Accessed June 4, 2018. www.realinstitutoelcano.org/wps/wcm/connect/6363d9e8-c223-4387-9937-d852b74bc3a1/ARI102-2017-Arteaga-Strategic-autonomy-European-defence.pdf?MOD=AJPERES&CACHEID=6363d9e8-c223-4387-9937-d852b74bc3a1.

Arteaga, Félix, Tomas Jermalavicius, Alessandro Marrone, Jean-Pierre Maulny and Marcin Terlikowski. *Appropriate Level of European Strategic Autonomy*. ARES Report (ARES, 2016). Accessed June 13, 2018. www.iris-france.org/wp-content/uploads/2016/11/ARES-Group-Report-Strategic-autonomy-November-2016.pdf.

Bartels, Hans-Peter, Anna Maria Kellner and Uwe Optenhögel. *Strategic Autonomy and European Defense. On the Way to a European Army?* Bonn: Dietz, 2017.

Billon-Galland, Alice, and Martin Quencez. "Can France and Germany Make PESCO Work as a Process toward EU Defense?" GMF Policy Brief 33. German Marshall Fund, 2017. Accessed June 13, 2018. www.gmfus.org/publications/can-france-and-germany-make-pesco-work-process-toward-eu-defense.

Billon-Galland, Alice, and Adam Thomson. "European Strategic Autonomy: Stop Talking, Start Planning." *European Defence Policy Brief*. European Leadership Network, 2018. Accessed July 20, 2018. www.europeanleadershipnetwork.org/wp-content/uploads/2018/05/ELN-Policy-Brief-European-Strategic-Autonomy-Stop-Talking-Start-Planning.pdf.

Biscop, Sven. "Letting Europe Go Its Own Way. The Case for Strategic Autonomy." *Foreign Affairs* (2018). Accessed July 24, 2018. www.foreignaffairs.com/articles/2018-07-06/letting-europe-go-its-own-way.

"Brussels Declaration on Transatlantic Security and Solidarity." NATO website. July 11, 2018. Accessed July 12, 2018, www.nato.int/cps/en/natohq/official_texts_156620.htm.

Brustlein, Corentin. "L'entrée en Premier et L'avenir de L'autonomie Stratégique." Études de l'IFRI / Focus stratégique 70 (2016). Accessed June 15, 2018. www.ifri.org/fr/publications/etudes-de-lifri/focus-strategique/lentree-premier-lavenir-de-lautonomie-strategique.

Bundesministerium der Verteidigung. *Die Konzeption der Bundeswehr. Ausgewählte Grundlinien der Gesamtkonzeption* (2018). Accessed August 25, 2018. www.bmvg.de/resource/blob/26546/befaf450b146faa515e19328e659fa1e/20180731-broschuere-konzeption-der-bundeswehr-data.pdf.

Bundesregierung. *Weißbuch 2016 zur Sicherheitspolitik und zur Zukunft der Bundeswehr* (2016). Accessed January 14, 2017. https://m.bundesregierung.de/Content/Infomaterial/BMVg/Weissbuch_zur_Sicherheitspolitik_2016.pdf;jsessionid=F19A4B313E2F99D32B0FFD92D205F944.s7t1?__blob=publicationFile&v=4.

Departamento de Seguridad Nacional. *Estrategia de Seguridad Nacional* (2017). Accessed February 17, 2019. www.dsn.gob.es/es/estrategias-publicaciones/estrategias/estrategia-seguridad-nacional-2017.

Directorate-General for External Policies of the Union (European Parliament). *The Development of a European Defence Technological and Industrial Base (EDTIB)* (EXPO/B/SEDE/2012/20). Brussels: European Parliament, 2013. Accessed July 4, 2018. www.europarl.europa.eu/RegData/etudes/etudes/join/2013/433838/EXPO-SEDE_ET%282013%29433838_EN.pdf.

Eddy, Melissa. "In Era of Trump, Germany Seeks a Stronger Role Abroad." *New York Times*, December 5, 2017. Accessed July 10, 2018. www.nytimes.com/2017/12/05/world/europe/germany-trump-sigmar-gabriel.html.

European Commission. "Action Plan on Military Mobility: EU Takes Steps towards a Defence Union." Brussels: European Union, March 28, 2018. Accessed June 15, 2018. http://europa.eu/rapid/press-release_IP-18-2521_en.htm.

European Commission. *European Defence Action Plan*. COM(2016) 950 final. Brussels: European Union, November 11, 2016. Accessed June 6, 2018. https://eeas.europa.eu/sites/eeas/files/com_2016_950_f1_communication_from_commission_to_inst_en_v5_p1_869631.pdf.

European Commission. *Launching the European Defence Fund*. COM(2017) 295 final. Brussels: European Union, June 7, 2017. Accessed June 6, 2018. https://eeas.europa.eu/sites/eeas/files/launching_the_european_defence_fund.pdf.

European Commission. *Reflection Paper on the Future of European Defence*. Brussels: European Union, June 7, 2017. Accessed June 6, 2018. https://ec.europa.eu/commission/sites/beta-political/files/reflection-paper-defence_en.pdf.

European Commission. *White Paper on the Future of Europe. Reflections and Scenarios for the EU27 up to 2025*. Brussels: European Union, March, 1 2017. Accessed June 6, 2018. https://ec.europa.eu/commission/sites/beta-political/files/white_paper_on_the_future_of_europe_en.pdf.

European Council. Conclusions of the European Council EUCO 217/13. Brussels: European Union, December 20, 2013. Accessed June 4, 2018. http://data.consilium.europa.eu/doc/document/ST-217-2013-INIT/en/pdf.

European External Action Service. *Shared Vision, Common Action: A Stronger Europe. A Global Strategy for the European Union's Foreign and Security Policy*. European External Action Service, 2016. Accessed November 11, 2016. https://eeas.europa.eu/top_stories/pdf/eugs_review_web.pdf.

European Parliament. *Annual Report on the Implementation of the European Security Strategy and the Common Security and Defence Policy* (2009/2198(INI)). Brussels: European Union, March 10, 2010. Accessed July 4, 2018. https://eur-lex.europa.eu/LexUriServ/LexUriServ.do?uri=OJ:C:2010:349E:00.

Howorth, Jolyon. "Strategic Autonomy and EU-NATO Cooperation: Squaring the Circle." Security Policy Brief 85. Egmont, 2017. Accessed June 20, 2018. www.egmontinstitute.be/content/uploads/2017/05/SPB85.pdf?type=pdf.

Jaklin, David Christopher. "The EU's Steps towards More Strategic Autonomy: The European Defence Action Plan." *AIES Fokus* 2 (2018). Accessed June 8, 2018. www.aies.at/download/2018/AIES-Fokus-2018-02.pdf.

Joint Declaration on European Defence. Saint-Malo: British-French Summit, 1998. Accessed June 6, 2018. www.cvce.eu/content/publication/2008/3/31/f3cd16fb-fc37-4d52-936f-c8e9bc80f24f/publishable_en.pdf.

Kempin, Ronja, and Barbara Kunz. "France, Germany and the Quest for European Strategic Autonomy: Franco-German Defence Cooperation in a New Era." Notes de l'IFRI/Notes du CERFA 141 (2017).

Accessed July 11, 2018. www.ifri.org/sites/default/files/atoms/files/ndc_141_kempin_kunz_france_germany_european_strategic_autonomy_dec_2017.pdf.
Kempin, Ronja, and Barbara Kunz. "Washington Should Help Europe Achieve 'Strategic Autonomy,' Not Fight It." *War on the Rocks* (2018). Accessed July 20, 2018. https://warontherocks.com/2018/04/washington-should-help-europe-achieve-strategic-autonomy-not-fight-it/.
Kettle, Martin. "Trump Is Hell-bent on Destroying the NATO Alliance." *Guardian*, June 27, 2018. Accessed July 15, 2018. www.theguardian.com/commentisfree/2018/jun/27/donald-trump-nato-europe-ally.
Kleine-Brockhoff, Thomas, et al. "In Spite of It All, America." *New York Times*, October 11, 2017. Accessed July 10, 2018. www.nytimes.com/2017/10/11/world/europe/germany-united-states-trump-manifesto.html.
Koenig, Nicole. "The European Intervention Initiative: A Look behind the Scenes." Jacques Delors Institut–Berlin (2018). Accessed July 6, 2018. www.delorsinstitut.de/en/all-publications/the-european-intervention-initiative-a-look-behind-the-scenes/.
Kundnani, Hans. "The Necessity and Impossibility of 'Strategic Autonomy.'" The German Marshall Fund of the United States, January 10, 2018. Accessed July 24, 2018. www.gmfus.org/blog/2018/01/10/necessity-and-impossibility-strategic-autonomy.
Kundnani, Hans, and Jana Puglierin. "Atlanticist and 'Post-Atlanticist' Wishful Thinking." GMF Policy Essay 1 (The German Marshall Fund of the United States, 2018). Accessed July 10, 2018. www.gmfus.org/publications/atlanticist-and-post-atlanticist-wishful-thinking.
Kunz, Barbara. "The Three Dimensions of Europe's Defense Debate." GMF Policy Brief 24 (The German Marshall Fund of the United States, 2018). Accessed August 22, 2018. www.gmfus.org/publications/three-dimensions-europes-defense-debate.
Kunz, Barbara, and Ronja Kempin. "The Treaty of Aachen. New Impetus for Franco-German Defense Cooperation?" Éditoriaux de l'Ifri, January 2019. Accessed January 31, 2019. www.ifri.org/en/publications/editoriaux-de-lifri/treaty-aachen-new-impetus-franco-german-defense-cooperation.
Macron, Emmanuel. *Discours du Président de la République lors de la Conférence des Ambassadeurs*. August 27, 2018. Accessed August 28, 2018. www.elysee.fr/videos/discours-du-president-de-la-republique-emmanuel-macron-lors-de-la-conference-des-ambassadeurs-et-des-ambassadrices/.
Macron, Emmanuel. *Initiative pour l'Europe – Discours d'Emmanuel Macron pour une Europe souveraine, unie, démocratique*. Paris: University of Sorbonne, 2017. Accessed June 6, 2018. www.elysee.fr/declarations/article/initiative-pour-l-europe-discours-d-emmanuel-macron-pour-une-europe-souveraine-unie-democratique/.
Mauro, Frédéric. "Strategic Autonomy under the Spotlight: The New Holy Grail of European Defence." *GRIP Report* (2018). Accessed June 6, 2018, www.grip.org/sites/grip.org/files/RAPPORTS/2018/Rapport_2018-1_EN.pdf.
"Merkel hält USA für nicht mehr verlässlich." *Süddeutsche Zeitung*, May 28, 2017. Accessed September 10, 2017. www.sueddeutsche.de/politik/g-gipfel-merkel-haelt-usa-fuer-nicht-mehr-verlaesslich-1.3524283.
Ministère de la Défense. *Défense et Sécurité Nationale: Le Livre Blanc*. Ministère de la Défense, 2008.
Ministère de la Défense. *Livre Blanc sur la Défense 1994*. Accessed June 6, 2018. www.ladocumentationfrancaise.fr/var/storage/rapports-publics/944048700.pdf.
Ministère de la Défense. *Livre Blanc sur la Défense et la Sécurité*. Ministère de la Défense, 2013.
Ministère des Armées. *Revue stratégique de défense et de sécurité nationale*. Ministère des Armées, 2017.
Ministero della Difesa. *Libro Bianco per la Sicurezza Internazionale e la Difesa*. 2015. Accessed June 15, 2018. www.difesa.it/Primo_Piano/Documents/2015/04_Aprile/LB_2015.pdf.
Poushter, Jacob, and Dorothy Manevich. "Globally, People Point to ISIS and Climate Change as Leading Security Threats: Concern about Cyberattacks, World Economy Also Widespread." Pew Research Center, 2017. Accessed July 10, 2018. www.pewglobal.org/2017/08/01/globally-people-point-to-isis-and-climate-change-as-leading-security-threats/.
Rehrl, Jochen. *Handbook for Decision Makers. The Common Security and Defence Policy of the European Union*. Wien: Federal Ministry of Defence and Sports of the Republic of Austria, 2014.
Sanger, David E., and Mark Landler. "Obama's Strategic Shift to Asia Is Hobbled by Pressure at Home and Crises Abroad." *New York Times*, April 21, 2014. Accessed August 22, 2018. www.nytimes.com/2014/04/22/world/asia/obamas-strategic-shift-to-asia-is-hobbled-by-pressure-at-home-and-crises-abroad.html.
"Trump vs. Merkel: Blistering Salvo Meets Quiet Rejoinder." *New York Times*, July 11, 2018. Accessed July 12, 2018. www.nytimes.com/2018/07/11/world/europe/germany-merkel-russia-trump-nato.html.

Varga, Gergely. "Towards European Strategic Autonomy: Evaluating the New CSDP Initiatives." KKI Studies-Institute for Foreign Affairs and Trade, 2017. Accessed June 6, 2018. http://kki.hu/assets/upload/07_KKI-Studies_CSDP_VargaG_20171003.pdf.

Wagner, Wolfgang, and Rosanne Anholt. "Resilience as the EU Global Strategy's New Leitmotif: Pragmatic, Problematic, or Promising?" *Contemporary Security Policy* 37 (2016): 414–30.

"We Europeans really have to take our fate into our own hands." *Süddeutsche Zeitung*, May 28, 2017. Accessed September 10, 2017. www.sueddeutsche.de/politik/g-gipfel-merkel-haelt-usa-fuer-nicht-mehr-verlaesslich-1.3524283.

Whitney, Nick. "Macron and the European Intervention Initiative: Erasmus for Soldiers?" *ECFR Commentary* (2018). Accessed July 6, 2018. www.ecfr.eu/article/commentary_macron_and_the_european_intervention_initiative_erasmus_for_sold.

6

BUDGET AND EU SECURITY

What are the current reasons to increase the budget? The Multiannual Financial Framework 2021–2027

Fernando Serrano Antón

Introduction

There is no doubt of the European commitment to peace. Today we have unprecedented social and economic opportunities in our societies, but we are also facing new threats and challenges. Peace and security in Europe should not be taken for granted in a changeable world in which global and regional powers rearm, terrorists strike in Europe and cyberattacks escalate.

Within this framework, the European Union (EU) has an obligation and responsibility to protect its citizenship and promote European interests and values. Therefore, security and defence have become one of the biggest concerns for Europeans, who trust the European Union for protection, security and defence. The consequence is that security and defence must play a more prominent role in the European project for the coming years, in parallel with the North Atlantic Treaty Organization (NATO).

The threats and challenges that Europe faces today do not respect national borders. Notwithstanding that Member States remain on the front line and are responsible for deploying security and armed forces when needed, these new types of threats and challenges are best prevented and tackled by the EU Member States together, within the framework of the European institutions. In addition, the capacity of individual states on their own could be easily overwhelmed when facing such modern threats.[1]

Concerning the development and maintaining of defence capabilities, collaboration and cooperation within the European Union should be the general rule, since they are much more effective than a state acting alone. More systematic cooperation and the joint development of technologies and capabilities could be good mechanisms to foster EU security and defence.

So far, the European Union has been acting as a player with a soft power approach promoting peace, inclusive growth and environmental protection. But the mechanisms of diplomacy, sanctions, development cooperation and trade, aimed at preventing conflict, are not enough. This is the reason why the Union at this stage, with the conditions above described, has decided to develop a hard approach to security and defence instruments alongside its existing approach.

Taking into consideration such a hard approach, the European Union has to cooperate and collaborate on security and defence with its partners such as NATO and the United Nations

(UN). The EU and its Member States put in place a set of new measures and tools to increase the effectiveness of their actions, e.g. through new command structures for military training missions or policies to strengthen the civilian dimension of the Common Security and Defence Policy (CSDP). At the same time, a stronger foundation with new tools and instruments has been built to continuously develop and strengthen security and defence capabilities. Cooperation and coordination is thereby at the very heart of the EU's approach. The EU must take strategic responsibility for acting alone when necessary and with partners whenever possible. This is why the EU strengthens its cooperation with other international partners such as NATO or the UN.

The first occasion in which security and defence changed its role in the EU was probably in the 2016 *State of the Union*, in which President Juncker called for a "Europe that protects and defends, at home and abroad." This reflection paper considers the issues that matter for the future of our security and defence.[2]

The aim of this paper is to consider how to finance the new approach to policy on security and defence and the opportunities which opened with the new Multiannual Financial Framework 2021–2027.

A new budget for 2021–2027: modernizing the budget

Every seven years, the European Union decides on its future long-term budget – the Multiannual Financial Framework. It is an opportunity for Member States and the European institutions to design the European vision for the near future.[3] A new seven-year EU budget always consists of a crucial financial element to implement the EU agenda, in this case agreed by the Leaders of the 27 Member States in Bratislava on 16 September 2016, as well as in the Rome Declaration of 25 March 2017.

Negotiations on the next Multiannual Financial Framework will have a significant impact on how the EU deals with the challenges ahead. Choices taken in the coming months will shape the Union for decades to come. In particular, new security threats require new responses. The refugee crisis, caused by war in Europe's neighbourhood, has shown the need to reinforce the capacity to manage migratory pressures and to address their root causes. Geopolitical instability is increasing and the values and democratic principles on which the European Union is founded are being tested.

The European Commission (EC) has set out options for the future EU budget in its Communication of 14 February 2018.[4] The Commission is proposing a new, modern long-term budget. The proposed budget combines new instruments with modernized programmes to deliver efficiently on the Union's priorities and to rise to new challenges. The European Commission's proposal of 2 May 2018 concerning the Multiannual Financial Framework (MFF) of the EU starting in 2021 contains a whole chapter on "security and defence." The following sections set out the main reforms and programmes under each of the spending priorities. We will focus on the security and defence priorities as contained in this communication:

Part V. Security and Defence
12. Security
Internal Security Fund
Nuclear Decommissioning (Lithuania)
Nuclear Safety and Decommissioning (including for Bulgaria and Slovakia)

13. Defence
European Defence Fund
Connecting Europe Facility – Military Mobility

14. Crisis Response
Union Civil Protection Mechanism (rescEU)

Security and defence as spending priorities

Over recent years, security threats have intensified and diversified in Europe. They have come in the form of terrorist attacks, organized crime and cybercrime. Security has an inherently cross-border dimension and therefore a strong, coordinated EU response is required. Beyond internal security challenges, Europe faces complex external threats that no Member State can tackle on its own. To be ready to protect its citizens, Europe also needs a step change to enhance its strategic autonomy and to build well-designed and streamlined instruments in relation to defence.[5]

One of the reasons for the European Union to expand its responsibility for defending and protecting its citizens and their values is the increasing geopolitical instability in the neighbourhood. In addition, another reason deals with the ultimate instability of the traditional EU allies, particularly the United States of America (USA). The European Union is stepping up its contribution to Europe's collective security and defence, working closely with its partners, beginning with NATO, avoiding any type of suspicious of unilateralism.

While the Union cannot substitute for Member States' efforts in defence, it can, within the limits of the Treaties, complement and leverage their collaboration in developing the defence products and technologies needed to address common security challenges.[6] This would reduce duplication and allow for a more efficient use of taxpayers' money. The lack of cooperation between Member States in the field of defence and security is estimated to cost annually between EUR 25 billion and EUR 100 billion. More than 80 per cent of public procurement and more than 90 per cent of research and technology are run on a national basis. The European levels of investment in the development and the procurement of future capabilities are insufficient and lag behind the investments of other countries.[7] There is also a wide difference between the defence spending levels among the Member States. In addition, the costs of defence equipment are rising faster than defence national budgets. A high degree of fragmentation remains, with, for example, 178 different weapon systems in Europe compared to 30 in the United States. The low level of coordination of the national defence planning leads to inefficient use of taxpayers' money and unnecessary duplication. In addition, weak cooperation, fragmentation and systematic duplication of resources affect deployability and hamper the EU's ability to act and protect.

European defence faces significant market inefficiencies linked to untapped economies of scale (fragmentation of national markets with a single buyer) and duplication of resources at national level. The demand comes almost exclusively from Member States, but their defence budgets, in particular for research and development (R&D), have seen major budget cuts in the past ten years. Although there are recent positive indications as regards stabilization and increases of national defence funding, significant further efforts are needed to maximize the efficiency of these investments. At the same time, the costs of defence equipment and in particular R&D have increased, while cooperation between Member States in R&D and defence equipment investments has remained limited. In 2015, only 16 per cent of defence equipment was procured through European collaborative procurement, far from the collective benchmark of 35 per cent agreed in the framework of the European Defence Agency (EDA). The estimated share of European collaboration in the earlier stage of defence research was of only 7.2 per cent against a benchmark of 20 per cent.

These trends are reflected in the difficulties that the sector faces, which are substantial as regards defence research and defence development projects. The development of prototypes is particularly costly and there is a significant risk of failure. Also, bridging the gap between research and development entails considerable technical and financial risks that individual Member States may not wish to bear on their own.

The sector is fragmented across national borders, with substantial duplication and resulting inefficiencies in terms of failure to capture economies of scale and learning. Despite the combination of increasing costs and stagnating or shrinking defence budgets, planning, R&D spending and the procurement and maintenance of equipment have remained largely matters for individual Member States, with very limited cooperation between them. The existing situation is not sustainable and the development of a major next generation defence system is increasingly beyond the reach of individual Member States.

This lack of cooperation between Member States further weakens the ability of the EU defence industry to sustain the industrial and technological capabilities necessary to preserve the EU's strategic autonomy and meet its current and future security needs. In response, the Commission has taken a number of initiatives in support of greater defence cooperation.

The European Commission, taking into account the conditions above explained, has proposed several mechanisms in order to step up the defence budget:

- To reinforce the Internal Security Fund in order to develop networks and common systems for efficient cooperation between national authorities and to improve the capacity of the Union to face these security threats.[8]
- To strengthen cybersecurity in all relevant programmes focused on digital technologies, infrastructures and networks, research and innovation as well as targeted defence against cybercrime, notably through the Digital Europe Programme[9] and Horizon Europe.[10]
- To reinforce the European Union Agency for Law Enforcement Cooperation (Europol). This will increase its ability to support the work of national authorities and provide for a European response to security threats.
- To provide strictly targeted financial support for the decommissioning and safety of nuclear activities in some Member States (Lithuania, Bulgaria and Slovakia), as well as its own nuclear installations.
- To provide lasting support for the health of workers and the general public, preventing environmental degradation and contributing to nuclear safety and security.

In the area of defence, the Union will need to take greater responsibility for protecting its interests, values and the European way of life, complementing the work of NATO. As mentioned, even if Europe cannot substitute Member States' efforts in defence, it can encourage and leverage their collaboration in developing the defence capabilities needed to address common security challenges. For instance, the UK is arguably the EU's strongest defence power. It is one of only two Member States possessing "full-spectrum" military capabilities (including a nuclear deterrent),[11] and one of only three Member States meeting the NATO target of spending 2 per cent of gross domestic product on defence. Therefore, taking into consideration the previous reasons, the Commission proposes:

- A strengthened European Defence Fund that will aim to foster the competitiveness and innovative capacity of the defence industry throughout the Union by supporting collaborative actions at each stage of the industrial cycle, starting with research. This will avoid duplication, allow for economies of scale and ultimately result in a more efficient use of taxpayers' money.
- To enhance its strategic transport infrastructures so as to make them fit for military mobility, through the Connecting Europe Facility.[12]

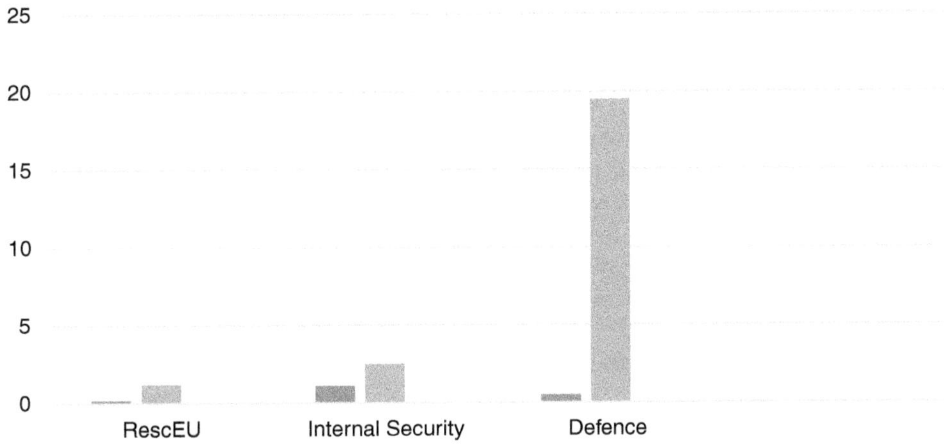

Figure 6.1 EU budget on defence and security – comparative 2014–2020 and 2021–2027.

Note: EUR billions.

Developments at the European level in recent years have shown that the EU must be able to deploy operational assistance rapidly to deal with unexpected developments of any kind. The criticism of the absence of EU response in some of the latter security events has affected EU credibility. This is why the Commission is proposing to increase the resources available for crisis response. This will be achieved through a reinforced Civil Protection Mechanism (rescEU)[13] and an enlarged Emergency Aid Reserve,[14] to provide financial means above the ceilings set in the Financial Framework in case of emergencies inside and outside the Union. The Commission also proposes maintaining unallocated reserves in certain programmes, such as the Asylum and Migration Fund and the Internal Security Fund, to be used in the event of crisis and emergency situations.

In total, for security and defence, there is an estimation for the framework 2021–2027, current prices, of 27.51 billion euros.

Defence budget: European Defence Fund and mobility

In the context of the implementation of the EU Global Strategy (EUGS), the European Commission proposed a European Defence Action Plan (EDAP) with a European Defence Fund (EDF) tailored to common European priorities to support technical development in the EU – from research to development to procurement – in 2016. In preparation for this, the Preparatory Action on Defence Research (PADR) was initiated within the Research Window in 2017 with a total budget of EUR 90 million, and a European Defence Industrial Development Programme (EDIDP) was created with a funding amount of EUR 500 million to be used within the Capability Window in 2019 and 2020.[15]

European Defence Fund[16]

The Commission proposes a European Defence Fund to promote cooperation and cost savings among Member States in producing state-of-the-art and interoperable defence technology and equipment. Offering support for the research and development parts of the lifecycle will make sure that the results of research are not lost due to lack of funding for developing and testing the technology. The Fund will encourage the participation of small and medium-sized enterprises in collaborative projects.

For the EDF, the amount of EUR 4.1 billion is proposed to be used to provide 100 per cent funding for projects in the research phase, and EUR 8.9 billion are proposed to be used during the development phase as subsidies in varying amounts depending on the stage of development (20 to 80 per cent). With the necessary co-financing by the Member States or the industry, this should lead to an investment of up to EUR 50 billion. The new proposal of the EC does not include separation of programmes but separate budgetary approaches. The integrated approach will bring new opportunities as well as new challenges for all involved stakeholders.

The EDF is a comparatively large and important EU initiative to strengthen the European Defence Technological and Industrial Base (EDTIB) and also to contribute to the faster development of capacities under the CSDP. In particular, it is supposed to contribute to the improvement of the EU's autonomous ability to act by preserving important (key) technologies in Europe, and to thus contribute to the long-term competitiveness of the EU. The Fund will coordinate, supplement and amplify national investments in defence. By pooling resources, individual Member States can achieve greater output and develop defence technology and equipment that may not be feasible on their own. Increased collaboration reduces duplication costs, promotes standardization of equipment and ensures better interoperability between European armed forces. The Fund will also foster innovation and allow economies of scale, thus reinforcing the competitiveness of the EU defence industry.[17]

The EU's future research framework programme "Horizon Europe" provides for a total amount of around EUR 100 billion.[18] Since the EDF is legally a part of "Horizon Europe," a total amount of about EUR 113 billion will be available for civil and military research and development, more than 10 per cent of which is for the first time specifically available for military research and development.

To apply for the EDF, only collaborative projects are eligible, and they must have at least three participants from several Member States. The European Union will only co-fund development of prototypes where Member States commit to buying the final product.

The European Defence Fund links to projects implemented within the framework of the Permanent Structured Cooperation in defence (PESCO). Once assessed eligible, a "PESCO bonus," in the form of an increased financing rate, will be granted to projects developed in the framework of the Permanent Structured Cooperation. In other words, projects conceived by Member States in the framework of PESCO will benefit from a higher EU co-financing rate (10 per cent bonus). Early pre-consultation with the Commission will be required to help assess possible eligibility of Permanent Structured Cooperation projects under the Fund.[19]

The EDF will take into account the EU Capability Development Plan and the Coordinated Annual Review on Defence of the European Defence Agency, notably as regards the implementation of priorities and the identification of new cooperative opportunities. Implementation will take into account relevant activities of North Atlantic Treaty Organization and other partners.

The Fund also complements defence activities implemented through the European Peace Facility (EPF), an off-budget instrument proposed outside the Multiannual Financial Framework (MFF).[20]

The Commission proposes a budget of EUR 13 billion (over the seven-year period 2021–2027) be dedicated to the European Defence Fund. This will place the EU among the top four defence research and technology investors in Europe. The figures are shown in Figure 6.2.

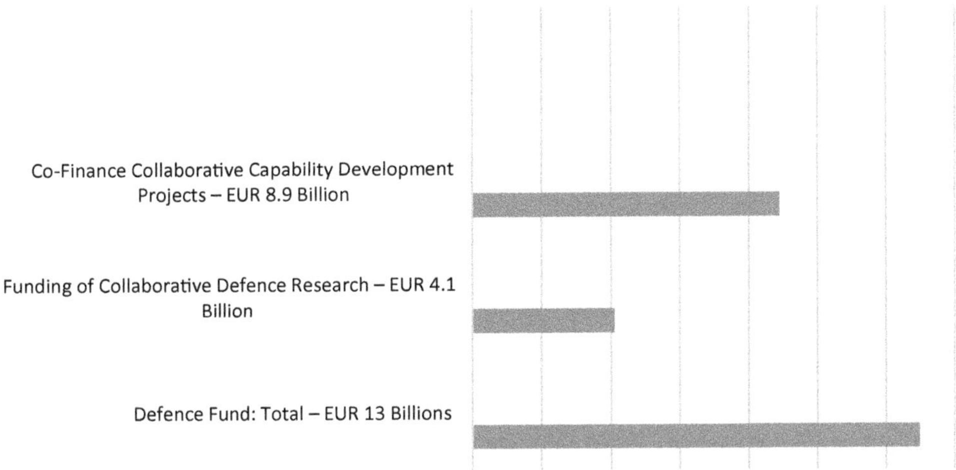

Figure 6.2 Defence fund: research & development (EUR billions).

Up to 5 per cent of the financial envelope of EUR 13 billion is to be devoted to supporting disruptive technologies for defence.

An eligible action for funding must relate to one or more of the following items:[21]

(a) activities aiming to create, underpin and improve new knowledge and defence technology which can achieve significant effects in the area of defence;
(b) activities aiming to increase interoperability and resilience, including secured production and exchange of data, master critical defence technologies, strengthen the security of supply or enable effectively exploitation of results for defence products and technologies;
(c) studies, such as feasibility studies to explore the feasibility of a new or improved technology, product, process, service, solution or statistics on the defence industry and projects to pilot the collection of data;
(d) the design of a defence product, tangible or intangible component or technology as well as the definition of the technical specifications on which such design has been developed which may include partial tests for risk reduction in an industrial or representative environment;
(e) the development of a model of a defence product, tangible or intangible component or technology, which can demonstrate the element's performance in an operational environment (system prototype);
(f) the testing of a defence product, tangible or intangible component or technology;
(g) the qualification of a defence product, tangible or intangible component or technology. Qualification is the entire process of demonstrating that the design of a defence product, tangible or intangible component or technology meets the specified requirements. This process provides objective evidence by which particular requirements of a design are demonstrated to have been achieved;
(h) the certification of a defence product, tangible or intangible component or technology. Certification is the process according to which a national authority certifies that the defence product, tangible or intangible component or technology complies with the applicable regulations;

(i) the development of technologies or assets increasing efficiency across the life cycle of defence products and technologies;
(j) dissemination activities, networking events and awareness-raising activities.

Military mobility

In addition, the second part of the defence budget, namely "military mobility," is planned with EUR 6.5 billion and is supposed to mainly contribute to the improvement of infrastructural measures. Military mobility is another recent achievement based on closer cooperation among EU Member States but also with NATO allies. Be it for the purpose of military exercises, joint training or preparation for deployments in third countries, mobility of the armed forces of EU Member States is crucial in combining their strengths and in the accomplishment of tasks.

The Commission proposes that the Union enhance its strategic transport infrastructures to make them fit for military mobility. A dedicated budget will be earmarked in the Connecting Europe Facility.

Final reflections

Therefore, for the first time in the history of the EU, the defence sector will be supported with significant financial resources (EUR 19.5 billion: EUR 13 billion EDF + EUR 6.5 billion mobility) from the common EU budget for the timing 2021–2027, as well as through the provision of several financing instruments by the EC.

In addition, the EU budget for defence and security will support other defence-related activities through the European Peace Facility,[22] an off-budget instrument proposed outside the Multiannual Financial Framework. The Facility will aim to increase the EU's support to peace operations by third parties worldwide; to cover joint costs of Common Security and Defence Policy military missions (now covered under the Athena mechanism); and to enable the EU to engage in broader actions aimed at supporting non-EU countries' armed forces with infrastructure, equipment and supplies or military technical assistance. The European Peace Facility helps improve the EU's ability to prevent conflicts, build peace and guarantee international security. The EPF increases the effectiveness of financing for Common Security and Defence Policy military missions and operations. It also facilitates the EU's contributions to peace operations led by partners and it will broaden the scope of the military and defence support the EU can offer. The EPF will cover expenditure that cannot be financed under the EU's budget because of its military and defence implications.

The European budget for defence will also help reduce reliance on Washington. Once the European defence industry is ready, EU Member States will be in a position to choose between US and EU products. While these initial steps on the EDF may seem small, they represent a radical shift after decades of inaction.[23] The European Commission has found its way into the European security and defence sector, even though this sector has long been considered a *domaine réservé* of the Member States, and ambitious Commission initiatives have come to fruition.

Security EU budget

The Internal Security Fund

The Internal Security Fund contributes to ensuring a high level of security in the Union by tackling terrorism and radicalization, organized crime and cybercrime and by assisting and protecting victims of crime.[24] The proposed budget allocation for 2021–2027 reaches EUR 2,500 million.

Over recent years, security threats have intensified and diversified in Europe. Terrorist attacks, organized crime and growing cybercrime have a cross-border dimension which demands an EU response. EU action has provided a comprehensive reaction to these challenges and the general policy response was formulated in 2015 by the Agenda on Security.[25] That issue will remain for years to come and Europe and national governments have the duty to deliver security in a fast-changing and uncertain world.

The challenges the EU is facing, bearing in mind the international character of terrorism, cannot be managed by individual Member States alone and without the financial and technical support of the EU. In an era in which terrorism and other serious crime operates across borders, both the European Union and its Member States have a responsibility towards their citizens to deliver in the area of security. In this regard, the European Treaties envisage the need to ensure a high level of security, through preventive measures and through coordination and cooperation between police, judicial and other competent authorities. These needs should be provided for at EU level.

EU support provides added value to national funding by stimulating cooperation and exchange of information between Member State law enforcement officials and other relevant authorities including Europol and other relevant Union bodies, third countries and international organizations, in particular by:

- enabling the interoperability of the different security systems and making EU information systems more effective and efficient;
- facilitating and intensifying cross-border joint operational actions;
- providing support for training, for the construction of essential security-relevant facilities and the purchase of necessary technical equipment; and,
- ensuring collective responses to security threats by increasing capabilities and enhancing EU preparedness and resilience, including by increasing cooperation among public authorities, civil actors and private partners from across EU Member States and third countries.

The Internal Security Fund is mainly implemented through shared management via multiannual programmes implemented by Member States and, in addition, through direct or – to a limited extent also – indirect management. Emergency Assistance can complement the programmes of Member States by responding to an emergency situation.[26] Shared management allows for funding predictability and long-term planning; it guarantees an allocation to all Member States, while securing the ability to implement common priorities across the Union. However, for a better steer of funds towards the EU priorities, shared management is complemented by a Thematic Facility that would be available to channel funds to support action.[27]

Several decentralized agencies such as Europol (EU Agency for Law Enforcement Cooperation) and CEPOL (Agency for Law Enforcement Training), play key operational, coordination and advisory roles in the implementation of the EU priorities and objectives in the area of security. They have their own budgets to carry out their tasks, separate from the Fund.

Drawing on the experience of the current programme, the future Fund will further simplify the rules for its beneficiaries. The key operational features include an increased flexibility to respond to unforeseen developments, a common feature of the area of security. A part of funding will be allocated upfront, while a significant envelope will be allocated subsequently to specific priorities, periodically allowing reaction to changed circumstances or urgencies (via the Thematic Facility).

Security is a cross-cutting issue and the new Internal Security Fund cannot provide an effective EU response without other funding instruments, including the European Structural and Investment Funds and external instruments. Synergies of the Internal Security Fund with other related instruments must be established in particular in relation to the following aspects: border management and customs control equipment; security of infrastructure and public spaces; cybersecurity (cybersecurity is a key theme of the Digital Europe Programme, with the Fund focusing on cybercrime); the prevention of radicalization; and the external dimension of security.

Security budget: nuclear decommissioning in Lithuania

The programme provides support to Lithuania to safely decommission first-generation nuclear reactors. As a condition for its accession to the European Union, Lithuania made the commitment to close and subsequently decommission two Soviet-designed first-generation nuclear reactors for which an upgrade to Western safety standards was deemed uneconomical. Correspondingly, the EU committed itself in Article 3 of Protocol No. 4 of the Act of Accession of 2003 to financially support the decommissioning.

The proposed EU budget allocation for 2021–2027 reaches EUR 552 million.

To date, the decommissioning activity is progressing, with an end foreseen in 2038. It is in the interest of the Union to continue providing strictly targeted financial support, contributing to ensuring the highest level of safety of the operation. The programme provides substantial and lasting support for the health of workers and the general public, preventing environmental degradation and ensuring real progress in nuclear safety and security.

The programme has a high potential for becoming a benchmark within the EU for safely managing technological issues in nuclear decommissioning, such as the decommissioning of graphite-moderated reactors.

Keeping the decommissioning of these reactors under a dedicated spending programme ensures that implementation continues seamlessly through the established implementing body (a dedicated Lithuanian agency).

Synergies with the Cohesion Policy will be strengthened in the next programming period. In particular, the policy will have the potential to support the development of the region concerned by creating jobs and promoting sustainable growth and innovation. Similarly, synergies will be explored with Horizon Europe in areas such as technology development and testing, as well as training and education.

Security budget: nuclear safety and decommissioning

The aim is to support Bulgaria and Slovakia to safely decommission first-generation nuclear reactors and, separately, to finance the decommissioning process and final disposal of waste of the Commission's own nuclear installations.

As a condition for their accession to the EU, Bulgaria and Slovakia made the commitment to close and to subsequently decommission six Soviet-designed first-generation nuclear reactors for which an upgrade to Western safety standards was deemed uneconomical.

Correspondingly, the EU committed itself in the frame of Article 203 of the Euratom Treaty to financially support the decommissioning. The decommissioning activity is progressing with an end foreseen in 2025 for Bohunice, Slovakia and 2030 for Kozloduy, Bulgaria. It is in the interest of the Union to continue providing financial support for decommissioning, contributing to ensuring the highest level of safety of the operation. Substantial and durable support will be provided for the health of workers and the general public, preventing environmental degradation and ensuring real progress in nuclear safety and security.

The aim is to continue assisting Bulgaria and Slovakia in managing the radioactive safety challenges of the decommissioning process. Additionally, the decommissioning of the Commission (Joint Research Centre, or JRC) sites will help explore and develop options for the anticipated transfer of decommissioning and waste management liabilities to the JRC host Member States.

The management of the programme for Bulgaria and Slovakia is entrusted (indirect management mode) to the European Bank for Reconstruction and Development and a national agency in Slovakia. Keeping the decommissioning of these reactors under a dedicated spending programme ensures that implementation continues seamlessly through the established implementing bodies.

Synergies with the Cohesion Policy will be strengthened in the next programming period. In particular, the policy will have the potential to support the development of the region concerned by creating jobs, promoting sustainable growth and innovation. Similarly, synergies should be explored with Horizon Europe in areas such as technology development and testing, as well as training and education.

The proposed budget allocation for 2021–2027 reaches EUR 626 million, and specifically is as follows:

- Assistance to Bulgaria: EUR 63 million.
- Assistance to Slovakia: EUR 55 million.
- Decommissioning of Commission sites: EUR 348 million.
- Nuclear safety and nuclear safeguards: EUR 160 million.

European Peace Facility as an extra-budgetary tool[28]

The European Peace Facility aims to finance the common costs of military operations under the Common Security and Defence Policy; contribute to the financing of military peace support operations led by other international actors; and provide support to third states' armed forces to prevent conflicts, build peace and strengthen international security.

The EU aims to be recognized as a credible global actor. This gives it a competitive advantage in terms of conflict prevention and peace-keeping. EU interventions in these areas can take different forms, ranging from providing support to peace-keeping operations by third countries or international organizations (such as under the African Peace Facility), to direct support to partners' capacities, to deploying troops for operations under the Common Foreign and Defence Policy. This ability of the EU to contribute to the prevention of crisis, restoration of peace or public order or stabilization of countries or regions faced with conflict or disorder is essential. It does not only serve to protect the EU and its citizens, but also to stabilize countries, enable development and prevent massive displacement of persons.

The EU has engaged in or assisted peace support operations, including through the deployment of EU military forces, in a variety of locations – from Africa to the Middle-East and the Western Balkans.[29] These operations have demonstrated the added value of a European dimension, allowing participating Member States to pool resources, share costs and show a genuine European engagement on the ground. However, over recent years, the number of security and stability challenges in the neighbourhood and beyond has grown – and so have the demands for peace-keeping.

This calls for an enhanced engagement of the EU to respond to external conflicts and crises, through peace-keeping and conflict management which is achieved more efficiently and effectively at EU level. Very few Member States have sufficient resources to support or conduct effective military operations on their own and the Member States that do so should not be expected to bear the entire cost of operations which benefit the EU as a whole. Solidarity between Member States and pooling of resources is therefore essential. Moreover, EU-level involvement can facilitate cooperation with international and regional organizations and countries worldwide through its network of EU delegations.

The objective of the Facility is to enable the EU to do more and to act more swiftly to prevent conflicts, promote human security, address instability and work towards a safer world, also using military and defence means if required.

The Treaty on European Union (TEU) does not allow for Common Foreign and Security Policy operations that have military or defence implications to be financed under the EU budget. The primary objective of the Facility will therefore be the pursuit of EU foreign and security policy activities with military and/or defence implications which cannot be funded under the EU budget. Except when the Council decides otherwise, actions under the Common Foreign and Security Policy that can be financed under the EU budget must continue to be financed under the EU budget. The implementation of the Facility will require full consistency and coherence with the EU budget to be ensured at each and every level of the Facility's functioning.

The Facility is a new single extra-budgetary instrument. It will combine support which, under the Multiannual Financial Framework 2014–2020, is partly covered by the Africa Peace Facility (financed from the extra-budgetary European Development Fund),[30] and the Athena mechanism.[31] Military Common Security and Defence Policy operations are funded outside of the EU budget primarily by the participating Member States, while a limited percentage of common costs are financed through the Athena mechanism.

These existing funding mechanisms, while of clear added value, have up to now only partially addressed the expectations of partners and the need to ensure the EU's external stability in light of unprecedented external challenges. The Facility therefore seeks to:

- enhance the financing of military operations under the Common Security and Defence Policy, which should be made more flexible and efficient;
- widen the scope of the EU's support to peace-supporting military operations led by third countries and international organizations worldwide, and build the military capacities of third countries and international organizations to prevent conflicts, build peace and strengthen international security;
- facilitate the financing of other operational actions under the Common Foreign and Security Policy having military or defence implications when so decided by the Council.

The Facility will be established through a Council Decision under the Common Foreign and Security Policy. As an instrument under the Common Foreign and Security Policy, its implementation will be ensured by the High Representative. With regard to the financial implementation of the Facility in line with the Financial Regulation, the High Representative will be assisted by the Commission's Service for Foreign Policy Instruments.

The Facility will be financed through yearly contributions by Member States based on a Gross National Income distribution key. It will improve flexibility and responsiveness to crisis, drawing on lessons learned from the current instruments and mechanisms. It will ensure that EU funding is available on a permanent basis, while allowing for a rapid response to crises and other urgent requests. It will also facilitate the provision of integrated packages with military training provided by EU military training missions, military equipment and support. The European

Peace Facility is designed in an efficient, flexible manner to take into account the different nature of its activities. The important role of partners will be clearly reflected.

The Facility will be governed by the principles of coherence and complementarity, ensuring full consistency and synergy with relevant external action instruments and measures under the EU budget, in particular the Common Foreign and Security Policy, capacity building for security and development and other forms of security-related assistance and action under the Security and Peace objectives of the EU's neighbourhood and development policies. Flexibility and responsiveness will ensure that support is available in a timely manner and caters to external military needs as agreed. Simplification and streamlining of funding sources and structures will also be ensured. The Facility will be subject to a strong political steer, to ensure its effectiveness and coherence with the EU's overall external policy approach.

The Facility reflects the need to find expression for the EU's role in defence but is clearly distinct from the European Defence Fund, which aims to supplement and amplify national investments in defence research and industrial development. Nevertheless, the European Defence Fund has the potential to provide a significant boost to the EU's strategic autonomy and the competitiveness of Europe's defence industry, thus indirectly allowing the EU to provide more efficient support to military peace-keeping operations abroad.

The European Peace Facility is an "extra-budgetary" instrument. The proposed budget allocation for 2021–2027 reaches EUR 10,500 million.

Conclusions

The European Union has been acting as a player with a soft power approach promoting peace, inclusive growth and environmental protection. The mechanisms of diplomacy, sanctions, development cooperation and trade, aimed at preventing conflict, are not enough. This is the reason why the European Union at this stage, with the conditions above described, has decided to develop a hard approach on security and defence instruments alongside that.

Taking into consideration such a hard approach, the European Union has to cooperate and collaborate on security and defence with its partners such as NATO and the United Nations. The EU and its Member States have put in place a set of new measures and tools to increase the effectiveness of their actions.

Following the new role assumed by the EU, in June 2018 the European Commission presented a legislative proposal on a European Defence Fund, including a budget allocation of EUR 13 billion in current prices for the 2021 to 2027 period. The proposal aims to streamline and simplify the current legislation by integrating the Preparatory Action on Defence Research and the European Defence Industrial Development Programme into a single fund. The main aims of the fund are to foster the competitiveness and innovativeness of European defence and to contribute to the EU's strategic autonomy. In this regard, the fund would support collaborative industrial projects; co-finance the costs of prototype development; encourage the participation of small and medium-sized enterprises; and promote projects in the framework of Permanent Structured Cooperation. Synergies are expected with other EU initiatives in the field of cybersecurity, maritime transport, border management, Horizon Europe, the space programme and the European Peace Facility.

This is a major step in making European defence cooperation a reality. The new defence budget will help Member States get better value for taxpayers' money, promote a strong and innovative defence industry and raise the EU's autonomy and technological leadership in defence.

The MFF 2021–2027 on Defence should ensure that Europe becomes a stronger security provider for its citizens. The budget will foster technological innovation and cooperation in the

European defence sector, so that Europe benefits from cutting-edge, interoperable defence technology and equipment in novel areas like artificial intelligence, encrypted software, drone technology or satellite communication.

Notes

1 Bernardo de Miguel, "La UE lanza una ofensiva para reducir la dependencia de la OTAN," *El País*, November 19, 2018, accessed November 19, 2018, https://elpais.com/internacional/2018/11/16/actualidad/1542390635_431550.html.
2 Jean-Claude Junker, *State of the Union – 2016* (Brussels: European Commission, 2016), accessed October 10, 2018, https://publications.europa.eu/en/publication-detail/-/publication/c9ff4ff6-9a81-11e6-9bca-01aa75ed71a1/language-en/format-PDF/source-30945725.
3 European Commission, Communication from the Commission to the European Parliament, the European Council and the Council: A New, Modern Multiannual Financial Framework for a European Union that Delivers Efficiently on Its Priorities Post-2020, COM(2018) 98 final (Brussels: European Union, February 14, 2018), accessed September 10, 2018, https://ec.europa.eu/commission/sites/beta-political/files/communication-new-modern-multiannual-financial-framework_en.pdf.
4 Ibid.
5 European Parliament, Resolutions of 14 March 2018 on "The next MFF: Preparing the Parliament's position on the MFF Post-2020 (2017/2052(INI))" and on the "Reform of the European Union's System of Own Resources (2017/2053(INI))" (Brussels: European Union, 2018).
6 The security of European citizens is first and foremost a European responsibility. Recognizing this, Member States are reinvesting in defence. The current 28 Member States are spending 1.34 per cent of GDP on defence (for the EU27, the figure is 1.32 per cent), and there is a clear need to do more. European Commission, Communication from the Commission to the European Parliament, the Council, the European Economic and Social Committee and the Committee of the Regions: Launching the European Defence Fund, COM(2017) 295 final (Brussels: European Union, June 7, 2018). See also European Parliament, "EU Defence Policy: The Sleeping Giant," December 2016, accessed April 14, 2019, www.europarl.europa.eu/EPRS/EPRS_BRIE_593791_defence_policy_final.pdf.
7 In budget terms alone, the US spends twice as much as European defence efforts. Jean-Claude Junker, "Speech by President Jean-Claude Juncker at the 54th Munich Security Conference" (Munich, 2018), accessed March 20, 2019, http://europa.eu/rapid/press-release_SPEECH-18-841_en.htm.
8 The Internal Security Fund (ISF) was set up for the period 2014–2020, with a total of EUR 3.8 billion for the seven years' period. The Fund will promote implementation of the Internal Security Strategy, law enforcement cooperation and management of the Union's external borders. The ISF is composed of two instruments: (1) ISF Borders and Visa; and (2) ISF Police. More information on the official website: https://ec.europa.eu/home-affairs/financing/fundings/security-and-safeguarding-liberties/internal-security-fund-police_en, accessed March 20, 2019.
9 The Digital Europe programme is part of the EU's long-term budget presented by the Commission for 2021–2027. The programme will invest in five key digital sectors: high performance computing; artificial intelligence; cybersecurity and trust; advanced digital skills; ensuring wide use and deployment of digital technologies across the economy and society, in order to strengthen European industrial technological leadership. More information on the official website: https://ec.europa.eu/digital-single-market/en/news/commission-welcomes-agreement-digital-europe-programme-2021-2027, accessed March 20, 2019.
10 Horizon 2020 reflects the policy priorities of the Europe 2020 strategy and addresses major concerns shared by citizens in Europe and elsewhere. Funding will focus on the different challenges. Areas of interest in this connection will cover Secure Societies – protecting the freedom and security of Europe and its citizens, consisting of provision of enhanced cybersecurity, ranging from secure information sharing to new assurance models. More information on the official website: https://ec.europa.eu/programmes/horizon2020/en/h2020-section/secure-societies-%E2%80%93-protecting-freedom-and-security-europe-and-its-citizens, accessed March 20, 2019. See also "2018/0254 (COD) EP Procedure File on the European Defence Fund 2021–2027," Legislative Observatory, accessed April 14, 2019, https://oeil.secure.europarl.europa.eu/oeil/popups/ficheprocedure.do?reference=2018/0254(COD)&l=en.
11 Military capability could be defined as "the ability to achieve a desired effect in a specific operating environment." It is defined by three interdependent factors: combat readiness, sustainable capability

and force structure. Australian Government: Department of Defence, *Defence Capability Development Manual*, accessed March 20, 2019, www.defence.gov.au/publications/dcdm.pdf.

12 The Connecting Europe Facility (CEF) is a key EU funding instrument to promote growth, jobs and competitiveness through targeted infrastructure investment at European level. It supports the development of high performing, sustainable and efficiently interconnected trans-European networks in the fields of transport, energy and digital services. CEF investments fill the missing links in Europe's energy, transport and digital backbone, including cybersecurity. More information on the official website: https://ec.europa.eu/inea/en/connecting-europe-facility, accessed March 20, 2019.

13 The aim of the EU Civil Protection Mechanism is to strengthen cooperation between participating States in the field of civil protection, with a view to improving prevention, preparedness and response to disasters. Through the Mechanism, the European Commission plays a key role in coordinating the response to disasters in Europe and beyond. More information on the official website: https://ec.europa.eu/echo/what/civil-protection/mechanism_en, accessed March 20, 2019. Any country in the world can call on the EU Civil Protection Mechanism for help and it has intervened in some of the most devastating disasters and complex emergencies. Examples include the Ebola outbreak in West Africa (2014) and in the Democratic Republic of the Congo (2018), the conflict in Ukraine (2014), the earthquake in Nepal (2015), the refugee and migration crisis in Europe (2015) and forest fires in the Mediterranean region (2017) and Sweden (2018).

14 The Emergency Aid Reserve was designed to enable a rapid response to specific aid requirements for non-EU countries that were unforeseeable when the budget was drawn up. Priority is given to humanitarian operations, but the reserve may also be used for civil crisis management and protection if necessary. More information on the official website: http://ec.europa.eu/budget/explained/budg_system/flex/flex_en.cfm, accessed March 20, 2019.

15 The European Defence Fund aims at fostering the competitiveness and innovativeness of the Union's defence technological and industrial base by supporting defence-oriented R&D activities. It is based on the Treaty on the Functioning of the European Union (TFEU) (Articles 173, 182, 183 and 188). European Commission, Proposal for a Regulation of the European Parliament and of the Council Establishing the European Defence Industrial Development Programme, Aiming at Supporting the Competitiveness and Innovative Capacity of the EU Defence Industry, COM(2017) 294 final, 2017/0125(COD) (Brussels: European Union, June 7, 2017).

16 European Commission, Proposal for a Regulation of the European Parliament and of the Council Establishing the European Defence Fund, COM(2018) 476 final, 2018/0254(COD) (Brussels: European Union, 2018). See also "EU Budget: Stepping Up the EU's Role as a Security and Defence Provider," European Commission website, June 13, 2018, accessed April 14, 2019, https://ec.europa.eu/growth/content/eu-budget-stepping-eus-role-security-and-defence-provider_en.

17 Clear cases of consistency between the EDF and other European policies are the EU initiatives in the field of cybersecurity, such as those announced in the Joint Communication on Cybersecurity (JOIN(2017) 0450 final of 13 September 2017). In particular, the Cyber Security Competence Centre to be set up should seek synergies between the civilian and defence dimensions of cybersecurity. It could actively support Member States and other relevant actors by providing advice, sharing expertise and facilitating collaboration with regard to projects and actions as well as, when requested by Member States, acting as a project manager in relation to actions under the European Defence Fund.

18 See note 10.

19 The Permanent Structured Cooperation is a practical EU framework, although in the framework of the EU Member States only, that enables participating Member States to pursue cooperation with each other on concrete projects in defence and security. Out of the 28 EU Member States, 25 have joined PESCO and have agreed to binding commitments. So far, 34 projects have been put forward by a group of Member States and adopted by the Council. The respective Member States now work together on, for example, military training and exercises, military capabilities on land, air and sea, but also the ever more important area of cyberdefence. Some examples of such projects are the European Military Space Surveillance/Awareness Network; the EU Radio Navigation Solution; Eurodrone; European Attack Helicopters; the Counter Unmanned Aerial System; the Land Battlefield Missile System; the Armoured Infantry Fighting Vehicle; the Deployable Module Underwater Intervention Capability Package; the Joint EU Intelligence School; the Cyber Threats and Incident Response Information Sharing Platform; and Cyber Rapid Response Teams and Mutual Assistance in Cyber Security.

20 The European Peace Facility is a proposal by the High Representative, to set up a new off-budget fund, a fund outside of the Union's multiannual budget, worth EUR 10.5 billion. It will enable the financing

of operational actions under the Common Foreign and Security Policy that have military or defence implications. The EPF will only cover expenditure that cannot be financed under the Union's budget because of its operational military or defence implications, as set out in the EU Treaty (art. 41.2 TEU). It will thus help maximize the impact, effectiveness and sustainability of the EU's external actions in peace and security. Through the EPF, the EU will be able to do more and to act more swiftly by using military and defence means as required. The EPF will be financed through contributions by EU Member States based on a Gross National Income distribution key. Its proposed ceiling is EUR 10.5 billion over a period coinciding with the next Multiannual Financial Framework.

21 Article 11 of the Proposal for a Regulation of the European Parliament and of the Council Establishing the European Defence Fund, COM/2018/476 final, 2018/0254(COD).

22 See note 20.

23 Chantal Lavallée, *The European Commission: an Enabler for the European Security and Defence Union* (Madrid: Real Instituto Elcano, 2018), accessed November 10, 2018, www.realinstitutoelcano.org/wps/portal/rielcano_es/contenido?WCM_GLOBAL_CONTEXT=/elcano/elcano_in/zonas_in/ari59-2018-lavallee-european-commission-enabler-for-european-security-defence-union.

24 See note 8.

25 European Commission, Communication from the Commission to the European Parliament, the Council, the European Economic and Social Committee and the Committee of the Regions: The European Agenda on Security, COM(2015) 185 final (Strasbourg: European Union, April 28, 2015), accessed March 20, 2019, https://ec.europa.eu/home-affairs/sites/homeaffairs/files/e-library/documents/basic-documents/docs/eu_agenda_on_security_en.pdf.

26 The Emergency Assistance applies in urgent and exceptional circumstances, such as the sudden influx of refugees in Europe, so the EU can fund emergency humanitarian support for people in need within the EU territory. The emergency support within the EU, adopted in March 2016, aims to preserve life, prevent and alleviate human suffering and maintain human dignity. This type of support can be provided for exceptional disasters in the European Union with severe humanitarian consequences. The provision of such assistance is decided collectively by Member States within the Council. More information on the official website: https://ec.europa.eu/echo/what-we-do/humanitarian-aid/emergency-support-within-eu_en, accessed March 21, 2019.

27 The EU contributions (Justice, Home Affairs Funds) should be disbursed either through programmes in Member States or through a Thematic Facility under various implementation methods. This facility includes emergency assistance, Union actions and specific actions which can top up national programmes. The Thematic Facility could be mobilized for any actions considered necessary to meet the objectives defined at EU level, including actions in third countries such as actions with the purpose of stemming illegal migration. Dedicated components for tackling the external dimension of migration are explicitly included in the Thematic Facility. This option provides enough flexibility to channel funds to the right component (either as emergency assistance, as Union action or through national programmes). Under this scenario, the Thematic Facility could dedicate a share of its financial envelope for external migration management. Council of the European Union, Reinforcing the External Dimension of Migration in Home Affairs Funds: A Challenge for Flexibility, Coherence and Complementarity? (Brussels: European Union, 2018), accessed March 21, 2019, http://data.consilium.europa.eu/doc/document/ST-12777-2018-INIT/en/pdf.

28 "European Peace Facility – An EU Off-budget Fund to Build Peace and Strengthen International Security," EEAS website, June 13, 2018, accessed November 10, 2018, https://eeas.europa.eu/headquarters/headquarters-homepage/46285/european-peace-facility-eu-budget-fund-build-peace-and-strengthen-international-security_en.

29 European Commission, Communication from the Commission to the European Parliament, the European Council, the Council and the European Investment Bank: Towards a More Efficient Financial Architecture for Investment outside the European Union, COM(2018) 644 final (Brussels: European Union, September 12, 2018), accessed November 10, 2018, https://ec.europa.eu/commission/sites/beta-political/files/soteu2018-investment-outside-eu-communication-644_en_0.pdf.

30 The African Peace Facility was established in 2004 in response to a request by African leaders. Financed through the European Development Fund, it constitutes the main source of funding to support the African Union's and African Regional Economic Communities' efforts in the area of peace and security with an overall amount of more than EUR 2.7 billion since 2004. Official website: https://ec.europa.eu/europeaid/regions/africa/continental-cooperation/african-peace-facility_en.

31 Athena is a mechanism which handles the financing of common costs relating to EU military operations under the EU's Common Security and Defence Policy (CSDP). Official website: www.consilium.europa.eu/en/policies/athena/.

References

"2018/0254 (COD) EP Procedure File on the European Defence Fund 2021–2027." Legislative Observatory. Accessed April 14, 2019. https://oeil.secure.europarl.europa.eu/oeil/popups/ficheprocedure.do?reference=2018/0254(COD)&l=en.

Australian Government: Department of Defence. *Defence Capability Development Manual*. Accessed March 20, 2019. www.defence.gov.au/publications/dcdm.pdf.

Council of the European Union. Reinforcing the External Dimension of Migration in Home Affairs Funds: A Challenge for Flexibility, coherence and complementarity? Brussels: European Union, 2018. Accessed March 21, 2019. http://data.consilium.europa.eu/doc/document/ST-12777-2018-INIT/en/pdf.

De Miguel, Bernardo. "La UE lanza una ofensiva para reducir la dependencia de la OTAN." *El País*, November 19, 2018. Accessed November 19, 2018. https://elpais.com/internacional/2018/11/16/actualidad/1542390635_431550.html.

"EU Budget: Stepping Up the EU's Role as a Security and Defence Provider." European commission website, June 13, 2018. Accessed April 14, 2019. https://ec.europa.eu/growth/content/eu-budget-stepping-eus-role-security-and-defence-provider_en.

European Commission. Communication from the Commission to the European Parliament, the Council, the European Economic and Social Committee and the Committee of the Regions: Launching the European Defence Fund. COM(2017) 295 final. Brussels: European Union, June 7, 2018.

European Commission. Communication from the Commission to the European Parliament, the Council, the European Economic and Social Committee and the Committee of the Regions: The European Agenda on Security. COM(2015) 185 final. Strasbourg: European Union, April 28, 2015. Accessed March 20, 2019. https://ec.europa.eu/home-affairs/sites/homeaffairs/files/e-library/documents/basic-documents/docs/eu_agenda_on_security_en.pdf.

European Commission. Communication from the Commission to the European Parliament, the European Council and the Council: A New, Modern Multiannual Financial Framework for a European Union that Delivers Efficiently on Its Priorities Post-2020. COM(2018) 98 final. Brussels: European Union, February 14, 2018. Accessed September 10, 2018. https://ec.europa.eu/commission/sites/beta-political/files/communication-new-modern-multiannual-financial-framework_en.pdf.

European Commission. Communication from the Commission to the European Parliament, the European Council, the Council and the European Investment Bank: Towards a More Efficient Financial Architecture for Investment outside the European Union. COM(2018) 644 final. Brussels: European Union, September 12, 2018. Accessed November 10, 2018. https://ec.europa.eu/commission/sites/beta-political/files/soteu2018-investment-outside-eu-communication-644_en_0.pdf.

European Commission. Joint Communication to the European Parliament and the Council: Resilience, Deterrence and Defence: Building Strong Cybersecurity for the EU. JOIN(2017) 0450 final. Brussels: European Union, September 13, 2017.

European Commission. Proposal for a Regulation of the European Parliament and of the Council Establishing the European Defence Fund. COM(2018) 476. Brussels: European Union, 2018.

European Commission. Proposal for a Regulation of the European Parliament and of the Council Establishing the European Defence Industrial Development Programme, Aiming at Supporting the Competitiveness and Innovative Capacity of the EU Defence Industry. COM(2017) 294 final, 2017/0125(COD). Brussels: European Union, June 7, 2017.

European Parliament. European Parliament Resolution of 14 March 2018 on Reform of the European Union's System of Own Resources (2017/2053(INI)). Brussels: European Union, 2018.

European Parliament. "EU Defence Policy: The Sleeping Giant." December 2016. Accessed April 14, 2019. www.europarl.europa.eu/EPRS/EPRS_BRIE_593791_defence_policy_final.pdf.

European Parliament. European Parliament Resolution of 14 March 2018 on the Next MFF: Preparing the Parliament's Position on the MFF Post-2020 (2017/2052(INI)). Brussels: European Union, 2018.

European Parliament. "Europe of Defence? Views on the Future of Defence Cooperation." July 2016. Accessed April 14, 2019. www.europarl.europa.eu/RegData/etudes/BRIE/2016/586607/EPRS_BRI(2016)586607_EN.pdf.

"European Peace Facility – An EU Off-budget Fund to Build Peace and Strengthen International Security." EEAS website. June 13, 2018. Accessed November 10, 2018. https://eeas.europa.eu/headquarters/headquarters-homepage/46285/european-peace-facility-eu-budget-fund-build-peace-and-strengthen-international-security_en.

Junker, Jean-Claude. "Speech by President Jean-Claude Juncker at the 54th Munich Security Conference" (Munich, 2018). Accessed March 20, 2019. http://europa.eu/rapid/press-release_SPEECH-18-841_en.htm.

Junker, Jean-Claude. *State of the Union – 2016*. Brussels: European Commission, 2016. Accessed October 10, 2018. https://publications.europa.eu/en/publication-detail/-/publication/c9ff4ff6-9a81-11e6-9bca-01aa75ed71a1/language-en/format-PDF/source-30945725.

Lavallée, Chantal. *The European Commission: An Enabler for the European Security and Defence Union*. Madrid: Real Instituto Elcano, 2018. Accessed November 10, 2018. www.realinstitutoelcano.org/wps/portal/rielcano_es/contenido?WCM_GLOBAL_CONTEXT=/elcano/elcano_in/zonas_in/ari59-2018-lavallee-european-commission-enabler-for-european-security-defence-union.

PART II

Risks and Challenges facing the EU

7

EU MONETARY AND ECONOMIC INTEGRATION

Security dilemma between competitiveness and sustainability

Marta Gómez-Puig and Simón Sosvilla-Rivero

Introduction

In this chapter we offer a general overview of the economic integration process in the European Union (EU), with special emphasis on the Economic and Monetary Union (EMU) and the sovereign debt crisis, as well as exploring the different scenarios about its further evolution. To that end, we survey the relevant empirical research in this area so as to illustrate the academic results regarding the evaluation of the European experience.

We analyze the challenge of reinvigoration of the integration process completed to achieve the Lisbon Agenda's goal of becoming the world's most competitive economy while re-orienting the regulatory framework to monitor the financial system and identify potential risks and vulnerabilities.

The rest of this chapter is structured as follows: the next section describes the evolution of the European integration from 1957 to 1998, followed by an assessment of the rise and fall of the euro (1999–2015) and some considerations of the future of the euro. The last section offers some concluding remarks.

The long road to the euro (1957–1998)

The stages of European economic integration

One of the most outstanding features of the recent economic evolution has been the progressive widening of national economies, as shown by the great expansion recorded in the volume of international transactions (both goods and services and financial assets), which has been translated to an unprecedented increase in economic integration amongst different countries.

The EU has long been the most developed model of regional integration, with 60 years of history of economic integration, characterized by a progressive increase in membership (initially 6, currently 28) and a gradual advancement in the modality (from a customs union to an EMU) (see Box 7.1).

Box 7.1 The stages of European economic integration

1. Preferential trade zone, which implies a reduction of customs tariffs between countries, thus facilitating trade between them.
2. Free trade zone, which implies the elimination of tariffs on some or all of the goods among the participating countries, thus contributing to boost trade in goods among its partners.
3. Customs Union, which goes one step further and imposes the application of common customs tariffs to third countries and a common commercial policy.
4. Single market, which involves the establishment of common regulations for products and freedom of movement of goods, capital, labor and services.
5. Economic and monetary union, which, by combining a single market with a common currency and monetary policy, implies a deepening of economic integration among the participating countries.
6. Complete economic integration, in which, in addition to an economic and monetary union implies the harmonization of fiscal policy and other economic policies.

After the Second World War, in a context of economic difficulties and distrust between countries, a firm political decision was implemented to guarantee peace in Europe by promoting international trade, cooperation and coordination.[1]

In 1951, the European Coal and Steel Community (ECSC) was set up by the six founding members (Belgium, the Federal Republic of Germany, France, Italy, Luxembourg and the Netherlands) and, in 1957, those countries signed the Treaties of Rome, setting up the European Economic Community and the European Atomic Energy Community (Euratom). Apart from the political objectives of securing peace and regaining international influence, the economic objectives were the creation of a common market covering a wide range of goods and services and the achievement of an economic union in the future. Although there were significant advances in the common market (customs duties between the six countries were abolished on July 1, 1968), the same change was not mirrored in the EMU.

In 1973, Denmark, Ireland and the United Kingdom joined the Communities and new social and environmental policies were introduced.

The genesis of the euro: the European Monetary System and the Maastricht Treaty

Relatively soon, it became relevant that the excessive volatility of the exchange rates was detrimental to the integration process under way, so in 1979 the European Monetary System (EMS) was established. The key element of this was the Exchange Rate Mechanism (ERM), which established a system of fixed, but adjustable, exchange rates, in which each participating currency had a central parity vis-à-vis the European Currency Unit (ancestor of the euro, of which the value was determined as a weighted average of the participating currencies) and some bands within which exchange rates could fluctuate, establishing an agreement of mutual support to keep currencies in the fluctuation bands. Occasionally, variations were allowed in the central parities (called realignments) which tried to reflect the changing economic conditions and the relative evolution of the participating countries.

The ERM was the first attempt to define a totally European exchange agreement, without reference to the US dollar, being, in principle, symmetrical, given that no currency played a preponderant role. However, the German mark became the reference currency. In addition, the ERM provided an explicit framework for coordinating macroeconomic policies among Member States, imposing some monetary discipline upon them.

Meanwhile, Greece had joined the EU in 1981 followed by Spain and Portugal in 1986, while Austria, Finland and Sweden acceded to the EU in 1995.

The strategy, initially chosen to coordinate closely the monetary policies of the member countries of the ERM, was to gradually reduce the margin of fluctuation of their currencies (±6 percent, ±2.5 percent, ±1 percent) until reaching fixed exchange rates (0 percent) (Figure 7.1). However, the evolution actually observed in the exchange rates of the participating countries was very different due to an excessive use of realignments, increasingly distancing the exchange rate from its initial target value. Indeed, there were 58 realignments during the 1979–1998 period, implemented in 19 discrete adjustments. It should be noted that 38 of such realignments were made prior to the currency turmoil of 1992/1993. Likewise, for some currencies there were no reductions in the fluctuation margin, with it being originally set at ±2.25 percent, but there was a ±6 percent band for Italy and the newcomers (Spain, the UK and Portugal). Moreover, after almost a year of unprecedented turmoil in the history of the EMS, the fluctuation bands of the ERM were broadened to ±15 percent in August 1993 (except for the Dutch guilder and the Deutschmark, which remained within the narrow bands of ±2.25 percent).

Following Krugman,[2] a growing theoretical literature attempted to explain exchange rate movements inside official fluctuation bands such as those of the ERM with the help of target zone models.[3] The main result of the target zone model is that, with perfect credibility, the zone exerts a stabilizing effect (the so-called "honeymoon" effect), reducing the sensitivity of exchange rates to a given change in fundamentals. Nevertheless, in a target zone with credibility problems, expectations of future interventions tend to destabilize the exchange rate (the so-called "divorce" effect), making it less stable than its underlying fundamentals.[4] Gómez-Puig and Montalvo

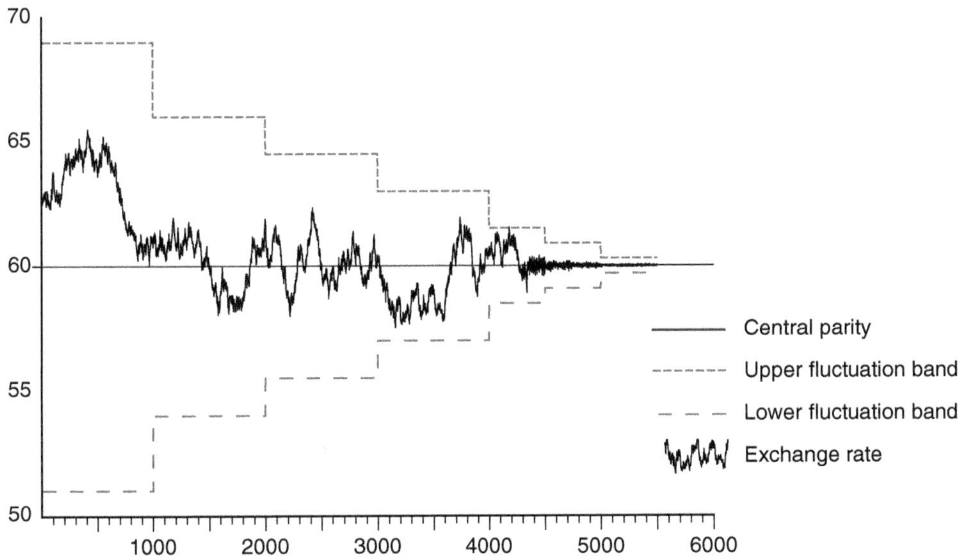

Figure 7.1 The expected behaviour of the exchange rate in the ERM.

propose a credibility indicator for the EMS using the inferred probabilities of realignment derived from the estimation of a Markov-switching regime model.[5] Ledesma-Rodríguez et al. offer an empirical examination of exchange rate credibility in the EMS using several credibility indicators.[6] Their results suggest that: (i) before the currency crisis in late 1992, for most of the countries, the exchange rate policy was credible, except for the Italian case; (ii) the 1992 currency turbulence was accompanied, initially, by credibility losses in all countries, except Belgium and the Netherlands; (iii) after the widening of the fluctuation bands, a gain in credibility was established for the currencies participating in the ERM, with the exception of the Belgian franc and the Irish pound. Ledesma-Rodríguez et al. examined the determinants of the exchange rate credibility in the EMS, finding that the level of international reserves, the real interest rate and right-wing governments would have positively affected the credibility of a given central parity, while the unemployment rate and the inflation rate would have negatively influenced such credibility.[7] Finally, Sosvilla-Rivero and Pérez-Bermejo study the factors explaining regime changes in the ERM using duration analysis.[8] Their results indicate that both economic and political factors are important determinants of European currency policy. As for the economic factors, they find that the money supply, the real exchange rate, the interest in Germany and the central parity deviation would have negatively affected the duration of a given regime, while credibility and the price level in Germany would have positively influenced this duration. Regarding political factors, elections, central bank independence and left-wing government influence increase the probability of maintaining the current regime, while less stable governments would be associated with a regime change. These results were robust to the distinction of core and periphery countries.

The failure of this gradual approach until reaching fixed exchange rates was exacerbated by the abolition of capital controls on July 1, 1990, since according to the well-known Mundell's "impossible trinity" among the three desirable objectives – stabilization of the exchange rate; free international capital mobility; and an effective monetary policy oriented towards domestic goals – only two can be mutually consistent.[9] The impossible trinity or trilemma means that independent monetary policy and unrestricted international capital flows can coexist only if the exchange rate is allowed to fluctuate. This leads to an important question. Which one of the three objectives should be given up? In the European context, the question imposed by the trilemma can, in fact, be further narrowed down. If policymakers were willing to take for granted the achievements of the European common market, then clearly restriction of international capital mobility was no longer a viable policy choice for the EU. The trilemma was thereafter reduced to a dilemma. Policymakers had to choose between mutually inconsistent policy of exchange rate stabilization and monetary policy oriented towards domestic goals. Since the exchange rate volatility was detrimental to the integration process under way and in view of problems accompanying the ERM as well as the political constraints, EMU appeared as the obvious option for Europe (it was a credible arrangement for achieving exchange rate stability and ensuring continuation of the integration process). So, policymakers chose the option of giving up independent monetary policy and stabilizing the exchange rates and adopted a two-stage plan for EMU:

1. The first stage began on January 1, 1994. It involved setting up the European Monetary Institute (EMI, made up of the governors of the central banks of the EU countries), making (or keeping) national central banks independent of government control, and introducing rules to curb national budget deficits.
2. The second stage was the creation process of the euro. To this extent, economic and legal requirements (the so-called "Maastricht criteria") were established, which had to be fulfilled

a year before the incorporation by the candidate countries to join the EMU to ensure their convergence:

a) Price stability: the rate of inflation may not exceed by more than 1.5 percentage points the average rates of inflation of the three Member States with the lowest inflation;
b) Interest rates: long-term interest rates may not vary by more than 2 percentage points in relation to the average interest rates of the three Member States with the lowest interest rates;
c) Deficits: national budget deficits must be below 3 percent of Gross Domestic Product (GDP);
d) Public debt: this may not exceed 60 percent of GDP;
e) Exchange rate stability: exchange rates must have remained in the ERM within the authorized margin of fluctuation for the previous two years.

After meeting each of the criteria, from January 1, 1999, eleven countries joined the EMU (Austria, Belgium, Finland, France, Germany, Ireland, Italy, Luxembourg, the Netherlands, Portugal and Spain), and the European Central Bank (ECB) took over from the EMI and became responsible for monetary policy, which was now defined and implemented in the new currency. Three countries (Denmark, Sweden and the United Kingdom) decided, for political and technical reasons, not to adopt the euro when it was launched.

With the start-up on January 1, 1999 of the EMU, the EMS ceased to exist, being replaced by a new ERM (called ERM-II), which regulates the dependency between the exchange rates of the euro and the countries of the EU that do not belong to the EMU. In 2002, the euro notes and coins were introduced.

The ERM-II also constitutes a system of fixed exchange rates, but its central parities are set against the euro and not against the other participating currencies. This new bilateral design aims to reduce the frequency and magnitude of realignments, by establishing central parities and bands in common agreement between the euro zone ministers, the ECB and the governors of the National Central Banks of the countries involved.

In this period, eight Central and Eastern European countries (the Czech Republic, Estonia, Hungary, Latvia, Lithuania, Poland, Slovakia and Slovenia) and two Mediterranean countries (Malta and Cyprus) joined the EU in 2004 and Croatia acceded to the EU in 2013.

The ERM-II was expected to play a determining role in the design and execution of economic policies in the participating countries, actively aiming to stabilize their economies (especially in terms of prices and sanitation of public accounts) and increase the reputation of their governments.[10]

Greece joined the EMU in 2001, followed by Slovenia in 2007, Cyprus and Malta in 2008, Slovakia in 2009, Estonia in 2011, Latvia in 2014 and Lithuania in 2015. The euro area thus embraces 19 EU countries, and each of the other Member States is expected to join once they have fulfilled the necessary conditions, except those that have obtained an exemption during treaty negotiations.

There are several benefits seen in a common currency (reduction of transaction costs and economic uncertainty, strengthening discipline and credibility, improvement of the functioning of the monetary mechanism), but also some costs (loss of monetary policy autonomy and increase in macroeconomic instability).[11]

The theory of optimum currency areas (OCU), pioneered by Mundell,[12] and further complemented by McKinnon[13] and again by Kenen,[14] addresses the question of under which circumstances a country benefits from membership in a currency union such as the EMU, offering a set of criteria in order to assess a country's suitability for membership:

1 Criteria that reduce the exposure of member countries to asymmetric shocks: similarity of economic structure, openness/intraregional trade and a low degree of specialization.
2 Criteria that facilitate the adjustment to asymmetric shocks: homogeneity of preferences, factor mobility and transfer payments.

In this respect, the EMU consists of a heterogeneous group of countries with different geographic realities, different institutions, different economic and demographic structures and different cultures and traditions. In particular, the distinction between EMU central (Austria, Belgium, Finland, France and The Netherlands) and peripheral (Greece, Ireland, Italy, Portugal and Spain) countries has been extensively used in the empirical literature. The seminal paper by Bayoumi and Eichengreen[15] stresses the existence of a core–periphery pattern already in the run-up to the EMU using 1963–1988 data. More recently, results in Ahlborn and Wortmann[16] confirm the existence of a persistent core cluster, as opposed to clusters on the Eastern and Southern European peripheries, highlighting the inadequate composition of the EMU, while Botta et al.[17] further document the widening divergence between the macroeconomic performances of core EMU countries and peripheral economies.

The dissimilarities in economic structure combined with economic cycles that observed high degrees of industrial specialization increased the EMU's vulnerability to asymmetric shocks. Moreover, the lack of labor mobility or a transfer payment system limits the EMU's crisis adjustment capabilities. Therefore, EMU is a unique experiment, in which a large group of developed, but structurally heterogeneous economies have created a monetary union.

Rise and fall of the euro (1999–2015)

The first years and the "honeymoon" effect

After the Treaty of Maastricht and the launching of the EMU a process of convergence began, reinforced by the desire of governments to participate in the euro from 1999. In the financial markets, the elimination of exchange rate risk and the costs associated with banking transactions between currencies facilitated investment across borders and led to a greater liquidity. Market participants entered a "honeymoon" phase with the euro, as the German reputation was exported to other member countries and the ECB inherited (reinforced) the credibility of the Bundesbank. The initial financial conditions masked vulnerabilities and macroeconomic imbalances, not to mention the risks involved in lending more and more to the States.

As can be seen in Figure 7.2, during the years of stability that preceded the crisis (1999–2007):

1 On average, the ratio of public debt over GDP in the euro area was reduced from 86 percent to 79 percent;
2 The debt of households increased from 45 percent to 66 percent of GDP;
3 Non-financial corporations increased their debt levels from 93 percent of GDP to about 120 percent.

In particular, the peripheral EMU economies registered a strong increase in credit as their banks had access to international funds in their own currency at lower interest rates with

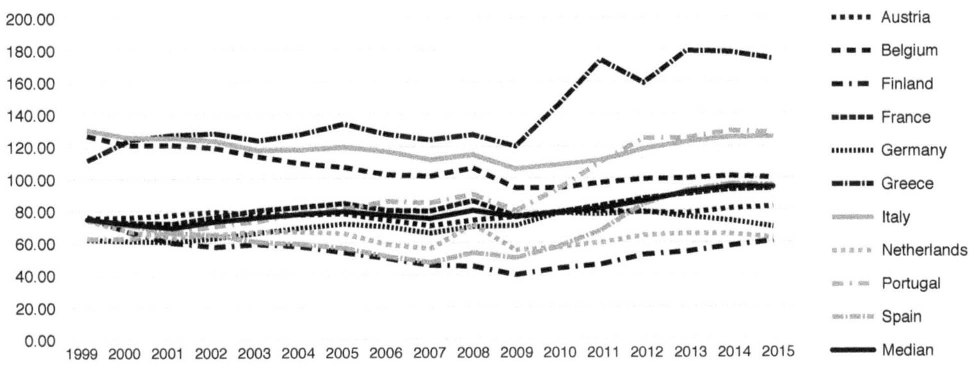

Figure 7.2.1 Government debt-to-GDP in EMU countries: 1999–2015.

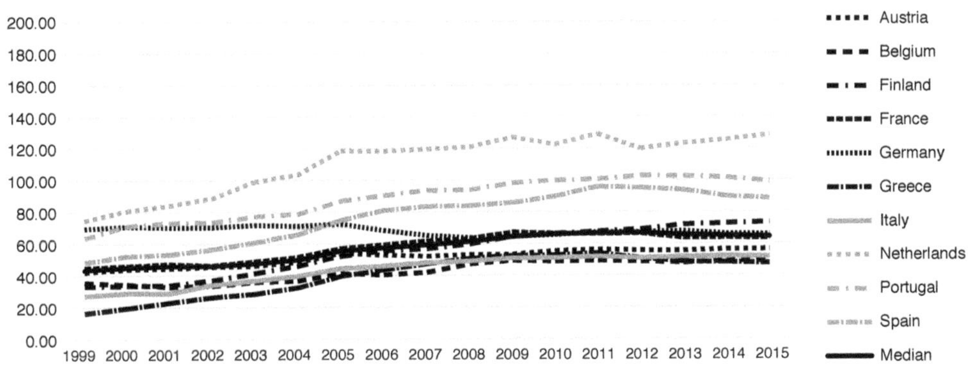

Figure 7.2.2 Household debt-to-GDP in EMU countries: 1999–2015.

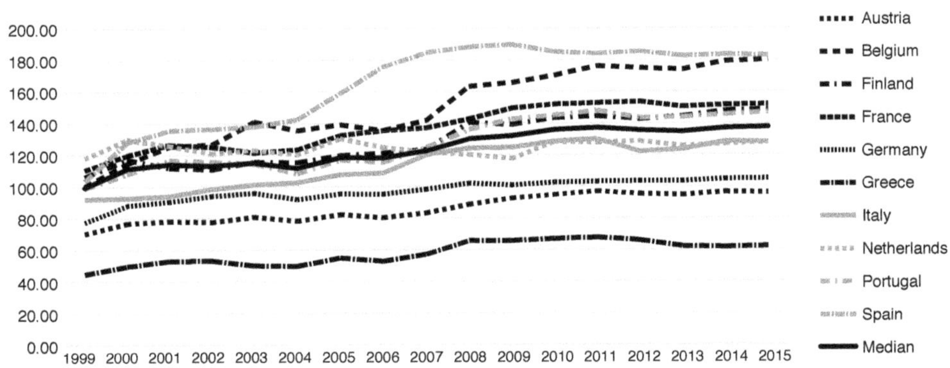

Figure 7.2.3 Non-financial corporations debt-to-GDP in EMU countries: 1999–2015.

respect to the pre-euro situation, increasing consumption and investment, as well as deteriorating their current account balances. The increase in credit translates into a housing bubble, an impulse to the construction sector, higher tax revenues for the government and a large mortgage boom.

The crisis of the euro

After ten years of stability, tension emerged in the international financial markets in August 2007, resulting in the European sovereign debt crisis, initially triggered by developments in the US banking sector.

As the US economy slowed down, many Americans stopped paying their mortgage, and banks around the world with investments tied to those mortgages started losing money. The collapse of Lehman Brothers in September 2008 led to a global financial crisis, affecting the productivity of the economy and causing a revision of asset prices and growth perspectives.

The announcement of the existence of serious problems with Greece's debt at the end of 2009 caused a sudden loss of investor confidence and marked the beginning of the euro zone sovereign debt crisis, since governments had accumulated debts almost double the size of the economy, generating fear of contagion, due to the high exposure of EU banks to Greece.

Investors began to look closely at the finances of governments, with severe scrutiny of the state of the economies, particularly the peripheral ones, paying special attention to macroeconomic and fiscal imbalances, which had largely been ignored until then.

The threat of bank failures meant that the need for sound public finances became more important than ever and what started as a banking crisis turned into a sovereign debt crisis.[18] The high cost of bank bailouts led financial markets to question whether governments could really support the banking sector and a vicious circle appeared, as financial instability hindered economic growth. The recession, in turn, reduced tax revenues; the fall in revenues and the increase in expenses increased the public debt; and higher levels of public debt then translated into higher costs for loans to governments, which, eventually, fueled financial instability.

Adverse conditions were immediately reflected in the sovereign debt markets, all denominated in euros (regardless of the issuing country), with differences in expected returns, representing perceived risks and differences in volatility. The increased debt resulted in an increase in vulnerability, an increase in the required return (relative to the risk-free German bonds) and an increase in the possibility of default, triggering a "divorce effect" as small deviations from fundamentals were followed by significant falls in bond demand and by a flight toward quality. As a result, since the end of 2009, yield spread on public debt, with respect to Germany, has skyrocketed.

As seen in Figure 7.3, the EMU sovereign debt crisis is characterized by a simultaneous surge in the cost of borrowing for peripheral European governments after 2008. The crisis revealed several shortcomings in the economic governance system of the EU and important weaknesses in the EMU design:

1. Too much emphasis on the deficit and not on the public debt;
2. Lack of supervision of macroeconomic imbalances and competitiveness;
3. Little firmness with countries that do not comply with the Stability and Growth Pact (SGP);
4. Less decision-making capacity;
5. Lack of an emergency financing mechanism to deal with the specific problems of each country and to provide a "firewall" to avoid problems of propagation to other countries that are at risk.

In order to avoid a total collapse of the banking system, European governments came to the rescue of their banks with urgent support on an unprecedented scale: 1.6 billion euros between 2008 and 2011 (13 percent of the annual EU GDP).

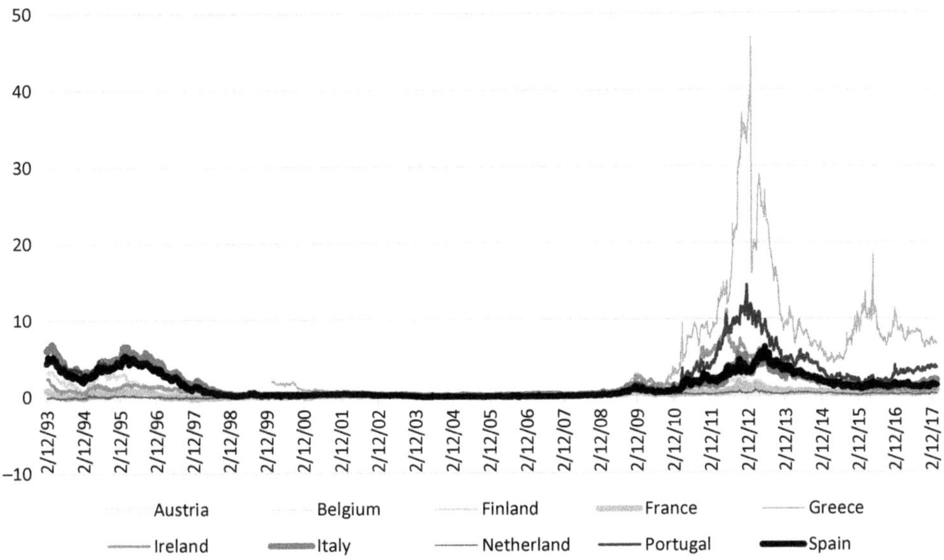

Figure 7.3 Ten-year sovereign yield spreads over Germany: 1993–2017.

Between 2010 and 2013, five countries (Cyprus, Greece, Ireland, Portugal and Spain) made agreements with several of the EU bodies and the International Monetary Fund to gain financial assistance.

Forensic analysis of the euro crisis

The increase in the risk premium in the euro area during the European sovereign debt crisis raised some important questions: Was it solely due to the sustainability of the deteriorated debt in the member countries? Did contagion play any important role?

Two groups of theories (not necessarily mutually exclusive) explain the transmission mechanisms of the crisis:

1 Macroeconomic fundamentals of different countries are interconnected by their cross-border flows of goods, services and capital via "externalities,"[19] "interdependence"[20] or "foundation-based contagion."[21]
2 "Pure contagion":[22] spread from one country to another due to market imperfections, behavior of international investors, or sudden changes in market confidence and expectations.

The results of Gómez-Puig and Sosvilla-Rivero[23] and Fernández-Rodríguez et al.[24] suggest that the episodes of the intensification of causality/connectedness were concentrated around the inception of the EMU in 1999–2000, the introduction of euro coins and banknotes in 2002 and the global financial crisis. When analyzing the determinants of these episodes, they find a significant role both for the variables that capture the "market sentiment" and for the macroeconomic fundamentals, indicating that the increase in the sovereign risk premium in the euro area during the European sovereign crisis was not solely attributed to the sustainability of the deteriorated debt in the member countries, nor can it be explained only by herd behavior or sudden changes in market confidence and expectations.[25] Furthermore, between April 1999 and March 2009, the core countries are found to be the triggers of the episodes of volatility intensification, while as from April 2009, the peripheral countries were the origin of the uncertainty transmissions.

Furthermore, Verstegen et al.[26] quantify the benefits from participation in the EMU for individual euro-area countries. Using the synthetic control method, they estimate how real GDP per capita would have developed for the EMU Member States, if those countries had not joined the EMU. Their results indicate that most countries have profited from having the euro, at least until the start of the financial crisis. During and after the crisis, some countries would have been better off if they had not joined the EMU. Small open economies profit the most from having the euro, and the peripheral countries would have been better off if they had not been an EMU member during the crisis.[27]

In an attempt to create a common narrative on the causes of the Eurozone crisis, Baldwin and Giavazzi[28] collected the views of eighteen prominent economists. The different arguments conducted by the invited authors can be summarized by the following list of potential causes: (i) accumulation of public debt; (ii) unregulated expansion of the banking sector; (iii) capital flows and current account imbalances; (iv) loss of competitiveness, due to diverging inflation rates; (v) institutional differences across countries.

The European sovereign debt crisis not only was one of the most severe post-World War II economic crises in the developed economies, but it also threatened the continued existence of the EMU, and undermined European integration in general. Despite the high output and unemployment costs experienced during the crisis, we have not observed any departures, yet, from the EMU. The absence of an exit realization from the EMU could be the result of a high expected cost associated with departing the union. Such costs could be the direct short-term cost in the form of output loss, or financial turmoil and the operational cost of introducing a new currency, or the long-term cost of foregone international trade, facilitated by a pegged currency.

New times for the euro

The EMU crisis clearly demonstrates that a debt-based economy is not sustainable, implying the need to ensure that the limits of debts and deficits apply and that national budgets do not put other European economies at risk.

The European response was twofold:

1 The ECB assumed new functions, implementing unconventional monetary policy, providing bank supervision, favoring financial stability through macroprudential policies and defending the integrity of the euro;[29]
2 The Banking Union was created, representing a qualitative leap for the monetary union and an important step towards financial integration and the completion of the stabilization of the euro.

As presented, monetary policy was the main public instrument to support the activity, but its effectiveness was reduced by the fragmentation of financial markets along national lines as the crisis deepened. Therefore, a banking union was introduced to sever the links between banks and their sovereigns.

After questioning its own pillars (Is the euro irreversible? Does it make sense to deepen the integration?), Europe adopted a positive tone to its questions (What Europe do we want?).

Jean Monnet, one of the founding fathers of the EU, once stated "Europe will be forged in crises, and will be the sum of the solutions adopted for those crises." The recent European crisis would be an opportunity to make countries grow closer together, to give up gradually larger pieces of their sovereignty and move towards a more effective Union.

The future of the euro (since 2015)

In June 2015, the five presidents (European Commission, European Council, Eurogroup, ECB, European Parliament) established an ambitious and pragmatic roadmap for the full realization of the EMU, advancing on four fronts in parallel:[30]

1 Genuine Economic Union, ensuring that each economy has the structural features to prosper within the EMU, increasing specific support for reforms through EU funds and technical assistance, strengthening the political dialogue between the EU and the Member States and reinforcing economic policy coordination.
2 Financial Union, guaranteeing the integrity of the currency across the Monetary Union and increasing risk-sharing with the private sector, reducing the EMU's dependence on the banking sector, strengthening the integration of EU financial markets and supporting economic growth in Europe. A full Financial Union entails a Banking Union and a Capital Markets Union (CMU).[31]
3 Fiscal Union, that delivers both fiscal sustainability and fiscal stabilization, with the creation of an independent European Fiscal Council, the improvement of transparency, the reduction of the complexity of current tax regulations and the implementation of a process of reinforced macroeconomic imbalance.[32]
4 Political Union, that provides the foundation for all of the above, through genuine democratic accountability, legitimacy and institutional strengthening. This will require the involvement of the European Parliament, national parliaments and social partners so as to adopt a unified representation for the euro area in international financial institutions and to improve coordination between the EMU Member States.

All four Unions depend on each other and must develop in parallel, with the overall aim of enhancing the unity, efficiency and democratic accountability of the EMU by 2025. The process has been organized in two consecutive stages:

1 Stage 1 (2017–2019): implementing risk reduction measures and a strategy to reduce non-performing loans and to help banks diversify their investments in sovereign bonds; establishing a backstop for the Single Resolution Fund (SRF), implementing the European deposit insurance scheme, and completing the CMU to accelerate capital market integration, help absorb asymmetric shocks and reduce the need for government support in times of crises.
2 Stage 2 (2020–2025): formalizing and establishing an institutional framework in the convergence process; setting up a macroeconomic stabilization function for the euro area, turning the European Stability Mechanism (EMU sovereign bailout fund) into a European Monetary Fund (EMF); establishing a euro-area Treasury accountable at European level, and moving towards the issuance of a European safe asset; and introducing changes to the regulatory treatment of sovereign exposures, as well as a European minister of economy and finance in charge of introducing the bounds of EMU budget rules setting an overall EMU fiscal stance and of both the implementation of the new Multiannual Financial Framework and the simplification of the rules of the SGP.

The European Commission has also proposed to integrate the substance of the Treaty on Stability, Coordination and Governance into the Union's legal framework, taking into account the appropriate flexibility built into the Stability and Growth Pact in order to support sound fiscal frameworks on a national level.

A common fiscal policy would help to free the ECB of some functions assumed during the crisis:

1 The EMU Treasury would assume the economic and fiscal surveillance, being responsible for macroeconomic stabilization, the issuance of safe assets (Eurobonds) and the protection of investments in the event of large asymmetric shocks;
2 The EMF would provide the common backstop to the SRF and act as a last resort lender in order to facilitate an orderly resolution of distressed banks.

Deepening the EMU is a means to an end: more jobs, growth, investment, social fairness and macroeconomic stability. The single currency offers protection and opportunities to Europeans, and a strong and stable EMU is essential for its members as well as for the EU as a whole. The time is right, since there is a renewed citizens' confidence in the single currency.[33]

From 2025, the European Commission (2017) considers five scenarios for the 27 Member States (EU27) after the withdrawal of the United Kingdom to move forward together as a Union:[34]

1 Carrying on: The EU27 focuses on delivering its positive reform agenda, strengthening the single market and stepping up investment in digital, transport and energy infrastructure.
2 Nothing but the single market: The EU27 is gradually re-centered on the single market, with further progress depending on the capacity to agree related policies and standards.
3 Those who want more do more: The EU27 allows willing Member States to do more together in specific areas such as defense, internal security, taxation or social matters.
4 Doing less more efficiently: The EU27 focuses its attention and limited resources on delivering more and faster in selected policy areas, while doing less elsewhere. For chosen priority areas, stronger tools are given to directly implement and enforce collective decisions.
5 Doing much more together: The EU27 decides to do much more together across all policy areas. As a result, cooperation between all Member States goes further than ever before in all domains, decisions being agreed faster at European level and being rapidly implemented.

These scenarios look at how Europe will change in the next decade, from the impact of new technologies on society and jobs, to doubts about globalization, security concerns and the rise of populism. They aim to steer a debate on the future of Europe, opening the possibility of a multi-speed Europe where some EMU countries can accelerate towards a fiscal and political union, while the other countries can initially maintain a certain degree of independence through a more functional integration, enabling groups of countries to be involved in different degrees of involvement with the EU.

Finally, in the Rome Declaration, adopted at the end of the celebrations of the sixtieth anniversary of the Rome Treaties, the leaders set out a joint vision for the years to come, pledging to work towards:

1 A safe and secure Europe: where all citizens can move freely; with secured external borders and an efficient migration policy;

2 A prosperous and sustainable Europe: promoting sustainable growth, with a strong single market;
3 A social Europe: tackling unemployment, discrimination, social exclusion and poverty; and
4 A stronger Europe on the global scene: developing existing partnerships and building new ones, committed to strengthening its common security and defense.

Therefore, there is an ongoing process of a creative rethink of the entire European project, including the possibility of dropping the rigid one-size-fits-all model and adopting a wider flexibility of a network.

Concluding remarks

The EU is a unique project in which domestic priorities have been combined with sovereignty being voluntarily shifted to better serve national and collective interests. This project has conveyed enormous historical success and despite challenging difficulties, it has strengthened the economy and fostered prosperity as a result.

Seventy-two years of European integration and twenty years of EMU have created significant interconnectivity between the political, economic and social fates of Member States. At the same time, however, their fortunes have started to diverge dramatically, taking the EMU crisis as an example of deep structural imbalances observed across the Union.

Despite the remarkable progress, it is necessary to further strengthen the institutional and legal European framework so as to ensure a more united and solid Europe in the face of a challenging future. Accelerating the process of increasing the efficiency of the EU and the EMU would be a necessary condition to rejoin the path of strong, sustainable and inclusive growth and job creation. There are as many opportunities as there are challenges, requiring structural rethinking of the European project in accordance with the principles of subsidiarity and of sustainable and shared development enshrined in the Treaties.

Populist movements have called into question the value of European integration. Political difficulty does not absolve from economic necessity. The main focus of the EU's mission has always been inclusivity even in challenging circumstances, creating a very ambitious and hopeful frontier for the future stance of its members.

Notes

1 Tony Judt, *Postwar: A History of Europe since 1945* (New York: Penguin, 2006).
2 Paul Krugman, "Target Zones and Exchange Rate Dynamics," *Quarterly Journal of Economics* 106 (1991): 669–82.
3 For a review, see: Bernd Kempa and Michael Nelles, "The Theory of Exchange Rate Target Zones," *Journal of Economic Surveys* 13 (1999): 173–210.
4 Giuseppe Bertola and Ricardo Caballero, "Target Zones and Realignments," *American Economic Review* 82 (1992): 520–36.
5 Marta Gómez-Puig and José G. Montavo, "A New Indicator to Assess the Credibility of the EMS," *European Economic Review* 41 (1997): 1511–35.
6 Francisco Ledesma-Rodríguez, Manuel Navarro Ibáñez, Jorge Pérez-Rodríguez and Simón Sosvilla-Rivero, "Assessing the Credibility of a Target Zone: Evidence from the EMS," *Applied Economics* 37 (2005): 2265–87.
7 Francisco Ledesma-Rodríguez, Jorge Pérez-Rodríguez and Simón Sosvilla-Rivero, "An Empirical Examination of Exchange-Rate Credibility Determinants in the EMS," *Applied Economics Letters* 13 (2006): 847–50.

8 Simón Sosvilla-Rivero and Francisco Pérez-Bermejo, "Political and Institutional Factors in Regime Changes in the ERM: An Application of Duration Analysis," *The World Economy* 31 (2008): 1049–77.

9 Maurice Obstfeld, Jay C. Shambaugh and Alan M. Taylor, "The Trilemma in History: Tradeoffs among Exchange Rates, Monetary Policies, and Capital Mobility," *Review of Economics and Statistics* 87 (2005): 423–38.

10 These potential gains could have significantly affected the decision of EU Member States and candidates to participate even de facto in the ERM-II, establishing implicit bands and maintaining the exchange rate around a central parity while permitting enough flexibility to adjust to fundamental disequilibrium and allowing some degree of monetary policy discretion. Carmen Ramos-Herrera and Simón Sosvilla-Rivero, "Detection of Implicit Fluctuation Bands and Their Credibility in EU Candidate Countries," *Baltic Journal of Economics* 15 (2015): 18–37.

11 Paul De Grauwe, *Economics of Monetary Union*, 11th ed. (Oxford: Oxford University Press, 2016).

12 Robert Mundell, "A Theory of Optimum Currency Areas," *American Economic Review* 51 (1961): 657–65.

13 Ronald McKinnon, "Optimum Currency Areas," *American Economic Review* 53 (1963): 717–25.

14 Peter Kenen, "The Theory of Optimum Currency Areas: An Eclectic View," in *Monetary Problems of the International Economy*, ed. Robert Mundell and Aaron Swoboda (Chicago: University of Chicago Press, 1969), 41–60.

15 Tamim Bayoumi and Barry Eichengreen, "Shocking Aspects of European Monetary Integration," in *Adjustment and Growth in the European Monetary Union*, ed. Francisco Torres and Francesco Giavazzi (Cambridge: Cambridge University Press, 1993).

16 Marcus Ahlborn and Marcus Wortmann, "The Core Periphery Pattern of European Business Cycles: A Fuzzy Clustering Approach," *Journal of Macroeconomics* 55 (2018): 12–27.

17 Alberto Botta, Ben Tippet and Özlem Onaran, *Divergence between the Core and the Periphery and Secular Stagnation in the Eurozone*, Greenwich Papers in Political Economy 63 (University of Greenwich: Greenwich Political Economy Research Centre, 2018).

18 Manish Singh, Marta Gómez-Puig and Simón Sosvilla-Rivero, "Sovereign-Bank Linkages: Quantifying Directional Intensity of Risk Transfers in EMU Countries," *Journal of International Money and Finance* 63 (2016): 137–64.

19 Paul Masson, "Contagion, Monsoonal Effects, Spillovers, and Jumps between Multiple Equilibria," in *The Asian Financial Crisis: Causes, Contagion and Consequences*, ed. Peter Agenor, Marcus Miller, David Vines and Axel Weber (Cambridge: Cambridge University Press, 1999), 265–84.

20 Kristin Forbes and Roberto Rigobon. "No Contagion, Only Interdependence: Measuring Stock Market Comovements," *Journal of Finance* 57 (2002): 2223–61.

21 Graciela Kaminsky and Carmen Reinhart, "On Crises, Contagion, and Confusion," *Journal of International Economics* 51 (2000): 145–68.

22 Masson, "Contagion."

23 Marta Gómez-Puig and Simón Sosvilla-Rivero, "Causes and Hazards of the Euro Area Sovereign Debt Crisis: Pure and Fundamentals-based Contagion," *Economic Modelling* 56 (2016): 133–47.

24 Fernando Fernández-Rodríguez, Marta Gómez-Puig and Simón Sosvilla-Rivero, "Using Connectedness Analysis to Assess Financial Stress Transmission in EMU Sovereign Bond Market Volatility," *Journal of International Financial Markets, Institutions and Money* 43 (2016): 126–45.

25 Marta Gómez-Puig, Simón Sosvilla-Rivero and María del Carmen Ramos-Herrera, "An Update on EMU Sovereign Yield Spread Drivers in Times of Crisis: A Panel Data Analysis," *North American Journal of Economics and Finance* 30 (2014): 133–53. Using panel data techniques, the authors empirically investigate the determinants of EMU sovereign bond yield spreads with respect to the German bund. Their results suggest that the rise in sovereign risk can only be partially explained by the evolution of local macroeconomic variables. Besides, without exception, the marginal effects of sovereign spread drivers (specifically, the variables that measure global market sentiment) increased during the crisis compared to the pre-crisis period, especially in peripheral countries.

26 Loes Verstegen, Bas van Groezen and Lex Meijdam, *Benefits of EMU Participation: Estimates Using the Synthetic Control Method*. CentER Discussion Paper 2017-032 (Tilburg University: Center for Economic Research, 2017).

27 Marta Gómez-Puig and Simón Sosvilla-Rivero, "Nonfinancial Debt and Economic Growth in Euro-area Countries," *Journal of International Financial Markets, Institutions and Money* 56 (2018): 17–37. The authors examine the effects of non-financial debt (household, corporate as well as government) accumulation on economic growth in EMU countries.

28 Richard Baldwin and Francesco Giavazzi, *The Eurozone Crisis – A Consensus View of the Causes and a Few Possible Remedies* (London: CEPR Press, 2015).
29 Hans-Werner Sinn, *The ECB's Fiscal Policy*, NBER Working Paper 24613 (Cambridge, MA: National Bureau of Economic Research, 2018). The financial market reaction to the ECB president's statement in July 2012 that the ECB was ready to do whatever it takes to preserve the euro revealed that the markets had previously been unsure whether the ECB would be willing or able to play a similar role to that of a national central bank supporting a sovereign state, and by extension its currency regime. The ECB went further in supporting the euro in 2015 with the launch of a stimulus program for the real economy. Not only has this program created fiscal breathing space for euro zone governments by pushing down yields, but together with the ECB's commitment to the euro it has significantly reduced the risk of contagion in the case of serious issues in any Member State.
30 European Commission, *The Five Presidents' Report: Completing Europe's Economic and Monetary Union* (Brussels: European Commission, 2015).
31 For a description of the key features of the Commission's plan to build a CMU in Europe and for a discussion on the economic rationale behind it, see: Franklin Allen and Luboš Pástor, *The Capital Markets Union: Key challenges*. CEPR Discussion Paper 12761 (London: Centre for Economic Policy Research, 2018).
32 For an analytical discussion of a fiscal union in the euro area, see: Helge Berger, Giovanni Dell'Ariccia and Maurice Obstfeld, *Revisiting the Economic Case for Fiscal Union in the Euro Area*, Departmental Paper 18/03 (Washington, DC: International Monetary Fund, 2018).
33 The Flash Eurobarometer on the euro area published in December 2017 shows that 64 percent of respondents say the euro is a good thing for their country. Indeed, Roth et al. explore the evolution and determinants of public support for the euro since its creation in 1999 until the end of 2017, finding a majority of citizens support the euro in nearly all 19 euro-area Member States. Their results suggest that crisis reduces support while periods of recovery from unemployment bode well for public support. Felix Roth, Edgar Baake, Lars Jonung and Felicitas Nowak-Lehmann. *Revisiting Public Support for the Euro, 1999–2017: Accounting for the Crisis and the Recovery*, Discussion Paper 1/18 (Hamburg: Institute for European Integration, 2018).
34 European Commission, *White Paper on the Future of Europe* (Brussels: European Commission, 2017).

References

Ahlborn, Marcus, and Marcus Wortmann. "The Core-Periphery Pattern of European Business Cycles: A Fuzzy Clustering Approach." *Journal of Macroeconomics* 55 (2018): 12–27.

Allen, Franklin, and Luboš Pástor. *The Capital Markets Union: Key Challenges*. CEPR Discussion Paper 12761. London: Centre for Economic Policy Research, 2018.

Baldwin, Richard, and Francesco Giavazzi. *The Eurozone Crisis – A Consensus View of the Causes and a Few Possible Remedies*. London: CEPR Press, 2015.

Bayoumi, Tamim, and Barry Eichengreen. "Shocking Aspects of European Monetary Integration." In *Adjustment and Growth in the European Monetary Union*, edited by Francisco Torres and Francesco Giavazzi, 193–235. Cambridge: Cambridge University Press, 1993.

Berger, Helge, Giovanni Dell'Ariccia and Maurice Obstfeld. *Revisiting the Economic Case for Fiscal Union in the Euro Area*. Departmental Paper 18/03. Washington, DC: International Monetary Fund, 2018.

Bertola, Giuseppe, and Ricardo Caballero. "Target Zones and Realignments." *American Economic Review* 82 (1992): 520–36.

Botta, Alberto, Ben Tippet and Özlem Onaran. *Divergence between the Core and the Periphery and Secular Stagnation in the Eurozone*. Greenwich Papers in Political Economy 63. University of Greenwich: Greenwich Political Economy Research Centre, 2018.

De Grauwe, Paul. *Economics of Monetary Union*. 11th edition. Oxford: Oxford University Press, 2016.

European Commission. *The Five Presidents' Report: Completing Europe's Economic and Monetary Union*. Brussels: European Commission, 2015.

European Commission. *White Paper on the Future of Europe*. Brussels: European Commission, 2017.

Fernández-Rodríguez, Fernando, Marta Gómez-Puig and Simón Sosvilla-Rivero. "Using Connectedness Analysis to Assess Financial Stress Transmission in EMU Sovereign Bond Market Volatility." *Journal of International Financial Markets, Institutions and Money* 43 (2016): 126–45.

Forbes, Kristin, and Roberto Rigobon. "No Contagion, Only Interdependence: Measuring Stock Market Comovements." *Journal of Finance* 57 (2002): 2223–61.

Gómez-Puig, Marta, and José G. Montavo. "A New Indicator to Assess the Credibility of the EMS." *European Economic Review* 41 (1997): 1511–35.
Gómez-Puig, Marta, Simón Sosvilla-Rivero and María del Carmen Ramos-Herrera. "An Update on EMU Sovereign Yield Spread Drivers in Times of Crisis: A Panel Data Analysis." *North American Journal of Economics and Finance* 30 (2014): 133–53.
Gómez-Puig, Marta, and Simón Sosvilla-Rivero. "Causes and Hazards of the Euro Area Sovereign Debt Crisis: Pure and Fundamentals-based Contagion." *Economic Modelling* 56 (2016): 133–47.
Gómez-Puig, Marta, and Simón Sosvilla-Rivero. "Nonfinancial Debt and Economic Growth in Euro-area Countries." *Journal of International Financial Markets, Institutions and Money* 56 (2018): 17–37.
Judt, Tony. *Postwar: A History of Europe since 1945*. New York: Penguin, 2006.
Kaminsky, Graciela, and Carmen Reinhart. "On Crises, Contagion, and Confusion." *Journal of International Economics* 51 (2000): 145–68.
Kempa, Bernd, and Michael Nelles. "The Theory of Exchange Rate Target Zones." *Journal of Economic Surveys* 13 (1999): 173–210.
Kenen, Peter. "The Theory of Optimum Currency Areas: An Eclectic View." In *Monetary Problems of the International Economy*, edited by Robert Mundell and Aaron Swoboda, 41–60. Chicago: University of Chicago Press, 1969.
Krugman, Paul. "Target Zones and Exchange Rate Dynamics." *Quarterly Journal of Economics* 106 (1991): 669–82.
Ledesma-Rodríguez, Francisco, Jorge Pérez-Rodríguez and Simón Sosvilla-Rivero. "An Empirical Examination of Exchange-Rate Credibility Determinants in the EMS." *Applied Economics Letters* 13 (2006): 847–50.
Ledesma-Rodríguez, Francisco, Manuel Navarro Ibáñez, Jorge Pérez-Rodríguez and Simón Sosvilla-Rivero. "Assessing the Credibility of a Target Zone: Evidence from the EMS." *Applied Economics* 37 (2005): 2265–87.
Masson, Paul. "Contagion, Monsoonal Effects, Spillovers, and Jumps between Multiple Equilibria." In *The Asian Financial Crisis: Causes, Contagion and Consequences*, edited by Peter Agenor, Marcus Miller, David Vines and Axel Weber, 265–84. Cambridge: Cambridge University Press, 1999.
McKinnon, Ronald. "Optimum Currency Areas." *American Economic Review* 53 (1963): 717–25.
Mundell, Robert. "A Theory of Optimum Currency Areas." *American Economic Review* 51 (1961): 657–65.
Obstfeld, Maurice, Jay C. Shambaugh and Alan M. Taylor. "The Trilemma in History: Tradeoffs among Exchange Rates, Monetary Policies, and Capital Mobility." *Review of Economics and Statistics* 87 (2005): 423–38.
Ramos-Herrera, Carmen, and Simón Sosvilla-Rivero. "Detection of Implicit Fluctuation Bands and Their Credibility in EU Candidate Countries." *Baltic Journal of Economics* 15 (2015): 18–37.
Roth, Felix, Edgar Baake, Lars Jonung and Felicitas Nowak-Lehmann. *Revisiting Public Support for the Euro, 1999–2017: Accounting for the Crisis and the Recovery*. Discussion Paper 1/18. Hamburg: Institute for European Integration, 2018.
Singh, Manish, Marta Gómez-Puig and Simón Sosvilla-Rivero. "Sovereign-Bank Linkages: Quantifying Directional Intensity of Risk Transfers in EMU Countries." *Journal of International Money and Finance* 63 (2016): 137–64.
Sinn, Hans-Werner. *The ECB's fiscal policy*. NBER Working Paper 24613. Cambridge, MA: National Bureau of Economic Research, 2018.
Sosvilla-Rivero, Simón, and Francisco Pérez-Bermejo. "Political and Institutional Factors in Regime Changes in the ERM: An Application of Duration Analysis." *The World Economy* 31 (2008): 1049–77.
Verstegen, Loes, Bas van Groezen and Lex Meijdam. *Benefits of EMU Participation: Estimates Using the Synthetic Control Method*. CentER Discussion Paper 2017-032. Tilburg University: Center for Economic Research, 2017.

8

THE ECONOMIC CONSEQUENCES OF *BREXIT*

A brief overview of the literature

Bruce Morley

Introduction

On June 23, 2016, the United Kingdom (UK) voted to leave the European Union (EU), a process usually termed *Brexit*, which was a momentous event with implications for the future stability of the EU and the UK. Following this decision, the UK has been negotiating with the EU on what type of economic relationship it wants with the EU and the rest of the world. There are a number of economic and political issues that complicate the decision and the negotiating position with the EU. The EU is wary about offering the UK too beneficial an arrangement, as they fear it may encourage other countries to leave; however, they are also aware that the EU and UK enjoy strong trading relations, with the EU having a strong advantage in terms of trade flows between them. There are also many political considerations to take into account in terms of future UK and EU security, such as the need to prevent any economic border between Northern Ireland and the rest of the UK as well as the border between Northern Ireland and the Irish Republic, so that frictionless trade continues between them after *Brexit*. This issue has important implications regarding the legal and security integrity in these countries. During the negotiations, one of the main areas of disagreement between the UK and EU has been over economic relations and trade between Ireland and Northern Ireland, in particular attempts to avoid a hard border. But the problem is more complicated than trade relations alone, encompassing important legal and security issues; for instance, as part of the *Good Friday Agreement* in 1997, it requires avoiding a hard border between them. As Inkster points out, there are implications for the security situation in Northern Ireland resulting from whether there is a hard border or not, not least because of the role the EU played in the agreement and ending of the "troubles."[1] There are similar issues with the legal implications of *Brexit*, affecting not only Northern Ireland but also the UK as a whole, especially in the role of financial services regulations.

Over recent years there have been myriad studies on how *Brexit* will affect the UK and EU economies, from both a macroeconomic and a microeconomic perspective. The macroeconomic studies have tended to analyse the effects on trade and output in various forms, using gravity type models and simulations to produce estimates of potential effects on the main macroeconomic variables under differing assumptions on future trade relations and economic scenarios.

The microeconomic studies have concentrated on specific industries, in particular the agricultural sector, due to the common policy across the EU and the importance of food security; the financial sector, due to its importance to the UK; and the motor industry, due to its integration across the EU. This is not an exhaustive review of all aspects of *Brexit* on the economy, but an attempt to provide a discussion of some of the highest profile economic issues that have arisen and an analysis of their potential impacts on EU security.

Following the introduction, there is a discussion of the main points of contention during the negotiations, which tend to revolve around whether the UK should stay in a customs union with the EU. There is then an examination of the types of analysis used, followed by a brief analysis of the main macroeconomic studies. The next section reviews the main sectors of importance to the UK, which are the financial sector, agriculture and the motor industry. Finally, there are some conclusions and suggestions for future studies.

Trading relations and the customs union

Among the most contentious decisions are whether the UK remains in some form within the European single market and also whether it should stay in the customs union.[2] As one aim of the UK before and after *Brexit* is to negotiate its own trade relations with the rest of the world, it means remaining in both would be difficult, especially the single market. But what form of customs relations is eventually chosen is potentially the most difficult decision for both the UK and the EU. One option being debated would be to follow Norway and retain membership of the European Economic Area (EEA), although this would still require contributions to the EU budget and free movement of labour, which have been ruled out by the UK government. They could have a negotiated bilateral agreement, by which the UK would retain access to aspects of the EU, such as the financial passport system.[3] Finally, the UK could exit without a specific agreement, but trade under World Trade Organization (WTO) rules, as discussed in Sampson along with other potential trading scenarios.[4] The options are usually referred to as "soft *Brexit*" for the Norway variant of the options, and "hard *Brexit*" for the WTO rule based option.[5]

Currently, the members of the EU maintain a customs union of which the UK is a member, but it has the opportunity to leave after *Brexit*. A customs union requires member states to be able to trade without tariffs or barriers, whilst having a common external tariff with the non-members. In addition, the apportionment of revenues is distributed between the member states in accordance with a specific agreement. The consequences of a customs union are that member states are unable to reach trade agreements with external states and are subject to the requirements of the customs union.

Customs unions have always been a controversial topic, with some economists such as Viner arguing that they are not always beneficial to the member states, although for various reasons both supporters of free trade and protectionists have supported them over the years (this also tends to be the case in the studies discussed later in this chapter).[6] However, the controversy is arguably even older, as the classical economist J.R. McCulloch argued against the *Methuen Treaty* of 1703 between Portugal and the UK, as he suggested it produced the need to buy Portuguese wine which he felt was inferior to French wine.[7] More recently, Facchini et al. have tried to explain why most preferential trade agreements involve free trade agreements rather than customs unions, suggesting that free trade areas have welfare and political advantages over customs unions.[8]

With the recent analyses of the UK leaving and how it affects the UK economy, the different scenarios considered for the analyses have tended to be based on different types of trading relationships, with membership of a customs union being one of the main differentiating factors considered. There are many studies that have attempted to measure the effects of membership within a customs union, mostly based on the standard gravity model and using dummy variables to measure the effects of membership on trade, investment and other economic measures. However, when studies have attempted to measure the effects of the hard and soft scenarios, whether the UK is a member or not varies across studies.

The costs and benefits to the UK and EU of *Brexit*

Many of the studies have analysed the effects on measures of welfare in the UK following it leaving the EU. These studies tend to use simulations to model likely scenarios for the UK economy, usually from two perspectives, a "soft *Brexit*," where the UK remains within the European single market and a "hard *Brexit*," where it leaves the single market and trades with the EU using the WTO rules on tariffs. In addition, they differ in how welfare can be measured, with some studies, such as Dhingra et al. using real per capita consumption as the measure of welfare.[9] Other studies have analysed the effects on incomes and employment, whilst still others have assessed the effects on trade between the UK and EU as well as foreign direct investment flows (FDI). Figure 8.1 depicts the trade between the UK and EU over recent years, showing how both exports and imports have grown and how the trade deficit between the UK and EU has steadily widened.

Approaches to analysing the Brexit *effect*

There have been a number of different approaches to analysing the effects on the UK and EU economies following the UK leaving. The forms of analysis differ in terms of complexity, assumptions and time scale; however, they tend to have a similar goal which involves measuring

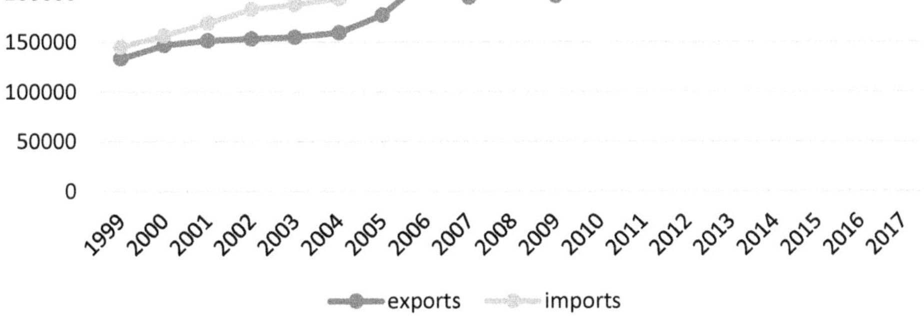

Figure 8.1 Exports in goods and services from the UK to the EU and imports to the UK from the EU (£ million).

Note: Data from Office for National Statistics, UK (ONS).

changes in welfare to the UK economy once it leaves. The simplest approaches assess the trends in the data and the use of case studies.

Perhaps the most basic approach is to assess the differing effects on the UK economy before and after its joining the common market in 1973. Simply viewing trends in the data, such as per capita real Gross Domestic Product (GDP) growth, as in Figure 8.2, suggests that little has changed before and after the UK's decision to join. For instance, looking at 1946–1972 and 1973–2016, average real per capita GDP growth was approximately 1.8 per cent before 1973 and 1.7 per cent afterwards.[10] Conducting a simple hypothesis test that the two series are equal, using a *t*-test based on a student's *t*-distribution and testing for whether the series are significantly different to each other, the result indicates that there is no significant difference between them. The results are the same whether using real per capita GDP growth with 2011 as the benchmark real per capita Gross Domestic Product (RGDPPC) or real per capita GDP with multiple benchmarks (CGDPPC).

In any case, viewing the main economic series before and after the UK joined the EU is problematic as there are many factors that affected the UK economy before 1973 that weren't important afterwards, for instance, changes to technology and environmental policies that have had a far greater effect on GDP growth over recent decades. There have also been differing monetary conditions before and after 1973. The decision to join the EU coincided with the decision to allow the Bretton-Woods exchange rate system to collapse and move largely to the managed floating exchange rates in many Western economies.

In a similar way, case studies of the value of UK membership have tended to analyse the UK macroeconomy for a set number of years before and after the UK joined in 1973. For instance, Crafts concluded that membership of the EU could have increased UK per capita GDP growth through increases in productivity as a result of the increased competition from abroad.[11] Campos et al. used a synthetic control technique to produce the result that UK per capita GDP would have been 8.6 per cent higher after ten years than what it would have been otherwise following

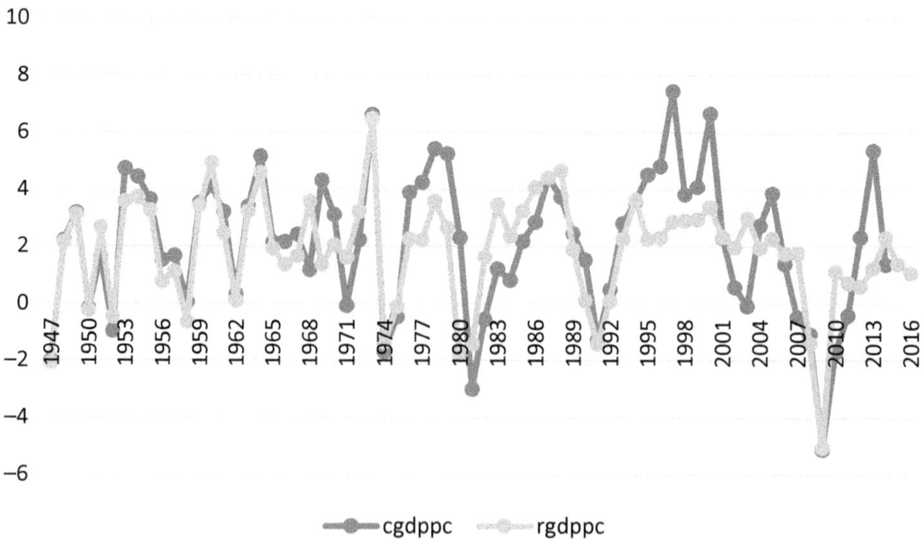

Figure 8.2 UK trends in per capita economic growth between 1947 and 2016.

Note: Data from the Madison dataset.

the UK joining the EU.[12] Still, it is probably difficult to compare this with leaving the EU, because the effects of leaving will inevitably differ to those of joining it.

A further approach has involved the use of event studies which use the stock market return of a firm to determine if a specific event such as *Brexit* has had a positive or negative effect on the stock price. For instance, Davies and Studnicka have used this approach with the Financial Times Stock Exchange (FTSE) 350 returns to determine the effect of *Brexit* on certain industries.[13] This approach involves estimating abnormal returns (AR) or cumulative abnormal returns (CAR) following a specific event. Nonetheless, this approach also has its limitations as it assumes semi-strong market efficiency and the length of event window can also affect the results.

The most common approach to modelling the impact of *Brexit* on the UK and EU economies has involved the use of estimation and simulations using general equilibrium trade models. These models are based on assuming certain conditions affecting trade between the UK and EU following *Brexit*, which then generate predictions of how the UK economy will react in terms of future trade, output and welfare measures. This approach also enables the effects of trade diversion between the UK and non-EU countries to be considered as a result of *Brexit*, whilst accounting for varying scenarios in terms of the form that *Brexit* takes. Therefore, it is possible to compare whether leaving the EU but remaining in the customs union would produce a more favourable result than leaving the EU completely. However, the use of simulations to predict future economic outcomes, having been employed extensively to analyse economic outcomes across a wide range of economic studies, is notoriously complex. For example, Bosquet highlights the inherent uncertainties of using simulation results in his study of environmental tax reform and its effects on the macroeconomy and suggests care when using simulations for policy decision making for a number reasons, such as the margin of error in the assumptions of the models used.[14] One problem is that there has been no similar economic event to *Brexit* to base these assumptions and values on. A further technique used to analyse *Brexit* has involved the use of reduced form estimation approaches, using gravity type models. The results are then combined with the elasticities of per capita income to trade in order to determine the effects on income under various scenarios related to EU membership.

The main test of how well a prediction works is usually through some form of prediction error, where the difference between the actual and forecast values are compared. In terms of the long-run predictions, this is not possible due to the event not having yet occurred. But it is possible to compare what actually happened with the short-term predictions produced by HM Treasury (2016).[15] This short-term analysis suggested three effects would have a negative impact immediately, which were, the uncertainty effect, the transition to the new position effect and the financial conditions effect. These predictions concluded that in the event of a 'no' vote, after two years the exchange rate would lose about 12 per cent of its value, GDP would be 3.6 per cent lower than if the UK had voted to remain in and unemployment would have been about 500,000 higher. Although it is not possible to say what would have happened in the event of a vote to remain, two years and half after the vote was taken, the exchange rate did initially lose about 10 per cent of its pre-vote value, although economic growth was roughly in line with the long-run UK trend growth and unemployment had continued to fall at the pre-vote trend rate. In consequence, the performance of the model has been mixed.

Analysis of other previous related studies of the UK and its relationship to the EU

There has also been a substantial amount of literature on the economic relationship between the UK and EU relating not just to whether the UK should be a member or not, but also to whether it should be more integrated within the EU. This literature is also relevant and is worth comparing with the recent studies on UK membership. It includes studies on aspects of increased monetary union, such as membership of the European exchange rate mechanism in the 1980s, as well as whether the UK should join the euro. This culminated in a series of reports published by HM Treasury in 2003, which assessed the costs and benefits of the UK joining the euro.[16] Even so, the difference with that analysis and much of the current analysis is that the 2003 studies were based on a set of published criteria which would be used to decide if the UK would join, whereas the criteria this time are less explicit than in the 2003 analysis and vary between studies. The aims, as stipulated by the UK government in terms of what they want to achieve from leaving the EU, tend not to include specific targets, except on some subjects such as migration, but even here to reduce numbers to the UK government's promised levels would also require changes to wider legislation, such as the 2002 Act.

In terms of techniques, the types of study used to determine whether the UK should join the euro were similar to those used in the studies to assess the effects of *Brexit*, in that macroeconometric analysis and simulations were used.[17] Overall, these studies concluded it was not possible to confirm whether economic volatility would increase or decrease if the UK took part in the EMU (Economic and Monetary Union). The UK government decided not to join in 2003, due to structural differences between the UK and EU economy and a lack of convergence, in particular with regard to housing and the inherent differences between the UK and EU housing situation.[18]

Main macroeconomic analysis of Brexit

There have been a number of advanced studies that have analysed the impact on the UK and EU, using structural gravity models to analyse the effects on bilateral trade between the UK and EU and how this would affect output, consumption and employment when the UK leaves. The gravity model mainly used by these studies was developed by Anderson and Wincoop and suggests that the distance between countries has a negative relationship with the levels of trade between them.[19] The model includes other factors such as output, prices and exchange rates as well as policy dummies. One of the first attempts to quantify the effect of *Brexit* on trade flows was the HM Treasury study of 2016 and much of the subsequent analysis has been based on this approach.[20] It uses the National Institute Global Econometric Model (NIGEM), which is comprised of an econometric model along with simulations to determine the economic outcomes from various shocks and different economic scenarios. It includes the estimation of a gravity model in a panel data context and predominantly using a fixed effects approach to overcome the unobserved heterogeneity. The data comprises bilateral trade flows and the *Brexit* effects are measured by a series of *Brexit* dummy variables measuring trade creation and diversion as a result of the membership of the EU. The study finds that in the case of a hard *Brexit*, potential trade falls by as much as 20 per cent, but the decline is 17 per cent in the case of a soft *Brexit*. Although, as this study notes, there could be some offsetting of the fall in exports due to a potential depreciation in Sterling, which is not specifically modelled, much would depend on the reaction of the currency markets.

Other studies following a similar approach to the HM Treasury study include Kierzenkowski et al. who used slightly different data over varying time periods to estimate the gravity model, but came up with similar conclusions to HM Treasury.[21] Gudkin et al. also follow a similar approach to HM Treasury, but check the robustness of their findings with varying specifications and time periods.[22] They also overcome the problem of bias due to zero trade flows between countries by using the Pseudo Poisson Maximum Likelihood estimator. Their results again suggest negative effects, although it is worth noting that the Treasury estimates were in the upper bound of their results using different specifications. Dhingra et al. used a similar approach with a quantitative general equilibrium model.[23] They use trade in value added data for 40 economies and 35 industrial sectors from the World Input Output Database from 2011. According to this analysis welfare losses amount to 2.7 per cent for a hard *Brexit* and 1.3 per cent for a soft *Brexit*; however, after using reduced form estimation in which as a result of a reduction in FDI the UK loses competitiveness, this generates an income loss for the UK up to three times the initial estimates.

Other studies include the effects of *Brexit* on the EU countries as well as the UK. Vandenbussche et al. use the World Input Output data starting in 2014 and also find a negative result, with value added production declining by about 1.2 per cent in the event of a soft *Brexit* and 4.5 per cent if there were a hard *Brexit* in the UK.[24] This would produce a loss in employment of between 140,000 and 530,000 in the UK depending on whether it is a hard or soft *Brexit* and in the EU the loss of employment would be from about 280,000 to 1.2 million. Similarly, Brakman et al., using a more complex estimation technique, but the same dataset, find large falls in value added exports after *Brexit*, which would still be negative even if the UK signed bilateral trade agreements with all the non-EU countries in the dataset.[25] Felbermayr et al. also find negative effects arising from Brexit, but much lower than the previous studies.[26] Most recently, Oberhofer and Pfaffermayr have again used the structural gravity model, but with a different dataset.[27] They use the OECD's STAN and UNIDO database which includes data on production for 65 countries between 1994 and 2012, incorporating some recent trade agreements. This produces a negative effect on the UK's level of real income, but little effect on the EU's. A study not based on the gravity model, but instead using the Liverpool economic model by Minford, and incorporating a fall in tariff equivalents, improvements in the terms of trade and a reduction in regulation, finds an increase in consumer living standards of about 3.2 per cent after *Brexit*.[28]

The effects on the UK's financial sector

A particular feature of the UK economy is the reliance on financial services in general and the City of London financial sector in particular for its financial security, output, employment and substantial amounts of tax revenue. As an example, according to the City of London Corporation, in the year to March 2017, UK financial services contributed £72.1 billion in tax revenue, or 11 per cent of total tax receipts in the UK, with the industry employing approximately 1.1 million people.[29] As a member of the single market, the UK's financial services sector has access to a "single passport" to conduct financial services across all the member states with minimal amounts of additional authorisation. As Dhingra et al. suggest, this is important, as not only do UK firms have the right to carry out financial services across the EU, but also any foreign financial firms, such as US banking subsidiaries, have the same right.[30] They argue that not having this right would impose significant extra costs on the sector, negatively affecting output. Moreover, a key area of business in the City concerns the settlement and clearing for euro-denominated products and services, and some have argued that these could leave if the UK lost access to the passport. In the event of a hard Brexit for financial services, it is difficult to say for certain what effect there would be on employment in the City of London, as it is not clear what framework would replace it and what levels of access the UK would be granted by the EU. However, Tata, using client proximity as the determinant of location, suggests that up to 28,500 jobs in corporate and investment banking could be moved to Frankfurt and Paris, in the event of a simple hard *Brexit*.[31] Yet, as with most studies, they believe that even if this scenario occurred, London would remain the prominent financial hub.

The relationship between the UK's financial sector and the EU would depend on whether it is a "soft *Brexit*" or a "hard *Brexit*," as discussed in Armour.[32] As just mentioned, if there is a "hard *Brexit*," the UK could lose its automatic passporting rights in the financial sector. However, even if this occurs a bilateral agreement with the EU could still be negotiated. As such, the UK could follow the example of Switzerland, which has a bilateral agreement including areas of financial services. The problem for the UK is that the EU requires the free movement of people between the EU and Switzerland, which the UK has ruled out. Canada has a similar agreement, the Comprehensive Economic and Trade Agreement (CETA) between this country and the EU, which does not include the free movement of people, but its financial services agreement does not go anywhere near as far as the rights under the EU passport. The other option is for the UK to negotiate a third-country equivalence whereby centralised authorisation occurs for a specific third party covering much of the EU's current regulatory regime. Anyway, this requires that the levels of regulation in the third party country are equivalent to those in the EU. Armour details a number of G20 nations and the main financial centres across the world that have already negotiated these types of agreements, as well as his concerns over whether the UK would be able to reach similar agreements.[33] In spite of that, there has been a long-term difference between the EU and UK in terms of the levels of regulation required, with the UK fearing that excessive regulations and financial taxes could deter overseas trade being conducted in the City. Reynolds argues that it is possible for a compromise solution which he has termed "enhanced equivalence," whereby the UK would enjoy similar access arrangements to the present but have the freedom to draft its own rules and regulations.[34]

The UK financial services sector has over recent years been affected by both the UK's domestic legal and regulatory regime and, increasingly, the Eurozone's regulators as the approach to regulation changed following the 2007/08 financial crisis. This has been an area in which the UK's relationship with the Eurozone is particularly important, as it is moving towards some common regulation across EU members. Traditionally, EU financial regulation was done by issuing directives, even though this left substantial differences over the way that individual countries regulated their financial institutions. It has been argued that some countries have coped better than others with the crisis: Spain did not suffer to the same extent as the UK, as Spanish banks were limited in their ability to hold mortgage-backed securities off balance sheet, so were subject to more effective prudential requirements than banks in the UK. This has led to the formation of a single rule book of financial regulations, which aims to provide a set of prudential controls over the financial institutions across the whole of the EU. This has coincided with the creation of the *Basel III Accord*, which aims to strengthen prudential controls across the world's banking system.[35] Under the single rule book, the European Banking Authority (EBA) will ensure that Basle III is implemented in a consistent manner across the EU.[36]

There are some fears in the City of London that the EBA would impose excessive controls on activities, making it uncompetitive and ensuring that it loses business to other financial centres around the world. However, there have been reassurances regarding the relationship between the UK financial sector and the EBA, such as a double majority vote requirement to change regulations. Even more, the member states have broadly accepted the basic tenets of the new financial regulatory system, such as the need to hold more tier 1 capital made up of the bank's equity capital and reserves, although the UK is not in favour of increased transaction taxes. There is, in any case, a clear potential for future problems. For instance, what would happen in the event of a crisis to a Eurozone headquartered bank, which does much of its business in the City of London? So the negotiations over the future of financial services are complex, with a potential trade-off to consider between ease of access to EU markets and fears over the potential regulatory burden the EU could impose.

The effects of *Brexit* on individual industries

After *Brexit*, the effect on individual industries will vary, but the agricultural sector is one industry that will experience the most impact, as there is a comprehensive policy for managing the market for agricultural products across the member states. After *Brexit* becomes a reality, the EU's Common Agricultural Policy (CAP) will no longer apply in the UK and an alternative policy based on the needs of the UK agricultural and food sector will need to be developed. Currently, the subsidy is based on a single farm payment, largely based on land under agricultural use, with a lesser payment based on environmental aspects of farming. Over recent years, the EU has sought to encourage more environmentally friendly forms of agriculture, which were encompassed in the 2003 changes to the CAP and assessed in Maye et al.[37] The 2003 changes to the CAP moved financial support away from direct produce subsidies, towards single farm payments which were linked to the size of the farm and included measures to ensure protection of the wider environment, such as maintaining hedgerows and woodland. In the UK, the application of the 2003 changes has varied between the constituent nations. In England, the payments depend on an area based system, whereas in Northern Ireland, Scotland and Wales the payments have been allocated to farms on a historic basis. The overall aim for all countries has involved a single farm payment to ensure that the farm is kept in a cultivatable condition, whilst additional payments are possible if the land is kept in a specified environmentally friendly way. The future post-*Brexit* plan appears to continue with this approach and levels of subsidy in the short term, although the EU has concerns over the levels of support and whether they could give the UK a future advantage.

With the UK leaving the EU, the emphasis will be on its own forms of governance for both the environment and agriculture, although as these are closely inter-related, the governance of both will overlap on many issues. The most pressing short-term need will be to ensure the systems of financial support to UK agriculture are continued to ensure the country's food security, although in the long term these can be developed to meet the needs of the constituent nations, such as to increase domestic food production in the UK so as to reduce the current trade imbalance between the UK and EU. The financial support is not just an issue relating to farm profitability, but has effects on trade policy and wider economic goals in terms of food security and rural communities. Helm suggests that the UK leaving the CAP after *Brexit* is a positive move in terms of economic efficiency and for the environment.[38] He suggests three outcomes are possible: first, continuing on with the current policy, which has most of the subsidy directed to each farm based on the amount of land under cultivation, with a smaller amount for environmental schemes; the second option is to continue with the current scheme, but direct more subsidy to the environmental aspects; the third option is termed public payments for public goods and involves paying the subsidy more for the environmental aspects, but initially developing a statement of the objectives of the policy and drawing up the necessary policy instruments. There are few quantitative studies of the effects on UK agriculture of leaving the CAP. One exception is Boulanger and Philippidis, who argue that the UK could financially gain by leaving the CAP, although factoring in to the analysis the trade facilitation costs could lead to a loss for both the UK and EU, with the EU loss being substantially bigger.[39] What is more, when the study is limited just to trade in the agri-food sector and CAP budget then the effect on the UK is beneficial regardless of the assumptions regarding trade facilitation.

Other sectors that have received particular attention are the car manufacturing industries, in which the manufacturers in the UK are often dependent on the EU component manufacturers and are particularly sensitive to tariffs. The UK builds over one and a half million cars a year; about three-quarters are exported, with just under 40 per cent going to the EU.

It employs about 800,000 people across the UK, particularly in less affluent areas such as the West Midlands. Many are overseas owned firms that have located in the UK due to the skilled workforce and access to the EU markets. As Figure 8.3 indicates, there are substantial levels of imports and exports of cars between the UK and EU. Bailey and De Propris assess the effects of *Brexit* on this industry, suggesting that there are a number of ways it could impact it negatively.[40] These impacts might come through foreign direct investment (FDI), which could be adversely affected due to the complex nature of the global value chains (GVC) in this industry that cross a number of EU borders in many cases.[41] Additionally, the UK has been used as a base by multinationals to access the EU single market. Moreover, one of the main ways *Brexit* will impact the industry is through the uncertainty it has created, which could also deter investment. Dhingra et al. indicate that there is potentially a high cost to the motor industry as a result of *Brexit*, although this depends on the type of trade deal reached. In the event of a hard *Brexit*, they find that there could be a 12 per cent reduction in car production, whilst in the event of a soft *Brexit* the reduction would be about 2.4 per cent.[42]

In a related area to the microeconomic studies, the main event studies including Davies and Studnicka, have conducted a two stage event study in which firms in the Financial Times Stock Exchange index (FTSE) 350 of top 350 companies initially have their abnormal return estimated in the days after the *Brexit* vote.[43] These abnormal returns are then regressed on factors such as the firms' GVC, measuring the extent of the dependency on supplies from around the world. They find that firms with a GVC orientated towards the EU perform worse than the main UK market, suggesting the market expects them to underperform when the UK leaves. These findings as a whole provide evidence of within-industry heterogeneity and the need to assess the effects of *Brexit* on specific industries on an individual basis. Ramiah et al. have also conducted a post-*Brexit* based event study across the UK industrial and main UK stock market returns, finding considerable heterogeneity in the performance of different industries following the *Brexit* vote.[44] In their study, banking had a cumulative abnormal return (10 day CAR), which is

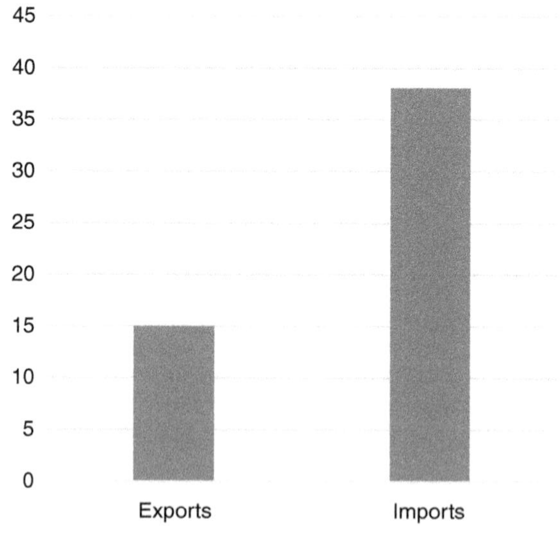

Figure 8.3 UK exports and imports of motor vehicles and parts to/from the top seven EU destinations (2018).

Note: Billions of euros. Data from Eurostat.

the return above what would normally be expected, of −15 per cent, whereas with aerospace and defence it was a positive return of about 7 per cent and food production showed no significant effect.

Conclusion

The results from the macroeconomic and microeconomic analyses have mostly tended to show that the economic repercussions of *Brexit* are potentially negative to the UK and to a lesser extent the EU and likely to reduce the stability of both, although the effects will be heterogeneous across different industries and firms. But, arguably, all studies on the economy in this area are limited by the lack of any similar precedent to base the analysis on. Attempts to predict the consequences of *Brexit* based on the models of the recent economy are difficult in that there is going to be a sizeable structural break in the economic series, which makes it problematic to predict through and what happens after *Brexit*. In any case, the UK will need to prepare future economic policies to account for the likely scenarios after *Brexit*, including the worst case scenarios discussed in this review, such as a sizeable fall in trade and output.

One of the possible limitations of some of the studies discussed, is that the emphasis tends to be on trade, output and associated measures of economic welfare. In this vein, there are no studies that attempt to explain how the trade balance between the UK and EU will be affected by *Brexit*, or what policies should be followed to ensure that it is rebalanced. Given that one explanation for the 2007/08 financial crisis was the presence of fundamental imbalances across different macroeconomies, this is an important area to consider. The analysis as a whole tends to omit the effects on the exchange rate or limit the inclusion of this important variable. If the effects of *Brexit* are as negative as some studies suggest, there is likely to be a substantial depreciation of the pound against the world's main currencies. A more competitive exchange rate would encourage UK exports and growth, potentially offsetting the negative effects.

There are many other features of the *Brexit* campaign that have not received as much attention in the literature relative to the debates during the referendum campaign, such as the security implications and effects of regulation or migration between the UK and EU. In addition to a more specific inclusion of the exchange rate, it would also be interesting to factor in the performance of the EU and its feedback effect on the UK. Further research could also include greater analysis of the interaction between the economy, the legal framework, policy and security issues following *Brexit*.

Notes

1 Nigel Inkster, "*Brexit* and Security," *Survival* 60, no. 6 (2018): 28.
2 Since July 2018, the UK's negotiating position has revolved around a document termed the "Chequers agreement." This involves the UK and EU continuing with a common rulebook for all goods but not services. It includes a backstop to prevent a hard border between the UK and Ireland, which has proven to be controversial.
3 The financial passport system enables any bank or financial institution that is authorised in any EU member country to trade freely in financial services in any other member state, with minimal extra requirements.
4 Thomas Sampson, "*Brexit*: The Economics of International Disintegration," *Journal of Economic Perspectives* 31, no. 4 (2017): 163–84.
5 Much of the negotiation surrounds the nature of the future trading agreements between the UK and EU. The negotiation process follows the principles of game theory; in terms of Nash bargaining the most successful negotiator will be the one with the most credible "no deal" threat.
6 Jacob Viner, *The Customs Union Issue* (Oxford: Oxford University Press, 1950), xvii.

7 The Methuen Treaty of 1703 was a military and trade treaty between Portugal and England, in which Portuguese wine and English cloth had preferential trading status, making Portuguese wine cheaper than French wine.
8 Giovanni Facchini, Giovanni, Peri Silva and Gerald Willmann, "The Customs Union Issue: Why Do We Observe So Few of Them?," *Journal of International Economics* 90, no. 1 (2013): 136–47.
9 Swati Dhingra, Hanwei Huang, Gianmarco Ottaviano, Joao Pessoa, Thomas Sampson and John Van Reenen, *The Costs and Benefits of Leaving the EU: Trade Effects* (CEP Discussion Paper, 2017).
10 The data was taken from the Madison dataset and refers to real per capita GDP in 2011 US$ (2011 benchmark): Jutta Bolt, Robert Inklaar, Herman de Jong and Jan Luiten van Zanden, *Rebasing "Maddison": New Income Comparisons and the Shape of Long-run Economic Development*, Maddison Project Working Paper, 2018. Using the same series but with multiple benchmarks gives similar conclusions in terms of similarity between the series.
11 Nicholas Crafts, *The Growth Effects of EU Membership for the UK: A Review of the Evidence* (University of Warwick, 2016).
12 Nauro Campos, Fabrizio Coricelli and Luigi Moretti, *Norwegian Rhapsody? The Political Economy Benefits of Regional Integration* (CEPR Discussion Paper, 2015).
13 Ronald Davies and Zuzanna Studnicka, "The Heterogeneous Impact of *Brexit*: Early Indications from the FTSE," *European Economic Review* 110 (2018): 1–17.
14 Benoit Bosquet, "Environmental Tax Reform: Does It Work? A Survey of the Empirical Evidence," *Ecological Economics* 34 (2000): 19–32.
15 *The Long-term Economic Impact of EU Membership and the Alternatives* (London: HM Treasury, 2016).
16 *Modelling Shocks and Adjustment Mechanisms in EMU* (London: HM Treasury, 2003).
17 Ibid.
18 Duncan Maclennan, John Muellbauer and Mark Stephens, "Asymmetries in Housing and Financial Market Institutions and EMU," *Oxford Review of Economic Policy* 14 (1998): 54–80.
19 James Anderson and Eric Van Wincoop, "Gravity with Gravitas: A Solution to the Border Puzzle," *American Economic Review* 93, no. 1 (2003): 170–92.
20 *The Long-term Economic Impact of EU Membership and the Alternatives.*
21 Rafal Kierzenkowski, Nigel Pain, Elena Rusticelli and Sanne Zwart, *The Economic Consequences of Brexit: A Taxing Decision* (OECD Economic Policy Paper, 2016).
22 Graham Gudgin, Ken Coutts, Neil Gibson and Jordan Buchanan, *The Role of Gravity Models in Estimating the Economic Impact of Brexit* (Cambridge: Centre for Business Research, 2017).
23 Dhingra et al., *The Costs and Benefits of Leaving the EU.*
24 Hylke Vandenbussche, William Connell and Wouter Simons, *Global Value Chains, Trade Shocks and Jobs: An Application to Brexit* (CEPR Working Paper, 2017).
25 Steven Brakman, Harry Garretsen and Tristan Kohl, *Consequences of Brexit and Options for a Global Britain* (CESifo Working Paper, 2017).
26 Gabriel Felbermayr, Jasmin Groschl and Marina Steininger, *Britain Voted to Leave the EU: Brexit through the Lens of New Quantitative Trade Theory* (Unpublished manuscript, 2017).
27 Harald Oberhofer and Michael Pfaffermayr, *Estimating the Trade and Welfare Effects of Brexit: A Panel Data Structural Gravity Model* (CESifo Working Papers, 2018).
28 Patrick Minford, *The Economy after Brexit* (London: Economists for Free Trade, 2016).
29 The total tax contribution of UK financial services can be consulted on the following website: www.cityoflondon.gov.uk (last modified January 10, 2019).
30 Dhingra et al., *The Costs and Benefits of Leaving the EU.*
31 Fidelio Tata, "Client-Proximity-based Spatial Clustering of European and Corporate and Investment Banking after a Hard *Brexit*," *Finance Research Letters* 27 (2018): 241–46.
32 John Armour, "*Brexit* and Financial Services," *Oxford Review of Economic Policy* 33 (2017): s54-s69.
33 Ibid.
34 Barnabas Reynolds, *A Template for Enhanced Equivalence: Creating a Lasting Relationship for Financial Services between the EU and the UK* (London: Politeia, 2017).
35 The *Basel III Accord* refers to a set of international financial sector regulations produced by the Bank for International Settlements based in Basel in Switzerland in the wake of the 2007/08 financial crisis.
36 The EBA is an independent EU institution which safeguards the stability and security of the banking system across the EU. The common regulations for banking and the financial system across the EU are compiled in the single rule book.

37 Damian Maye, Brian Ilbery and David Watts, "Farm Diversification, Tenancy and CAP Reform: Results from a Survey of Tenant Farmers in England," *Journal of Rural Studies* 25, no. 3 (2009): 333–42.
38 Dieter Helm, "Agriculture after Brexit," *Oxford Review of Economic Policy* 33 (2017): s124–s133.
39 Pierre Boulanger and George Philippidis, "The End of a Romance? A Note on the Quantitative Impacts of a '*Brexit*' from the EU," *The Journal of Agricultural Economics* 66 (2015): 832–42.
40 David Bailey and Lisa De Propris, "*Brexit* and the UK Automotive Industry," *National Institute Economic Review* 241, no. 1 (2017): R51–R59.
41 Companies around the world, especially in the EU are increasingly reliant on these global value chains, and there are concerns with the security of these supply chains after *Brexit* for many multinationals based in the UK.
42 Swati Dhingra, Gianmarco Ottaviano, Thomas Sampson and John Van Reenen. *The Consequences of* Brexit *for UK Trade and Living Standards* (London: London School of Economics and Political Science, 2016).
43 Davies and Studnicka, "The Heterogenous Impact of Brexit."
44 Vikash Ramiah, Huy Pham and Imad Moosa, "The Sectoral Effects of *Brexit* on the British Economy: Early Evidence from the Reaction of the Stock Market," *Applied Economics* 49 (2017): 2508–14.

References

Anderson, James, and Eric van Wincoop. "Gravity with Gravitas: A Solution to the Border Puzzle." *American Economic Review* 93, no. 1 (2003): 170–92.
Armour, John. "*Brexit* and Financial Services." *Oxford Review of Economic Policy* 33 (2017): s54–s69.
Bailey, David, and Lisa de Propris. "*Brexit* and the UK Automotive Industry." *National Institute Economic Review* 241, no. 1 (2017): R51–R59.
Bolt, Jutta, Robert Inklaar, Herman de Jong and Jan Luiten van Zanden. *Rebasing "Maddison": New Income Comparisons and the Shape of Long-run Economic Development.* Maddison Project Working Paper, 2018.
Bosquet, Benoit. "Environmental Tax Reform: Does It Work? A Survey of the Empirical Evidence." *Ecological Economics* 34 (2000): 19–32.
Boulanger, Pierre, and George Philippidis. "The End of a Romance? A Note on the Quantitative Impacts of a '*Brexit*' from the EU." *The Journal of Agricultural Economics* 66 (2015): 832–42.
Brakman Steven, Harry Garretsen and Tristan Kohl. *Consequences of Brexit and Options for a Global Britain.* CESifo Working Paper, 2017.
Campos, Nauro, Fabrizio Coricelli and Luigi Moretti. *Norwegian Rhapsody? The Political Economy Benefits of Regional Integration.* CEPR Discussion Paper, 2015.
Crafts, Nicholas. *The Growth Effects of EU Membership for the UK: A Review of the Evidence.* University of Warwick, 2016.
Davies, Ronald, and Zuzanna Studnicka. "The Heterogeneous Impact of *Brexit*: Early Indications from the FTSE." *European Economic Review* 110 (2018): 1–17.
Dhingra, Swati, Gianmarco Ottaviano, Thomas Sampson and John van Reenen. *The Consequences of* Brexit *for UK Trade and Living Standards.* London: London School of Economics and Political Science, 2016.
Dhingra, Swati, Hanwei Huang, Gianmarco Ottaviano, Joao Pessoa, Thomas Sampson and John van Reenen. *The Costs and Benefits of Leaving the EU: Trade effects.* CEP Discussion Paper, 2017.
Facchini, Giovanni, Peri Silva and Gerald Willmann. "The Customs Union Issue: Why Do We Observe So Few of Them?" *Journal of International Economics* 90, no. 1 (2013): 136–47.
Felbermayr, Gabriel, Jasmin Groschl and Marina Steininger. *Britain Voted to Leave the EU: Brexit through the Lens of New Quantitative Trade Theory.* Unpublished manuscript, 2017.
Gudgin, Graham, Ken Coutts, Neil Gibson and Jordan Buchanan. *The Role of Gravity Models in Estimating the Economic Impact of Brexit.* Cambridge: Centre for Business Research, 2017.
Helm, Dieter. "Agriculture after *Brexit*." *Oxford Review of Economic Policy* 33 (2017): s124–s133.
Inkster, Nigel. "*Brexit* and Security." *Survival* 60, no. 6 (2018): 27–34.
Kierzenkowski, Rafal, Nigel Pain, Elena Rusticelli and Sanne Zwart. *The Economic Consequences of Brexit: A Taxing Decision.* OECD Economic Policy Paper, 2016.
The Long-term Economic Impact of EU Membership and the Alternatives. London: HM Treasury, 2016.
Maclennan, Duncan, John Muellbauer and Mark Stephens. "Asymmetries in Housing and Financial Market Institutions and EMU." *Oxford Review of Economic Policy* 14 (1998): 54–80.

Maye, Damian, Brian Ilbery and David Watts. "Farm Diversification, Tenancy and CAP Reform: Results from a Survey of Tenant Farmers in England." *Journal of Rural Studies* 25, no. 3 (2009): 333–42.
Minford, Patrick. *The Economy after Brexit.* London: Economists for Free Trade, 2016.
Modelling Shocks and Adjustment Mechanisms in EMU. London: HM Treasury, 2003.
Oberhofer, Harald, and Michael Pfaffermayr. *Estimating the Trade and Welfare Effects of Brexit: A Panel Data Structural Gravity Model.* Cesifo Working Papers, 2018.
Ramiah, Vikash, Huy Pham and Imad Moosa. "The Sectoral Effects of *Brexit* on the British Economy: Early Evidence from the Reaction of the Stock Market." *Applied Economics* 49 (2017): 2508–14.
Reynolds, Barnabas. *A Template for Enhanced Equivalence: Creating a Lasting Relationship for Financial Services between the EU and the UK.* London: Politeia, 2017.
Sampson, Thomas. "*Brexit*: The Economics of International Disintegration." *Journal of Economic Perspectives* 31, no. 4 (2017): 163–84.
Tata, Fidelio. "Client-Proximity-based Spatial Clustering of European and Corporate and Investment Banking after a Hard Brexit." *Finance Research Letters* 27 (2018): 241–46.
Vandenbussche, Hylke, William Connell and Wouter Simons. *Global Value Chains, Trade Shocks and Jobs: An Application to Brexit.* CEPR Working Paper, 2017.
Viner, Jacob. *The Customs Union Issue.* Oxford: Oxford University Press, 1950.

9

FINANCING BUSINESS IN THE DIGITAL ECONOMY

Some challenges[1]

Briseida Sofía Jiménez-Gómez

Introduction

This chapter provides an insight into some of the challenges that enterprises face in the digital economy when trying to access credit. Despite the increasing ratio of intangible assets in companies, there are still obstacles for businesses whose value is based on intangible assets to a greater extent. A general overview of the main shortcomings of the under-use of intangible assets as resources is offered. The existing valuation risks and the territorial limitations of using intangible assets are presented in order to gain understanding of the lack of legal certainty in international business.

However, it is claimed that the European regulatory framework could be improved. The disharmony of national laws considering secured transactions on intangibles is an issue for legal certainty. The action taken in conflict of laws on securities in the field of financial collateral arrangement illustrates a critical step for legal certainty at the European level. It is argued that further legal developments concerning substantive laws of security interests plus conflict of law rules would be beneficial to improve legal certainty and predictability of use of intangible assets in financing transactions in Europe. Finally, the outcome of this analysis offers some recommendations to outweigh the legal risks associated with intangible property.

Financial crisis and digital economy

During the last economic crisis, financing institutions were cutting access to credit to enterprises. This fact has had devastating consequences for many businesses. At present, companies are less based on a bricks-and-mortar business and more technologically based. Access to sources of financing is still considered an issue for most businesses and companies in Europe, in particular for small and medium enterprises (SMEs) and start-ups. The usual problem is the high cost of finance and whether there is a lack of guarantees and security rights.[2]

In today's digital economy, financing institutions, banks and investors have come to acknowledge that intangible assets have considerable influence on the value of enterprises and on the stability of business models. However, the ability to leverage this presumed value is impaired by some valuation risks and a complicated regulatory landscape for international transactions.

Intangible assets consist of intellectual property rights (patents, trademarks, designs, plant variety rights, copyright, domain names, computer software), know-how, contracts, trained workforce and distribution networks.[3] However, access to funding is a real constraint, especially at the business stage from technology to the market.[4]

SMEs and start-ups with a technological base, especially software, have been financed in greater proportion with venture capital. Some studies show that enterprises with higher R&D intensity issue more equity and the use of debt for financing declines.[5] The reason behind this is that venture capital and equity look into the company as a unit and do not value specific intangible assets belonging to the company. The greatest disadvantage of this financing system is that the founders of the technological start-up have to transfer ownership and control over the shares of the company to receive financing.[6] This is perceived as a great sacrifice on the part of the owners of the technology company. One of the consequences that can become undesirable by relying exclusively on risk capital is the influence of investors in the management of the company. An increase in control in the hands of investors whose interests may be contrary to those of the creators of the start-up is the price they have to pay in exchange for financing.

Under-use of intangible assets as resources

The rise of intangible assets is staggering, starting at 17 percent in 1975 and amounting to 84 percent of the value of companies in 2015.[7] Intangible assets could be a source of security, in particular when they have the potential to create a stream of revenue in the future. For instance, consider royalties arising from licensing contracts of intellectual property rights. The use of intellectual property also represents an opportunity for development for the poorest countries by opening the door to a type of secured financing with intellectual property.

On the one hand, secured transactions allow financial institutions to return the loaned amounts more safely. This benefits not only the financial institutions, but also the clients that come to carry out this type of transaction, who will benefit from better credit conditions, for example, a lower interest rate, longer repayment terms or more possibilities of debt restructuring. In short, access to credit is expanded as a consequence of the security interests granted on intellectual property. For example, the Ford company obtained $18 billion in 2006 at a time when Ford had negative operating cash flows, using as security rights for the loan not only real estate, but also patents and trademarks owned by Ford.[8] Consequently, the company did not require a taxpayer bailout to survive the 2008–2009 credit crisis, in contrast with General Motors and Chrysler.

On the other hand, the importance of intellectual property rights is now more relevant than ever, especially for technology companies. Intellectual property rights have become a source of technological transfer in innovation processes, since they are more commercialized, showing a change of static perspective in a dynamic vision that affects business strategy. However, the financing market is still in its infancy in Europe as regards the use of intangible assets. Two alternatives to access to finance may be explored: secured transactions and securitization of rights derived from intangible assets.[9]

Main shortcomings

Having recourse to intangible assets could be problematic for several reasons. From a legal perspective, the lack of a harmonized regime for security rights is the most stinging concern.[10] Besides that, legal risks may arise from uncertainties regarding ownership of intangibles assets and intellectual property rights may be subject to legal actions, namely declaration of revocation or declaration of invalidity of the encumbered intellectual property rights. As a result, the declaration of invalidity of the patent involves the termination of the chattel mortgage on that patent.

In addition to legal risks, several market inefficiencies could be the cause of the lack of use of intangibles for financing purposes: valuation issues, rapid market changes, asymmetric information, poor knowledge of the functioning of markets for intangible assets or lack of link between registries.

Territoriality issues

Concerning the legal basis for creating of security interests, the territoriality principle should be considered. Intangible assets are not protected in a uniform way worldwide; instead, the protection of intangible assets is territorially fragmented. The territory of protection of rights is limited to a State or a certain geographical area, for instance, the European Union. The consequences of the independence of intellectual property rights affect the creation of security interests. Therefore, there could be issues related to the legal basis for creating security interests on several intangible assets. Modern secured transaction laws implement a flexible concept of security interest and encumbered assets. On the other hand, traditional laws seem to be more rigid and there must be a specific legal basis for the creation of security interests over specific intellectual property rights.

Thus it is necessary to examine the specific rules of intellectual property rights, which are different in the whole territory of the European Union. Relevant questions vary across jurisdictions; for example, it may be not possible to create security interests on certain intangibles under the law of many jurisdictions, such as trade secrets or domain names.

Ownership uncertainties

Another risk to be considered could be related to the existence of uncertainties about ownership of intangible assets. It may be determined who is the owner of the intangible assets and the conditions to exploit by others, like licensees. Following the *nemo dat quod not habet* rule, it means that it must be clear the type of rights of use in case the grantor of the security is a licensee instead of the owner.

The delimitation of property rights over assets seems to be the key to being able to use them in financing operations.[11] The "property" on intellectual property rights is the starting point for its accommodation to the use as economic goods in commercial business, for example, through contracts of assignment, license or collaboration.[12] Ownership over the patent, trademark or copyright influences the acceptance by creditors of industrial and intellectual property rights as collateral. It has been argued that mortgage loans can reduce the costs of the debtor's default, but there are also costs of entry into the transaction and administration of the encumbered assets, which can determine the choice of unsecured credit.[13]

Lack of publicity

The registration of the rights in a specialized registry enables the verification of the ownership that the prospective granting has over the patents, trademarks or copyright considered. However, the option to register is not always available, for instance, regarding copyright in some countries. At the same time, the effects of the rights registered vary depending on some jurisdictions. Therefore, it is not possible to give an answer that is practical for all type of intangible assets:

instead, national rules must be scrutinized for each type of protected right. The specialized registries such as patents, trademarks and copyright and related rights could remedy the problem of the lack of information regarding the true ownership of rights.

Trend change

The obsolescence of certain products may affect the effective value of intangible assets, such as patents or copyrights on computer programs. On the one hand, new products in the market made with more advanced technology reduce the value of previous patents under which similar products were manufactured. Despite the legal protection of certain signs perhaps being unlimited, as happens with trademarks if they are renewed in due time, consumer trends vary with time, so that the value of the trademarks is not insured in a timely manner.[14] On the other hand, the tastes of consumers change over time depending on fashion trends. However, the risks of obsolescence or changes in the market can be minimized with certain loan structures.[15]

Obscure markets

It is considered that one way to mitigate risks to the creditor is to avoid creating security interests in patents that are positioned in a consolidated market, not to take intangible assets as collateral that have already been taxed or to focus on intangible assets of higher technical quality.[16] However, intellectual property markets are not characterized by transparency. The existence of a specific intellectual property market has a decisive influence on granting a loan with security interests on these rights. In principle, it seems that markets for tangible goods are more stable than those for intangible goods. Therefore, the existence of reference values with respect to intellectual property rights that are purported to be usable as a security is a determining factor in accepting them as a security. In any eventual enforcement of the security on intangible assets, there must be third parties interested in acquiring the intangible assets. Nevertheless, the lack of a transparent market for transactions in intangible assets makes it difficult to create security interests on them.[17]

However, acquisitions and mergers of companies show that there is a market with respect to intellectual property. Some studies have tried to quantify the economic benefits of the transfer of patents in the market, its consequences in the development of a technological market and, even, to warn of a future technological change.[18] Contrary to what might appear, these economic studies confirm that there is a large patent market, taking into account the registered transactions in the US Patent Office (USPTO). It can be stated that 30 percent of European patents between 1998 and 2012 changed at least once from the owner in the European context.[19]

Valuation risks

There are two methods to value intangible assets: qualitative methods and quantitative methods.

Qualitative methods

Qualitative methods assign a score to the intellectual property, which is based on factors representing the value of the rights of intellectual property. In the case of patents, the factors used are, among others, remaining years of the legal protection or period of the license, previous royalties received by the patent owner, royalties paid by the potential licensee for other patents, nature and scope of the license (exclusive or simple), license policy established by the owner, prior commercial relations established between the owner and the potential licensee, and effects of the sale of the patented product in the promotion and or commercialization of other products.[20] For example, some license agreements provide more the right that establishes freedom to operate the patent, when they integrate knowledge expertise. In case of mixed agreements where patents plus know-how (for example material necessary to use the patent in a given way, databases or research data) are provided, the value of the rate of the license agreement is generally higher than naked patents.[21]

Quantitative methods

Quantitative methods are more advisable for financing purposes. The different methods can be grouped into three approaches: first, the cost approach; second, the market approach; and third, the income approach.

Cost approach

The cost approach involves calculating the cost of supporting the development or purchase of the asset plus its protection (administrative costs). It takes into consideration how to develop an asset identically with or alternatively to a potentially similar utility or service. Therefore, value is defined as acquisition price when assets are bought. However, this approach has many disadvantages when the value is created internally, as usually the internal cost of an asset cannot be equivalent to its real value. At the same time, the cost approach disregards any expected profits that assets can generate. It could be used for computer software, although the cost approach value may have to be adjusted to reflect obsolescence.[22]

Market approach

The second, market approach estimates the value calculated from real market transactions. The value is not only for the owner of the company but the asset value for third parties. Prices derived from market transactions that include the sale of comparable assets are used in the market approach. Several conditions are necessary to assess the value of intangibles. It is essential that there exist a dynamic market, a sufficient number of cases to compare, as purchase-sale of assets, and access to the public information about transactions and contracts. However, some obstacles exist to using this method, as perhaps when it comes to unique assets or in case of absence of comparable databases and very heterogeneous data. Normally, intellectual property transactions are part of a bigger deal and details are confidential.[23] The usefulness of this approach could serve to contrast results achieved by other methodologies, such as value from damages estimated in court judgments.

Income approach

The third, income approach considers value from all the profits or benefits that the asset can generate.[24] Different methods exist: the royalty method, the premium profit method and the excess earning method.[25] The most used of them is the royalty method, which calculates the present value of the net costs imposed by royalties or licenses saved by owning the intangible asset. It is very useful for patents and trademarks. There are available databases with public information on patent licensing contracts.[26] It is necessary to conduct a sector analysis, to know some information on the rate of royalties in the considered sector and to estimate future sales of products and services marketed under the trademarks for a specific period (for example ten years). As usual, it must be considered for the useful life of the asset. An estimate of the royalty rate is also required to multiply by the expected sales and discount future flows with a discount rate, but it could be difficult to determine an adequate royalty rate based on assets in FRAND terms (fair, reasonable and non-discriminatory royalty estimate).

It follows that information should be gathered regarding the strength of the asset, terms and conditions, exclusivity or not, life cycle of the assets, level of operating margins and existence of rights retained by the licensor. For example, the difference between patented and unpatented technology must be considered in the royalty rate: it has been estimated in the pharmaceutical, biotechnology and medical products field that the royalty in an unpatented technology is lower by 50 percent compared to a valid patented technology.[27] Thus, it could be a benchmark for know-how and trade secrets. In practice, a combination of income approaches is used, verified with the market value or the cost of the assets.

Implement the recommendations from the group of experts

Several measures have already been suggested by a group of experts in the European Union. The *Final Report from the Expert Group on Intellectual Property Valuation* (IP Valuation report) was published in 2013.[28] The expert group appointed by the European Commission proposed some recommendations. In our view, four recommendations could improve the financing business in the digital economy, involving taking into account intellectual property rights.

Due to non-disclosure contracts, important details on market transactions remain confidential. First, the establishment of a data source that contains anonymous information about transactions relating to intellectual property could overcome barriers of information asymmetry and facilitate a more reliable source for decision takers on intellectual property asset-based lending.[29] Data can only be gathered from market participants; therefore, they must be convinced that publication of data boosts these types of transactions. It could be made mandatory for companies whose benefits from tax reliefs related to innovation investments, or some tax incentives could be linked to companies that provide data.[30]

Second, the creation of an organization to supervise the practice of valuation of intellectual property (including education and training) could be a good solution to increase trust and transparency. Therefore, a proposal has been made to create a register of accredited expert valuers and enhance education and training standards in Europe.[31]

Third, the setting up of a risk-sharing loan guarantee plan for banks in order to facilitate secured loans with intellectual property rights could be considered. The loan guarantee plan would be shared by the bank and an institution in order to diminish financial risks. The aim of the scheme would be to address the market failure in the provision of low cost debt finance by providing a guarantee to banks in cases where a business with a viable business plan is unable to raise finance because they cannot offer tangible security for their debt or lack a track record. Besides, some service providers to value intangible assets could overcome the knowledge gap related to intangible assets and bank expertise. The appraiser service provider can benefit the bank because it shortens the lending risk of financing institutions temporarily.[32]

Fourth, introduction of an additional information section on intangible assets and intellectual property assets in financial reports could be a source of reliable information for investors and valuers. Inspiration from the available information in case of initial public offerings (IPOs) could be relevant. Among others, some specifications of type of assets, the level of protection, jurisdictions included, development stage of intellectual property and estimated cost to bring the intellectual property to the market could enhance the understanding of the value and upgrade users and decision takers.[33]

Regulatory framework

Disharmony in Europe: is it desirable?

The substantive rules concerning security interests in intellectual property rights vary significantly across the territory of the European Union. The diversity of national regimes is a consequence of the principle of territoriality; accordingly, with respect to the patrimonial aspects of the security interests, it is not possible to perfect a single secured transaction when the assets are located in different States. The "nationality" of rights currently reflects the way that security interests are granted with respect to a legal system. The Spanish chattel mortgage and pledge without possession Act admits the creation of a chattel mortgage on intellectual property rights.[34] The requirements for the creation of a chattel mortgage are the constitution of a chattel mortgage in public deed plus entry in the Registry of Personal Property. Under some legal systems, such as Spanish law or Italian law, creation and perfection are treated as a unitary concept. Therefore, it is not possible that a security interest comes into existence without being effective against third parties.[35]

In contrast to these frameworks, under other legal systems it may be possible to enforce a security against the debtor with lower requirements, for instance under common law. It does not mean that common law would be easier to deal with in comparison with civil law jurisdictions.[36] However, some jurisdictions are most prone to admit all type of assets as security, in particular when there is not a *numerus clausus* list to admit movable assets suitable for security interests.

Businesses with intangible assets located in several countries in the European Union have difficulties accessing secured credit as it is costly to scrutinize different relevant rules across countries. For example, domain names could be subject to a chattel mortgage under a specific law that requires notarized documents and entries in several registries,[37] but it does not assure that these registries are linked with foreign registries or that it would be possible to accept domain names as security in all pertinent countries. In fact, proper registries to register the transactions may not even exist in some jurisdictions when, according to their laws, it is not necessary to register a secured transaction.[38] Therefore, publicity across Europe could be a concern that requires a harmonized policy to solve the current inefficiencies in the legal landscape.[39]

Moreover, it seems clear that a secured transaction registry at a low fee must exist to incentivize lenders to acquire priority over any other competing claimant to the collateral. The recommendation by the Model Law[40] of UNCITRAL (United Nations Commission on International Trade Law) includes an electronic register of security interests that can strike the balance between different perspectives in the EU.

Finally, it becomes evident that the current situation is far from optimal. It could be good for companies to create unified rules for security interests on intangible assets, in particular regarding the value that intangible assets have in the digital economy. The lack of legal certainty in cross-border transactions of securities in intangible assets is a legal deterrent to access to finance for enterprises in Europe. It could even be argued that it is not helping the proper functioning of the internal market.

Conflict of laws rules

Action taken

The European Union has only unified conflict of laws on securities in the field of financial collateral arrangement. The Financial Collateral Directive[41] on the one hand enhances legal certainty of financial collateral arrangements because it ensures a harmonized system of creation and enforcement of financial collateral. So, Member States do not apply the provisions of insolvency law.

On the other hand, this Directive regulates a conflict of law rule based on the Settlement Finality Directive.[42] This conflict rule provides that the law applicable to book entry securities as collateral is the law of the country in which the relevant account is maintained, extending the rule previously set in the Settlement Finality Directive. The wording of the conflict of law rule is not exactly the same, but the interpretation must be equivalent according to the European Commission.[43] The matters to which this conflict rule refers are proprietary aspects, such as the legal nature and proprietary effects of book entry securities collateral, the requirement for perfection, the priority between competing titles and the realization process of the security.[44] The unification establishes *lex rei sitae* for determining perfection of financial collateral; however, the interpretation of where the account or register is located or maintained could differ when implementing it in national law.

Future developments

In private international law a widely recognized principle for intellectual property is the *lex loci protectionis*.[45] *Lex loci protectionis* is the law of the State for which protection is sought.[46] This law is established in international treaties for the existence and effects of intellectual property. Despite territoriality being usually supported in the field of applicable law in the *Paris Convention for the Protection of Industrial Property* (1883) and in the *Berne Convention for the Protection of Literary and Artistic Works* (1886), it is not so clear that international agreements have been drawn up to regulate the applicable law to security interest on intellectual property.

The Rome I Regulation on the Law Applicable to Contractual Obligations only harmonized conflict of law rules at Union level with regard to the contractual elements.[47] By the same token, the Rome II Regulation is not applicable to property aspects of security rights.[48] Therefore, there is a lack of regulation to govern property aspects of security interests over intellectual property rights at the European level. Consequently, it is necessary to examine national conflict of laws rules, and most of them consider *lex loci protectionis* in a general way, but not expressly for security interests.[49]

Whether *lex loci protectionis* is a suitable law for secured transactions is a question not easy to answer.[50] In principle, this law creates efficiency and certainty in business transactions where the whole bunch of intellectual property rights is protected in a single country. However, this law is not so appropriate in case of transactions of intellectual property rights protected in several countries.[51] *Lex loci protectionis* may impose administrative burdens for each country in case of a cross-border transaction. It means that for creation, effectiveness against third parties, priority and enforcement of security interests over intellectual property, the transaction must comply with the requirements of each country of protection of the intellectual property used as security.[52]

The alternative to *lex loci protectionis* is following a modern secured transactions approach. The law that provides the highest level of certainty for operators dealing with assets situated in many States is the law of the State in which the grantor is located.[53] A similar approach to that taken by UNCITRAL has been proposed from the European Max Planck Group. The law of the State of residence of the grantor could apply to the security agreement that creates or transfers the security right, any registration requirements in general security rights registers, the security right's dependence on the existence of the secured obligation, and the transferability and the enforcement of the security right.[54]

The law of the State of the grantor is not a general rule in Europe, where the *lex rei sitae* applies. However, when considering intangibles, some risks of application of the *lex rei sitae* appear. The Commission's 2018 Proposal for a Regulation on the Law Applicable to the Third-Party Effects of Assignments of Claims[55] shows interest in regulating an area traditionally inconsistent among Member States. The legal risks associated with cross-border assignments of claims have been considered in order to unify conflict of laws in this area. The applicable law for the third-party effects of an assignment of claims would be the law of the country in which the assignor has its habitual residence at the material time (art. 4.1 Proposal for a Regulation). Likewise the United Convention on the Assignment of Receivables in International Trade provides support for the law of the State of the assignor.[56] Nevertheless, the above mentioned rule does not apply in case of assignment of cash credited to an account in a credit institution or claims arising from a financial instrument and in case of a securitization where the parties may choose the law applicable to the assigned claim for purposes of third-party effects of an assignment of claims (art. 4.2 Proposal for a Regulation).

Although the assignor's approach is not for all cases, it consolidates the idea that it is good to regulate at the European level for the internal market and that the applicable law can be tailored to specific types of transactions.[57] However, this Proposal is limited to assignment of claims, including transfer of claims by way of security or pledges but not applicable to intellectual property rights. So far, there is no action regarding conflict of laws on security interests over intellectual property rights in Europe, which undermines the use of these transactions in the internal market.

Concluding remarks

Some recommendations could be suggested to improve the current economic and legal landscape of financing in Europe.

First, to foster a better valuation of intellectual property, specialized registers of each country could make available to the public quantitative data on transfers, licenses and security interests of intellectual property rights, especially patents, trademarks or copyrights, since the ignorance of the market about intellectual property rights does not favor the use of them in secured transactions.

Second, a greater cooperation between national and international offices could also be established. It may not be necessary to create a European register, but at least recording in a national register should be coordinated and accessible throughout the European Union.

Third, it would be positive to consider rules concerning security interests for the whole territory of the European Union. These rules should also contain provisions related to intangibles ,and in particular intellectual property rights, as these are valuable assets in the digital economy. In our view, European enterprises need a better understanding of their problems for financing. A harmonized regime could alleviate the present legal risks in European secured transactions. In particular, it could increase cross-border transactions using intellectual property rights as security rights, as clarity and predictability would be better for the creation of security rights. These actions will promote financing and innovation in our economy. Therefore, harmonization of substantive law and conflict of laws regarding security interests in intellectual property rights should be included in the European Commission Agenda.

Notes

1 This contribution has been made within the framework of the research project DER-2015–64063-P, MINECO-FEDER.

2 For figures in Spain: *VII Informe: La financiación de la PYME en España: Resultados de septiembre de 2018*, accessed January 13, 2019, www.cesgar.es/wp-content/uploads/2018/12/VII-Informe-financiaci%C3%B3n-de-la-pyme-9-2018-2.pdf.

3 The definition of intangible asset by UNCITRAL is broad: "all types of movable assets other than tangible assets and includes incorporeal rights, receivables and rights to the performance of obligations other than receivables." The *UNCITRAL Legislative Guide on Secured Transactions (the Secured Transactions Guide)* (UNCITRAL, 2007), 10, accessed January 13, 2019, www.uncitral.org.

4 European Commission, *Towards Enhanced Patent Valorisation for Growth and Jobs* (Brussels: European Union, 2012), 11.

5 Carl Benedikt Frey, *Intellectual Property Rights and the Financing of Technological Innovation* (Cheltenham: Edward Elgar Publishing, 2013), 4–5.

6 Janice Denoncourt, "IP Debt Finance and SMEs: Revealing the Evolving Conceptual Framework Drawing on Initiatives from around the World" in *Security Interests in Intellectual Property*, ed. Toshiyuki Kono, Springer Perspectives in Law, Business and Innovation (Singapore: Springer, 2017), 7.

7 As the report of a US consultancy Ocean Tomo shows, taking into account the US S & P 500 index, accessed January 13, 2019, www.oceantomo.com/intangible-asset-market-value-study/.

8 Gerald B. Halt Jr., John C. Donch, Amber R. Stiles and Robert Fesnak, *Intellectual Property and Financing Strategies for Technology Startups* (Springer, 2017), 29–30.

9 Robert Laverty, "Alice-Backed Securitization: Start-ups' New Alternative to Venture Capital," *John Marshall Review of Intellectual Property Law* 16, no. 2 (2017): 246–71.

10 See section entitled "Regulatory framework," below.

11 Hernando De Soto, *The Mystery of Capital* (London: Black Swan, 2000), 27–34.

12 William W. Fisher and Felix Oberholzer-Gee, "Strategic Management Intellectual Property: An Integrated Approach," *California Management Review* 33, no. 5 (2013): 157–83.

13 Ronald J. Mann, "Explaining the Pattern of Secured Credit," *Harvard Law Review* 110 (1997): 633–34.

14 Julio Cerviño Fernández, "Valoración y cuantificación de la dilución de marcas: un encuentro entre el ámbito jurídico y económico," *Estudios de Derecho Judicial* 99 (2006): 467–508.

15 Brian W. Jacobs, "Using Intellectual Property to Secure Financing after the Worst Financial Crisis since the Great Depression," *Marquette Intellectual Property Law Review* 15, no. 2 (2011): 459.

16 Bruce W. Burton, Emma Bienias and Candice K. Quinn, "Financing Alternatives for Companies: Using Intellectual Property as Collateral," (Stout/Risius/Rous, 2014), 1–6, accessed January 13, 2019, www.hilcoglobal.com.

17 Liina Tonisson, Raymond Millien and Lutz Maicher, *Shortcomings on the Market for Intellectual Property* (Leipzig: Fraunhofer Center for International Management and Knowledge Economy, 2016), 17, accessed January 13, 2019, www.imw.fraunhofer.de/.

18 Carlos J. Serrano, *The Market for Intellectual Property: Evidence from the Transfer of Patents* (University of Toronto, 2006), accessed January 13, 2019, http://citeseerx.ist.psu.edu/viewdoc/download?doi=10.1.1.583.7564&rep=rep1&type=pdf.

19 Laurie Ciaramella, Catalina Martínez and Yann Ménière, "Tracking Patent Transfers in Different European Countries: Methods and a First Application to Medical Technologies," *Scientometrics* 112, no. 2 (2017): 817–50.

20 *George Pacific Corp.* v. *U.S. Plywood Corp* (S.D.N.Y.1970).

21 Russell L. Parr and Gordon V. Smith, "Determining Royalty Rates," in *Intellectual Property, Valuation, Exploitation and Infringement Damages: 2017 Cumulative Supplement*, ed. Russell L.L. Parr, and Gordon V. Smith, 4th ed. (Hoboken: John Wiley & Sons, 2017), 129.

22 Russell L. Parr and Gordon V. Smith, "Market and Cost Approach," in *Valuation of Intellectual Property and Intangible Assets*, ed. Russell L.L. Parr, and Gordon V. Smith, 3rd ed. (Nueva York: John Wiley & Sons, 2000), 193–94.

23 Kelvin King, "The Value of Intellectual Property," *Journal of Intellectual Property Rights* 7 (2002): 247.
24 Russell L. Parr and Gordon V., Smith, "When Theory Meets Practice," in *Valuation of Intellectual Property and Intangible Assets*, ed. Russell L.L. Parr and Gordon V. Smith, 3rd ed. (New York: John Wiley & Sons, 2000), 312.
25 European Commission, *Final Report from the Expert Group on Intellectual Property Valuation* (Brussels: European Union, 2013), 75–79, accessed January 13, 2019, https://ec.europa.eu/research/innovation-union/pdf/Expert_Group_Report_on_Intellectual_Property_Valuation_IP_web_2.pdf.
26 For example, RoyaltySource IP Database, ktMINE, Royalty connection.
27 Parr and Smith, "Determining Royalty Rates," 131–32.
28 European Commission, *Final Report from the Expert Group on Intellectual Property Valuation*, 75–79.
29 Ibid., 57.
30 Ibid., 58.
31 Ibid., 60.
32 Ibid., 61–65.
33 Ibid., 65–69.
34 Ley de hipoteca mobiliaria y prenda sin desplazamiento de 16 de diciembre de 1954, BOE núm. 352 de 18 de diciembre.
35 Andrea Tosato, "Security Interests over Intellectual Property Rights in Italy: Critical Analysis and Reform Proposals," in *International and Comparative Secured Transactions Law, Essays in Honour of Roderick A Macdonald*, ed. Orkun Akseli and Spyridon Bazinas (Oxford, Portland: Hart Publishing, 2017), 265.
36 Martin Brassell and Kevin King, *Banking on IP? The Role of Intellectual Property and Intangible Assets in Facilitating Business Finance* (UK Intellectual Property Office, 2013), 169–74, accessed January 13, 2019, www.gov.uk/government/publications/banking-on-ip.
37 For a development in Spanish law concerning domain names: Briseida Sofía Jiménez-Gómez, "La nueva Ley de Patentes y sus implicaciones en materia de garantías internacionales," *Anuario Español de Derecho Internacional Privado* XVI (2016): 555.
38 Briseida Sofía Jiménez-Gómez, *Las garantías reales sobre derechos de propiedad industrial e intelectual en Derecho internacional privado*, PhD dissertation, Complutense University of Madrid, 2018, 204–5.
39 Giuliano G. Castellano, "Reforming Non-Possessory Secured Transactions Laws: A New Strategy," *Modern Law Review* 78, no. 4 (2015): 614.
40 UNCITRAL Model Law on Secured Transactions (2016), accessed January 13, 2019, www.uncitral.org/.
41 European Parliament and Council of the European Union, Directive 2002/47/EC of the European Parliament and of the Council of 6 June 2002 on Financial Collateral Arrangements ("Financial Collateral Directive"), OJ L 168, June 27, 2002.
42 European Parliament and Council of the European Union, Directive 98/26/EC of the European Parliament and of the Council of 19 May 1998 on Settlement Finality in Payment and Securities Systems ("Settlement Finality Directive"), OJ L 166/45, June 11, 1998.
43 European Commission, Communication from the Commission to the European Parliament, the Council, the European Economic and Social Committee and the Committee of the Regions on the Applicable Law to the Proprietary Effects of Transactions in Securities, COM(2018) 089 final (Brussels: European Union, March 12, 2018).
44 Directive 98/26/EC, art. 9.2.
45 European Max Planck Group on Intellectual Property, *The CLIP Principles and Commentary* (Oxford: Oxford University Press, 2013); American Law Institute, *Intellectual Property: Principles Governing Jurisdiction. Choice of Law, and Judgments in Transnational Disputes* (American Law Institute Publishers, 2008).
46 Jürgen Basedow, *The Law of Open Societies, Private Ordering and Public Regulation in the Conflict of Laws* (The Hague Academy of International Law, Brill/Nijhoff, 2015), 212–6.
47 European Parliament and Council of the European Union, Regulation (EC) No 593/2008 of the European Parliament and of the Council of 17 June 2008 on the Law Applicable to Contractual Obligations (Rome I), OJ L 177, July 4, 2008.
48 European Parliament and Council of the European Union, Regulation (EC) No 864/2007 of the European Parliament and of the Council of 11 July 2007 on the Law Applicable to Non-contractual Obligations (Rome II), OJ L 199, July 31, 2007.
49 On the considerations of territoriality for security interests: Raymond T. Nimmer and Lorin Brennan, "Modernizing Secured Financing Law for International Information Financing: Conceptual Framework," *Houston Business and Tax Law Journal* 6 (2005–2006): 46–49.

50 UNCITRAL, *The Supplement on Security Rights in Intellectual Property to the UNCITRAL Legislative Guide on Secured Transactions* (UNCITRAL, 2010), accessed January 13, 2019, www.uncitral.org.
51 Toshiyuki Kono and Kazuaki Kagami, "Functional Analysis of Private International Law for Security Interests in Intellectual Property," in *Security Interests in Intellectual Property*, ed. Toshiyuki Kono (Singapore: Springer, 2017), 119–53.
52 Stefania Bariatti, "The Creation and Enforcement of Security Interests in Intellectual Property Rights: Choice-Law Issues," in *Research Handbook on Cross-Border Enforcement of Intellectual Property* ed. Paul Torremans (Cheltenham: Edward Elgar Publishing, 2014), 528.
53 Recommendation 208, UNCITRAL Guide.
54 Christian Heinze, "Section 8: Security Rights in Intellectual Property," in *Conflict of Laws in Intellectual Property: The CLIP Principles and Commentary*, ed. the European Max Planck Group. (Oxford: Oxford University Press, 2013), 354.
55 European Commission, Proposal for a Regulation on the Law Applicable to the Third-Party Effects of Assignments of Claims, COM(2018) 096 final, 2018/0044(COD) (Brussels: European Union, March 12, 2018).
56 United Convention on the Assignment of Receivables in International Trade (New York, 2001), art. 22, available at: www.uncitral.org.
57 In favor of regulation on the European level: Christian Heinze and Cara Janine Warmuth, "The Law Applicable to Proprietary Effects of Assignment and its Interplay with Insolvency," *Uniform Law Review* 22 (2017): 808–25. Against the Commission's Proposal: Hendric Labonté, "Third-Party Effects of the Assignment of Claims: New Momentum from the Commission's Capital Markets Union Action Plan and the Commission's 2018 Proposal," *Journal of Private International Law* 14, no. 2 (2018): 319–42.

References

American Law Institute. *Intellectual Property: Principles Governing Jurisdiction. Choice of Law, and Judgments in Transnational Disputes*. American Law Institute Publishers, 2008.

Bariatti, Stefania. "The Creation and Enforcement of Security Interests in Intellectual Property Rights: Choice-Law Issues." In *Research Handbook on Cross-Border Enforcement of Intellectual Property*, edited by Paul Torremans, 526–48. Cheltenham: Edward Elgar Publishing, 2014.

Basedow, Jürgen. *The Law of Open Societies, Private Ordering and Public Regulation in the Conflict of Laws*. The Hague Academy of International Law, Brill/Nijhoff, 2015.

Brassell, Martin, and Kevin King. *Banking on IP? The Role of Intellectual Property and Intangible Assets in Facilitating Business Finance*. Intellectual Property Office, 2013. Accessed January 13, 2019. www.gov.uk/government/publications/banking-on-ip.

Burton, Bruce W., Emma Bienias and Candice K. Quinn. "Financing Alternatives for Companies: Using Intellectual Property as Collateral." Stout/Risius/Rous, 2014. Accessed January 13, 2019. www.hilcoglobal.com.

Castellano, Giuliano G. "Reforming Non-Possessory Secured Transactions Laws: A New Strategy." *Modern Law Review* 78, no. 4 (2015): 611–40.

Cerviño Fernández, Julio. "Valoración y cuantificación de la dilución de marcas: un encuentro entre el ámbito jurídico y económico." *Estudios de Derecho Judicial* 99 (2006): 467–508.

Ciaramella, Laurie, Catalina Martínez and Yann Ménière. "Tracking Patent Transfers in Different European Countries: Methods and a First Application to Medical Technologies." *Scientometrics* 112, no. 2 (2017): 817–50.

Denoncourt, Janice. "IP Debt Finance and SMEs: Revealing the Evolving Conceptual Framework Drawing on Initiatives from around the World." In *Security Interests in Intellectual Property*, edited by Toshiyuki Kono, Springer Perspectives in Law, Business and Innovation, 1–38. Singapore: Springer, 2017.

De Soto, Hernando. *The Mystery of Capital*. London: Black Swan, 2000.

European Commission. *Final Report from the Expert Group on Intellectual Property Valuation*. Brussels: European Union, 2013. Accessed January 13, 2019. https://ec.europa.eu/research/innovation-union/pdf/Expert_Group_Report_on_Intellectual_Property_Valuation_IP_web_2.pdf.

European Commission. *Towards Enhanced Patent Valorisation for Growth and Jobs*. Brussels: European Union, 2011.

European Max Planck Group on Intellectual Property. *The CLIP Principles and Commentary*. Oxford: Oxford University Press, 2013.

Fisher, William W., and Felix Oberholzer-Gee. "Strategic Management Intellectual Property: An Integrated Approach." *California Management Review* 33, no. 5 (2013): 157–83.
Frey, Carl Benedikt. *Intellectual Property Rights and the Financing of Technological Innovation*. Cheltenham: Edward Elgar Publishing, 2013.
Halt, Gerald B. Jr., John C. Donch, Amber R. Stiles and Robert Fesnak. *Intellectual Property and Financing Strategies for Technology Startups*. Springer, 2017.
Heinze, Christian. "Section 8: Security Rights in Intellectual Property." In *Conflict of Laws in Intellectual Property: The CLIP Principles and Commentary*, edited by the European Max Planck Group, 352–69. Oxford: Oxford University Press, 2013.
Heinze, Christian, and Cara Janine Warmuth. "The Law Applicable to Proprietary Effects of Assignment and its Interplay with Insolvency." *Uniform Law Review* 22 (2017): 808–25.
Jacobs, Brian W. "Using Intellectual Property to Secure Financing after the Worst Financial Crisis since the Great Depression." *Marquette Intellectual Property Law Review* 15, no. 2 (2011): 449–64.
Jiménez-Gómez, Briseida Sofía. "La nueva Ley de Patentes y sus implicaciones en materia de garantías internacionales." *Anuario Español de Derecho Internacional Privado* XVI (2016): 535–63.
Jiménez-Gómez, Briseida Sofía. *Las garantías reales sobre derechos de propiedad industrial e intelectual en Derecho internacional privado*, PhD dissertation. Complutense University of Madrid, 2018.
King, Kelvin. "The Value of Intellectual Property." *Journal of Intellectual Property Rights* 7 (2002): 245–8.
Kono, Toshiyuki, and Kazuaki Kagami. "Functional Analysis of Private International Law for Security Interests in Intellectual Property." In *Security Interests in Intellectual Property*, edited by Toshiyuki Kono, 119–53. Singapore: Springer, 2017.
Labonté, Hendric. "Third-Party Effects of the Assignment of Claims: New Momentum from the Commission's Capital Markets Union Action Plan and the Commission's 2018 Proposal." *Journal of Private International Law* 14, no. 2 (2018): 319–42.
Laverty, Robert. "Alice-Backed Securitization: Start-ups' New Alternative to Venture Capital." *John Marshall Review of Intellectual Property Law* 16, no. 2 (2017): 246–71.
Mann, Ronald J. "Explaining the Pattern of Secured Credit." *Harvard Law Review* 110 (1997): 625–83.
Nimmer, Raymond T., and Lorin Brennan. "Modernizing Secured Financing Law for International Information Financing: Conceptual Framework." *Houston Business and Tax Law Journal* 6 (2005–2006): 1–53.
Parr, Russell L., and Gordon V. Smith. "Determining Royalty Rates." In *Intellectual Property, Valuation, Exploitation and Infringement Damages: 2017 Cumulative Supplement*, edited by Russell L. Parr and Gordon V. Smith, 4th edition, 101–48. Hoboken: John Wiley & Sons, 2017.
Parr, Russell L., and Gordon V. Smith. "Market and Cost Approach." In *Valuation of Intellectual Property and Intangible Assets*, edited by Russell L. Parr and Gordon V. Smith, 3rd edition, 193–94. New York: John Wiley & Sons, 2000.
Parr, Russell L., and Gordon V. Smith. "When Theory Meets Practice." In *Valuation of Intellectual Property and Intangible Assets*, edited by Russell L. Parr and Gordon V. Smith, 3rd edition, 307–31. New York: John Wiley & Sons, 2000.
Serrano, Carlos J. *The Market for Intellectual Property: Evidence from the Transfer of Patents*. University of Toronto, June 2006. Accessed January 13, 2019. http://citeseerx.ist.psu.edu/viewdoc/download?doi=10.1.1.583.7564&rep=rep1&type=pdf.
Tonisson, Liina, Raymond Millien and Lutz Maicher. *Shortcomings on the Market for Intellectual Property*. Leipzig: Fraunhofer Center for International Management and Knowledge Economy, 2016. Accessed January 13, 2019. www.imw.fraunhofer.de/.
Tosato, Andrea. "Security Interests over Intellectual Property Rights in Italy: Critical Analysis and Reform Proposals." In *International and Comparative Secured Transactions Law, Essays in Honour of Roderick A Macdonald*, edited by Orkun Akseli and Spyridon Bazinas, 259–85. Oxford, Portland: Hart Publishing, 2017.
UNCITRAL. *Legislative Guide on Secured Transactions (the Secured Transactions Guide)*. UNCITRAL, 2007. Accessed January 13, 2019. www.uncitral.org.
UNCITRAL. Model Law on Secured Transactions. UNCITRAL, 2016. Accessed January 13, 2019. www.uncitral.org.
UNCITRAL. "Supplement on Security Rights in Intellectual Property" in the *UNCITRAL Legislative Guide on Secured Transactions*. UNCITRAL, 2010. Accessed January 13, 2019. www.uncitral.org.

10
EU REGULATION OF VIRTUAL CURRENCIES[1]

Xesús Pérez López

Introduction

In many respects, virtual currencies remain a controversial phenomenon as of yet. Their resistance to being easily apprehended by conclusive statements first manifested in the issue of their very denomination. Obviously, the name chosen by the promoters of the first wide-spread virtual currency, "bitcoin," conveyed an implied qualification of it as "cash" or, more precisely, as "hard cash," thus presenting such a character as a *fait accompli*. More recent virtual currencies, complying with the model presented by bitcoin to a greater or lesser extent, have mostly assumed a similar *Selbstdarstellung* in this particular point.

In the last decade, this character of "cash" – or even of "currency" in proper sense – of virtual currencies has been subjected to an intense cross-cutting debate involving scholars, promoters of (specific) virtual currencies, industry actors, jurists, user communities, economists and – last, but not least–EU and national public sector instances, such as law enforcement authorities or financial system supervisors. As of today, a single solid statement could be made: EU jurists and regulators, following wider, global trends, have reached a firm consensus on the non-equivalence as a principle of virtual currencies to fiat currencies, given their lack of legal tender status.[2] As self-evident as it might seem, this statement is far from being of no consequence: even if the scholarly support of the opposite position may well be considered as residual,[3] the conception of virtual currencies as "money" or "cash" is always strongly endorsed by promoters[4] and community actors,[5] in spite of some recent differentiation attempts made by the promoters of particular virtual currencies.[6]

Further insight can be obtained through a closer analysis of the various approaches represented in the *opinio generalis* of non-equivalence of virtual currencies to fiat money. On one hand, this non-equivalence has been formulated by European state and supranational (EU) actors negating any superposition whatsoever between virtual currencies and fiat currencies, especially from a juridical point of view. These formulations lean towards avoiding any ambiguity resulting from the denomination of virtual currencies as "money" or "cash," as much as it could lead to an erroneous perception of their validity as "money" in the sense of "legal tender money."[7] The European Central Bank (ECB), following the opinion of the European Bank Authority (EBA), has conveyed this position by insisting specifically on denying both the character of "currencies" in proper sense and of "payment means" to virtual currencies;[8] the main EU bodies have aligned themselves with the EU financial supervisor's approach to this matter.[9]

On the other hand, a number of technical reports commissioned by international bodies and State financial supervisors have pointed out the ideal adequacy of virtual currencies to fulfill the functions traditionally attributed to money by economic theory (medium of exchange, unit of account, store of value). Building on that, some of these reports have established, albeit in a theoretical, hypothetical framework, a direct parallelism between virtual currencies and fiat money.[10] Some other reports, setting these theoretical results against the background of everyday practice, take as a point of departure the adequacy of virtual currencies to fulfill the economic functions of money, but pointing out the limited extent to which they achieve that as of now.[11]

The first, more theoretical, ECB understanding of the virtual currencies' problematics seemed to be aligned with this sort of approach.[12] Later, its position on the matter (and thus the position of other EU bodies) drifted towards the foremost consideration on later instances of the virtual currencies' relation to legal tender money. This difference of position may have been determined by the different demeanor with which the ECB has approached the problem in each instance, that is, whether, as a relatively detached observer of a new phenomenon, it should supposedly furnish some initial insights on it at the beginning, or whether, later, as a financial system supervisory body, it is deemed to take a clear position on the matter and is expected to supply firm counsel to other EU bodies, especially for regulatory purposes.

This shift of demeanor entailed a tendency to define virtual currencies, not only considering the theoretical coherence of the definition, but rather looking forward to the regulatory consequences of it. First, the ECB reasoned in terms of theoretical possibility, then, later on, in terms of regulatory feasibility. In other words, the theoretical adequacy of virtual currencies to fulfill the functions of money does not necessarily entail their recognition by supervisory bodies and regulators. On this latter point, by avoiding the qualification of virtual currencies as "money" in official texts and by clearly stating their lack of legal tender status in the EU, the EU bodies have adopted the same general direction taken by national regulators globally.

As important as the controverted economic, societal and political aspects involved in virtual currencies are,[13] our work focuses on regulatory matters. Without any intent of diminishing the weight of the ongoing discussions on other aspects, we will thus analyze virtual currencies mainly in the light of their regulatory consideration by EU bodies. For the same reason, we will not attempt here any thorough technical characterization or description of the working of typical virtual currencies and, especially, bitcoin (a task best left to specialists[14]). Instead, we will limit ourselves to a brief hint of the technical traits most likely to be relevant from a regulatory point of view:

1 First, as the transactions are verified and registered by the user community as a whole, no centralized supervision would be possible.
2 Second, and owing to this very decentralization trait, no intermediaries are required for transactions (that is, from a strictly technical point of view: the economic functioning of the system has inevitably led to the proliferation of financial intermediation products and services).
3 Third, in as much as every transaction may (and it often does) involve more than one sending address (payer/s) and/or more than one receiving address (receivers), the very architecture of the system makes it difficult to relate the account units (for instance, bitcoins or ethers) sent by a specific set of sending addresses and the account units received by a specific set of receiving addresses to a given transaction.
4 Fourth, and for the same reason, no individual account unit can be "singled out" by means of a "serial number," thus further increasing the difficulty of tracing a given transaction.

5 Fifth, and in the same order of consideration, the data accessible to the users in the public ledger do not allow the establishment of the bounds of a given wallet, that is, to relate a wallet to a specific user.
6 Sixth, once validated, the transactions cannot be cancelled or reverted, thus narrowing the feasibility of a devolution of the value received through a given transaction by a certain account to a voluntary, backwards transaction *a posteriori* by the controller of the receiving address(es).
7 Seventh, as the loss of the cryptographic tokens allows control of an address amounting to the loss of the account units attributed to that address, the loss of the data conforming the token's alphanumeric chain amounts to the destruction of said account units, while the theft of these data amounts to the theft of the aforementioned account units.[15]

The broad picture

Both from a jurisprudential and from a regulatory point of view, virtual currencies have stirred the attention of the relevant bodies of the EU in general and of those of its Member States in particular. In light of the societal and economical relevance of virtual currencies in the last few years, this attention is far from being surprising. However, if we compare the progress made by the EU with that achieved by other major global economic players such as the USA (boasting, as of now, a clear statutory regulation and a consolidated line of jurisprudence on the matter), the results of the aforementioned attention appear to be relatively meager.

Even specifically jurisprudential approaches – both by courts and by State agencies giving binding decisions – to the law applicable to virtual currencies in the EU are relatively timid. They pertain first and foremost to the fiscal consideration of economic activity associated with virtual currencies and, in particular, to virtual currencies' exchanging and mining. The issue in question has consisted invariably in the ascertainment of the tax regulations when applied to this kind of activity, the first approaches to the matter being inevitably accompanied by a certain bewilderment of the courts and agencies on the juridical qualification of the facts. Such ascertainment has necessitated, in certain cases, some measure of analogical interpretation due to the lack of specific regulations applied in order to rule out the issues raised.[16] Only very few Member States of the EU have already taken a definitive stance on the fiscal aspects of the matter through direct, straightforward official statements of Government bodies, whereby they have explicitly declared virtual currencies as being conclusively valid.[17] Given the lack of specific regulatory responses to virtual currencies (at least, until the AMLD – Anti-Money Laundering Directive – reform), the scholarly efforts to theorize their inclusion in the systematic frame of private law had to settle for the possibility of analogical interpretation of general rules to virtual currencies.[18] At best, these endeavors lead to hypothesizing a general set of rules applicable to contractual relationships, specifically pertaining to virtual currencies, possibly apt to substantiate a proposal *de lege ferenda*.[19]

The only ruling on the matter of the EUCJ (EU Court of Justice) to this moment[20] may be included in this trend of tentative decisions. The issue was raised by the Supreme Administrative Court of Sweden, which requested a preliminary ruling on the applicability of the pertinent EU derivative law relative to the VAT on bitcoin exchange activities. The case on trial motivating the request had its origin in a decision dictated by the Swedish Revenue Law Commission at the request of a citizen, on the matter of the applicability of the VAT regulations to bitcoin exchange activity. The decision was appealed by the Swedish Tax Authority, and it was in the context of the subsequent proceedings that the preliminary ruling request was elevated to the EUCJ.

The Supreme Administrative Court of Sweden raised, in particular, two questions: whether bitcoin exchange activity would constitute the supply of a service, effected for consideration in the sense of the Directive 2006/112/CE (the "VAT Directive") or not; and whether the article 135(1) of the aforementioned Directive should be interpreted as connoting that bitcoin exchange activity was exempt of that tax. The Court answered affirmatively to both questions, with the answer to the second formidably including some nuances proposed by Advocate General Kokott in her Opinion.[21]

The EUCJ resolved the first question with the focus on declaring bitcoin exchange activity to constitute the supply of services for consideration within the meaning of article 2(1)(c) of the VAT Directive, which concludes that the supply of goods and services for consideration within the territory of a Member State by a taxable person acting as such is to be subject to VAT. Given the specific nature of the services in question (the exchange rates offered by the concerned exchanger clearly foreseeing a margin of profit for him), it was convenient for the Court to do so.[22] In order to answer the second question, the EUCJ differentiated between the causes of VAT exemption possibly applicable to bitcoin exchange activity as per the article 135(1) of the VAT Directive. The Court, thus, explicitly negated the applicability to bitcoin exchange activities of the causes of exemption enunciated in letters (d) and (f) of the aforementioned article and paragraph, whereas expressly declaring these activities to be exempted of the VAT on the basis of letter (e).

This answer could be thought to amount to a jurisprudential definition of sorts of what a bitcoin would be (or possibly, any close-related virtual currency) from the point of view of EU regulations: as it stands, this second answer envisages bitcoin exchange activities to constitute "transactions [...] concerning currency, bank notes and coins used as legal tender," rather than "transactions [...] concerning deposit and current accounts, payments, transfers, debts, cheques and other negotiable instruments" or "transactions [...] in shares, interests in companies or associations, debentures and other securities."[23] Certainly, inasmuch as this second answer prefers some exemption cause to others, it provides both positive and negative delimitation of the consideration of bitcoin exchange activity in the case at stake.

However, the impact of this ruling on the legal encompassing of virtual currencies in EU Law is probably not as ground-breaking as it could seem (that is, putting aside it's providing some relatively safe interpretative grips for the national jurisdictions to cling to). It must be stressed that the ruling, pertaining to a preliminary question, concerns the applicability of a particular EU norm to the issue at hand. Properly speaking, it concerns only the interpretation of articles 2(1) and 135(1) of the VAT Directive, and only as to their applicability to bitcoin exchange at that: exchange activities of any other virtual currency are not concerned in the ruling, as it explicitly states on several occasions.[24] In one instance, the EUCJ further narrows the reach of the ruling, narrowing its applicability to other cases pertaining to bitcoin exchange services such as those at issue in the main proceedings.[25] Given the lack of specific EU regulations on the subject, the cautious attitude adopted by the Court was not only adequate, but almost unavoidable. However, the very need for such ruling provided a plain example of the involvement of virtual currencies in key EU regulatory fields.

The EU main bodies' taking notice of this involvement resulted in the launch of a broad EU regulatory initiative in 2016, with a relatively modest outcome as of yet. The origin of this initiative lies in a European Parliament resolution on virtual currencies, suggesting a number of lines of action to the Commission and to the Council – in particular, regulatory action.[26] The suggestions made by the European Parliament took into account virtual currencies as well as, more generally, distributed ledger technologies (DLT). In light of the general expectations of the development of further applications of DLT to finance and other fields of activity, the broadness of scope encouraged by this resolution can only be welcome, due to the risk of premature obsolescence of a narrow-minded regulation on the matter.

The necessity for regulatory action was sustained by the Parliament on the basis of a twofold argumentation, which highlighted the urge of regulating existing applications of DLT related to payments (including therein virtual currencies), as well as the need of taking into account any other DLT developments being liable to acquire societal relevance.[27] Obviously, the European Parliament's call for regulatory action dedicated special attention to payment-related DLT applications, given their current societal relevance. On that matter, the resolution first stressed the substantial potential of virtual currencies, as well as of DLT in general, being particularly apt to contribute to the welfare and economic development of the EU.[28] Thereafter, it emphasized the risks underlying DLT in general and virtual currencies in particular, including issues associated with consumer protection, legal and economic uncertainty, and, very specifically, money laundering and terrorism financing possibilities.[29]

Setting aside the suggestion of other various, "softer" measures,[30] the resolution charged the Commission with the regulatory initiative for two matters directly related to virtual currencies. First and foremost, the Commission was to take on the inclusion (that is, as obliged entities) of virtual currency exchange platforms in the Directive (EU) 2015/849 of 20th May 2015 (the so-called "Anti-Money Laundering Directive" or "AMLD"), the European Parliament thus accepting the suggestion to this effect previously made by the Commission itself.[31] Second, the Commission was to conduct a thorough analysis of the impact of virtual currencies, in order to evaluate the opportunity of revising "the relevant EU legislation on payments, including the Payment Accounts Directive (PAD), the Payment Services Directive (PSD) and the Electronic Money Directive (EMD)."[32] As much as the second, broad task the European Parliament gave into the charge of the Commission seems to be still in an embryonic state as of yet, the first one has been accomplished: Directive (EU) 2018/843 of the European Parliament and the Council of 30 May 2018, Amending Directive (EU) 2015/849 on the Prevention of the Use of the Financial System for the Purposes of Money Laundering or Terrorist Financing, and Amending Directives 2009/138/EC and 2013/36/EU.

Virtual currencies and money laundering in the EU

The relatively rapid advance of this first task can be easily explained when taking into account that the risks related to the use of virtual currencies in criminal finances are a primary concern for law enforcing authorities, financial supervisors and regulators both on a national and a supranational (EU) level.

It is hardly necessary to insist on how this concern is far from being exclusive to European countries.[33] As for the EU, the first institutional alarms regarding these kinds of risks were raised in the EU mainly by financial supervisory bodies (as they were in the international context). The European Central Bank pointed out the potential use of virtual currencies by criminals (and, in particular, by money launderers) to be a challenging factor already for 2012, due to the lack of regulation on the matter.[34] In the report accompanying its Opinion of 2014 on virtual currencies, the European Banking Authority identified, out of a total of 70 potential risks affecting the use of virtual currencies, a dozen risks specifically associated with their criminal uses.[35]

The reality of the use of virtual currencies in criminal finances seems to justify the concern of the European supervisors. As much as no financial product or service is safe from illegitimate, malicious use in a criminal context (from a simple credit card to high complexity financial products), in recent years virtual currencies have become a prevalent payment method in criminal finances.[36]

It may be worth the effort to summarize now the foremost reasons for virtual currencies' attraction and appeal for criminal finances. We have already mentioned some of them in relation to the virtual currencies' relevant technical characteristics. Again, we will refer our discourse mainly to bitcoins as they remain the single most used virtual currency in criminal finances,[37] even if ether and other widely used virtual currencies are getting ever-increasing attention from law enforcement agencies in Europe.[38]

1 First, the very decentralization principle underlying bitcoin (and many other virtual currencies) carries with it an intrinsic lack of external transaction supervision mechanisms (that is, "external" as opposed to the "internal" supervision mechanism constituted by the distributed ledger itself). Granted, the various intermediaries operating in the virtual currencies market (especially exchangers and virtual currency-related application developers) might accept voluntarily or be constrained to accept (as it were) some supervision mechanisms. In 2015, EUROPOL provided regulatory advice to this effect, in order to cope with virtual currencies' criminal use;[39] as we will see, the revision of the AMLD has furthered this advice.

However, serious doubt may be formulated against the sufficiency of regulation-imposed supervision mechanisms to compensate for the advantages offered by virtual currencies' decentralization. Putting aside the cultural reticence of the virtual currency community to the imposition of any external supervision, the distributed, peer-to-peer functioning of decentralized virtual currencies will continuously allow direct transaction between users, thus limiting intermediaries. As the imposition of traffic surveillance obligations on electronic communication service providers can be ruled out (above all, and obviously, due to strong human rights concerns, but also because of economic reasons), peer-to-peer, no-intermediary virtual currency transactions can remain an accessible, affordable, unsupervised payment method for criminals.

2 Second (and mainly, but not only, as a consequence of the very architecture of the address system in the case of bitcoin and other widely used cryptocurrencies), virtual currencies offer a high degree of privacy for transactions, due to the inherent complexity of relating a given transaction to a given user, then further tracking the route followed by a "particular" unit of value changing "proprietary" (controller) by comparing "accounts." Granted, no perfect privacy and anonymity is provided by the bitcoin network: enough, adequate resources coupled with accomplished, complex methods may allow, within certain bounds, tracking of a given bitcoin transaction.[40] In proper sense, the term "pseudonymity," rather than "anonymity," might better be applied to bitcoin transactions, as some data (i.e., bitcoin addresses) may (dauntingly) be related to the parties of each transaction.

However, a substantial part of the bitcoin community continually struggles to improve the transaction privacy offered by the systems. Moreover, new virtual currencies compete with more established virtual currencies by offering potential users an increased level of privacy, tending to the ideal of technically proper, "perfect" anonymity.[41]

3 Third, the irreversibility of transactions in the more widely adopted virtual currencies (bitcoin, ether) contributes to their allure for criminal finances.[42] Such irreversibility is especially useful for victim-to-criminal payments: most probably, it contributes substantially to the fact of virtual currencies being the preferred victim-to-criminal payment method in online extortion cases (typically those committed through ransomware[43]). Additionally, in order to prevent or to revert such payments, law enforcement authorities are constrained either to effectively intervene in the computer used to control bitcoin addresses in a given moment (a difficult feat at best), or to trust that providers of services of

virtual currency exchange and storage will willingly collaborate in a prosecution (that is, only if such services are engaged by criminals in a particular case).

4 Fourth, the use of virtual currencies is particularly pertinent to the classical characteristics of cybercrime: instantaneity, as per transaction quickness; physical distance between the offender and a substantial part of the *iter* conducting to the perpetration of the crime; trans-frontier character and consequent set of problems in order to determine jurisdiction and effectively enforce prosecution; immateriality, facilitating evidence disposal (somewhat mitigated by the ledger's publicity, however).

5 Fifth, and related to the previous item, particular flexibility: a token allowing control of a given set of bitcoin addresses may instantaneously circulate online, but may also circulate physically when the need arises (for instance, when the organization suspects that its online channels are being compromised by law enforcement activity): frontier agencies are hardly able to attentively browse through the contents of every pendrive carried by persons traversing national and/or EU boundaries, barring a specific suspicion of a particular individual in that perspective.

Regardless of their preeminent use as a victim-to-criminal payment method in cybercriminal extortion, the characteristics we have just summed up contribute to virtual currencies being the main criminal-to-criminal payment method as of yet.[44] Virtual currencies have become widely known to the general public, and they constitute a readily available, relatively accessible means of money laundering. Consequently, and despite their main illegitimate users remaining cybercriminals, virtual currencies are known to be used as criminal finance enablers even by petty, non-specialized criminals.[45]

Given the aforementioned possibilities, plain sending of tokens to a fiscal paradise country allows criminals to easily overcome the initial phase of money laundering, that is, the placement phase. Virtual currencies may be there exchanged against legal tender currency, so as to enable further layering and final integration of the laundered proceeds of criminal activity.

Virtual currency mining also provides attractive opportunities for money laundering: tight supervision of virtual currency "production" of a given mining operation requires specific surveillance. In its absence, a production lower than really attained may be disclosed in order to evade taxes, or so as to launder illicit money by investing it in more equipment and energy than openly declared to tax authorities. To similar ends, virtual currencies obtained by illicit means (for instance, as proceeds of a ransomware extortion, or through the use of botnets of infected computers) may be falsely disclosed to be the produce of a licit mining operation.

The AMLD reform

The first EU major regulatory action to affect virtual currencies[46] consists in the Directive (EU) 2018/843 of the European Parliament and the Council of 30 May 2018, amending Directive (EU) 2015/849 on the prevention of the use of the financial system for the purposes of money laundering or terrorist financing, and amending Directives 2009/138/EC and 2013/36/EU. The text is of capital interest to our means, as it reforms the AMLD in the sense of taking into account virtual currency storage and exchange activities. As stated before, the dispositions pertaining to virtual currencies included in this reform are intended to be but the point of departure of a wide, ambitious reform front aiming to modify EU payment regulations to take into account present and potential DLT applications.

Since the first proposal of the EU Commission in July 2016, the reform project has been the object of substantial discussion before the competent EU regulatory and advisory bodies,[47] bearing fruit in the relatively short terms of less than two years. The heading of the Directive (EU) 2018/843 suggests the comparative importance of the amendments introduced to the AMLD:[48] those made to Directive 2009/138/EC and Directive 2013/36/EU are relatively meager in extension (only a letter of a paragraph modified for each one of them), essentially working as enablers for the expansion, operated by the core reform of the AMLD itself, of information exchange possibilities between the national Financial Intelligence Units (FIUs).[49]

Obviously, the amendments introduced through the Directive (EU) 2018/843 to the Directive (EU) 2015/849 (that is, the AMLD) are not confined to taking into account virtual currencies.[50] Putting aside the dispositions pertaining virtual currencies, the AMLD reform, amongst other things: a) reinforces the information access powers corresponding to the FIUs;[51] b) enlarges the applicability of customer due diligence measures to obliged entities or third-country issuers issuing prepaid cards;[52] c) enhances customer due diligence measures for any transaction involving high-risk third countries and introduces dispositions aiming to reinforce the cooperation with the latter;[53] d) commands Member States to take measures in order to ensure that corporate and other legal entities embedded within their territory are required to obtain and hold adequate, accurate and current information on their beneficial ownership, including trusts and other types of legal arrangements, such as, *inter alia*, *fiducie*, certain types of *Treuhand* or *fideicomiso*, where such arrangements have a structure or functions similar to trusts.[54]

The dispositions of the reformed AMLD specifically pertaining to virtual currencies consist of:

- a long awaited legal definition of "virtual currencies" (at least, for AML intents and purposes), as well as one of "custodian wallet provider";[55]
- the inclusion of specific service providers operating in the virtual currencies' market (namely, exchangers and custodian wallet providers) in the list of AMLD-obliged entities;[56]
- the requirement for the aforementioned specific service providers to be registered before the Member States in which they would operate.[57]

Such dispositions are to be understood not only in the light of the European Parliament resolution of 26 May 2016 on virtual currencies, but also against the background of the whole AMLD reform. On the one hand, such dispositions accomplish the objective of "including VC exchange platforms in the Anti-Money-Laundering Directive (AMLD) in order to end the anonymity associated with such platforms" as encouraged by the aforementioned Parliament resolution,[58] according to its risk-based approach.[59] On the other hand, the new rules on virtual currencies are coherent with the general expansion of EU financial supervision authorities' powers directly and indirectly enforced by the reformed AMLD. Notwithstanding, and however necessary and salutary culling the money laundering and terrorism financing risks associated to virtual currencies may be (essentially, for the reasons we have already stated in the previous section of this chapter), some doubt can be raised to the specific *ratio legis* advanced by the EU legislator as motivation for our rules, as we will later see.

Regarding the definition of "virtual currencies" introduced by the reform in article 3, letter 18 of the AMLD, its final extent is largely the consequence of the observations formulated by the ECB in its opinion on the reform project:

> "Virtual currencies" means a digital representation of value that is not issued or guaranteed by a central bank or a public authority, is not necessarily attached to a legally established currency and does not possess a legal status of currency or money, but is

accepted by natural or legal persons as a means of exchange and which can be transferred, stored and traded electronically.[60]

In order to understand the precise extent of the definition, we must turn to the particulars of the legislative process leading to its promulgation. In the original proposal of the EU Commission, the purport of the definition stirred the hopes of the sector's stakeholders, by defining virtual currencies through their acceptance "as a means of payment."[61] Even if defining virtual currencies through their acceptance as a means of payment is far from being the same as defining virtual currencies as a means of payment outright, the wording of the original proposal conveyed a certain ambiguity. Such ambiguity pushed set stakeholders to conceive some expectation for the EU regulations on payments to be applied to virtual currencies through an extensive interpretation of the definition.

However, the twofold observation made by the ECB on the tenor of the Commission's proposed definition was final on the matter. First, the ECB's opinion held the term "currency" as meaning, in proper sense, "legal tender status currency," such a term thus indicating a legally binding payment method (which virtual currencies are not, at least at the moment); consequently, the ECB insisted on the denial of the status of "currency" in proper sense to virtual currencies. Second, and regarding the general use of virtual currencies, the ECB pointed out that virtual currencies can be used for purposes other than that of a means of payment, as demonstrated by everyday practice. As a consequence, the European financial system supervisor encouraged insistence and particular explicitness on denying legal tender status to them in the final definition – the preferred expression is "means of exchange" rather than "means of payment" as applicable to virtual currencies – and suggested that the definition should contain some specific reference to their "other uses."[62]

The subsequent report of the European Parliament on the project, incorporated all of the three suggestions of the ECB on the matter into its proposal of amendment to the Commission's original definition.[63] Besides some minor formal changes, two substantial further modifications were made to the definition during the legislative process.

First, the reference to the "other uses" of virtual currencies was finally eliminated from the definition.[64] In doing so, the European legislator clearly outlined that any scheme otherwise responding to the AMLD's definition can be held as "virtual currency" in the sense of the said definition only when it is accepted as a means of exchange, putting aside the question of any other uses being plausible or not. In this manner, the acceptance as a means of exchange came to be the main and only social-use based criterion provided by the definition in order to consider a virtual currency as such per the AMLD. No precise indication is made as to a minimum extent of such acceptance, maybe so as to not hinder the virtual currencies in process of being launched (typically through an ICE) and included in the scope of the AMLD. The definition only states that virtual currencies should be "accepted by natural or legal persons as a means of exchange"; some further precision could still come through the national transpositions to be of the amendments to the AMLD.

Second, the EU Parliament's amended proposal for the definition stated that virtual currencies would be not be "attached to a legally established fiat currency"; the following proposals down to the definitive version preferred the wording "not necessarily attached to a legally established currency." Both wordings are meant to clearly highlight the difference between "electronic money" as defined by the article 2.2 of Directive 2009/110/EC and "virtual currencies" as defined by the AMLD. The adding of the word "necessarily" allows for the possibility of a given virtual currency scheme attaching its units' value to that of any fiat currency, otherwise not responding to the aforementioned definition of electronic money, but still responding to the definition of "virtual currency" of the amended AMLD. Even if the definition could concern any virtual currency (including, for instance, massive multiplayer online video game – MMO – "gold" and similar value units), the EU legislator seems to have laid it down primarily thinking of the "proper" cryptocurrencies.[65]

As for the definition provided in the amended AMLD of "custodian wallet providers," it adopts a terminology of common use in the sector: " 'custodian wallet provider' means an entity that provides services to safeguard private cryptographic keys on behalf of its customers, to hold, store and transfer virtual currencies."[66]

A "custodian" (or sometimes "custodial") virtual currency wallet commonly designates any virtual currency wallet in which the private cryptographic keys, enabling control by a given person of the related value units, are kept in logical storage devices by a third party. The ends of the services thus provided by such third party to the concerned person (hence, the "customer") consist primarily of the purpose of securing the cryptographic tokens against any malicious intrusion (possibly amounting, as we have already pointed out, to outright theft or loss of the controlled value units). As it stands, the amended AMLD definition encompasses both "cold storage" providers (that is, providers offering a secure storage of the tokens in offline logical storage devices, much in a similar way to a "traditional" bank offering strongboxes to its customers) and "hot storage" service providers (providers securing the keys in online servers, usually allowing the customer to readily and remotely access and operate with the controlled value units, much like a bank offering online account access services), "hot storage" services being more frequently used as of now.

As much as these definitions could contribute to the gradual development of a European legal framework pertaining to virtual currencies, the realization of their potential will only come by recurrent use of both definitions in further EU and national legislation to come, as they remain as of now strictly applicable only in the cadre of the AMLD. Meanwhile, the lack of specific regulations adequate to cope with the contentious, raised in the everyday practice by the use of virtual currencies, can only result in a "jurisprudential voracity" of sorts for (sufficiently) firm interpretative holds in the (scarcely) existing legal terminology. Such "voracity" could possibly lead to some analogical application of the AMLD definitions by EU and national courts.

At any rate, the aforementioned definitions can be considered instrumental to the primary end of the new AMLD dispositions on virtual currencies, including the primary legitimate stakeholders of the virtual currencies' market in the list of obliged entities as per the AMLD, in order to allow identification of suspicious activity and, ultimately, to avoid criminal financial operations being conducted under the cover offered by the lack of monitoring and the anonymity of virtual currency markets.[67] While such expansion of the obliged entities' list to key virtual currency market stakeholders was envisaged since the very origin of the reform project,[68] the precise extent of it was the object of some discussion during the legislative process. At some point, a proposal was advanced for the inclusion in the list not only of exchangers and custodian wallet providers, but also of "issuers, administrators, intermediaries and distributors of virtual currencies."[69] The incertitude of the proposed terminology as applied to virtual currencies made the proposal unrealistic: in the case of decentralized virtual currencies, should the whole community be considered as "issuer"? In any case, could the communication service providers be held as "distributors" of virtual currencies?

What is maybe more interesting, such a proposal evinced (perhaps involuntarily) the intrinsic limits to any regulatory approach to virtual currencies. Virtual currencies often work on the basis of a decentralization principle and can be stored and held locally by controlling users and then can be traded P2P. The intervention of custodian wallet providers or of "intermediaries," such as exchangers, can be thus *convenient* (even *highly* convenient in profitability terms), but it is not technically *unavoidable*, in order to operate with virtual currencies. From the optic of an authority willing to avoid any possibility of illegitimate use of virtual currencies (and passing itself of any proportionality issues, that is), the imposition of specific obligations to any subject able to operate with virtual currencies might be held to be *sufficient*; however, it would be *unrealistic*, because of the very architecture of virtual currency schemes.

These efficacy issues have been accounted for in the final text: the imposition of such obligations to legitimate third parties offering storage and exchange services can be considered a more realistic approach to the problem, as it stands in the final version of the amended Directive, through the addition to the list of obliged entities dressed by the article 2.1.3 of the AMLD of:

(g) providers engaged in exchange services between virtual currencies and fiat currencies;
(h) custodian wallet providers.[70]

An evaluation of this particular extension of the list of obliged entities from the point of view of efficacy leads inevitably to mixed results. As for sufficiency, there can be no doubt as to the usefulness of such an approach to facilitate the prevention of money laundering and terrorism financing: the obligations of customer due diligence and disclosure attributed to the obliged entities are far from being trivial in that sense. A wide range of conditions require diligence due measures to be applied by the obliged entities, including positive customer identification; specific transaction monitoring, up to the verification of the origin of the concerned value involved in specific, high-risk transactions; and (not the lesser of these obligations) conservation of the information so obtained and disclosure to FIUs and national and EU jurisdictions.[71] The obligation for virtual currency exchangers and custodian wallet providers to be registered before the Member States, set in the amended article 47.1 of the AMLD, is to be interpreted as complementary to their addition to the list of obliged entities;[72] the specific national sets of rules applicable to this register could vary widely.[73]

However, no magic regulatory wand can completely avert the risk associated with illegitimate use of virtual currencies, as already pointed out by EUROPOL.[74] This can be said, *mutatis mutandis*, by any financial product or service, but may be more true of virtual currencies due to their decentralized, privacy-oriented technical nature. As it stands, increased awareness and implication of promoters and user communities of virtual currencies could be suited to better contributing to reducing their use as criminal finance enablers – a collaboration is to be fostered in the best interests of the aforementioned legitimate stakeholders, as the broad illegitimate use of virtual currencies remains a key question for their long-term societal and economic viability.

As the obligations imposed on third parties offering virtual currency-related services involve personal data disclosure, a further order of concerns beyond efficacy pertain to the respect of data protection principles. On that matter, the opinion of the European Data Protection Supervisor (EDPS) on the reform project specifically addressed the compliance of each of the text proposals advanced by the EU bodies to that moment (Commission, Council) to the data protection principles of limitation of purpose and proportionality.[75] On that occasion, the EDPS considered contrary to the principle of limitation of purpose the notion of leaving to the Member States a broad margin of discretion in setting the requirements for the access to the data disclosed by the obliged entities.[76] These concerns are far from being allayed by the final text of the amended AMLD, now in force.[77]

Moreover, no specific provisions have been laid down by the reformed AMLD, leaving any difference as to the limits of data collection and access depending on which of the two main purposes justifying such data collection and access according to the very AMLD would cover data collection and access in each given case. In our opinion, such indistinct consideration of money laundering and terrorism financing purposes raises proportionality questions. From the point of view of the European Court of Human Rights, any State measure involving interference with the exercise of a given Human Right (such as the right to privacy) must be proportionate to the legitimate aim pursued in order to be deemed as justified according to the Convention.[78] When the legitimate aim consists of the "the prevention of disorder or crime,"[79] the gravity of the offenses to be prevented by the concerned measure gives a measure of the public interest to be weighed against the interference with the individual rights at stake. Consequently, applying the very same measure in the same conditions to offenses of different gravity may substantially contribute to the disproportion between the public and private interests at stake, possibly determining the illegitimacy of the measure.[80]

Given the substantial divergence between money laundering and terrorism financing in terms of gravity of offenses, the new AMLD should clearly differentiate the measures justified by the prevention and fighting of each one to both. The fact of the new AMLD not laying any rule directed to such differentiation raises substantial concerns from the point of view of proportionality of the measure. Now it may be worth recalling that the European Union Court of Justice (EUCJ) has already declared invalid a Directive involving the imposition onto private service providers (for the sake of crime prevention) of specific obligations of data collection and disclosure on one occasion – this judgment basing itself, *inter alia*, on the pertinent ECHR (European Court of Human Rights) jurisprudence.[81] In that, the EDPS cited this very judgment when expressing concern towards the compliance of the AMLD reform project to the principle of proportionality consecrated by the article 52.1 of the Charter of Fundamental Rights of the European Union.[82]

In the context of lacking EU legislation on virtual currencies, the inclusion of the providers of financial, virtual currency-related services in the scope of the AMLD must be saluted, in spite of its deficiencies. Needless to say, such inclusion shall contribute to the diminishing of the incertitude entailed by the lack of regulations only in a limited manner, given the very confinement of the new rules and definitions to AML issues, as well as the need for national transposition of the AMLD reform.[83]

Notwithstanding, the importance of these rules and definitions as building blocks for the consideration of virtual currencies in further EU legislation must not be spurned. In particular, such rules and definitions might be instrumental to the further construction of an in-depth set of rules on virtual currencies on occasion of the EU legislation on payment revision fostered by the EU Parliament, already mentioned. Other occurrences in the fluid everyday economic and technical practice related to virtual currencies may require a swift reaction on the EU bodies' part. For instance, Europe is no stranger to the public concern raised on a global scale[84] by reckless or fraudulent Initial Coin Offerings (ICOs): institutional attention[85] might as well be followed by a legislative reaction.

Notes

1 The research activity leading to the elaboration of this work is a result of the author's participation in the research project "*CyberLaundry*" (ref. DER2014–58257-R), financed by the *Programa Estatal de I+D+i Orientada a los Retos de la Sociedad* of the Spanish MINECO and led from the UDIMA under the successive direction of C. Mallada Fernández and D. Fernández Bermejo.

2 Putting aside the European Central Bank (ECB) reports on this matter (followed by the incipient EU regulations on cryptocurrencies), we might refer, *mutatis mutandis*, to the considerations on the juristic qualification of virtual currencies made by Paulina J. Pesch, *Cryptocoin-Schulden. Haftung und Risikoverteilung bei den Verschaffung von Bitcoins und Alt-Coins* (Munich: C.H. Beck, 2017), 71ff.

3 Tulio Rosembuj, *Bitcoin* (Barcelona: El Fisco, 2015), 69.

4 As of June 2018, the front page of the English version of the site *bitcoin.org* defined bitcoin as *a new kind of money*. The very designation adopted by the promoters of the alternative version of bitcoin created by the hard fork of the bitcoin blockchain put into place August 1, 2017, "BitcoinCash," is no less than a hyperbolic reiteration of the very idea of this cryptocurrency being "hard cash."

5 For instance, the blog of the Spanish bitcoin exchange site *bit2me*:

> Ningún gobierno ni banco central puede controlarlo o interferir en la valoración del bitcoin, ni en su creación ni en su distribución. Con Bitcoin se despolitiza el dinero, se hace de la gente, eliminando de esta forma el control que con el dinero FIAT [sic] se ejerce sobre la población.
>
> See: "*Ventajas de bitcoin*," accessed June 10, 2018, https://blog.bit2me.com/es/ventajas-bitcoin/.

6 According to the self-definition of ether given by the promoters of the Ethereum project as of June 10, 2018, "Ether is to be treated as 'crypto-fuel', a token whose purpose is to pay for computation, and is not intended to be used as or considered a currency, asset, share or anything else." Leaving out the intention of the promoters (whose sincerity we do not question), some serious doubt could be raised, however, about the practical truth of this statement when applied to the market behavior of ether (essentially and mostly used by its community as an exchange asset, both P2P and on exchange sites).

7 No State as of now has recognized the legal tender status of any virtual currency in proper sense, the case of the *petro* in the Republic of Venezuela notwithstanding. As the *petro* is a centralized virtual currency with a direct value correlation to the market price of an existing commodity (the Venezuelan petrol barrel), the Venezuelan State ideally guaranteeing its exchangeability against this asset of reference, it might be closer to a kind of e-money than it is to virtual currencies (in the commonly accepted sense of the latter). The emission of *petros*, directly controlled by the Venezuelan authorities, might also be assimilated more to a (perhaps particularly marketable) blunt emission of debt, rather than to the non-State sponsored "emission" procedures characterizing virtual currencies (stereotypically, the "free mining," but not only).

8 European Banking Authority, *EBA/Op/2014/08: EBA Opinion on virtual Currencies*, 2014, 11ff.; European Central Bank, *Virtual Currency Schemes – A Further Analysis*, 2015, p. 24; ECB Opinion of 12th October 2016 (CON/2016/49), 3ff.

9 Despite some initial inconsistency: Skatteverket vs. D. Hedqvist (2015) EUCJ Preliminary Ruling, Case C-264/14, §24: "virtual currency has no purpose other than to be a means of payment." As we will see, however, both the EU Parliament and the EU Council have followed the guidelines furnished by the ECB in this regard during the preparatory works for the Anti-Money Laundering Directive reform.

10 Dirk G. Baur, Kihoon Hong and Adrian D. Lee, *Virtual Currencies: Media of Exchange or Speculative Asset?*, SWIFT Institute Working Paper 2014-007 (SWIFT Institute, 2016), 10: "[Bitcoin] … can be defined as synthetic commodity money (Selgin, 2015) sharing features with both commodity monies such as gold and fiat monies … Bitcoin is a hybrid of commodity money and fiat money."

11 Robleh Ali, John Barrdear, Roger Clews and James Southgate. "The economics of digital currencies," *Bank of England Quarterly Bulletin* 54, no. 3 (2014): 278–79: "In theory, digital currencies could serve as money for anybody with an internet-enabled computer or device. At present, however, digital currencies fulfil the roles of money only to some extent and only for a small number of people."

12 European Central Bank, *Virtual Currency Schemes*, 2012, 13ff., 21ff.

13 From different points of view: Erik Voorhees, "What Is Bitcoin? Welcome to Cryptocurrency," *yBitcoin Magazine* 2, no. 2 (2015), 14–15; Nigel Dodd, "The Social Life of Bitcoin," *Theory, Culture & Society* 35, no. 3 (2017): 35–56; Jens Ekkenga, "Bitcoin und andere Digitalwährungen – Spielzeug für Spekulanten oder Systemveränderung durch Privatisierung der Zahlungssysteme?" *Computer und Recht* 33, no. 11 (2017): 762–68.

14 Anton Badev and Matthew Chen, *Bitcoin. Technical Background and Data Analysis* (Washington, DC: Federal Reserve Board, 2014), 5ff.; Félix Brezo Fernández and Yaiza Rubio Viñuela, *Bitcoin. La tecnología blockchain y su investigación* (Móstoles: ØxWord, 2017), 23ff. and 63ff.

15 No hundred-percent theft-proof solution exists: not even stocking private keys in a dedicated, secured "bank" online site ("hot storage") guarantees the absolute imperviousness of a given set of assets to malicious activity, as shown by well-known cases such as those of Mt. Gox (2014) or BitFinex (2016).

16 The case of Spain may serve as an example: the first decisions related to virtual currencies (anti-money laundering regulations to exchange activities and the taxation of such activities) were highly tentative

(Provincial Audience of Oviedo, Sección Cuarta, nº 37/2015, 6th February 2015; or Binding Opinion of the Dirección General de Tributos nº V1028–15, 3rd Mars 2015), while the latter decisions on the matter remain mainly confined to very specific basic taxation issues (for instance, DGT Binding Opinions nº V3625–16, 8th August 2016, or nº V-2908/17, 18th November 2017).

17 Such is the case of Austria and Germany.

18 María del Carmen Pastor Sempere, "Criptodivisas, ¿una disrupción jurídica en la eurozona?" *Revista de Estudios Europeos* 70 (2017): 284–318. The analysis is centered on the Skatteverket vs. D. Hedqvist (2015) EUCJ Preliminary Ruling, Case C-264/14.

19 Of particular note are the results achieved on this direction by Pesch, *Cryptocoin-Schulden*, 215 ff.

20 Skatteverket vs. D. Hedqvist (2015) EUCJ Preliminary Ruling, Case C-264/14.

21 Opinion of AG Kokott delivered on 16th July 2015, on the Skatteverket vs. D. Hedqvist (2015) EUCJ Preliminary Ruling, Case C-264/14, §§12 through 18 regarding the first question and §§19 through 53 regarding the second question.

22 Skatteverket vs. D. Hedqvist (2015) EUCJ Preliminary Ruling, Case C-264/14, §§22 through 31.

23 Respectively, letters (e), (d) and (f) of the art. 135(1) of European Council Directive 2006/112/CE: on the two latter see Skatteverket vs. D. Hedqvist (2015) EUCJ Preliminary Ruling, Case C-264/14, §§38 through 43 and 54 through 56.

24 Skatteverket vs. D. Hedqvist (2015) EUCJ Preliminary Ruling, Case C-264/14, §§24, 31, 52, 55 and 57.

25 Ibid, §52.

26 European Parliament, Resolution of 26 May 2016 on Virtual Currencies (2016/2007(INI)) (Brussels: European Parliament, 2016).

27 Ibid, §§1 through 4, and §§5 through 13.

28 Ibid, §1.

29 Ibid, §2.

30 In particular, calling for the creation of a Task Force on DLT and urging the Commission to develop, together with the concerned societal actors, guidelines apt to ensure that correct information is provided to virtual currency users. See: European Parliament, Resolution of 26 May 2016 on Virtual Currencies, §§22 and 23.

31 Ibid, §19.

32 Ibid, § 20. That is to say: Directive 2014/92/EU of 23rd July 2014; Directive 2007/64/EC of 13th November 2007; and Directive 2009/110/EC of 16th September 2009.

33 GAFI FATF, *Virtual Currencies. Key Definitions and Potential AML/CTF Risks* (GAFI FATF, 2014); FATF, *Report to the G20 Finance Ministers and Central Bank Governors* (FATF, 2018); UNODC, *Basic Manual on the Detection and Investigation of the Laundering of Crime Proceeds Using Virtual Currencies* (UNODC, 2014).

34 ECB Opinion of 12th October 2016 (CON/2016/49), 42–47.

35 European Banking Authority, *EBA/Op/2014/08: EBA Opinion on Virtual Currencies*, 2014, 32ff., §§117 through 133.

36 Europol, *Internet Organized Crime Threat Assessment* (Europol, 2017), 60ff.; Europol, *Internet Organized Crime Threat Assessment* (Europol, 2016), 42ff.; Europol, *Internet Organized Crime Threat Assessment* (Europol, 2015), 46 ff.

37 Europol, *Internet Organized Crime Threat Assessment* (2017), 61.

38 Ibid; Europol, *Internet Organized Crime Threat Assessment* (2016), 43.

39 European Central Bank, *Virtual Currency Schemes – A Further Analysis* (2015), 30, citing Europol's advice.

40 Sarah Meiklejohn, Marjori Pomarole, Grant Jordan et al., *A Fistful of Bitcoins: Characterizing Payments between Men with No Names* (San Diego: University of California, 2013), accessed September 6, 2018, https://cseweb.ucsd.edu/~smeiklejohn/files/imc13.pdf.

41 Europol, *Internet Organized Crime Threat Assessment* (2016), 43 ff.

42 UNODC, *Basic Manual*, 39 ff.

43 Europol, *Internet Organized Crime Threat Assessment* (2016), 43. For practical analysis IMPERVA, *The Secret behind Cryptowall's Success* (IMPERVA, 2016).

44 Europol, *Internet Organized Crime Threat Assessment* (2016), 42; Europol, *Internet Organized Crime Threat Assessment* (2017), 61.

45 Europol, *Internet Organized Crime Threat Assessment* (2017), 61ff.: "Some European law enforcement already report that even street level drug dealers are converting to crypto-currencies."

46 For a prehistory of sorts of the consideration of virtual currencies by EU law: Niels Vandezande, "Virtual Currencies Under EU Anti-Money Laundering Law," *Computer Law and Security Review* 33, no. 3 (2017): 343 ff.

47 As highlights of the reform project, and putting aside the European Parliament Resolution of 26 May 2016 on virtual currencies itself (origin of the reform process), we may point to:

- the EU Commission's Proposal of July 5, 2016 for a Directive of the European Parliament and of the Council Amending Directive (EU) 2015/849 on Prevention of the Use of the Financial System for the Purposes of Money Laundering or Terrorist Financing and Amending Directive 2009/101/EC, COM(2016) 450 final;
- the ECB Opinion of October 12, 2016 on a Proposal for a Directive of the European Parliament and of the Council Amending Directive (EU) 2015/849 on the Prevention of the Use of the Financial System for the Purposes of Money Laundering or Terrorist Financing and Amending Directive 2009/101/EC, CON/2016/49;
- the Opinion of the European Data Protection Supervisor of February 2, 2017 on a Commission Proposal Amending Directive (EU) 2015/849 and Directive 2009/101/EC;
- the EU Parliament's preliminary position of March 9, 2017 on the Commission's original proposal, presented in the Report on the Proposal for a Directive of the European Parliament and of the Council Amending Directive (EU) 2015/849 on the Prevention of the Use of the Financial System for the Purposes of Money Laundering or Terrorist Financing and Amending Directive 2009/101/EC, COM(2016) 0450, C8–0265/2016–2016/0208(COD);
- the counter-proposal of the EU Council to the EU Parliament's preliminary position of December 19, 2017, as per the Note of the EU Commission's Presidency to the Permanent Representatives Committee on the Proposal for a Directive of the European Parliament and of the Council Amending Directive (EU) 2015/849 on the Prevention of the Use of the Financial System for the Purposes of Money Laundering or Terrorist Financing and Amending Directive 2009/101/EC – Analysis of the Final Compromise Text with a View to Agreement, 15849/17;
- the definitive approval of the text by the European Parliament legislative Resolution of April 19, 2018 on the Proposal for a Directive of the European Parliament and of the Council Amending Directive (EU) 2015/849 on the Prevention of the Use of the Financial System for the Purposes of Money Laundering or Terrorist Financing and Amending Directive 2009/101/EC.

48 The very heading of the Directive (EU) 2018/843 implies the prominence of the anti-money laundering aspect, by fully quoting, out of the three Directives being modified, the whole heading of the AMLD.

49 The Directive (EU) 2018/843 thus adds the FIUs:

- to the list dressed by article 56, paragraph 1, of the Directive 2013/36/EU of the European Parliament and the Council of 26 June 2013 on Access to the Activity of Credit Institutions and the Prudential Supervision of Credit Institutions and Investment Firms, Amending Directive 2002/87/EC and Repealing Directives 2006/48/EC and 2006/49/EC, list containing the authorities excepted of the limits to information exchange established by articles 53 and 54 of the same Directive;
- to the list dressed by article 68, paragraph 1, letter b, of the Directive 2009/128/EC of the European Parliament and of the Council of 25 November 2009 on the Taking-up and Pursuit of the Business of Insurance and Reinsurance (so-called "Solvency II"), list containing the authorities excepted of the limits to information exchange established by articles 64 and 67 of the same Directive.

50 See the original EU Commission's Proposal of July 5, 2016, COM(2016) 450 final, 12 ff.

51 Directive (EU) 843/2018, recitals 16ff., with its art. 1 introducing abundant amendments to AMLD to this effect.

52 Ibid, recitals 14 f., with its art. 1 introducing amendments to art. 12 of the AMLD.

53 Ibid, recitals 12 and 13, with its art. 1 introducing amendments to arts. 6 and 9 of the AMLD and inserting the new arts. 18a and 57a into it.

54 Ibid, recitals 25ff., with its art. 1 introducing amendments to arts. 30 and 31 of the AMLD and inserting a new art. 31a to it. As per most of the preparatory works for the reforming Directive, these dispositions were conceived as amendments to the Directive 2009/101/EC, but were, in the end, directly integrated into the AMLD.

55 Art. 3.18 & 3.19 AMLD (new version, as modified by art. 1(2)(c) of Directive (EU) 843/2018).
56 Art. 2.1.3.g & 2.1.3.h AMLD (new version, as modified by art. 1(1)(c) of Directive (EU) 843/2018).
57 Art. 47.1 AMLD (new version, as modified by art. 1(29) of Directive (EU) 843/2018).
58 European Parliament, Resolution of 26 May 2016 on Virtual Currencies, §19.
59 European Parliament, Resolution of 26 May 2016 on Virtual Currencies, §2.
60 Art. 3.18 AMLD (new version, as modified by art. 1(2)(c) of Directive (EU) 843/2018).
61 EU Commission's Proposal of July 5, 2016, COM(2016) 450 final, art. 1.2.c.:

> "virtual currencies" means a digital representation of value that is neither issued by a central bank or a public authority, nor necessarily attached to a fiat currency, but is accepted by natural or legal persons as a means of payment and can be transferred, stored or traded electronically.

62 ECB Opinion of 12th October 2016 (CON/2016/49), § 1.1.3.
63 Report of the EU Parliament of March 9, 2017, on the Proposal for the Directive, COM(2016) 0450, C8–0265/2016–2016/0208(COD), 26.
64 Such elimination figured already in the definition's wording as per the EU Council's text of compromise, presented in the Note of the EU Commission's Presidency of December 19, 2017 on the proposal for the reforming Directive (15849/17), 28 (art. 1.2.c of the Directive's proposal).
65 Vandezande, "Virtual Currencies," 350.
66 Art. 3.19 AMLD (new version, as modified by art. 1(2)(c) of Directive (EU) 843/2018).
67 Directive (EU) 843/2018, recitals 8 f.
68 European Parliament, Resolution of 26 May 2016 on Virtual Currencies, § 19 (initially, only exchangers were foreseen); EU Commission's Proposal of July 5, 2016, COM(2016) 450 final, 7 (custodian wallet providers added).
69 Report of the EU Parliament of March 9, 2017 on the Proposal for the Directive, COM(2016) 0450, C8–0265/2016–2016/0208(COD), 99 (amendment 21 out of those suggested to the competent EU Parliament's Committees by the EU Parliament's Committee on Legal Affairs).
70 Art. 2.1.3.g and h of the AMLD (new version, as modified by the art. 1.1.c of the Directive (EU) 843/2018).
71 As specified by the Chapter II of the AMLD, which has been the object of substantial amendment by Directive (EU) 843/2018.
72 Art. 47.1 AMLD (new version, as modified by art. 1.29 of Directive (EU) 843/2018). Some of the project text proposals left to Member States the choice of requiring registering or licensing to the involved virtual currency stakeholders.
73 Vandezande, "Virtual Currencies," 351.
74 Europol, *Internet Organized Crime Threat Assessment* (2015), 47:

> Any regulation of cryptocurrencies would likely only be applicable and enforceable when applied to identifiable users such as those providing exchange services. The inability to attribute transactions to end users makes it difficult to imagine how any regulation could be enforced for everyday users. It is clear that cybercriminals will continue to use whichever payment mechanism is convenient, familiar or perceived to be safe, including those that are already regulated and maintain anti-money laundering controls.

75 EDPS Opinion 1/2017, 8 ff.
76 EDPS Opinion 1/2017, § 41, on the Council's position.
77 Directive (EU) 843/2018, recitals 20 and 21. The sole specific guideline for transposition provided by the recitals lies in the five-year conservation term suggested to national legislators, without discarding its possible extension by them.
78 We deliberately use the terminology adopted by the ECHR in its standing jurisprudence on the justification of State interference on the exercise of the rights consecrated by the Convention and, in particular, by its arts. 8 through 11. Concerning specifically the right to respect for private and family life, see for instance: Klass vs. Germany (1987) EUCJ Judgment 5029/71, §§42ff.; Malone vs. United Kingdom (1984) EUCJ Judgement 8691/79, §§65 through 89; Rotaru vs. Romania (2000) EUCJ Judgement 28341/95, §§47 through 63; Weber and Saravia vs. Germany (2006) EUCJ Judgement 54934/00, §§80 through 138; Uzun vs. Germany (2010) EUCJ Judgement 35623/05, §§54 through 81; M.K. vs. France (2013) EUCJ Judgment 19522/09, §§30 through 47; etc.
79 EConvHR, art. 8.2.

80 ECHR Judgment (Grand Chamber) S. and Marper vs. United Kingdom, n. 30562/04 and 30566/04, of 4th December 2008, §119.

81 EUCJ Judgment (Grand Chamber) Digital Rights Ireland et al., joined cases C-293/12 and C-594/12, of 8th April 2014, §§45, 57, 54 and 55

82 EDPS Opinion 1/2017, §§44 ff.

83 As of end August 2019, eight EU Member states had already taken national transposition measures to different degrees.

84 As an example of the cautious attitude of U.S. authorities on the matter see U.S. Security Exchanges Commission, *Investor Bulletins: Initial Coin Offerings*, 2017; as is well-known, the People's Bank of China reached the point of banning ICOs in September 2017.

85 Besides the warnings of national supervisory authorities, we might refer to the statements of ESMA, in particular the Statement ESMA50–157–829, "ESMA Alerts Investors to the High Risks of Initial Coin Offerings (ICOs)" and the Statement ESMA50–157–828, "ESMA Alerts Firms Involved in Initial Coin Offerings (ICOs) to the Need to Meet Relevant Regulatory Requirements," both of November 13, 2017.

References

Ali, Robleh, John Barrdear, Roger Clews and James Southgate. "The Economics of Digital Currencies." *Bank of England Quarterly Bulletin* 54, no. 3 (2014): 276–86.

Badev, Anton, and Matthew Chen. *Bitcoin. Technical Background and Data Analysis*. Washington, DC: Federal Reserve Board, 2014.

Baur, Dirk G., Kihoon Hong and Adrian D. Lee. *Virtual Currencies: Media of Exchange or Speculative Asset?* SWIFT Institute Working Paper 2014-007. SWIFT Institute, 2016.

Brezo Fernández, Félix, and Yaiza Rubio Viñuela. *Bitcoin. La tecnología blockchain y su investigación*. Móstoles: ØxWord, 2017.

Ekkenga, Jens. "Bitcoin und andere Digitalwährungen – Spielzeug für Spekulanten oder Systemveränderung durch Privatisierung der Zahlungssysteme?" *Computer und Recht* 33, no. 11 (2017): 762–68.

European Banking Authority. *EBA/Op/2014/08: EBA Opinion on Virtual Currencies*. EBA, 2014.

European Central Bank. Opinion of the European Central Bank of 12 October 2016 on a Proposal for a Directive of the European Parliament and of the Council Amending Directive (EU) 2015/849 on the Prevention of the Use of the Financial System for the Purposes of Money Laundering or Terrorist Financing and Amending Directive 2009/101/EC (CON/2016/49). ECB, 2016.

European Central Bank. *Virtual Currency Schemes*. ECB, 2012.

European Central Bank. *Virtual Currency Schemes – A Further Analysis*. ECB, 2015.

Europol. *Internet Organized Crime Threat Assessment*. Europol, 2017.

Europol. *Internet Organized Crime Threat Assessment*. Europol, 2016.

Europol. *Internet Organized Crime Threat Assessment*. Europol, 2015.

FATF. *Report to the G20 Finance Ministers and Central Bank Governors*. 2018.

GAFI FATF. *Virtual Currencies. Key Definitions and Potential AML/CTF Risks*. GAFI FATF, 2014.

IMPERVA. *The Secret behind Cryptowall's Success*. IMPERVA, 2016.

Meiklejohn, Sarah, Marjori Pomarole, Grant Jordan et al. *A Fistful of Bitcoins: Characterizing Payments between Men with No Names*. San Diego: University of California, 2013. Accessed September 6, 2018. https://cseweb.ucsd.edu/~smeiklejohn/files/imc13.pdf.

Pastor Sempere, María del Carmen. "Criptodivisas, ¿una disrupción jurídica en la eurozona?" *Revista de Estudios Europeos* 70 (2017): 284–318.

Pesch, Paulina J. *Cryptocoin-Schulden. Haftung und Risikoverteilung bei den Verschaffung von Bitcoins und Alt-Coins*. Munich: C.H. Beck, 2017.

Rosembuj, Tulio. *Bitcoin*. Barcelona: El Fisco, 2015.

Skatteverket vs. D. Hedqvist (2015) EUCJ Preliminary Ruling, Case C-264/14.

UNODC. *Basic Manual on the Detection and Investigation of the Laundering of Crime Proceeds Using Virtual Currencies*. UNODC, 2014.

Vandezande, Niels. "Virtual Currencies Under EU Anti-Money Laundering Law." *Computer Law and Security Review* 33, no. 3 (2017): 341–53.

Voorhees, Erik. "What Is Bitcoin? Welcome to Cryptocurrency." *Bitcoin Magazine* 2, no. 2 (2015), 14–15.

11

DYNAMICS OF ORGANIZED CRIME IN THE EUROPEAN UNION IN THE CONTEXT OF GLOBAL INSECURITY

Concepción Anguita Olmedo

Introduction

Since the end of the Cold War, the international system has undergone a transformation accompanied by a globalization process. Similarly, the concept of security has undergone significant changes, leaving behind the concept of national security based on East–West confrontation in which the main actor was the State as guarantor of independence and territorial integrity, to focus on other actors of a global or transnational nature that put at risk the current international society because their illegal actions affect the lives of citizens, prevent economic development and hinder the efforts of States to avoid their consequences.

The challenges to international security have evolved since the attacks of 2001. While terrorism and armed conflicts play an important role among the major concerns of international society, other threats such as organized crime in all its manifestations have been incorporated into the security agendas, which are mainly focused on the deterritorialization of risks and threats.

Within the framework of the United Nations Organization, the adoption of the Convention against Transnational Organized Crime (UNTOC, also known as the Palermo Convention) in the year 2000[1] represented progress in the fight against organized crime, because for the first time most of the States agreed that this was a transnational threat that should be addressed globally. This Convention vaguely established a definition of international crime, articulated around the elements and purposes of a criminal group;[2] this was a minimum agreement that allowed harmonization to advance against a phenomenon that until then had demonstrated the difficulty of adopting a common perspective to combat it. Despite the limitations and questions that can be raised about the Convention in its maturity, there is no doubt that it required the necessary awareness to address this problem with a certain degree of commitment, identifying different instruments of cooperation that, although they would not put an end to organized crime, did at least allow the initiation of common synergies in response to a global phenomenon, providing the States with instruments of formal and informal cooperation. In this sense,

> the international community took a very significant step in the global fight against transnational organized crime (TOC), because the states committed themselves, among

> other issues, to criminalize participation in an organized criminal group, money laundering, corruption and the obstruction of justice; to eliminate the safe territories for TOC in the world; to strengthen the protection of victims and witnesses; as well as to facilitate the investigation and prosecution of cross-border crimes.[3]

In addition, this treaty would suppose as explained by Ruiz Díaz:

> the conformation of transnational criminal law as an instrument to fight against transnational organized crime (TOC) in a wide variety of new aspects with regard to the previous scenario, with the entailed consequences it had and still has in the preventive, repressive and international cooperation areas, contributing to the transformation of criminal law in the last decades – in particular, regarding the establishment of the individual's criminal responsibility and the exceptional investigation procedures.[4]

During the debates for the drafting of the Convention, the European Union was more concerned that the standards of the Convention were in line with the regulations approved by the Member States regarding TOC than in actively participating in its debate.[5] The reason for this has much to do with the initial construction of the EU because it was based on economic and political considerations, given the misgivings raised by the incorporation of areas such as security that affect national sovereignty. It is in this context that the debates of the Convention are framed. Moreover, after its approval, not all the crimes contained in the Convention have been adopted by the EU, nor can it be affirmed that the Member States have transposed the European provisions adequately; there exists, even today, a lack of harmonization that makes the struggle against and repression of organized crime more difficult, in both the European and the international framework. However, with the passage of time and the advance of threats, Member States have been more and more aware of the danger posed by transnational organized crime and, therefore, since 1990, have been normatively active in this area, designing a multilevel security model in which different instruments are combined to deal with organized crime that is no longer considered a domestic threat. Therefore, and in spite of the difficulties already expressed, there is no doubt that there are important reasons for the European Union to work on underpinning the principles of the Convention, which would imply, in the first place, a strengthening of global governance in the region and the fight against organized crime; in the second, the EU remaining a global player of reference in the initiatives against TOC; and, finally, the tackling of the increasing threats jeopardizing the area of freedom, security and justice within the European Union.[6]

To these mechanisms of a juridical–political nature, we must incorporate operational capacities, especially in relation to the security forces, law enforcement authorities and intelligence. However, in this context of global insecurity and in correlation with what is happening in other regions of the world, such as Latin America, where the use of the Armed Forces has been one of the instruments in the fight against organized crime when the police have been unable to stop it, there are also voices in Europe in favor of a similar implementation, since it is considered that the actions of the police forces are not enough to put a stop to this type of activity, especially when there is an indisputable link between organized crime and terrorism.

In this sense, and although we cannot currently speak of a change in the nature, motivations and aims of both illegal actors, there is evidence that both share operational links and organizational dynamics that may converge in what Makarenko calls a "*Black Hole syndrome*," whereby the activities of organized crime acquire a political aspect and those of terrorism a commercial aspect, both exhibiting criminal and terrorist characteristics.[7] "In Europe, terrorist organisations have worked with and sometimes emulated organised crime syndicates through involvement in the trafficking of drugs, people, weapons and antiquities."[8] In addition, both illegal actors perceive the benefits derived from cooperation in the commission of criminal acts, with three elements identified as fundamental to generate dynamics of cooperation between organized crime and terrorist groups: "the current financing of terrorist groups, the dynamics of decentralization presented by both actors and, finally, the state contexts of fragility in which they can act."[9]

The security structure of the European Union

> is organized around three large interconnected areas: i) the common legal framework (...) ii) the establishment of rules regarding the exchange of information and intelligence as an element of prevention and repression of crimes committed by criminal groups; and iii) the intervention of European actors, promoters of a supranational management of risks and mutual trust between the competent national authorities.[10]

However, numerous obstacles still exist that make it difficult to share coordinated measures and effective policies that combat organized crime. We must bear in mind that in the current international system there is a need to combat organized crime outside the borders of the States, which means greater difficulties in having to involve different international bodies, prepare joint actions, provide them with resources and also work in coordination, making it very difficult to have successful outcomes. On the other hand, an optimal degree of legal or police harmonization has yet to be reached, and it is the same at a political level, where more proactive responses should be adopted instead of reactive actions.

The first movements to deal with common security problems occurred with the approval of the Maastricht Treaty in 1992, when Justice and Home Affairs (JHA) were incorporated into the competences of the European Union. As a consequence, the first initiatives against organized crime, incorporated into the European Agenda as one of the main threats, are found in the Agreement on Cooperation in Justice and Home Affairs, concluded after the 1997 Treaty of Amsterdam, in the 1997 Action plan to combat organized crime, in the 1998 Council Resolution on the prevention of organized crime and in the 1999 Vienna Action Plan. But it was not until the European Council of Tampere, held in October 1999, when it was assumed as one of the priority issues of the European Union. Under the Finnish presidency, the document "The Prevention and Control of Organized Crime: A European Union Strategy for the Beginning of the New Millennium," which modified the 1997 Action Plan and included the decisions of Tampere, was produced. Since then, The Hague Programme and its successor, the Stockholm Programme, have served to strengthen the area of freedom, security and justice, establishing the priorities for the next ten years. After the Stockholm Programme, the European Union equipped itself with other instruments such as the Policy Cycle,[11] during which a strategy against TOC is adopted and action plans are implemented in the form of projects under EMPACT (the European Multidisciplinary Platform against Criminal Threats), which we will discuss later. These projects have served to reinforce and advance the European fight against organized crime.

With these premises, the chapter that we address has as objectives to determine the nature of the current threats focused on organized crime, to establish how it affects the political, social and economic development of the States and the European Union and to verify what are the measures implemented against this threat to protect the area of freedom, security and justice, all with a mid-scale projection that allows the advancement of critical issues that must be addressed in the immediate future of the European Union.

Current dimensions of organized crime in the EU

The evolution of transnational organized crime is conditioned by the globalization process and, in this sense, economic interdependence, the dynamism of communications and the porosity of borders, as well as pockets of poverty, massive displacements or the instability of some regions, all of which are factors favoring the emergence and development of transnational criminal organizations. These organizations are capable of creating new models of illegal businesses that oblige States to adapt to these new circumstances in order to avoid the development of criminality and the conquest of governmental institutions.

Among the fundamental characteristics of current criminal organizations, we can highlight their great capacity to adapt to new technologies, the execution of increasingly complex operations, a flexible but at the same time complex structure, which makes its detection difficult, and their penetration into the international economic system. As criminal organizations adapt to the environment in which they develop, they have also undergone an evolution of criminal manifestations. Although the crime of human trafficking[12] could be considered an inheritance of the slave trade, being one of the "first crimes in acquiring considerable international dimensions, not only because of the cross-border nature of the phenomenon, but also because of the response of the national and international authorities,"[13] there are others of which the origin also goes back to ancient time but which have adapted to the new international reality – such as piracy, drug trafficking, arms trafficking, and other new ones, such as cybercrime and many other expressions of organized crime.

The exponential increase of organized crime in the European Union, which has gone from 3,600 groups operating in Europe in 2013 to more than 5,000 in 2017, with an increase of 39 percent, shows the importance of the phenomenon and the risks that it entails. On the other hand, it should be noted that "30% to 40% of the OCGs operating on an international level feature loose network structures. An approximate 20% of these networks only exist for a short period of time and are set up to support specific criminal ventures."[14] In the EU, 45 percent of OCGs (organized crime groups) are involved in more than one criminal activity, and 65 percent of OCGs are involved in the drug trade and other criminal activities such as smuggling migrants or human trafficking, Another one of their characteristics is that the "OCGs operating on an international level are typically active in more than three countries (70%). A limited number of groups is active in more than seven countries (10%)."[15]

Criminal activities in the European Union do not respond to a single typology of criminal organization; there are criminal networks formed by traditional bands, but also by small groups or independent networks and by large economic networks. These organizations work in a network and incorporate new technologies, which gives them more invisibility, an overcoming of geographical limits, allowing them greater connection between groups and, above all, greater benefits and less vulnerability. The most important manifestation of organized crime is drug trafficking, but also human trafficking, the smuggling of migrants and crimes committed on the internet.[16]

Among the fundamental characteristics of criminal organizations are the involvement in more than one criminal activity, high geographic mobility, cybercrime that affects both European citizens and public sector organizations and, of course, money laundering. It is important to highlight that one-third of the criminal organizations in the European Union involve drug trafficking, either as producers or distributors of illicit drugs. However, it is worth saying that most of the organizations are engaged in more than one criminal activity, hence they are defined as "policriminals."[17]

Organized crime groups behave like legal companies with their own commercial strategies the purpose of which is to obtain the greatest benefits at the minimum cost. To do this, they take advantage of all the human and material resources available to them, such as routes or contacts, making the most of the benefits, diversifying the catalogue of illegal activities and the client portfolio.[18] This business model not only moves on the level of illegality, but also needs a legal structure to camouflage or whitewash its benefits, establishing links with corrupt or failed state institutions and with other organizations that provide coverage. The complex business networks and the relationships between criminal organizations constitute a true crime industry, whose fundamental characteristics are the horizontality of their structures (network structures), the dynamism and operational capacity and, where control of the territory is no longer profitable, the economic and political influence. This criminal cooperation forces States to react to the narrow and weak line that separates the legal from the illegal. The corruption and infiltration capacities, both political and financial, in the State and the international system pose a risk to international security.

Although it is impossible to establish exactly the profits generated by organized crime worldwide, these are estimated at two trillion dollars, equivalent to 3.6 percent of world GDP. These figures suggest that criminal organizations are transcendental illegal actors for geopolitics and geoeconomics. Although, drug trafficking continues to be the most lucrative business, other illegal businesses – such as human trafficking, mainly for sexual exploitation, but also migrant smuggling – have shown significant growth. It seems that this trend will continue in the coming years in the international arena and within the borders of the EU. Along with these areas, we can point out others that require new technologies – such as cybercrime. Undoubtedly, the complex dynamics of organized crime go beyond the borders of the European Union.

Drug trafficking in the European Union[19]

Drug trafficking is one of the most lucrative businesses on a global scale, having become a security issue, as it not only affects the health of citizens, but also poses a threat to global governance. One of the greatest challenges for States is to dismantle organized crime groups that engage in drug trafficking and money laundering, as well as other types of crime. To this end, the producing, transit and consumer States must join forces to understand the functioning of the markets and the actions of the illegal actors, in order to make strategic decisions that favor the prevention and neutralization of this type of illicit business. Both the range of drugs and the drug markets are expanding and diversifying as never before.

The European Union has been an important region for the drug market for decades, mainly cannabis, heroin, cocaine and synthetic stimulants, a business estimated at 24,000 million euros annually. Thirty-five percent of criminal gangs operating in Europe are engaged in producing or trafficking drugs and three out of four do so with different types of narcotics.[20]

It is estimated that EU citizens spend annually between 21,000 and 31,000 million euros on illegal drugs. Of all of them, cannabis as herb (marihuana) and resin (hashish) is the most consumed in Europe; its retail market represents 38 percent, with a value of between 8,400 and 12,900 million euros and with around 22 million adult consumers. The heroin market is the second largest in the European Union. It is estimated that it has a value of around 6,800 million euros per year. These products are followed by cocaine, the most consumed illegal product in Europe, with a retail market that ranges between 4,500 and 7,000 million euros. Finally, there is the market of synthetic drugs: amphetamine, methamphetamine and MDMA, the value of which fluctuates between 1,200 and 2,500 million euros, and which is the most recent and sophisticated market.[21]

Regarding cocaine, 100 percent of it comes from Latin America, mainly from Colombia, where 68 percent of the total crops are found, but also from Peru and Bolivia. These countries dominate the chain of the drug business: production, processing, trafficking, distribution and sale, positioning the South American hemisphere on the world map of drugs.[22] The cocaine market is increasing due mainly to a greater availability of the drug and the maintenance of prices. This situation is worrisome, as the data reveal that 2.3 million young Europeans between 15 and 34 years old have tried cocaine between 2017 and 2018. In 2016, cocaine seizure exceeded 1,000 tons, with Spanish ports in the Mediterranean being the main gateway to Europe, but also Holland and Belgium, where 30 tons of drugs were seized. In terms of consumption, the United Kingdom is the third largest consumer (2.3 percent of its population consumes), followed by Spain with a 2 percent consumer population. The South America–Europe connection until recently passed by Galicia, which is a traditional route for the smuggling of tobacco and other substances. However, at present, although not exclusively, the cocaine routes reach the African continent in what is known as the Highway 10 of the drug, which follows the 10th parallel, and

> without a doubt, the lack of border control and the West African States facilitate the commercialization of narcotics (fishing and merchant vessels and airplanes execute the transfer). Mali, Gambia and Guinea Bissau appear as the favorite destinations of the South American drug traffickers.[23]

It should be noted that, although the African route is not new, there are reasons why drug trafficking groups are using this route as an alternative to traditional routes. In the first place, the institutional weakness, corruption, poverty and the many kilometers of coast without surveillance allow the drug traffickers to step onto African soil without any great obstacle and in this way avoid the pressure exerted from Spain by the action of the security forces and bodies as well as the Customs Surveillance Service along traditional routes. In the second, it allows the adoption of the "swarming attack" strategy that basically consists in

> avoiding exposing a single macro load (several tons) to government interdiction. Now such macro loads arrive at diverse points of the western coast of Africa (marine route) or to clandestine airstrips located in desert zones of the interior (aerial route), and from there they are stored ashore in diverse locations. Subsequently, from these locations they are redistributed into smaller shipments to be sent, following a constant flow, by land, sea and air, through various routes.[24]

However, cocaine is not the only drug that enters Europe through the hand of organized crime groups.

Regarding cannabis, there are different approaches within the framework of the European Union, since very restrictive approaches coexist with more tolerant ones, following the line set by some countries in Latin America or Canada, where their medicinal or recreational use has opened the door of the legal market. In the case of Europe, "the European cannabis market has evolved considerably in recent years, motivated, in part, by a shift towards domestic production."[25] The cannabis herb destined for the illegal market is produced inside the European Union mainly in closed spaces, in plantations controlled by criminal groups, although they coexist with crops from abroad. Spain is one of the main producers along with the Netherlands, Belgium and the United Kingdom, while other countries of the EU such as Slovakia or the Czech Republic cannot be ruled out as producers. The grass that comes from outside the European borders comes from Morocco, the main exporter of cannabis resin, although the pressure on this route is causing an increase in traffic along the Western Balkan route. Data on this drug reveal that 17.2 million young people across Europe have consumed it between 2017 and 2018; leading the figures are France (21.5 percent), Italy (20.7 percent) and the Czech Republic (19.4 percent), while Spain is placed in fourth place (17.15 percent).

With regard to heroin, most of the production entering the European Union comes from Afghanistan following four main routes:

> … "the Balkan route" and the "southern route". The first of these crosses Turkey and reaches the countries of the Balkans (Bulgaria, Romania or Greece) and central, southern and western Europe. There has also been a branch of this route that passes through Syria and Iraq. The southern route, through which shipments of Iran and Pakistan enter Europe by air or sea, either directly or transiting through African countries, has gained importance in recent years. Other routes are the "northern route" and a heroin route through the South Caucasus and through the Black Sea.[26]

The market for synthetic products, mainly amphetamines, interacts with that of cocaine and some new substances. "In the EU, the Netherlands and Belgium are important countries for MDMA and amphetamines production, while it seems that most of the methamphetamine is produced in the Czech Republic."[27]

As can be seen, the European Union represents a space for production, sale and consumption that is fundamental for drug markets, which has negative repercussions for its citizens and for the region's own governance, in which organized crime groups proliferate and can get huge benefits from this situation. In addition, in recent years, due to technological development, online drug markets have been generated coinciding with traditional drugs, where precursor chemicals, new psychoactive substances and even counterfeit medicines can be purchased. Criminals are hidden in the network through data anonymization and encrypted communication services, making them more difficult to trace. The European Union must act to prevent the problems associated with drug trafficking from affecting not only the quality of life of European citizens, but also the institutionalization and the governance of the region.

Trafficking in human beings and smuggling of migrants in the European Union

Human trafficking and smuggling, although of a different nature, are phenomena that imply a violation of human rights and are among the most serious crimes that originate in today's international society.

> Both phenomena involve the movement of human beings to obtain some benefit. However, in the case of trafficking there must be two additional elements compared to smuggling: it must be a form of undue capture and the activity must be carried out with some purpose of exploitation, even though it would not be finally fulfilled.[28]

In the phenomenon of trafficking there is an exploitation of the victims, either through labor or sexually, or through other types of exploitation, such as organ trade or other forms of abuse. In the smuggling of persons, on the other hand, the migrant pays for a service and the relationship almost never persists after reaching the destination. There are fundamental differences that must be taken into account in order to identify both crimes: the consent that occurs in the migrant trade, but not in the trafficking of human beings, which is always done by scam or coercion; the exploitation, which occurs in the case of trafficking, but not in smuggling, although it may happen once the relationship between migrants and criminals is established; and transnationality, which always occurs in smuggling, but not necessarily in trafficking, since the movements can be intra-state.

Although the phenomena of human trafficking and smuggling are not the same crime, they do share their main characteristics: both are illegal businesses that provide important benefits and are expanding. The vulnerabilities offered by the international system, such as socioeconomic instability, demographic pressure, political crises, armed conflicts, poverty, inequality, natural and humanitarian disasters, etc., are factors that favor these manifestations of organized crime. It should be noted that the current irregular migration has a mixed character, because "it consists of flows of people who are in movement for different reasons but who share the same routes, modes of transport and boats."[29] In this sense, the European Union is a human trafficking destination, mainly of women and girls who are sexually exploited, but also a destination for the smuggling of migrants who seek to reach the external borders of the European Union, and end up being subjected to criminal organizations in the face of the difficulties they encounter to reach European soil.

Trafficking

The European Union is not immune to human trafficking, a phenomenon that is expressly prohibited in Article 5 of the EU Charter of Fundamental Rights and which has as its frame of reference the Directive 2011/36/EU[30] of the European Parliament and the Council against trafficking in human beings and the EU Strategy towards the Eradication of Trafficking in Human Beings (2012–2016). The phenomenon of human trafficking is constantly evolving and expanding because of the benefits it provides and the few risks involved, especially in criminal matters. In the 2015–2016 period, 5,979 prosecutions were notified for crimes related to trafficking and 2,927 convictions were attained,[31] a number that is still insufficient if we take into account the volume of business and the organized crime groups involved. Despite the efforts, the crime of trafficking is still very profitable. In trafficking there is an interaction conditioned by supply and demand among the perpetrators, the exploiters, the beneficiaries and the users,[32] all of whom are necessary for the crime to occur. The demand is, without a doubt, one of the fundamental factors, because in the sex industry, there is no trafficking in human beings to satisfy the demand of the traffickers, but rather that of the buyers, who define the characteristics of this business.

The International Labour Organization estimates that there are more than 21 million people exploited throughout the world, so the European Union is not immune to this phenomenon. In the 2015–2016 period, 20,532 victims of human trafficking were registered in the EU, of which registrations 65 percent were for sexual exploitation, 15 percent for labor exploitation and the remaining 20 percent for other purposes such as organ harvesting and forced begging.[33] The complexity of the phenomenon prevents establishing the exact number of victims, but it is estimated that for each identified victim, there are more than 20 unidentified victims.[34] Another of the fundamental characteristics of trafficking is the number of women exploited, which makes this phenomenon a gender issue. Of the victims of trafficking registered in the EU, 77 percent were women and 23 percent were minors. One of the consequences of the migrant crisis in 2015 has been the increase in victims of trafficking for sexual exploitation on the central Mediterranean route, especially women from sub-Saharan Africa.

> According to UNODC, 67% of the 12,775 victims detected in Western and Southern Europe between 2012 and 2014, whose form of exploitation was reported, were trafficked for this purpose. Likewise, in Central and South Eastern Europe, more than two thirds of the 6,870 victims detected were subjected to sexual exploitation.[35]

These figures give an account of the risks involved in reaching European borders, especially for the most vulnerable migrants.

The lack of harmonization in the European Union regarding the practice of prostitution is a stumbling block for the detection of trafficking, since, according to Europol (2016), the traffickers transfer their victims to those countries where prostitution is legal, being able to camouflage in legal businesses the adult and minor women who are victims of human trafficking.[36] Among the patterns of trafficking in the EU, we should point out the increase in internal trafficking and exploited children, but also the increase in pregnant women for the purpose of selling her baby once born, or trafficking in order to sell human organs or tissues.[37] Trafficking in human beings and migrant smuggling must be addressed in the context of migration, as criminal groups, in a constant mutation to adapt to the circumstances, explore the possibilities they have of drawing in their victims through asylum procedures. Organized crime groups are characterized by dominating the entire trafficking process, from the capture in the countries of origin, the transfer with the control of the routes through the countries of transit and the exploitation in the countries of destination. Between 2012 and 2014, more than 500 types of trafficking flows were detected, within the same country, between neighboring countries and even between different continents,[38] which accounts for the difficulties in the detection and eradication of this phenomenon.

Migrant smuggling

The migratory movements are not a new phenomenon nor specific to the current international society. Throughout history there have been massive movements and these have been exacerbated by the Industrial Revolution of the nineteenth century. Although economic reasons derived from lack of development or the inequality between regions could be indicated as the main cause of the displacements, there can also be political or ideological reasons for them, persecutions based on race, religion or gender and warlike causes, or ecological reasons such as natural catastrophes.

During the last years of the twentieth century and the first years of the current century, international migrations have increased at a significant rate, with the number of international migrants rising to 244 million people in 2015,[39] of whom, according to 2017 figures, 25.4 million are refugees.[40] In these figures, organized crime groups perceive a significant volume of business.

> There is evidence that, at a minimum, 2.5 million migrants were smuggled for an economic return of US$5.5–7 billion in 2016. This is equivalent to what the United States of America (some US$7 billion) or the European Union countries (some US$6 billion) spent on humanitarian aid globally in 2016. This is a minimum figure as it represents only the known portion of this crime.[41]

In this sense, the European Union is one of the main destination regions, taking into account that economic prosperity and political stability are the reasons that cause a "pull effect." Along with this, it is important to note the role played by the previous diaspora communities already living in some cities of the EU, which act as attractive elements.[42] The difficult situation experienced by some neighboring countries of the European Union after the Arab uprisings along with the war in Syria have caused the massive arrival of migrants to the European external borders, causing one of the biggest crises suffered since its creation. The arrivals of these migrants amounted to one million people between 2015 and 2016, a figure to which the community partners have responded with security migration policies, rather than with policies of support and assistance to the migrant, and to this end the EU Action Plan 2015–2020 was implemented.

Although these policies led to a decline of migrants by 60 percent in 2017, organized crime has not declined, since smuggling of migrants follows the same dynamics of other transnational organized markets.

The closing of the external land borders (mainly the eastern border), the impossibility of obtaining regular travel documents and the difficulty of reaching southern Europe in the face of controls in the Mediterranean provide more opportunities to profit for smugglers. Consequently, well-organized and more sophisticated hierarchical crime networks with transnational links are proliferating, taking advantage of the vulnerability of migrants and moving them along increasingly dangerous routes. It is worth highlighting the increase in the number of women who are transferred by the central Mediterranean route and who end up being sexually exploited, to which reference has already been made. These illegal groups are flexible and resilient, adapting to law enforcement actions by quickly changing the routes. More than ever before, law enforcement authorities have to rely on situational awareness and the criminal intelligence that can be maintained only through effective intelligence sharing.[43]

Although it is difficult to establish the exact number of migrants smuggled in the EU, the number of detections that were made at the eastern land borders in 2016 amounted to 1,350, which indicates that this flow is lower than that which is made by sea, although it is possible to think that these figures only represent a small part of the real number of migrants smuggled across the borders of the EU.[44] Similarly, in the Western Balkans that same year 10,000 people were detected crossing the European border illegally, of whom the exact number of who used organized crime groups is unknown. However, although it is not possible to know with precision the exact profits generated by migrant smuggling, the three main routes of the Mediterranean, eastern, central and western, may represent benefits of between 320 and 550 million dollars per year.[45]

In October 2018, European leaders committed themselves to intensifying efforts to fight migrant smuggling networks, since 90 percent of migrants seeking to reach European borders use these networks.[46] The proposal for this in the short and medium term is to act on several vectors: first, to reinforce Frontex and increase the returns of irregular migrants; second, to create a joint working group at Europol's European Migrant Smuggling Centre, which should work to prevent criminal networks from continuing to smuggle migrants to the EU; and third, to reinforce cooperation with countries of origin and transit, especially in Africa, and strengthen bilateral agreements with other countries, as was done with Turkey. In addition, fighting against migrant networks is one of EMPACT's priorities, under the 2018–2021 EU Policy Cycle.

The services offered by criminal groups vary depending on the routes and countries of origin of the migrants. For the eastern Mediterranean route, a package with guaranteed delivery is offered, which includes several attempts in case the migrant does not reach the European borders. Likewise, transfer fees may vary according to nationality or sex. In this sense, migrants who come from Syria have to pay a higher rate than other migrants who use the same route, because of the high demand for services by Syrian nationals.[47]

This eastern route is made up of more sophisticated and very professional criminal groups, which distinguishes it from other routes. In this framework of ideas, migrant smugglers are not necessarily part of a large hierarchical structure, but belong to differentiated groups that establish commercial relationships and regular contacts to facilitate the illegal crossing of borders. Between 2015 and 2016, the EU increased the resources available to combat this crime, and more than 2,000 traffickers and smugglers were arrested and 375 vessels withdrawn.[48] These are important but insufficient figures.

The European Commission adopted in June 2016 the Migration Partnership Framework (MPF)[49] which had short-term objectives to strengthen the links with external partners, end the networks of traffickers, rescue migrants at sea and facilitate the return of irregular migrants. In the longer term, it was proposed to address the root causes that in the countries of origin imply an expulsion effect and constitute push factors for migrants. However, security policies have prevailed over migrant protection, which should not be a model for the rest of the international community to follow.

The current state of affairs requires cooperative mechanisms to put an end to organized crime networks and the insecurity of migrants, not only European ones, but also international ones. In this context, the Global Compact for Safe, Orderly and Regular Migration, the mandate for which is found in the New York Declaration for Refugees and Migrants of September 2016,[50] and which reflected the intention of the States to prepare global agreements on migration and refugees before the end of 2018, was approved in Marrakech under the auspices of the United Nations General Assembly in December 2018.

Although work is still underway on refugees, the Global Compact for Migration, which is non-binding in its intergovernmental nature, implies a first step to generate a global framework for the protection of human rights for migrants "that can build, frame and ensure cooperation between countries and more adequately protect people from transnational risks to their human security and the human rights violations they so often face."[51] As can be observed, the manifestations of organized crime are not specific to a State or a region, and therefore measures must be implemented to combat it at a transnational level.

Cybercrime in the European Union

Organized crime represents a challenge to the current international society, due to the volume of business it moves and the damage it generates with the violation of human rights. One of its most recent manifestations, which is related to the globalization process and to information technologies is cybercrime, understood as the criminal behavior that is practiced while taking advantage of network use, which represents a global, transboundary and unprecedented threat and presents a new challenge for the security forces of the States. The Center for Strategic and International Studies (CSIS) suggested that "the combination of high value, low risk, and low 'work factor' (the amount of effort it takes to break into a network) makes cybercrime a winning proposition."[52] In this sense, citizens, companies and States are affected by new types of crimes and infractions that endanger security. One of the factors that favors these crimes is the high degree of connectivity of the current international society. The high number of connected devices and sensors as part of the Internet of Things creates new opportunities for cybercriminals. Criminal groups, although also the terrorists,

> are exploiting the functionalities of social media along all parts of their enterprise chains, from the identification of allies and victims, to the execution of operational capacities such as logistics and fundraising, the procurement of services, and the development of their technical capacity.[53]

In this respect, it is estimated that there were nearly 4 billion internet users in 2018 (nearly half of the world's population of 7.7 billion), up from 2 billion in 2015. The figures show the importance of internet use and, as a consequence, the considerable legal and illegal business volume that may be involved, since other figures estimate that in 2022 there will be 6 billion internet users (75 percent of the projected world population of 8 billion), and more than 7.5 billion internet user in 2030.[54]

Cybercrime is a low risk crime that provides high payoffs. A smart cybercriminal can make hundreds of thousands, even millions of dollars with almost no chance of arrest or jail. In terms of monetary value, in 2014, the global cost of cybercrime was estimated to be $445 billion per year[55] or about 0.7 percent of global income. But,

> the current estimate is that cybercrime may now cost the world almost $600 billion, or 0.8% of global GDP. The reasons for this growth are as follows: Quick adoption of new technologies by cybercriminals; the increased number of new users online (these tend to be from low-income countries with weak cybersecurity); the increased ease of committing cybercrime, with the growth of Cybercrime-as-a-Service; an expanding number of cybercrime "centers" that now include Brazil, India, North Korea, and Vietnam and a growing financial sophistication among top-tier cybercriminals that, among other things, makes monetization easier.[56]

The internet has revolutionized the *modus operandi* of the criminal groups that can commit crimes without moving out of the office. In this sense, every user is susceptible to digital crime. As noted by Samani, there are different types of illegal network products that can be classified into four categories:

> 1 Research-as-a-Service. Unlike other categories, buying in research does not have to originate from illegal sources; there is room for a gray market (...).
> 2 Crimeware-as-a-Service. Once criminals have identified their target, in many cases they will attempt to install malicious software on the victim's computer. (...) This category also includes the availability of hardware that may be used for financial fraud (e.g., card skimming) or equipment used to hack into physical platforms.
> 3 Cybercrime Infrastructure-as-a-Service. Once the toolset has been developed, cybercriminals are faced with the challenge of delivering their exploits to their intended victims. An example is rental of a network of computers to carry out a denial-of-service (DoS) attack.
> 4 Hacking-as-a-Service. Acquiring the individual components of an attack remains an option; alternatively, there are services that allow for outsourcing of the attack entirely. This path requires minimal technical expertise, although it is likely to cost more than acquiring individual components.[57]

These are some of the categories but there are many more that will not nearly fit within these descriptions, the reason being that the environment is fluid and new products and services emerge on a constant basis.

Criminal activity on the internet is much broader than cybercrime as essentially all elements of human criminal activity have moved into cyberspace. For example, half of all reported crime in the UK is cyber-related, and only 13 percent of cybercrimes are reported. Government figures "indicate that almost half of all UK businesses suffered a cyberattack or data breach in 2016, with the costs ranging from an average of $26,700 up to a maximum of millions of dollars in the most damaging instances."[58] In Germany,

> more than half of all German companies have been the victims of cybercrime, causing damages of more than $64 billion per year. These costs are rapidly increasing, with the total number of cybercrime instances reported to German law enforcement almost doubling between 2015 and 2016 to a total of 82,000.[59]

In Spain, computer crimes are on the rise. In 2017, 22.1 percent more were registered than in the previous year, with a total of 62,419 registered victimizations, which is 14.65 percent more than in the previous year, corresponding to crimes of computer fraud, threats and coercion, and illegal interception. Regarding the victims, computer fraud is the highest incidence of crime and the age range is between 24 and 40 years. "However, if we analyze the global distribution of known incidents by scope and sex, women exceed male victims in percentage when it comes to incidents related to unlawful access and interception, against honor, sexual crimes and computer falsification."[60]

The increase and the importance of the crimes and, above all, the difficulties in attribution of the crimes committed on the internet force the European Union to equip itself with instruments and organisms that contribute to the prevention and detection of aggressions committed mainly by organized criminal groups, such as malware crimes, hacking, phishing, theft or identity theft, fraud, online sexual exploitation and any other that occurs in the network, including cyberterrorism or crimes such as sexual abuse, sexual exploitation of minors and child pornography. It is to be noted that in Europe and Central Asia the cost of cybercrime is between 160 and 180 billion dollars, with losses of 0.79 percent to 0.89 percent of GDP in both regions.[61] The data for 2017 indicate that the European countries with the highest percentage of cyberattacks are Malta (42 percent), Greece (41 percent), Romania (41 percent), Slovakia (40 percent), Spain (40 percent) and Lithuania (39 percent).[62]

Data theft is one of the most widespread crimes in the network. Eighty percent of European companies have suffered at least one cybersecurity incident, with cyberattacks multiplying in recent years. In 2016 alone, there were more than 4,000 attacks per day with file hijacking programs. But crimes do not only affect companies or public administrations, they can also target the fundamental infrastructures of a State with the aim of destabilizing it, and can operate against the freedoms and rights of citizens as well. As many as 85 percent of internet users feel at risk of becoming a victim of cybercrime.[63]

One of the crimes that occur in the network and cause great concern in society is the exploitation of minors on the internet. Europol has identified key threats in the area of child sexual exploitation:

> Peer-to-peer (P2P) networks and anonymised access like Darknet networks (e.g. Tor). These computer environments remain the main platform to access child abuse material and the principal means for non-commercial distribution. These are invariably attractive for offenders and easy to use. The greater level of anonymity and the strong networking possibilities offered by hidden internet that exists beneath the "surface web" appear to make criminals more comfortable in offending and discussing their sexual interests.
>
> Live-streaming of child sexual abuse. Facilitated by new technology, one trend concerns the profit-driven abuse of children overseas, live in front of a camera at the request of westerners."[64]

The ease of using technology, especially for minors and young people, but also the possibility of anonymization and encryption tools to conceal offenders facilitates the increased number of cases of online sexual coercion and extortion of minors, because it is easier to avoid law enforcement detection. In this sense, 60 percent of Members States report an increase in the online distribution of Child Sexual Exploitation Material (CSEM).

Online child sexual exploitation is not an organized crime phenomenon in the traditional sense of the world.

> Offenders are often lone actors and there is little or no involvement of traditional OCGs. However, offenders do organize themselves. They congregate on online

> forums, where they not only distribute and share CSEM, but also discuss techniques and teach each other how to avoid law enforcement detection.[65]

With the intention of avoiding being discovered, the criminals have modified their *modus operandi*. Although previously they were using a great variety of sites and forums, now a decrease of these can be observed, as they are making best use of the technologies, managing multiple platforms and moving towards the formation of smaller groups of criminals exchanging CSEM and information in mobile messaging applications with end-to-end encryption.

Technological advances favor criminals as an increase in the crimes committed in the network can be observed. Therefore, it is necessary that EU partners along with third partners work together to prevent and reduce risks.

The European Union against organized crime: the security architecture

The security of the European Union cannot be understood outside the scope of international security. Working cooperatively and jointly is essential to face the threats of organized crime in all its manifestations, bearing in mind that this is one of the challenges that the EU must face today and in the coming years. In this logic, the European Union has equipped itself with instruments, means and institutions to respond to this threat, being essential to establish strategic objectives and coordinated operational actions. In the area of freedom, security and justice, cooperation is the formula that guarantees an important degree of security. In the fight against organized crime, police cooperation (based on the principle of availability) and judicial cooperation, among others, are fundamental. In 2010, the European Union adopted the Policy Cycle to tackle organized crime, which came to give continuity to the Stockholm Programme (2010–2014) that was a successor to the Tampere and The Hague Programmes.[66] Each cycle, with a duration of four years, translates strategic objectives at the European level into concrete operational actions against serious and organized crime and it sustains its decisions in criminal intelligence, which constitutes a fundamental tool to determine which threats have to be counteracted and what means are the most appropriate.[67] According to Ruiz Díaz, "the main advantage of this model is the construction of a common perception of the threats and the coordination of the different actors at the different levels and phases of evaluation, prevention and repression."[68]

This instrument for the processing and exchange of information is the responsibility of the European Police Office, Europol, which has been converted into an EU Agency in the Treaty of Lisbon, compared to other entities operating under Title VI of the TEU (Treaty on European Union), such as EuroJust or Cepol.[69] Europol is responsible for assessing the threat posed by international crime and other serious forms of crime, and presenting it in different reports. First, it has responsibility for the SOCTA (Serious and Organized Crime Threat Assessment), which is

> the most comprehensive study of serious and organized crime in the EU ever undertaken. It is the outcome of a detailed analysis of the threat of serious and organized crime facing the EU providing information for practitioners, decision-makers and the wider public. As a threat assessment, the SOCTA (Serious and Organized Crime Threat Assessment) is a forward-looking document that assesses shifts in the serious and organized crime landscape.[70]

Second, Europol produces the IOCTA (Internet Organized Crime Threat Assessment); and lastly, it issues the early warning notifications of new organized crime threats (from Europol's Scanning, Analysis and Notification (SCAN) team).

On March 27, 2017, the Council decided to continue the EU Policy Cycle for organized and serious international crime for the period 2018–2021. Subsequently, at its meeting of May 18, 2017, the EU Council catalogued the priorities in the fight against organized crime during this period: cybercrime, drug trafficking, facilitation of illegal immigration, trafficking in human beings, organized property crime, criminal finances and money laundering, among others. Once the threats have been defined, Europol develops multi-annual strategic plans (MAPs) to combat them and subsequently defines actions or initiatives that must be developed in projects known under the name EMPACT, which are operational action plans (OAPs) against crime that are established and coordinated by all the Member States. Without a doubt, the Political Cycles require an important collaboration not only of the law enforcement agencies, but also of the other EU agencies, EU institutions and other relevant third parties. In this line of action, agreements have been established with other States or regions. As has been observed, the main threats are related to drug trafficking and especially to the Latin American region, where production, trafficking and consumption is the main business of organized crime groups, a phenomenon that poses an obstacle to the development of this region. For this reason, the European Union, through different programs and agreements, promotes cross-border cooperation. In this sense, it is worth mentioning El PacCTO, the Europe Latin America Assistance Programme Against Organized Transnational Crime, an initiative that was launched in 2017, lasting 60 months. Its objective is to strengthen the fight against crime in this region, and 18 States have joined up. The program is financed by the European Commission, with a total budget of 19 million euros, and implemented by the FIIAPP (International and Ibero-American Foundation for Administration and Public Policies) and Expertise France with the collaboration of the Italo-Latin American Institute (IILA) and the Camoes Institute of Portugal. This program is divided into three fundamental pillars – cooperation between the police and the law enforcement forces, judicial cooperation and the penitentiary system[71] – and it works in five transversal axes: corruption, money laundering, gender, cybercrime and human rights.[72]

Another of the regional programs launched by the European Union in Latin America is the ICRIME project, which aims to improve cooperation in criminal investigation and the prosecution of organized crime cases and drug trafficking, supporting the Member States of the Central American Integration (SICA).[73] The EU will provide financing of 20 million euros, while Spain and the General Secretariat of SICA will contribute one million euros and 500 thousand euros respectively. This program will strengthen the exchange of information, the mutual recognition of forensic evidence and the coordination of operations in the field, for which the police forces, forensic institutes, prosecutors and magistrates will have to coordinate transnationally.[74]

Regarding the exchange of strategic information on organized crime between Latin America and the EU, it is essential to mention AMERIPOL (The American Police Community), which is a hemispheric cooperation mechanism the purpose of which is to promote police cooperation in training, doctrine and exchange of information to neutralize criminality. Thirty-three police bodies and 26 observer organizations belong to this Community, which dates back to 2007. In the line of cooperation initiated with El PacCTO, AMERIPOL occupies a prominent role, since the transnationality of crime requires the strengthening of police services to "optimize the operational capabilities of the institutions in their fight against international criminal groups engaged in trafficking of human beings, drugs, weapons or cultural property, among others."[75]

Another phenomenon that the European Union has experienced in recent years has been the massive arrival of migrants who fled their countries for different reasons and who have ended up subject to organized crime groups. In this regard, the European Union has adopted some measures that, although they have served to mitigate the number of irregular migrants arriving at the external borders of the European Union, have not been able to resolve the issue. Consequently, the European Union must address in the short and medium term the structural causes that originate the migratory movements mainly in the neighboring regions. Although the EU works with five key countries of origin and transit in Africa (Ethiopia, Mali, Niger, Nigeria and Senegal), satisfactory results cannot yet be said to have been achieved, as it has been observed that organized crime groups continue to act with impunity. In view of this phenomenon, the EU has responded with the European Agenda on Migration and the European Agency for the Border and Coast Guard that will come to turn Frontex[76] into a fully operational European system of coastal and border guards, with an emphasis on more security and redefining migration policy and border management towards a security aspect.

Regarding the European Agenda on Migration, proposed by the Commission in 2015, its objective is to act on three axes. The first axis, outside the EU, is assisting and resettling the refugees, besides addressing the structural causes that cause irregular migration by signing agreements with third countries, essentially of origin and transit. In this regard, it is worth mentioning the EU–Turkey Agreement, the purpose of which is to discourage irregular migration flows while breaking the business model of organized crime groups.[77] The second axis, at the borders of the EU, involves acting, first of all, at sea, not only to save lives, but also to put an end to organized crime networks that take advantage of the vulnerability of migrants; and second, by better managing the borders, identifying those who reach European soil to establish the relevance of the asylum procedure or the return and readmission procedure. The third and last axis is inside the EU. The objective here is to relocate the refugees and simplify and harmonize the asylum system.[78] These axes are fundamental to address the current crisis but they are not enough to face the migration challenges in the coming years, taking into account the needs of migrants and the benefits obtained by organized crime groups with this business. The reinforcement of borders is a joint responsibility. The European Agency for the Border and Coast Guard has assessed the vulnerable points at the EU's external borders. The Member States must act to avoid situations of risk, both for the organization itself and for migrants who, in desperate actions, end up in the hands of criminal groups. Given the current limitations of Frontex, this new reinforced and strengthened Agency could address new challenges and political realities such as the migrant crisis or threats to internal security by terrorist or organized crime groups.

Regarding the fight against cybercrime, the European Union launched in 2013 the European Cybercrime Centre (EC3), based in The Hague, which provides the EU with a public body against cybercrime. However, prior to its creation, the EU had already begun to build a framework of prevention and combat, establishing the European Network and Information Security Agency[79] and the Community Program for the promotion of safer use of the internet and new technologies.[80] Also in 2013, it published the *Cybersecurity Strategy of the European Union: an Open, Safe and Secure Cyberspace*, reinforced in September 2017 with a Strategic Cybersecurity Plan, consisting of a package of measures presented to Parliament and the Council with the aim of strengthening cybersecurity. It has also adopted a European Security Agenda (2015) in order to make a common front against cybercrime, but also against terrorism and organized crime. The European Union is working to provide itself with initiatives and instruments to advance cybersecurity. In this line, it has created the European Union Agency for Network and Information Society (ENISA), the Single Digital Market Strategy and the Bratislava Roadmap.[81]

More recently, in 2016, the Directive (EU) 2016/1148, known as the NIS (Network and Information Security) Directive,[82] was adopted with the aim of strengthening the security of the European Union's networks and information systems, since current capacities are not sufficient to guarantee the level of security of networks and information systems. On December 19, 2018, a Cybersecurity Act was provisionally approved, which is a piece of legislation that will establish a cybersecurity certification framework for the entire European area and will also lead to the consolidation of an EU Cybersecurity Agency with a permanent mandate. The Strategic Cybersecurity Plan, adopted in 2017, aims to strengthen EU capacities at three levels: the building of resilience, the reinforcement of response capacities and the definition of new penal instruments.[83]

Conclusions

Organized crime is a threat to international security and to the European Union. This phenomenon surpasses all security dimensions. For this reason, it is necessary to be equipped with mechanisms and instruments for its prevention and combat.

However, the current instruments do not prevent the perpetration of illegal actions such as drug trafficking, migrant smuggling, human trafficking or cybercrime. Through all of them, organized crime obtains immense benefits and almost always at a low criminal cost. The law of supply and demand governs the markets, which favors the proliferation of groups of dissimilar characteristics but that establish connections because of the possibilities for obtaining money with little risk. Together with the legal–political mechanisms provided by States and organizations, operational capabilities must be incorporated, especially by the security forces and intelligence corps. All this forms a necessary security architecture but is still insufficient to face the challenges to international security with guarantees of success. To end organized crime, which takes advantage of the globalization process and creates illegal business models that are difficult to detect, international cooperation is important.

Drug use has grown substantially in the European Union, which is the destination and passage of the main routes. Spain has become the gateway for cocaine that comes from Latin America and cannabis that comes from Africa. As has been observed, Europe is not only a transit and consumption region, but in the last few years it has also become a producer, especially of the cannabis herb which aims to satisfy both the illegal and the recreational use markets. This new situation undoubtedly has repercussions at the individual, national and community levels. It is proven that wherever there is drug production or trafficking, its consumption increases, an illicit market is generated and governance is impaired. One of the fundamental actions that could be decisive in the fight against organized crime groups is undoubtedly the pursuit of money laundering. The European Union must work more intensively in the tracing, seizure, freezing and confiscation of all illegally obtained benefits. It must be equipped with adequate instruments and mechanisms. In this sense, the EU has begun to take the steps to face the threats with a more modern and effective security structure. It has been strengthened in terms of border control and maritime surveillance to prevent crime networks from trafficking with migrants. It has reinforced the systems of analysis and information exchange to fight against drug traffickers and prevent the drug from reaching European soil. It has set up centers against cybercrime and taken measures that, although they will not stop criminal activities, will at least hinder it.

The fact that transnational organized crime is a strategic threat to security is an unquestionable reality; therefore, it is necessary that both the international community and the European Union equip themselves with all the necessary instruments to face effectively and efficiently the challenge that transnational organized crime represents, in the short and medium term, prioritizing responses not only within the EU but also on a global scale.

Notes

1 The Convention entered into force in September 2003 and included 179 States Parties.
2 The Palermo Convention defines an organized criminal group as

a structured group of three or more persons, existing for a period of time and acting in concert with the aim of committing one or more serious crimes or offenses established in accordance with this Convention, in order to obtain, directly or indirectly, a financial or other material benefit.

See United Nations Organization, *United Nations Convention against Transnational Organized Crime and the Protocols Thereto* (Palermo: United Nations Office on Drugs and Crime, 2000).

3 Juan Pablo Soriano, "Gobernanza global contra la delincuencia transnacional: la UE y la Convención de Palermo," *CIDOB d'Afers Internacionals* 108 (2014): 141–63.

4 Lucas J. Ruiz Díaz, *La lucha contra el crimen organizado en la Unión Europea. Aspectos internos y dinámicas externas del discurso securitario* (Granada: Universidad de Granada, 2015), 84.

5 In March 1999, the European Council approved the development of a Common Position (1999/235/JHA) in the negotiations on the Convention to avoid its incompatibility with existing instruments of the European Union, as well as ensuring that the Convention is consistent with the measures of the Council of Europe and the Financial Action Task Force on money laundering. Soriano, "Gobernanza global contra la delincuencia transnacional."

6 Ibid.

7 Tamara Makarenko, "The Crime-Terror Continuum: Tracing the Interplay between Transnational Organised Crime and Terrorism," *Global Crime* 6, no. 1 (2004): 129–45.

8 Cameron Sumpter and Joseph Franco, "Migration, Transnational Crime and Terrorism: Exploring the Nexus in Europe and Southeast Asia," *Perspectives on Terrorism* 12, no. 5 (2018): 36–50.

9 Inmaculada Marrero Rocha, "Nuevas dinámicas en las relaciones entre crimen organizado y grupos terroristas," *Revista Española de Derecho Internacional* 69, no. 2 (2017): 145–69.

10 Ruiz Díaz, *La lucha contra el crimen organizado en la Unión Europea.*

11 "The action cycle of the European Union (EU) is a method adopted in 2010 by the European Union to deal with the most important threats that crime poses to the EU. Each cycle lasts four years and optimizes coordination and cooperation on established priorities. To determine which threats are to be addressed, criminal intelligence is used and then a political agreement is reached." Council of the European Union, *The EU Policy Cycle to Tackle Organised and Serious International Crime* (Brussels: The Publications Office, 2014), accessed December 28, 2018. www.consilium.europa.eu/media/30232/qc0114638enn.pdf. On March 27, 2017, the Council decided to continue the EU Policy Cycle for organised and serious international crime for the period 2018–2021.

12 Concepción Anguita Olmedo, "El tráfico ilegal de seres humanos para la explotación sexual y laboral: La esclavitud del siglo XXI," *Nómadas: Revista de Ciencias Sociales* 15 (2007): 3–16.

13 Ruiz Díaz, *La lucha contra el crimen organizado en la Unión Europea.*

14 Europol. *Serious and Organised Crime Threat Assessment. Crime in the Age of Technology* (The Hague: Europol, 2017).

15 Ibid.

16 Ibid.

17 Carolina Sampó, "Porque no todo es terrorismo: Notas sobre la actividad del Crimen Organizado en España," *Relaciones Internacionales* 51 (2016): 1–14.

18 Phil Williams, "Organizing Transnational Crime: Networks, Markets and Hierarchies," in *Combating Transnational Crime: Concepts, Activities and Responses*, ed. Phil Williams and Dimitri Vlassis (London: Frank Cass Publishers, 2001), 61–98.

19 In this section, reference will only be made to drug trafficking as a manifestation of organized crime, since in the book there is a chapter on drugs in the European Union.

20 Europol. *Serious and Organised Crime Threat Assessment.*

21 European Monitoring Centre for Drugs and Drug Addiction and Europol, *EU Drug Markets Report: Strategic Overview* (Luxembourg: The Publications Office, 2016).

22 Mariano Bartolomé, "Las drogas ilegales, elemento central del crimen organizado en América Latina," in *El Crimen Organizado en América Latina: Manifestaciones, Facilitadores y Reacciones*, ed. Carolina Sampó and Valeska Troncoso (Madrid: Instituto Universitario General Gutiérrez Mellado, 2017), 89–122.

23 Sampó, "Porque no todo es terrorismo."

24 Daniel Sansó-Rubert Pascual, *¿Por qué África: desentrañando la geopolítica criminal del tráfico ilícito de cocaína entre América Latina y Europa (vía España)*, Documento de Trabajo 7/2018 (Madrid: Real Instituto Elcano, 2018).

25 European Monitoring Centre for Drugs and Drug Addiction and Europol, *EU Drug Markets Report.*

26 Ibid.

27 Ibid., 8.
28 Juan Andrés Romero Bermejo, "Formas e instrumentos de cooperación judicialinternacional en el delito de trata de personas," Fiscal.es, accessed January 27, 2019, www.fiscal.es/fiscal/PA_WebApp_SGNTJ_NFIS/descarga/Ponencia%20de%20Juan%20Andr%C3%A9s%20Bermejo%20Romero%20de%20Terreros.pdf?idFile=c0bbf9b3-a2c2-4675-ba40-ad541c6d5d9f.
29 Judith Kumin, "El desafío de la migración mixta por vía marítima," *Revista Migraciones Forzadas* (2014): 49–51.
30 This Directive replaces Framework Decision 2002/629/JHA of the Council (OJ L 101, April 15, 2011).
31 European Commission, Report from the Commission to the European Parliament and the Council, COM(2018) 777 final (Brussels: European Union, 2018), December 3, 2018, accessed January 27, 2019, https://eur-lex.europa.eu/LexUriServ/LexUriServ.do?uri=COM:2018:0777:FIN:ES:PDF.
32 Ibid.
33 Ibid. The Commission data that have been used exclude those provided by the United Kingdom, since it records a high percentage of labor exploitation, which distorts data from the rest of the EU, as stated in the report.
34 Concepción Anguita Olmedo and Cecilia Della Penna, "La trata en América Latina y la Unión Europea. Características, factores e instrumentos de detección y erradicación. Un estudio comparado," in *El Crimen Organizado en América Latina: Manifestaciones, Facilitadores y Reacción*, ed. Carolina Sampó and Valeska Troncoso (Madrid: Instituto Universitario General Gutiérrez Mellado, 2017), 251–82.
35 Frontex, *Risk Analysis for 2018* (Warsaw: Risk Analysis Unit, 2018), accessed January 24, 2019, https://frontex.europa.eu/assets/Publications/Risk_Analysis/Risk_Analysis/Risk_Analysis_for_2018.pdf.
36 Europol, *Situation Report: Trafficking in Human Beings in the EU* (The Hague: Europol, 2016), accessed January 28, 2019, www.europol.europa.eu/publications-documents/trafficking-in-human-beings-in-eu.
37 European Commission, Report from the Commission to the European Parliament and the Council.
38 Anguita Olmedo and Della Penna, "La trata en América Latina y la Unión Europea."
39 International Organization for Migration, *World Migration Report 2018* (Geneva: International Organization for Migration, 2018).
40 United Nations High Commissioner for Refugees, *The Global Compact on Refugees: UNHCR Quick Guide* (Geneva: United Nations High Commissioner for Refugees, 2018), accessed January 26, 2019, www.acnur.org/5bbe32564.pdf.
41 United Nations Office on Drugs and Crime, *Global Study on Smuggling of Migrants 2018* (New York: United Nations Publications, 2018).
42 Frontex, *Risk Analysis for 2018*.
43 Europol. *Situation Report*.
44 United Nations Office on Drugs and Crime, *Global Study on Smuggling of Migrants 2018*.
45 According to some conservative estimates, the smuggling fee to cross to Italy from Libya fluctuates between US$700 and $1,000 per migrant (International Organization for Migration, "IOM Monitors Italy Arrivals during Busy Smuggling Week in Mediterranean," online briefing, February 2015). In 2016, the smuggling activity along this route would range between US$127 million and US$181.5 million. In the same year, the passage along the eastern Mediterranean route involved smuggling fees between US$1,000 and US$2,000. For 2016, the revenues for smugglers along this route could range between US$182 million and US$364 million. In 2016, the fee recorded to reach the Spanish mainland shores ranged around US$1,000. For this route, the smugglers' revenues could range around US$8 million. United Nations Office on Drugs and Crime, *Global Study on Smuggling of Migrants 2018*.
46 Europol, "Crime Areas and Trends," Europol website, accessed January 27, 2019. www.europol.europa.eu/crime-areas-and-trends/crime-areas/facilitation-of-illegal-immigration.
47 Depending on the point of departure, citizenship and smuggling method, smuggling fees to reach different parts of the Horn of Africa and from here to Sudan, reportedly range from US$200 to a few thousand dollars. Smuggling fees to cover the journey from Khartoum to Libya or Egypt range around US$1,500. Smuggling income for smuggling within the Horn of Africa, and from there to North Africa could range between US$300 million and US$500 million per year. United Nations Office on Drugs and Crime, *Global Study on Smuggling of Migrants 2018*.
48 European Commission, *The EU and the Migratory Crisis* (Brussels: European Union, 2017), accessed January 29, 2019, http://publications.europa.eu/webpub/com/factsheets/migration-crisis/es/.
49 Establishment of the new Partnership Framework with third countries under the European Agenda on Migration. European Commission, COM(2018) 385 final, June 1, 2016.

50 On September 19, 2016, the General Assembly of the United Nations adopted Resolution 71/1 containing the text of the *New York Declaration for Refugees and Migrants*. The Declaration was approved by 193 States.

51 Office of the United Nations High Commissioner for Refugees, "Italy/Migrants: A Humanitarian Crisis Must Have a Global Humanitarian Response." Press release, United Nations Special Rapporteur on the Rights of Migrants, accessed January 26, 2019. www.ohchr.org/EN/NewsEvents/Pages/DisplayNews.aspx?NewsID=15386.

52 Center for Strategic and International Studies, "Net Losses: Estimating the Global Cost of Cybercrime. Economic Impact of Cybercrime II," CSIS website, accessed February 2, 2019. https://csis-prod.s3.amazonaws.com/s3fs-public/legacy_files/files/attachments/140609_rp_economic_impact_cybercrime_report.pdf.

53 Tuesday Reitano and Andrew Trabulsi, "Virtually Illicit: The Use of Social Media in a Hyper-Connected World," in *Beyond Convergence: World Without Order*, ed. Hilary Matfess and Michael Miklaucic (Washington: Centre for Complex Operations, Institute for National Strategic Studies, National Defense University, 2016), 222.

54 Steve Morgan, "Cybercrime Magazine," Cybersecurity Ventures, December 7, 2018, accessed February 2019, 6. https://cybersecurityventures.com/cybercrime-damages-6-trillion-by-2021/.

55 Chris Strohm, "Cybercrime Remains Growth Industry with $445 Billion Lost," Bloomberg, June 9, 2014, accessed February 2, 2019, www.bloomberg.com/news/articles/2014-06-09/cybercrime-remains-growth-industry-with-445-billion-lost.

56 James Lewis, "Economic Impact of Cybercrime – No Slowing Down," McAfee, accessed February 2, 2019, www.mcafee.com/enterprise/en-us/assets/reports/restricted/rp-economic-impact-cybercrime.pdf?utm_source=Press&utm_campaign=bb9303ae70-EMAIL_CAMPAIGN_2018_02_21&utm_medium=email.

57 Raj Samani, "Cybercrime: The Evolution of Traditional Crime," in *Beyond Convergence: World Without Order*, ed. Hilary Matfess and Michael Miklaucic (Washington: Centre for Complex, Operations Institute for National Strategic Studies, National Defense University, 2016), 276–77.

58 Department for Culture Media and Sport, "Cyber Security Breaches Survey 2017," Government of United Kingdom, accessed February 2, 2019, https://assets.publishing.service.gov.uk/government/uploads/system/uploads/attachment_data/file/609186/Cyber_Security_Breaches_Survey_2017_main_report_PUBLIC.pdf.

59 Lewis, "Economic Impact of Cybercrime – No Slowing Down."

60 Secretaria de Estado de Seguridad, "Estudio sobre la ciberdelincuencia en España," Ministerio del Interior, accessed February 6, 2019, www.interior.gob.es/documents/10180/5791067/Estudio+Cibercriminalidad+2016.pdf/456576b2-9ce8-4f3c-bbcc-ca0dbf3bb3cf.

61 Lewis, "Economic Impact of Cybercrime – No Slowing Down."

62 Tom Watts, "Which EU Country Is Most Vulnerable to Cybercrime?" Website Builder Expert, accessed January 3, 2019, www.websitebuilderexpert.com/blog/eu-cybercrime-risk/.

63 Europol, *Serious and Organised Crime Threat Assessment*.

64 Europol, *Internet Organised Crime Threat Assessment (IOCTA)* (The Hague: European Cybercrime Centre, 2018).

65 Ibid.

66 Council of the European Union, *The Stockholm Programme – An Open and Secure Europe Serving and Protecting Citizens* (Brussels: European Union, 2009).

67 Council of the European Union, *The EU Policy Cycle to Tackle Organised and Serious International Crime*.

68 Ruiz Díaz, *La lucha contra el crimen organizado en la Unión Europea*, 222.

69 Juana Goizueta Vértiz, "La cooperación policial en el seno de Europol: el principio de disponibilidad y la confidencialidad de la información," *Revista Española de Derecho Constitucional* 110 (2017): 75–103.

70 Europol, *Serious and Organised Crime Threat Assessment*, 8.

71 Andreea Marica, "Unión Europea y Latinoamérica: Cooperación estratégica en el ámbito de la seguridad," *Revista Electrónica IberoAmericana* 11, no. 2 (2017): 1–18.

72 "El PacCTO," FIIAP, accessed February 7, 2019. www.fiiapp.org/proyectos/lucha-crimen/#titulo-seccion-proyectos.

73 Belize, Costa Rica, El Salvador, Guatemala, Honduras, Nicaragua, Panama and the Dominican Republic.

74 "Nuevo programa regional ICRIME contribuirá a lucha contra el crimen organizado," European External Action Service, accessed February 7, 2019. https://eeas.europa.eu/delegations/peru/36779/nuevo-programa-regional-icrime-contribuir%C3%A1-lucha-contra-el-crimen-organizado_es.
75 "El PacCTO Europa-América Latina," FIIAPP, accessed February 8, 2019, www.fiiapp.org/proyectos_fiiapp/apoyo-a-ameripol-ue/#ancla-contenido-proyectos.
76 European Border and Coast Guard Agency. It was created in 2004, and its function is to help the EU Member States to manage their external borders, offering technical support and experience. Frontex is currently not allowed to acquire its own resources; it does not have its own operational staff, so it depends on the contributions of the Member States; it cannot carry out its own return or border management operations without the prior authorization of a Member State; and does not have an explicit mandate to develop search and rescue operations.
77 "Declaración UE-Turquía," European Council, March 18, 2016, accessed February 8, 2019, www.consilium.europa.eu/es/press/press-releases/2016/03/18-eu-turkey-statement/.
78 European Commission, *The EU and the Migratory Crisis.*
79 Regulation (EC) No 460/2004 of the European Parliament and of the Council.
80 Decision 854/2005/EC of the European Parliament and Council.
81 Javier Alonso Lecuit, *Relanzamiento del Plan de Ciberseguridad de la UE* ARI 97/2017 (Madrid: Real Instituto Elcano, 2017).
82 European Parliament and the Council of the European Union, Directive (EU) 2016/1148 of the European Parliament and of The Council of 6 July 2016 Concerning Measures for a High Common Level of Security of Network and Information Systems across the Union (Brussels: European Union, 2016), accessed February 9, 2019, https://eur-lex.europa.eu/legal-content/ES/TXT/?uri=uriserv:OJ.L_.2016.194.01.0001.01.SPA&toc=OJ:L:2016:194:TOC.
83 European Commission, Joint Communication to the European Parliament and the Council: Resilience, Deterrence and Defence: Building Strong Cybersecurity for the EU, JOIN(2017) 450 final (Brussels: European Union, September 13, 2017), accessed February 9, 2019, https://eur-lex.europa.eu/legal-content/en/TXT/?uri=CELEX%3A52017JC0450.

References

Alonso Lecuit, Javier. *Relanzamiento del Plan de Ciberseguridad de la UE* ARI 97/2017. Madrid: Real Instituto Elcano, 2017.

Anguita Olmedo, Concepción. "El tráfico ilegal de seres humanos para la explotación sexual y laboral: La esclavitud del siglo XXI." *Nómadas: Revista de Ciencias Sociales* 15 (2007): 3–16.

Anguita Olmedo, Concepción, and Cecilia Della Penna. "La trata en América Latina y la Unión Europea. Características, factores e instrumentos de detección y erradicación. Un estudio comparado." In *El Crimen Organizado en América Latina: Manifestaciones, Facilitadores y Reacción*, edited by Carolina Sampó and Valeska Troncoso, 251–82. Madrid: Instituto Universitario General Gutiérrez Mellado, 2017.

Bartolomé, Mariano. "Las drogas ilegales, elemento central del crimen organizado en América Latina." In *El Crimen Organizado en América Latina: Manifestaciones, Facilitadores y Reacciones*, edited by Carolina Sampó and Valeska Troncoso, 89–122. Madrid: Instituto Universitario General Gutiérrez Mellado, 2017.

Center for Strategic and International Studies. "Net Losses: Estimating the Global Cost of Cybercrime. Economic Impact of Cybercrime II." CSIS website. Accessed February 2, 2019. https://csis-prod.s3.amazonaws.com/s3fs-public/legacy_files/files/attachments/140609_rp_economic_impact_cybercrime_report.pdf.

Council of the European Union. *The EU Policy Cycle to Tackle Organised and Serious International Crime.* Brussels: The Publications Office, 2014. Accessed December 28, 2018. www.consilium.europa.eu/media/30232/qc0114638enn.pdf.eport.pdf.

Council of the European Union. *The Stockholm Programme – An Open and Secure Europe Serving and Protecting Citizens.* Brussels: European Union, 2009.

"Declaración UE-Turquía." European Council. March 18, 2016. Accessed February 8, 2019, www.consilium.europa.eu/es/press/press-releases/2016/03/18-eu-turkey-statement/.

Department for Culture Media and Sport. "Cyber Security Breaches Survey 2017." Government of United Kingdom. Accessed February 2, 2019. https://assets.publishing.service.gov.uk/government/uploads/system/uploads/attachment_data/file/609186/Cyber_Security_Breaches_Survey_2017_main_report_PUBLIC.pdf.

"El PacCTO Europa-América Latina." FIIAPP. Accessed February 8, 2019. www.fiiapp.org/proyectos_fiiapp/apoyo-a-ameripol-ue/#ancla-contenido-proyectos.
"El PacCTO." FIIAP. Accessed February 7, 2019. www.fiiapp.org/proyectos/lucha-crimen/#titulo-seccion-proyectos.
European Commission. Joint Communication to the European Parliament and the Council: Resilience, Deterrence and Defence: Building Strong Cybersecurity for the EU. JOIN(2017) 450 final. Brussels: European Union, September 13, 2017. Accessed February 9, 2019, https://eur-lex.europa.eu/legal-content/en/TXT/?uri=CELEX%3A52017JC0450.
European Commission. Report from the Commission to the European Parliament and the Council. COM(2018) 777 final. Brussels: European Union, 2018. Accessed January 27, 2019. https://eur-lex.europa.eu/LexUriServ/LexUriServ.do?uri=COM:2018:0777:FIN:ES:PDF.
European Commission. *The EU and the Migratory Crisis*. Brussels: European Union, 2017. Accessed January 29, 2019. http://publications.europa.eu/webpub/com/factsheets/migration-crisis/es/.
European Monitoring Centre for Drugs and Drug Addiction and Europol. *EU Drug Markets Report: Strategic Overview*. Luxembourg: The Publications Office, 2016.
European Parliament and the Council of the European Union. Directive (EU) 2016/1148 of the European Parliament and of The Council of 6 July 2016 Concerning Measures for a High Common Level of Security of Network and Information Systems across the Union. Brussels: European Union, 2016. Accessed February 9. 2019. https://eur-lex.europa.eu/legal-content/ES/TXT/?uri=uriserv:OJ.L_.2016.194.01.0001.01.SPA&toc=OJ:L:2016:194:TOC.
Europol. "Crime Areas and Trends." Europol website. Accessed January 27, 2019. www.europol.europa.eu/crime-areas-and-trends/crime-areas/facilitation-of-illegal-immigration.
Europol. *Internet Organised Crime Threat Assessment (IOCTA)*. The Hague: European Cybercrime Centre, 2018.
Europol. *Serious and Organised Crime Threat Assessment. Crime in the Age of Technology*. The Hague: Europol, 2017.
Europol. *Situation Report: Trafficking in Human Beings in the EU*. The Hague: Europol, 2016. Accessed January 28, 2019. www.europol.europa.eu/publications-documents/trafficking-in-human-beings-in-eu.
Frontex. *Risk Analysis for 2018*. Warsaw: Risk Analysis Unit, 2018. Accessed January 24, 2019. https://frontex.europa.eu/assets/Publications/Risk_Analysis/Risk_Analysis/Risk_Analysis_for_2018.pdf.
Goizueta Vértiz, Juana. "La cooperación policial en el seno de Europol: el principio de disponibilidad y la confidencialidad de la información." *Revista Española de Derecho Constitucional* 110 (2017): 75–103.
International Organization for Migration. *World Migration Report 2018*. Geneva: International Organization for Migration, 2018.
Kumin, Judith. "El desafío de la migración mixta por vía marítima." *Revista Migraciones Forzadas* (2014): 49–51.
Lewis, James. "Economic Impact of Cybercrime – No Slowing Down." McAfee. Accessed February 2, 2019, www.mcafee.com/enterprise/en-us/assets/reports/restricted/rp-economic-impact-cybercrime.pdf?utm_source=Press&utm_campaign=bb9303ae70-EMAIL_CAMPAIGN_2018_02_21&utm_medium=email.
Makarenko, Tamara. "The Crime-Terror Continuum: Tracing the Interplay between Transnational Organised Crime and Terrorism." *Global Crime* 6, no. 1 (2004): 129–45.
Marica, Andreea. "Unión Europea y Latinoamérica: Cooperación estratégica en el ámbito de la seguridad." *Revista Electrónica IberoAmericana* 11, no. 2 (2017): 1–18.
Marrero Rocha, Inmaculada. "Nuevas dinámicas en las relaciones entre crimen organizado y grupos terroristas." *Revista Española de Derecho Internacional* 69, no. 2 (2017): 145–69.
Morgan, Steve. "Cybercrime Magazine." Cybersecurity Ventures. December 7, 2018. Accessed February 2019. https://cybersecurityventures.com/cybercrime-damages-6-trillion-by-2021/.
"Nuevo programa regional ICRIME contribuirá a lucha contra el crimen organizado." European External Action Service. Accessed February 7, 2019. https://eeas.europa.eu/delegations/peru/36779/nuevo-programa-regional-icrime-contribuir%C3%A1-lucha-contra-el-crimen-organizado_es.
Office of the United Nations High Commissioner for Refugees. "Italy/Migrants: A Humanitarian Crisis Must Have a Global Humanitarian Response." Press release, United Nations Special Rapporteur on the Rights of Migrants. Accessed January 26, 2019. www.ohchr.org/EN/NewsEvents/Pages/DisplayNews.aspx?NewsID=15386.
Reitano, Tuesday, and Andrew Trabulsi. "Virtually Illicit: The Use of Social Media in a Hyper-Connected World." In *Beyond Convergence: World Without Order*, edited by Hilary Matfess and Michael Miklaucic,

215–34. Washington: Centre for Complex Operations, Institute for National Strategic Studies, National Defense University, 2016.

Romero Bermejo, Juan Andrés. "Formas e instrumentos de cooperación judicialinternacional en el delito de trata de personas." Fiscal.es. Accessed January 27, 2019. www.fiscal.es/fiscal/PA_WebApp_SGNTJ_NFIS/descarga/Ponencia%20de%20Juan%20Andr%C3%A9s%20Bermejo%20Romero%20de%20Terreros.pdf?idFile=c0bbf9b3-a2c2-4675-ba40-ad541c6d5d9f.

Ruiz Díaz, Lucas J. *La lucha contra el crimen organizado en la Unión Europea. Aspectos internos y dinámicas externas del discurso securitario.* Granada: Universidad de Granada, 2015.

Samani, Raj. "Cybercrime: The Evolution of Traditional Crime." In *Beyond Convergence: World Without Order*, edited by Hilary Matfess and Michael Miklaucic, 274–95. Washington: Centre for Complex, Operations Institute for National Strategic Studies, National Defense University, 2016.

Sampó, Carolina. "Porque no todo es terrorismo: Notas sobre la actividad del Crimen Organizado en España." *Relaciones Internacionales* 51 (2016): 1–14.

Sansó-Rubert Pascual, Daniel. *¿Por qué África: desentrañando la geopolítica criminal del tráfico ilícito de cocaína entre América Latina y Europa (vía España)*, Documento de Trabajo 7/2018. Madrid: Real Instituto Elcano, 2018.

Secretaria de Estado de Seguridad. "Estudio sobre la ciberdelincuencia en España." Ministerio del Interior. Accessed February 6, 2019. www.interior.gob.es/documents/10180/5791067/Estudio+Cibercriminalidad+2016.pdf/456576b2-9ce8-4f3c-bbcc-ca0dbf3bb3cf.

Soriano, Juan Pablo. "Gobernanza global contra la delincuencia transnacional: la UE y la Convención de Palermo." *CIDOB d'Afers Internacionals* 108 (2014): 141–63.

Strohm, Chris. "Cybercrime Remains Growth Industry with $445 Billion Lost." Bloomberg, June 9, 2014. Accessed February 2, 2019. www.bloomberg.com/news/articles/2014-06-09/cybercrime-remains-growth-industry-with-445-billion-lost.

Sumpter, Cameron, and Joseph Franco. "Migration, Transnational Crime and Terrorism: Exploring the Nexus in Europe and Southeast Asia." *Perspectives on Terrorism* 12, no. 5 (2018): 36–50.

United Nations High Commissioner for Refugees. *The Global Compact on Refugees: UNHCR Quick Guide.* Geneva: United Nations High Commissioner for Refugees, 2018. Accessed January 26, 2019. www.acnur.org/5bbe32564.pdf.

United Nations Office on Drugs and Crime. *Global Study on Smuggling of Migrants 2018.* New York: United Nations Publications, 2018.

United Nations Organization. *United Nations Convention against Transnational Organized Crime and the Protocols Thereto.* Palermo: United Nations Office on Drugs and Crime, 2000.

Watts, Tom. "Which EU Country Is Most Vulnerable to Cybercrime?" Website Builder Expert. Accessed January 3, 2019. www.websitebuilderexpert.com/blog/eu-cybercrime-risk/.

Williams, Phil. "Organizing Transnational Crime: Networks, Markets and Hierarchies." In *Combating Transnational Crime: Concepts, Activities and Responses*, edited by Phil Williams and Dimitri Vlassis, 61–98. London: Frank Cass Publishers, 2001.

12
THE CHALLENGES OF EXTREMISM AND TERRORISM

Irene Rodríguez Ortega

Introduction

In 2002, following the attacks of September 11 in New York, the European Union (EU) offered a definition of violent radicalization through the adoption of a Framework Decision on combating terrorism. Thus, in its Article 1, it understood violent radicalization as a "phenomenon by virtue of which people adhere to opinions, points of view and ideas that may lead them to commit terrorist acts."[1] Today, however, radicalization is understood as a process within other processes within the cycle of terrorism. Likewise, as a product of globalization and modernity, reality becomes more confusing and so does terrorism.

Since the 1970s, scholars have tried to answer the difficult question of why an individual becomes a radical or religious extremist.[2] The terrorist attacks that have taken place on European territory in recent years have once again shown that the threat of religious extremism is present in today's European political and social reality. With the self-proclamation of the Caliphate of the Islamic State in 2014,[3] its rapid territorial extension, its operational capacity, its strategy of recruiting combatants of European origin and its extremist ideology,[4] Europe faced a difficult scenario to address in which religious extremism seemed to become an endemic problem that jeopardized social stability and generated violence.

According to data from Europol,[5] whose latest 2018 *EU Terrorism Situation and Trend Report* will be used as an analysis reference for this chapter, the number of attacks perpetrated on European soil has increased considerably since 2015, generating a feeling of uncertainty, hysteria and insecurity among European citizens. The problem is even more serious if one considers that those responsible for attacks, such as those that took place in Nice[6] in 2016 or Barcelona[7] in 2017, were European citizens. Problems and flaws in integration policies are more present than ever. In any case, the fall and loss of relevance of terrorist organizations such as Al-Qaeda or ISIS does not mean the end of the problem of radicalization and religious extremism facing the European Union. Moreover, according to the latest Eurobarometer, security is one of the main concerns for Europeans and 80 percent want the EU to do more to fight terrorism.

The terrorist threat in the EU: trends and overview

According to data from the European Commission, there were a total of 1,010 failed, frustrated or consummated attacks in European territory between 2009 and 2013. However, as mentioned above, with the emergence of the Islamic State in 2014, there has been a radical shift in statistics, making terrorism a priority issue on the Member States' agendas.[8] In 2017 alone, 62 people were killed in 33 religious terrorist attacks in the EU.

In the latest annual edition of the TE-SAT (*Terrorism Situation and Trend Report*), published on June 20, 2018, Europol provided an in-depth overview of the number of terrorist attacks that took place in 2017, as well as the number of arrests and convictions for terrorist offenses.

The European Commissioner for the Security Union, Julian King, pointed out in 2018 the following:

> as this latest progress report and EU trend against terrorism shows, Europe remains a target for terrorism: we must maintain our collective vision and strengthen our efforts at EU level to deny terrorists the means to carry out attacks including weapons, explosives and funds, work in evolving areas such as CBRN threats and continue to tackle radicalisation and all kinds of violent extremism.[9]

In the years following the first edition of TE-SAT, the total number of terrorist attacks in the Union decreased, largely due to a substantial drop in the number of attacks of secessionist origin, which over a period of ten years had accounted for the largest proportion of attacks reported by Member States. In contrast to this situation, the threat of jihadist terrorism has increased considerably since 2006, culminating in major propaganda attacks such as those in Paris in 2015 and in Brussels, Nice and Berlin in 2016.

The recent attacks by jihadist terrorists share common characteristics: preference for attacking people, attacks on Western symbols and attacks on Western lifestyle symbols. The 2018 TE-SAT report also identifies the following 12 key trends:[10]

- The increase in jihadist attacks in recent years is accompanied by a decrease in the sophistication of their preparation and execution. Nevertheless, they have become more impactful attacks, with more casualties and deaths.
- Jihadist terrorist attacks in Europe followed three patterns: indiscriminate assassinations (London, March and June 2017; Barcelona, August 2017), attacks on authority symbols (Paris, February, June and August 2017); attacks on European lifestyle symbols (Manchester, May 2017).
- Attacks committed on European territory are characterized by being committed by radicalized individuals in their country of residence, without having traveled.[11]
- The attacks demonstrate a preference for attacking people rather than facilities in order to cause greater emotional damage.
- Those responsible for jihadist terrorist attacks are often solitary actors, but they can operate as a group.
- The number of European citizens traveling to conflict zones to join terrorist groups, such as the foreign terrorist combatants of the Islamic State, has fallen considerably since 2016.[12]
- Social networks remain essential for terrorist groups such as the Islamic State in order to disseminate older and older material by new means in order to recruit, radicalize and raise funds.

- It has been realized that young people's scarce or fragmented knowledge of Islam makes them more vulnerable to being manipulated by those groups that use religious texts to adapt to a violent ideology.
- Despite the degradation of the Islamic State, the threat of jihadist terrorism remains present in the EU, above all among members and sympathizers who reside in Member States and who are likely to continue to defend jihadist beliefs.
- Ethno-nationalist and separatist terrorist attacks continue to outnumber attacks by violent extremists inspired by other ideologies or motivations.
- The extreme right is becoming increasingly violent, fueled by fears of the perception of an "Islamization" of society and immigration.[13]
- There is no record of chemical, biological, radiological or nuclear weapons being used by terrorists in the EU.[14]

Terrorist and violent extremist activities

In the latest 2018 Europol report on terrorism, the main activities of terrorism and violent extremism in Europe are analysed. It is these activities that the EU security agencies have identified as security threats to be analysed.

Financing of terrorism[15]

It is estimated that terrorist attacks on European territory have been financed by a mixture of lawful and unlawful sources.

It is believed that at least 40 percent of the attacks were financed with money from crime, especially drug trafficking, theft, fraud or the sale of counterfeit goods. For example, telephone scams are known to impersonate banks or law enforcement authorities in order to obtain financial information from individuals and access their accounts and money.

Many cases of financial fraud have also been found such as bank credits, SMS credits, VAT fraud or car theft and insurance fraud. They also obtain financing through ISIS's own funds from the illegal marketing of oil. In the case of the FTFs (foreign terrorist fighters[16]), European security services have discovered that the jihadists had illegally claimed social aid amounting to more than two million euros in Europe between 2012 and 2016.[17]

From lawful sources, many received some form of social assistance, and some even obtained bank loans. There are also known initiatives of crowdfunding, raising money through charities or supporting networks that provide legal business funds.[18] It is also known that a large proportion of jihadists of European origin have acquired computer skills and use technology to obtain funding, as well as to conceal money transfers. In any case, the sources of terrorist financing are one of the main threats, as well as concerns for European governments.[19]

That is why, as we shall see later in this chapter, the fight against the financing of terrorism is one of the main actions within the measures adopted by the EU in its fight against terrorism.

Explosives

Although a wide range of resources that can be used as weapons are readily available, explosive devices remain one of the most widely used in terrorist attacks due to their impact and symbolic power.

In 2016, the transfer of terrorist tactics, techniques and procedures (TTPs) from conflict zones was reported. It has been observed that jihadists seeking to attack in the EU have knowledge and instructions for bomb making. The availability of explosive precursors has facilitated the use of homemade explosives (HME). Of particular concern are improvised explosive devices (IEDs) against easy targets and the use of conventional firearms.

Travel for terrorist purposes

At December 2015, estimates of the number of foreign combatants who have joined the Islamic State stood at around 30,000 combatants.[20] Although the vast majority of IS recruits come from the Middle East and the Arab world in general, many foreign fighters also come from Western states.

A large number of these Western fighters belong to countries of the European Union. Sixty percent of European jihadists come from three countries: France, the United Kingdom and Germany. According to Europol data, around 7,500 people from the EU have traveled to conflict zones in Syria and Iraq.[21] At the end of 2017 the registered number was about 2,500. Europol has also noted that **women**[22] are assuming an increasing operational role in jihadist terrorist operations, as well as **minors and adolescents**, as has been demonstrated above all in avoided attacks.

It is also estimated that 1,500 of them, or 25 per cent of European citizens and residents participating in total, have returned to their country of origin. France currently has the largest contingent of foreign fighters from Europe in Syria and Iraq. More than 2,000 French citizens and residents participate in the Syrian and Iraqi jihadist networks. Among them, 600 are believed to be fighting alongside terrorist organizations abroad and 250 are believed to have returned. France alone accounts for a third of all Europeans involved. However, by 2017 the number of European citizens traveling to join IS was much lower, and the number of returnees was also lower. However, the threat is still present. In 2017, cases were reported, for example in Poland, of individuals who had attempted to travel to conflict zones to join IS. As indicated in the aforementioned Europol report, "[d]espite this apparent reduction in travellers, it should be underlined that IS, al-Qaeda and other jihadist groups, continue to pose a major threat. They have the ongoing intent and capability to conduct terrorist attacks."

Returning fighters

A problematic issue to be dealt with by European leaders and security services is what will happen to combatants of European origin who joined the ranks of the Islamic State and return.

Despite the fact that the latest Europol reports state that knowledge of the number of returnees was low, the return still poses a serious threat to the EU. In particular, those individuals who have been radicalized into violent extremism or jihadism and who have been trained in terrorist techniques, tactics and procedures represent a threat. Many of them are unlikely to return, but due to the high number of Europeans who joined the ranks of the ISIS,[23] the chances of return grow no matter how minimal.[24] Many others may be likely to return but do not pose a threat to their home states.

The question arises as to what happens to the small but realistic percentage of returning combatants. Among the measures that some States are putting on the table are:

a *Deprivation of citizenship*: countries such as Austria, Australia, France, the Netherlands and Norway are discussing passing legislation to increase their power to cancel citizenship.
b *Limitation of movement*: some States have taken or are taking measures to limit the freedom of movement of persons intending to travel abroad for the purpose of being a combatant in

an armed conflict. Other States are considering increasing their power to revoke or suspend passports. However, freedom of movement is a right recognized in the European Convention on Human Rights or the International Covenant on Civil and Political Rights, so any interference with the right to freedom of movement must take account of the particular situation of the person concerned, which means that general and automatic restrictions, for which no reasons are given, are not justified.

Many Western European governments have introduced more repressive measures into their legislation on terrorism-related offenses.[25] In doing so, they seek to counter violent extremism and address the potential threat posed by returning foreign fighters.[26] Such legislation includes improvements in prosecutorial powers, extending the scope of extradition measures and revocation of travel documents, as well as increased intelligence powers for surveillance or criminalization of travel to foreign conflict zones. Recently the governments of the United Kingdom, the Netherlands, Germany, Austria, France and other countries have adopted measures in relation to foreign fighters, both in terms of outward and inward flows.[27]

In the European Union, Islamic State terrorism and the refugee crisis resulting from the Syrian conflict are putting the policy of freedom of movement in a serious dilemma. For the first time since its creation, the Schengen area has been called into question. Countries of the Union such as France have affirmed the need to rethink the Schengen area, which they claim is becoming a black hole. However, talking about reforming the Schengen area is sensitive if we bear in mind that this is one of the fundamental pillars of the Union. To question its effectiveness is to question the Union. However, it is proving that there are serious problems in curbing the radicalization of European citizens and terrorism, so that the European security crisis is currently one of the biggest in the history of the Union.

Radicalization factors

In its fight against terrorism, the European Union, through Europol, has tried to establish a profile of citizens susceptible to radicalization, in order to establish measures to prevent it, as well as to be able to detect them more easily.

In the European case, when building a profile of radicalized individuals, possible inducing factors are studied, such as political, cultural, ideological, economic factors, etc.[28] However, concrete cases have demonstrated and confirmed that factors commonly associated with radicalism do not function as sufficient causes despite the causal impact. Therefore, there is no single profile that predisposes a person to violent radicalism or religious extremism.

The motivations that lead a person of European origin to join a terrorist organization or perpetrate an attack have also been analysed. In each specific case, several motivations intervene at the same time. However, understanding motivations is relevant because they act on the person in two ways: a) feeding the radicalization process, and b) generating new motivations.

Much of the research into why people join violent extremist groups boils down to a distinction between external and internal motives. External motives have to do with the individual's perception of large-scale events in the world. While many analysts and politicians have pointed to factors such as weak states, education, and social and economic disadvantage as external motivating factors, among experts who study extremism in depth there is little consensus and much discussion about the importance of these factors. Jihadist propaganda often relies exactly on these factors as radicalization enhancers. It has been shown, however, that these enhancers do not provide all the necessary motivation.

Recruitment and propaganda

As Europol warns in its report, the new dynamics of Islamist terrorism are closely related to recruitment and recruitment taking place through digital media. Terrorist organizations such as the Islamic State have turned technology into their main strategic tool to achieve diffusion and radicalization and subsequent recruitment.

Already in 2012, through Islamist forums, a call was made in which "any Muslim who tries to make jihad against the enemy by electronic means is considered in one sense or another a *mujahideen*."[29] For the first time anyone, from anywhere in the world, had the possibility to actively participate in the jihad without having to be part of any violent act, yet this electronic jihad leads to incitement, recruitment and radicalization.[30]

In Europe, recruitment has mainly taken place through social networks (Twitter, Facebook, Kik, Tumblr, Ask.fm, etc.); however, it should be noted that there does not seem to be a recruitment structure, but rather groups of volunteers who carry it out independently.

The use of digital media by terrorist groups is not new – 20 years ago al-Qaeda launched its first website (Azzam.com) – but, with the evolution of technology and the emergence of social networks, terrorist organizations have been adapting and evolving at the same time to get their message to as many people as possible.

The Islamic State has been able to take advantage of new technologies and social networks for its own benefit in order to reach as many people as possible. This has been achieved thanks to the development of a shocking and sophisticated propaganda campaign that cannot be compared with that of other groups. Since the Europol reports, the propaganda carried out by the Islamic State is considered important because it is through it that potential future terrorists come into contact for the first time with the jihadist world. It is also propaganda that is the greatest factor inducing radicalization, that incites and motivates a certain person to begin the process of radicalization.

Propaganda is therefore for Islamist terrorism one of its main weapons for recruiting new combatants, as well as for spreading terror and setting the political agenda of the EU.[31]

The European Union's response

In recent years the EU has taken a number of measures with the aim of preventing further terrorist attacks.

The main issues on which the EU has taken decisions in its fight against terrorism in the EU have been:[32]

- Reinforcement of controls at external borders;
- Intensified exchange of information between countries;
- Detection of the flow of foreign fighters of European origin;
- The establishment of a European register of air passenger data;
- Stopping the financing of terrorism;
- Limiting the possession of weapons in civilian hands and the control of firearms; and
- Prevention of radicalization, especially online.

In June 2013, the first significant steps were taken by the Justice and Home Affairs Council. A series of proposals for action against the threat of terrorism was agreed. The Council encouraged the counter-terrorism coordinator to present a report on the implementation of these measures at its meeting in December 2013. In that report, the counter-terrorism coordinator identified four areas considered to be of particular relevance, and on which the EU should act in support of the Member States in their efforts:

- Prevention;
- Penal response;
- Exchange of information on the identification and detection of movements; and
- Cooperation with third countries.

In its conclusions of August 30, 2014, the European Council called for accelerated implementation of the 22 measures contained in the report. The recognition of the Islamic State as a major threat to European security led to the adoption of a specific EU strategy against Islamist terrorism. The outline of the counter-terrorism strategy for Syria and Iraq, with special attention to foreign fighters, is summarized as the:[33]

- Urgency of adopting the Directive on passenger name records;
- Need to improve the judicial response and, in particular, to update the Framework Decision on combating terrorism;
- Need to improve controls at the Schengen external borders;
- Need to improve the exchange of information (Europol/Eurojust); and
- Implementation of identified actions in order to accelerate the implementation of agreed measures.

The attacks in Paris in 2016 or in Barcelona in 2017 showed major flaws in the European border control policy and the exchange of information between the States of the Union with the other European members. The fact that most attackers and facilitators were able to travel and move around undetected in the heart of Europe, going back and forth between Belgium and France to prepare for attacks, raised significant concerns about the ability of European law enforcement agencies to detect and investigate transnational threats, and raises questions about the viability of the current situation in the European security paradigm.[34]

Therefore, following these terrorist attacks, the ministers of justice and home affairs presented a joint declaration, the *Riga Joint Declaration on Combating Terrorism*. This declaration served as a basis for EU States to take internal measures such as:

- Adopting a framework for the Passenger Name Record Directive;
- Cooperating with the Internet industry to eliminate extremist content;
- Creating effective alternative discourses to prevent radicalization;
- Making full use of the existing Schengen framework, e.g. through systematic checks on EU citizens at external borders;
- Improving the information exchange through Europol and EuroJust; and
- Combating illicit trafficking in firearms and the financing of terrorism.

In March 2015 another meeting was arranged. At that meeting, ministers discussed the implementation of agreed measures, focusing in particular on:[35]

- Enhanced application of the Schengen framework: to apply systematic controls on the basis of risk assessment;
- Firearms trafficking: urging the Commission and Europol to propose ways of combating firearms trafficking and to intensify information exchange and operational cooperation;

- Internet content that encourages violent extremism or terrorism: Europol to set up an EU Internet Content Notification Unit; and
- *EU Passenger Name Record Directive*: to maintain active contacts with the European Parliament in order to make decisive progress in the coming months.

On March 7, 2017, the Council also adopted a Directive on combating terrorism. The new rules strengthen the EU legal framework to prevent terrorist attacks and tackle the phenomenon of foreign terrorist combatants. The Directive introduces the criminalization of acts such as:

- Training or travel for terrorist purposes;
- Organization or facilitation of such trips; and
- Contribution or raising of funds in connection with terrorist groups or activities.

In addition to this, Parliament agreed on November 30, 2017 on a new entry and exit registration system[36] in order to have a register of the movements of non-EU citizens in the Schengen area and thus speed up controls. These new external border controls are expected to be operational by 2020.

On the financing of terrorism, MEPs completed the latest update[37] of the EU Anti-Money Laundering Directive, which strengthens rules on virtual currency platforms and anonymous prepaid cards. An effective measure to stop terrorists is to cut off their sources of income and disrupt their logistics.[38] The European Parliament wants EU countries to track suspicious financial transactions and charities and also investigate trafficking in oil, cigarettes, gold, precious stones and works of art. MEPs also secured additional resources in the EU budget for 2018[39] to better combat terrorism and organized crime.

European Counter-Terrorism Centre

Among the measures taken to prevent and combat terrorism is the creation of the European Counter-Terrorism Centre. This center, which is part of Europol, is one of the proposals adopted at the extraordinary Justice and Home Affairs (JHA) Council held following the attacks in Paris[40] on November 13, 2015. The European Counter-Terrorism Centre (ECTC)[41] responds to the European Union's need to strengthen the anti-terrorist response to the possibility of new attacks within the European space.

The ECTC is a centralized and strengthened information center through which Member States can increase information exchange and operational coordination between law enforcement agencies, making new tools available to them and maximizing information exchange capacity. The Centre combines information, intelligence and support resources to tackle terrorism.

Among other functions, its mission is to improve operational analysis, analysis of incident cases and coordinated responses to Terrorism Analysis Files (AWFs), incorporating: Travel Focal Point (foreign terrorist combatants traveling to or returning from conflict zones); Terrorist Finance Tracking Programme (TFTP); website tracking (analysis of Internet propaganda material including threat analysis); EU Internet Reference Unit and the Europol Information System (EIS). In addition, it is important to note that it is capable of deploying an Immediate Response Team in the event of a terrorist attack.

The new European Counter-Terrorism Centre (ECTC) therefore arises from the need for the European Union to strengthen its anti-terrorist response in the face of the possibility of new attacks occurring within the European space. An effective fight against terrorism requires joint action, as well as cooperation and coordination among Member States. The ECTC is designed to fulfill these functions as the central axis in the EU's fight against terrorism.

Migration and Islamophobia

Migration has been a constant throughout history and has been one of the sources of progress in many countries. However, the immigration that is currently heading for Europe, especially that deriving from the conflict in Syria and Iraq, is generating unusual tensions and confrontations that point to differentiating elements, absent a century ago, which give these migrations a more controversial and conflictive character within the European Union. These migratory phenomena towards Europe are perceived by the population as a threat of Islamization, a fact reiterated by Europol in its latest report.

In countries such as the Netherlands, Germany or Finland, groups of "vigilantes," volunteer citizens who organize themselves to patrol the streets, have been created. They argue that the police authorities are incapable of protecting civil society from terrorist threats, as exemplified by New Year's events in Cologne[42] or Berlin.[43]

Likewise, police stations in countries such as Germany have experienced an increase in reports of attacks related to racism and xenophobia. The Europol report mentioned in previous sections devotes a section to the phenomenon of Islamophobia in Europe, and warns that since 2015 there has been a 41 percent increase in crimes related to religious or racial motives.

According to data from the Pew Research Center,[44] an American organization that studies social problems and conflicts in the West, the rejection of the Muslim community in EU member countries has increased considerably. In Hungary it is 72 percent, and there are similar feelings in Italy, Poland and Greece. And it is also there where there is the greatest fear that the arrival of refugees will lead to an increase in terrorist attacks.

Right wing

Many citizens have echoed their concern about immigration in the political sphere. The rise of extreme right-wing discourses as an unjustified response to phenomena such as immigration makes us reflect on the future of democracy in the West and the rise of populism. When dictatorships fell in Europe and democracies were re-established, the extreme right was relegated to an almost non-existent presence in the institutions. However, the last decade has been characterized by concern about the rise of extreme right-wing radicalism, which has also found, for the first time in democracy, electoral support from the population, becoming part of the executive in the respective countries.

In most of the cases in which we find ourselves in Europe where the extreme right is booming, experts agree that the origin of this panorama is the economic crisis. However, finding an answer for the consolidation of this type of extremism in Europe is not so simple. Each country has a complex reality with its own economic, social, historical and political variables that make up the fabric of the country. However, these phenomena show that the integration of immigrants is still a pending issue which is beginning to take its toll in all the countries of the Union.

Although it may be difficult for part of the population to explain the rise of a discourse based on the past and intolerance, we are faced with various factors, not only economic but also cultural. This opposition to immigration, in more ethnically diverse societies, responds to the desire of some sectors that their country "return to the way it was." Thus arises a hatred for the different and a nostalgia for a world that never existed and never will return. It must also be understood, according to economist Kaufmamn,[45] that populism comes to break the growing homogeneity of political discourses. With the end of communism, the parties got closer in economic matters and now their differences have to do with a cultural division.

Of course, extreme right-wing speeches are spreading all over Europe. Thus, we can talk about Golden Dawn in Greece, the Northern League or New Force in Italy, the Great Romania Party in Romania, the Swedish Democrats, the True Finns party, the Danish People's Party in Denmark and, in Croatia, the Croatian Pure Rights Party. All of them are characterized by defending xenophobic, anti-European, anti-immigration and, some of them, openly fascist programs.

To this list must be added phenomena such as *Brexit* at the hands of the former leader of the UKIP, Nigel Farage, who defended a discourse of excluding nationalism, a strong rejection of immigration, and the exit of the United Kingdom from the European Union, something that has finally been achieved. The rise of the xenophobic Alternative Party for Germany and the rise of the Freedom Party in the Netherlands are also discussed. In Austria, the far-right, xenophobic, populist and Eurosceptic candidate of the Freedom Party has run an election campaign marked by a strong xenophobic and islamophobic discourse in which pride in being Austrian and zero tolerance of difference and immigration were highlighted.

In general, the political landscape in Europe is delicate. While it is true that we cannot know how these phenomena are going to evolve, there is a consolidation of the European extreme right in the institutions and an increase in its voting intention.

Has European integration failed?

In both the political and academic spheres, the debate on integration is present. The European Union is defined by the values of democracy, freedom and equality. These are values that defend the multiculturalism of the European Union. However, in recent years we have witnessed an increase in the processes of radicalization of European citizens, an example of which has been the unprecedented movement of European combatants who joined the ranks of the Islamic States. As well as the increase in terrorist attacks on European territory, attacks of a religious extremist nature have aimed at sowing chaos and hatred. At the same time, we have witnessed an increase in racist and xenophobic discourses in response to these realities, which coincided with the entry of refugees into European territory because of the conflict in Syria and Iraq. In a state of latent insecurity and economic crisis, the correlation between extremism, terrorism and immigration has been exploited in far-right political and social discourses. All this has had a serious impact on the European coexistence pact, which has been threatened.

The social sciences have tried to respond to the causes of religious extremism, radicalization and terrorism within Europe. Some argue that the reasons for the growth of Islamic radicalism can be found in social policies. Something has failed in European integration. The existence of different communities in the different Member States of the Union and the failure of immigration and integration policies are two of the causes that have given rise to uprooted, frustrated youth with very few possibilities for the future within European societies, a generation much more vulnerable to the discourses of religious extremism.

Conclusion

The threat posed by the radicalization of European citizens, many of whom have ended up traveling abroad to fight, is likely to continue in the coming years. An effective response to these issues requires a comprehensive approach and long-term commitment. The primary responsibility for combating terrorism lies with the Member States. However, the EU can and should play a supportive role in helping to respond to the cross-border nature of the threat.

Religious extremism and the threat of terrorism within Europe have jeopardized European values and the principles of the rule of law. There is right now a tension between the principles of freedom and security that must be alleviated. One thing the decisions taken seem to agree on is that the fight against terrorism and religious extremism must be a fight based on legislation and political and social instruments, and not on intolerance and force.

Notes

1 Council of the European Union, *Framework Decision on combating terrorism* 2002/475/JHA (Brussels: European Union, 2002).
2 Rik Coolsaet, *What Accounts for the Rise of Violent Extremism in European Cities?* (Barcelona: Barcelona Centre for International Affairs, 2017).
3 Yasmine Haflz, "What Is a Caliphate? ISIS Declaration Raises Questions," *Huffington Post*, June 6, 2014, accessed February 24, 2019, www.huffingtonpost.com/2014/06/30/what-is-a-caliphatemeaning_n_5543538.html?guccounter=1.
4 Jessica Stern and John M. Berger, *ISIS: The State of Terror*, 1st ed. (New York: Ecco, 2015).
5 "Terrorism in the EU: Terror Attacks, Deaths and Arrests," European Parliament News, July 25, 2018, accessed February 24, 2019, www.europarl.europa.eu/news/en/headlines/security/20180703STO07125/terrorism-in-the-eu-terror-attacks-deaths-and-arrests.
6 "Truck Attack in Nice," *Aljazeera*, July 10, 2018, accessed February 24, 2019, www.aljazeera.com/programmes/aljazeeraworld/2018/07/truck-attack-nice-180710132318265.html.
7 "Barcelona Attacks News," *Independent*, accessed February 24, 2019, www.independent.co.uk/topic/barcelona-attack; "Barcelona Terror Attack," *CBS news*, accessed February 24, 2019, www.cbsnews.com/pictures/barcelona-terror-attack-van-crashes-into-pedestrians/.
8 Europol, *EU Terrorism Situation and Trend Report 2017* (The Hague: European Union Agency for Law Enforcement Cooperation, 2017).
9 "Terrorist Threat in the EU Remains High Despite the Decline of IS in Iraq and Syria," Europol press release, June 20, 2018, accessed February 24, 2019, www.europol.europa.eu/newsroom/news/terrorist-threat-in-eu-remains-high-despite-decline-of-in-iraq-and-syria. CBRN (chemical, biological, radiological and nuclear) defense is protective measures taken in situations in which chemical, biological, radiological or nuclear warfare (including terrorism) hazards may be present.
10 Europol, *EU Terrorism Situation and Trend Report 2018* (The Hague: European Union Agency for Law Enforcement Cooperation, 2018).
11 The profile of these actors is analysed and dealt with in the following sections.
12 Darryl Li, "A Universal Enemy? 'Foreign Fighters' and Legal Regimes of Exclusion and Exemption under the 'Global War on Terror,'" *Columbia Human Rights Law Review* 41, no. 2 (2010): 355.
13 This will be dealt with in the following paragraphs.
14 "Chemical, Biological, Radiological and Nuclear (CBRN) Protection." The Netherlands Organisation, accessed February 24, 2019, www.tno.nl/en/focus-areas/defence-safety-security/expertise-groups/chemical-biological-radiological-and-nuclear-cbrn-protection/.
15 "Fight against Money Laundering and Terrorist Financing," European Council Policies database, October 25, 2018, accessed February 24, 2019, www.consilium.europa.eu/en/policies/fight-against-terrorism/fight-against-terrorist-financing/.
16 According to United Nations Security Council Resolution 2178 of 2014, foreign terrorist fighters are defined as "Individuals who travel to a State other than their State of residence or nationality for the purpose of the perpetration, planning or preparation of, or participation in, terrorist acts or the providing or receiving of terrorist training, including in connection with armed conflict."
17 David Chazan, "French Jihadists Regularly Received Welfare Payments after Joining Isil, Police Reveal," *The Telegraph*, October 26, 2017, accessed February 24, 2019, www.telegraph.co.uk/news/2017/10/26/french-jihadists-regularly-received-welfare-payments-joining/.
18 Magnus Ranstorp, "La financiación del terrorismo: principales actores, estrategias y fuentes," *Estudios de Política Exterior* 57 (2018), accessed February 24, 2019, www.politicaexterior.com/articulos/afkar-ideas/la-financiacion-del-terrorismo-actores-estrategias-fuentes/.

19 "Terrorism Funding: 'If We Tackle the Logistics, We Fix the Issue,'" European Parliament News, February 28, 2018, accessed February 24, 2019, www.europarl.europa.eu/news/en/headlines/priorities/terrorism/20180222STO98436/terrorism-funding-if-we-tackle-the-logistics-we-fix-the-issue.
20 "Foreign Fighters: An Updated Assessment of the Flow of Foreign Fighters into Syria and Iraq," The Soufan Group, December 2015, accessed February 24, 2019, http://soufangroup.com/wp-content/uploads/2015/12/TSG_ForeignFightersUpdate3.pdf.
21 "How to Stop Terrorism: EU Measures Explained (Infographic)," March 22, 2018, accessed February 24, 2019, www.europarl.europa.eu/news/en/headlines/security/20180316STO99922/how-to-stop-terrorism-eu-measures-explained-infographic.
22 It is worth mentioning at this point that the proliferation of women of European origin who traveled to Syria and Iraq during the conflict in order to join the cause of the Islamic State has also been highlighted and studied. Europol and other institutions investigating the phenomenon estimate that the number of European women and girls who have traveled to Syria to join the Islamic State may exceed 550. This number is alarming given that there are no precedents. Until the Islamic State, no terrorist organization had aimed to recruit women to join their ranks as well. As mentioned earlier, this may be mainly due to the fact that, after the Syrian civil war, the country was left desolate, facing serious demographic problems.
23 Lorenzo Vidino, "European Foreign Fighters in Syria: Dynamics and Responses," *European View* 13, no. 2 (2014): 217–24.
24 Global Center on Cooperative Security, Human Security Collective, and International Centre for Counter-Terrorism, *Addressing the Foreign Terrorist Fighters Phenomenon from a European Union Perspective* (The Hague: International Centre for Counter-Terrorism, 2014), accessed February 24, 2019, www.icct.nl/download/file/Dec2014_EU-FTFS_GCCS_HSC_ICCT.pdf.
25 Christophe Paulussen and Eva Entenmann, "Addressing Europe's Foreign Fighter Issue: Legal Avenues at the International and National Level," *Security and Human Rights* 25, no. 1 (2014): 86–118.
26 Orla Hennessy, *The Return of Europe's Foreign Fighters* (The Hague: International Centre for Counter-Terrorism, 2014), accessed February 24, 2019, http://icct.nl/publication/the-return-of-europes-foreign-fighters.
27 Charles Lister, *Returning Foreign Fighters: Criminalization or Reintegration?* (Doha: Brookings Doha Center, 2015), 4, accessed February 24, 2019, www.brookings.edu/wp-content/uploads/2016/06/En-Fighters-Web.pdf.
28 Anne Speckhard, "Talking Terrorism: What Drives Young People to Become Foreign Fighters for ISIS and Other Terrorism Groups and What Can Be Done in Response?" *Freedom from Fear* 2 (2015): 24–28.
29 Gabriel Weimann, "New Terrorism and New Media," Wilson Center Research Series 2 (Wilson Center, 2014), 3.
30 James P. Farwell, "The Media Strategy of ISIS," *Survival* 56, no. 6 (2014): 49–55.
31 "State of the Union 2018: Commission Proposes New Rules to Get Terrorist Content off the Web." European Commission Press, September 12, 2018, accessed February 24, 2019, http://europa.eu/rapid/press-release_IP-18-5561_en.htm.
32 "Response to the Terrorist Threat and the Recent Terrorist Attacks in Europe," *European Council and Council of the European Union website*, November 30, 2018, accessed February 24, 2019, www.consilium.europa.eu/en/policies/fight-against-terrorism/foreign-fighters/.
33 "Response to the Phenomenon of Foreign Terrorist Combatants and Recent Terrorist Attacks in Europe," *European Council and Council of the European Union website*, April 4, 2016, accessed February 24, 2019, www.consilium.europa.eu/es/policies/fight-against-terrorism/foreign-fighters/.
34 Jean-Charles Brisard, "The Paris Attacks and the Evolving Islamic State Threat to France," *CTC Sentinel* 8, no. 11 (2015): 5–8.
35 Ibid.
36 "Schengen: New Rules for Stronger Protection," European Parliament News, October 25, 2017, accessed February 24, 2019, www.europarl.europa.eu/news/en/headlines/security/20171023STO86604/schengen-new-rules-for-stronger-protection-video.
37 "Public to Get Access to Information on Beneficial Owners of Firms in EU," European Parliament News, January 29, 2018, accessed February 24, 2019, www.europarl.europa.eu/news/es/press-room/20180129IPR96112/public-to-get-access-to-information-on-beneficial-owners-of-firms-in-eu.
38 "Cutting Cash Flows to Terrorists," European Parliament News, February 26, 2018, accessed February 24, 2019, www.europarl.europa.eu/news/en/press-room/20180226IPR98617/cutting-cash-flows-to-terrorists.

39 "EU Budget 2018 Approved Support for Youth Growth Security," European Parliament News, November 27, 2017, accessed February 24, 2019, www.europarl.europa.eu/news/en/headlines/priorities/2018-budget/20171127IPR88936/eu-budget-2018-approved-support-for-youth-growth-security.
40 "2015 Paris Terror Attacks Fast Facts," *CNN Library*, November 12, 2018, accessed February 24, 2019, https://edition.cnn.com/2015/12/08/europe/2015-paris-terror-attacks-fast-facts/index.html.
41 Official website: www.europol.europa.eu/about-europol/european-counter-terrorism-centre-ectc.
42 Rick Noack, "2,000 Men Sexually Assaulted 1,200 Women at Cologne New Year's Eve Party," *Independent*, July 11, 2016, accessed February 24, 2019, www.independent.co.uk/news/world/europe/cologne-new-years-eve-mass-sex-attacks-leaked-document-a7130476.html.
43 "Berlin Christmas Market Attack," *Guardian*, May 2018, accessed February 24, 2019, www.theguardian.com/world/berlin-christmas-market-attack.
44 Pew Research. www.pewresearch.org/.
45 Eric Kaufmann, *Whiteshift: Populism, Immigration and the Future of White Majorities* (Penguin, 2018).

Bibliography

"2015 Paris Terror Attacks Fast Facts." CNN Library. November 12, 2018. Accessed February 24, 2019. https://edition.cnn.com/2015/12/08/europe/2015-paris-terror-attacks-fast-facts/index.html.

"Barcelona Attacks News." *Independent*. Accessed February 24, 2019. www.independent.co.uk/topic/barcelona-attack.

"Barcelona Terror Attack." CBS News. Accessed February 24, 2019. www.cbsnews.com/pictures/barcelona-terror-attack-van-crashes-into-pedestrians/.

Barros, Carlos P., and Isabel Proença. "Mixed Logit Estimation of Radical Islamic Terrorism in Europe and North America: A Comparative Study." *The Journal of Conflict Resolution* 49, no. 2 (2005): 298–314.

"Berlin Christmas Market Attack." *Guardian*, May 2018. Accessed February 24, 2019. www.theguardian.com/world/berlin-christmas-market-attack.

Braun, Aurel, and Stephen Scheinberg. *The Extreme Right: Freedom and Security at Risk*. New York: Westview Press, 1997.

Brisard, Jean-Charles. "The Paris Attacks and the Evolving Islamic State Threat to France." *CTC Sentinel* 8, no. 11 (2015): 5–8.

Chazan, David. "French Jihadists Regularly Received Welfare Payments after Joining Isil, Police Reveal." *The Telegraph*, October 26, 2017. Accessed February 24, 2019. www.telegraph.co.uk/news/2017/10/26/french-jihadists-regularly-received-welfare-payments-joining/.

"Chemical, Biological, Radiological and Nuclear (CBRN) Protection." The Netherlands Organisation. Accessed February 24, 2019, www.tno.nl/en/focus-areas/defence-safety-security/expertise-groups/chemical-biological-radiological-and-nuclear-cbrn-protection/.

Coolsaet, Rik. *What Accounts for the Rise of Violent Extremism in European Cities?* Barcelona: Barcelona Centre for International Affairs, 2017.

Council of the European Union. Framework Decision on Combating Terrorism (2002/475/JHA). Brussels: European Union, 2002.

"Cutting Cash Flows to Terrorists." European Parliament News, February 26, 2018. Accessed February 24, 2019. www.europarl.europa.eu/news/en/press-room/20180226IPR98617/cutting-cash-flows-to-terrorists.

"EU Budget 2018 Approved Support for Youth Growth Security." European Parliament News, November 27, 2017. Accessed February 24, 2019. www.europarl.europa.eu/news/en/headlines/priorities/2018-budget/20171127IPR88936/eu-budget-2018-approved-support-for-youth-growth-security.

Europol. *EU Terrorism Situation and Trend Report 2017*. The Hague: European Union Agency for Law Enforcement Cooperation, 2017.

Europol. *EU Terrorism Situation and Trend Report 2018*. The Hague: European Union Agency for Law Enforcement Cooperation, 2018.

"Extremism and the EU." *Daily Telegraph*. August 30, 2018. Accessed February 24, 2019, http://0-search.proquest.com.cisne.sim.ucm.es.bucm.idm.oclc.org/docview/2096278151?accountid=14514.

Farwell, James P. "The Media Strategy of ISIS." *Survival* 56, no. 6 (2014): 49–55.

"Fight against Money Laundering and Terrorist Financing." European Council Policies database. October 25, 2018. Accessed February 24, 2019. www.consilium.europa.eu/en/policies/fight-against-terrorism/fight-against-terrorist-financing/.

"Foreign Fighters: An Updated Assessment of the Flow of Foreign Fighters into Syria and Iraq." The Soufan Group, December 2015. Accessed February 24, 2019. http://soufangroup.com/wp-content/uploads/2015/12/TSG_ForeignFightersUpdate3.pdf.

Global Center on Cooperative Security, Human Security Collective, and International Centre for Counter-Terrorism. *Addressing the Foreign Terrorist Fighters Phenomenon from a European Union Perspective*. The Hague: International Centre for Counter-Terrorism, 2014.

Haflz, Yasmine. "What Is a Caliphate? ISIS Declaration Raises Questions." *Huffington Post*, June 6, 2014. Accessed February 24, 2019. www.huffingtonpost.com/2014/06/30/what-is-a-caliphate meaning_n_5543538.html?guccounter=1.

Hennessy, Orla. *The Return of Europe's Foreign Fighters*. The Hague: International Centre for Counter-Terrorism, 2014. Accessed February 24, 2019. http://icct.nl/publication/the-return-of-europes-foreign-fighters.

"How to Stop Terrorism: EU Measures Explained (Infographic)." European Parliament News, March 22, 2018. Accessed February 24, 2019. www.europarl.europa.eu/news/en/headlines/security/20180316STO99922/how-to-stop-terrorism-eu-measures-explained-infographic.

Jegan, Vlad. "Interfering with Democracy: the Coalition between Right-Wing Extremism and Terrorism inside a Globalized World." *Research and Science Today* 2 (2016): 69–77.

Kaufmann, Eric. *Whiteshift: Populism, Immigration and the Future of White Majorities*. Penguin, 2018.

Koehler, Daniel. "Right-Wing Extremism and Terrorism in Europe: Current Developments and Issues for the Future." *PRISM* 6 2 (2016): 84–105.

Li, Darryl. "A Universal Enemy? 'Foreign Fighters' and Legal Regimes of Exclusion and Exemption under the 'Global War on Terror.'" *Columbia Human Rights Law Review* 41, no. 2 (2010): 355.

Lister, Charles. *Returning Foreign Fighters: Criminalization or Reintegration?* Doha: Brookings Doha Center, 2015.

Martín, Teresa Marcos. "Legal Instruments and Specific Actions in the EU's Fight against Terrorism." In *Radicalism and Terrorism in the 21st Century: Implications for Security*, edited by Anna Sroka, Fanny Castro-Rial Garrone and Rubén Darío Torres Kumbrián, 247–60. Frankfurt Am Main: Peter Lang AG, 2017.

Minkenberg, Michael. "The Rise of the Radical Right in Eastern Europe: Between Mainstreaming and Radicalization." *Georgetown Journal of International Affairs* 18, no. 1 (2017): 27–35.

Noack, Rick. "2,000 Men Sexually Assaulted 1,200 Women at Cologne New Year's Eve Party." *Independent*, July 11, 2016. Accessed February 24, 2019. www.independent.co.uk/news/world/europe/cologne-new-years-eve-mass-sex-attacks-leaked-document-a7130476.html.

Paulussen, Christophe, and Eva Entenmann. "Addressing Europe's Foreign Fighter Issue: Legal Avenues at the International and National Level." *Security and Human Rights* 25, no. 1 (2014): 86–118.

"Public to Get Access to Information on Beneficial Owners of Firms in EU." European Parliament News, January 29, 2018. Accessed February 24, 2019. www.europarl.europa.eu/news/es/press-room/20180129IPR96112/public-to-get-access-to-information-on-beneficial-owners-of-firms-in-eu.

Ranstorp, Magnus. "La financiación del terrorismo: principales actores, estrategias y fuentes." *Estudios de Política Exterior* 57 (2018).

"Response to the Phenomenon of Foreign Terrorist Combatants and Recent Terrorist Attacks in Europe." European Council and Council of the European Union website, April 4, 2016. Accessed February 24, 2019. www.consilium.europa.eu/es/policies/fight-against-terrorism/foreign-fighters/.

"Response to the Terrorist Threat and the Recent Terrorist Attacks in Europe." European Council and Council of the European Union website. November 30, 2018. Accessed February 24, 2019. www.consilium.europa.eu/en/policies/fight-against-terrorism/foreign-fighters/.

"Schengen: New Rules for Stronger Protection." European Parliament News, October 25, 2017. Accessed February 24, 2019. www.europarl.europa.eu/news/en/headlines/security/20171023STO86604/schengen-new-rules-for-stronger-protection-video.

Speckhard, Anne. "Talking Terrorism: What Drives Young People to Become Foreign Fighters for ISIS and Other Terrorism Groups and What Can Be Done in Response?" *Freedom from Fear* 2 (2015): 24–28.

"State of the Union 2018: Commission Proposes New Rules to Get Terrorist Content off the Web." European Commission Press, September 12, 2018. Accessed February 24, 2019. http://europa.eu/rapid/press-release_IP-18-5561_en.htm.

Stern, Jessica, and John M. Berger. *ISIS: The State of Terror*, 1st edition. New York: Ecco, 2015.

"Terrorism Funding: 'If We Tackle the Logistics, We Fix the Issue.'" European Parliament News, February 28, 2018. Accessed February 24, 2019. www.europarl.europa.eu/news/en/headlines/.priorities/terrorism/20180222STO98436/terrorism-funding-if-we-tackle-the-logistics-we-fix-the-issue.

"Terrorism in the EU: Terror Attacks, Deaths and Arrests." European Parliament News, July 25, 2018. Accessed February 24, 2019. www.europarl.europa.eu/news/en/headlines/security/20180703STO07125/terrorism-in-the-eu-terror-attacks-deaths-and-arrests.

"Truck Attack in Nice." *Aljazeera*, July 10, 2018. Accessed February 24, 2019. www.aljazeera.com/programmes/aljazeeraworld/2018/07/truck-attack-nice-180710132318265.html.

Verkuyten, Maykel. "Religious Fundamentalism and Radicalization among Muslim Minority Youth in Europe." *European Psychologist* 23, no. 1 (2018): 21–31.

Vidino, Lorenzo. "European Foreign Fighters in Syria: Dynamics and Responses." *European View* 13, no. 2 (2014): 217–24.

Weimann, Gabriel. "New Terrorism and New Media." Wilson Center Research Series 2. Wilson Center, 2014.

13
EU SPACE SECURITY POLICY

Marco Pedrazzi

Introduction: the relevance of space security

In the context of space security, it is advisable to give the term security a broad meaning, so as to include safety, since the two concepts are tightly connected, especially in the field of space activities.[1] Space security has three fundamental facets, which are all important for the following reasons.

First, space activities provide essential tools for security on earth. Let us only think of the essential telecommunication, surveillance, early warning, navigation and positioning infrastructures in which satellites play a fundamental role, contributing to life-sustaining and life-saving activities on our planet (and to military security/defence).

Second, and as a direct consequence of the first facet, for exactly the same reason that makes space activities so important for many activities that compose our daily life, the security of space assets – i.e. their protection from threats coming from space and/or earth – becomes vital. This is so not only to ensure space security, but also to safeguard the security of all of us on earth. This is true even more when we are dealing with space assets specifically devoted to security purposes. Threats take various forms, including, among many, possible physical attacks launched by States or by non-State actors against satellites and spacecrafts, using different kinds of weapons based on earth or in space; cyberattacks, which are a concrete, high-level threat for space activities, and require the strict coordination of efforts in the space security and cybersecurity domains; the risk of accidents due to collisions with other space objects and particularly with space debris; and other risks arising out of the harshness of the space environment, such as the ones deriving from space weather occurrences.

Third, as much as space activities can contribute to security on earth, so can they contribute to threatening our security: military uses that are traditionally security/defence oriented can be turned to threaten the security of others. That is why space weaponization could represent a major threat. Among the threats originating from space, along with those of human origin, there are also natural hazards.[2]

The institutional setting of space activities in Europe: ESA and the EU

A preliminary note on the institutional setting of space activities in Europe is necessary in order to understand the European Union's interest and the role it can play in the area of space security.

While space activities are still, especially in their military component, in the hands of States, private entities and international (or supranational) entities also play a role in Europe.

The role of private entities is becoming more relevant every day, although the situation in Europe is not yet comparable to the one in the United States.[3] In legal terms, private entities act under the authorization, control, and responsibility of their national State.[4] The launching State, in turn, is liable, according to different criteria, for any damage caused by space objects on earth, to aircraft in flight, or to other space objects.[5]

In Europe, however, national roles are complemented by those of two fundamental international (or supranational) players, which are the European Space Agency (ESA) and the European Union (EU). ESA is an international organization made up of twenty-two member States (twenty of them are also EU members, soon to be nineteen after Brexit enters into effect, unless there are any new accessions), set up in order to organize and handle space cooperation among European States. It has an important scientific program and makes an essential contribution to boosting European space activities through research and development, building space systems (such as launchers and telecommunication or observation satellites) that are later transferred to other private or public entities, which will own and operate them.

The EU, as a global economic power, is naturally interested in space activities, and this interest has grown over time with the extension of EU competences to new fields, such as the protection of the environment and the development of a common foreign and security policy. For quite some time, this has made the EU a regulator of certain aspects of space activities (such as satellite telecommunications), and a customer of space.

Today, after the Treaty of Lisbon, the spread of EU interests into space finds its legal basis in the Treaty on the Functioning of the European Union (TFEU). According to Article 4.3:

> In the areas of research, technological development and space, the Union shall have competence to carry out activities, in particular to define and implement programmes; however, the exercise of that competence shall not result in Member States being prevented from exercising theirs.

According to Article 189, (paragraph 1) the Union "shall draw up a European space policy," in order to "promote scientific and technical progress, industrial competitiveness and the implementation of its policies," and to this end "it may promote joint initiatives, support research and technological development and coordinate the efforts needed for the exploration and exploitation of space." And, in order to contribute to these objectives (paragraph 2),

> the European Parliament and the Council, acting in accordance with the ordinary legislative procedure, shall establish the necessary measures, which may take the form of a European space programme, excluding any harmonisation of the laws and regulations of the Member States.

The article adds (paragraph 3) that the EU "shall establish any appropriate relations with the European Space Agency."[6]

Therefore the EU and member States enjoy parallel competences regarding outer space activities.[7] As for the relationship with ESA, an attempt was made some years ago within the EU to radically modify it, and the idea was even floated to transform ESA into the space agency of the European Union.[8] For the time being, however, ESA does not intend to lose its status as an independent international organization. In 2003, the EU and ESA concluded a Framework Agreement, setting out the basic parameters for their cooperation, which has been automatically renewed ever since.[9] A European Space Policy was elaborated within this framework and approved by the Space Council, a body resulting from joint meetings of the ESA and EU Councils, in 2007.[10] More recently, in October 2016 the European Commission and ESA issued a joint statement, in which they expressed their "intention to reinforce their cooperation in the future [...] and further develop it."[11]

The most important aspect of this cooperation is the fact that the EU is implementing some major space programs of particular interest for the realization of its policies, mostly utilizing ESA as the agency in charge of the research and development phases. These programs are of direct relevance to our topic, as the pursuit of security, on earth and in space, is one of their most important objectives. Here, I am referring to the following components of the European space program identified in the latest proposal of the European Commission, issued in June 2018: Galileo, an autonomous global navigation satellite system under civil control but with relevant security implications; EGNOS, a regional satellite navigation system augmenting and correcting the open signals emitted by Galileo and by other global navigation satellite systems (GNSSs) (above all, the American GPS); Copernicus (the former Global Monitoring for Environment and Security (GMES)), an autonomous earth observation system, once again under civil control but with relevant security implications; a space surveillance and tracking (SST) system, mainly based on member States' capabilities, intended to identify and track orbiting spacecraft and debris, in order to better protect Europe and its satellites against related risks. The future objective is to reach a full space situational awareness (SSA) capacity, including the detection of space weather phenomena and near earth objects (NEOs) approaching our planet.[12] Finally, there is a new initiative, GOVSATCOM, i.e. "a governmental satellite communications service enabling the provision of satellite communications services to Union and Member State authorities managing security critical missions and infrastructures."[13] In order to achieve these ambitious objectives, the Commission envisages a modification in the existing governance structure, projecting the substitution of the current European GNSS Agency, which manages the European GNSS programme (EGNOS and Galileo), with a European Union Agency for the Space Programme, in charge of a broader set of tasks, which would also relate to other components of the programme. While it is true that the proposal does not intend to touch on the competences of ESA, with which the EU intends to sign a Financial Framework Partnership Agreement, and that ESA officially welcomes the proposal as fully in line with the common arrangements,[14] it should come as no surprise that backstage reactions to the projected creation of a second European space agency have proven to be more concerned.[15]

The UK has been one of the main actors, all through the years, in the European space and security arenas. Therefore, *Brexit*, which should take effect on 31 October 2019, will significantly affect the UK and the EU in these areas, although the UK will remain a member State of ESA. Deep uncertainties still surround the whole process. Nonetheless, it is clear that the continuing participation of the UK in programs such as Copernicus and Galileo, and especially in some security-related aspects of these programs, is open to question.[16]

EU attempts to regulate in the field of space security

In recent years, the EU has also pursued more ambitious plans in regulatory, and not merely operational, terms in relation to space security. The international legal framework, apart from some important (although far from comprehensive) limitations in the military field (the prohibition against positioning nuclear weapons and other weapons of mass destruction in outer space; the prohibition of military activities on celestial bodies),[17] only contains some general, broad prescriptions in terms of space security, a term that does not appear in any treaty as such.[18] In the last two decades, there have been important developments with regard to the prevention and limitation of debris, which is the factor most endangering the safety of all objects in earth's orbit. However, these developments have not taken the form of new treaty rules, but are rather acts of soft law. The most important of these are the Space Debris Mitigation Guidelines adopted by the UN Committee on the Peaceful Uses of Outer Space (COPUOS) in 2007, and endorsed by the UN General Assembly (UNGA).[19]

Similar recommendations are contained in the Report on Transparency and Confidence-Building Measures (TCBMs) in Outer Space Activities presented in 2013 by a Group of Governmental Experts (GGE) established by the Secretary-General. In one of the final recommendations of the Report, the Group endorsed "efforts to pursue political commitments, for example, in the form of unilateral declarations, bilateral commitments or a multilateral code of conduct, to encourage responsible actions in, and the peaceful use of, outer space." It concluded "that voluntary political measures can form the basis for consideration of concepts and proposals for legally binding obligations."[20] In reality, the UNGA had already invited member States to submit proposals on TCBMs in outer space in 2006 and 2007 (resolutions 61/75 and 62/43[21]). Following these invitations, in 2008 the EU Council decided to propose a draft Code of Conduct for Space Activities to the international community.[22] The draft was revised a few times, partly on the basis of other States' reactions, and the last revision dates from 2014.[23]

The Code's aim was to function like a TCBM, able to enhance the safety, security and sustainability of outer space activities.

The Code consists of a set of non-binding measures, complementary to the existing international legal framework governing space activities, that all States (and not only EU member States!) are invited to voluntarily subscribe to. The provisions are not all entirely new. First, States are to engage in promoting and implementing existing treaties and the most important soft law documents, including those relating to the use of nuclear power sources (NPS) in outer space[24] and COPUOS's Space Debris Mitigation Guidelines. Paragraph 4.2, on space debris mitigation measures, is particularly important. Under it, States would resolve to:

> refrain from any action which brings about, directly or indirectly, damage, or destruction, of space objects unless such action is justified:
>
> - by imperative safety considerations, in particular if human life or health is at risk; or
> - in order to reduce the creation of space debris; or
> - by the Charter of the United Nations, including the inherent right of individual or collective self-defence.
>
> and where such exceptional action is necessary, that it be undertaken in a manner so as to minimise, to the greatest extent practicable, the creation of space debris.

It is worth recalling that the first version of this rule was proposed one year after China had effected an anti-satellite (ASAT) test, destroying one of its satellites in orbit, with disastrous effects in terms of production of space debris, and worrisome consequences in terms of the spread and possible future uses of ASAT weapons.[25] Although important, the rule would remain subject to different interpretations of, for example, what would constitute the situations giving rise to the right of self-defence and which actions would be justified as measures of self-defence. This ambiguity is not confined to outer space. However, the dual nature of most objects in outer space would render the rules relating to the use of force in such an environment (whether *ius ad bellum* or *ius in bello*) particularly contentious.[26]

The Code, in addition to rules concerning the mitigation of space debris, includes a series of provisions relating to transparency requirements,[27] providing for notification of launches and of all relevant occurrences in orbit to all other states, for example through a specially constituted point of contact, information sharing concerning space activities and safety and security measures adopted, and consultation procedures.[28]

The proposal is complementary to a series of efforts going on in particular within the UN and specifically within COPUOS. In addition to the documents already mentioned, these include the draft guidelines for the long-term sustainability of space activities that the respective Working Group within COPUOS's Scientific and Technical Subcommittee has been developing in recent years.[29]

This document is particularly interesting because, unlike the COPUOS documents, which are confined to dealing with the non-military uses of outer space, since the military ones fall under the competence of the Conference on Disarmament (CD),[30] the EU Code, as previously highlighted, openly covers all potential uses of space, including military ones.

Here, it is worth recalling that the legal basis for EU action with regard to space is found not only in the TFEU rules previously mentioned, but also in the Treaty on European Union (EU Treaty) rules concerning the common foreign and security policy (CFSP), and, more specifically, the common security and defence policy (CSDP). Although space is not explicitly mentioned there, it is obviously fully included in this policy, along with all other dimensions. We must bear in mind that in this case we are dealing with an EU competence which continues to rest on substantially intergovernmental forms of cooperation.

Actually, the proposed Code is perfectly consonant with the objectives of the Union's external action as defined in the EU Treaty:

> The Union … shall work for a high degree of cooperation in all fields of international relations, in order to: (a) safeguard its values, fundamental interests, security, independence and integrity; … (c) preserve peace, prevent conflicts and strengthen international security, …; … (f) help develop international measures to preserve and improve the quality of the environment and the sustainable management of global natural resources, in order to ensure sustainable development; … (h) promote an international system based on stronger multilateral cooperation and good global governance (art. 21.2);

and with the fact that, according to Article 24 EU, the Union's competence in matters of CFSP shall cover "all questions relating to the Union's security."[31]

The Code was proposed to nearly 100 States, through an intense diplomatic effort that took place by means of a series of meetings organized outside the formal UN framework, since the EU is not a UN member, but substantially within the UN context. Many, including the US, expressed their interest or support.[32] However, States such as China and Russia, which are pursuing their own international space security political agenda through their draft treaty on prevention of the placement of weapons in outer space (PPWT) proposed within the CD,[33] have opposed the project from the outset. This opposition was one of the main elements that effectively drowned the document,[34] although the draft Code remains officially on the table.

The fact is that the Chino-Russian proposal is strongly opposed by the US, and the prospects of adopting a binding treaty for the prevention of an arms race in outer space (PAROS) are, at the moment, rather slim. The issue is, nonetheless, under discussion: the General Assembly, by resolution 72/250, adopted on 24 December 2017, has given a mandate to the Secretary-General to establish a new Group of Governmental Experts, "to consider and make recommendations on substantial elements of an international legally binding instrument on the prevention of an arms race in outer space, including, inter alia, on the prevention of the placement of weapons in outer space."[35] The Group held a two-week session in Geneva in 2018 and will hold a second session in 2019.

The EU proposal has had the merit of putting important issues on the table, which can only be satisfactorily dealt with through intense and open international cooperation, and possibly by means of voluntary non-binding measures for the time being. The EU did so with the strength of its voice, and with the fragility of its voice, especially in the space arena. Here, the EU does not yet have a fully recognized position, since it is not a party to the relevant treaties, and neither is it a member of the UN or COPUOS, and it coexists in its own physical space with other powerful actors, even more powerful than itself in certain respects, such as ESA and some of its member States. Furthermore, the cooperation among these different actors does not always function at its best.

Despite the de facto rejection of its proposal, the EU continues to pursue (albeit in a less visible way) the path of promoting the adoption of non-binding measures, at least as a first step, in all fora. It does so in its efforts concerning the sustainability of space activities, in its involvement with TCBMs or in the PAROS debate, and in its support of initiatives such as the Principles of Responsible Behavior in Outer Space (PORBOS), all of which have the same underlying concept: to devise rules for the responsible and transparent handling of outer space activities, minimizing security risks and guaranteeing the orderly and safe development of space ventures for all.[36]

Concluding remarks

The times do not breed optimism, especially in Europe. However, the hope is that maximal coordination among all European space actors can be achieved in order to produce a coherent and comprehensive intra-European space security policy with a visible and coherent external projection, whatever the international, extra-EU reception of the EU positions will be. A further goal is that this policy will be used for security, and not for other purposes, such as, for example, building a fortress Europe totally impermeable to migrants (and refugees…). A big question mark, at the moment, relates to the uncertain future position of the UK, one of the most important space actors in Europe, particularly from the security point of view, after Brexit enters into effect. The Draft Withdrawal Agreement or the Political Declaration of 14 November 2018 do not clarify the issue. What is clear, however, and emerges from these documents, is that the two parties wish to continue cooperating as much in the security field as in that of defence and in the area of space, and that the participation of the UK in specific EU programs is anticipated.[37] However, as Brexit is approaching, the fate of such texts would seem to be definitely compromised.

Notes

1 The Space Security Index defines space security as: "the security and sustainability of outer space as an environment that can be used safely and responsibly by all." Jessica West, *Space Security Index 2017*, 14th edition, (Waterloo: Project Ploughshare, 2017), 5.

2 European Space Policy Institute, *Security in Outer Space: Rising Stakes for Europe*, ESPI Report 64 (August 2018), 5–81, 6–7.

3 Ibid., 9ff.

4 Treaty on Principles Governing the Activities of States in the Exploration and Use of Outer Space, including the Moon and Other Celestial Bodies (best known as *Outer Space Treaty*), adopted by the UN General Assembly by res. 2222 (XXI) of 19 December 1966, opened for signature on 27 January 1967, entered into force on 10 October 1967, art. VI, UNTS 610 (1967): 205.

5 According to the Convention on International Liability for Damage Caused by Space Objects, adopted by the UN General Assembly by res. 2777 (XXVI) of 29 November 1971, opened for signature on 29 March 1972, entered into force on 1 September 1972, UNTS 961 (1975): 187. The "launching State" is defined as the State "which launches or procures the launching of a space object" or "from whose territory or facility a space object is launched" (Article I (c)). Liability is absolute for damage on the surface of the earth or to aircraft in flight (Article II), based on fault for damage caused in airspace or in outer space to a space object of another launching State (Article III).

6 Annette Froehlich, "Vertrag von Lissabon und seine Folgen für die ESA-EU-Beziehungen: von Luxemburg bis Luzern," *Zeitschrift für Luft- und Weltraumrecht* 66 (2017): 58.

7 On the legal conundrum of this notion see, among others, Florent Mazurelle, Jan Wouters, and Walter Thiebaut, "The Evolution of European Space Governance: Policy, Legal and Institutional Implications," *International Organizations Law Review* 6 (2009): 155–89, 22; Frans G. von der Dunk, *The EU Space Competence as per the Treaty of Lisbon: Sea Change or Empty Shell? Proceedings of the International Institute of Space Law* (The Hague: Eleven International, 2011), 382–92, accessed May 6, 2019, http://digitalcommons.unl.edu/spacelaw/66.

8 European Commission, White Paper – Space: A New European Frontier for an Expanding Union. An Action Plan for Implementing the European Space Policy, COM(2003) 673 (Brussels: European Union, November 11, 2003), 35ff.; and, again, European Commission, Communication to the Council and the European Parliament, Establishing Appropriate Relations between the EU and the European Space Agency, COM(2012) 671 final (Brussels: European Union, November 14, 2012).

9 Council Decision of 29 April 2004 on the conclusion of the Framework Agreement between the European Community and the European Space Agency (signed 25 November 2003, entered into force 28 May 2004), OJ L261, August 6, 2004.

10 Council of the European Union, 4th Space Council, Resolution on the European Space Policy, Competitiveness (Internal Market, Industry and Research) Council meeting, Brussels, May 22, 2007. For a short survey on ESA and these developments, and for further bibliographic references, see Marco Pedrazzi, "European Space Agency (ESA)," *Max Planck Encyclopedia of Public International Law*, 2010, accessed May 6, 2019, www.mpepil.com.

11 European Commission, Joint Statement on Shared Vision and Goals for the Future of Europe in Space by the European Union and the European Space Agency (Brussels: European Union, October 26, 2016), accessed May 6, 2019, http://ec.europa.eu/DocsRoom/documents/19562/. On the same day, the European Commission issued a Communication to the European Parliament, the Council, the European Economic and Social Committee and the Committee of the Regions: Space Strategy for Europe, COM(2016) 705 final (Brussels: European Union, October 26, 2016).

12 European Parliament and Council of the European Union, Decision No 541/2014/EU of the European Parliament and of the Council of 16 April 2014 Establishing a Framework for Space Surveillance and Tracking Support, OJ L 158, May 25, 2014. See also the Report from the Commission: European Commission, Report from the Commission to the European Parliament and the Council on the Implementation of the Space Surveillance and Tracking (SST) Support Framework (2014–2017), COM(2018) 256 final (Brussels: European Union, May 3, 2018).

13 European Commission, Proposal for a Regulation of the European Parliament and of the Council Establishing the Space Programme of the Union and Repealing Regulations (EU) No 912/2010, (EU) No 1285/2013, (EU) No 377/2014 and Decision 541/2014/EU, COM(2018) 447 final (Brussels: European Union, June 6, 2018). The quoted paragraph is from art. 3 (e) of the proposed Regulation.

14 European Space Agency, "The European Space Agency Welcomes European Commission's Proposal on Space Activities," European Space Agency press release 13–2018, June 6, 2018, accessed May 6, 2019, www.esa.int/For_Media/Press_Releases/The_European_Space_Agency_welcomes_European_Commission_s_proposal_on_space_activities.

15 Daniel Boffey, "Space Agency Boss Warns EU of Rival Agency Risks," *Guardian*, June 6, 2018, accessed May 6, 2019, www.theguardian.com/science/2018/jun/06/european-space-agency-boss-warns-eu-over-star-wars.

16 European Space Policy Institute. "Brexit and Space." ESPI Briefs 24, July 24, 2018, accessed May 6, 2019, www.espi.or.at; Jean-Jacques Tortora, "The potential implications of Brexit for EU space

policy;" European Parliament, *Brexit and Industry and Space Policy*, Workshop proceedings, Study requested by the ITRE committee, PE 626.084, November 2018: 10–11; Leslie Jane Smith and Ruairidh J.M. Leishman, "Up, Up and Away: An Update on the UK's Latest Plans for Space Activities," *Air & Space Law* 44, no. 1 (2019): 1–26, 22–4.

17 Article IV, Outer Space Treaty: "States Parties to the Treaty undertake not to place in orbit around the earth any objects carrying nuclear weapons or any other kinds of weapons of mass destruction, install such weapons on celestial bodies, or station such weapons in outer space in any other manner. The Moon and other celestial bodies shall be used by all States Parties to the Treaty exclusively for peaceful purposes. The establishment of military bases, installations and fortifications, the testing of any type of weapons and the conduct of military manoeuvres on celestial bodies shall be forbidden. The use of military personnel for scientific research or for any other peaceful purposes shall not be prohibited. The use of any equipment or facility necessary for peaceful exploration of the Moon and other celestial bodies shall also not be prohibited." For a comment, see Kai-Uwe Schrogl and Julia Neumann, "Article IV," in *Cologne Commentary on Space Law, Volume 1, Outer Space Treaty*, eds. Stephan Hobe, Bernhard Schmidt-Tedd and Kai-Uwe Schrogl (Cologne: Carl Heymanns Verlag, 2009), 70.

18 Among the norms having a relevance in a space security perspective, we may mention the provisions relating to the principle of due regard for the interests of other States and the prevention of contamination, transparency in the conduct of space activities and the means of verification contained in Articles I, IX, XI and XII, Outer Space Treaty and in the Convention on Registration of Objects Launched into Outer Space, adopted by UN General Assembly res. 3235 (XXIX) of 12 November 1974, opened for signature on 14 January 1975, entered into force on 15 September 1976, UNTS 1023 (1976): 15.

19 United Nations Committee on the Peaceful Uses of Outer Space, *Space Debris Mitigation Guidelines*, Vienna, 2007. The Guidelines were adopted by COPUOS' Scientific and Technical Subcommittee (STSC) in its 44th session (Vienna, 12–23 February 2007: see the STSC Report, UN Doc. A/AC.105/890 issued on March 6, 2007), endorsed by the Committee in its 50th session (Vienna, 6–15 June 2007: see COPUOS Report, UN Doc. A/62/20 (2007)). The text of the Guidelines is published in the Annex and later by the General Assembly with res. 62/217 of 22 December 2007.

20 United Nations General Assembly, *Report of the Group of Governmental Experts on Transparency and Confidence-Building Measures in Outer Space Activities*, UN Doc. A/68/189, issued on 29 July 2013, reissued for technical reasons on 27 September 2013, para. 69.

21 United Nations General Assembly, Resolution 61/75, UN Doc. A/RES/61/75 of 6 December 2006; United Nations General Assembly, Resolution 62/43, UN Doc. A/RES/62/43 of 5 December 2007.

22 The draft Code was approved by the Council on 8–9 December 2008: see Council of the European Union, Council Conclusions and Draft Code of Conduct for Outer Space Activities, 17175/08, PESC 1697, CODUN 61 (Brussels: European Union, December 17, 2008).

23 The version of 31 March 2014 is available at https://eeas.europa.eu/headquarters/headquarters-homepage/14715/eu-proposal-international-space-code-conduct-draft_en. See, among others, Sergio Marchisio, "Security in Space: Issues at Stake," *Space Policy* 33 (August 2015): 67–69.

24 Reference is made to the following documents: United Nations General Assembly, *Principles Relevant to the Use of Nuclear Power Sources in Outer Space*, UN Doc. A/RES/47/68 of 14 December 1992; and to United Nations General Assembly, *Safety Framework for Nuclear Power Source Applications in Outer Space*, UN Doc. A/AC.105/934 of 19 May 2009, jointly prepared by COPUOS' STSC and by the International Atomic Energy Agency (IAEA), endorsed by COPUOS in its 52nd session (Vienna, 3–12 June 2009: see its Report, UN Doc. A/64/20 (2009), paragraph 138), and "welcome[d] with satisfaction" by UNGA res. 64/86 of 10 December 2009.

25 Among others, David A. Koplow, "ASAT-isfaction: Customary International Law and the Regulation of Anti-Satellite Weapons," *Michigan Journal of International Law* 30 (2008–2009): 1187–272, 1203.

26 Michael N. Schmitt, "International Law and Military Operations in Space," *Max Planck UNYB* 10 (2006): 89–125; Michel Bourbonnière and Ricky J. Lee, "*Jus ad Bellum* and *Jus in Bello* Considerations on the Targeting of Satellites: The Targeting of Post-Modern Military Space Assets," *Israel Yearbook on Human Rights* 44 (2014): 167–217.

27 According to Paul B. Larsen, "Outer Space Arms Control: Can the USA, Russia and China Make This Happen?" *Journal of Conflict and Security Law* 23, no. 1 (Spring 2018): 137–59, insuring transparency in order to allow States to avoid accidental war in outer space is the main purpose of the draft Code.

28 In particular, paragraphs 5, 6, 7 and 9.

29 See the text of the agreed-upon guidelines and of those still under discussion in United Nations General Assembly, *Guidelines for the Long-term Sustainability of Outer Space Activities*, UN Doc. A/AC.105/L.135 of

23 February 2018. It would appear, however, that the Working Group has run aground at the moment (see COPUOS Report on its 73rd session, 20–29 June 2018, UN Doc. A/73/20, paragraphs 194 and ff.), due to the lack of agreement on the most politically sensitive provisions, and the fact that there are no prospects for a final approval of the whole document.

30 This is the reason apparently thwarting the efforts to conclude the Sustainability Guidelines.

31 On the scope and the ambiguities of Article 24: Enzo Cannizzaro, "Art. 24," in *Trattati dell'Unione Europea*, ed. Antonio Tizzano. (Milan: Giuffrè, 2014): *I. Trattato sull'Unione Europea*, 232; on the operative side: European External Action Service, *Shared Vision, Common Action: A Stronger Europe. A Global Strategy for the European Union's Foreign and Security Policy* (Brussels: European Union, 2016), 42, accessed May 6, 2019, http://europa.eu/globalstrategy/en.

32 On the US support, expressed during the Obama administration, see Jameson Rohrer, "Deciphering and Defending the European Union's Non-Binding Code of Conduct for Outer Space Activities," *Duke Journal of Comparative & International Law* 23 (2012): 187–216, 209.

33 For an overview, see, Fabio Tronchetti and Hao Liu, "The 2014 Updated Draft PPWT: Hitting the Spot or Missing the Mark?" *Space Policy* 33 (2015): 38–49.

34 Michael J. Listner, "The International Code of Conduct: Comments on changes in the latest draft and post-mortem thoughts," *The Space Review*, October 26, 2015, accessed May 6, 2019, www.thespacereview.com/article/2851/1.

35 United Nations General Assembly, Resolution 72/250, UN. Doc. A/RES/72/250, adopted on 24 December 2017.

36 European External Action Service, *Conference on Disarmament – Working Group on the "Way Ahead" – EU Statement on the Prevention of an Arms Race in Outer Space* (Brussels: European Union, 2017), accessed May 6, 2019, http://eueuropaeeas.fpfis.slb.ec.europa.eu:8084/delegations/un-geneva/28329/conference-disarmament-working-group-way-ahead-eu-statement-prevention-arms-race-outer-space_en; European External Action Service, *Conference on Disarmament – Subsidiary Body 3 – Prevention of an Arms Race in Outer Space (PAROS): EU Statement* (Brussels: European Union, 2018), accessed May 6, 2019, http://eueuropaeeas.fpfis.slb.ec.europa.eu:8084/delegations/un-geneva/46129/conference-disarmament-subsidiary-body-3-prevention-arms-race-outer-space-paros-eu-statement_en; European Space Policy Institute, *Security in Outer Space*, 53.

37 European Commission, *Draft Agreement on the withdrawal of the United Kingdom of Great Britain and Northern Ireland from the European Union and the European Atomic Energy Community* (Brussels: European Union, November 14, 2018); and the Political declaration setting out the framework for the future relationship between the European Union and the United Kingdom, adopted on the same date, and, in particular, the following paragraphs of the Political declaration: paragraph 11, according to which the parties will establish the conditions for the UK's participation in Union programmes, in areas such as, inter alia, "science and innovation, … external action, defence capabilities, civil protection and space"; paragraph 80, where it is stated that "the Parties should establish a broad, comprehensive and balanced security partnership," comprising "law enforcement and judicial cooperation in criminal matters, foreign policy, security and defence, as well as thematic cooperation in areas of common interest"; paragraph 92, where the "Parties support ambitious, close and lasting cooperation on external action to protect citizens from external threats, including new emerging threats"; paragraph 104, in relation to defence capabilities cooperation; paragraph 107 ("The Parties should consider appropriate arrangements for cooperation on space"). Council of the European Union, *Political Declaration Setting out the Framework for the Future Relationship between the European Union and the United Kingdom* (Brussels: European Union, November 22, 2018).

References

Boffey, Daniel. "Space Agency Boss Warns EU of Rival Agency Risks." *Guardian*, June 6, 2018.

Bourbonnière, Michael, and Ricky J. Lee. "*Jus ad Bellum* and *Jus in Bello* Considerations on the Targeting of Satellites: The Targeting of Post-Modern Military Space Assets." *Israel Yearbook on Human Rights* 44 (2014): 167–217.

Cannizzaro, Enzo. "Art. 24." In *Trattati dell'Unione Europea*, edited by Antonio Tizzano, *I. Trattato sull'Unione Europea*, 232. Milan: Giuffrè, 2014.

Convention on International Liability for Damage Caused by Space Objects, adopted by the UN General Assembly by res. 2777 (XXVI) of 29 November 1971, opened for signature on 29 March 1972, entered into force on 1 September 1972, *UNTS* 961 (1975).

Convention on Registration of Objects Launched into Outer Space, adopted by UN General Assembly res. 3235 (XXIX) of 12 November 1974, opened for signature on 14 January 1975, entered into force on 15 September 1976, *UNTS* 1023 (1976).
Council of the European Union. Council Conclusions and Draft Code of Conduct for Outer Space Activities, 17175/08, PESC 1697, CODUN 61. Brussels: European Union, December 17, 2008.
Council of the European Union. Council Decision of 29 April 2004 on the Conclusion of the Framework Agreement between the European Community and the European Space Agency (signed 25 November 2003, entered into force 28 May 2004). *Official Journal of the European Union* L261, August 6, 2004, 63–68.
Council of the European Union. *Political Declaration Setting out the Framework for the Future Relationship between the European Union and the United Kingdom*. Brussels: European Union, November 22, 2018.
Council of the European Union, 4th Space Council. Resolution on the European Space Policy, Competitiveness (Internal Market, Industry and Research). Council meeting, Brussels, May 22, 2007.
European Commission. Communication from the Commission to the Council and the European Parliament, Establishing Appropriate Relations between the EU and the European Space Agency. COM(2012) 671 final. Brussels: European Union, November 14, 2012.
European Commission. Communication to the European Parliament, the Council, the European Economic and Social Committee and the Committee of the Regions: Space Strategy for Europe. COM(2016) 705 final. Brussels: European Union, October 26, 2016.
European Commission. *Draft Agreement on the Withdrawal of the United Kingdom of Great Britain and Northern Ireland from the European Union and the European Atomic Energy Community*. Brussels: European Union, November 14, 2018.
European Commission. Joint Statement on Shared Vision and Goals for the Future of Europe in Space by the European Union and the European Space Agency. Brussels: European Union, October 26, 2016.
European Commission. Proposal for a Regulation of the European Parliament and of the Council Establishing the Space Programme of the Union and Repealing Regulations (EU) No 912/2010, (EU) No 1285/2013, (EU) No 377/2014 and Decision 541/2014/EU. COM(2018) 447 final). Brussels: European Union, June 6, 2018.
European Commission. Report from the Commission to the European Parliament and the Council on the Implementation of the Space Surveillance and Tracking (SST) Support Framework (2014–2017). COM(2018) 256 final Brussels: European Union, May 3, 2018.
European Commission. *White Paper – Space: A New European Frontier for an Expanding Union. An Action Plan for Implementing the European Space Policy*. COM(2003) 673. Brussels: European Union, November 11, 2003.
European External Action Service. *Conference on Disarmament – Subsidiary Body 3 – Prevention of an Arms Race in Outer Space (PAROS): EU Statement*. Brussels: European Union, 2018.
European External Action Service. *Conference on Disarmament – Working Group on the "Way Ahead" – EU Statement on the Prevention of an Arms Race in Outer Space*. Brussels: European Union, 2017.
European External Action Service. *Shared Vision, Common Action: A Stronger Europe. A Global Strategy for the European Union's Foreign and Security Policy*. Brussels: European Union, 2016.
European Parliament and Council of the European Union. Decision No 541/2014/EU of the European Parliament and of the Council of 16 April 2014 Establishing a Framework for Space Surveillance and Tracking Support. *Official Journal of the European Union* L 158, May 25, 2014, 227–34.
European Space Agency. "The European Space Agency Welcomes European Commission's Proposal on Space Activities." European Space Agency press release 13–2018, June 6, 2018.
European Space Policy Institute. "Brexit and Space." ESPI Briefs 24, July 24, 2018.
European Space Policy Institute. *Security in Outer Space: Rising Stakes for Europe*. ESPI Report 64 (ESPI, 2018).
Froehlich, Annette. "Vertrag von Lissabon und seine Folgen für die ESA-EU-Beziehungen: von Luxemburg bis Luzern." *Zeitschrift für Luft- und Weltraumrecht* 66 (2017).
Koplow, David A. "ASAT-isfaction: Customary International Law and the Regulation of Anti-Satellite Weapons." *Michigan Journal of International Law* 30 (2008–2009): 1187–272.
Larsen, Paul B. "Outer Space Arms Control: Can the USA, Russia and China Make This Happen?" *Journal of Conflict and Security Law* 23, no. 1 (Spring 2018): 137–59.
Listner, Michael J. "The International Code of Conduct: Comments on Changes in the Latest Draft and Post-Mortem Thoughts." *The Space Review*, October 26, 2015.
Marchisio, Sergio. "Security in Space: Issues at Stake," *Space Policy* 33 (August 2015): 67–69.

Mazurelle, Florent, Jan Wouters and Walter Thiebaut. "The Evolution of European Space Governance: Policy, Legal and Institutional Implications." *International Organizations Law Review* 6 (2009): 155–89.
Pedrazzi, Marco. "European Space Agency (ESA)." *Max Planck Encyclopedia of Public International Law*, 2010.
Rohrer, Jameson. "Deciphering and Defending the European Union's Non-Binding Code of Conduct for Outer Space Activities." *Duke Journal of Comparative & International Law* 23 (2012): 187–216.
Schmitt, Michael N. "International Law and Military Operations in Space." *Max Planck UNYB* 10 (2006): 89–125.
Schrogl, Kai-Uwe, and Julia Neumann. "Article IV." In *Cologne Commentary on Space Law, Volume 1, Outer Space Treaty*, edited by Hobe Stephan, Bernhard Schmidt-Tedd and Kai-Uwe Schrogl. Cologne: Carl Heymanns Verlag, 2009.
Smith, Leslie Jane, and Ruairidh J.M. Leishman. "Up, Up and Away: An Update on the UK's Latest Plans for Space Activities." *Air & Space Law* 44, no. 1 (2019): 1–26.
Tortora, Jean-Jacques. "The Potential Implications of Brexit for EU Space Policy." European Parliament, *Brexit and Industry and Space Policy*, Workshop proceedings, Study requested by the ITRE committee, PE 626.084, November 2018, 10–11.
Treaty on Principles Governing the Activities of States in the Exploration and Use of Outer Space, including the Moon and Other Celestial Bodies, adopted by the UN General Assembly by res. 2222 (XXI) of 19 December 1966, opened for signature on 27 January 1967, entered into force on 10 October 1967, art. VI, *UNTS* 610 (1967).
Tronchetti, Fabio, and Hao Liu. "The 2014 Updated Draft PPWT: Hitting the Spot or Missing the Mark?" *Space Policy* 33 (2015): 38–49.
United Nations Committee on the Peaceful Uses of Outer Space. *Space Debris Mitigation Guidelines*. Vienna, 2007.
United Nations General Assembly. *Guidelines for the Long-term Sustainability of Outer Space Activities*. UN Doc. A/AC.105/L.135 of 23 February 2018.
United Nations General Assembly. *Principles Relevant to the Use of Nuclear Power Sources in Outer Space*. UN Doc. A/RES/47/68 of 14 December 1992.
United Nations General Assembly. *Report of the Group of Governmental Experts on Transparency and Confidence-Building Measures in Outer Space Activities*. UN Doc. A/68/189, issued on 29 July 2013, reissued for technical reasons on 27 September 2013.
United Nations General Assembly. Resolution 61/75. UN Doc. A/RES/61/75 of 6 December 2006.
United Nations General Assembly. Resolution 62/43. UN Doc. A/RES/62/43 of 5 December 2007.
United Nations General Assembly. Resolution 72/250. UN. Doc. A/RES/72/250, adopted on 24 December 2017.
United Nations General Assembly. *Safety Framework for Nuclear Power Source Applications in Outer Space*. UN Doc. A/AC.105/934 of 19 May 2009.
Von Der Dunk, Frans G. *The EU Space Competence as per the Treaty of Lisbon: Sea Change or Empty Shell? Proceedings of the International Institute of Space Law*. The Hague: Eleven International, 2011.
West, Jessica. *Space Security Index 2017*, 14th edition. Waterloo: Project Ploughshare, 2017.

14
THE EU'S COMPREHENSIVE APPROACH TO FISHERIES, GLOBAL COMMONS AND SECURITY*

Carlos Teijo García

Introduction

The overfishing of living marine resources, especially in areas beyond national jurisdiction, as is the case with the High Seas, is a classic example of problems posed by "common-pool resources," public goods which are limited, non-excludable and rivalrous. In accordance with the paradigmatic vision of Hardin's[1] "tragedy of the commons," the combination of rivalry among users and freedom of access to resources leads to the fact that each individual has incentives to extract as much of the resource as possible in the shortest possible amount of time, thereby generating a spiral which inevitably ends up in the collapse of the common-pool resource. This view is often expressed about fisheries and, if we consider official data, it would seem to be partially correct. According to the UN Food and Agriculture Organization (FAO), 59.9 per cent of stocks for which information is available are fully exploited; another 33.1 per cent are exploited at biologically unsustainable levels, because fish are being caught at a rate that exceeds their regeneration potential; and only 7.0 per cent of the total stocks assessed remain underfished.[2]

The metaphor of the "tragedy of the commons" supposes a simplification of reality and has been the object of widespread academic criticism.[3] However, in the field of the fishing industry, this idea proves to be useful as it allows two aspects to be explained which have come to characterise the contemporary Law of the Sea. On the one hand, the jurisdiction of coastal States over their Exclusive Economic Zones (EEZs) has been recognised in order to let them restrict access to resources. On the other hand, mechanisms of limited efficiency (such as RFMOs, Regional Fisheries Management Organisations) have been established with the aim of promoting cooperation in different areas of the High Seas. The coexistence of both opposing dynamics (appropriation versus cooperative management) has not, however, been enough to achieve an efficient global governance of living marine resources that are beyond the control of the coastal States.

Bearing this general perspective in mind, this chapter proposes an approach to the contribution made by the EU towards the preservation of fishery resources considered as global commons, that is, focusing on the fishing that takes place in areas beyond the jurisdiction of any

State or in the EEZ of developing States that lack a real capacity to control their jurisdictional waters. Before addressing the processes of international fisheries cooperation promoted by the EU, we shall, first, highlight the link which exists between fisheries issues and security matters, both from the perspective of *human security* and from the more traditional approach of *military security*. Subsequently, we shall address the role of the EU in the promotion of international fisheries cooperation via the mechanism of RFMOs and through the analysis of the Sustainable Fisheries Partnership Agreements (SFPAs) signed by the EU with, mainly, developing countries with weak policies regarding fisheries. And, finally, we shall examine the role played by the EU in the worldwide struggle against Illegal, Unreported and Unregulated (IUU) fishing. This latter aspect will be dealt with in more detail as in strategies to repress illegal fishing, the socio-economic and military dimensions of international security are directly linked.[4] Although IUU fishing has not traditionally been viewed as a security issue – because it is most often treated as a regulatory matter and deemed a trivial issue in many states insofar as it relates to national security – our analysis shares the argument that this diagnosis is flawed, because a great deal of IUU fishing takes place on a systematic and industrial scale, across multiple jurisdictions, as a form of transnational organised crime.[5] From this perspective, we consider that the commercial approach adopted by the EU in the fight against IUU fishing must be complemented by a strengthening of international cooperation allowing for an increase in the monitoring and vigilance of fishing activities carried out outside of EU waters.

Fishing and security

The first factor which must be highlighted is that the exhaustion of living marine resources due to overfishing has a highly negative impact on human security,[6] as it endangers the sustenance and livelihoods of individuals who depend on marine ecosystems. A significant proportion of the dynamics of overexploitation of resources derives from the administrative difficulties generated by the governance of widely used fishing assets. However, the overexploitation of fisheries does not arise only from the daily problems related to the inadequate management of fishery resources (due to the lack of technical capacity or political will of the States responsible), but it also originates from criminal activity related to fishing.

The implications of overfishing, in relation to the different aspects of security, for the European Union can be systematised in five levels of analysis. The first stage is ecological in nature. The total capture fishery in 2016 was 93 million tonnes, and aquaculture production was 79.3 million tonnes, having undergone exponential growth in the last two decades, with the total of fishery production reaching 170.9 tonnes;[7] the FAO estimates that this figure will reach 196 million tonnes in 2025.[8] Therefore, the pressure on living marine resources will increase, as will the competition for access to them. Over the course of the next few decades, the importance of living marine resources will continue to increase and the relevance of the issue of their international protection will become greater within the framework of collective security strategies, as the recent prospective exercises of the EU[9] and the UN have shown, particularly in relation to the implementation of SDG 14 – Conserve and sustainably use the oceans, seas and marine resources for sustainable development.[10]

The second aspect to be considered in terms of human security is the need to guarantee internal European supply in the medium term. The EU is the world's largest market for fishery products. Hence, despite being a superpower in terms of distant water fishing, it continues to be a net importer of fish. The internal demand for seafood in the EU is mostly met through imports, as they cover around 60 per cent of the total supply.[11] Three out of every five fish bought by European consumers come from outside of EU waters. Therefore, for the EU, guaranteeing both the extractive capacity of the EU fleet and access to fisheries located in the High Seas and in the EEZs of third States is a strategic issue, particularly in the light of the increase in global competition for access to fisheries resources.

The third dimension to be taken into account from the perspective of human security – including the issue of employment – is to guarantee the economic competitiveness of the EU fleet in the medium term, due to the fact that its subsistence depends on access to fisheries outside of EU waters. Although the distant waters sector accounts for less than 1 per cent of the EU fleet, with only 285 of the 84,420 vessels registered, it provides 14 per cent of the total catch and 19 per cent of the total gross tonnage.[12] From the social and economic point of view, fisheries agreements with third States constitute a fundamental source of supply for the European processing sector, which receives more than 60 per cent of the products it processes from outside of EU waters, and generates a significant volume of employment, given that 35,000 jobs depend directly on these agreements. For some countries like Spain, which is the most important State in terms of European distant water fishing, the socio-economic relevance of this activity is even greater.[13]

In fourth place, a connection between the classic security problems affecting the EU (border control, migratory crises, etc.) and the protection of the human security of the populations of neighbouring regions can also be observed. In western Africa and the Gulf of Guinea, the improvement of food security is directly related to an increase in the intake of protein of marine origin among the population; in countries such as Sierra Leone, Gambia, Senegal and Mali more than 60 per cent of protein consumption comes from eating fish.[14] In socio-economic terms, the combination of inadequate fisheries governance and the proliferation of IUU fishing generates a huge negative impact. In western Africa, where more than 3 million people make their living directly from the fishing industry (600,000 of them in Senegal alone), the true catch is 40 per cent higher than the declared one and has a cost of between $820 million and $1.6 billion per year.[15] Of course, this illicit aspect undermines the fragile human security of the countries in the region. In accordance with existing estimations, the resolution of the issue of IUU fishing and the development of the local fishing industry could generate more than 300,000 jobs in the countries of West Africa.[16] The promotion of small-scale and industrial fishing in this region is a fundamental challenge for the EU. The establishment of a constructive fishing relationship with its main partners in the region (the EU has fisheries agreements in force with Morocco, Mauritania, Senegal, Cape Verde, Guinea-Bissau, Liberia, Sierra Leone and Sao Tomé) is key to generating stability, which would strengthen the perspectives of development in the region and reduce the flow of migration.

The fifth and final aspect in summarising the connections between fisheries issues and the concept of security concerns the relationship between illegal fishing activities and the dynamics of transnational criminality. INTERPOL and the United Nations Office on Drugs and Crime (UNODC) have documented both the existence of criminal organisations involved in IUU fishing and the incorporation of criminal techniques, such as human trafficking, slavery, tax evasion, money laundering, customs fraud, corruption and the trafficking of stolen goods, into fishing activity.[17] There has traditionally been a strong resistance to treating large-scale IUU fishing as a serious security threat rather than a simple fisheries management problem. Thus, "a disconnect exists at both national and international levels, between the response to IUU fishing as a minor technical issue in policy terms and its large-scale and highly damaging manifestations in reality,"[18] although this tendency seems to be in the process of being turned around at present given that it is becoming more common to describe – at least in the academic discourse – illegal fishing as a form of transnational crime.[19]

From the beginning, the concept of "IUU fishing" has been problematic because it was adopted in the FAO's International Plan of Action to Deter, Prevent and Eliminate IUU Fishing

(IPOA IUU) as a catch-all term to describe all instances of unfulfillment of international or domestic fisheries management regulations.[20] Therefore, the term IUU fishing encompasses the main subcategory of "illegal fishing" that refers to activities conducted by national or foreign vessels in waters under the jurisdiction of a state or in the area of competence of RFMO, in contravention of the laws and regulations of that state or of the RFMO's conservation and management measures; the "unreported fishing," that is a form of illegal fishing that refers to activities that have not been reported, or have been misreported, to proper authorities; and finally the "unregulated fishing" that covers activities conducted in areas under the authority of RFMOs "by vessels without nationality, or by those flying the flag of a State not party to that organization, or by a fishing entity, in a manner that is not consistent with or contravenes the conservation and management measures of that organization," as well as fishing in "areas or for fish stocks in relation to which there are no applicable conservation or management measures."[21] This last subcategory's results are particularly controversial since unregulated fishing does not necessarily represent a breach of national or international norms.[22] Despite these conceptual ambiguities, it is possible to conclude that the concept of IUU fishing aims to cover all forms of fishing that contribute to the impoverishment of fishery resources that are carried out either on the margin or in violation of international and national mechanisms that guarantee responsible fishing.[23]

To complicate further this terminological confusion, the term "illegal fishing" is frequently also used in literature and international documents as an abbreviation referring to the broad range of fishing activities covered by the IUU concept. As the meaning of the term IUU is so broad and ambiguous, this analysis is only limited to its connection with the concept of "fisheries crime" that can be defined as those criminal offences committed within the fisheries sector, with the "fisheries sector" referring to the entire value chain from vessel registration to the sale of the commodity.[24] In this analytical framework, the organised criminal nature of large-scale IUU fishing is thus more often explicitly recognised, alongside that of other, better-established organised criminal practices.[25]

The EU and the protection of living marine resources in non-EU waters

The core of the EU's reform of fisheries policy was formed in 2013, when it was stated that

> the Common Fisheries Policy (CFP) shall apply the precautionary approach to fisheries management and shall aim to ensure that exploitation of living marine biological resources restores and maintains populations of harvested species above levels which can produce the maximum sustainable yield (article 2.2)[26]

Evidently, this operational principle was conceived to be applied, above all, in EU waters.[27] However, the new Regulation (EU)1380/2013 also points out that "the Union also should promote the objectives of the CFP internationally, ensuring that Union fishing activities outside Union waters are based on the same principles and standards as those applicable under Union law" (paragraph 50). This new philosophy, aimed at protecting fisheries resources as "common-pool resources," is designed on three independent, but interconnected, planes: the involvement of the EU in RFMOs; the signing of fisheries agreements with third States; and, finally, the regulation of the access of the EU fleet to the fishing grounds of third States via private agreements.

The first field on which the EU's approach to international fishery cooperation is built is the RFMOs. The Regulation (EU) 1380/2013 on the CFP has established the mandate that "the

Union should seek to lead the process of strengthening the performance of RFMOs in order to better enable them to conserve and manage marine living resources under their purview" (art. 29.2). The EU contributes economically to the functioning of the RFMOs but its main contribution to these organisations lies in "promot(ing) the establishment and the strengthening of compliance committees of RFMOs, periodical independent performance reviews and appropriate remedial actions, including effective and dissuasive penalties" (art. 28.2.d).

RFMOs are international organisations formed by countries with fishing interests in an area. Some of them manage all the fish stocks found in a specific area, while others focus on particular highly migratory species, notably tuna, throughout vast geographical areas. The organisations are open both to countries in the region ("coastal States") and countries with interests in the fisheries concerned. While some RFMOs have a purely advisory role, most have management powers to set catch and fishing effort limits, technical measures and control obligations. The EU, represented by the Commission, currently plays an active role in six tuna organisations and eleven non-tuna organisations.

In RFMOs with greater powers, the EU is really leading institutional reform – in accordance with the mandate of Regulation (EU) 1380/2013 – by means of the establishment of trade-related sanctioning mechanisms and joint inspection schemes, such as those adopted by the Northwest Atlantic Fisheries Organization (NAFO), the North-East Atlantic Fisheries Commission (NEAFC), the International Commission for the Conservation of Atlantic Tunas (ICCAT), the Convention on Conservation of Antarctic Marine Living Resources (CCAMLR) or the General Fisheries Commission for the Mediterranean (GFCM). A recent empirical study has shown that, although the EU has received criticism for years due to some of the positions it has defended in RFMOs like NAFO and ICCAT "more recent conduct in both RFMOs proves that the claim [of EU leadership] is instead an indication for changing policy."[28] Along the same lines, the WWF (World Wildlife Fund) has concluded, after analysing the EU's participation in the Indian Ocean Tuna Commission (IOTC) and the Western and Central Pacific Fisheries Commission (WCPFC) that "the EU is positively active in the two RFMOs examined and makes proposals that can address several crucial areas to ensure the good governance of fisheries through RFMOs. The EU proposals also relate to important objectives under the CFP, such as improving the data available, promoting the precautionary principle, reducing discards, strengthening RFMOs, and increasing consistency between measures adopted in different fora."[29] For countries with a low rate of development, the strengthening of the RFMOs is essential as the assessments show that the best regulated fisheries are those which fall under the mandate of these organisations, as occurs in the case of Africa with the IOTC and the ICCAT.[30]

The second field in which we can observe the EU's contribution to the global management of fisheries lies in the growing control exerted by the European Commission over the European fleet which carries out its activities in the waters of third countries with a poor governance of fisheries resources. In this case, the idea of fisheries as a "common-pool resource" seems to be weakened given that these marine living resources are, at least in theory, subject to the jurisdiction of a State. However, it is relevant to analyse the role of the EU fleet (when it fishes under the protection of a fisheries agreement or when it enters the EEZ of a State via a private licence issued by that country's authorities in favour of the European ship-owner) because of the absence of an effective control exerted by developing coastal States over these waters.

Regarding the subscription to *fisheries agreements* with third countries, it should be remembered that, in 2018, the EU maintains in force twelve Sustainable Fisheries Partnership Agreements (SFPAs), mainly with African States.[31] Although the commercial nature of these treaties has traditionally been the object of harsh criticism,[32] the 2013 reform of the CFP has led to substantial progress with regard to the environmental, economic and social sustainability of these agreements. The structure of the SFPAs is based on the financial compensation paid by the EU to the associated countries in exchange for allowing the EU fleet access to their waters. In this exchange, it is possible to distinguish an initial element linked to obtaining access rights to the EEZ of the coastal State and a second aspect which consists of "sectoral" financial support for the promotion of sustainable fishing in the associated country, aimed at strengthening the management, supervision and monitoring of fishing activity. Following the 2013 reform, the commitments to development included in the agreements (which refer, among other aspects, to supporting the fishing industry of the country, employment of local people in vessels, unloading catches in the ports of the coastal States and investment) have been strengthened.[33]

The new SFPAs have also been designed to reach a higher level of environmental sustainability. The evaluations made of the fisheries agreements subscribed to by the EU have traditionally stated that one of the main limits to their ecological sustainability was the limited capacity of coastal States to determine the surplus of resources which can be put at the disposition of fleets from third States.[34] In order to overcome this deficit, the SFPAs signed since the reform have strengthened the indirect or cooperative role played by the EU in the process of the identification of the surplus made by the third State.[35] In order to achieve this aim, the SFPAs have introduced three measures which contribute towards reducing the uncertainty surrounding the process of the determination of the surplus; the inclusion of an exclusivity clause, by virtue of which EU vessels will only be able to fish in the EEZs of States counterpart to the protection of the agreement;[36] restrictions on the reflagging of vessels, with the aim of avoiding EU vessels obtaining additional opportunities to fish by acquiring the flag of a third State;[37] and, finally, the promotion of rules to increase the transparency of fishing operations carried out both by EU vessels and by those of third States relating to distant water fishing. A good example of the latter solution can be found in the Protocol signed with Mauritania for the period 2015–2019, in which the authorities of the coastal State agreed to publish all the agreements with States and private bodies giving foreign vessels access to its EEZ.[38]

The empirical analyses show that cooperation with the EU via fisheries agreements generates a more positive impact for coastal States (in spite of their limitations) than the establishment of purely trade-related relations with other long-distance fishing States such as China, Russia or South Korea.[39]

Finally, it is necessary to mention a third element of reform in the EU's actions in non-EU waters which also has the objective of protecting fisheries as a common-pool resource: external monitoring of the EU fleet entering the fishing grounds of third States via private licences. Until the beginning of 2018, the European Commission only had power to supervise the activity of European vessels fishing in waters of third countries under public fisheries agreements. However, both the general evolution of international law[40] and Regulation (EU) 1380/2013 itself have established the principle that the European Union must supervise its fleet wherever it is operating and, above all, independently of the public or private framework to which vessels are subscribed in their fishing activity. For this reason, the European legislative body has proceeded to adopt a new Regulation (EU) 2017/2403 on the sustainable management of external fishing fleets,[41] allowing the Commission to monitor the private agreements signed directly by European ship-owners with coastal States.[42]

The EU as a global leader in the fight against illegal fishing and the limits of commercial strategy

IUU fishing causes enormous environmental, economic and social damage, especially in developing countries such as Sierra Leone, Senegal and Mali. The most frequently quoted estimates state that illegal fishing generates losses of between \$10 billion and \$23.5 billion per year, with an especially negative impact in regions with a low level of development, such as western Africa where the true catch is 40 per cent higher than that which is declared.[43]

Notwithstanding the seriousness of the situation, the international regulations that allow fighting against it are scarce. Along with the general rules on fisheries sustainability defined by the United Nations Conference of the Law of the Sea (UNCLOS), it is also possible to take into consideration the binding provisions that establish, for the States parties, both the 1993 FAO Agreement to Promote Compliance with International Conservation and Management Measures by Fishing Vessels on the High Seas and the 1995 UN Agreement for the Implementation of the Provisions of UNCLOS relating to the Conservation and Management of Straddling Fish Stocks and Highly Migratory Fish Stocks. In addition to these treaties, other soft law instruments like the FAO Code of Conduct for Responsible Fisheries have also been important – although insufficient – for the regulation of international fisheries. In order to limit the negative consequences of illegal fishing, FAO promoted the adoption of the Agreement on Port State Measures to Prevent, Deter and Eliminate IUU Fishing (PSMA) which entered into force in 2016 and is the first international binding treaty specifically devoted to this issue. The EU has been one the main drivers of the ratification of the PSMA, although it has concurrently carried out a strategy of its own to combat illegal fishing, also based on its centrality as a port state since it is the world's largest market for fishery products.

The EU's response to IUU fishing has been extremely successful and has placed the region at the forefront of this struggle on a worldwide level. The legislative framework defining this strategy is contained in Council Regulation 1005/2008, which establishes the following measures: 1) fishing vessels from third countries can only land their catches in ports designated by member States; 2) port States must monitor imported fishery products, and check licences and compliance with fishing quotas; 3) flag States of the vessels must issue catch certificates in order to guarantee the traceability of fishery products; and 4) if problems are noted in the process of checking the legality of catches, the Regulation enables the Commission to draw up two black lists, the first including vessels practising IUU fishing and the second including States which tolerate this activity.[44]

The EU has strictly applied this monitoring regime, imposing trade sanctions upon non-cooperative countries such as Sri Lanka, Guinea and Cambodia, and issuing warnings (albeit without imposing sanctions) to others like Thailand, Curaçao, Ghana, the Solomon Islands, Tuvalu or Papua New Guinea. Among the different participants involved in the process of implementation of EU fisheries policy (governments, fishermen and NGOs), there is a broad consensus concerning the opinion that the EU's fight against IUU fishing has been a success.[45]

The commercial and administrative sanctions imposed by the EU have made it a world leader in the combat against IUU fishing. However, the exclusively commercial approach of the strategy remains insufficient. The ex-post evaluations of the fisheries agreements show that in areas in which a higher rate of IUU fishing is detected, such as western Africa, monitoring of fishing activity continues to be deficient. The lack of technical means for monitoring, particularly in the area closest to the Gulf of Guinea (as highlighted in the analyses relating to Sierra Leone, Guinea and Guinea-Bissau), leads to the proliferation of *blind spots*.

Faced with this situation, the ineffectiveness of the EU (and of specific countries with direct interests in the issue, such as Spain) to integrate monitoring activities of IUU fishing into the maritime security strategies which it has adopted is paradoxical. The European Union Maritime Security Strategy includes fisheries issues among the interests which should be the object of protection[46] but it lacks specific proposals to respond to this problem from the perspective of an increase in the monitoring of fishing activity. In other words, issues regarding fishing occupy a secondary position within the complex mosaic of maritime security, in which the decision is taken to highlight those risks (piracy, drug trafficking and the control of migratory flow) which unequivocally require a response implying the use of coercive measures. In the case of the EU, even the documents on maritime security with a regional focus which have been passed, such as the EU Strategy for the Gulf of Guinea, avoid including operational measures for the monitoring of fishing activity. Rather, they restrict themselves to affirming that the EU already acts in these countries via the bilateral fisheries agreements.[47] This conclusion does not provide a sufficient or a strategic response to the problem.

As far as the resources aimed at strengthening supervision mechanisms are concerned, neither the EU's development programmes (such as ACP Fish II) nor the sectoral support included in the SFPAs, which is reserved for the strengthening of the local fisheries sector, have been sufficient to articulate an effective system of governance for fisheries in the associated countries, particularly those located in the Gulf of Guinea. In fact, over recent years, the appearance of cooperation processes on a regional level can be observed with the aim of mitigating these insufficiencies, as can be seen in the initiative adopted by the Fisheries Committee for the West Central Gulf of Guinea (FCWC), the New Partnership for Africa's Development (NEPAD) and the Sub-Regional Fisheries Commission (SRFC), which, funded by the World Bank, is developing the West Africa Regional Fisheries Program.[48] As far as the Indian Ocean is concerned, the States participating in the Djibouti Code of Conduct, promoted by the IMO (International Maritime Organization), have also broadened the scope of the agreement in order to include IUU fishing among the illicit activities which should be controlled.[49] However, as Standing has pointed out "technological advances, such as satellite monitoring or the use of drones, may help improve effectiveness in detecting some forms of crime and bring surveillance cost down but they are unlikely to replace the need for more traditional and expensive law enforcement activities, including paying form inspectors, patrol boats, and the undertaking of complex financial investigations."[50]

However, developing States cannot face the costs of maintaining and equipping a large fleet of maritime surveillance vessels and, in this context, it is possible to observe that the efforts for international cooperation which have been made are still not enough. The gradual increase in awareness of the need to strengthen the fight against illegal fishing by way of increasing surveillance and monitoring has not led to operational results in African waters. Pursuant to different types of bilateral agreements, EU member States participate in surveillance activities in waters under the jurisdiction of third States, fundamentally in the fight against piracy, drug trafficking and irregular migration; nevertheless, the repression of illegal fishing continues to be excluded from international cooperation activities in terms of maritime security.[51] The example of Spain, which is the European country with the largest fleet of vessels operating in African waters, is revealing as far as this tendency is concerned. Although Spain has signed technical agreements regarding maritime security with Cape Verde, Senegal, Mauritania, Gambia, Guinea and Guinea-Bissau, through which the exchange of information and the carrying out of joint patrols are promoted, the fight against illegal fishing has been excluded from the coverage of these agreements.

In contrast, the United States has proceeded to sign shiprider agreements with several States in the region (such as Sierra Leone, Senegal, Cape Verde, Gambia and Ghana), which enable law enforcement agents of the coastal States to board US vessels with the aim of applying the laws of the State in question.[52] In the time that these agreements have been in force, significant detentions of vessels and confiscations of illegal catches have been carried out.[53] A recent report on the security implications of IUU fishing recommends the United States Government to not only promote complementary measures of a civil nature in order to repress this illegal activity (such as dedicating resources to increase monitoring and enforcement capacities, encouraging greater transparency of the fishing industry or mandating the use of vessel tracking systems to track fishing fleets), but also to insist on the need for the direct involvement of military vessels in the fight against illegal fishing activity. Thereby, the report suggests that "strategic planners at the Department of Defense should include IUU fishing and its acute threats to maritime security in their military planning efforts." It also states that "shiprider agreements are an important tool in combatting IUU fishing and other maritime threats" and that, as a consequence, "the U.S. government should pursue establishing new shiprider agreements with countries to help deter and enforce against IUU fishing across the globe."[54]

Conclusion

In the light of what has been mentioned, it can be stated that the EU's contribution towards the resolution of the management problems posed by the issue of fisheries as a *global common* (principally in cases in which the resources lie outside of State jurisdiction) is significant and that the EU is in the vanguard of the cooperation mechanisms being established on a global level in order to achieve this aim.

However, the EU's position in the multilateral context should not only be understood as an altruistic stance. In addition to environmental commitments, the political behaviour of the EU in the debate on international fisheries can also be explained in commercial terms. The European fleet cannot compete in terms of prices with the largest long-distance fleets in the world (such as China, Russia or South Korea), which have lower labour costs and are under less pressure to apply international fishing regulations. Therefore, the comparative advantage of the EU fleet lies in the restriction of access to the European fishing market (the largest in the world) of products originating from IUU fishing, along with promoting awareness amongst European consumers that fish captured by EU vessels fulfils all the attributes of quality, sustainability and traceability. For these reasons, European ship-owners (that is, the business sector) are becoming the principal champions of the EU's promotion of sustainable fishing on a global scale, through SFPAs or RFMOs, given that this policy enables them to be more competitive. This is a fine example, therefore, of the synergy which can arise between industry and environmentalism.

Although the success of the administrative and commercial strategy of the repression of illegal fishing promoted by the EU must be recognised, it must be also admitted that the increase in the surveillance and monitoring of extractive activities should also form part of the formula to be implemented in order to eradicate this illegal activity in the waters where it takes place. Academics have pointed out that, to combat the robbery of fisheries resources in countries which are not able to monitor fishing in their territorial and jurisdictional waters, the application of international procedures similar to those being adopted to combat maritime piracy could be envisaged, "in other words, the authorization of the Security Council so that official vessels of third States can intervene in those waters adopting the necessary measures for combatting illegal fishing … for many coastal States, the possibility that, with their agreement, official vessels from third States could proceed to pursue such crimes could be a solution, albeit a provisional one."[55] Even without resorting to such an extreme solution as that proposed by the organised international community to confront the challenges existing in terms of security posed by piracy in the Gulf of Aden, there is room enough for EU member States to include bilateral military support in the fight against IUU fishing in the terms of the relationship of constructive cooperation which they maintain with third States, in particular in Africa.

Notes

* Chapter 14 is the result of the collaboration developed by the author within the framework of the research project "Spain in the face of the new challenges of maritime security: Instruments and strategies in the international, European and Iberian framework", DER2016-78272-R, financed by the Spanish Ministry of Economy and Competitiveness.

1 Garret Hardin, "The Tragedy of the Commons," *Science* 162, no. 3859 (1968): 1243–8.

2 Food and Agriculture Organization, *The State of World Fisheries and Aquaculture, SOFIA 2018 – Meeting the Sustainable Development Goals* (Rome: FAO, 2018), 6.

3 Elinor Ostrom, *Governing the Commons: The Evolution of Institutions for Collective Action* (New York: Cambridge University Press, 1990).

4 As Shaver and Yozell have pointed out

> the perpetrators of IUU fishing are not just the local fisherman catching a bit more than his quota allows, but include a range of offenders: from foreign vessels fishing illegally in another nation's sovereign waters to criminal networks that participate in a variety of illicit activities, including trafficking in drugs, arms, and humans, as well as utilizing shell companies to launder money and slaves to carry out their operations. For these reasons and many others (...) IUU fishing poses a risk to national security and dealing with it will require more effort and focus than can be addressed by the conservation community and natural resource management agencies alone.
>
> *See Amanda Shaver and Sally Yozell, Casting a Wider Net. The Security Implications of Illegal, Unreported and Unregulated Fishing (Washington, DC: The Stimson Center, 2018), 2.*

5 Cathy Haenlein, *Below the Surface. How Illegal, Unreported and Unregulated Fishing Threatens our Security* (London: Royal United Services Institute, 2017), 1.

6 The 1994 Human Development Report argued that the concept of security has "for too long been interpreted narrowly: as security of territory from external aggression, or as protection of national interests in foreign policy, or as global security from a nuclear holocaust. It has been related more to nation states than to people." This narrow approach was widened to include the safety of individuals and groups from such threats as hunger, disease and political instability, and protection from "sudden and hurtful disruptions in patterns of daily life." United Nations Development Programme, *Human Development Report 1994: New Dimensions of Human Security* (New York: UNDP, 1994), 22–23.

7 Food and Agriculture Organization, *SOFIA 2018*, 4.

8 Food and Agriculture Organization, *The State of World Fisheries and Aquaculture, SOFIA 2016 – Contributing to food security and nutrition for all* (Rome: FAO, 2016), 183.

9 European Commission and High Representative of the EU for Foreign Affairs and Security Policy, Joint Communication: International Ocean Governance: An Agenda for the Future of Our Oceans, JOIN(2016) 49 final (Brussels: European Union, November 10, 2016).

10 UN General Assembly, *Transforming Our World: The 2030 Agenda for Sustainable Development*, UN Doc. A/RES/70/1 of 21 October 2015. On the implementation process of SDG 14, see the outcome document of the UN Ocean Conference, UN General Assembly, *Our Ocean, Our Future: Call For Action*, UN Doc. A/RES/71/312 of 14 July 2017.

11 In accordance with the data of the European Commission,

> a market's self-sufficiency rate is the ratio of domestic supply (what is produced) over domestic demand (what is consumed). The self-sufficiency of a market is calculated on a scale of 0 to 100%, where 0 and 100 are theoretical conditions: at a 0% self-sufficiency rate, a market would depend solely on imports, while at a 100% rate, a market would be independent from external resources and fully satisfy demand through domestic production. In the EU, this ratio decreased from 47,4% (2014) to 46,0% (2015), meaning that more of the consumed fisheries and aquaculture products were supplied through products imported from non-EU countries than through EU catches or aquaculture production.
>
> *European Market Observatory for Fisheries and Aquaculture Products (EUMOFA),* The EU Fish Market 2017 *(Brussels: European Commission, 2018), 13.*

12 European Commission, Scientific, Technical and Economic Committee for Fisheries (STECF), *The 2017 Annual Economic Report on the EU Fishing Fleet (STECF-17–12)* (Luxembourg: Publications Office of the European Union, 2017), 63.

13 In Spain, the distant water fleet and the long-distance water fleet are made up of 194 vessels, out of the 9,299 fishing vessels included in the national registry, although these vessels account for 56 per cent of the total catch, CEPESCA, *Informe del sector pesquero español 2017* (Madrid: CEPESCA, 2017), 9.
14 Pauline Guibbaud, *Pêche Illicite: Quel avenir pour l'Afrique de l'Ouest?* (Brussels: GRIP, 2014).
15 FAO. *The State of World Fisheries and Aquaculture, SOFIA 2014 – Opportunities and challenges* (Rome: FAO, 2014), 39.
16 Alfonso Daniels, Miren Gutiérrez, Gonzalo Fanjul, Arantxa Guereña, Ishbel Matheson and Kevin Watkins, *Western Africa's Missing Fish: The Impacts of Illegal, Unreported and Unregulated Fishing and Under-Reported Catches by Foreign Fleets* (London: Overseas Development Institute, 2016).
17 United Nations Office on Drugs and Crime, *Transnational Organized Crime in the Fishing Industry* (Vienna: UNDOC, 2011); Interpol Environmental Security Sub-Directorate, *Study on Fisheries Crime in the West African Coastal Region* (Lyon: Interpol, 2014); Teale N. Phelps, Tuesday Reitano, Wietse van der Werf, *The Illegal Fishing and Organized Crime Nexus: Illegal Fishing as Transnational Organized Crime* (Geneva: The Global Initiative Against Transnational Organized Crime and The Black Fish, 2015).
18 Haenlein, *Below the Surface*, 37.
19 Don Liddick, "The Dimensions of a Transnational Crime Problem: The Case of IUU Fishing," *Trends in Organised Crime* 17 (2014): 290–312.
20 FAO, *International Plan of Action to Deter, Prevent and Eliminate Illegal, Unreported and Unregulated Fishing* (IPOA IUU) (Rome: FAO, 2001).
21 Ibid., paragraphs 3.1, 3.2 and 3.3.
22 Paragraph 3.4 of the IPOA IUU refers precisely to this issue when establishing, as a safeguard clause, that "notwithstanding paragraph 3.3, certain unregulated fishing may take place in a manner which is not in violation of applicable international law and may not require the application of measures envisaged under the International Plan of Action."
23 Tullio Treves, "La pesca ilegal, no declarada y no reglamentada: Estado del pabellón, Estado costero y Estado del puerto," in *La cooperación internacional en la ordenación de mares y océanos*, coord. Jorge Pueyo Losa and Julio Jorge Urbina (Madrid: Iustel, 2009), 135.
24 Eve de Coning and Emma Witbooi, "Towards a New 'Fisheries Crime' Paradigm: South Africa as an Illustrative Example," *Marine Policy* 60 (2015): 208–15, 209. As Coning and Witbooi have pointed out it implies not only concern with "illegal fishing" per se (that is, the extraction of marine living resources in contravention of law, which is the current concern of the mainstream fisheries management discourse), but a whole range of criminal offences, including document fraud, customs and tax evasions, human trafficking, money laundering and insurance fraud.
25 Haenlein, *Below the Surface*, 14.
26 Regulation (EU) No 1380/2013 of the European Parliament and of the Council of 11 December 2013 on the Common Fisheries Policy, Amending Council Regulations (EC) No 1954/2003 and (EC) No 1224/2009 and repealing Council Regulations (EC) No 2371/2002 and (EC) No 639/2004 and Council Decision 2004/585/EC, OJ L 354, December 28, 2013, 22.
27 The main obligations which includes Regulation (EU)1380/2013, derived from the application of the precautionary principle in communitarian waters, are to achieve the Maximum Sustainable Yield (MSY) in the exploitation of marine biological resources, through the execution of multiannual plans based on criteria of joint – rather than individual – management of the stocks; accomplishing a gradual elimination, until 2019, of discards; improving fisheries governance through the decentralisation of decision-making processes and the strengthening of Regional Advisory Councils; as well as controlling overcapacity of the fleet and improving knowledge of the marine environment, through the reform of the European Maritime and Fisheries Fund.
28 Anna Antonova, "Reforming EU Participation in Fisheries Management and Conservation on the High Seas," *Ocean Yearbook Online* 29 (2015): 125–43.
29 World Wildlife Fund, *Is Europe Ready to Lead on International Fisheries Governance?* (Surrey: WWF UK, 2018), 24.
30 André Standing, *Criminality in Africa's Fishing Industry: A Threat to Human Security*, Africa Security Brief, no. 33 (Washington, DC: Africa Center for Strategic Studies, 2017), 7.
31 Cape Verde (from 23 December 2014 to 22 December 2018), Ivory Coast (from 1 July 2013 to 30 June 2018), Greenland (from 31 December 2020), Cook Islands (from 25 October 2015 to 24 October 2019, in provisional application), Liberia (from 5 June 2015 to 8 December 2020, in provisional application from 9 December 2015, Council Decision (EU) 2015/2312 of 30 November 2015, OJ L 328 of 12 December 2015), Madagascar (from 01 January 2015 to 31 December 2018), Morocco (from

15 July 2014 to 14 July 2018), Mauritius (from 28 January 2014 to 27 January 2017), Mauritania (from 16 November 2015 to 15 November 2019, in provisional application), Sao Tomé and Príncipe (from 23 May 2014 to 22 May 2018), Senegal (from 20 November 2014 to 19 November 2019), the Seychelles (from 18 January 2014 to 17 July 2020).

32 Vlad M. Kaczynski and David L. Fluharty, "European Policies in West Africa: Who Benefits from Fisheries Agreements?" *Marine Policy* 26 (2002): 75–93.

33 José M. Sobrino and Gabriela Oanta, "The Sustainable Fisheries Partnership Agreements of the European Union and the Objectives of the Common Fisheries Policy: Fisheries and/or Development?" *Spanish Yearbook of International Law* 19 (2015): 61–85.

34 European Court of Auditors, *Are the Fisheries Partnerships Agreements Well Managed by the Commission?* Special Report 11/2015, par. 31.

35 Regulation (EU) 1380/2013 (recital 51) states that

> sustainable fisheries partnership agreements with third countries should ensure that Union fishing activities in third-country waters are based on the best available scientific advice and relevant information exchange, ensuring a sustainable exploitation of the marine biological resources, transparency as regards the determination of the surplus and, consequently, a management of the resources that is consistent with the objectives of the CFP.

36 Carlos Teijo, "An Analysis of the Legal Problems Arising from the Application of Exclusivity Clauses in the European Union's Dormant Fisheries Agreements," *Marine Policy* 95 (2018): 174–79.

37 Article 31, Regulation (EU) 1380/2013.

38 Article 1.6, OJ L 315, 1 December 2015. Regarding this issue, the European Parliament has emphasised that it "strongly encourages the Commission to ensure that similar transparency provisions are included in other future protocols, leading to much-improved transparency regarding total fishing effort and conditions of access." European Parliament, *Report on Common Rules in Respect of Application of the External Dimension of the CFP, Including Fisheries Agreements*, A8-0052/2016 (Brussels: European Union, March 10, 2016), par. 49.

39 S.F. Walmsley, C.T. Barnes, I.A. Payne, C.A. Howard, *Comparative Study of the Impact of Fisheries Partnership Agreements. Technical Report* (London: MRAG, 2007); Hubert Zimmermann, "Balancing Sustainability and Commerce in International Negotiation: The EU and its Fisheries Partnership Agreements," *Journal of European Public Policy* 24 (2017): 135–55. A comparative of the fisheries agreements reached by various distant water fishing powers with developing countries concludes along these lines, stating that "while European, US- and Japanese distant water operations have contributed to overfishing in many occasions, their distant-water politics are gradually moving towards more responsible fishing. This, however, is not yet the case for the rising Asian distant water fleets." Antonius Gagern, Jeroen Van Den Berg, "Critical review of Fishing Agreements with Tropical Developing Countries," *Marine Policy* 38 (2013): 375–86, 384.

40 FAO, *Voluntary Guidelines for Flag State Performance* (Rome: FAO, 2015); International Tribunal for the Law of the Sea (ITLOS), Request for an Advisory Opinion Submitted by the Sub-Regional Fisheries Commission, Advisory Opinion of April 2, 2015.

41 Regulation (EU) 2017/2403 of the European Parliament and of the Council of 12 December 2017 on the Sustainable Management of External Fishing Fleets, and Repealing Council Regulation (EC) No 1006/2008, OJ L 347, December 28, 2017, 81.

42 There is an average of 180 licences per year: European Commission, Impact Assessment Accompanying the Document: Proposal for a Regulation of the European Parliament and of the Council on the Sustainable Management of External Fishing Fleets, Repealing Council Regulation (EC) No 1006/2008, SWD(2015) 279 final (Brussels: European Union, December 10, 2015), 15.

43 David J. Agnew, John Pearce, Ganapathiraju Pramod, Tom Peatman, Reg Watson, John R. Beddington and Tony J. Pitcher, "Estimating the Worldwide Extent of Illegal Fishing," *PLoS ONE* 4, no. 2 (2009): e4570.

44 Council Regulation (EC) No 1005/2008 of 29 September 2008 Establishing a Community System to Prevent, Deter and Eliminate Illegal, Unreported and Unregulated Fishing, OJ L 286, October 29, 2008, 1.

45 EJF, OCEANA, PEW, WWF, *The EU IUU Regulation Building on Success: EU Progress in the Global Fight against Illegal Fishing*, February 2016.

46 Among the strategic maritime security interests mentioned in the document are

> the protection of economic interests, including the safeguarding of maritime energy resources, the sustainable exploitation of natural and marine resources in the different maritime zones

and the high seas, the control of illegal, unregulated and unreported (IUU) fishing, the security of Member States' fishing fleets and the delimitation of maritime zones

Council of the EU, European Union Maritime Security Strategy, *11205/14 (Brussels: European Union, June 24, 2014), 8.*

47 Council of the EU, *EU Strategy on the Gulf of Guinea* Foreign Affairs Council Meeting, Brussels, March 17, 2014, 7.
48 Interpol Environmental Security Sub-Directorate, *Study on Fisheries Crime*, 31–40.
49 A high-level meeting of signatories held in Jeddah, Saudi Arabia (10 to 12 January 2017) adopted a revised Code of Conduct, which will be known as the "Jeddah Amendment to the Djibouti Code of Conduct 2017."
50 Standing, *Criminality in Africa's Fishing Industry*, 9.
51 With regard to this issue, it has been pointed out that only France has included the fight against IUU fishing in its naval exercises, named NEMO, which it has carried out with African States European – see EU, European Commission, *Second Report on the Implementation of the EU Maritime Security Strategy Action Plan*, SWD(2017) 238 final (Brussels: European Union, June 14, 2017), 18.
52 On shiprider agreements, see Douglas Guilfoyle, *Shipping Interdiction and the Law of the Sea* (Cambridge: Cambridge University Press, 2009), 91.
53 Interpol Environmental Security Sub-Directorate, *Study on Fisheries Crime*, 40.
54 Shaver and Yozell, *Casting a Wider Net*, 28.
55 José Manuel Sobrino, "La tensión entre la gobernanza zonal y la gobernanza global en la conservación y gestión de los recursos pesqueros," in *The Contribution of the United Nations Convention on the Law of the Sea to Good Governance of the Oceans and Seas*, coords. José Manuel Sobrino and Giuseppe Cataldi (Napoli: Scientifica, 2014) 455–83, 481.

References

Agnew, David J., John Pearce, Ganapathiraju Pramod, Tom Peatman, Reg Watson, John R. Beddington and Tony J. Pitcher. "Estimating the Worldwide Extent of Illegal Fishing." *PLoS ONE* 4, no. 2 (2009): e4570.

Antonova, Anna. "Reforming EU Participation in Fisheries Management and Conservation on the High Seas." *Ocean Yearbook Online* 29 (2015): 125–43.

CEPESCA. *Informe del sector pesquero español 2017*. Madrid: CEPESCA, 2017.

Council of the European Union. Council Regulation (EC) No 1005/2008 of 29 September 2008 Establishing a Community System to Prevent, Deter and Eliminate Illegal, Unreported and Unregulated Fishing, *Official Journal of the European Union* L 286, October 29, 2008, 1.

Council of the European Union. *European Union Maritime Security Strategy* (11205/14). Brussels: European Union, June 24, 2014.

Council of the European Union. *EU Strategy on the Gulf of Guinea*. Foreign Affairs Council Meeting. Brussels: European Union, March 17, 2014.

Daniels, Alfonso, Miren Gutiérrez, Gonzalo Fanjul, Arantxa Guereña, Ishbel Matheson and Kevin Watkins. *Western Africa's Missing Fish: The Impacts of Illegal, Unreported and Unregulated Fishing and Under-Reported Catches by Foreign Fleets*. London: Overseas Development Institute, 2016.

De Coning, Eve, and Emma Witbooi. "Towards a New 'Fisheries Crime' Paradigm: South Africa as an Illustrative Example." *Marine Policy* 60 (2015): 208–15.

EJF, OCEANA, PEW and WWF. *The EU IUU Regulation Building on Success: EU Progress in the Global Fight against Illegal Fishing*. February 2016.

European Commission. Proposal for a Regulation of the European Parliament and of the Council on the Sustainable Management of External Fishing Fleets, repealing Council Regulation (EC) No 1006/2008. SWD(2015) 279 final. Brussels: European Union, December 10, 2015.

European Commission. *Second Report on the Implementation of the EU Maritime Security Strategy Action Plan*. SWD(2017) 238 final. Brussels: European Union, June 14, 2017.

European Commission and High Representative of the EU for Foreign Affairs and Security Policy. Joint Communication to the European Parliament, the Council, the European Economic and Social Committee and the Committee of the Regions: International Ocean Governance: An Agenda for the Future of Our Oceans. JOIN(2016) 49 final. Brussels: European Union, November 10, 2016.

European Commission Scientific, Technical and Economic Committee for Fisheries (STECF). *The 2017 Annual Economic Report on the EU Fishing Fleet (STECF-17–12)*. Luxembourg: Publications Office of the European Union, 2017.

European Court of Auditors. *Are the Fisheries Partnerships Agreements Well Managed by the Commission?* Special Report 11/2015.

European Market Observatory for Fisheries and Aquaculture Products (EUMOFA). *The EU Fish Market 2017*. Brussels: European Commission, 2018.

European Parliament. *Report on Common Rules in Respect of Application of the External Dimension of the CFP, Including Fisheries Agreements* (A8-0052/2016). Brussels: European Union, March 10, 2016.

European Parliament and Council of the European Union. Regulation (EU) 2017/2403 of the European Parliament and of the Council of 12 December 2017 on the Sustainable Management of External Fishing Fleets, and Repealing Council Regulation (EC) No 1006/2008, *Official Journal of the European Union* L 347, December 28, 2017, 81.

European Parliament and Council of the European Union. Regulation (EU) No 1380/2013 of the European Parliament and of the Council of 11 December 2013 on the Common Fisheries Policy, Amending Council Regulations (EC) No 1954/2003 and (EC) No 1224/2009 and Repealing Council Regulations (EC) No 2371/2002 and (EC) No 639/2004 and Council Decision 2004/585/EC. *Official Journal of the European Union* L 354, December 28, 2013, 22.

Food and Agriculture Organization. *International Plan of Action to Deter, Prevent and Eliminate Illegal, Unreported and Unregulated Fishing* (IPOA IUU). Rome: FAO, 2001.

Food and Agriculture Organization. *The State of World Fisheries and Aquaculture, SOFIA 2014 – Opportunities and Challenges*. Rome: FAO, 2014.

Food and Agriculture Organization. *The State of World Fisheries and Aquaculture, SOFIA 2016 – Contributing to Food Security and Nutrition for All*. Rome: FAO, 2016.

Food and Agriculture Organization. *The State of World Fisheries and Aquaculture, SOFIA 2018 – Meeting the Sustainable Development Goals*. Rome: FAO, 2018.

Food and Agriculture Organization. *Voluntary Guidelines for Flag State Performance*. Rome: FAO, 2015.

Gagern, Antonius, and Jeroen Van Den Berg. "Critical Review of Fishing Agreements with Tropical Developing Countries." *Marine Policy* 38 (2013): 375–86.

Guibbaud, Pauline. *Pêche Illicite: Quel avenir pour l'Afrique de l'Ouest?* Brussels: GRIP, 2014.

Guilfoyle, Douglas. *Shipping Interdiction and the Law of the Sea*. Cambridge: Cambridge University Press, 2009.

Haenlein, Cathy. *Below the Surface. How Illegal, Unreported and Unregulated Fishing Threatens our Security*. London: Royal United Services Institute, 2017.

Hardin, Garret. "The Tragedy of the Commons." *Science* 162, no. 3859 (1968): 1243–48.

International Tribunal for the Law of the Sea. Request for an Advisory Opinion Submitted by the Sub-Regional Fisheries Commission. Advisory Opinion of April 2, 2015.

Interpol Environmental Security Sub-Directorate. *Study on Fisheries Crime in the West African Coastal Region*. Lyon: Interpol, 2014.

Kaczynski, Vlad M., and David L. Fluharty. "European Policies in West Africa: Who Benefits from Fisheries Agreements?" *Marine Policy* 26 (2002): 75–93.

Liddick, Don. "The Dimensions of a Transnational Crime Problem: The Case of IUU Fishing." *Trends in Organised Crime* 17 (2014): 290–312.

Ostrom, Elinor. *Governing the Commons: The Evolution of Institutions for Collective Action*. New York: Cambridge University Press, 1990.

Phelps, Teale N., Tuesday Reitano and Wietse van der Werf. *The Illegal Fishing and Organized Crime Nexus: Illegal Fishing as Transnational Organized Crime*. Geneva: The Global Initiative against Transnational Organized Crime and the Black Fish, 2015.

Shaver, Amanda, and Sally Yozell. *Casting a Wider Net. The Security Implications of Illegal, Unreported and Unregulated Fishing*. Washington, DC: The Stimson Center, 2018.

Sobrino, José Manuel. "La tensión entre la gobernanza zonal y la gobernanza global en la conservación y gestión de los recursos pesqueros." In *The Contribution of the United Nations Convention on the Law of the Sea to Good Governance of the Oceans and Seas*, coordinated by José Manuel Sobrino and Giuseppe Cataldi, 455–83. Napoli: Scientifica, 2014.

Sobrino, José Manuel, and Gabriela Oanta. "The Sustainable Fisheries Partnership Agreements of the European Union and the Objectives of the Common Fisheries Policy: Fisheries and/or Development?" *Spanish Yearbook of International Law* 19 (2015): 61–85.

Standing, André. *Criminality in Africa's Fishing Industry: A Threat to Human Security*. Africa Security Brief 33, Washington, DC: Africa Center for Strategic Studies, 2017.

Teijo, Carlos. "An Analysis of the Legal Problems Arising from the Application of Exclusivity Clauses in the European Union's Dormant Fisheries Agreements." *Marine Policy* 95 (2018): 174–79.

Treves, Tullio. "La pesca ilegal, no declarada y no reglamentada: Estado del pabellón, Estado costero y Estado del puerto." In *La cooperación internacional en la ordenación de mares y océanos*, coordinated by Jorge Pueyo Losa and Julio Jorge Urbina, 135–58. Madrid: Iustel, 2009.

United Nations Development Programme. *Human Development Report 1994: New Dimensions of Human Security*. New York: UNDP, 1994.

United Nations General Assembly. *Our Ocean, Our Future: Call for Action*. UN Doc. A/RES/71/312 of 14 July 2017.

United Nations General Assembly. *Transforming Our World: The 2030 Agenda for Sustainable Development*. UN Doc. A/RES/70/1 of 21 October 2015.

United Nations Office on Drugs and Crime. *Transnational Organized Crime in the Fishing Industry*. Vienna: UNDOC, 2011.

Walmsley, S.F., C.T. Barnes, I.A. Payne and C.A. Howard. *Comparative Study of the Impact of Fisheries Partnership Agreements*. London: MRAG, 2007.

World Wildlife Fund. *Is Europe Ready to Lead on International Fisheries Governance?* Surrey: WWF UK, 2018.

Zimmermann, Hubert. "Balancing Sustainability and Commerce in International Negotiation: The EU and Its Fisheries Partnership Agreements." *Journal of European Public Policy* 24 (2017): 135–55.

15

INTEGRATING CLIMATE CHANGE ACTION INTO EU SECURITY POLICY[1]

Lara Lázaro Touza and Ángel Gómez de Ágreda

Introduction

Climate change has been portrayed as a 'threat multiplier' that could partially reverse development gains and fuel instability. The security-related reasons to fight climate change are many. Crop productivity losses, disruptions to trade in agricultural and non-agricultural commodities, more frequent and severe extreme weather events, increased water scarcity, loss of territory and 'environmentally induced' migration, political radicalisation, tensions over energy security and challenges to global governance are some of the key impacts of failing to tackle climate change effectively.[2]

Avoiding the worst consequences of climate change requires that the global mean temperature increase should be limited to well below 2°C above preindustrial temperatures, while striving to limit such temperature increase to 1.5°C. Net zero emissions must be achieved during the second half of this century and financial flows have to be aligned with the goals set in the Paris Agreement.[3]

Actions required to meet the goals of the Paris Agreement include: the reduction of greenhouse gas emissions (GHG) through the complete overhaul of the energy systems and land-use practices (mitigation), fostering spontaneous and planned adaptation to the impacts that will occur, even if all greenhouse emissions are halted, and addressing the limits to adaptation. Additionally, technology transfer, capacity building and climate finance will be essential to deliver effective climate action, especially in less developed economies.[4]

Despite the fact that the Armed Forces are known to be one of the largest energy consumers, neither the Kyoto Protocol nor the Paris Agreement specify GHG emission reduction requirements for the military. Similarly, adaptation, technology transfer, capacity building or climate finance goals are expected from Parties to these agreements, but not from the military and intelligence communities. The Kyoto Protocol, at the request of the US negotiating team, excluded military emissions from its scope. The Paris Agreement is silent as regards the Armed Forces and their contribution to globally concerted climate action.[5]

And yet, not only are the Armed Forces a significant contributor to climate change, they can also expect to be impacted by it. Climate impacts on military infrastructure, facilities and operations substantiate the inclusion of climate change in security policies,[6] both nationally and internationally.[7]

Climate action is also a natural area of concern for the defence community if it wants to be perceived as a 'force for good' that acts as the first line of defence against threats to national security, human security and in cases where disaster relief is provided.[8]

However, how the climate–security nexus is conceptualised is still up for debate[9] with unanswered questions regarding which climate impacts pose a security threat, whose security is imperilled and what should be done to address climate-security concerns.[10] Beyond the conceptualisation of the climate–security nexus, however, militaries from around the world and external action services (in the case of the EU) have taken steps to integrate climate action into their activities. Reductions in GHG emissions have been planned by the Armed Forces, not only on the energy consumption front but also through better management of land that falls under the authority of the military. Furthermore, adaptation to climate change has historically been part of operational resilience in missions.

Security communities (and the foreign policy community in the case of the EU) have integrated, to a certain extent, climate change as a security concern in their strategies and actions. One of the key reasons for considering climate change as a security issue is its potential for exacerbating existing conditions that help ignite, worsen or change the dynamics of socioeconomically contingent occurrences such as migration and conflict.[11]

The present chapter will analyse climate change and its integration into the EU's security policy. In setting the above-mentioned integration into a broader context, the next section will delve into the security dimension of climate change and its impacts from the global to the EU level. The third section will discuss the unresolved debates revolving around the climate–security nexus from a theoretical and policy perspective. Then the fourth section will analyse how the EU has integrated climate change into its security strategies and publications from 2003 to 2018. The following, fifth, section will reflect on the future research agenda. The final section will conclude by summarising some of the key ideas discussed throughout the text.

Climate impacts and the security dimension of climate change

The Intergovernmental Panel on Climate Change (IPCC) stated in its latest report (the Fifth Assessment Report or AR5) that climate change is unequivocal, with some of the observed changes being unprecedented in decades to millennia, its anthropogenic component being clear and its consequences for humans, societies and ecosystems already being felt.[12] The impacts of climate change include global mean temperature increases, sea-level rise, acidification of the oceans, variability in precipitation (with wet areas getting wetter and arid regions becoming drier), melting of glaciers, reductions in the extent of sea ice and snow cover, variations in crop productivity, increases in the frequency and severity of extreme weather events, biodiversity losses and changes in species ranges, among others. Table 15.1 summarises some of the key impacts of a changing climate.

As described in Table 15.1, the key areas that represent a joint climate-security challenge include water and food security, sea-level rise and coastal degradation in densely populated low-lying areas, extreme weather events and weather-related disasters, and socially contingent outcomes such as migration and conflict.[13] Furthermore, it is the interaction of the joint climate-security challenges with existing governance structures, and with pre-existing socio-economic and environmental conditions, which helps explain the impact of climate change on security. Developed, wealthy and resilient societies will be best suited to cope with climate change and its impacts.

As regards the EU, its size and its wealth of bioclimatic regions explain the myriad of climate change impacts that can be observed. For instance, southern European countries are more

Table 15.1 Key climate change impacts

Area	*Climate change impacts*
Temperature increases	The summary for policy makers of the AR5 states that there is high confidence that for a doubling of CO_2, the global *mean surface temperature* increase is likely to be in the range of 1.5°C to 4.5°C. According to the Potsdam Institute for Climate Impact Research[1] if no additional mitigation occurs, the world is likely to warm more than 3°C compared to preindustrial levels by the end of the century. This is well above the 2°C mark that the scientific and policy community have agreed to be the threshold above which there is dangerous interference with the climate system. More frequent and extreme heat waves will accompany these mean temperature increases.
Sea level rise	Sea level rise data analysed in the AR5 has been narrowed down compared to previous analyses and it is expected to increase between 0.4 to 0.63 meters on average by the end of the century.
Water	In terms of mean annual precipitation, changes vary depending on the region. In many mid-latitudes and dry regions, mean precipitation is likely to decrease. Additionally, extreme precipitation will become more intense as global mean surface temperature increases. The area encompassed by monsoon systems will increase over the 21st century. There will also be a potential lengthening of the monsoon season in many regions. Countries located in the Mediterranean region are likely to suffer more severe climate change impacts than other EU nations.[2] Droughts could become more intense and frequent, and rivers' run-off may decrease.[3]
Extreme weather events (EWE)	More frequent and severe extreme weather events have been observed since the 1950s and the IPCC expects that by the end of the 21st century, this trend will continue. Higher certainty exists regarding the increase in the number of hot days and heatwaves. Less data is available on hurricanes and flooding.
Ecosystems, food and agriculture	Ecosystems could lose up to 30% of plants and animal species for temperature increases ranging from 1.5°C to 2.5°C according to the IPCC's Fourth Assessment Report (AR4). The structure and function of ecosystems are expected to be impacted. This could imply, among other things, reductions in the capacity of forests to absorb CO_2, impacts on coral reefs, and polar, glacier and alpine ecosystems disappearing. Adaptation of species is agreed to be increasingly difficult and costly beyond 2°C. Food security could be threatened globally if temperature increases are above 4°C.[4]
Health	According to the World Health Organization (WHO), 'Climate change affects the social and environmental determinants of health – clean air, safe drinking water, sufficient food and secure shelter. Many of the major killers such as diarrhoeal diseases, malnutrition, malaria and dengue are highly climate-sensitive and are expected to worsen as the climate changes.'[5]
Security	Climate change is expected to be one of the variables[6] that may ignite or aggravate *future conflicts*. The intelligence community has furthermore warned that climate change will have a significant geopolitical impact worldwide. This implies 'contributing to poverty, environmental degradation, and the further weakening of fragile governments. Climate change will contribute to food and water scarcity, will increase the spread of disease, and may spur or exacerbate mass migration.'[7]

Source: Adapted from Lázaro Touza and López Gunn, p. 3.[8]

Notes

1 Potsdam Institute for Climate Impact Research and Climate Analytics, *Turn Down the Heat: Why a 4°C Warmer World Must be Avoided* (Washington: World Bank, 2012).

2 Bryson C. Bates et al., *Climate Change and Water*, Technical Paper of the Inter-Governmental Panel on Climate Change (Geneva: IPCC Secretariat, 2008).

3 Günther Fischer et al., "Climate Change Impacts on Irrigation Water Requirements: Effects of Mitigation, 1990–2080," *Technol. Forecast Soc.* 74, no. 7 (2007): 1083–1107. Also, J. Lorenzo-Lacruz et al., "Recent Trends in Iberian Stream Flows (1945–2005)," *Journal of Hydrology* 414–415 (2012): 463–475.

4 Potsdam Institute, *Turn Down the Heat.*

5 World Health Organisation, "Climate Change and Health" World Health Organization, February 1, 2018. www.who.int/mediacentre/factsheets/fs266/en/.

6 Other variables include: cultural tensions, resource scarcity, disease and rapid urbanization of coastal regions.

7 Department of Defense, *Quadrennial Defense Review Report* (Washington, DC: Department of Defense, 2010), 85.

8 Lara Lázaro Touza and Elena López-Gunn, "Climate Change Diplomacy in Spain's Future Foreign Policy," SFS (EEE) 18/2014 - 9/6/2014. www.realinstitutoelcano.org/wps/portal/rielcano_en/contenido?WCM_GLOBAL_CONTEXT=/elcano/elcano_in/zonas_in/spanishforeignpolicy/eee18-2014-lazaro-lopezgunn-climate-change-in-spain-future-foreign-policy.

exposed than the rest of Europe to the adverse impacts of climate change. For Mediterranean countries, observed and expected climate impacts include: increases in extreme temperatures, with higher risk of heatwaves and droughts, enhanced risks of forest fires and electricity blackouts, losses of ecosystem services, increases in vector borne diseases, adverse economic impacts for a number of sectors (including tourism) and exposure to 'spillover' climate impacts from other regions, among other things.[14]

The key issues to watch concerning Europe's vulnerability to climate impacts coming from other regions include potential disruptions to trade and trade routes, impacts to infrastructures and transport, geopolitical risks and migration. Overall, Europe's vulnerability to external shocks is expected to increase in the future. Figure 15.1 summarises the impacts of climate change across Europe.

Despite the above, and compared to other more vulnerable regions, the European Union has been largely insulated from the worst impacts of climate change by its latitude and western position in the continent[15] (with most extreme weather events (EWE) being local and seasonal) and

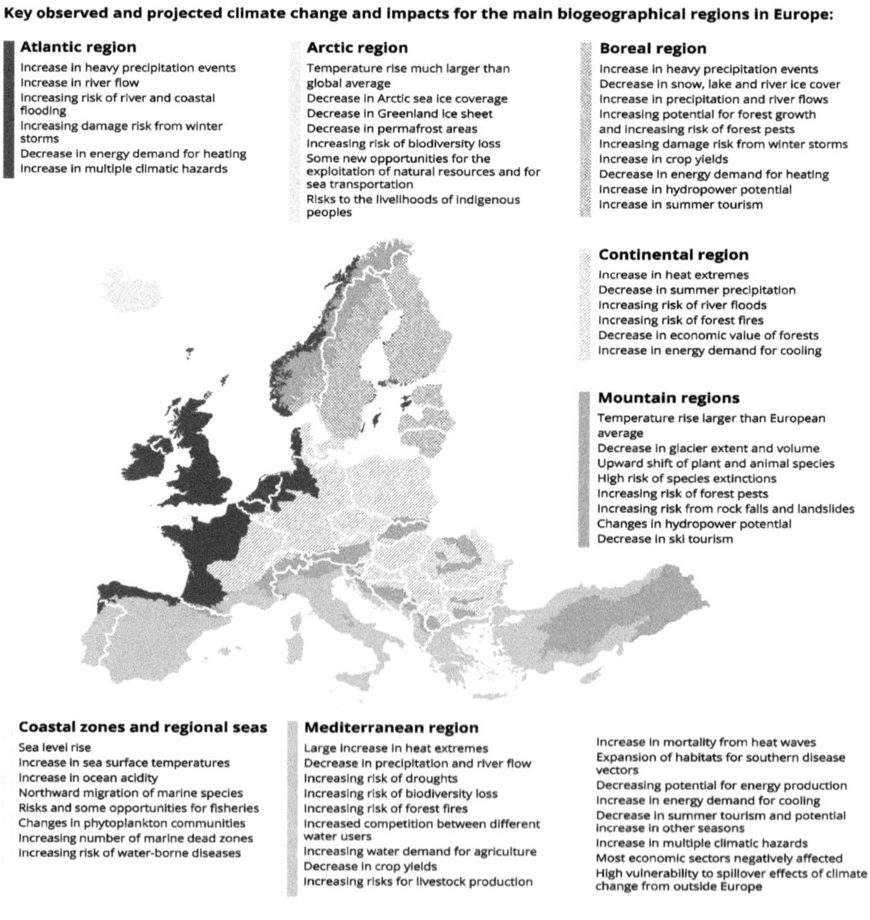

Figure 15.1 Climate change impacts in Europe.

Source: European Environment Agency, *Climate Change, Impacts and Vulnerability in Europe 2016: An Indicator-based Report*, EEA Report 1 (Luxembourg: European Union, 2017), 25.

due to its economic development. The European Environment Agency, however, warns that the impacts of climate change can be expected to rise in the future, although more data is needed to precisely quantify expected climate change losses.[16]

Beyond the physical impacts described above, the empirical climate-security literature focuses primarily on conflict and migration as key security threats that can be enhanced by climate change. Angela Oels[17] and Donald Wallace,[18] for instance, point out that climate change is considered to be one of the factors that can ignite or exacerbate these socially contingent outcomes. In a meta-analysis of 55 studies Marshall Burke et al.[19] argue that variations in temperature and precipitation patterns lead to increased risk of conflict. Marshall Burke et al.[20] had previously analysed the case of Africa, finding that warmer years lead to a significant increase in the likelihood of wars. On the other hand, Halvard Buhaug[21] claims that climate change is a poor predictor of wars. The author finds that pre-existing socioeconomic and political conditions better explain armed conflicts. While Halvard Buhaug[22] acknowledges the existence of a climate–conflict link, he calls for more sophisticated analyses that seek to understand indirect (conditioned) pathways from climate change to conflict.

Other authors rightly point out that the worst effects of climate change have not yet been experienced.[23] Future climate impacts, in particular the increase in the frequency and severity of extreme weather events, may provide further evidence that could support more direct links between climate change and conflict, although pre-existing socioeconomic conditions, institutional frameworks and political circumstances are expected to continue to play a key role in the climate–conflict pathway.

A much larger impact on the EU's security may come from abroad. Many large European corporations are more exposed to extreme weather events. A shift in the areas capable of growing produce can be expected to diminish productivity and push food prices up.[24] While this will have a limited impact in most European nations and its relevance is disputed by some scholars and politicians,[25] similar phenomena already set the Arab Spring in motion – or contributed to it – in the last decade. Widespread conflict in key areas of interest could demand that European forces intervene outside our borders or risk losing access to them.

On the security implications of migration, Michael Brzoska and Christiane Fröhlich argue that 'large migration movements, regardless of their causes, have frequently been presented as a threat to national and international security, particularly when crossing into the United States and Europe'.[26] The IPCC for instance has warned since 1990 that migration is one of the most significant impacts of climate change.[27] In 2014, the IPCC's *Fifth Assessment Report* concluded that there is a broad agreement among scientists that there is a high probability of an increase in climate-induced migration during this century,[28] especially if no robust mitigation, adaptation and development policies are implemented.[29]

The potential number of forced migrants due to climate change is, however, heavily disputed,[30] as is the direct link between resource scarcity and migration and between migration and conflict.[31] The literature provides wide-ranging estimates of climate-induced migration, ranging from 50 million to 1 billion people by the end of the century, depending on the scope of the study. Recent literature reviews warn, however, that existing data can be misleading, lacking empirical rigour, and can be published in order to raise awareness and to spur climate action by governments.[32] Caution is therefore advised when evaluating climate-induced migration data.

There is more consensus in the literature supporting the view that climate change is one factor, among many socioeconomic and political variables, that may enhance the likelihood of migration.[33] However, the social and political fallout of current migration policies in the EU (and elsewhere) is a powerful enough reason to be concerned with the security consequences of climate-induced migration.[34] This is so despite the uncertainty as regards the number of potential climate migrants, and the limited academic literature analysing the direct link between climate change and migration, which according to Michael Brzoska and Christiane Fröhlich[35] largely fails to support this direct link at present.

On a policy level, in spite of national policies that seek to restrict migration, the role of the military and security forces in the management of climatic crises seems to have shifted from that of shielding their nations from illegal migration towards supporting its channelling and management when it happens.[36] Even the most outspoken political leaders have so far refrained from sealing their borders altogether, although they have become very vocal in requesting migrants be allotted evenly among all nations.[37]

These antimigratory discourses seem to build on popular sentiment against immigration by some sectors of the population in certain countries but fail to address the issue from a holistic perspective. Most of those affected by climate change consider migrating only as their last option.[38] The hardships of the process and the significant expenses they need to incur are only some of the deterrents. Family and attachment to the land weigh heavily in the decision as to whether to migrate, especially in tribal cultures, which are the most affected. People tend to remain as close to home as possible. Only a fraction of potential migrants will actually embark on the journey to Europe.[39]

Integrating climate and security: a theoretical overview and political considerations

The desire to broaden the security agenda, along with worsening environmental conditions, led scholars during the 1980s and 1990s to incorporate modern threats such as environmental problems as potential security issues.[40] Climate change, however, only entered into the security realm recently.[41] It was not until the early 2000s that security strategies and political discourses[42] included the impacts of a changing climate in their remits.

Mainstream academic research began to analyse climate change as a security issue after defence ministries and political actors put climate security on the agenda. However, early work in the 1990s by Norman Myers, Tomas Homer-Dixon and Robert Kaplan already warned about migration and conflict being potentially triggered by environmental degradation and resources exhaustion.[43] Various discourses are used in the literature to conceptualise the climate–security nexus. However, no consensus has been achieved to date as regards the *type of threat* that climate change poses to security, *whose security* is at stake or the *actions to be taken* to halt climate change.[44]

Analysed through a securitisation[45] lens,[46] some of the key security narratives discussed in the literature include the Copenhagen School, the individual security discourse that is based on the concept of human security, and the ecological security discourse.[47] These narratives offer diverging views regarding the referent object (*whose security is at stake* – whether the nation, the individual or the planet), the *type of threat* (existential or non-existential), and on the *prognosis* (fostering reactive and extraordinary measures *versus* proactive and long-term sustainable management of resources, ecosystems and societies). See Table 15.2 for a succinct summary of the security discourses analysed above.

The Copenhagen School

As regards *whose security is at risk* and *how to deal with climate change* the *Copenhagen School* considers the referent object of security to be the State. This school of thought seeks to answer the question of whether there has been a securitisation of climate change. Securitisation according to the

Table 15.2 Some key climate security discourses

Discourse	*Referent object*	*Level*	*Conflict*	*Agent*	*Response*
Copenhagen School/ National Security	State	Territorial	Conflict, sovereignty, economic interests	State	Adaptation
Individual security/ Human security	People	Individual	Life and livelihoods, core values and practices	State, NGOs, the international community, communities	Mitigation and adaptation
Ecological security	Ecosystems	Planetary	Challenges to current socio-political equilibria	People	Reorientation of production and consumption systems and behaviours

Sources: based on Matt McDonald, "Climate Change and Security: Towards Ecological Security?," *International Theory* 10, no. 2 (2018), 163; Franziskus von Luke et al., "What's at Stake in Securitising Climate Change? Towards a Differentiated Approach," *Geopolitics* 19 (2014), 864; Angela Oels, "From 'Securitization' of Climate Change to 'Climatization' of the Security Field: Comparing Three Theoretical Perspectives," in *Climate Change, Human Security and Violent Conflict*, ed. Jürgen Scheffran et al., 185–203 (Berlin: Springer, 2012).

Copenhagen School would mean that climate change poses an existential threat to national security in that it can affect the existing social order. The threat posed by climate change is also judged uninsurable, which can lead to exceptional measures, including military intervention, to prevent threats to industrialised countries.[48] These exceptional measures can potentially escape the democratic policy processes of dealing with environmental problems, which entail the passing of laws and making use of climate policy instruments.[49]

In short, securitisation 'empowers political actors to breach the boundaries of normal politics'[50] in order to attain politically motivated climate action goals that need not be supported by citizens. Additionally, as Matt McDonald contends,[51] the problem with a national security perspective is that it addresses the provision of a global public good (a stable atmosphere), and that requires coordinated action by all countries, from an individual nation-state perspective. Furthermore, this state-centric approach turns other nations into threatening entities as potentially causing, *inter alia*, migration and conflict. As regards the prognosis, the conceptualisation of climate change as a national security issue would primarily call for adaptation responses,[52] rather than mitigation of climate change, hence tackling the consequences but not the root causes of the problem.

While concluding that, to date, securitisation of climate has not been a widespread phenomenon, the Copenhagen School cautions against securitisation, as do other authors.[53] In any case, the literature contends that securitisation of climate change is more likely in countries, such as the US, in which political gridlock prevents climate action at the national level, but where national security concerns afford some leeway for the military to address climate impacts.[54]

Individual security discourse

The second perspective called *individual security discourse*[55] considers climate change as a threat to human security, understood from World War II onwards to be the 'freedom from fear and freedom from want'.[56] Human security enables individuals – as the referent object – to cope with stress that can affect their 'needs, rights and values'.[57] Anything that endangers lives and livelihoods such as impacts on food security, water shortages, access to energy, etc. which can threaten values and practices of individuals, should be addressed through mitigation[58] as well as through reducing vulnerability and adapting to climate impacts.[59]

Hence, mitigation and adaptation actions to address climate change are justified in order to ensure human security as an extension of traditional security concerns regarding the nation's territory. The individual security discourse calls for international financial transfers (i.e. increasing development aid), supporting capacity building programmes in vulnerable areas, enhancing technology transfer etc.[60] While focusing on a population that is vulnerable to climate change at present, the individual security discourse ignores future generations and other living organisms and ecosystems.[61]

The EU and international organisations such as the United Nations (UN) consider climate change primarily as an *individual security* issue[62] that rests on enabling human security.[63] In geographical regions and institutions where climate action is feasible, as is the case with the EU, the literature concludes that it is mostly the individual security (human security) narrative that drives the inclusion of climate change in security strategies.[64] Additionally, the theoretically non-confrontational nature of the individual security discourse, compared to the Copenhagen School discourse, reinforces the EU's values-based and soft power approach to conflict resolution.

Ecological security discourse

A more holistic, future inclusive and other-regarding narrative, although supported by a minority of scholars, is provided by the *ecological security* discourse.[65] While using ecosystems as a referent object, it shares with the individual security discourse the view that climate change poses a long-term threat, while acknowledging the uncertainty that riddles the science regarding the exact timing, nature and location of impacts. It also renders climate change as insurable, in contrast to the Copenhagen School. However, the distinct feature of the ecological security discourse is that it seeks to achieve dynamic equilibria and resilience across the socioeconomic and environmental domains.[66]

The prognosis from the ecological security perspective advocates for both mitigation and adaptation actions. It does, however, contemplate 'radical changes' if we are to ensure operating within planetary boundaries[67] while fostering a symbiosis between humans and the environment.[68] A full-fledged transition towards a low carbon economy is to be sought according to this perspective if ecosystem resilience is to be maintained.[69] Hence, the appropriate response is a complete overhaul of production and consumption patterns.

Having presented the key climate-security discourses, the following section will delve into the integration of climate change in the EU's security strategies, bearing in mind that it is the human security narrative that is overall used in the EU to refer to the climate–security nexus.

Climate change action in the EU and integration as a security issue

The transnational nature of the causes and impacts of climate change make intergovernmental organisations (IGOs) such as the EU key players in climate governance.[70] The EU, as a 'civilian power' with limited coercive potential,[71] decreasing weight as a percentage of global emissions, and shrinking economic weight and power[72] enacts climate action through various means. These include the use of climate diplomacy and economic incentives (at home and abroad) and the passing of rules and regulations. This section will analyse the key drivers of the EU's climate action, it will provide a brief overview of the commitments made since the 1990s and it will conclude by analysing the extent to which there has been an integration of climate change into the EU's security strategies.

According to Alina Averchenkova et al.[73] and Guri Bang, Arild Underdal and Steinar Andersen,[74] some of the key factors behind the EU's long-lasting climate ambition are:

- The expected impacts of climate change[75] as described above.
- The historical responsibility of the EU in emitting GHGs, which amount to over a quarter of all anthropogenic emissions.[76]
- High energy dependence, especially from Russia[77] (see Figure 15.2).
- Concern about energy security, i.e. uninterrupted access to energy at affordable prices,[78] that is related to the EU's high energy dependence from Russia.
- An institutional setup that enables ambitious action, especially through a stable body of civil servants and the push of the European Parliament, ambitious Member States[79] and (although to a lesser extent in certain issues) the European Commission.
- Citizen concern for climate change and support for ambitious climate action.[80] Not only are European citizens historically concerned about climate change, they also demand that their governments address climate change as the second foreign policy priority after fighting terrorism in countries like France and Germany.[81] In Spain, for instance, climate change is ranked as the first foreign policy priority.[82]

The EU has historically been, and has prided itself on being, a directional climate leader and bridge-builder.[83] The EU Commission's Directorate-General for Environment commissioned reports on climate change as far back as the late 1970s. The EU Parliament showed interest in climate change around the same period as the Commission, but the interest to enact climate policies was not widespread at the time. Despite the limited action on climate policies until the 1990s, the EU has been instrumental in international climate negotiations since they started over a quarter of a century ago.[84] During the 1992 Earth Summit in Rio de Janeiro, and despite internal asymmetries and disagreements, the EU strengthened the negotiating text that was to become the first global climate action framework, the United Nations Framework Convention of Climate Change (UNFCCC).[85] The EU enabled the entry into force of the Kyoto Protocol in 2005, after the US failed to ratify it in 2001. The mediation of the EU to support Russian accession to the World Trade Organisation (WTO) led to Russia's ratification of the Kyoto Protocol,[86] which helped meet the conditions of entry into force of the Protocol.[87]

After the diplomatic setback in Copenhagen (COP15) in 2009,[88] the EU worked relentlessly towards the adoption of the Paris Agreement COP21,[89] along with other members of the High Ambition Coalition. In 2016, it was the EU's ratification of the Paris Agreement, after the joint US–Chinese ratification, that allowed the accord to enter into force.[90]

The EU's directional leadership has materialised in several commitments. Internationally, the EU committed to limiting temperature increases first to 2°C, well before the Kyoto Protocol and the Paris Agreement entered into force,[91] and later on to well below 2°C with the ratification of the Paris Agreement.[92] Under the Kyoto Protocol, the EU committed to jointly reduce its GHG emissions by 8 per cent by 2012 compared to its 1990 emissions. Internally, the adoption of the climate and energy package in 2008 meant that the EU committed to reducing its emissions by 20 per cent compared to 1990 levels, established a 20 per cent share of renewable energy in gross final energy consumption and agreed to reduce energy consumption by 20 per cent compared to business as usual (BAU) projections by 2020.[93]

Building on the 2008 climate and energy package, in October 2014 the EU Council published its conclusions on the 2030 climate and energy policy framework. The EU committed to achieve a 40 per cent GHG emission reduction target by 2030 compared to 1990 levels, at least 27 per cent of renewables in EU energy consumption and at least 27 per cent increase in energy efficiency compared to future energy consumption projections.[94]

Ahead of the Paris Agreement the EU submitted its Nationally Determined Contribution (NDC) that stated the EU would reduce its GHG emissions by 40 per cent by 2030 compared to 1990 levels, based on the previous agreement within the EU.[95] In June 2018, after the EU agreed to raise its renewable energy and energy efficiency targets for 2030 to 32 per cent and 32.5 per cent respectively, Climate Action and Energy Commissioner Miguel Arias Cañete stated the EU was in a position to raise its ambition in the next round of NDCs and to reduce its emissions by over 45 per cent by 2030 compared to 1990 levels.[96]

The EU has so far delivered on its emission reduction promises and is on track to achieve its 2020 goals. With a 53 per cent GDP growth and a drop in GHG emissions of 23 per cent between 1990 and 2016, the EU has shown that climate action has been growth-compatible.[97] As regards the EU's economic incentives for third parties to tackle climate change, it should be noted that, as is the case for development aid, the EU is the largest contributor to international climate finance.[98] According to Commissioner Arias Cañete, the EU contributed to international public climate finance with over €20 billion in 2017.[99] Overall, the EU is seen as a credible climate partner.

Europe's capacity to deliver on its 2030 goals will, however, be subject to significantly higher efforts. The need for enhanced climate action comes at a complex time for the EU. It will lose one of its climate champions, the UK, post-Brexit. Germany has admitted it will fail to reach its GHG emission goals for 2020. France's ecological transition minister, Nicolas Hulot, resigned for lack of real ambition and commitment by the French government, whom he accused of caving in to anti-environmental lobbies. The three largest GHG emitters in Europe are expected to be engaged, in the short to medium term, in matters that could delay the low carbon transition and endanger the EU's green competitive edge. Additionally, Poland, the host of the key Conference of the Parties (COP24) in Katowice, is one of the bedrocks of coal in the EU. There are doubts about a real push for a robust Paris rulebook from the COP Presidency given its recent focus on showcasing clean coal initiatives (UNFCCC, 2018) as well as its laggard positioning in European climate negotiations.[100]

The EU's commitments are not at present aligned with the goals of the Paris Agreement,[101] despite its commendable efforts, bridge-building capacity and credibility. This is the case for all the big emitters. In fact, even if fully implemented, the current NDCs will only take us a third of the way towards the temperature goals of the Paris Agreement.[102] Engagement by other sectors and actors like the Armed Forces is urgently required.

Integrating climate change and security in the EU

The EU's security and global strategies will be the focus of our analysis in order to understand the extent to which climate change has been integrated into EU security. Institutionally, the European External Action Service (EEAS) has a mandate to develop the Common Foreign and Security Policy (CFSP), and within it the Common Security and Defence Policy (CSDP).[103]

The security implications of climate change, the mandate to include environmental considerations in all European policies and the large amounts of energy consumed (and GHGs emitted) by the Armed Forces, beg the question of how climate change is being dealt with by the EU's security institutions. The need for integrating climate change across policy areas stems from the fact that it is a cross-cutting issue that fails to conform to the silo approach that is the norm across government departments. Given the complex nature of climate change, and the insufficient action to arrest it at present, integration seems a necessary, if insufficient, tool to tackle one of the greatest challenges of the twenty-first century.[104]

Theoretically, Climate Policy Integration (CPI) is considered to be an application of Environmental Policy Integration (EPI).[105] Integration implies the inclusion of climate change in decision making across policy areas, in our case study within security and foreign policy strategies. Following Lenschow[106] and Nilsson and Persson,[107] CPI could be thought of as a learning process, based on available knowledge regarding climate impacts and enhanced concern about climate change, that leads to new policies and practices.

In order to understand the extent to which climate change has been integrated into the EU's security strategies Jacob, Volkery and Lenschow's[108] analysis of Environmental Policy Integration tools will be adapted. Said tools include:

1 *Communicative instruments* which would entail including climate change in sectoral strategies such as the European Security Strategy of 2003 (ESS) and the European Union Global Strategy (EUGS, 2016).
2 *Organisational reforms* that amount to a deeper level of institutionalisation and would entail reorganising departments, establishing environmental units or establishing interdepartmental working groups.
3 *Procedural instruments* such as establishing green budgets, requiring climate-resilient peace building or conflict-sensitive climate programming[109]

Since the Single European Act of 1987 all policies in the EU have to be conducive to a high level of environmental protection. Preventive and restorative approaches should be pursued, and the precautionary principle[110] as well as the polluter pays principle should guide European policies.[111] These requirements provide the basis for integrating climate action across policy domains, including security policies. The first European Security Strategy (henceforth ESS) adopted in 2003, the Solana report published in 2008 and the European Security Strategy published in 2016, will be briefly discussed to illustrate the extent to which the EU has integrated climate change into the security arena.

The first European Security Strategy was published in 2003.[112] The main goals of the strategy were to reinforce safety in neighbouring countries and to help build an international order based on multilateralism. The key threats that were highlighted in this security strategy were terrorism, the proliferation of weapons of mass destruction, regional conflicts, state failure and organised crime. The ESS does, however, stress the need for a more proactive approach than was the case during the Cold War. One of the consequences of a move towards a more preventive security strategy was to call for coherence of security, development and environmental policies.[113] Global warming is mentioned in the strategy twice, as a security concern that will have to be addressed, and as one of the drivers that would indirectly aggravate competition for scarce resources such as water, having an impact on 'turbulence and migration'.[114]

Closely related to climate-security concerns, it can be argued that, in the EU, energy security concerns have long been recognised as a clear threat to the EU and as one of the drivers of the recent concern for climate change in security circles. Climate change and energy security concerns have reinforced each other[115] and have helped substantiate the need for a low carbon transition. Policies such as the Energy Union have benefitted from the climate–energy security nexus. The main driver of the energy security concern is the dependence on the Gulf, Russia and North Africa as Europe's main hydrocarbon suppliers.

In 2008 Javier Solana, the High Representative for the Common Foreign and Security Policy and Secretary General of the Council of the European Union from 1999 to 2009, commissioned a report analysing climate change and international security.[116] In that report, mitigation and adaptation are seen as preventive strategies that should be undertaken to avoid the worst consequences of climate change. A changing climate was seen, as was discussed earlier, as a threat multiplier that could wipe out development gains, fuelling instability. Losses in crop productivity, increased water scarcity, loss of territory and 'environmentally induced' migration, political radicalisation, tensions over energy security and challenges to global governance are mentioned as some of the key impacts of failing to tackle climate change effectively. Individual security (human security) as well as State security are believed to be at stake because of climate change.

The Solana report states that the EU is well placed to respond to the threat of climate change due to its 'comprehensive approach to conflict prevention, crisis management and post-conflict reconstruction',[117] a message that is reiterated in the 2016 European Union Global Strategy. The Solana report furthermore calls on the EU and its Member States to plan and enhance their civil and military capabilities in order to respond to crises and disasters. And yet, it is surprising to see that there are no calls for developing the loss and damage mechanisms that will be needed, should mitigation be insufficient to avoid dangerous climate change, as is the case at present, and should adaptation capabilities be exceeded.

A revision of the 2003 strategy was expected by 2008.[118] Instead, however, the *Report on the Implementation of the European Security Strategy: Providing Security in a Changing World* was published.[119] In this report, both energy security and climate change feature more prominently than in the 2003 ESS as threats to the EU. Despite leaving its key messages unchanged, climate change is addressed in that report with a renewed sense of urgency. There are calls for strengthening early warning capabilities as well as for maintaining cooperation with like-minded partners within the UN system. It can, however, be argued that no real integration of climate change and security was considered at the time.[120]

In 2016 the new European Union Global Strategy (henceforth EUGS) was published. The document was titled *Shared Vision, Common Action: A Stronger Europe*. From the outset, the document provides a dire vision of the current global context, while also stressing the opportunities for concerted global action to address current threats. The EU's Global Strategy for Foreign and Security Policy states that we live in times of existential crises spanning terrorism to demographic tensions. Climate change is considered as one of the elements causing additional 'disruption'. Based on principled pragmatism,[121] the strategy seeks to promote peace and security by promoting resilience within the EU and abroad. In short, the EUGS aims to protect EU citizens and territory, improve the wellbeing of EU citizens, strengthen democracies across Europe and continue building a rule-based multilateral world order.

The EUGS' *first priority* is ensuring the security of the EU. This entails addressing threats that affect both people and territory including, *inter alia*, energy insecurity and climate change. In order to promote energy security, the EUGS calls for diversifying energy sources and suppliers, a plea that has not materialised to date as Figure 15.2 clearly shows. It also supports working towards an integrated energy market that has sustainable energy and energy efficiency at its core.

The *second priority* in the EUGS is achieving State and social resilience, especially in Central Asia and Central Africa. The key elements to achieving a resilient society include a well-functioning

	2006	2007	2008	2009	2010	Solid fuels 2011	2012	2013	2014	2015	2016
Russia	25.0	24.8	26.1	30.0	26.9	26.0	25.5	28.8	29.1	28.9	30.2
Colombia	11.4	12.7	12.3	17.4	19.9	23.5	24.1	21.8	21.1	23.9	23.4
Australia	12.0	13.0	11.7	7.5	10.5	8.7	7.3	7.5	6.3	9.8	14.6
United States	7.8	9.1	14.0	13.5	16.8	17.9	22.9	22.4	20.5	16.1	14.1
South Africa	23.1	20.1	16.5	15.8	9.6	7.8	6.3	6.7	9.8	7.7	5.1
Indonesia	9.3	7.8	7.3	7.0	5.5	5.0	4.5	3.1	3.4	3.5	3.0
Canada	2.8	3.0	2.6	1.4	2.0	2.2	1.6	1.8	2.5	1.6	2.0
Mozambique	0.0	0.0	0.0	0.0	0.0	0.1	0.0	0.3	0.3	0.5	0.8
Kazakhstan	0.2	0.1	0.3	0.2	0.2	0.3	0.3	0.3	0.5	0.5	0.8
Others	8.5	9.4	9.2	7.3	8.6	8.6	7.4	7.5	6.4	7.4	6.0
	2006	**2007**	**2008**	**2009**	**2010**	**Crude oil 2011**	**2012**	**2013**	**2014**	**2015**	**2016**
Russia	33.8	33.7	31.8	33.6	34.7	34.8	33.7	33.7	30.4	29.1	31.9
Norway	15.4	15.0	15.0	15.1	13.7	12.5	11.2	11.8	13.1	12.0	12.4
Iraq	2.9	3.4	3.3	3.8	3.2	3.6	4.1	3.6	4.6	7.7	8.3
Saudi Arabia	9.0	7.2	6.8	5.7	5.9	8.0	8.8	8.7	8.9	7.9	7.8
Kazakhstan	4.6	4.6	4.8	5.3	5.5	5.7	5.1	5.7	6.4	6.6	6.8
Nigeria	3.6	2.7	4.0	4.5	4.1	6.1	8.2	8.1	9.1	8.4	5.7
Azerbaijan	2.2	3.0	3.2	4.0	4.4	4.9	3.9	4.8	4.4	5.2	4.5
Iran	6.2	6.2	5.3	4.7	5.7	5.8	1.3	0.0	0.1	0.0	2.9
Algeria	2.5	1.9	2.5	1.6	1.2	2.6	2.9	3.9	4.2	4.2	2.8
Others	19.7	22.4	23.3	21.8	21.6	16.1	20.9	19.7	18.7	19.0	17.0
	2006	**2007**	**2008**	**2009**	**2010**	**Natural gas 2011**	**2012**	**2013**	**2014**	**2015**	**2016**
Russia	39.3	38.7	37.4	33.0	31.9	34.4	34.9	41.1	37.4	37.6	39.9
Norway	25.9	28.1	28.5	29.7	27.9	27.6	31.8	30.4	32.1	32.0	24.8
Algeria	16.3	15.3	14.7	14.1	13.9	13.1	13.3	12.6	12.0	10.8	12.4
Qatar	1.8	2.2	2.3	5.9	9.7	11.6	8.3	6.5	6.8	7.7	5.6
Nigeria	4.3	4.6	4.0	2.4	4.0	4.4	3.1	1.7	1.5	2.0	2.0
Libya	2.5	3.0	2.9	2.9	2.7	0.7	1.9	1.7	2.1	2.1	1.3
Peru	0.0	0.0	0.0	0.0	0.0	0.0	0.8	0.5	0.5	0.3	0.5
Trinidad and Tobago	1.2	0.8	1.7	2.0	1.4	1.2	0.9	0.7	0.9	0.6	0.2
Turkey	0.0	0.0	0.1	0.2	0.2	0.2	0.2	0.2	0.2	0.2	0.2
Others	8.8	7.3	8.3	9.7	8.2	6.8	4.8	4.5	6.5	6.7	13.1

eurostat

Figure 15.2 EU energy imports by country (2006–2016): % of extra EU-28 imports.

Source: Eurostat, "Energy Production and Imports," 2018 (online data codes: nrg_122a, nrg_123a and nrg_124a).

democracy, credible institutions and sustainable development. Energy transition is seen as one of the greatest challenges for the EU's neighbours. Development aid, research and development (R&D) and diplomacy are the key tools mentioned in the EUGS to encourage a low carbon transition and manage climate impacts that can help exacerbate conflicts.

The EU considers supporting different 'paths to resilience' in cases where severe fragility can be expected due to socioeconomic, institutional or 'climate/energy' related factors. For instance, the EU is supporting both public and private investments through the use of instruments such as the External Investment Plan (EIP) and the new European Fund for Sustainable Development contained in the EIP. At the One Planet Summit organised by President Emmanuel Macron in December 2017, marking the second anniversary of the Paris Agreement, the EU announced that its support through the EIP could be expected to reach €9 billion in 2020 in three key areas: 'sustainable cities, sustainable energy and connectivity and sustainable agriculture, rural entrepreneurs and agribusiness'.[122]

The *third priority* in the EUGS is providing an integrated approach to conflicts with both enhanced prevention and deeper post-conflict engagement. As part of EU's pre-emptive peace building efforts, the EUGS seeks to monitor and prevent climate change and act swiftly to limit its impacts. In the EUGS, early warnings regarding climate change and its impacts are to be complemented with early actions to arrest it. The *fourth priority* is supporting cooperative regional institutions, akin to the EU, that are conducive to peace building.

The *fifth priority* calls for supporting multilateralism, especially through the UN system, the G20 and in *liaison* with non-state actors. Investing in climate change action, achieving sustainable development and, more generally, ensuring long-term access to the global commons is seen as an investment in the EU's security.

Despite its proactive and all-encompassing approach, the EUGS has been criticised for being more aspirational than transformational, lacking concrete targets, timetables and progress indicators.[123] Despite its vagueness and aspirational nature, for those concerned with climate change as a security issue it should be highlighted that the EUGS addresses energy and climate change concerns directly or indirectly throughout the strategy. The contrast with the first European Security Strategy is significant. However, the full array of Environmental Policy Integration (EPI) or Climate Policy Integration (CPI) instruments[124] cannot yet be seen either in the EUGS or across European countries' security strategies. In fact, in countries such as Spain for instance, the integration of climate change in the National Security Strategy is very recent, and there is still considerable work to be done in order to engage in mitigation and adaptation measures, both internally and abroad, from a security perspective.[125]

Two years after the publication of the EUGS, during a high-level event HR/VP Mogherini captured the essence of the link between climate and national security when she said:

> Here in Europe, experience tells us that peace and security are not only about peace treaties and defence budgets. Peace has to be sustainable in time. And sustainable peace requires good jobs, decent access to natural resources, and sustainable development. Sustainable peace needs climate action … So let us keep this in mind: when we invest in the fight against climate change, we invest in our own security.[126]

The present section has highlighted that diplomacy, rules, regulations and economic incentives in the EU are increasingly aligned with climate action, while acknowledging insufficient climate action to limit global mean temperature increases to well below 2°C compared to pre-industrial levels. In the security realm communicative instruments such as the ESS, the Solana report and the EUGS have integrated climate change. Deeper forms of integration, such as widespread organisational reforms or the use of procedural instruments, have yet to be fully materialised.

Future research

According to the literature, the novel field of climate security will benefit from further research in areas ranging from theoretical clarification regarding the climate–security nexus[127] to institutional responses to climate security. The theoretical research frontier is striving to develop models that accurately capture the complex interrelations between pre-existing socioeconomic conditions, the vulnerability to climate impacts and the increased likelihood of socially contingent outcomes such as migration and armed conflict.[128]

From a policy-making perspective, the European Environment Agency calls for quantitative projections of European vulnerability to cross-border effects of climate change, while also demanding EU funded research to close adaptation knowledge gaps and to support climate-smart innovation.[129] Additionally, Niklas Bremberg[130] adds to the research agenda the need to understand how Intergovernmental Organisations (IGOs) such as the EU address climate-security concerns.

A further issue that has not been widely explored in the climate-security literature is related to the need for an expansion of the adaptation agenda to include the analysis of uncompensated losses and damages.[131] Current mitigation policies will only take us one-third of the way towards the well-below-2°C guardrail established in the Paris Agreement. And yet, the limits to adaptation, beyond crisis management, do not feature prominently in security strategies. Analysing and preparing for losses and damages that will disproportionately affect vulnerable populations is arguably a low cost strategy to minimise the threat-enhancing effect of climate change.

Given the limits of current climate action and the potentially disastrous consequences of climate change, it is arguably logical to also invest in high-impact, low-probability technological solutions to address it, while being mindful of potential side-effects of such technologies. The Armed Forces' experience in R&D has resulted in a century of leadership in the development of energy technologies that have been used in military operations. This expertise has recently expanded to encompass advancements in energy efficiency, developments in renewable energy and improvements in transportation fuels.[132]

The Armed Forces' capabilities therefore seem well suited to address this significant security concern. Furthermore, the EU has already explored a myriad of potential breakthrough energy technologies, from artificial photosynthesis to low energy nuclear reactions in condensed matter.[133] Additional basic research funding is needed in order to provide the world with scalable, carbon free and cost efficient energy sources. This funding need is aligned with the EUGS that calls for 20 per cent of the defence budget to be allocated to procuring 'equipment, research and technology'.[134]

Conclusion

Climate change is purported by the EU to be 'a threat multiplier that catalyses water and food scarcity, pandemics and displacement'.[135] Destabilising impacts of climate change are expected both inside Europe and in neighbouring regions, affecting Europe's vulnerability to climate change. Within the borders of the Union, we are concerned about water and food security, sea-level rise and coastal degradation, extreme weather events and weather-related disasters. Beyond Europe's limits disruptions to trade and trade routes, infrastructures, transport, geopolitical risks and migration will have an impact on other nations' assets and will affect European interests.

Migration is one of the most immediate risks to be addressed, even if models establishing direct or indirect links between migration and conflict are yet to be fully fleshed out. Be it through Turkey, the central Mediterranean or the Strait of Gibraltar towards Spain, Europe needs to deal with migration with a single voice before the impacts of climate change are in full swing. In addition to regulating the influx of migrants the EU will foster sustainable development in countries of origin.

Popular sentiment is highly volatile regarding security. Most people tend to stress the importance of short-term, high-impact and low-probability threats[136] such as terrorism, which tend to be widely reported by the media, but for which a direct climate–conflict development path has not been established to date.[137]

Most scholars agree that there is no longer a risk of securitising climate change.[138] And yet, security policies in the aftermath of 9/11 terrorist attacks on US soil and the above-mentioned national(istic) policies in Europe regarding migration show signs of toughening. The radical change in scale that climate-triggered migrations might experience is likely to make many governments change course and toughen their present positions as numbers become unmanageable. We already saw that happening during the first Schengen crisis following a dispute between Italy and France back in 2011.

Europe has managed to play a leading role in adopting ambitious climate commitments. Its climate and energy policies have so far been at the cutting edge of the ongoing low carbon transition. Additionally, the EU's negotiation and bridge-building skills have been pivotal at international climate conferences since the 1990s.[139] Europe should also aim at capitalising on this innovation effort. Other major low carbon transition players such as China are heavily engaged in developing their strategic industries in the areas of energy efficiency, the electric vehicle and renewable energies, among others.

Finally, the EU has integrated, to a certain extent, climate change as a security issue, first in the 2003 European Security Strategy and more recently throughout the EU Global Strategy. As Federica Mogherini recently said, addressing climate change will help strengthen EU security. As the impacts of climate change manifest themselves more vividly, the EU's preemptive approach to climate action will prove increasingly necessary to ensure a stronger Europe.

Notes

1 The authors would like to acknowledge the helpful comments and suggestions by Michel Zoghby. The usual disclaimer applies.

2 European Council, *Climate Change and International Security: Paper from the High Representative and the European Commission to the European Council* (Brussels: European Union, 2008), accessed July 15, 2018, file:///Volumes/NEWHD/Google%20Drive/MIS%20ARTI%CC%81CULOS/Routledge%20Climate%20Change%20and%20Security%20in%20the%20EU/Lit%20rev/EU%20Consilium%202008%20Climate%20change%20and%20security%20Solana.pdf. Also, European Environment Agency, *Climate Change, Impacts and Vulnerability in Europe 2016: An Indicator-based Report*, EEA Report 1 (Luxembourg: European Union, 2017), accessed September 21, 2018, www.eea.europa.eu/publications/climate-change-impacts-and-vulnerability-2016.

3 United Nations, Paris Agreement, adopted on 12 December 2015, entered into force on 4 November 2016, TIAS no. 16–1104.

4 Ibid.

5 Ignacio García Sánchez, "Cambio climático y Fuerzas Armadas. La cultura de la transformación permanente," in *Cuadernos de Estrategia 193. El cambio climático y su repercusión en la defensa*, eds. Instituto Español de Estudios Estratégicos e Iberdrola (Madrid: Ministerio de Defensa, 2017).

6 Joshua S. Goldstein, "Climate Change as a Global Security Issue," *Journal of Global Security Studies* 1, no. 1 (2016): 95–98.

7 A salient example of the potential impacts of climate change on military infrastructure and facilities is the closure of Homestead AFB in Florida after Hurricane Andrew completely destroyed it in 1992.

8 Specific military units are being created to deal with emergency situations and complement civil protection services when their resources are insufficient. One such example is Spain's Military Emergency Unit (UME, in Spanish), a 3,000 strong Brigade fully equipped with heavy vehicles and a fire-fighting aircraft, which has become the role model for many similar units throughout the World. These formations have proved especially efficient on the field and have also become the seeds of a totally new approach to security. See UME (Unidad Militar de Emergencias), www.ume.mde.es. See also Juan A. Rico Palma and Francisco Rodríguez, "El cambio climático y las Fuerzas Armadas españolas," in *Cuadernos de Estrategia 193. El cambio climático y su repercusión en la defensa*, eds. Instituto Español de Estudios Estratégicos e Iberdrola (Madrid: Ministerio de Defensa, 2018).

9 Matt McDonald, "Climate Change and Security: Towards Ecological Security?" *International Theory* 10, no. 2 (2018): 153–80.

10 Franziskus Von Luke, Zehra Wellmann, and Thomas Diez, "What's at Stake in Securitising Climate Change? Towards a Differentiated Approach." *Geopolitics* 19 (2014): 857–84.

11 Department of Defense, *Quadrennial Defense Review* (Washington, DC: Department of Defense, 2014), accessed on August 12, 2018, http://archive.defense.gov/pubs/2014_quadrennial_defense_review.pdf; Department of Defense, *Quadrennial Defense Review Report* (Washington, DC: Department of Defense, 2010), accessed on August 12, 2018, https://dod.defense.gov/Portals/1/features/defenseReviews/QDR/QDR_as_of_29JAN10_1600.pdf; European External Action Service, *Shared Vision, Common Action: A Stronger Europe. A Global Strategy for the European Union's Foreign And Security Policy* (Brussels: European Union, 2016), accessed on September 27, 2018, http://europa.eu/globalstrategy/sites/globalstrategy/files/regions/files/eugs_review_web_0.pdf; European External Action Service, *A Secure Europe in a Better World. European Security Strategy* (Brussels: European Union, 2003), accessed on August 1, 2018, https://europa.eu/globalstrategy/en/european-security-strategy-secure-europe-better-world; European Council, *Climate Change and International Security*; European Council, *Report on the Implementation of the European Security Strategy.*

Providing Security in a Changing World (Brussels: European Union, 2008), accessed on August 31, 2018, https://europa.eu/globalstrategy/en/report-implementation-european-security-strategy-providing-security-changing-world.

12 Intergovernmental Panel on Climate Change, "Summary for Policymakers," in *Climate Change 2013: The Physical Science Basis. Contribution of Working Group I to the Fifth Assessment Report of the Intergovernmental Panel on Climate Change*, eds. Thomas F. Stocker et al. (Cambridge, New York: Cambridge University Press, 2013).

13 Malin Mobjörk, "Integrated Policy Responses for Addressing Climate Related Security Risks," SIPRI Policy Brief, Stockholm Resilience Centre, Stockholm University, 2016, accessed on September 28, 2018, www.sipri.org/sites/default/files/Integrated-policy-responses-for-addressing-climate-related-security-risks.pdf.

14 European Environment Agency, *Climate Change, Impacts and Vulnerability in Europe.*

15 Flooding and the potential consequences of changes in AMOC (the Gulf Current) are the main threats in Europe.

16 European Environment Agency, *Climate Change, Impacts and Vulnerability in Europe.*

17 Angela Oels, "From 'Securitization' of Climate Change to 'Climatization of the Security Field: Comparing Three Theoretical Perspectives," in *Climate Change, Human Security and Violent Conflict*, eds. Jürgen Scheffran et al. (Berlin: Springer, 2012), 185–203.

18 Donald Wallace, "Security and Global Climate Change," in *Climate Change, Policy and Security*, eds. Donald Wallace and Daniel Silander (London: Routledge, 2018), 1–40.

19 Marshall Burke, Solomon Hsiang and Edward Miguel, "Climate and Conflict," *Annual Review of Economics* 7 (2015): 577–618.

20 Marshall Burke et al., "Warming Increases the Risk of Civil War in Africa," *PNA* 106, no. 49 (2009): 20670–74.

21 Halvard Buhaug, "Climate Not to Blame for African Civil Wars," *Proceedings of the National Academy of Sciences of the United States of America* 107, no. 38 (2010): 16477–82.

22 Halvard Buhaug, "Climate Changes Affect Conflict Dynamics." NewSecurityBeat podcast. Wilson Center, 2018, accessed on September 11, 2018, www.newsecuritybeat.org/2018/05/halvard-buhaug-climate-affect-conflict-dynamics/; Halvard Buhaug, "Climate Change and Conflict: Taking Stock," *Peace Economics, Peace Science and Public Policy* 22, no. 4 (2016): 331–38.

23 Oli Brown, Anne Hammill and Robert McLeman, "Climate Change as the 'New' Security Threat: Implications for Africa," *International Affairs* 83, no. 6 (2007): 1141–54.

24 Food and Agriculture Organization (FAO), FAO website, accessed on October 14, 2018, www.fao.org/prices/en/.

25 Diána Szoke, "Weaponizing the Weather? The Implications of Treating Climate Change as a Security Issue," KKI Policy Brief (Institute for Foreign Affairs and Trade, 2017), 10.

26 Michael Brzoska and Christiane Fröhlich, "Climate Change, Migration and Violent Conflict: Vulnerabilities, Pathways and Adaptation Strategies," *Migration and Development* 5, no. 2 (2015): 1–20.

27 Nuria Arenas-Hidalgo, "Climate Change and Human Mobility. The National and International Approach to Native Community Relocation in the Arctic." in *Global Challenges in the Arctic Region. Sovereignty, Environment and Geopolitical Balance*, eds. Elena Conde and Sara Iglesias Sánchez (London: Routledge, 2017), 254–77.

28 Neil Adger et al., "Human Security," in *Climate Change 2014: Impacts, Adaptation, and Vulnerability. Part A: Global and Sectoral Aspects. Contribution of Working Group II to the Fifth Assessment Report of the Intergovernmental Panel on Climate Change*, eds. Christopher B. Field et al. (Cambridge: Cambridge University Press, 2014), 755–91.

29 Kanta Kumari Rigaud et al., *Groundswell: Preparing for Internal Climate Migration* (Washington, DC: World Bank, 2018).

30 Juan Marcos Gamero Rus, "Las migraciones humanas inducidas por el Cambio Climático como un fenómeno multicausal: la respuesta desde las políticas sociolaborales y los mecanismos de Protección Social" (PhD dissertation, Universidad Carlos III, 2014).

31 Brzoska and Fröhlich, "Climate Change, Migration and Violent Conflict."

32 Gamero Rus "Las migraciones humanas."

33 Wallace, "Security and Global Climate Change."

34 Lara Lázaro Touza and Ángel Gómez de Ágreda "Gobernanza climática y empresa," *Revista de Responsabilidad Social de la Empresa* 24 (2016): 139–70.

35 Brzoska and Fröhlich, "Climate Change, Migration and Violent Conflict."

36 European Commission, *Managing Migration in All Its Aspects* (Brussels: European Union, 2018), accessed on October 14, 2018, https://ec.europa.eu/commission/sites/beta-political/files/euco-migration-booklet-june2018_en_1.pdf.
37 John Henley, "Italy's Coalition on Collision Course with EU after Migration Standoff," *Guardian*, June 11, 2018, www.theguardian.com/world/2018/jun/11/italy-coalition-collision-course-eu-migration-standoff-matteo-salvini; Lorenzo Tondo, "Matteo Salvini and Viktor Orbán to Form Anti-migration Front," *Guardian*, August 28, 2018, www.theguardian.com/world/2018/aug/28/matteo-salvini-viktor-orban-anti-migrant-plan-brussels.
38 Brzoska and Fröhlich, "Climate Change, Migration and Violent Conflict."
39 Note that Africa will be responsible for most of human population growth during the next half century. Doubling its population every 30 years may render its resources insufficient. Migratory pressure from Africa could be expected to increase in the absence of development gains that are on par with the expected population growth.
40 Wallace, "Security and Global Climate Change"; Lisa M. Dellmuth et al., "Intergovernmental Organizations and Climate Security: Advancing the Research Agenda," *WIREs Climate Change* 9:e496 (2017). doi:10.1002/wcc.496.
41 McDonald, "Climate Change and Security."
42 Backed by commissioned reports such as the Stern Report (Stern, 2007) in the UK, the report on *Climate Change as a Security Risk* commissioned by Germany (German Advisory Council on Climate Change (WBGU), 2008) or the report commissioned by the US and written by the Center for Naval Analysis (CNA) titled *National Security and the Threat of Climate Change.*
43 Oels, "From 'Securitization' of Climate Change."
44 McDonald, "Climate Change and Security."
45 Securitisation is defined by von Luke, Wellmann and Diez as 'a series of speech acts ultimately accepted by the wider societal audience – through which an issue could be represented as an existential threat to a specific referent object legitimising extraordinary measures'. See von Luke, Wellmann and Diez, "What's at Stake in Securitising Climate Change?," 859.
46 Ole Wæver, "Securitization and Desecuritization," in *On Security*, ed. Ronnie Lipschutz (New York: Columbia University Press, 1995).
47 McDonald, "Climate Change and Security"; Oels, "From 'Securitization' of Climate Change"; Von Luke, Wellmann and Diez, "What's at Stake in Securitising Climate Change?"; Wallace, "Security and Global Climate Change."
48 McDonald, "Climate Change and Security."
49 Note that the key climate policy instruments are: command and control (CAC) which is the most widely used environmental policy instrument across the world, environmental taxes, subsidies, deposit-refund systems, emission trading systems, voluntary agreements and moral suasion. Robert N. Stavins, "Policy Instruments for Climate Change: How Can National Governments Address a Global Problem?," Resources for the Future, Discussion Paper, 1997, 97–11. Accessed September 14, 2018, www.rff.org/files/sharepoint/WorkImages/Download/RFF-DP-97-11.pdf.
50 Jarrod Hayes and Janelle Knox-Hayes, "Security in Climate Change Discourse: Analyzing the Divergence between US and EU Approaches to Policy," *Global Environmental Politics* 14, no. 2 (2014): 85.
51 McDonald, "Climate Change and Security."
52 Ibid.; Wæver, "Securitization and Desecuritization."; Von Luke, Wellmann and Diez, "What's at Stake in Securitising Climate Change?"
53 Gonzalo Escribano and Lara Lázaro Touza, "Gobernanza, integración y securitización del cambio climático," *Revista de Economía. Información Comercial Española (ICE)*, no. 892 (2016). In addition, Angela Oels states that according to the Paris School, rather than climate change being securitised, there has been a climatisation of security. This means that the failure of securitisation of climate change has resulted in climate change being legitimised as a security threat. Climatisation also implies that security practices, such as using early warning systems, are now applied to climate action. It could hence be argued that, according to the Paris School, there has been a cross-fertilisation between the climate change and security fields. See Oels, "From 'Securitization' of Climate Change," 185–204.
54 Hayes and Knox-Hayes, "Security in Climate Change Discourse," 85. A recent example of this was the signing into law of the John S. McCain National Defense Authorization Act (NDAA) for Fiscal Year 2019 in August 2018 by President Trump (see McCain, 2019). According to this Act, the

Armed Forces are directed to ensure energy and climate resilience of its installations to the potential impacts of extreme weather events (see Udvardy, 2018), despite public opposition to climate action by the forty-fifth president of the United States, and his depiction of climate change as a hoax invented by the Chinese to damage US interests (see Trump, 2012).

55 Von Luke, Wellmann, and Diez, "What's at Stake in Securitising Climate Change?"

56 United Nations Development Programme, *Human Development Report 1994*. (New York: Oxford University Press, 1994), 24.

57 Oels, "From 'Securitization' of Climate Change," 188.

58 McDonald, "Climate Change and Security."

59 Von Luke, Wellmann, and Diez, "What's at Stake in Securitising Climate Change?"

60 Ibid.

61 McDonald, "Climate Change and Security."

62 Note that despite the fact that the EU is generally aligned with the human security discourse, there have been attempts to securitise certain issues such as migration. Dellmuth et al., "Intergovernmental Organizations and Climate Security." Martin Nilsson, "The European Union and Global Climate Change," in *Climate Change, Policy and Security*, eds. D. Wallace and D. Silander, 131–49 (London: Routledge, 2018).

63 United Nations Development Programme, *Human Development Report 2007/8* (New York: UNDP, 2008).

64 Hayes and Knox-Hayes, "Security in Climate Change Discourse," 85.

65 McDonald, "Climate change and Security."

66 Dennis Pirages, "From Resource Scarcity to Ecological Security," in *From Resource Scarcity to Ecological Security*, eds. Dennis Pirages and Ken Cousins (Cambridge, MA: MIT Press, 2005).

67 Will Steffen, et al., "Planetary Boundaries: Guiding Human Development on a Changing Planet," *Science* 347, no. 6223 (2015).

68 Von Luke, Wellmann, and Diez, "What's at Stake in Securitising Climate Change?"

69 McDonald, "Climate Change and Security."

70 Dellmuth et al., "Intergovernmental Organizations and Climate Security."

71 Mobjörk et al., "Integrated Policy Responses."

72 Daniela Schwarzer, "Europe, the End of the West and Global Power Shifts," *Global Policy* 8, no. 4 (2017).

73 Alina Averchenkova et al., "Climate Policy in China, the European Union and the United States: Main Drivers and Prospects for the Future In-depth Country Analyses," Policy Paper (Grantham Research Institute on Climate Change and the Environment, 2016), accessed on September 14, 2018, www.lse. ac.uk/GranthamInstitute/wp-content/uploads/2016/11/Averchenkova-et-al_2106-in-depth-country-analysis-v2.pdf.

74 Guri Bang, Arild Underdal and Steinar Andersen (eds.), *The Domestic Politics of Global Climate Change. Key Actors in International Climate Cooperation* (Cheltenham and Northampton: Edward Elgar Publishing, 2015).

75 European Environment Agency, *Climate Change, Impacts and Vulnerability in Europe*.

76 Andrew Jordan et al., *Climate Change Policy in the European Union. Confronting the Dilemmas of Mitigation and Adaptation* (Cambridge: Cambridge University Press, 2010).

77 Eurostat, "Energy Production and Imports" (Luxembourg: European Union, 2018), accessed on September 17, 2018. https://ec.europa.eu/eurostat/statistics-explained/index.php/Energy_production_and_imports#The_EU_and_its_Member_States_are_all_net_importers_of_energy.

78 International Energy Agency, *Energy Security* (IEA, 2018), available on-line at www.iea.org/topics/energysecurity/.

79 Jordan et al., *Climate Change Policy in the European Union*. Also, Green Growth Group, *Common statement on the long-term strategy and the climate ambition of the EU* (Luxembourg, June 25, 2018), accessed on September 17, 2018, www.ecologique-solidaire.gouv.fr/sites/default/files/2018.06.25_statement_ggg_climat.pdf.

80 European Commission, *Special Eurobarometer 459. Climate Change – Wave EB87.1 – TNS opinion & social* (Brussels: European Union, 2017), accessed on September 17, 2018. https://ec.europa.eu/clima/sites/clima/files/support/docs/report_2017_en.pdf.

81 Real Instituto Elcano, *Barómetro de la Imagen de España. 7ª oleada*, Mayo 2017, accessed on October 14, 2018. www.realinstitutoelcano.org/wps/wcm/connect/7cb3a69f-1f93-4dd3-b0dd-0b7c0d7d6

672/7BIE_Informe_mayo2017.pdf?MOD=AJPERES&CACHEID=7cb3a69f-1f93-4dd3-b0dd-0b7c0d7d6672.

82 Real Instituto Elcano, *Barómetro del Real Instituto Elcano (BRIE), 39ª oleada*, January 2018, accessed on October 14, 2018. www.realinstitutoelcano.org/wps/wcm/connect/3ba1221c-fd41-4195-bbb1-aa35ed625fe4/39BRIE_Informe_Enero2017.pdf?MOD=AJPERES&CACHEID=3ba1221c-fd41-4195-bbb1-aa35ed625fe.

83 Nilsson, "The European Union and Global Climate Change"; Jordan et al., *Climate Change Policy in the European Union*; Lara Lázaro Touza, "Governing the Geopolitics of Climate Change after the Paris Agreement," in *Handbook of Energy Politics*, ed. Jennifer Considine (Cheltenham: Edward Elgar, 2018).

84 Jordan et al., *Climate Change Policy in the European Union.*

85 United Nations, United Nations Framework Convention on Climate Change, adopted on 9 May 1992, entered into force on 21 March 1994, 1771 UNTS 107.

86 United Nations, Kyoto Protocol to the United Nations Framework Convention on Climate Change, adopted on 11 December 1997, entered into force on 16 February 2005, 37 ILM 22.

87 Scott Barrett, *Environment and Statecraft. The Strategy of Environmental Treaty Making.* (Oxford: Oxford University Press, 2005); Jordan et al., *Climate Change Policy in the European Union.*

88 Where the high expectations of adopting an international agreement to supersede the Kyoto Protocol were temporarily frustrated. See: Lara Lázaro Touza, "Cambio climático: frenazo en Copenhague; próxima estación: México 2010 (COP 16)." *ARI* no. 9 (2010).

89 United Nations, *Paris Agreement.*

90 Lázaro Touza, "Governing the Geopolitics of Climate Change after the Paris Agreement."

91 Jordan et al., *Climate Change Policy in the European Union.*

92 European Commission, *Paris Agreement to Enter into Force as EU Agrees Ratification* (Brussels: European Union, 2016), accessed on September 15, 2018. https://ec.europa.eu/clima/news/articles/news_2016100401_en.

93 European Commission, Communication from the Commission: 20 20 by 2020: Europe's Climate Change Opportunity, COM(2008) 30 final (Brussels: European Union, January 23, 2008), accessed on October 17, 2018, https://eur-lex.europa.eu/legal-content/EN/TXT/PDF/?uri=CELEX:52008DC0030&from=EN.

94 European Council, European Council (23 and 24 October 2014) – Conclusions (EUCO 169/14) (Brussels: European Council, 2014), www.consilium.europa.eu/uedocs/cms_data/docs/pressdata/en/ec/145397.pdf.

95 Council of the European Union, *Intended Nationally Determined Contribution of the EU and its Member States* (Brussels: European Union, 2015), accessed on September 17, 2018. http://www4.unfccc.int/ndcregistry/PublishedDocuments/European%20Union%20First/LV-03-06-EU%20INDC.pdf.

96 European Commission, "Opening Remarks by Climate Action and Energy Commissioner Miguel Arias Cañete at the Second Ministerial on Climate Action (MoCA) by the EU, China and Canada," press release (Brussels: European Union, 2018), accessed September 17, 2018. http://europa.eu/rapid/press-release_SPEECH-18-4236_en.htm.

97 European Commission, Report from the Commission: Two Years after Paris – Progress towards Meeting the EU's Climate Commitments, COM(2017) 646 final (Brussels: European Commission 2017), https://ec.europa.eu/clima/sites/clima/files/strategies/progress/docs/swd_2017_xxx_en.pdf (accessed on September 17, 2018).

98 MobJörk et al., "Integrated Policy Responses."

99 European Commission, "Speech by Commissioner Arias Cañete at the Climate Action EU for Talanoa Conference," press release (Brussels: European Union, 2018), accessed on September 27, 2018. europa.eu/rapid/press-release_SPEECH-18-4154_en.pdf.

100 Jon Birger Skjærseth, "Implementing EU Climate and Energy Policies in Poland: Policy Feedback and Reform," *Environmental Politics* 27, no. 3 (2018).

101 With emissions in the EU having increased in 2017, which is unwelcome news given the need to significantly reduce our emissions if we are to meet our climate and energy commitments. Climate Action Tracker (CAT), EU, update September 7, 2018, accessed on September 11, 2018, https://climateactiontracker.org/countries/eu/.

102 United Nations Environmental Programme, *The Emissions Gap Report 2017* (Nairobi: United Nations Environment Programme, 2017).

103 Mobjörk, "Integrated Policy Responses."
104 Sam Fankhauser and Nicholas Stern, "Climate Change, Development, Poverty and Economics," Centre for Climate Change Economics and Policy Working Paper no. 284. Grantham Research Institute on Climate Change and the Environment. Working Paper no. 253 (CCCEP, 2016), accessed on September 27, 2018, http://personal.lse.ac.uk/sternn/ClimateChangeDevelopmentPoverty&Economics.Fankhauser-Stern.Oct16.pdf.
105 Camilla Adelle and Duncan Russel, "Climate Policy Integration: a Case of Déjà Vu?" *Environmental Policy and Governance* 23, no. 1 (2013).
106 Andrea Lenschow, "Greening the European Union: An Introduction," in *Environmental Policy Integration: Greening Sectoral Policies in Europe*, ed. Andrea Lenschow (London: Earthscan, 2012), 3–21.
107 Måns Nilsson and Assa Persson, "A Framework for Analysing Environmental Policy Integration," *Journal of Environmental Policy and Planning* 5, no. 49 (2003), 333–59.
108 Kalus Jacob, Axel Volkery, and Andrea Lenschow, "Instruments for Environmental Policy Integration in 30 OECD Countries," in *Innovation in Environmental Policy? – Integrating the Environment for Sustainability*, eds. A. Jordan and A. Lenschow (Cheltenham: Edward Elgar, 2008), 24–48.
109 Mobjörk, "Integrated Policy Responses."
110 According to principle 15 of the Rio Declaration, the Precautionary Principle states that when there are 'threats of serious or irreversible damage, lack of full scientific certainty shall not be used as a reason for postponing cost-effective measures to prevent environmental degradation'. European Commission, Communication from the Commission on the Precautionary Principle, COM(2000) 1 final (Brussels: European Union, February 2, 2000), 8, accessed on October 17, 2018, https://eur-lex.europa.eu/legal-content/EN/TXT/PDF/?uri=CELEX:52000DC0001&from=EN.
111 Nilsson, "The European Union and Global Climate Change." For the Act, see Single European Act (1987), O.J. L 169/1, (amending Treaty Establishing the European Economic Community, Mar. 25, 1957, 298 U.N.T.S. 11).
112 European External Action Service, *A Secure Europe in a Better World.*
113 Javier de Carlos Izquierdo, "La nueva estrategia de Seguridad Europea 2016," *Instituto Español de Estudios Estratégicos* 16, 2016, accessed on September 11, 2018, www.ieee.es/Galerias/fichero/docs_marco/2016/DIEEEM16-2016_EstrategiaSeguridad_DeCarlos.pdf.
114 European External Action Service, *A Secure Europe in a Better World*, 3.
115 Maria Julia Trombetta, "Environmental Security and Climate Change: Analysing the Discourse," *Cambridge Review of International Affairs* 21, no. 4, 2008.
116 European Council, *Climate Change and International Security.*
117 Ibid., 2.
118 Javier de Carlos Izquierdo, "La nueva estrategia de Seguridad Europea 2016."
119 European Council, *Report on the Implementation of the European Security Strategy.*
120 Nilsson, "The European Union and Global Climate Change."
121 European External Action Service, *Shared Vision, Common Action.* It should be noted, however, that the academic literature has criticised the 'principled pragmatism' approach of the EUGS as being a contradiction in terms. For instance, Juncos argues that

> theoretically, principled pragmatism implies that the EU should act in accordance with universal values (liberal ones in this case), but then follow a pragmatic approach which denies the moral imperatives of those universal categories. The EU needs to be either pragmatic or principled; it cannot have it both ways.

The risk in this principled priority approach would be that the EU can be criticised by other actors as using either principles or pragmatism to suit its own interests and, by doing so it risks losing its normative power. Ana E. Juncos, "Resilience as the New EU Foreign Policy Paradigm: A Pragmatist Turn?," *European Security* 26, no. 1 (2017): 1–18, 2.

122 European Commission, "EU External Investment Plan: Climate-Smart Investments Worth €9bn Unveiled at 'One Planet Summit'" (Brussels: European Union, 2017), accessed on September 17, 2018, https://ec.europa.eu/clima/news/eu-external-investment-plan-climate-smart-investments-worth-eur-9bn-unveiled-one-planet-summit_en.
123 Félix Arteaga, "European Defence between the Global Strategy and Its Implementation," *Real Instituto Elcano Working Paper* 4, 2017, accessed on September 24, 2018, www.realinstitutoelcano.

org/wps/wcm/connect/1e698ba2-2ff0-4a6a-8b5f-0fad2dc0d122/WP4-2017-Arteaga-European-defence-between-Global-Strategy-implementation.
pdf?MOD=AJPERES&CACHEID=1e698ba2-2ff0-4a6a-8b5f-0fad2dc0d122.
124 Adelle and Russel, "Climate Policy Integration: a Case of Déjà Vu?"; Klaus Jacob, Axel Volkery and Andrea Lenschow, "Instruments for Environmental Policy Integration in 30 OECD Countries," in *Innovation in Environmental Policy? Integrating the Environment for Sustainability*, ed. Andrew Jordan and Andrea Lenschow (Cheltenham: Edward Elgar, 2008), 24–48; Lázaro Touza and López-Gunn, "Climate Change Policies – Mitigation and Adaptation at the Local Level"; Åsa Persson, Hens Runhaar, Sylvia Karlsson-Vinkhuyzen, Gerard Mullally, Duncan Russel and Alexander Widmer, "Environmental Policy Integration: Taking Stock of Policy Practice in Different Contexts," *Environmental Science & Policy* 85 (2018): 113–15.
125 Juan Antonio Rico Palma and Francisco Rodríguez, "El cambio climático y las Fuerzas Armadas españolas."
126 European External Action Service, *Climate, Peace and Security: The Time for Action* (Brussels: European Union, 2018), accessed on October 1, 2018, https://eeas.europa.eu/headquarters/headquarters-homepage/47165/climate-peace-and-security-time-action_en.
127 McDonald, "Climate Change and Security."
128 Buhaug, "Climate Changes Affect Conflict Dynamics"; Buhaug, "Climate Change and Conflict: Taking Stock"; Malin Mobjörk et al., "The Role of Multilateral Organisations in Addressing Climate Change and its Security Risks," SIPRI Policy Brief, Stockholm Resilience Centre. Stockholm University, 2015, accessed on September 28, 2018, www.statsvet.su.se/polopoly_fs/1.264072.1461241894!/menu/standard/file/Policy%20brief,%20Addressing%20climate-related%20security%20risks,%20November%202015.pdf.
129 European Environment Agency, *Climate Change, Impacts and Vulnerability in Europe.*
130 Niklas Bremberg, "European Regional Organisations and Climate-related Security Risks: EU, OSCE and NATO," SIPRI Insights on Peace and Security no. 1 (2018), accessed on September 29, 2018, www.sipri.org/sites/default/files/2018-02/sipriinsight_1802_01_igos_and_climate_change.pdf.
131 See for instance Lázaro Touza and Atkinson (2013) for an applied case study of how losses and damages can be compensated, based on scientific advice, politically feasible compensation choices and citizen preferences. Lara Lázaro Touza and Giles Atkinson, "Nature, Roads or Hospitals? An Empirical Evaluation of 'Sustainable Development Preferences'," *Ecological Economics* 95 (2013).
132 William J. Nuttall, Constantine Samaras and Morgan Bazilian, "Energy and the Military: Convergence of Security, Economic, and Environmental Decision-Making." EPRG Working Paper 1717. Cambridge Working Paper in Economics 1752 (EPRG, 2017), accessed on September 21, 2018, www.eprg.group.cam.ac.uk/wp-content/uploads/2017/11/1717-Text.pdf.
133 European Commission, *Forward Looking Workshop on Materials for Emerging Energy Technologies* (Brussels: Directorate-General for Research and Innovation Industrial Technologies Material Unit, 2012), accessed on September 3, 2018, www.gppq.fct.pt/h2020/_docs/brochuras/nmpb/emerging-materials-report_en.pdf.
134 European External Action Service, *Shared Vision, Common Action: A Stronger Europe*, 44.
135 Ibid., 29.
136 Damien J. Williams and Jan M. Noyes, "How Does Our Perception of Risk Influence Decision-Making? Implications for the Design of Risk Information," *Theoretical Issues in Ergonomics Science* 8, no. 1 (2007).
137 Larissa A. Brunner, "Low-Probability, High-Impact Events: Why Are People Afraid of Terrorism?" *Global Risk Insights*, November 25, 2015, accessed on September 22, 2018, https://globalriskinsights.com/2015/11/low-probability-high-impact-events-why-are-people-afraid-of-terrorism/.
138 Oels, "From 'Securitization' of Climate Change."
139 Rosa Giles Carnero, "La contribución de la Unión Europea al desarrollo del régimen internacional en materia de cambio climático: el paquete europeo sobre clima y energía en el contexto de la acción internacional," *Cuadernos Europeos de Deusto*, no. 57 (2017).

References

Adelle, Camilla, and Duncan Russel. "Climate Policy Integration: a Case of Déjà Vu?" *Environmental Policy and Governance* 23, no. 1 (2013): 1–12.

Adger, Neil et al. "Human Security." In *Climate Change 2014: Impacts, Adaptation, and Vulnerability. Part A: Global and Sectoral Aspects. Contribution of Working Group II to the Fifth Assessment Report of the Intergovernmental Panel on Climate Change*, edited by Christopher B. Field et al., 755–91. Cambridge: Cambridge University Press, 2014.

Arenas-Higaldo, Nuria. "Climate Change and Human Mobility. The National and International Approach to Native Community Relocation in the Arctic." In *Global Challenges in the Arctic Region. Sovereignty, Environment and Geopolitical Balance*, edited by Elena Conde and Sara Iglesias Sánchez, 254–77. London: Routledge, 2017.

Arteaga, Félix. "European Defence between the Global Strategy and Its Implementation." Real Instituto Elcano Working Paper 4, 2017.

Averchenkova, Alina, et al. "Climate Policy in China, the European Union and the United States: Main Drivers and Prospects for the Future In-depth Country Analyses." Policy Paper. Grantham Research Institute on Climate Change and the Environment, 2016.

Bang, Guri, Arild Underdal and Steinar Andersen (eds.). *The Domestic Politics of Global Climate Change. Key Actors in International Climate Cooperation.* Cheltenham and Northampton: Edward Elgar Publishing, 2015.

Barrett, Scott. *Environment and Statecraft. The Strategy of Environmental Treaty Making.* Oxford: Oxford University Press, 2005.

Bates, Bryson C., Z.W. Kundzewicz, S. Wu and J.P. Palutikof. *Climate Change and Water, Technical Paper of the Inter-Governmental Panel on Climate Change.* Geneva: IPCC Secretariat, 2008.

Bremberg, Niklas. "European Regional Organisations and Climate-related Security Risks: EU, OSCE and NATO." SIPRI Insights on Peace and Security no. 1. SIPRI, 2018.

Brown, Oli, Anne Hammill and Robert McLeman. "Climate Change as the 'New' Security Threat: Implications for Africa." *International Affairs* 83, no. 6 (2007): 1141–54.

Brunner, Larissa A. "Low-Probability, High-Impact Events: Why Are People Afraid of Terrorism?." *Global Risk Insights*, November 25, 2015.

Brzoska, Michael, and Christiane Fröhlich. "Climate Change, Migration and Violent Conflict: Vulnerabilities, Pathways and Adaptation Strategies." *Migration and Development* 5, no. 2 (2015): 1–20.

Buhaug, Halvard. "Climate Change and Conflict: Taking Stock." *Peace Economics, Peace Science and Public Policy* 22, no. 4 (2016): 331–38.

Buhaug, Halvard. "Climate Changes Affect Conflict Dynamics." NewSecurityBeat podcast. Wilson Center, 2018.

Buhaug, Halvard. "Climate Not to Blame for African Civil Wars." *Proceedings of the National Academy of Sciences of the United States of America* 107, no. 38 (2010): 16477–82.

Burke, Marshall, Solomon Hsiang and Edward Miguel. "Climate and Conflict." *Annual Review of Economics* 7 (2015): 577–618.

Burke, Marshall, Edward Miguel, Shanker Satyanath, John A. Dykema and David B. Lobell. "Warming Increases the Risk of Civil War in Africa." *PNA* 106, no. 49 (2009): 20670–74.

Campiglio, Emanuele. "Beyond Carbon Pricing: The Role of Banking and Monetary Policy in Financing the Transition to a Low-carbon Economy." Centre for Climate Change Economics and Policy Working Paper no. 181. Grantham Research Institute on Climate Change and the Environment Working Paper no. 160, 2014.

CAN. National Security and the Threat of Climate Change. 2007. Last accessed July 25, 2019. https://www.cna.org/CNA_files/pdf/National%20Security%20and%20the%20Threat%20of%20Climate%20Change.pdf.

Council of the European Union. *Intended Nationally Determined Contribution of the EU and Its Member States.* Brussels: European Union, 2015.

De Carlos Izquierdo, Javier. "La nueva estrategia de Seguridad Europea 2016." *Instituto Español de Estudios Estratégicos* 16, 2016.

Dellmuth, Lisa M., et al. "Intergovernmental Organizations and Climate Security: Advancing the Research Agenda." *WIREs Climate Change* 9:e496 (2017): 1–13.

Department of Defense. *Quadrennial Defense Review.* Washington, DC: Department of Defense, 2014.

Department of Defense. *Quadrennial Defense Review Report.* Washington, DC: Department of Defense, 2010.

Escribano, Gonzalo, and Lara Lázaro Touza. "Gobernanza, integración y securitización del cambio climático." *Revista de Economía. Información Comercial Española (ICE)*, no. 892 (2016): 33–48.

European Commission. Communication from the Commission on the Precautionary Principle. COM(2000) 1 final. Brussels: European Union, February 2, 2000.

European Commission. Communication from the Commission to the European Parliament, the Council, the European Economic and Social Committee and the Committee of the Regions: 20 20 by 2020: Europe's Climate Change Opportunity. COM(2008) 30 final. Brussels. European Union, January 23, 2008.

European Commission. "EU External Investment Plan: Climate-Smart Investments Worth €9bn Unveiled at 'One Planet Summit.'" Brussels: European Union, 2017.

European Commission. *Forward Looking Workshop on Materials for Emerging Energy Technologies*. Brussels: Directorate-General for Research and Innovation Industrial Technologies Material Unit, 2012.

European Commission. *Managing Migration in All Its Aspects*. Brussels: European Union, 2018.

European Commission. "Opening Remarks by Climate Action and Energy Commissioner Miguel Arias Cañete at the Second Ministerial on Climate Action (MoCA) by the EU, China and Canada." Press release. Brussels: European Union, 2018.

European Commission. "Paris Agreement to Enter into Force as EU Agrees Ratification." Brussels: European Union, 2016.

European Commission. Report from the Commission to the European Parliament and the Council: Two Years after Paris – Progress towards Meeting the EU's Climate Commitments. COM(2017) 646 final. Brussels: European Commission, 2017.

European Commission. Special Eurobarometer 459. Climate Change – Wave EB87.1 – TNS opinion & social. Brussels: European Union, 2017.

European Commission. "Speech by Commissioner Arias Cañete at the Climate Action EU for Talanoa Conference." Press release. Brussels: European Union, 2018.

European Council. *Climate Change and International Security: Paper from the High Representative and the European Commission to the European Council*. Brussels: European Union, 2008.

European Council. European Council (23 and 24 October 2014) – Conclusions (EUCO 169/14). Brussels: European Council, 2014.

European Council. *Report on the Implementation of the European Security Strategy. Providing Security in a Changing World*. Brussels: European Union, 2008.

European Environment Agency. *Climate Change, Impacts and Vulnerability in Europe 2016: An Indicator-based Report*. EEA Report 1. Luxembourg: European Union, 2017.

European External Action Service. *Climate, Peace and Security: The Time for Action*. Brussels: European Union, 2018.

European External Action Service. *A Secure Europe in a Better World. European Security Strategy*. Brussels: European Union, 2003.

European External Action Service. *Shared Vision, Common Action: A Stronger Europe. A Global Strategy for the European Union's Foreign and Security Policy*. Brussels: European Union, 2016.

European Union. Consolidated Version of the Treaty on the Functioning of the European Union. *Official Journal of the European Union* C 202, June 7, 2016, 51. EUR-Lex website, accessed March 9, 2019. https://eur-lex.europa.eu/legal-content/EN/TXT/?uri=CELEX:12016E/TXT.

European Union. Single European Act (Amending Treaty Establishing the European Economic Community, Mar. 25, 1957, 298 U.N.T.S. 11) *Official Journal of the European Communities* L 169, 1987, 1.

Eurostat. "Energy Production and Imports." Luxembourg: European Union, 2018.

Fankhauser, Sam, and Nicholas Stern. "Climate Change, Development, Poverty and Economics." Centre for Climate Change Economics and Policy Working Paper no. 284. Grantham Research Institute on Climate Change and the Environment. Working Paper no. 253. CCCEP, 2016.

Fischer, Günther, Francesco N. Tubiello, Harrij van Velthuizen and David, A. Wiberg. "Climate Change Impacts on Irrigation Water Requirements: Effects of Mitigation, 1990–2080." *Technol. Forecast Soc.* 74, no. 7 (2007): 1083–107.

Food and Agriculture Organization (FAO). www.fao.org/prices/en/.

Gamero Rus, Juan Marcos. "Las migraciones humanas inducidas por el Cambio Climático como un fenómeno multicausal: la respuesta desde las políticas sociolaborales y los mecanismos de Protección Social." PhD dissertation, Universidad Carlos III, 2014.

García Sánchez, Ignacio. "Cambio climático y Fuerzas Armadas. La cultura de la transformación permanente." In *Cuadernos de Estrategia 193. El cambio climático y su repercusión en la defensa*, edited by Instituto Español de Estudios Estratégicos e Iberdrola. Madrid: Ministerio de Defensa, 2017.

German Advisory Council on Climate Change (WBGU). *Climate Change as a Security Risk*. London: Earthscan, 2008.

Giles Carnero, Rosa. "La contribución de la Unión Europea al desarrollo del régimen internacional en

materia de cambio climático: el paquete europeo sobre clima y energía en el contexto de la acción internacional." *Cuadernos Europeos de Deusto*, no. 57 (2017): 193–208.
Goldstein, Joshua S. "Climate Change as a Global Security Issue." *Journal of Global Security Studies* 1, no. 1 (2016): 95–98.
Green Growth Group. *Common Statement on the Long-term Strategy and the Climate Ambition of the EU*. Luxembourg, June 25, 2018.
Hayes, Jarrod, and Janelle Knox-Hayes. "Security in Climate Change Discourse: Analyzing the Divergence between US and EU Approaches to Policy." *Global Environmental Politics* 14, no. 2 (2014): 82–101.
Henley, John. "Italy's Coalition on Collision Course with EU after Migration Standoff." *Guardian*, June 11, 2018.
Intergovernmental Panel on Climate Change (IPCC). "Summary for Policymakers." In *Climate Change 2013: The Physical Science Basis. Contribution of Working Group I to the Fifth Assessment Report of the Intergovernmental Panel on Climate Change*, edited by Thomas F. Stocker et al., 3–29. Cambridge: Cambridge University Press, 2013.
International Energy Agency. *Energy Security* (IEA, 2018).
Jacob, K., Axel Volkery and Andrea Lenschow. "Instruments for Environmental Policy Integration in 30 OECD Countries." In *Innovation in Environmental Policy? Integrating the Environment for Sustainability*, edited by Andrew Jordan and Andrea Lenschow, 24–48. Cheltenham: Edward Elgar, 2008.
Jordan, Andrew, et al. *Climate Change Policy in the European Union. Confronting the Dilemmas of Mitigation and Adaptation*. Cambridge: Cambridge University Press, 2010.
Juncos, Ana, E. "Resilience as the New EU Foreign Policy Paradigm: A Pragmatist Turn?" *European Security* 26, no. 1 (2017): 1–18.
Lázaro Touza, Lara. "Cambio climático: frenazo en Copenhague; próxima estación: México 2010 (COP 16)." *ARI* no. 9 (2010): 1–15.
Lázaro Touza, Lara. "Governing the Geopolitics of Climate Change after the Paris Agreement." In *Handbook of Energy Politics*, edited by Jennifer Considine, 435–82. Cheltenham: Edward Elgar, 2018.
Lázaro Touza, Lara, and Giles Atkinson. "Nature, Roads or Hospitals? An Empirical Evaluation of 'sustainable development preferences'." *Ecological Economics* 95 (2013): 63–72.
Lázaro Touza, Lara, and Ángel Gómez de Ágreda. "Gobernanza climática y empresa." *Revista de Responsabilidad Social de la Empresa* 24 (2016): 139–70.
Lázaro Touza, Lara, and Elena López-Gunn. "Climate Change Diplomacy in Spain's Future Foreign Policy." SFS (EEE) 18/2014 - 9/6/2014. http://www.realinstitutoelcano.org/wps/portal/rielcano_en/contenido?WCM_GLOBAL_CONTEXT=/elcano/elcano_in/zonas_in/spanishforeignpolicy/eee18-2014-lazaro-lopezgunn-climate-change-in-spain-future-foreign-policy.
Lázaro Touza, Lara, and Elena López-Gunn. "Climate Change Policies – Mitigation and Adaptation at the Local Level: The Case of the City of Madrid (Spain)." In *Sustainable Systems and Energy Management at the Regional Level: Comparative Approaches*, edited by Marco Tortora (Hershey: IGI Global, 2014): 261–87.
Lenschow, Andrea. "Greening the European Union: An Introduction." In *Environmental Policy Integration: Greening Sectoral Policies in Europe*, edited by Andrea Lenschow, 3–21. London: Earthscan, 2012.
Lorenzo-Lacruz, J., S.M. Vicente-Serrano, J.I. López Moreno, E. Morán-Tejeda and J. Zabalza. Recent Trends in Iberian Stream Flows (1945–2005). *Journal of Hydrology* 414–415 (2012): 463–75.
McCain, John. "John S. McCain National Defense Authorization Act for Fiscal Year 2019." 115th Congress of the United States of America. US Government, 2018.
McDonald, Matt. "Climate Change and Security: Towards Ecological Security?" *International Theory* 10, no. 2 (2018): 153–80.
Mobjörk, Malin. "Integrated Policy Responses for Addressing Climate Related Security Risks." SIPRI Policy Brief. Stockholm Resilience Centre, Stockholm University, 2016.
Mobjörk, Malin, et al. "The Role of Multilateral Organisations in Addressing Climate Change and Its Security Risks." SIPRI Policy Brief. Stockholm Resilience Centre. Stockholm University, 2015.
Nilsson, Måns, and Assa Persson. "A Framework for Analysing Environmental Policy Integration." *Journal of Environmental Policy and Planning* 5, no. 49 (2003): 333–59.
Nilsson, Martin. "The European Union and Global Climate Change." In *Climate Change, Policy and Security. State and Human Impacts*, edited by D. Wallace and D. Silander, 131–49. London: Routledge, 2018.
Nuttall, William J., Constantine Samaras and Morgan Bazilian. "Energy and the Military: Convergence of Security, Economic, and Environmental Decision-Making." EPRG Working Paper 1717. Cambridge Working Paper in Economics 1752. EPRG, 2017.

Oels, Angela. "From 'Securitization' of Climate Change to 'Climatization' of the Security Field: Comparing Three Theoretical Perspectives." In *Climate Change, Human Security and Violent Conflict*, edited by Jürgen Scheffran et al., 185–203. Berlin: Springer, 2012.

Persson, Åsa, Hens Runhaar, Sylvia Karlsson-Vinkhuyzen, Gerard Mullally, Duncan Russel and Alexander Widmer. "Environmental Policy Integration: Taking Stock of Policy Practice in Different Contexts." *Environmental Science & Policy* 85 (2018): 113–15.

Pirages, Dennis. "From Resource Scarcity to Ecological Security." In *From Resource Scarcity to Ecological Security*, edited by Dennis Pirages and Ken Cousins. Cambridge, MA: MIT Press, 2005.

Potsdam Institute for Climate Impact Research and Climate Analytics. *Turn Down the Heat: Why a 4°C Warmer World Must be Avoided*. Washington: World Bank, 2012.

Real Instituto Elcano. *Barómetro de la Imagen de España. 7ª oleada*. Madrid: Real Instituto Elcano, 2017.

Real Instituto Elcano. *Barómetro del Real Instituto Elcano (BRIE), 39ª oleada*. Madrid: Real Instituto Elcano, 2018.

Rico Palma, Juan A., and Francisco Rodríguez. "El cambio climático y las Fuerzas Armadas españolas." In *Cuadernos de Estrategia 193. El cambio climático y su repercusión en la defensa*, edited by Instituto Español de Estudios Estratégicos e Iberdrola. Madrid: Ministerio de Defensa, 2018.

Rigaud, Kanta Kumari, et al. *Groundswell: Preparing for Internal Climate Migration*. Washington, DC: The World Bank, 2018.

Schwarzer, Daniela. "Europe, the End of the West and Global Power Shifts." *Global Policy* 8, no. 4 (2017): 18–26.

Skjærseth, Jon Birger. "Implementing EU Climate and Energy Policies in Poland: Policy Feedback and Reform." *Environmental Politics* 27, no. 3 (2018): 498–518.

Stavins, Robert N. "Policy Instruments for Climate Change: How Can National Governments Address a Global Problem?" Resources for the Future Discussion Paper, 1997, 97–11.

Steffen, Will, et al. "Planetary Boundaries: Guiding Human Development on a Changing Planet." *Science* 347, no. 6223 (2015): 736–47.

Stern, N. The Economics of Climate Change. The Stern Review. Cambridge: Cambridge University Press, 2007.

Szoke, Diána. "Weaponizing the Weather? The Implications of Treating Climate Change as a Security Issue." KKI Policy Brief. Institute for Foreign Affairs and Trade, 2017.

Tondo, Lorenzo. "Matteo Salvini and Viktor Orbán to Form Anti-migration Front." *Guardian*, August 28, 2018.

Trombetta, Maria Julia. "Environmental Security and Climate Change: Analysing the Discourse." *Cambridge Review of International Affairs* 21, no. 4 (2008): 585–602.

Trump, Donald. Donald J. Trump Twit @realDonaldTrump on Climate change, 2012. https://twitter.com/realDonaldTrump/status/265895292191248385?ref_src=twsrc%5Etfw%7Ctwcamp%5Etweetembed%7Ctwterm%5E265895292191248385&ref_url=https%3A%2F%2Fwww.vox.com%2Fenergy-and-environment%2F2017%2F1%2F18%2F14313126%2Ftrump-pruitt-climate-hoax-lukewarmism.

Udvardy, Shana. *New Defense Bill Strengthens the Military's Flood & Energy Readiness and Saves Taxpayer Dollars – All While Addressing Climate Change*. Union of Concerned Scientists, 2018.

UME (undated). Madrid: Unidad Militar de Emergencias. www.ume.mde.es.

United Nations. Kyoto Protocol to the United Nations Framework Convention on Climate Change, adopted on 11 December 1997, entered into force on 16 February 2005, 37 ILM 22.

United Nations. Paris Agreement. Adopted on 12 December 2015, entered into force on 4 November 2016., TIAS no. 16–1104.

United Nations. United Nations Framework Convention on Climate Change, adopted on 9 May 1992, entered into force on 21 March 1994, 1771 UNTS 107.

United Nations Development Programme. *Human Development Report 1994*. New York: Oxford University Press, 1994.

United Nations Development Programme. *Human Development Report 2007/8*. New York: UNDP, 2008.

United Nations Environmental Programme. *The Emissions Gap Report 2017*. Nairobi: United Nations Environment Programme, 2017.

Von Luke, Franziskus, Zehra Wellmann and Thomas Diez. "What's at Stake in Securitising Climate Change? Towards a Differentiated Approach." *Geopolitics* 19 (2014): 857–84.

Wæver, Ole. "Securitization and Desecuritization." In *On Security*, edited by Ronnie Lipschutz, 1–31. New York: Columbia University Press, 1995.

Wallace, Donald. "Security and Global Climate Change." In *Climate Change, Policy and Security*, edited by Donald Wallace and Daniel Silander, 1–40. London: Routledge, 2018.
Williams, Damien J., and Jan M. Noyes. "How Does Our Perception of Risk Influence Decision-Making? Implications for the Design of Risk Information." *Theoretical Issues in Ergonomics Science* 8, no. 1 (2007): 1–35.
World Health Organisation. "Climate Change and Health." World Health Organization, February 1, 2018. www.who.int/mediacentre/factsheets/fs266/en/.

16
ENERGY SECURITY IN THE EU

Miriam Solera Ureña

Introduction

In the field of International Relations, the concept of security is still undergoing debate. For Arnold Wolfers, security refers to both the objective "absence of threats" to core values and the subjective "absence of fear."[1] David Baldwin's reformulation of security as "a low probability of damage to acquired values" focuses on reducing vulnerability and increasing resilience in anticipation of potential risks.[2] In the context of political and military rivalries, access to fossil energy resources has been traditionally an unquestionable keystone of national security policies. The 1970s oil crisis broadened the concept of energy security to include economic risks arising from supply interruptions or price volatility. These events also reshaped the geopolitical and trade leverage between suppliers and importers, thus stressing increasingly tight interdependences in the world energy market. The establishment in 1992 of the *United Nations Framework Convention on Climate Change* and the ensuing *Kyoto Protocol* were prominent milestones in promoting awareness beyond geopolitics and economics leading to the *Paris Agreement* in 2015.

The concept of energy security has evolved differently through history and geography for supplier and consumer countries. Currently, there is no consensus on the definition of energy security and which dimensions this concept should comprise. Surveys compiling conceptualisations of energy security in the scholarly literature and expert discussion fora consider a wide range of these.[3] Though different, most conceptualisations share specific importer's approaches focussing on the procurement of supplies (availability) and supply affordability. This fact has slowed both the understanding of existing interdependences and the effective deployment of multi-sector initiatives at global and regional levels by stakeholders. Nonetheless, more extensive interpretations are becoming prominent that embrace sustainability, technological innovation and societal components, such as energy poverty and governance. Such understandings highlight the difference between energy security at large and the more constrained concept of security of energy supply. In particular, following the 2015 Paris Agreement a separation of energy policy and the climate, renewable energies and efficiency policies has become inconceivable.

The semantic progress of the energy security concept reflects the increasing complexity and transversality of the issue and it has certainly paved the way for more comprehensive legislation as well as new investments and innovation around the globe. Furthermore, because the scope of energy policies supersedes the national and regional levels, a treatment of energy security demands multidisciplinary, multiagency and multilevel approaches.

Security of supply is one of the dimensions included under the concept of energy security and may refer to short as well as medium and long terms. From an import perspective, the first is related to the ability to deal with the physical and economic upshots of unanticipated supply shocks by adopting emergency measures and collective responses.[4] On the other hand, medium and long term security policies aim at guaranteeing a continuous supply of affordable energy by reducing vulnerabilities and increasing resilience in a sustainable way. It is not the aim of this chapter to review the numerous theoretical proposals of energy security, nor to explore their quantitative assessment from the European Union (EU) perspective.[5] Moreover a detailed analysis of the various existing approaches and their policies is a complex task that exceeds the scope of this section. This chapter intends to provide an overview of some relevant issues concerning the medium to long term security of supply of oil and gas, as well as the deployment of renewable energies in the EU in the forthcoming years.

Energy: the cornerstone of the European Union

Both the European Coal and Steel Community (1952) and the European Atomic Energy Community (1957) were pioneering supranational institutions devoted to regional energy cooperation. Paradoxically, following their creation, the energy integration process abated and failed to reach the same course of maturity as the vigorous economic development that ensued upon the creation the European Economic Community in 1957. The European internal energy market has striven for integration, transparency and competitiveness since the first liberalising electricity and gas directives of 1996 and 1998.

In 2009, the TFEU (Treaty on the Functioning of the European Union), Article 4, conferred on the EU and the Member States (MS) shared competences on energy policy subject to co-decision by the European Parliament and the Council, according to ordinary legislative procedure.[6] According to Article 194 under Title XXI on energy, the functioning of the energy market, security of energy supply, improved efficiency and savings, the fostering of new and renewable energies and the interconnection of energy networks all fall within the remit of the EU. The TFEU also links energy and environment (art. 194 and 192) together with the solidarity principle among MS (art. 122) as essential pillars of the Energy Union.

The reluctance of national governments to transfer energy competences to the EU has been actively endorsed by the TFEU. Article 194 guarantees national sovereignty on the selection of energy mix, the structure of energy supply and conditions to exploit its natural resources without prejudice to Article 192 (2)(c) devoted to environment. Although it is rather improbable that it should be recalled due to the requirement of unanimity, Article 192 (2)(c) allows the Council to intervene in the above-specified MS competences according to a special legislative procedure pursuant to environmental goals defined under Title XX, Article 191.

EU energy policies aim to ensure that European citizens can access secure, affordable and sustainable energy supplies.[7] Geopolitical events, worldwide energy competition and the impact of climate change are all triggering a rethinking of the EU energy and climate strategy. With an average monthly value of extra-EU imports in energy products of €22.7 billion in 2017 and €26.1 billion in the first semester of 2018, the European Union is facing unprecedented challenges arising from the transitional path to a low-carbon energy model while also securing competitiveness and energy supply under increasing dependence on energy imports with limited budgets.[8]

There are significant differences among MS in aspects concerning the security of supply, such as: energy mix and import dependences, efficiency, supply diversification, transport infrastructures, regional back-up and political and economic ties with supplier countries. Further differences concern structural features like energy/carbon intensity, energy consumption per capita and national regulation.[9] There is a plurality of intangible issues that hinder convergence in the EU. These may include historic sympathies or animosities among MS and with supplier countries; social rejection of nuclear power generation; ecological and environmental awareness; or national assertion, *Brexit* and increasing populist party support being two examples of the latter. Under these premises, devising common, one-size-fits-all policies to meet the physical demands and subjective grounds underlying MS national energy prospects seems rather daunting. Energy policy is likely to remain bound for contestation within the EU.

EU security in the context of global energy systems in transition

Energy systems are in transition with a long term shift towards digitalised, consumer centred and low emission alternatives driven by international environmental commitments and technology innovation. Technology developments, Asia's economic growth, changes in the geographical distribution of energy supply and demand, emergence of new energy players, ongoing regional conflicts and international environmental commitments are all fostering the emergence of new dynamics and interdependences, and an increasingly multi-polar energy system. All of these circumstances raise both uncertainty and challenges.

Handling such complexity demands the EU to articulate a comprehensive common approach to energy security, further multilevel cooperation within and beyond its borders, as well as joint external energy and climate actions by the MS. However, contentious energy issues among MS continue to challenge EU governance; the diverging positions in regard to the Nord Stream 2 project clearly illustrate this point.[10] Launched in 2015, the Energy Union seeks to deter such dynamics by unifying positions that allow further security of supply, by fostering solidarity, transparency and coordination among national energy plans and by deepening market integration and multilevel cooperation as prerequisites for a competitive, secure transition to low emission energy systems.[11] The Energy Union embodies the intertwining of energy and environment and the EU's aim to lead the global energy transition towards low-carbon energy systems. The European Commission presented its *Clean Energy Package for All Europeans* in 2016. It encompasses eight competitive calls for a stable legislative framework, though currently with uneven development.[12] These serve as a comprehensive umbrella for the deployment of the main Energy Union targets (governance, electricity markets, energy efficiency, energy performance in buildings, further deployment of renewable energies and market regulation) alongside the guarantee to deliver the Paris Agreement commitments.[13]

It is of foremost importance that the role of the EU in the global energy markets be strengthened in order to address the ongoing changes in the oil and liquefied natural gas (LNG) markets, energy trade flows and EU relations with Russia, which are increasingly deteriorating. This can only be achieved by empowering both the external common dimension of the energy and climate policies and by projecting the EU's soft power in favour of transparent, competitive global energy markets. The EU *Energy Diplomacy Action Plan* adopted in 2015 aims at strengthening the external dimension of energy, chiefly by focussing on the diversification of supply routes and suppliers, as well as the promotion of clean energies.[14] From a security of supply perspective, much of the EU external action ought to strive for stable and predictable energy regulatory frameworks abroad.[15] However, inasmuch as regional instability happens to be embedded in, and caused by, a wide range of interdependent issues, the EU should foster comprehensive projects which address physical and intangible concerns to enable sustained regional well-being.

The EU position in the world scene will also depend on its ability to lead the decarbonisation transition worldwide. This daunting enterprise is accompanied by a larger debate over momentum, paths and feasibility, among other aspects, which is beyond the scope of this work. But for the short and medium terms, the EU's advocacy for a clean transition serves MS's trade policies and the export of green technologies and services to foreign markets.

On the geopolitics of renewables

The 2030 *Climate and Energy Policy Framework* embraces post 2020 climate and energy goals.[16] Despite the *Clean Mobility package*,[17] there is widespread concern about the capability of the EU to reach the emission targets given that transport is the largest, non-declining green-house gas (GHG) emitter sector, the immaturity of the clean mobility market as well as the resistance of major European automotive manufacturers.[18]

The expansion of renewable energies also poses a wide range of challenges for the EU, which go beyond dissimilar national renewable energy shares (RES), uneven levels of governmental support and the differing pathways to decarbonisation taken by the EU members. Some of these challenges will become increasingly important in the long term. In particular, there is high uncertainty surrounding aspects such as: patenting as well as know-how and technology transfer to developing countries; carbon taxing, subsidies and industrial competitiveness; cybersecurity risks alongside the massive deployment of super grids and/or more decentralised topologies; stranded assets in supplier, transit and consumer countries; economic diversification in fossil fuel rich countries; regional integration with renewable energy exporting countries; shifts in the current geopolitical leverage, including North and South relations; or effect on energy poverty, among other long-range issues, of which an exhaustive discussion is beyond the scope of this chapter.[19]

Renewable technologies lead the transformation of energy systems. This process will modify the approaches to energy security, and in particular to security of supply as fossil fuels are gradually substituted by alternative energy sources. The exertion of political or economic pressure through hostile energy measures will increasingly be displaced by cyber-attacks as smart energy infrastructures become pervasive in the internal market. In the long run, as the world's overall consumption of fossil fuel energy declines, the current external interdependences of security of supply will dilute, giving rise to new security dynamics and leverages. One may foresee a scenario of "inward securitisation" of the energy system, in which analysis and policy making revolve around the control and operation of the super smart grids, the need for complex maintenance standards and the challenges arising from virtual threats.

The EU has to handle this proportionately to the magnitude of the associated risks. Effective cybersecurity measures together with ample human resources will have to be budgeted in the coming years in order to secure the supply of energy and energy related services. The *Energy Expert Cyber Security Platform* provides support to the Commission in order to adapt the Directive on security of network and information systems according to four priorities: threat and risk management, prompt response to cyber-attacks, increasing resilience, and the build-up of required capacities and competences.[20]

Most low-carbon technologies require the so-called "hi-tech" or "critical raw materials" for which the global demand is expected to rise sharply in coming years. Though restrictions in the critical-metal supply chain are not expected, prices may spike due to a number of factors, including geopolitical asymmetry and geographical concentration, with China leading the world production and processing; market speculation; technology constraints for capital investments due to low production rates or geographical unfeasibility; and low efficiency of recycling processes. Well aware of the growing importance, in 2008 the EU launched the *European Raw Materials Initiative*, which produces a list of critical raw materials for the European economies, which is periodically revised.[21]

New players in the oil market

At the present day, crude oil accounts for about 35 per cent of the overall EU gross inland energy consumption. Though the trend is towards a gradual decline of the overall oil demand due to efficiency improvements, its import dependence has progressively increased since the early 2000s by approximately 13 per cent up to around 88 per cent due to continuing indigenous production decline.[22] According to data for 2017, the EU aggregated regional import share was of Russian and Caspian Basin origin (38.76 per cent), followed by imports from the Middle East (21.01 per cent), Africa (17.93 per cent), Europe (16.54 per cent) and America (5.76 per cent). Russia is by far the most prominent EU supplier with around 27.62 per cent share in 2017 in the EU market, compared to 5 per cent of intra-EU imports including UK provision.[23] Though the overall import dependence approaches 90 per cent, EU Member States are less exposed to the risk of supply disruption due to a diversified portfolio of suppliers, flexibility of transport routes and market liquidity.[24] They are, however, rather vulnerable to price spikes ensuing from geopolitical instability further afield, the evolution of recent market developments and breakdowns in the supply chain.

A number of recent disruptive circumstances raise market uncertainty, namely production disruptions in Nigeria, Libya, Venezuela[25] or Angola; the oil dispute between the central government of Iraq and the Kurdistan Regional Government of Northern Iraq; the conflict of Saudi Arabia with Iran and Yemen also affecting shipping routes; Donald Trump's withdrawal of the *Joint Comprehensive Plan of Action*, and the restoration of sanctions on Iran as well as the application of tariffs to imports and the consequent dispute with China and other trade partners. Uncertainty also surrounds the prospect of major political, economic and energy related reforms of the Saudi Crown Prince as included in the plan *Vision 2030*, particularly those concerning Saudi Aramco's initial public offering (IPO), the rationalisation of fossil subsidies and the commissioning of refining and chemical manufacturing in order to become a world product exporter.[26] The new International Maritime Organisation fuel rule marine transport content, to be in force in 2020, may create new opportunities for the products market.[27]

The US non-conventional oil sector has significantly impacted global crude oil prices, trade flows and the production strategy of the Organization of the Petroleum Exporter Countries (OPEC) after tight oil production was boosted in 2011 and former president Obama revoked a 40-year crude oil export ban to third countries in 2015. OPEC members have been confronted with the dilemma of either allowing prices to plunge or losing market share by cutting down their own production levels. In November 2014, OPEC's decision to maintain a production level of 30 mb/d (millions of barrels a day) aimed at winning back market share by driving high cost producers out of the market.[28] In January 2016, crude prices fell, down to about $31/b (dollars per barrel) average.[29] This collaterally affected OPEC members with higher fiscal breakeven oil prices, thus threatening their national spending and internal stability. Simultaneously, falling prices led to investment constraints, in particular in upstream projects.[30] To offset this situation, in December 2016, OPEC and non-OPEC oil producers (OPEC Plus) led by Saudi Arabia and Russia committed to reduce production by 1.8 mb/d of crude oil from the beginning of 2017, propping up the oil prices to levels higher than $70/b by mid-September 2018.[31] At the time of this writing, OPEC has attained a balance of supply and demand in the oil market. However, this strategy succeeded partially in recovering market share because of tight oil producers' resilience to cope with low prices as further technology development eased the costs of hydraulic fracturing (fracking).[32]

At present the US, Russia and Saudi Arabia together represent around a third of world crude production, each producing circa 11.0 mb/d.[33] Although the US is likely to become the world's largest oil producer, there is less confidence that it will challenge Saudi Arabia as a new swing producer.[34] There are three main reasons for this: the lack of spare capacity, the regulatory framework and the production capacity forecast for the medium term.[35] Swing producers possess sufficient spare (idle) capacity to promptly adjust oil production in response to variations in the supply and demand. The International Energy Agency (IEA) and the US Energy Information Administration (EIA) estimate that Saudi Arabia holds about 1.5 to 2 mb/d of spare capacity, around two-thirds of the 2.8 mb/d spare capacity of OPEC.[36] By definition, swing producers are able to increase the production volume within 30 days and to sustain it for at least another 90 days.[37] However, for tight oil companies, it takes longer to ramp up oil production due to technical constraints.[38] In addition, OPEC members tend to act and manage spare capacity in a coordinated manner to effectively influence the oil market, whereas fracking companies operate within a regulated anti-cartel framework and strive for their own benefit maximisation. In the short term, the oil market is confronting production outages in Venezuela and Iran. US light tight oil cannot compensate by itself for the whole production drop due to mismatches in the quality of the oil demanded by refineries.[39] Therefore, and even with the prospect of the US becoming the largest oil producer for the next few years, the market still relies on the OPEC production to provide stability to the market.[40]

For the medium term, Chinese and Indian demand, together with petrochemical activity, will drive global demand to increase by 5.5 mb/d up to 104.7 mb/d and by 5.7 mb/d up to 104.5 mb/d by 2023, according to IEA and OPEC, respectively.[41] However, after an inter-annual peak growth was reached in 2017, the annual growth rate is foreseen to decelerate due to higher prices, efficiency measures, environmental constraints and stronger alternative transport support. On the supply side, the global production may reach 104.7 mb/d by 2023, spurred mainly by the developments in US tight production. The US may be able to deliver about 60 per cent of the, in relation to 2018, 6.3 mb/d increasing production capacity by 2023. As a result, for the medium term, US producers will be major players in a well-supplied market. However, the prospect of a deceleration in the US production growth following the early 2020s and leading to a peak in 2027–28, raises concerns.[42] Insofar as tight production floods the market with oil, OPEC will restrain its own production in order to keep prices stable. Declining rates in production capacity growth, insufficient investments in conventional projects and geopolitical disruptions might result in a drop of the world spare capacity, thus tightening the market by the mid-2020s.[43]

The OPEC Plus agreement highlights the difficulty for Saudi Arabia and OPEC to cope alone with the complexity of a transitional market with new players and dynamics. Furthermore, it is difficult to predict how long the strategic alliance between Saudi Arabia and Russia may hold on account of the fragile, complex scenario in the Middle East. Despite it all, OPEC and in particular Saudi Arabia remain pivotal actors for the stabilisation of the oil market in the short and medium terms.

Some considerations on the diversification of gas supply

At time of this writing, natural gas represents around a quarter of the overall EU gross inland energy consumption. The overall EU gas demand grew by 17 per cent up to 491 bcm (billion cubic metres) between 2014 and 2017. Economic activity and rising coal-to-gas switching in power generation, the latter growing by 28.5 per cent between 2015 and 2017, have been the main drivers of such an increase. This sector comprises about 26 per cent of the overall gas demand.[44] While the long-term gas demand is expected to gradually phase out due to the EU decarbonisation commitment, prospects for the medium term remain uncertain.[45] The course of gas consumption is dependent upon a number of factors which include the structural development of the market; the energy commodity prices – including the performance of EU carbon allowances; and political agency concerning a wide range of issues, such as Market Stability Reserve (MSR) and the EU ETS (Emissions Trading System) reinforcement or nuclear and coal shutdowns, among others.[46]

Crucial components leading to enhanced security include: promoting constraints in the gas demand, completing the transnational corridors, enhancing redundancy and cross-border interconnectivity and striving for a stable, transparent, competitive regulatory framework.[47] These measures aim at deepening the internal EU market and involve a number of action areas, some of which require further and faster development and of which the analysis is outside the scope of this section.[48] Rather, this section introduces specific issues related to the EU's search for diversified supply routes and suppliers, a central and complex issue of the overall EU security of supply strategy.

With an import volume reaching 360 bcm in 2017, the steadily growing trend of gas dependence has reached the 70 per cent threshold. Russia and Norway alone account for about 77 per cent of all extra-EU imports, the former supplying 43 per cent, the latter 34 per cent of total volume. LNG imports account for circa 14 per cent of the overall imports, with Qatar covering about 40 per cent of all LNG supplies.[49]

Unlike the oil market, the European natural gas markets still show distinct regional features owing to the prevalence of differentiated gas suppliers and transport infrastructures physically connected to consumer countries. Those MS relying on pipeline-based imports are more vulnerable to critical events affecting any of the parties in the supply chain, due to the lack of flexibility to diversify their imports in the short term. Therefore, the structural aspects of the MS's import systems are key factors for the security of supply.

There are, however, remarkable differences in the import dependence levels among the MS. These range from negative values as low as about –48 per cent and –32 per cent for the exporting countries, Denmark and the Netherlands respectively, to values higher than 95 per cent, the latter group including 16 countries.[50] However, in addition to the import dependence level, the vulnerability of individual MS to supply disruptions varies according to specific import supplier portfolios and route diversification, alongside the degree of interconnectivity with other MS. The share of Russian gas in the overall import volumes of Bulgaria, Estonia, the Czech Republic, Latvia, Austria, Poland, Romania, Slovenia, Slovakia and Finland was in excess of 75 per cent in 2017. Some of these MS rely entirely on Russian supplies.[51] According to the European Commission report for 2014, the countries most vulnerable to disruption from Russia were the Baltic States and Finland and several South Eastern European States (Bulgaria, Croatia, Greece, Hungary and Romania). However, it is worth noticing that the relation between the EU and Russia is not one of dependence, but one of mutual interdependence, since at present the EU is by far the largest Russian importer, a situation without clear perspectives of change.

These facts gain enormous relevance in the context of the joint developments that have occurred in Russia and Ukraine since the late 2000s. The ongoing military conflict with the annexation of Crimea to Russia in 2014 had much farther reaching consequences than all other gas disputes in the mid-2000s, with occasional disruption of gas deliveries. This has led to widespread awareness, particularly among the Eastern European countries suffering from insufficient diversification, about the risks of too high a reliance on Russian gas, and has urged the

EU to reduce gas imports from Gazprom. Paradoxically, the net annual gas volume imported from Russia by the EU increased by circa 16 per cent between 2014 and 2017, though the average value of the imported mass decreased by 31 per cent for the same period.[52]

Russia and the Nord Stream pipeline are at the centre of the energy strife. Nord Stream enables direct gas conveyance from Russian reservoirs to Germany, minimising transit supply risks and turning Germany into a transit country for Central and Western Europe. This has generated political controversy in Europe with some MS showing strong opposition based on geopolitical and security grounds, while other MS regard it as beneficial for the security of the whole of the Union.[53] The decision to double the transport capacity with two new lines by the end of 2019 has intensified the debate within the EU and beyond as it has become intertwined with two circumstances: the US energy and security concerns underlying the threat of sanctions to European companies involved in the project and the uncertainty surrounding the negotiation between Ukrainian Naftogaz and Gazprom on a new gas transit contract from 2020 onwards.[54] The European Commission has set forth its objections to the Nord Stream 2 project with the adoption of a legislative proposal to amend the Gas Directive 2009/73/EC, thus reacting to the conclusions of the EU legal services; the latter specify that common rules for the internal market are not applicable to any pipelines between the EU and third countries.[55] The Commission's proposal pursues the compliance of every upstream pipeline connecting the EU to third countries with the internal gas market regulation. This has led to earnest discussions concerning the conformity of the proposal to the principles of subsidiarity and proportionality (TFEU, Article 5) and eventual jurisdictional conflicts with third countries and international law.[56] Though Germany and Austria, among other MS, firmly objected to any amendment to the Gas Directive, the political compromise reached in February 2019 endorses the application of the Third Energy Package to the territory and the territorial sea of the MS where the first interconnection point with its network is located.[57] For all that Nord Stream 2 has to abide by Third Energy Package rules, the approved version reinforces the German position to negotiate the pipeline's legal framework with Russia and to enforce the EU Gas Directive, compared with the original proposal; this one would have further undermined Germany's negotiating autonomy or even jeopardised the completion of the project.[58]

Both the European Commission and the European Parliament are pushing ahead with the construction of the Southern Gas Corridor as an alternative to Russian gas despite an eventual surplus import infrastructure.[59] The Southern Gas Corridor (SGC) consists of the South-Caucasus Pipeline Future Expansion, the Trans Anatolian Natural Gas Pipeline and the Trans-Adriatic Pipeline (TAP). The SGC will convey gas from Azerbaijan, via Georgia and Turkey to the EU, beginning in 2020. The aim of the Southern Gas Corridor is to undermine the Gazprom market share in Central and Eastern Europe with the import of Azerbaijani gas. Simultaneously, Gazprom is working to supply gas to the South and South Eastern European countries via the Turkstream pipeline. This offshore pipeline has an overall capacity of 31.5 bcm and connects Russia and Turkey through the Black Sea near the border with Bulgaria and Greece. It is due to become operative at the end of 2019.[60]

There is an issue worth considering, if the above projects progress as planned. By 2020, the Nord Stream and Turkstream will undermine or even completely nullify Ukraine's role as a transit country; in addition, the SGC corridor aims to bypass Russia. Given EU rules on third party access, TAP capacity could be disputed by SGC and Turkstream. That means that despite TAP's initial exemption granted for the first 10 bcm of gas, EU strategy might backfire if Gazprom was to bid for capacity through open season auctions once TAP achieves its full capacity of 20 bcm. Simultaneously, Turkey would become a prominent transit country for the EU if Ukraine were to be bypassed. The implications of this eventuality ought to be assessed in the contexts of the current EU–Turkey and Cyprus–Turkey relations as well as other geopolitical aspects in the East Mediterranean Basin, related for example to the gas reservoirs, the Kurdish conflict and the war in Syria.

It is in the interest of the EU that LNG serves the objective of further diversification, with cheap US shale gas developing a central role. Rapid global LNG capacity expansion and the emergence of new portfolio players are reshaping the regional nature of the gas markets by fostering flexibility, competition and diversification. Prospects estimate a global production capacity growth estimated at 140 bcm by 2023 with the US and Australia playing a major role. This may result in oversupply and higher competition for market share with traditional major EU pipeline and LNG suppliers, such as Russia and Qatar. However, the future of the LNG scenario remains open due to the uncertain development of the Asian consumption rate, in particular that of China and India. As mentioned previously, in 2017 the EU imported circa 55 bcm (14 per cent of all EU gas imports). Nonetheless, new LNG projects are being deployed in the EU, although there is a current spare capacity of about 150 bcm.[61]

The EU's eager support for the capacity expansion of the current import infrastructure is likely to prove counterproductive for the energy and climate goals. Surpluses in infrastructure may lead to fossil fuel lock-in if stranded assets are to be minimised, thus contravening EU internal and international commitments. Budgetary resources should be rationally devoted to further network interconnection and to strengthen diversification through storage, reverse flows, decentralisation and digitalisation, thus striving for a reliable, transparent and optimally interconnected market, with a particular focus on the Eastern and South European regions.

Conclusions

Energy security is to be understood in a comprehensive manner referring to ample, interrelated dimensions, the security of supply being an important one. The chapter has provided an overview of some prominent issues concerning the medium to long term security of supply of oil and gas, as well as the deployment of renewable energies in the EU in forthcoming years. Energy systems are undergoing a transition to decarbonisation. Simultaneously, ongoing changes in the world energy markets cause uncertainty and reshape traditional market and consumer patterns. In this challenging context, the MS and the EU as a whole are committed to providing their citizens with secure, affordable access to energy services while advancing the energy transition.

This work has pointed out current aspects which are likely to influence the expansion of renewables and the supply of oil and gas in the coming years. Renewable technologies are the key elements for the decarbonisation of the energy system. This transition implies a change in the interpretation of security of supply, shifting from an approach based on third-country dependence to another with increasing competition for the control of infrastructures and critical metals, as well as of virtual challenges. US tight oil supply has proved capable of challenging OPEC's position in the global oil market since its boost in 2011. But even if the US becomes the world's largest oil producer, it is unlikely that it will influence the market in the same way as the swing producers, Saudi Arabia and OPEC, do. The EU internal market involves ample projects and initiatives, which are essential for the security of supply and diversification. However, the EU's internal contentiousness in the Nord Stream 2 project again shows how far the EU remains from speaking with a common voice towards the rest of the countries. It is a matter of utmost importance for the EU to enforce the common external energy and climate dimensions. The EU can exert a constructive influence worldwide by deepening bonds with main supplier and consumer countries, by exporting its acquis to neighbouring countries and by leading the energy transition. This approach must prevail, in particular, in regard to the relation with Russia, which at present is mainly driven by the geopolitical decision to weaken this country's market share. The current diversification policy aims at reducing Gazprom's geopolitical leverage in the European gas market and abating potential interferences with trade and transit flows, unaware of eventual leverage shifts regarding Turkey's new role. In addition, as long as the current deployment of new import infrastructures continues to be motivated, to a great extent, by the goal to help at-risk MS reduce dependence on Russia rather than by market outlook considerations, what remains at stake is the dilemma between potential stranded assets and a climate fiasco.

Notes

1 Arnold Wolfers, "'National Security' as an Ambiguous Symbol," *Political Science Quarterly* 67, no. 4 (1952): 485.
2 David A. Baldwin, "The Concept of Security," *Review of International Studies* 23, no. 1 (1997): 13.
3 B.W. Ang et al., "Energy Security: Definitions, Dimensions and Indexes," *Renewable and Sustainable Energy Reviews* 42 (2015): 1077–93; Christian Winzer, "Conceptualizing Energy Security," *Energy Policy* 46 (2012): 36–48; Benjamin K. Sovacool and Mukherjee Ishani, "Conceptualizing and Measuring Energy Security: A Synthesized Approach," *Energy* 36, no. 8 (2011): 5343–55; Benjamin K. Sovacool et al., "Evaluating Energy Security Performance from 1990 to 2010 for Eighteen Countries," *Energy* 36, no. 10 (2011): 5846–53; Shahnaz Sharifuddin, "Methodology for Quantitatively Assessing the Energy Security of Malaysia and Other Southeast Asian Countries," *Energy Policy* 65 (2014): 574–77.
4 International Energy Agency, "What Is Energy?," IEA website, accessed July 2, 2018, www.iea.org/topics/energysecurity/whatisenergysecurity/.
5 A comprehensive qualitative and quantitative assessment can be found in: José María Marín Quemada et al., *Energy Security for the EU in the 21st Century: Markets, Geopolitics and Corridors* (London: Routledge, 2012).
6 European Union, Consolidated Version of the Treaty on the Functioning of the European Union, OJ C 202/15, EUR-Lex website, June 7, 2016, accessed March 9, 2019, https://eur-lex.europa.eu/legal-content/EN/TXT/?uri=CELEX:12016E/TXT, 98, 132, 150.
7 European Commission, Communication from the Commission to the European Parliament, the Council, the European Economic and Social Committee and the Committee of the Regions: A Policy Framework for Climate and Energy in the Period from 2020 to 2030, COM(2014) 015 final, EUR-Lex website, January 22, 2014, accessed February 25, 2019, https://eur-lex.europa.eu/legal-content/EN/ALL/?uri=CELEX:52014DC0015.
8 Eurostat, "EU Imports of Energy Products–Recent Development," Eurostat website, October 2018, accessed February 25, 2019, https://ec.europa.eu/eurostat/statistics-explained/index.php?title=EU_imports_of_energy_products_-_recent_developments.
9 European Commission, *EU Energy in Figures: Statistical Pocketbook 2018* (Luxembourg: Publications Office of the European Commission, 2018), 173–231.
10 European Commission, *Nord Stream 2 – Divide et Impera Again? Avoiding a Zero-Sum Game*, European Commission website, October 27, 2017, accessed September 2018, https://ec.europa.eu/epsc/sites/epsc/files/epsc_-_nord_stream_-_divide_et_impera_again.pdf.
11 European Commission, Communication from the Commission to the European Parliament, the Council, the European Economic and Social Committee, the Committee of the Regions and the European Investment Bank: A Framework Strategy for a Resilient Energy Union with a Forward-Looking Climate Change Policy, COM(2015) 080 final, EUR-Lex website, February 25, 2015, accessed March 12, 2019, https://eur-lex.europa.eu/legal-content/EN/TXT/?uri=CELEX:52015DC0080.
12 European Commission, Communication from the Commission to the European Parliament, the Council, the European Economic and Social Committee, the Committee of the Regions and the European Investment Bank: Clean Energy for All Europeans, COM(2016) 0860 final, EUR-Lex website, November 30, 2016, accessed March 9, 2019, https://eur-lex.europa.eu/legal-content/en/TXT/?uri=CELEX:52016DC0860.

13 The *Paris Agreement*, in force since November 2016, provides a global framework to prevent climate change. A total of 197 countries signed this international treaty with the goal of limiting the global temperature rise to 1.5 to 2 degrees Celsius in relation to pre-industrial levels. The Paris Agreement requires countries to submit their national contributions to the reduction of emissions and climate change resilience to the UNFCC secretariat by 2020 and every five years thereafter. The US withdrew from the agreement in June 2017. United Nations, "The Paris Agreement," UNFCC website, accessed 12 March, 2019, https://unfccc.int/process-and-meetings/the-paris-agreement/the-paris-agreement.

14 Council of the European Union, Council Conclusions on Energy Diplomacy, ST 10995 15 INIT, Council of the European Union website, July 20, 2015, accessed July 25, 2018, http://data.consilium.europa.eu/doc/document/ST-10995-2015-INIT/en/pdf.

15 Matteo Barra and Martin Svec, "Reinforcing Energy Governance under the EU Energy Diplomacy: A Proposal for Strengthening Energy Frameworks in Africa," *European Journal of Risk Regulation* 9, no. 2 (2018): 248.

16 Updated binding 2030 targets have been proposed for a 32 per cent share of renewable sources in the EU final energy consumption and 32.5 per cent for energy efficiency savings (compared to a projected business-as-usual scenario for 2030). The target for GHG reduction remains at a 40 per cent lower than the GHG levels in 1990. European Commission, "One Step Closer towards Fulfilling the Energy Union: Commission Welcomes Parliament Committee Votes on Clean Energy Package," European Commission website, July 10, 2018, accessed July 25, 2018, https://ec.europa.eu/info/news/one-step-closer-towards-fulfilling-energy-union-commission-welcomes-parliament-committee-votes-clean-energy-package-2018-jul-10_en.

17 The Clean Mobility Package comprises three sets of initiatives towards low emission mobility systems. European Commission, "Europe on the Move: Commission Completes Its Agenda for Safe, Clean and Connected Mobility," European Commission website, May 17, 2018, accessed March 12, 2019, https://ec.europa.eu/transport/modes/road/news/2018-05-17-europe-on-the-move-3_en.

18 Eurostat, "Europe 2020 Indicators-Climate Change and Energy," Eurostat website, June 2018, accessed July 25, 2018, https://ec.europa.eu/eurostat/statistics-explained/index.php/Europe_2020_indicators_-_climate_change_and_energy#General_overview.

19 Meghan O'Sullivan, Indra Overland and David Sandalow, *The Geopolitics of Renewable Energy* (Harvard Kennedy School, 2017); Daniel Scholten, *The Geopolitics of Renewables* (Cham: Springer International Publishing, 2018); Sergey Paltsev, "The Complicated Geopolitics of Renewable Energy," *Bulletin of the Atomic Scientists* 72, no. 6 (2016): 390–95.

20 Energy Expert Cyber Security Platform, *Cyber Security in the Energy Sector. Recommendations for the European Commission on a European Strategic Framework and Potential Future Legislative Acts for the Energy Sector*, Energy Expert Cyber Security Platform website, February 2017, accessed August 10, 2018, https://ec.europa.eu/energy/sites/ener/files/documents/eecsp_report_final.pdf.

21 The European Commission defines the critical raw materials as those "of a high importance to the economy of the EU and whose supply is associated with a high risk." British Geological Survey et al., *Study on the Review of the List of Critical Raw Materials* (Luxembourg: Publications Office of the European Union, 2017), 7, 38–49.

22 Data extracted and calculated from: Eurostat, "Energy Balances in the MS Excel File Format (2018 Edition)," Eurostat website, May 2018, accessed July 5, 2018, https://ec.europa.eu/eurostat/documents/38154/4956218/ENERGY-BALANCES-May-2018-edition.zip/310265d9-6adf-45aa-ba41-2dce8e5f78eb.

23 Directorate-General for Energy, "Registration of Crude Oil Imports and Deliveries in the European Union," EU Open Data Portal, accessed May 17, 2018, https://data.europa.eu/euodp/data/dataset/eu-crude-oil-imports-and-supply-cost (more specifically: https://ec.europa.eu/energy/sites/ener/files/documents/crude-oil-imports2016.zip).

24 Eurostat, "Energy Balances in the MS Excel File Format (2018 Edition)."

25 At the time of this writing, Venezuela's political future is uncertain. Due to its political symbolism and its vast energy resources, any pacific solution to the current deadlock will require the acquiescence of the US and Russia in the foreseeable future. Venezuela has the world's largest proven crude oil reserves, which represent around 20 per cent of the whole. However, between the beginning of 2016 and February 2019, its oil production has decreased by about one-half, to less than 1.1 mb/d. Venezuela's State oil company PdVSA has been object of US sanctions since August 2017, being followed by further executive orders. In January 2019, all properties and interests belonging to PdVSA subject to US jurisdiction were blocked and US nationals are prohibited from participating in transactions with

PdVSA. OPEC, "OPEC Share of World Crude Oil Reserves, 2017," OPEC website, accessed March 22, 2019, www.opec.org/opec_web/en/data_graphs/330.htm; US Energy Information Administration, "Crude Oil Production, Venezuela, Monthly," US EIA website, accessed March 22, 2019, www.eia.gov/opendata/qb.php?category=1039874&sdid=STEO.COPR_VE.M; US Department of State, "Venezuela-Related Sanctions," US Department of State website, accessed March 22, 2019, www.state.gov/e/eb/tfs/spi/venezuela/.

26 "Vision 2030," Kingdom of Saudi Arabia, accessed June 20, 2018, http://vision2030.gov.sa/sites/default/files/report/Saudi_Vision2030_EN_2017.pdf.

27 Annex VI of the MARPOL Convention regulates airborne emissions from ships. From January 1, 2020, the global sulphur content of ship's fuel oil outside designated emission control areas will be reduced from current 3.5 per cent m/m (mass by mass) to 0.5 per cent m/m. International Maritime Organization, "Sulphur 2020 – Cutting Sulphur Oxide Emissions," IMO website, accessed March 15, 2019, www.imo.org/en/MediaCentre/HotTopics/Pages/Sulphur-2020.aspx.

28 OPEC, "OPEC 166th Meeting concludes," OPEC website, November 27, 2014, accessed July 10, 2018, www.opec.org/opec_web/en/press_room/2938.htm.

29 OPEC, "Monthly Oil Market Report February 2016," OPEC website, February 10, 2016, accessed July 10, 2018, www.opec.org/opec_web/static_files_project/media/downloads/publications/MOMR%20February%202016.pdf.

30 "With the Benefit of Hindsight: The Impact of the 2014–16 Oil Price Collapse," in *Global Economic Prospects: Broad-Based Upturn, but for How Long?* (Washington, DC: World Bank, 2018).

31 OPEC, "OPEC and Non-OPEC Ministerial Meeting," OPEC website, December 10, 2016, accessed July 10, 2018, www.opec.org/opec_web/en/press_room/3944.htm.

32 Irma Alonso Álvarez and Virginia Di Nino, "The Oil Market in the Age of Shale Oil," *ECB Economic Bulletin* 8 (2017): 69, accessed July 3, 2018, www.ecb.europa.eu/pub/pdf/ecbu/eb201708.en.pdf?098fecf8c32c2fc25cc6c334adde0f91.

33 US Energy Information Administration, "The United States Is Now the Largest Global Crude Oil Producer," US EIA website, September 12, 2018, accessed September 13, 2018, www.eia.gov/todayinenergy/detail.php?id=37053.

34 Richard G. Newell and Brian Prest, "Is the US the New Swing Producer? The Price Responsiveness of Tight Oil," *Resources for the Future* (2017): 1–2, 22, 24.

35 Robert McNally, "Shale Oil Will Contribute to Future Crude Price Instability," *Financial Times*, February 20, 2018, accessed July 2, 2018, www.ft.com/content/1b911cc8-1583-11e8-9e9c-25c814761640.

36 International Energy Agency, "World Oil Demand," IEA website, March 15, 2019, accessed March 19, 2019, www.iea.org/oilmarketreport/omrpublic/; US Energy Information Administration, "What Drives Crude Oil Prices," US EIA website, March 12, 2019, accessed March 19, 2019, www.eia.gov/finance/markets/crudeoil/supply-opec.php.

37 US Energy Information Administration, "What Drives Crude Oil Prices."

38 Newell and Prest, "Is the US the New Swing Producer?," 22–24.

39 According to the International Energy Agency, oil demand from the petrochemical sector will account for circa 25 per cent of the global oil demand growth by 2023. International Energy Agency, "Market Report Series: Oil 2018: Analysis and Forecasts to 2023," 11, IEA website, accessed March 15, 2019, https://webstore.iea.org/market-report-series-oil-2018.

40 US Energy Information Administration, "The United States Is Now the Largest Global Crude Oil Producer."

41 In relation to the oil demand in 2018. International Energy Agency, "Market Report Series: Oil 2018: Analysis and Forecasts to 2023," 16; OPEC, "2018 OPEC World Oil Outlook," 99, OPEC website, September 2018, accessed March 9, 2019, https://woo.opec.org.

42 OPEC, "2018 OPEC World Oil Outlook," 164, 182–3.

43 International Energy Agency, "Market Report Series: Oil 2018: Analysis and Forecasts to 2023," 13.

44 European Commission, "Quarterly Report on European Gas Markets," European Commission website, accessed July 12, 2018 https://ec.europa.eu/energy/sites/ener/files/documents/quarterly_report_on_european_gas_markets_q4_2017_final_20180323.pdf; Agora Energiewende and Sandbag, *The European Power Sector in 2017: State of Affairs and Review of Current Developments* (2018): 27, accessed May 4, 2018, https://sandbag.org.uk/wp-content/uploads/2018/01/EU-power-sector-report-2017.pdf.

45 Iulia Pisca, *Outlook for EU Gas Demand and Import Needs to 2025* (Clingendael International Energy Programme, 2016), accessed May 10, 2018, www.clingendaelenergy.com/inc/upload/files/CIEP_paper_2016_2A_Demand_web.pdf.

46 For an overview of the EU-Emission Trading System: Carbon Tracker Initiative, "Carbon Countdown: Prices and Politics in the EU-ETS," Carbon Tracker Initiative website, August 21, 2018, accessed September 2, 2018, www.carbontracker.org/reports/carbon-countdown/. On coal phase-out status as of June 22, 2018: Europe Beyond Coal, "Overview: National Coal Phase-out Announcements in Europe," Europe Beyond Coal website, June 22, 2018, accessed July 28, 2018, https://beyond-coal.eu/wp-content/uploads/2018/06/Overview-of-national-coal-phase-out-announcements-Europe-Beyond-Coal-22-June-2018.pdf.

47 The North–South interconnections in Central Eastern and South Eastern Europe (NSI East Gas), the North–South gas interconnections in Western Europe (NSI West Gas) and the Baltic Energy Market Interconnection Plan on gas (BEMIP gas).

48 It is worth mentioning the Regulation (EU) 2017/1938. It introduces a regional approach to the EU strategy of security of supply, the assessment of multiple transnational risks, the focus on protected customers and a solidarity principle among neighbour MS. European Parliament and Council of the European Union, Regulation (EU) 2017/1938 of the European Parliament and of the Council of 25 October 2017 Concerning Measures to Safeguard the Security of Gas Supply and Repealing Regulation (EU) No 994/2010, EUR-Lex website, October 28, 2017, accessed March 9, 2019, https://eur-lex.europa.eu/eli/reg/2017/1938/oj.

49 Import dependence value calculated from: Eurostat, "Energy Balances in the MS Excel File Format (2018 Edition);" European Commission, "Quarterly Report on European Gas Markets," 3, 11; European Commission, "Liquefied Natural Gas," European Commission website, accessed August 27, 2018, https://ec.europa.eu/energy/en/topics/oil-gas-and-coal/liquefied-natural-gas-lng.

50 European Commission, *EU Energy in Figures*, 72.

51 Eurostat, "EU Imports of Energy Products–Recent Development."

52 Data calculated from Eurostat, "EU Imports of Energy Products–Recent Development."

53 On Nord Stream: Andreas Goldthau, *Assessing Nord Stream 2: Regulation, Geopolitics & Energy Security in the EU, Central Eastern Europe & the UK* (European Center for Energy and Resource Security, 2016), accessed July 27, 2018, www.kcl.ac.uk/sspp/departments/warstudies/research/groups/eucers/pubs/strategy-paper-10.pdf; Kim Talus, "Application of EU Energy and Certain National Laws of Baltic Sea Countries to the Nord Stream 2 Pipeline Project," *The Journal of World Energy Law & Business* 10, no. 1 (2017): 30–42.

54 US Embassy and Consulates in Germany, "Deutschland Muss Unterstützung für Nord Stream 2 Beenden," US Embassy & Consulates in Germany website, December 20, 2018, accessed March 12, 2019, https://de.usembassy.gov/de/deutschland-muss-unterstutzung-fur-nord-stream-2-beenden/; Naftogaz, "Trilateral Talks on Post-2019 Russian Gas Transit Held in Brussels," Naftogaz website, January 21, 2019, accessed March 12, 2019, www.naftogaz.com/www/3/nakweben.nsf/0/48F5648BC10B833CC2258389007235D5?OpenDocument&Highlight=0,gas transit.

55 European Commission, Proposal to Amend Directive 2009/73/EC Concerning Common Rules for the Internal Market in Natural Gas, COM(2017) 660, EUR-Lex website, November 8, 2017, accessed March 9, 2019, http://eur-lex.europa.eu/legal-content/EN/TXT/?qid=1510840797001&uri=CELEX:52017PC0660.

56 European Commission, Proposal for a Directive of the European Parliament and of the Council Amending Directive 2009/73/EC Concerning Common Rules for the Internal Market in Natural Gas (14204/17, COM(2017) 660 final) – Reasoned Opinion on the Application of the Principles of Subsidiarity and Proportionality, ST 5276 2018 INIT–2017/0294 (COD), EUR-Lex website, January 12, 2018, accessed March 9, 2019, https://eur-lex.europa.eu/legal-content/EN/ALL/?uri=CONSIL%3AST_5276_2018_INIT; European Commission, Proposal for a Directive of the European Parliament and of the Council Amending Directive 2009/73/EC Concerning Common Rules for the Internal Market in Natural Gas – Information from the Presidency, ST 15029 2018 INIT–2017/0294 (COD), EUR-Lex website, December 14, 2018, accessed 16 March 2019, https://eur-lex.europa.eu/legal-content/EN/TXT/PDF/?uri=CONSIL:ST_15029_2018_INIT&qid=1553179535872&from=EN.

57 European Commission, Proposal for a Directive of the European Parliament and of the Council Amending Directive 2009/73/EC Concerning Common Rules for the Internal Market in Natural Gas – Analysis of the Final Compromise Text with a View to Agreement, ST 6351 2019 INIT-2017/0294 (COD), EUR-Lex website, February 14, 2019, accessed March 16, 2019, https://eur-lex.europa.eu/legal-content/DE/TXT/?uri=CONSIL:ST_6351_2019_INIT.

58 The MS where the first interconnection point is located has the possibility to concede derogations up to 20 years for existing gas pipelines and to negotiate exemptions for new ones without prejudice to

the European Commission's binding decision. The final document is less stringent than the Commission's initial proposal. Previous drafts regarded the applicability of the Gas Directive to the MS's territorial waters and Exclusive Economic Zone (EEZ) traversed by any section of an offshore pipeline, which would have been contrary to Articles 56 and 58 of the UN Convention on the Law of the Sea (UNCLOS). The original provisions provided powers to negotiate with a third country any MS for whose territorial waters or EEZ a pipeline from this third country would cross before reaching the first interconnection point in the territory of a MS. Since Nord Stream 2 runs from Russia through Finnish and Swedish EEZ as well as via Danish and German territorial waters, this might have resulted in the application of different regulatory frameworks to each section of the pipeline.

59 On the Southern Gas Corridor: Marco Siddi, "The EU's Botched Geopolitical Approach to External Energy Policy: The Case of the Southern Gas Corridor," *Geopolitics* (2017): 124–44; Mübariz Hasanov, "An Analysis of Economic Benefits of the Southern Gas Corridor," *Energy Sources, Part B: Economics, Planning, and Policy* 11, no. 11 (2016): 999–1005.

60 At the time of this writing, there is no decision on which route, via either Bulgaria or Greece, will connect to Turkstream. Gazprom, "Management Committee Reviews Progress of TurkStream Project," Gazprom website, September 5, 2018, accessed August 7, 2018, www.gazprom.com/press/news/2018/september/article458440/.

61 European Commission, "EU–U.S. Joint Statement: Liquefied Natural Gas (LNG) Imports from the U.S. Continue to Rise, Up by 181%," European Commission website, March 8, 2019, accessed March 19, 2019, http://europa.eu/rapid/press-release_IP-19-1531_en.htm.

References

Agora Energiewende and Sandbag. *The European Power Sector in 2017. State of Affairs and Review of Current Developments.* Agora Energiewende and Sandbag, 2018. Accessed 4 May 2018. https://sandbag.org.uk/wp-content/uploads/2018/01/EU-power-sector-report-2017.pdf.

Alonso Álvarez, Irma, and Virginia Di Nino. "The Oil Market in the Age of Shale Oil." *ECB Economic Bulletin* 8 (2017): 57–74. Accessed 3 July 2018. www.ecb.europa.eu/pub/pdf/ecbu/eb201708.en.pdf?098fecf8c32c2fc25cc6c334adde0f91.

Ang, B.W., et al. "Energy Security: Definitions, Dimensions and Indexes." *Renewable and Sustainable Energy Reviews* 42 (2015): 1077–93.

Baldwin, David A. "The Concept of Security." *Review of International Studies* 23, no. 1 (1997): 5–26.

Barra, Matteo, and Martin Svec. "Reinforcing Energy Governance under the EU Energy Diplomacy: A Proposal for Strengthening Energy Frameworks in Africa." *European Journal of Risk Regulation* 9, no. 2 (2018): 245–67.

British Geological Survey et al. *Study on the Review of the List of Critical Raw Materials*. Luxembourg: Publications Office of the European Union, 2017.

Carbon Tracker Initiative. "Carbon Countdown: Prices and Politics in the EU-ETS." Carbon Tracker Initiative website, August 21, 2018. Accessed September 2, 2018. www.carbontracker.org/reports/carbon-countdown/.

Council of the European Union. Council Conclusions on Energy Diplomacy. ST 10995 15 INIT. July 20, 2015. Accessed July 25, 2018. http://data.consilium.europa.eu/doc/document/ST-10995-2015-INIT/en/pdf.

Directorate-General for Energy. "Registration of Crude Oil Imports and Deliveries in the European Union." EU Open Data Portal. Accessed May 17, 2018. https://data.europa.eu/euodp/data/dataset/eu-crude-oil-imports-and-supply-cost.

Energy Expert Cyber Security Platform. *Cyber Security in the Energy Sector. Recommendations for the European Commission on a European Strategic Framework and Potential Future Legislative Acts for the Energy Sector.* EECSP Report. EECSP, February 2017. Accessed August 10, 2018. https://ec.europa.eu/energy/sites/ener/files/documents/eecsp_report_final.pdf.

European Commission. Communication from the Commission to the European Parliament, the Council, the European Economic and Social Committee and the Committee of the Regions: A Policy Framework for Climate and Energy in the Period from 2020 to 2030. COM(2014) 015 final. Brussels: European Union, January 22, 2014. Accessed February 25, 2019. https://eur-lex.europa.eu/legal-content/EN/ALL/?uri=CELEX: 52014DC0015.

European Commission. Communication from the Commission to the European Parliament, the Council, the European Economic and Social Committee, the Committee of the Regions and the European

Investment Bank: Clean Energy for All Europeans. COM(2016) 0860 final. Brussels: European Union, November 30, 2016. Accessed March 9, 2019. https://eur-lex.europa.eu/legal-content/en/TXT/?uri=CELEX:52016DC0860.

European Commission. Communication from the Commission to the European Parliament, the Council, the European Economic and Social Committee, the Committee of the Regions and the European Investment Bank: A Framework Strategy for a Resilient Energy Union with a Forward-Looking Climate Change Policy. COM(2015) 080 final. Brussels: European Union, February 25, 2015. Accessed March 12, 2019. https://eur-lex.europa.eu/legal-content/EN/TXT/?uri=CELEX:52015DC0080.

European Commission. *EU Energy in Figures: Statistical Pocketbook 2018*. Luxembourg: Publications Office of the European Commission, 2018.

European Commission. "Europe on the Move: Commission Completes Its Agenda for Safe, Clean and Connected Mobility." European Commission website, May 17, 2018. Accessed March 12, 2019. https://ec.europa.eu/transport/modes/road/news/2018-05-17-europe-on-the-move-3_en.

European Commission. "EU-U.S. Joint Statement: Liquefied Natural Gas (LNG) Imports from the U.S. Continue to Rise, Up by 181%." European Commission website, March 9, 2019. Accessed March 19, 2019. http://europa.eu/rapid/press-release_IP-19-1531_en.htm.

European Commission. "Liquefied Natural Gas." European Commission website. Accessed August 27, 2018. https://ec.europa.eu/energy/en/topics/oil-gas-and-coal/liquefied-natural-gas-lng.

European Commission. *Nord Stream 2 – Divide et Impera Again? Avoiding a Zero-Sum Game*. European Commission website, October 27, 2017. Accessed September 2018, https://ec.europa.eu/epsc/sites/epsc/files/epsc_-_nord_stream_-_divide_et_impera_again.pdf.

European Commission. "One Step Closer Towards Fulfilling the Energy Union: Commission Welcomes Parliament Committee Votes on Clean Energy Package." European Commission website, July 10, 2018. Accessed July 25, 2018. https://ec.europa.eu/info/news/one-step-closer-towards-fulfilling-energy-union-commission-welcomes-parliament-committee-votes-clean-energy-package-2018-jul-10_en.

European Commission. Proposal for a Directive of the European Parliament and of the Council Amending Directive 2009/73/CEC Concerning Common Rules for the Internal Market in Natural Gas – Analysis of the Final Compromise Text with a View to Agreement. ST 6351 2019 INIT-2017/0294 (COD). EUR-Lex website, February 14, 2019. Accessed March 16, 2019. https://eur-lex.europa.eu/legal-content/DE/TXT/?uri= CONSIL:ST_6351_2019_INIT.

European Commission. Proposal for a Directive of the European Parliament and of the Council Amending Directive 2009/73/EC Concerning Common Rules for the Internal Market in Natural Gas – Information from the Presidency. ST 15029 2018 INIT–2017/0294 (COD). EUR-Lex website, December 14, 2018. Accessed 16 March 2019. https://eur-lex.europa.eu/legal-content/EN/TXT/PDF/?uri=CONSIL:ST_15029_ 2018_INIT&qid=1553179535872&from=EN.

European Commission. Proposal for a Directive of the European Parliament and of the Council Amending Directive 2009/73/EC Concerning Common Rules for the Internal Market in Natural Gas, (14204/17, COM(2017) 660 final) – Reasoned Opinion on the Application of the Principles of Subsidiarity and Proportionality. ST 5276 2018 INIT–2017/0294 (COD). EUR-Lex website, January 12, 2018. Accessed March 9, 2019. https://eur-lex.europa.eu/legal-content/EN/ALL/?uri=CONSIL%3AST_5276_2018_INIT.

European Commission. Proposal to Amend Directive 2009/73/EC Concerning Common Rules for the Internal Market in Natural Gas. COM(2017) 660. EUR-Lex website, November 8, 2017. Accessed March 9, 2019. http://eur-lex.europa.eu/legal-content/EN/TXT/?qid=1510840797001&uri=CELEX:52017PC0660.

European Commission. "Quarterly Report on European Gas Markets." European Commission website. Accessed July 12, 2018. https://ec.europa.eu/energy/sites/ener/files/documents/quarterly_report_on_european_gas_markets_q4_2017_final_20180323.pdf.

European Parliament and Council of the European Union. Regulation (EU) 2017/1938 of the European Parliament and of the Council of 25 October 2017 Concerning Measures to Safeguard the Security of Gas Supply and Repealing Regulation (EU) No 994/2010. EUR-Lex website, October 28, 2017. Accessed March 9, 2019. https://eur-lex.europa.eu/eli/reg/2017/1938/oj.

European Union. Consolidated Version of the Treaty on the Functioning of the European Union. *Official Journal of the European Union* C 202/51, June 7, 2016. EUR-Lex website. Accessed March 9, 2019. https://eur-lex.europa.eu/legal-content/EN/TXT/?uri=CELEX:12016E/TXT.

Europe Beyond Coal. "Overview: National Coal Phase-out Announcements in Europe." Europe Beyond Coal website, June 22, 2018. Accessed July 28, 2018. https://beyond-coal.eu/wp-content/

uploads/2018/06/Overview-of-national-coal-phase-out-announcements-Europe-Beyond-Coal-22-June-2018.pdf.
Eurostat. "Energy Balances in the MS Excel File Format (2018 Edition)." Eurostat website, May 2018. Accessed July 5, 2018. https://ec.europa.eu/eurostat/documents/38154/4956218/ENERGY-BALANCES-May-2018-edition.zip/310265d9-6adf-45aa-ba41-2dce8e5f78eb.
Eurostat. "EU Imports of Energy Products–Recent Development." Eurostat website, October 2018. Accessed February 25, 2019, https://ec.europa.eu/eurostat/statistics-explained/index.php?title=EU_imports_of_energy products_-_recent_developments.
Eurostat. "Europe 2020 Indicators-Climate Change and Energy." Eurostat website, June 2018. Accessed July 25, 2018. https://ec.europa.eu/eurostat/statistics-explained/index.php/Europe_2020_indicators_-_climate_change_and_energy#General_overview.
Gazprom. "Management Committee Reviews Progress of TurkStream Project." Gazprom website, September 5, 2018. Accessed August 7, 2018. www.gazprom.com/press/news/2018/september/article458440/.
Goldthau, Andreas. *Assessing Nord Stream 2: Regulation, Geopolitics & Energy Security in the EU, Central Eastern Europe & the UK*. European Center for Energy and Resource Security, 2016. Accessed July 27, 2018. www.kcl.ac.uk/sspp/departments/warstudies/research/groups/eucers/pubs/strategy-paper-10.pdf.
Hasanov, Mübariz. "An Analysis of Economic Benefits of the Southern Gas Corridor." *Energy Sources, Part B: Economics, Planning, and Policy* 11, no. 11 (2016): 999–1005.
International Energy Agency. "Market Report Series: Oil 2018: Analysis and Forecasts to 2023." IEA website. Accessed March 15, 2019. https://webstore.iea.org/market-report-series-oil-2018.
International Energy Agency. "What Is Energy?" IEA website. Accessed July 2, 2018. www.iea.org/topics/energysecurity/whatisenergysecurity/.
International Energy Agency. "World Oil Demand." IEA website, March 15, 2019. Accessed March 19, 2019. www.iea.org/oilmarketreport/omrpublic/.
International Maritime Organization. "Sulphur 2020 – Cutting Sulphur Oxide Emissions." IMO website. Accessed March 15, 2019. www.imo.org/en/MediaCentre/HotTopics/Pages/Sulphur-2020.aspx.
McNally, Robert. "Shale Oil Will Contribute to Future Crude Price Instability." *Financial Times*, February 20, 2018. Accessed July 2, 2018. www.ft.com/content/1b911cc8-1583-11e8-9e9c-25c814761640.
Naftogaz. "Trilateral Talks on Post-2019 Russian Gas Transit Held in Brussels." Naftogaz website, January 21, 2019. Accessed March 12, 2019. www.naftogaz.com/www/3/nakweben.nsf/0/48F5648BC10B833CC2258389007235D5?OpenDocument&Highlight=0,gas transit.
Newell, Richard G., and Brian Prest. "Is the US the New Swing Producer? The Price Responsiveness of Tight Oil." *Resources for the Future* (2017).
OPEC. "2018 OPEC World Oil Outlook." OPEC website, September 2018. Accessed March 9, 2019. https://woo.opec.org.
OPEC. "Monthly Oil Market Report February 2016." OPEC website, February 10, 2016. Accessed July 10, 2018. www.opec.org/opec_web/static_files_project/media/downloads/publications/MOMR February 2016.pdf.
OPEC. "OPEC 166th Meeting concludes." OPEC website, November 27, 2014. Accessed July 10, 2018. www.opec.org/opec_web/en/press_room/2938.htm.
OPEC. "OPEC and Non-OPEC Ministerial Meeting." OPEC website, December 10, 2016. Accessed July 10, 2018. www.opec.org/opec_web/en/press_room/3944.htm.
OPEC. "OPEC Share of World Crude Oil Reserves, 2017." OPEC website. Accessed March 22, 2019. www.opec.org/opec_web/en/data_graphs/330.htm.
O'Sullivan, Meghan, Indra Overland and David Sandalow. *The Geopolitics of Renewable Energy*. Harvard Kennedy School, 2017.
Paltsev, Sergey. "The Complicated Geopolitics of Renewable Energy." *Bulletin of the Atomic Scientists* 72, no. 6 (2016): 390–95.
Pisca, Iulia. *Outlook for EU Gas Demand and Import Needs to 2025*. Clingendael International Energy Programme, 2016. Accessed May 10, 2018. www.clingendaelenergy.com/inc/upload/files/CIEP_paper_2016_2A_Demand_web.pdf.
Quemada, José María Marín, Javier García-Verdugoa and Gonzalo Escribano (eds.). *Energy Security for the EU in the 21st Century: Markets, Geopolitics and Corridors*. London: Routledge, 2012.
Scholten, Daniel. *The Geopolitics of Renewables*. Cham: Springer International Publishing, 2018.
Sharifuddin, Shahnaz. "Methodology for Quantitatively Assessing the Energy Security of Malaysia and Other Southeast Asian Countries." *Energy Policy* 65 (2014): 574–82.

Siddi, Marco. "The EU's Botched Geopolitical Approach to External Energy Policy: The Case of the Southern Gas Corridor." *Geopolitics* (2017): 124–44.
Sovacool, Benjamin K., and Mukherjee Ishani. "Conceptualizing and Measuring Energy Security: A Synthesized Approach." *Energy* 36, no. 8 (2011): 5343–55.
Sovacool, Benjamin K., Mukherjee Ishani, Ira Martina Drupady and Anthony L. D'Agostino. "Evaluating Energy Security Performance from 1990 to 2010 for Eighteen Countries." *Energy* 36, no. 10 (2011): 5846–53.
Talus, Kim. "Application of EU Energy and Certain National Laws of Baltic Sea Countries to the Nord Stream 2 Pipeline Project." *The Journal of World Energy Law & Business* 10, no. 1 (2017): 30–42.
United Nations. "The Paris Agreement." UNFCC website. Accessed 12 March, 2019. https://unfccc.int/process-and-meetings/the-paris-agreement/the-paris-agreement.
US Department of State. "Venezuela-Related Sanctions." US Department of State website. Accessed March 22, 2019. www.state.gov/e/eb/tfs/spi/venezuela/.
US Embassy and Consulates in Germany. "Deutschland Muss Unterstützung für Nord Stream 2 Beenden." December 20, 2018. Accessed March 12, 2019. https://de.usembassy.gov/de/deutschland-muss-unterstutzung-fur-nord-stream-2-beenden/.
US Energy Information Administration. "Crude Oil Production, Venezuela, Monthly." EIA website. Accessed March 22, 2019. www.eia.gov/opendata/qb.php?category=1039874&sdid=STEO.COPR_VE.M.
US Energy Information Administration. "The United States Is Now the Largest Global Crude Oil Producer." EIA website, September 12, 2018. Accessed September 13, 2018. www.eia.gov/todayinenergy/detail.php?id=37053.
US Energy Information Administration. "What Drives Crude Oil Prices." EIA website, March 12, 2019. Accessed March 19, 2019. www.eia.gov/finance/markets/crudeoil/supply-opec.php.
"Vision 2030." Kingdom of Saudi Arabia. Accessed June 20, 2018. http://vision2030.gov.sa/sites/default/files/report/Saudi_Vision2030_EN_2017.pdf.
Winzer, Christian. "Conceptualizing Energy Security." *Energy Policy* 46 (2012): 36–48.
"With the Benefit of Hindsight: The Impact of the 2014–16 Oil Price Collapse." In *Global Economic Prospects: Broad-Based Upturn, but for How Long?* Washington, DC: World Bank, 2018.
Wolfers, Arnold. " 'National Security' as an Ambiguous Symbol." *Political Science Quarterly* 67, no. 4 (1952): 481–502.

17

CYBERSECURITY IN THE EUROPEAN UNION

Resilience through regulation?

Ramses A. Wessel

"We must develop capabilities in trusted digital services and products and in cyber technologies to enhance our resilience"

(EU Global Strategy, 2016)

Introduction: defining cybersecurity in the EU context

> European security policy is changing in fundamental ways. The old threat scenario involving tank divisions from the East has been replaced by the challenge posed by invisible adversaries whose geographical source can often not be determined. Virtual attacks threatening critical infrastructure, government institutions and personal data form one of the key challenges to security policy in the 21st century.[1]

These words by Bendiek underline the need for the European Union to adapt its security strategy to new threats. Perhaps ironically, this has to be done in a period in which traditional EU defence cooperation finally seems to be progressing. After decades of attempts to establish defence cooperation alongside the EU's other policies, the careful introduction of the Common Security and Defence Policy (CSDP) in the 1992 Maastricht Treaty and its further adaptations through subsequent treaty revisions,[2] we now witness new and far-reaching initiatives, including the implementation of the notion of Permanent Structured Cooperation (PESCO), new structures and frameworks, and enhanced oversight and coordination mechanisms as well as financing tools to trigger joint defence research and development.[3]

At the same time, cybersecurity triggers the emergence of a new field of research in European law and policy (and perhaps also in European Studies more generally[4]). Whereas 'law and technology' in general has become an established field of study,[5] EU law and technology, and in particular 'EU cybersecurity law', still seems to be in its first infancy. As the present contribution will reveal, this is partly due to two distinct factors. First of all, cybersecurity can be seen as a cross-cutting policy area, which concerns not only the Union's security policy, but also policies related to, *inter alia*, the internal market and the Area of Freedom, Security and Justice (AFSJ). This makes it difficult for specialists in any of these EU policy areas to provide comprehensive analyses or even approach the topic as such. Second, despite the by now extensive number of policy documents, there is as yet not so much law for lawyers to analyse. Yet, a shift is visible: it is increasingly acknowledged that "Current literature on the regulation of cyberspace is no longer focused on whether cyberspace can be regulated. Instead, discussion focuses on how cyberspace is regulated and who are the regulators."[6]

Cybersecurity is not mentioned as such in the EU Treaties as an area to be dealt with by the European Union. The perhaps most obvious policy area to have mentioned cybersecurity, CSDP, largely developed (and intentionally so) as military and civilian cooperation to be used for "missions outside the Union for peace-keeping, conflict prevention and strengthening international security" as stated in Article 42(1) TEU. In addition, the more specific list of tasks in Article 43(1) TEU does not include a reference to cybersecurity.[7] The same holds true for the Treaty provisions on the internal market and on the AFSJ, which are equally silent on cybersecurity.

Nevertheless, after a number of earlier policy initiatives in cybersecurity,[8] cybersecurity is high on the EU's agenda, in particular with the adoption of the 2013 Cybersecurity Strategy (updated in 2017)[9] and the 2015 Council conclusions on cyber diplomacy.[10] It has been argued that "cybersecurity is now among one of the EU's most important priorities, with cyber security elements having been integrated transversally within other EU policies."[11] The reasons are obvious: over the past years the number of cyberattacks on States and critical infrastructure has been constantly growing,[12] and by its nature cybersecurity needs cross-border cooperation.[13] The EU measures aim to build resilience, fight cybercrime, build cyberdefence, develop industrial and technical resources and elaborate a diplomatic strategy for cyberspace.[14] Indeed, 'resilience' is a key-word in the EU's 2016 Global Strategy,[15] and this strategy seems far more aimed at responding to threats than at promoting values and transformation of its surroundings, which were the focus of the 2013 Security Strategy. Cybersecurity is now presented as a key element in the EU's security and resilience policies.[16]

The fact that the EU does not have an express competence to take measures to improve cybersecurity has led it to either use legal competences it has in other areas, or adopt soft law and coordination measures (see further below).[17] This piecemeal approach has made it difficult to understand what exactly is covered by cybersecurity and, on that basis, to allocate tasks and responsibilities.[18] The definition of cybersecurity that was included in the 2013 Cybersecurity Strategy of the European Union (EUCSS) has a broad scope:

> Cyber-security commonly refers to the safeguards and actions that can be used to protect the cyber domain, both in the civilian and military fields, from those threats that are associated with or that may harm its interdependent networks and information infrastructure. Cyber-security strives to preserve the availability and integrity of the networks and infrastructure and the confidentiality of the information contained therein.[19]

A narrower definition was provided by the special agency of the EU in this area, ENISA (European Union Agency for Network and Information Security):

> the protection of information, information systems, infrastructure and the applications that run on top of it from those threats that are associated with a globally connected environment.[20]

This relates to ensuring the resilience of networks to potential attacks and the capacity to respond to such attacks.

Yet, cyberspace policies usually also include 'cybercrime'. Indeed, both the broader notion of 'cybersecurity' and the criminal activities falling under 'cybercrime' form part of the EU's policies.[21] In the 2013 EU Strategy it is described as follows:

> Cybercrime commonly refers to a broad range of different criminal activities where computers and information systems are involved either as a primary tool or as a primary target. Cybercrime comprises traditional offences (e.g. fraud, forgery, and identity theft), content-related offences (e.g. on-line distribution of child pornography or incitement to racial hatred) and offences unique to computers and information systems (e.g. attacks against information systems, denial of service and malware).

Hence, while *cybersecurity* refers to the range of safeguards and actions that can be used to protect the cyber domain, *cybercrime* reflects to the actual criminal activities, thus following the descriptions laid down in the Council of Europe Convention on Cybercrime.[22] Debates on activities in cyberspace also refer to many more phenomena. Where cybercrime involves offences against property rights of non-state actors (e.g., phishing), *cyber espionage* concerns breaches in the databases of state or non-state enterprises by foreign government agencies, and *cyber war* involves state attempts to attack another state via electronic networks.[23] Given the Union's activities under the heading of CSDP, it is striking that the latter is hardly mentioned in the EU's documents on cybersecurity. Indeed, allegedly for reasons of Member State sovereignty in the military field, the term *cyberdefence* lacks a clear definition.[24] Nevertheless, over the past few years in particular, the EU has taken policy initiatives to include cyber threats in its CSDP (see further below).

EU objectives and ambitions in cybersecurity

As noted above, with the adoption of the 2016 Global Strategy for the European Union's Foreign and Security Policy the EU stressed the importance of 'resilience'.[25] In fact, the term is used more than 30 times in the 60-page Global Strategy, turning 'resilience' into a key objective of the EU security strategy. While the term as such is not defined by the Global Strategy, the context makes clear that the main ambition is to resist and overcome threats to the EU's security and democratic values:[26] "The Strategy nurtures the ambition of strategic autonomy for the European Union. This is necessary to promote the common interests of our citizens, as well as our principles and values."[27] Yet, the idea of autonomy should not be read as to isolate the EU; "Together with its partners, the EU will [also] promote resilience in its surrounding regions."[28] And, this is done in cooperation with international partners. Thus, in 2014, for instance, EU Members were asked to check their cyberdefence capabilities in the context of the Atlantic cooperation as well.[29] In addition, cybersecurity and cyberdefence cooperation between the EU and NATO has been intensified since 2015, formalised in the July 2016 Warsaw Declaration, and reinforced with concrete implementation proposals at the joint meeting of the EU and NATO foreign ministers in December 2016.[30] More generally, the Union has engaged in a number of strategic partnerships with third countries, also as part of its strategy to 'mainstream' cyber issues in the EU's external relations.[31]

In order to understand the EU's ambitions and plans related to cybersecurity, it is useful to quote the respective paragraph in the Global Strategy in full:

> The EU will increase its focus on cyber security, equipping the EU and assisting Member States in protecting themselves against cyber threats while maintaining an

> open, free and safe cyberspace. This entails strengthening the technological capabilities aimed at mitigating threats and the resilience of critical infrastructure, networks and services, and reducing cybercrime. It means fostering innovative information and communication technology (ICT) systems which guarantee the availability and integrity of data, while ensuring security within the European digital space through appropriate policies on the location of data storage and the certification of digital products and services. It requires weaving cyber issues across all policy areas, reinforcing the cyber elements in CSDP missions and operations, and further developing platforms for cooperation.[32]

Cybersecurity is thus presented as a 'cross-sectional' policy task, and should be a dimension of different EU policy areas related to both internal and external security and civilian as well as military cooperation.[33]

More concrete ambitions can be found in the 2013 Cybersecurity Strategy of the European Union: An Open, Safe and Secure Cyberspace,[34] that addresses different dimensions of cybersecurity, including network and information security (NIS), cybercrime and cyberdefence. The starting point is the following: "For cyberspace to remain open and free, the same norms, principles and values that the EU upholds offline, should also apply online."[35] The Cybersecurity Strategy can be seen as a continuation of the internal and external policies that have been developed by the EU in the area of NIS[36] – and in the framework of the EU–US Working Group on Cyber-Security and Cyber-Crime (WGCC).[37] Part of the Cybersecurity Strategy is related to linking core EU values that exist in the 'physical world' to the 'digital world': promoting fundamental rights, freedom of expression, personal data and privacy; access for all; democratic and efficient multi-stakeholder governance and a shared responsibility to ensure security. Other elements relate to other policy areas of the EU, including the internal market or defence policy. As an express legal basis cannot be found in the EU Treaties, the Strategy acknowledges that "it is predominantly the task of the Member States to deal with security challenges in cyberspace."[38] It lists five strategic priorities: achieving cyber-resilience; drastically reducing cybercrime; developing cyberdefence policy and capabilities related to the Common Security and Defence Policy; developing the industrial and technological resources for cybersecurity; and establishing a coherent international cyberspace policy for the European Union and promoting core EU values.

Relying on 28 Member States to take the necessary measures, however, risks fragmentation (see further below). Primarily to overcome this risk, the 2015 European Agenda on Security (EAS) was adopted, as "an effective and coordinated response at European level,"[39] providing a strategic framework for EU initiatives in the field of cybersecurity for the period 2015–2020. Specific policies in relation to CSDP had already been formulated in the 2014 EU Cyber Defence Policy Framework,[40] to further integrate cybersecurity and defence into CSDP. The focus on these policies is on enhancing the cyber-resilience of CSDP missions and operations through, for instance, standardised procedures and technical capabilities in both civilian and military missions and operations.

Most recently, the Commission laid down the EU ambitions in a comprehensive 'cybersecurity package': *Resilience, Deterrence and Defence: Building Strong Cybersecurity for the EU*.[41] This policy document further analyses the way forward and introduces a large number of new policy initiatives and actions by the EU, but also calls upon Member States to, *inter alia*, ensure full and effective implementation of the NIS Directive; apply the same rules to public administrations, given the role they play in society and the economy as a whole; provide cybersecurity-related training in public administration; prioritise cyber-awareness in information campaigns and include cybersecurity as part of academic and vocational training curricula; and use initiatives on 'Permanent Structured Cooperation' (PESCO) and the European Defence Fund to support the development of cyberdefence projects.

Overall, the conclusion is that the European Union is very active in developing policies related to all dimensions of cybersecurity, mainly by drafting policy frameworks and guidelines to enhance and synchronise Member State initiatives. The topic is clearly high on the agenda and the EU's ambition is to play a central coordinating role in this area. Indeed, there is one main goal in mind: resilience through policy-making and regulation. These policies are more internal than external.[42] This implies, as also rightfully concluded by Odermatt, that "Unlike some other states, the EU has not sought to develop any kind of hard or offensive cyber power. The EU's approach to cyberdefence is guided by the logic of protection."[43] This is not to say that the Union is completely passive in its external relations with regard to cybersecurity initiatives. The EU recently adopted a framework for a joint EU diplomatic response to malicious cyber activities (the so-called 'cyber diplomacy toolbox'), which sets out the measures under the broader Common Foreign and Security Policy (CFSP), including restrictive measures which can be used to strengthen the EU's response to activities that harm its political, security and economic interests.[44] The instrument makes a start with listing, primarily, non-military instruments that could contribute to "the mitigation of cybersecurity threats, conflict prevention and greater stability in international relations."[45] The question, however, remains, to what extent the EU has the competence to realise all these internal as well as external ambitions.

EU competences related to cybersecurity

> The EU is well placed to address cybersecurity, given the scope of its policies and the tools, structures and capabilities at its disposal. While Member States remain responsible for national security, the scale and cross-border nature of the threat make a powerful case for EU action providing incentives and support for Member States to develop and maintain more and better national cybersecurity capabilities, while at the same time building EU-level capacity.[46]

Irrespective of this statement by the Commission, the question is whether in a legal sense, too, the EU is "well placed" to address cybersecurity.[47] Given the inherent cross-border nature of cybersecurity, the complete absence of the issue in the EU Treaties is striking. One reason may be that cooperation by the EU Member States or a transfer of competences to the EU may not be sufficient, precisely because of the larger, global scope of the challenge and the involvement of multiple actors.[48] Indeed, initiatives such as the *Tallinn Manual on International Law Applicable to Cyber Warfare* reveal the struggle to formulate rules on 'non-physical' phenomena in a state structure based on national jurisdictions.[49]

Yet, given the EU's ambitions described in the previous section, concrete legal bases to at least also formally regulate cybersecurity need to be found. And in the absence of express powers, they will need to be found in relation to other policy sectors.[50] In 2016, this was also emphasised by the European Parliament:

> conflicts and crises in Europe and around are happening in both physical and cyber space, and [this] underlines that cyber security and cyber defence must therefore be integrated as the core elements of the CSDP and fully mainstreamed throughout all the EU's internal and external policies.[51]

Whereas this is understandable, it also entails a risk of fragmentation and inconsistency when different EU (and Member States') institutions, as well as private actors (industry, service providers, etc.) are involved, all with their own policy preferences and procedures. It is questionable whether the demands for consistency and effectiveness (Articles 13 and 21 TEU) can be met. Cybersecurity forms an excellent example of an area in which the different policy fields of the Union need to be combined (a requirement for *horizontal* consistency), and where measures need to be taken at the level of both the EU and the Member States (calling for *vertical* consistency). This possible fragmentation thus raises the question to what extent the above-mentioned ambitions aimed at ensuring resilience through regulation can actually be attained, both internally and in the framework of the EU's external relations. The fact that external competences often depend on the existence (and/or use) of internal competences,[52] has indeed limited the Union's legal powers as a global actor in this field.[53]

In an institutional sense, a number of initiatives have been taken to create specialised bodies, but again in specific fields only.[54] Thus, a special EU Cybercrime Centre was established in 2012.[55] This centre – named 'EC3' – is located at one of the EU's agencies, Europol in The Hague.[56] EC3 officially commenced its activities on 1 January 2013 with a mandate to tackle the following areas of cybercrime:

a That committed by organised groups to generate large criminal profits such as online fraud
b That which causes serious harm to the victim such as online child sexual exploitation
c That which affects critical infrastructure and information systems in the European Union.

EC3 thus aims to become the focal point in the EU's fight against cybercrime, through building operational and analytical capacity for investigations and cooperation with international partners in the pursuit of an EU free from cybercrime. Yet, for the development of actual legislation, it is necessary for the European Commission and the European External Action Service (EEAS) to be involved. For that reason EC3 liaison offices have been placed at those institutions and in other relevant agencies, including the European Union Agency for Cybersecurity (ENISA).[57] This latter agency also works to improve cooperation between Member States to implement emergency response plans, conduct regular emergency drills and develop a European Information Sharing and Alert System (EISAS) to guard against attacks on critical infrastructure.[58]

Overall, however, it is questionable whether this somewhat loose institutional framework will allow the Union to regulate the field of cybersecurity in any comprehensive fashion.[59] The following sub-sections will provide some examples of legal bases used to tackle different dimensions of cybersecurity.

The single digital market

In terms of EU competences, a number of measures with an economic dimension fall under initiatives in the framework of the so-called 'Single Digital Market'. The Digital Single Market strategy (DSM) was adopted on 6 May 2015. It includes 16 specific initiatives which were delivered by the Commission by January 2017.[60] The EU refers to an obvious economic element, which relates to the completion of the DSM: citizens need trust and confidence to engage in new connected technologies and to use e-commerce facilities.[61]

Indeed, the extensive internal market competences of the Union do provide some hooks for cybersecurity measures related to the functioning of the free movement or competition rules. This, for instance, allows the Union to harmonise national rules with a view to the functioning of the internal market. A concrete example is formed by using Article 114 TFEU, which formed the basis for the Directive on Security of Network and Information Systems ('NIS Directive').[62] The NIS Directive forms the first piece of EU-wide legislation on cybersecurity, aimed at boosting the overall level of cybersecurity in the EU. Member States had to transpose the Directive into their national laws by 9 May 2018, but it has become clear already that this deadline was not met by most Member States.[63] The Commission argued that under Article 114 TFEU, the EU can adopt "measures for the approximation of the provisions laid down by law, regulation or administrative action in Member States which have as their object the establishment and functioning of the internal market,"[64] and security of network and information systems is seen as essential for the functioning of the internal market. The Directive presents the 'internal market' rationale as follows:

> Network and information systems and services play a vital role in society. Their reliability and security are essential to economic and societal activities, and in particular to the functioning of the internal market. [...] Network and information systems, and primarily the internet, play an essential role in facilitating the cross-border movement of goods, services and people. Owing to that transnational nature, substantial disruptions of those systems, whether intentional or unintentional and regardless of where they occur, can affect individual Member States and the Union as a whole. The security of network and information systems is therefore essential for the smooth functioning of the internal market.[65]

The Directive thus aims at setting a high common level of network and information security across the EU in a number of ways. The first is by requiring Member States to be adequately prepared for cyber threats. This involves the establishment of national NIS Strategies and national Computer Security Incident Response Teams (CSIRTs). A second way is by promoting cooperation between the Member States, e.g. through requirements for security and notification. The NIS Directive thus aims at securing resilience in certain critical sectors, including energy, health, transport and banking.[66] The involvement of the private sector – including a system for certification and labelling to achieve a functioning single market in cybersecurity – returns in the 2016 Communication on Strengthening Europe's Cyber Resilience System and Fostering a Competitive and Innovative Cybersecurity Industry.[67]

Enhancing trust in the internal market is also pursued by the 2014 Regulation on electronic identification and trust services for electronic transactions in the EU internal market.[68] This Regulation is also based on Article 114 TFEU, which concerns the adoption of rules to remove existing barriers to the functioning of the internal market.

In general, these initiatives only seem to form the start of a range of new measures. The 2017 Mid-Term Review of the Single Digital Market process[69] lists a large number of contributing threats and reveals the complications the EU is facing, also in terms of competences:

> Cyberattacks are on the increase and tackling them faces the problem that while cyberattacks are often cross-border, law enforcement competences are strictly national. [...] This requires effective EU level response and crisis management, building upon dedicated cyber policies and wider instruments for European solidarity and mutual assistance.

Cybercrime

Another policy area in which the EU has been relatively active when it comes to the regulation of cybersecurity is 'cybercrime'. The 2005 Framework Decision on attacks against information systems is probably one of the first legal instruments adopted by the Union in relation to cybersecurity.[70] The main objective of that Decision was to improve cooperation between judicial and other competent authorities, including the police and other specialised law enforcement services of the Member States, through approximating rules on criminal law in the Member States in the area of attacks against information systems. With a view to the integration of the former Police and Judicial Cooperation in Criminal Matters (PJCC) in the Union's Area of Freedom, Security and Justice (AFSJ), in August 2013 this Decision was replaced by the Directive on attacks against information systems (the 'Cybercrime Directive').[71] The legal basis of this Directive is Article 83(1) TFEU, which underlines that it forms part of the judicial cooperation in criminal matters, currently laid down in that part of the Treaty. In fact, this is one of the areas where one may find a competence of the EU to legislate in the area of cybercrime (despite the fact that the term is not used as such). Article 83(1) TFEU provides:

> The European Parliament and the Council may, by means of directives adopted in accordance with the ordinary legislative procedure, establish minimum rules concerning the definition of criminal offences and sanctions in the areas of particularly serious crime with a cross-border dimension resulting from the nature or impact of such offences or from a special need to combat them on a common basis.
>
> These areas of crime are the following: terrorism, trafficking in human beings and sexual exploitation of women and children, illicit drug trafficking, illicit arms trafficking, money laundering, corruption, counterfeiting of means of payment, computer crime and organised crime.

The Cybercrime Directive establishes minimum rules on the definition of criminal offences and sanctions with respect to attacks against information systems.[72] It also provides minimum rules on the definitions of crimes included in the Directive.

Earlier instruments adopted in this area include the 2011 Directive on Combatting the Sexual Exploitation of Children Online and Child Pornography, the 2002 ePrivacy Directive, ensuring the confidentiality of client information,[73] and the 2001 Framework Decision on combating fraud and counterfeiting.[74]

In terms of international cooperation, it is important to note that the EU is not a party to the main international treaty in this area, the Council of Europe Convention on Cybercrime (Budapest Convention),[75] although it participates in the Cybercrime Convention Committee (T-CY).

Cyberdefence

Cyberdefence is still underdeveloped in comparison to the economic and criminal law aspects of cybersecurity discussed above; it is still characterised by a piecemeal approach. As Odermatt rightfully states: "there is no comprehensive EU approach to cyberdefence,"[76] despite the claim that "the next war will begin in cyberspace."[77]

The above-mentioned Cybersecurity Strategy also mentions one particular field of cooperation related to the so-called 'solidarity clause' laid down in Article 222 TFEU.[78] On the basis of that provision:

> The Union and its Member States shall act jointly in a spirit of solidarity if a Member State is the object of a terrorist attack or the victim of a natural or man-made disaster. The Union shall mobilise all the instruments at its disposal, including the military resources made available by the Member States, to:
>
> (a) prevent the terrorist threat in the territory of the Member States;
> - protect democratic institutions and the civilian population from any terrorist attack;
> - assist a Member State in its territory, at the request of its political authorities, in the event of a terrorist attack;
>
> (b) assist a Member State in its territory, at the request of its political authorities, in the event of a natural or man-made disaster.

Indeed, cybersecurity is not mentioned explicitly. Yet, it easily fits under some of the headings. In a 2012 Resolution, the European Parliament even explicitly mentioned cybersecurity as falling within the scope of the solidarity clause: it called for

> an adequate balance between flexibility and consistency as regards the types of attacks and disasters for which the clause may be triggered, so as to ensure that no significant threats, such as attacks in cyberspace, pandemics, or energy shortages, are overlooked.[79]

In fact, the European Parliament even went a step further and also mentioned cyberattacks as a reason to invoke the so-called 'mutual defence clause' laid down in Article 42(7) TEU, containing a provision comparable to Article 5 of the NATO Treaty:

> If a Member State is the victim of armed aggression on its territory, the other Member States shall have towards it an obligation of aid and assistance by all the means in their power, in accordance with Article 51 of the United Nations Charter. This shall not prejudice the specific character of the security and defence policy of certain Member States.

The European Parliament took the view

> that even non-armed attacks, for instance cyberattacks against critical infrastructure, that are launched with the aim of causing severe damage and disruption to a Member State and are identified as coming from an external entity could qualify for being covered by the clause, if the Member State's security is significantly threatened by its consequences, while fully respecting the principle of proportionality.[80]

While in the case of the solidarity clause it may be argued that there needs to be a link with 'terrorism', the mutual defence clause refers to 'armed aggression', which in international law terms may rule out certain cyberattacks.[81] Hence, in both cases the application of the clauses to situations of cybersecurity is not always obvious. In practice, however, invoking a solidarity or a mutual defence clause will most probably be driven more by political incentives than by legal doctrinal analysis.

Conclusion and assessment

The relatively slow acknowledgement of the need to regulate cyberspace is not related only to the absence of competences on the side of the EU, but also to the early notion that by its very nature 'cyberspace' could and should not be regulated. It could not be regulated because of the fact that the phenomenon sits uneasily with traditional notions of territorial jurisdiction and it should not be regulated because "regulatory efforts [...] would unduly restrict the great potential of the Internet."[82] Yet, "this 'first generation thinking' [...] proved to be a fallacy"[83] and both the EU and its Member States realised that "if information flows freely, it is because we allow it to do so."[84] As we have seen, the regulation of cybersecurity is high on the EU agenda.

Over the years, the European Union has put great efforts into formulating ambitious cybersecurity policies. While this has resulted in an impressive pile of policy papers produced by the various EU institutions (the Commission in particular), clear legal competences to actually regulate the field are hard to find and measures do not necessarily relate to traditional notions of 'security'. As also rightfully held by others,

> Most of the EU's action in the field of cybersecurity has dealt with internal EU policies (e.g. internal market and consumer protection) or is linked to criminal law (combatting cybercrime) and is tied to the goals of economic growth and the internal market.[85]

The focus on the social-economic dimension is understandable since in that area connections were easier to make and the internal market still forms the core of what the EU stands for. In the words of Dewar,

> The system of exclusive, shared, supporting and special competences established a policy framework in which the EU was restricted to non-military, socio-economic policy choices. The result of this restriction was that only socio-economic considerations in cyber security could be developed and implemented.[86]

This also led to path dependencies and made it more difficult to connect to newer policy areas (perhaps such as CSDP). At the same time, cyberdefence is now emerging as a key issue and the EU is clearly attempting to mainstream cyber issues throughout its exiting foreign and security policy. One reason is that it is increasingly difficult to separate internal and external threats in this field:

> Not only may Internet-based attacks on critical infrastructure originate in Ghana, Russia or elsewhere, but also often it is difficult (if not impossible) to identify the source of the attack. [...] An appropriate response to such an attack requires cross-border cooperation between authorities. It is here that the current division of responsibilities between civil defence, military defence, and law enforcement falters.[87]

This chapter points to the need for a comprehensive regulatory approach. However, whereas the EU is usually able to find a connection to existing competences, allowing it to produce new legislation in many different fields, it suffers from the fact that it is not always easy (and is sometimes even impossible) to combine the different cybersecurity dimensions in consistent or even connected policies. Despite the fact that the Lisbon Treaty integrated many policy fields by making an end to some diverging decision-making procedures, the field of 'security' is still characterised by a substantial degree of fragmentation (with security aspects being covered by the internal market, the Area of Freedom, Security and Justice (AFSJ) and the Common Foreign, Security and Defence Policy). It is the EU's complex division of powers and its diverging procedures and rules for different policy areas that seem to stand in the way of realising a comprehensive body of cybersecurity law, leaving us with a large number of partly overlapping, soft as well as hard law measures in a complex multi-actor and multi-level setting.

The current treaty regime only partly allows the EU to improve things. Despite the fact that foreign and security measures are no longer 'subordinate' to other policies (which is underlined both by Treaty provisions and recent case law[88]), a choice for the correct legal basis will still have to be made and combinations of CFSP and other policies remain difficult because of the different (and often incompatible) procedural requirements. Obviously, this is not always a problem. The EU can simply adopt different decisions related to the internal market, crime or defence issues. But maintaining (or in fact creating) consistency (or at least coherence) in EU cybersecurity policy might very well be the main challenge for the EU the coming years.[89] Yet, there is no denying of the fact that something like a body of EU cybersecurity law is slowly developing. Alongside the existing decisions, the EU has announced new legislative initiatives, partly following international (transatlantic) cooperation, partly because of a connection to internal objectives related to either fundamental rights or economic motives. The fact that many options are still open will allow the EU to take its own consistency requirements seriously and aim for a comprehensive and coherent development of this new body of law. There should be no doubt that over the coming years these developments will lead to the emergence of new sub-disciplines in the area of EU cybersecurity law.

Notes

1 Annegret Bendiek, "European Cyber Security Policy," SWP Research Paper 13 (SWP, 2012), 5.

2 For an overview: Ramses A. Wessel and Joris Larik (eds.), *EU External Relations Law: Text, Cases and Materials* (Oxford: Hart Publishing, 2020), Chapter 9.

3 Further on these initiatives: https://eeas.europa.eu/headquarters/headquarters-Homepage/34226/permanent-structured-cooperation-pesco-factsheet_en.

4 Helena Carrapico and André Barrinha, "European Union Cyber Security as an Emerging Research and Policy Field," *European Politics and Society* 19, no. 3 (2018), 300: "Although cyber security has now become part of our daily lives and concerns, European Studies as a discipline is yet to fully embrace the area as a subject of in-depth research." Robert Scott Dewar, "Cyber Security in the European Union: An Historical Institutionalist Analysis of a 21st Century Security Concern" (PhD dissertation, University of Glasgow, 2017).

5 For the many dimensions: Roger Brownsword, Eloise Scotford and Karen Yeung, *The Oxford Handbook of Law, Regulation, and Technology* (Oxford: Oxford University Press, 2017); Davis S. Wall, "Crime, Security, and Information Communication Technologies: The Changing Cybersecurity Threat Landscape and Its Implications for Regulation and Policing," in *The Oxford Handbook of Law, Regulation, and Technology*, ed. Roger Brownsword, Eloise Scotford and Karen Yeung (Oxford: Oxford University Press, 2017), 1075–96.

6 Lennon Y.C. Chang and Peter Grabosky, "The Governance of Cyberspace" in *Regulatory Theory: Foundations and Applications*, ed. Peter Drahos (Acton: ANU Press, 2017), 535.

7 Art. 43(1) TEU:

> The tasks referred to in Article 42(1), in the course of which the Union may use civilian and military means, shall include joint disarmament operations, humanitarian and rescue tasks, military advice and assistance tasks, conflict prevention and peace-keeping tasks, tasks of combat forces in crisis management, including peace-making and post-conflict stabilisation. All these tasks may contribute to the fight against terrorism, including by supporting third countries in combating terrorism in their territories.

8 For the early emergence of a European Union policy on cybercrime from a comparative perspective: Fernando Mendez, "The European Union and Cybercrime: Insights from Comparative Federalism," *Journal of European Public Policy* 13 (2006): 509–27. For a reference to some earlier documents: Ramses A. Wessel, "Towards EU Cybersecurity Law: Regulating a New Policy Field," in *Research Handbook on International Law and Cyber Space*, eds. Nicholas Tsagourias and Russell Buchan (Cheltenham: Edward Elgar Publishing, 2015), 403–25. Parts of the present contribution further build on that publication.

9 European Commission, *State of the Union 2017 – Cyber-Security: Commission Scales Up EU's Response to Cyber-Attacks* (Brussels: European Union, 2017).

10 European Commission, *Cybersecurity Strategy of the European Union: An Open, Safe and Secure Cyberspace*, JOIN(2013) 1 final (Brussels: European Union, 2013), accessed May 9, 2019, http://eeas.europa.eu/archives/docs/policies/eu-cyber-security/cybsec_comm_en.pdf; and European Commission, *A Digital Single Market Strategy for Europe*, COM(2015) 192 final (Brussels: European Union, 2015), accessed May 9, 2019, http://eur-lex.europa.eu/legal-content/EN/TXT/PDF/?uri=CELEX:52015DC0192.

11 Carrapico and Barrinha, "European Union Cyber Security."

12 Bendiek, "European Cyber Security Policy," 5; Jed Odermatt, "The European Union as a Cybersecurity Actor," in *Research Handbook on EU Common Foreign and Security Policy*, eds. Steven Blockmans and Panos Koutrakos (Cheltenham: Edward Elgar Publishing, 2018); N. Robinson et al., *Data and Security Breaches and Cyber-Security Strategies in the EU and its International Counterparts* (Brussels: European Union, 2013); Javier Argomaniz, "The European Union Policies on the Protection of Infrastructure from Terrorist Attacks: A Critical Assessment," *Intelligence and Security* 30 (2013): 259–80; Paul Cornish, *Cyber Security and Politically, Socially and Religiously Motivated Cyber Attacks* (Brussels: European Union, 2009).

13 The European Commission remarks that cybercrime is "by its very nature cross-border" and hence "proper cross-border arrangements" are required. European Commission, Communication on Critical Information Infrastructure – "Achievements and Next Steps: Towards Global Cyber-Security," COM(2011) 163 final (Brussels: European Union, March 31, 2011).

14 Annegret Bendiek, "A Paradigm Shift in the EU's Common Foreign and Security Policy: From Transformation to Resilience," SWP Research Paper (SWP 2017), 5–30.

15 European External Action Service. *Shared Vision, Common Action: A Stronger Europe – A Global Strategy for the European Union's Foreign and Security Policy* (Brussels: European Union, 2016), accessed May 9, 2019, https://europa.eu/globalstrategy/en.

16 The term 'cyber' appears 23 times in the EU's Global Strategy. George Christou, *Cybersecurity in the European Union: Resilience and Adaptability in Governance Policy* (Basingstoke: Palgrave MacMillan 2016).

17 Wessel, "Towards EU Cybersecurity Law," 425.

18 Odermatt, "The European Union as a Cybersecurity Actor"; Krzysztof F. Sliwinski, "Moving Beyond the European Union's Weakness as a Cyber-Security Agent," *Contemporary Security Policy* 35, no. 3 (2014): 470:

> There is no coherent European understanding of what the notion of cyber-security should include. Consequently, conceptualization differences are more than likely to produce different approaches to respective national capabilities catalogues. Such inconsistencies, when reinforced by national security narratives and traditional sovereignty claims, are more than likely to leave the EU toothless in the future.

See also Federica Di Camillo and Valérie Miranda, "Ambiguous Definitions in the Cyber Domain: Costs, Risks and the Way Forward," IAI Working Paper 11 (IAI, 2011), 2–23.

19 European Commission, Joint Communication to the European Parliament, the Council, the European Economic and Social Committee and the Committee of the Regions: Cybersecurity Strategy of the European Union: An Open, Safe and Secure Cyberspace, JOIN(2013 1 final (Brussels: European Union, February 7, 2013), abbreviated as EUCSS.

20 Udo Helmbrecht, Steve Purser, and Maj Ritter Klejnstrup, *Cyber Security: Future Challenges and Opportunities* (ENISA, 2012), 13.

21 For a discussion on definitional questions: Elaine Fahey, "The EU's Cybercrime and Cyber-Security Rulemaking: Mapping the Internal and External Dimensions of EU Security," *European Journal of Risk Regulation* 1 (2014): 47:

> Conceptually, cybercrime may be defined both narrowly, to include offences against computer data and systems but also more broadly, to include offences committed with the help

of computer data and systems. By contrast, cyber-security usually relates to four major societal threats – crime, cyberwar, cyber terrorism and espionage.

22 Convention on Cybercrime, CETS No. 185, Council of Europe, signed 23 November 2001 in Budapest, entry into force 1 July 2004.

23 Annegret Bendiek and Andrew L. Porter, "European Cyber Security Policy within a Global Multi-stakeholder Structure," *European Foreign Affairs Review* 18, no. 2 (2013): 158. This article also provides a good overview of the wide scope of the actual problems caused by a lack of cybersecurity.

24 Christou, *Cybersecurity in the European Union: Resilience and Adaptability in Governance Policy*, 6: "Cyber defence is not defined within the EU documents given the sensitivity among member states on this issue, and the reluctance of certain member states to participate given their own cyber defence strategies."

25 Bendiek, "A Paradigm Shift in the EU's Common Foreign and Security Policy," 6.

26 As phrased by the Global Strategy it is about: "the swift recovery of Members States in the event of attacks." Also Bendiek, "A Paradigm Shift in the EU's Common Foreign and Security Policy," 6:

> Resilience is generally understood as 'a capacity to resist and regenerate', as well as be 'crisis-proof'. The concept acknowledges that there are practical limits to the normative goal of external transformation as outlined in article 21 paragraph 2 of the TEU. Resilience therefore aims to enable the EU both to maintain its existing values and norms and to pursue its own interests.

27 EU Global Strategy, 4.

28 Ibid, 23.

29 Council of the European Union, *EU Cyber Defence Policy Framework* 15585/14 (Brussels: European Union, 2014), https://ccdcoe.org/sites/default/files/documents/EU-141118-EUCyberDefencePolicyFrame.pdf; Bendiek, "A Paradigm Shift in the EU's Common Foreign and Security Policy," 18.

30 Bendiek, "A Paradigm Shift in the EU's Common Foreign and Security Policy," 18; Bruno Lété and Daiga Dege, *NATO Cybersecurity: A Roadmap to Resilience* (Washington: The German Marshall Fund of the United States, 2017).

31 Thomas Renard, "EU Cyber Partnerships: Assessing the EU Strategic Partnerships with Third Countries in the Cyber Domain," *European Politics and Society* 19, no. 3 (2018): 321–37. Renard lists the following dialogues in the framework of strategic partnerships: Brazil (Dialogue on international cyber policy; Information society dialogue); Canada (EU–US–Canada Expert Meeting on Critical Infrastructure Protection China Cyber taskforce; Dialogue on IT, telecommunications and informatisation); India (Political dialogue on cybersecurity; Information society dialogue); Japan (Cyber dialogue; Dialogue on ICT policy); Mexico (Working Group on telecommunications; Dialogue on public security and law enforcement); Russia (Information society dialogue); South Africa (Information society dialogue); South Korea (Cyber dialogue; Information society dialogue); USA (Working Group on Cybersecurity and Cyber-crime (WGCC); Cyber dialogue; Information society dialogue; EU–US–Canada Expert Meeting on Critical Infrastructure Protection).

32 Global Strategy, 21–22; emphasis added.

33 Bendiek, "A Paradigm Shift in the EU's Common Foreign and Security Policy," at 18.

34 Ibid.

35 EU Cybersecurity Strategy, 1.

36 *Inter alia* resulting in the 2001 Commission Communication on Network and Information Security: Proposal for a European Policy Approach (COM(2001) 298) and the 2006 Strategy for a Secure Information Society (COM(2006) 251).

37 EU–US Summit 20 November 2010, Lisbon-Joint Statement, European Commission-MEMO/10/597 20/11/2010. See also Maria Grazia Porcedda, "Transatlantic Approaches to Cyber-Security and Cybercrime," in *The EU-US Security and Justice Agenda in Action*, ed. Patryk Pawlak, EUISS Chaillot Paper (EUISS, 2011); Fahey, "The EU's Cybercrime and Cyber-Security Rulemaking."

38 Emmanuel Darmois and Geneviève Schméder, "Cybersecurity: A Case for a European Approach," SiT Paper SiT/WP/11/16 (SiT, 2016), accessed May 9, 2019, www.securityintransition.org/wp-content/uploads/2016/02/WP11_Cybersecurity_FinalEditedVersion.pdf.

39 European Commission, Communication from the Commission to the European Parliament, the Council, European Economic and Social Committee and the Committee of the Regions: European Agenda on Security, COM(2015) 185 final.

40 www.consilium.europa.eu/en/workarea/downloadasset.aspx?id=40802190515.

41 European Commission, Joint Communication to the European Parliament and the Council: Resilience, Deterrence and Defence: Building Strong Cybersecurity for the EU, JOIN(2017) 450 final (Brussels: European Union, September 13, 2017).

42 The Cybersecurity Strategy clearly states that "The EU does not call for the creation of new international legal instruments for cyber issues."

43 Odermatt, "The European Union as a Cybersecurity Actor."

44 Council of the European Union, Council Conclusions on a Framework for a Joint EU Diplomatic Response to Malicious Cyber Activities (9916/17) ('Cyber Diplomacy Toolbox') (Brussels: European Union, 2017).

45 Annegret Bendiek, "The EU as a Force for Peace in International Cyber Diplomacy," *SWP Comment* 19 (2018).

46 2017 Joint Communication to the European Parliament and the Council.

47 The Union's activities partly build on the EU's engagement with the regulation of the Internet in a broader sense – with co-regulation as an important dimension. Franz C. Mayer, "Europe and the Internet: The Old World and the New Medium," *European Journal of International Law* 11, no. 1 (2000): 149–69. According to the European Commission, the EU's regulatory role has evolved over the years, to keep pace with the evolving ICT landscape: introducing rules covering all electronic communications networks and services ensuring fair access to basic services (phone, fax, Internet, free emergency calls) at affordable prices, for all customers – including people with disabilities – and stimulating competition by reducing the dominant position that former national telecom monopolies used to maintained for certain services, like high-speed Internet access. The rules are applied independently by the authorities in each EU country, with national regulators coordinating their policies at EU level through forums like the Body of European Regulators for Electronic Communications (BEREC). For a summary: http://europa.eu/pol/infso/index_en.htm. On the role of the EU in Internet governance: Communication from the Commission to the European Parliament and the Council of 18 June 2009: Internet Governance: the Next Steps, COM(2009) 277 final; as well as the overview of activities by the Commission on http://europa.eu/legislation_summaries/information_society/internet/index_en.htm. Also: Chris T. Marsden, *Internet Co-Regulation: European Law, Regulatory Governance and Legitimacy in Cyberspace* (Cambridge: Cambridge University Press, 2011).

48 Jan Kleijssen and Pierluigi Perri, "Cybercrime, Evidence and Territoriality: Issues and Options," *Netherlands Yearbook of International Law* 47 (2016): 147–73. Indeed, as mentioned by the authors, the Council of Europe in particular has been used to draft (even more broadly accepted) instruments, such as the 2001 Budapest Convention on Cybercrime (ETS No. 185) as well as a large number of treaties on international co-operation in criminal matters, including in particular the European Convention on Mutual Assistance in Criminal Matters (ETS No. 030), its Additional Protocol to the European Convention on Mutual Assistance in Criminal Matters (ETS No. 099), and the Second Additional Protocol to the European Convention on Mutual Assistance in Criminal Matters (ETS No. 182). Bendiek and Porter, "European Cyber Security Policy."

49 On some theoretical discussions: Lianne J.M. Boer, "'Spoofed Presence Does Not Suffice': On Territoriality in the Tallinn Manual," *Netherlands Yearbook of International Law* (2016): 131–45; Joachim Zekoll, "Jurisdiction in Cyberspace," in *Beyond Territoriality – Transnational Legal Authority in an Age of Globalization*, eds. Gunther Handl, Joachim Zekoll and Peer Zumbansen (Leiden: Martinus Nijhoff Publishers, 2012), 341–69; Uta Kohl, "Jurisdiction in Cyberspace," in *Research Handbook on International Law and Cyberspace*, ed. by Nicholas Tsagourias and Russell Buchan (Cheltenham: Edward Elgar Publishing, 2017), 30–54; Armando A. Cottim, "Cybercrime, Cyberterrorism and Jurisdiction: An Analysis of Article 22 of The COE Convention on Cybercrime," *European Journal of Legal Studies* (2010): 55–79.

50 Art. 5(2) TEU:

> Under the principle of conferral, the Union shall act only within the limits of the competences conferred upon it by the Member States in the Treaties to attain the objectives set out therein. Competences not conferred upon the Union in the Treaties remain with the Member States.

Indeed, the 'principle of conferral' may further complicate things and leaves the Union with two options: it either connects cybersecurity to existing competences in other fields, or it uses soft law instruments to stimulate Member States and other relevant actors to implement parts of its strategies.

51 European Parliament, European Parliament Resolution of 23 November 2016 on the Implementation of the Common Security and Defence Policy (2016/2067(INI)) (Strasbourg: European Union, 2016), accessed May 9, 2019, www.europarl.europa.eu/sides/getDoc.do?type=TA&reference=P8-TA-2016-0440&language=EN.
52 Wessel and Larik, *EU External Relations Law*, Chapter 3.
53 Renard, "EU Cyber Partnerships," 326: "But just like in many other policy areas, the EU aims to assert itself in the global arena through 'soft power' assets and diplomatic skills."
54 On the institutional developments: Jukka Ruohonen, Sami Hyrynsalmi, and Ville Leppänen, "An Outlook on the Institutional Evolution of the European Union Cyber Security Apparatus," *Government Information Quarterly* 33, no. 4 (2016): 746–56.
55 Council conclusions on the establishment of a European Cybercrime Centre, 3172nd Justice and Home Affairs Council meeting Luxembourg, 7 and 8 June 2012.
56 www.europol.europa.eu/about-europol/european-cybercrime-centre-ec3.
57 Regulation (EC) No 460/2004.
58 www.enisa.europa.eu/activities/cert/other-work/eisas_folder.
59 Wessel, "Towards EU Cybersecurity Law."
60 European Commission, Communication from the Commission to the European Parliament, the Council, the European Economic and Social Committee and the Committee of the Regions: A Digital Single Market Strategy for Europe, COM(2015) 192 final (Brussels: European Union, May 6, 2015).
61 Much earlier already the Electronic Commerce Directive, adopted in 2000, had introduced an Internal Market Framework for electronic commerce, providing legal certainty for business and consumers alike. It established harmonised rules on issues such as the transparency and information requirements for online service providers, commercial communications, electronic contracts and limitations of liability of intermediary service providers. Directive 2000/31/EC of the European Parliament and of the Council of 8 June 2000 on Certain Legal Aspects of Information Society Services, in Particular Electronic Commerce, in the Internal Market ('Directive on electronic commerce'), OJ L 178, July 17, 2000.
62 Directive (EU) 2016/1148 of the European Parliament and of the Council of 6 July 2016 Concerning Measures for a High Common Level of Security of Network and Information Systems across the Union, OJ L 194 (Brussels: European Union, 2016), 1, abbreviated as 'NIS Directive'.
63 "EU countries miss cybersecurity deadline," *EU Observer*, July 30, 2018, accessed May 9, 2019, https://euobserver.com/digital/142493.
64 "NIS Directive", Explanatory memorandum.
65 Preamble of the NIS Directive, points 1 and 3.
66 Odermatt, "The European Union as a Cybersecurity Actor."
67 Communication from the Commission to the European Parliament, the Council, the European Economic and Social Committee and the European Committee of the Regions: Strengthening Europe's Cyber Resilience System and Fostering a Competitive and Innovative Cybersecurity Industry, COM(2016) 410 final (Brussels: European Union, 2016).
68 Regulation (EU) No 910/2014 of the European Parliament and of the Council of 23 July 2014 on Electronic Identification and Trust Services for Electronic Transactions in the Internal Market and Repealing Directive 1999/93/EC; OJ L 257 (Brussels: European Union, 2014), 73–114.
69 Communications from the Commission to the European Parliament, the Council, the European Economic and Social Committee and the Committee of the Regions on the Mid-Term Review on the Implementation of the Digital Single Market Strategy, *A Connected Digital Single Market for All*, COM(2017) 228 final (Brussels: European Union, 2017).
70 Council Framework Decision 2005/222/JHA of 24 February 2005 on Attacks against Information Systems.
71 Ibid.
72 Directive 2013/40/EU of the European Parliament and of the Council of 12 August 2013 on Attacks against Information Systems and Replacing Council Framework Decision 2005/222/JHA, OJ L 218 (Brussels: European Union, 2013), 8. This Directive replaced the 2005 EU Framework Decision on Attacks against Information Systems.
73 Directive 2009/136/EC of the European Parliament and of the Council of 25 November 2009, OJ L 337 (Brussels: European Union, 2009), 11.
74 Council Framework Decision of 28 May 2001 combating fraud and counterfeiting of non-cash means of payment, OJ L 149 (Brussels: European Union, 2001), 1.

75 http://conventions.coe.int/Treaty/en/Treaties/Html/185.htm; Mike Keyser, "The Council of Europe Convention on Cybercrime," *Journal of Transnational Law & Policy* (2002–2003): 287–327.
76 Odermatt, "The European Union as a Cybersecurity Actor."
77 Gen. Keith B. Alexander, upon accepting the post to lead the first US Cyber-Command (USCYBERCOM). Quoted by Rex Hughes, "A Treaty for Cyberspace," *International Affairs* 86, no. 2 (2010): 523–41.
78 Malcom Ross and Yuri Bogmann-Prebil, *Promoting Solidarity in the European Union* (Oxford: Oxford University Press, 2010).
79 European Parliament Resolution of 22 November 2012 on the EU's Mutual Defence and Solidarity Clauses: Political and Operational Dimensions (2012/2223(INI)) (Brussels: European Union, 2012), par. 20.
80 Ibid, par. 13.
81 For examples of cyberattacks: Alexander Klimburg and Heli Tirmaa-Klaar, *Cyber Security and Cyber Power: Concepts, Conditions and Capabilities for Cooperation for Action within the EU*, study commissioned by the European Parliament, PE 433 828, 54 (Brussels: European Union, 2011). Marco Roscini, "Cyber operations as a Use of Force" in in *Research Handbook on International Law and Cyberspace*, ed. by Nicholas Tsagourias and Russell Buchan (Cheltenham and Northampton: Edward Elgar Publishing, 2017), 233–54; Carlo Focarelli, "Self-Defence in Cyberspace," in in *Research Handbook on International Law and Cyberspace*, ed. by Nicholas Tsagourias and Russell Buchan (Cheltenham: Edward Elgar Publishing, 2017), 255–83.
82 Zekoll, "Jurisdiction in Cyberspace," 342–3.
83 Ibid., 343.
84 Horatia Muir Watt, "Yahoo! Cyberspace-Collision of Cultures: Who Regulates?" *Michigan Journal of International Law* 24, no. 3 (2003): 683. Also quoted in Zekoll, "Jurisdiction in Cyberspace," 344.
85 Odermatt, "The European Union as a Cybersecurity Actor."
86 Dewar, "Cyber Security in the European Union," 212.
87 Bendiek and Porter, "European Cyber Security Policy," 156–7.
88 Steven Blockmans and Martina Spernbauer, "Legal Obstacles to Comprehensive EU External Security Action," *European Foreign Affairs Review* 18, no. 4 (2013): 23.
89 Helena Carrapico and André Barrinha, "The EU as a Coherent (Cyber)Security Actor?" *Journal of Common Market Studies* 55, no. 6 (2017): 1267:

> the EU has an explicit ambition to be a coherent security actor. However, both the architecture put in place under the [EU Cybersecurity Strategy] and the resistance from Member States to allow the EU to have a more stringent control over their cyber activities, limit the EU's coherence in the field. That said, both the rising political importance given to cybersecurity and the progressive consolidation of what is still a rather recent field of activity, means there are signs the EU might move towards a more coherent actorness in the field.

References

Argomaniz, Javier. "The European Union Policies on the Protection of Infrastructure from Terrorist Attacks: A Critical Assessment." *Intelligence and Security* 30 (2013): 259–80.

Bendiek, Annegret. "The EU as a Force for Peace in International Cyber Diplomacy." *SWP Comment* 19 (2018).

Bendiek, Annegret. "European Cyber Security Policy." SWP Research Paper 13 (SWP, 2012).

Bendiek, Annegret. "A Paradigm Shift in the EU's Common Foreign and Security Policy: From Transformation to Resilience." SWP Research Paper (SWP, 2017).

Bendiek, Annegret, and Andrew L. Porter. "European Cyber Security Policy within a Global Multistakeholder Structure." *European Foreign Affairs Review* 18, no. 2 (2013): 155–80.

Blockmans, Steven, and Martina Spernbauer. "Legal Obstacles to Comprehensive EU External Security Action." *European Foreign Affairs Review* 18, no. 4 (2013): 7–24.

Boer, Lianne J.M. "'Spoofed Presence Does Not Suffice': On Territoriality in the Tallinn Manual." *Netherlands Yearbook of International Law* (2016): 131–45.

Brownsword, Roger, Eloise Scotford and Karen Yeung. *The Oxford Handbook of Law, Regulation, and Technology*. Oxford: Oxford University Press, 2017.

Carrapico, Helena, and André Barrinha. "The EU as a Coherent (Cyber)Security Actor?" *Journal of Common Market Studies* 55, no. 6 (2017): 1254–72.

Carrapico, Helena, and André Barrinha. "European Union Cyber Security as an Emerging Research and Policy Field," *European Politics and Society* 19, no. 3 (2018): 300.
Chang, Lennon Y.C., and Peter Grabosky. "The Governance of Cyberspace." In *Regulatory Theory: Foundations and Applications*, edited by Peter Drahos, 533–52. Acton: ANU Press, 2017.
Christou, George. *Cybersecurity in the European Union: Resilience and Adaptability in Governance Policy*. Basingstoke: Palgrave Macmillan, 2016.
Cornish, Paul. *Cyber Security and Politically, Socially and Religiously Motivated Cyber Attacks* (Brussels: European Union, 2009).
Council of the European Union. *EU Cyber Defence Policy Framework* (15585/14). Brussels: European Union, 2014.
Cottim, Armando A. "Cybercrime, Cyberterrorism and Jurisdiction: An Analysis of Article 22 of The COE Convention on Cybercrime." *European Journal of Legal Studies* (2010): 55–79.
Darmois, Emmanuel, and Geneviève Schméder. "Cybersecurity: A Case for a European Approach." SiT Paper SiT/WP/11/16. SiT, 2016.
Dewar, Robert Scott. "Cyber Security in the European Union: An Historical Institutionalist Analysis of a 21st Century Security Concern." PhD dissertation, University of Glasgow, 2017.
Di Camillo, Federica, and Valérie Miranda. "Ambiguous Definitions in the Cyber Domain: Costs, Risks and the Way Forward." IAI Working Paper 11 (IAI, 2011).
European Commission. Communication from the Commission to the European Parliament, the Council, the European Economic and Social Committee and the Committee of the Regions: A Digital Single Market Strategy for Europe. COM(2015) 192 final. Brussels: European Union, May 6, 2015.
European Commission. Communication from the Commission to the European Parliament, the Council, the European Economic and Social Committee and the Committee of the Regions on Critical Information Infrastructure – "Achievements and Next Steps: Towards Global Cyber-Security." COM(2011) 163 final. Brussels: European Union, March 31, 2011.
European Commission. *Cybersecurity Strategy of the European Union: An Open, Safe and Secure Cyberspace.* JOIN(2013) 1 final. Brussels: European Union, 2013.
European Commission. Joint Communication to the European Parliament and the Council: Resilience, Deterrence and Defence: Building Strong Cybersecurity for the EU. JOIN(2017) 450 final. Brussels: European Union, September 13, 2017.
European Commission. Joint Communication to the European Parliament, the Council, the European Economic and Social Committee and the Committee of the Regions: Cybersecurity Strategy of the European Union: An Open, Safe and Secure Cyberspace. JOIN(2013) 1 final. Brussels: European Union, February 7, 2013.
European Commission. *State of the Union 2017 – Cyber-Security: Commission Scales Up EU's Response to Cyber-Attacks*. Brussels: European Union, 2017.
European External Action Service. *Shared Vision, Common Action: A Stronger Europe. A Global Strategy for the European Union's Foreign and Security Policy*. Brussels: European Union, 2016.
Fahey, Elaine. "The EU's Cybercrime and Cyber-Security Rulemaking: Mapping the Internal and External Dimensions of EU Security." *European Journal of Risk Regulation* 1 (2014): 46–61.
Focarelli, Carlo. "Self-Defence in Cyberspace." In *Research Handbook on International Law and Cyberspace*, edited by Nicholas Tsagourias and Russell Buchan, 255–83. Cheltenham: Edward Elgar Publishing, 2017.
Helmbrecht, Udo, Steve Purser and Maj Ritter Klejnstrup. *Cyber Security: Future Challenges and Opportunities*. ENISA, 2012.
Hughes, Rex. "A Treaty for Cyberspace." *International Affairs* 86, no. 2 (2010): 523–41.
Keyser, Mike. "The Council of Europe Convention on Cybercrime." *Journal of Transnational Law & Policy* (2002–2003): 287–327.
Kleijssen, Jan, and Pierluigi Perri. "Cybercrime, Evidence and Territoriality: Issues and Options." *Netherlands Yearbook of International Law* 47 (2016): 147–73.
Klimburg, Alexander, and Heli Tirmaa-Klaar. *Cyber Security and Cyber Power: Concepts, Conditions and Capabilities for Cooperation for Action within the EU*. Study commissioned by the European Parliament, PE 433 828, 54 (Brussels: European Union, 2011).
Kohl, Uta. "Jurisdiction in Cyberspace." In *Research Handbook on International Law and Cyberspace*, edited by Nicholas Tsagourias and Russell Buchan, 30–54. Cheltenham: Edward Elgar Publishing, 2017.
Lété, Bruno, and Daiga Dege. *NATO Cybersecurity: A Roadmap to Resilience*. Washington: The German Marshall Fund of the United States, 2017.

Marsden, Chris T. *Internet Co-Regulation: European Law, Regulatory Governance and Legitimacy in Cyberspace.* Cambridge: Cambridge University Press, 2011.

Mayer, Franz C. "Europe and the Internet: The Old World and the New Medium." *European Journal of International Law* 11, no. 1 (2000): 149–69.

Mendez, Fernando. "The European Union and Cybercrime: Insights from Comparative Federalism." *Journal of European Public Policy* 12 (2006): 509–27.

Odermatt, Jed. "The European Union as a Cybersecurity Actor." In *Research Handbook on EU Common Foreign and Security Policy*, edited by Steven Blockmans and Panos Koutrakos. Cheltenham: Edward Elgar Publishing, 2018.

Porcedda, Maria Grazia. "Transatlantic Approaches to Cyber-Security and Cybercrime." In *The EU-US Security and Justice Agenda in Action*, edited by Patryk Pawlak. EUISS Chaillot Paper. EUISS, 2011.

Renard, Thomas. "EU Cyber Partnerships: Assessing the EU Strategic Partnerships with Third Countries in the Cyber Domain." *European Politics and Society* 19, no. 3 (2018): 321–37.

Robinson, N., et al. *Data and Security Breaches and Cyber-Security Strategies in the EU and Its International Counterparts* (Brussels: European Union, 2013).

Roscini, Marco. "Cyber Operations as a Use of Force." In *Research Handbook on International Law and Cyberspace*, edited by Nicholas Tsagourias and Russell Buchan, 233–54. Cheltenham: Edward Elgar Publishing, 2017.

Ross, Malcom, and Yuri Bogmann-Prebil. *Promoting Solidarity in the European Union*. Oxford: Oxford University Press, 2010.

Ruohonen, Jukka, Sami Hyrynsalmi and Ville Leppänen. "An Outlook on the Institutional Evolution of the European Union Cyber Security Apparatus." *Government Information Quarterly* 33, no. 4 (2016): 746–56.

Sliwinski, Krzysztof F. "Moving Beyond the European Union's Weakness as a Cyber-Security Agent." *Contemporary Security Policy* 35, no. 3 (2014): 468–86.

Wessel, Ramses A., and Joris Larik (eds.). *EU External Relations Law: Text, Cases and Materials*. Oxford: Hart Publishing. 2020.

Wall, Davis S. "Crime, Security, and Information Communication Technologies: The Changing Cyber-security Threat Landscape and Its Implications for Regulation and Policing." In *The Oxford Handbook of Law, Regulation, and Technology*, edited by Roger Brownsword, Eloise Scotford and Karen Yeung, 1075–96. Oxford: Oxford University Press, 2017.

Watt, Horatia Muir. "Yahoo! Cyberspace-Collision of Cultures: Who Regulates?" *Michigan Journal of International Law* 24, no. 3 (2003): 673–95.

Wessel, Ramses A. "Towards EU Cybersecurity Law: Regulating a New Policy Field." In *Research Handbook on International Law and Cyber Space*, edited by Nicholas Tsagourias and Russell Buchan, 403–25. Cheltenham: Edward Elgar Publishing, 2015.

Zekoll, Joachim. "Jurisdiction in Cyberspace." In *Beyond Territoriality – Transnational Legal Authority in an Age of Globalization*, edited by Gunther Handl, Joachim Zekoll and Peer Zumbansen, 341–69. Leiden: Martinus Nijhoff Publishers, 2012.

PART III

Combatting Threats from the Human Side?

18

EU COUNTER-TERRORISM POLICY AND HUMAN RIGHTS

Are we on the right track?[1]

Milena Costas Trascasas

Introduction

There is no doubt that the 9/11 attacks have been one of the most prominent historical events of our era. With the launching of a global fight against terrorism, under the leadership of the US, a new security paradigm has been introduced. Under this new paradigm, human rights concerns and considerations are progressively becoming merely marginal aspects of the decision and policy-making processes.[2]

In the name of strengthening international peace and security, a number of structural and institutional adjustments have been introduced at the international level. Under the leadership of the UN Security Council (UNSC), virtually transformed into a legislator, a new global legal framework is being modelled.[3] UNSC Resolution 1373 (2001), adopted on 21 September 2001, marks the beginning of a set of obligations that Member States are called upon to implement under the supervisory authority of the newly established Counter-Terrorism Committee.

The role of the EU as an implementing actor for this new framework is decisive.[4] The concerted efforts made to fight against terrorism have, without any doubt, contributed to boosting existing cooperation as well as to harmonizing national policies and legislation on security issues.

EU new counter-terrorism framework

In the aftermath of the US attacks, counter-terrorism moved quickly to the forefront of the EU's policy agenda.[5] The pressing need to harmonize legislations and to foster cooperation to implement UNSC resolutions greatly facilitated the swift advancement of EU policies under both the external and the internal fronts. Given the cross-border character of the terrorist threat, EU leadership was seen as the most natural option to provide a concerted response.[6]

It is broadly admitted that the counter-terrorism agenda has been crisis-driven and primarily reflects the security concerns of some Member States around jihadism, which has become the main EU focus.[7] The EU strategy has been developed in response to the "shock" of four major terrorist attacks: the 2001 attacks in the US, the 2004 attacks in Madrid, the 2005 attacks in London and, finally, the 2015 attacks in Paris and in Brussels in 2016.[8] The perceived threat opened the opportunity to foster cooperation and push forward stalled legislative proposals, enabling the harmonization of national laws in the area of internal security. Under such an "exceptional legislative climate," national reluctance to act upon operational arrangements was progressively diminished.[9]

It must be clarified that Member States traditionally have kept the main responsibility of maintaining public order and national security.[10] However, under the Treaty of Lisbon, they share with the EU the goal of ensuring "a high level of security" within the EU.[11] Moreover, they are committed to act in solidarity in the event of a terrorist attack against any single member.[12]

This common goal has been pursued through the coordination of the Member State policies, the harmonization of its national legislation and by supporting the operational work conducted by national authorities.[13] Action has mainly sought to facilitate cooperation between national competent authorities to prevent, investigate and prosecute terrorist offences. This has required strengthening the operational instruments of both the Common Foreign and Security Policy (CFSP) and the Area of Freedom, Security and Justice (AFSJ). While the political strategy has been mainly developed through cooperation in the framework of the external action, its broad implications have required progress in a plethora of EU policies under the former first and third pillars.[14]

However, the response of the EU has been as effective as it has been fragmented and incoherent. Today, the "EU counter-terrorism policy" hashtag encapsulates a number of different fields of intervention along with a myriad of policies, strategies, action plans, programmes, subprogrammes and a great number of legal measures.[15] Member States are therefore called upon to implement this extensive and intricate arsenal of measures that come along with a number of dedicated strategies on specific issues.

Human rights constraints/safeguards

As is well-known, human rights obligations set the framework under which counter-terrorism policies, actions and measures must be pursued. These norms and principles bind EU institutions and Member States also while implementing EU law.[16] This particularly includes the 2000 EU Charter of Fundamental Rights and the EU Court of Justice-related case-law[17] but also the legal standards on law enforcement and human rights aspects of counter-terrorism developed in the framework of the Council of Europe by the European Court of Human Rights.[18] According to applicable standards, counter-terrorism measures need to be provided by law, respect the essence of the rights concerned and be both necessary and proportionate in view of the security interest.[19] Although adherence to these principles and standards is largely proclaimed, the expected EU accession to the 1950 European Convention for the Protection of Human Rights and Fundamental Freedoms (ECHR) would certainly bolster this compromise, as compliance would be more stringently monitored.[20]

Internal documents and strategies have sought to ensure the respect and promotion of these principles and rights as a cross-cutting issue all across the EU policies. The *Operational Guidance on Taking Account of Fundamental Rights in Commission Impact Assessments* developed in 2011, underscores the importance of properly assessing any impact on fundamental rights in the preparatory stages of new legislation as a way of strengthening "the defence of EU legislation against legal challenges before the European Court of Justice."[21] Within the framework of the EU external action the importance of framing policies around respect for rule of law and fundamental rights has also been clearly recognized. The 2012 EU Strategy and Plan of Action on Human Rights and Democracy unequivocally states the commitment to "promote human rights in all areas of its external action without exception."[22]

The great majority of policy documents examined in the research equally frame the EU action against terrorism within the strict respect of all these obligations and standards.[23] Council's conclusions have systematically called for comprehensive action "in full compliance with international law, fundamental values and international human rights standards."[24] In addition to the usual reference to "human rights law," and "international humanitarian and refugee law," other relevant instruments include a more specific reference to rights particularly affected such as the right to free and fair judicial proceedings as well as the protection of personal and private data.[25]

However, beyond these rather general political commitments, what really matters is the capability of EU institutions to translate them into practice. As has been observed, the aim is not only to ensure that in exercising its competences the EU is not violating fundamental rights or negatively affecting them, but also be certain whether the competences are exercised in a way that allows fundamental rights to make progress. So fundamental rights should not be presented merely as a set of requirements that limit, but more broadly as a set of values that should guide law and policy-making, and that are to be progressively realized.[26] Furthermore, the general duty to ensure compliance with human rights obligations presupposes ensuring a certain level of protection.

Counter-terrorism coordinator (2004)

The Madrid Attacks of 11 March 2004 galvanized the EU into renewed action. The European Council adopted a plan of action with seven specific strategic objectives, whereby particular emphasis was placed on the exchange of information between law enforcement agencies and on mechanisms underpinning the recruitment of individuals into terrorism. New operational arrangements were decided and an EU counter-terrorism coordinator (CCT) was appointed.[27]

The new position was created to monitor the implementation of the EU counter-terrorism strategy and to provide a "comprehensive and strongly coordinated approach in response to the threat posed by terrorism."[28] His main task is to ensure that "relevant actors work closely together, integrating the internal and external aspects of the fight against terrorism."[29]

The coordinator supports EU counter-terrorism efforts by facilitating cooperation among EU members and between the EU and third countries. He also fosters coordination with and between the relevant preparatory bodies of the Council, the Commission and the European Action External Service (EEAS). He reports to the Council every six months and is competent to make policy recommendations. It is on the basis of these recommendations that the EU has progressively expanded its action to new areas.

Less clear is how the CCT is contributing to a more coordinated effort of all involved actors towards enhanced human rights mainstreaming and protection throughout all EU policies and actions. This objective is not mentioned as part of its portfolio, which nevertheless focuses on issues with human rights implications, such as foreign fighters, returnees and the fight against on-line extremism.[30]

Strategy on counter-terrorism (2005)

A new impetus to the counter-terrorism agenda was given after the London bombings in July 2005. The European Council adopted a new EU Counter-Terrorism Strategy which effectively streamlines all the ad hoc measures into a single framework.[31] EU action is based on four pillars, namely: 1) Preventing people from turning to terrorism by tackling the factors or root causes which can lead to radicalization and recruitment (Prevent); 2) Protecting citizens and infrastructure and reducing vulnerability to attack (Protect); 3) Pursuing terrorists across borders, cutting off their support bases and financing (Pursue); and 4) Managing and minimizing the consequences of terrorist attacks by putting into practice the 2004 solidarity clause, and assisting the victims (Respond).[32]

The strategy proclaims that it "constitutes a comprehensive and proportionate response to the international terrorist threat" but quite strikingly does not include any general safeguard related to the need to respect human rights in its implementation. Its main focus has remained practically unchanged since 2005 policies developed policies developed.[33]

In early years the EU focused on the prevent and pursue elements, while policies in the last period have focused on the protect and respond dimensions, which in practice have been translated into an increasing number of generalized security, surveillance and crisis management initiatives (cybersecurity, border control, information management and measures designed to support the emerging security industry).[34] No comprehensive assessment of its efficacy, entailing a substantive evaluation of the policies developed, has been made so far.[35]

Directive on counter-terrorism (2017)

In 2017, the EU increased its counter-terrorism arsenal by adopting a Directive on combating terrorism.[36] The Directive provides a comprehensive framework aimed at harmonizing Member States' approaches by bringing together: 1) the 2002 Framework Decision on countering terrorism providing for a minimum definition of terrorist offences and their corresponding penalties, including those related to terrorist groups, as well as rules related to prosecution at national level;[37] 2) the 2008 Framework Decision which introduced three new offences in relation to the use of the Internet for terrorist purposes;[38] 3) more recent international standards and obligations in relation to the so-called "Foreign Terrorist Fighters," and terrorism financing.[39] The new Directive also seeks to render the rights of victims more visible.[40]

In the drafting process a number of concerns were already raised in relation to the initial text proposed by the Commission.[41] Main issues related to the lack of an express mention of human rights in the operative part, as well as a lack of real human rights sensitivity in the approach taken. Human rights are only expressly mentioned in the operative text in Article 23 which states that the Directive "shall not have the effect of modifying the obligations to respect fundamental rights and fundamental legal principles, as enshrined in Article 6 TEU."[42]

Agreement on a common approach to terrorist and terrorist-linked offences is one of the great achievements of the EU, as it will certainly facilitate international cooperation among Member States. The Directive offers a list of the serious crimes that can be qualified as terrorist attacks if committed with a specific terrorist aim, i.e. to seriously intimidate a population, to unduly compel a government or an international organization to perform or abstain from performing any act, or to seriously destabilize or destroy the fundamental political, constitutional, economic or social structures of a country or an international organization.[43]

The overly broad definition of terrorism provided by the Directive has been largely criticized on grounds it allows a wide leeway in its implementation and application.[44] As civil society organizations have pointed out, this may bring States to criminalize as terrorism situations that are in fact not akin to terrorism, such as public protest or other peaceful acts. As a result, the new regulation could be interpreted as a way of encouraging the suppression of freedom of expression, particularly dissenting political views.[45]

There is also a risk that the Directive will be applied and implemented in a way that discriminates against vulnerable and marginalized ethnic and religious communities.[46] Finally, the catch-all definition of terrorism provided in the Directive offers a means to exert control over those who associate in any way with a "terrorist group," who commis any acts that can be "linked to a terrorist offence" or who make any statements that may "provoke" terrorism.

Also problematic from the human rights perspective is the pre-emptive approach which the Directive contributes to the endorsement of. The definition of terrorist offences as "indirect incitement to terrorism" leaves a wide margin of interpretation, since an action would not need to pose a real risk to the public safety nor directly incite anyone to commit a terrorist offence to be considered as such.[47] This is problematic, as is the fact that the Directive allows States to criminalize a series of "preparatory acts" that have minimal or no direct link to a violent act of terrorism, and may never result in one being committed.[48] The criminalization of such preparatory acts represents a concerning development for the rule of law, as it has the ability to undermine traditional legal principles, such as legal certainty.[49]

Increasingly restrictive approach

Authors have sought to explain the EU's bias towards security as a way to reinforce its identity and projection, in both external and internal dimensions. According to these views, the EU would be trying to transform itself into a kind of "holistic" security actor. The pursuing of this track would bring about the "securitization" of social and political life.[50]

There is no doubt that the development of a purely counter-terrorism agenda has provided the basis for a more comprehensive agenda on security. It has also served to consolidate a "pro-security" approach in the EU's policy-making, as it is shown by the following patterns: 1) the choice of taking a mainly criminal approach by extending the scope of terrorism-related offences; 2) the trend to use administrative law to complement and/or to replace traditional criminal law responses with the result of reducing procedural guarantees and access to justice; 3) the focus towards pre-emptive measures which broadens the scope of criminal law to catch behaviours that previously were not considered legal.

All these approaches may certainly end up by eroding established legal principles and undermining traditional legal protections.[51] By putting the focus on control, pre-emptive measures contribute to eliminate legal certainty, challenging the idea that political violence must be addressed through clearly defined norms and sanctions. Civil law is also deployed in a more coercive and intrusive manner, with administrative sanctions used to control behaviour.[52] There is also a change in the scope of criminal laws, and consequently of law enforcement actions, that shifts from targetting acts already committed to actions that may be committed in the future. As a result, counter-terrorism measures are progressively moving away from the criminal act towards the "pre-crime space;" a track that may easily lead to criminalizing the beliefs people hold instead of their actual conduct. Such an outcome is in sharp contrast with established principles of both criminal and human rights law.

Change in the narrative

The counter-terrorism narrative has contributed to the quick acceptance of measures that otherwise could not have been introduced, at least in such an expedited and unchecked manner. Indeed, measures today are presented as less corrosive to the rule of law, broadly sympathetic to civil society engagement, aware of community sensitivities and unlikely to elicit serious human rights challenges. But the progressive modelling of the EU response does not "take into account the cumulative effect of sustained degrading of human rights norms as produced by the new regulatory matrix."[53] In the name of advancing security, full-scale limitations are being introduced, in a very subtle but consistent way. Moreover, without an objective and regular evaluation of the efficacy of those measures they may morph into permanent restrictions to rights and freedoms. As has been concluded, "the costs of this slow decline are substantive and consequential."[54]

Terrorism as an evolving threat

The configuration of terrorism as an "evolving threat" has contributed to a sustained continuity in the development of the security agenda.[55] An increasing number of pieces of legislation and programmes are being introduced as preventive measures. The 2018 Europol EU *Terrorism Situation and Trend Report* states that none of the Member States suffered any terrorist attack during the last year, but that nonetheless, "the human suffering and the threat of attacks remains high." In the same vein, the Commission considers that the EU must remain vigilant to other emerging threats or unexpected events "to anticipate and adapt to future trends and security risks."[56]

In reality, EU policy-makers seem to rely more on the general perception of the risk, often based on citizens' perception as measured by the EU Barometer, than on the real risk.[57] In fact, it is quite striking the lack of a regular centralized mechanism enabling an accurate assessment of the overall threat or specific threats the EU and its Member States are facing.[58]

The nexus between internal and external security

The European Agenda on Security adopted by the European Commission in April 2015 consolidates the interlinkage between internal and external dimensions of security within the EU. According to this new approach, since threats are no longer circumscribed by the EU borders there is a need of strengthening coherence between policies in the area of Justice and Home Affairs and those developed in the framework of the Common Security and Defence Policy. With that objective, the Commission has envisaged a number of actions that should be undertaken over the period 2015–2020.[59]

Another element of this new architecture is the appointment in 2016 of a new "Commissioner for the Security Union."[60] Fundamental rights are not mentioned among the main tasks of the commissioner, which are largely focused on supporting a swift implementation of the security road-map.[61] In spite of this, the Commission's 2017 *Comprehensive Assessment of EU Security Policy* states that "the overarching goal of EU policy in the field is to reinforce efforts to safeguard security while promoting the respect of our common values including the rule of law and respect for fundamental rights."[62]

Decreasing human rights mainstream and protection

Assessing the human rights impact stemming from the new counter-terrorism EU framework is not an easy task. This is well shown by the fact that there is no comprehensive study on the substance of the more than 239 (both legislative and non-legislative) EU binding instruments adopted so far.[63] Some conclusions have, however, been drawn by some studies that have analysed EU policies on counter-terrorism from a broader perspective. Research carried out by RAND Europe for the European Parliament found in 2018 that "the existing evidence and case studies point to a large number of infringements of fundamental rights." The study further underlines that counter-terrorism measures "can have a detrimental impact on the fundamental rights of suspects, particular groups and communities and society at large."[64] According to other reports, EU policies are not evidence-based and point to a lack of clarity in the objectives and the underlying assumptions. Moreover, these studies question the legitimacy of many of these measures due to the lack of systematic consideration of human rights as an intrinsic part of the mandate.[65]

It is abundantly clear that the vast majority of the EU's counter-terrorism legislation has not been subject to the kind of scrutiny that could be expected.[66] Research is also conclusive on the fact that consultative, legislative and review procedures that are at disposal of the EU are underutilized or applied in a manner that "ultimately ignores crucial issues of civil liberties and human rights, necessity and proportionality, accountability and democratic control."[67]

This conclusion is in sharp contrast with the Commission's positive assessment of its own performance regarding mainstreaming fundamental rights across its internal security policy. In a comprehensive assessment made in 2017 the Commission concluded that over the period considered it "had ensured that fundamental rights are fully respected in all its legislative and policy proposals," by specifying in general terms that assessments have been carried out "to ensure that instruments remain necessary, proportionate and fit for the purpose."[68]

Such a self-indulgent approach is at odds with what emerges from practice, and contributes to shed doubts on the legitimacy and rigorous assessment of the necessity and proportionality of most of the measures introduced in the name of the fight against terrorism. Furthermore, it shows a worrying trend to downplay repercussions for fundamental rights while taking for granted the "automatic human rights adequacy and respect" of all EU polices and initiatives.[69]

Legislative process

As the main promoter of EU legislation, the Commission should ensure that human rights concerns are properly taken into account in the planning and implementation of all counter-terrorism legal initiatives. The EU's commitment to "better law-making" compels it to include impact assessments, to carry out stakeholder consultations and to make ex-post evaluations of existing legislation.[70] Furthermore, all the Commission's proposals must include a memorandum explaining compatibility of the measures proposed with fundamental rights.[71]

A comprehensive analysis of the practice against this framework shows that these guidelines have not been sufficiently taken into account so far. Since 2001, only 3 out of the 88 counter-terrorism legislative proposals have been subject to public consultation, while only one-quarter of the whole set of legally binding measures have been preceded by ex-ante impact assessments.[72] We find one striking example in the 2017 Directive on Combating Terrorism, which was passed without previous impact assessment "given the urgent need to improve the EU framework to increase security."[73] Better Regulation guidelines regarding ex-post reviews or evaluations of existing measures are not usually observed either.

Both the Parliament and the Council have working parties specializing in dealing with specific policy areas. The Council does have the possibility of using a standardized, formalized procedure for checking the compatibility of a proposal with fundamental rights obligations.[74] The Parliament's role in the drafting process has been crucial to ensure alignment of proposals with human rights standards; however, it does not allow it to influence the way in which counter-terrorism policy is shaped and implemented.[75]

Human rights expertise offered by specialized bodies such as the Fundamental Rights Agency or the Data Protection Supervisor is completely undervalued.[76] EU institutions, particularly the European Parliament, only refer to them for targeted consultations or on requests for opinions on specific topics of proposals. But even in these rare cases, the implementation of any recommendations received is not ensured.

More should be done to ensure that the opinion and recommendation of these bodies contributes to the EU fundamental rights policies and legislation.[77] Their advisory competencies should go beyond monitoring developments to actually allow them to influence change. In this regard, the criticism has been made that much greater weight is given to the needs and assessments of law enforcement and security agencies with respect to other "stakeholders."[78]

Implementation

There is no doubt that the real impact on human rights of the EU legislation, and more specifically of EU Directives, relies on the way in which they are transposed at national level.[79] Taking as an example the Directive on terrorism, it is crucial that Member States palliate uncertainties related to the definition of terrorist offences and integrate explicitly the fundamental rights safeguards it contains.[80]

In this sense, it can be argued that the EU has an enhanced responsibility in avoiding the risk that human rights safeguards be diluted while being transposed into national legislations, by redoubling the emphasis on these issues. Such responsibility should materialize systematically, including ex-post review of the compatibility of national implementing laws with human rights safeguards and broader standards.

Oversight and accountability

Studies reveal that EU oversight and accountability do not seem to guarantee the systematic protection of fundamental rights in EU counter-terrorism action.[81] Arguably, such mechanisms should be reinforced and be extended to the private sector. Proposals point to a modification of the mandate of the Fundamental Rights Agency or to strengthening the role of the European Parliament's LIBE (Civil Liberties, Justice and Home Affairs Committee) Committee. Another possibility put forward is the appointment of an independent reviewer as in the UK.[82] The establishment of a specific body or creating synergies with existing bodies could also be considered.[83]

Fostering accountability mechanisms to deal with cases of major human rights violations committed by the EU Member States, particularly in the framework of the fight against terrorism, remains problematic. The investigation of the involvement of nearly half of EU Member States in the CIA renditions and secret detention programme, and difficulties in putting into practice the mechanism foreseen by Article 7 TEU (Treaty on European Union) reflect a political deadlock to progressing in that direction.[84]

Assessing the specific impact of EU counter-terrorism policy

The analysis of two particular EU counter-terrorism instruments, the targeted sanctions regime, and the new proposal for a regulation to prevent the dissemination of terrorist content on-line, illustrates some of the patterns highlighted before as well as the concrete human rights impact of such measures.

Due process guarantees

The EU has developed in the framework of the CFSP an autonomous sanctions regime to target individuals and entities.[85] Guidelines were developed in 2005 to ensure that the system was aligned with human rights requirements.[86] However, litigation before the EU Court of Justice has revealed important failures in the process through which individuals and entities are included in the EU "back list." The consistent annulment of listing decisions demonstrates that, at the time this system was set up, little attention was payed to overarching human rights principles and standards.

In fact, the sanction system has been shaped as an exceptional regime that tends to elude ordinary procedures. Targets are persons who are subject to terrorism-related investigations or proceedings in a Member State or a third country.[87] Restrictive measures (i.e. sanctions) may consist of the imposition of harsh limitations, such as travel bans and asset freezing, and are aimed at limiting the target's capability to act, or at triggering a change in his or her behaviour. Since individuals targeted are not formally accused of any offence, sanctions are treated as administrative and not criminal measures; this provides a justification for making an exception to the procedural rights guaranteed to the accused by criminal law.

The EU Court of Justice has obliged the Council to delist persons and entities and to reform procedures with the view of complying with minimum standards of due process and the right to an effective remedy. The Court has also annulled "risk-based designations" decisions, i.e. decisions based on speculative and unspecified allegations.[88] In some cases it has even awarded the applicant compensation for the reputational damage the decision of the Council caused and in view of the seriousness of the breach.[89]

All these features do not only shed doubts on the legality of designations and the fairness of the listing and de-listing procedures but also raise questions about the grounds on which this system has been built. In fact, despite the regime having been reformed, critics consider that it does not meet with accepted standards yet.[90] But despite all these remaining concerns, everything indicates that the sanctions system is progressively being consolidated as an external policy tool. The EU actually envisages its extension to new situations not necessarily related to the fight against terrorism.[91]

Freedom of expression and information

Recently, the Commission has launched a proposal for a Regulation on preventing the dissemination of terrorist content on-line.[92] The draft sets up a procedure by means of which the provider of Internet services is obliged to remove the targeted material at the request of national authorities. Again, concerns refer to the lack of a proper assessment of the degree of interference against the right to freedom of expression and information, and the necessity and proportionality of the proposed measures.[93]

The proposed rules seek to prevent Internet services from being misused to disseminate terrorism content, particularly in radicalizing and inspiring new attacks on EU soil from so-called "lone wolves." But in doing so, the draft proposal provides for too broad a definition of terrorist content that risks it being used to unduly interfere in rights and freedoms.[94] Moreover, it may also impact on the important role that the Internet must play as the means for facilitating the dissemination of information and access by the public.

There are other issues, such as the one-hour time frame given to the hosting service providers to remove content or disable access after receiving a request from a national "competent authority." Warnings have been given that such an unrealistic deadline does not allow for a meaningful assessment of the contents, and may lead to the removal of legitimate or lawful content. Another concerning feature is the broad obligation upon hosting service providers to adopt "proactive measures" to assess and delete content. It is feared that automated means and artificial intelligence software, which would not be able to distinguish accurately between users, will be used by service providers in order to comply with this obligation.

To finish, the proposal does not foresee any mechanism allowing a challenge to the removal order by the content provider or the hosting service. Furthermore, the involvement of the judiciary in the process is not guaranteed.[95] Removal orders should be based on an independent and impartial assessment and should be issued (or reviewed) by an independent judicial authority.[96] Furthermore, the competent authority should have to ensure the immediate restoration of the content, should the removal order's legality not be confirmed.

The fact that this new legislative initiative comes without prior assessment of its impact, including on fundamental freedoms, confirms the Commission's failure in this regard. Moreover, the text does not contain any general reference to the obligation to respect human rights in its implementation. Such an obligation is only a requirement for the hosting services while putting in place "proactive measures."[97] The trend to strengthen the private sector's responsibilities for human rights protection should not, however, lead to the blurring or reduction of the States' primary responsibility in this regard. On the contrary, States should provide necessary guidance to hosting service providers to ensure that their content-restricting policies are drafted in a way that pays due regard to the relevant human rights standards.[98]

Democratic and judicial oversight deficit

The lack of a genuine and open public debate, along with the deficit in the oversight of counter-terrorism measures, represents a major departure from commitments on representative and participatory democracy undertaken over the past years. Secrecy surrounding the decision-making on security matters hinders democratic debate and curbs the dynamics needed to influence the EU policy orientation through a properly informed opinion.

The crucial role played by the EU Court of Justice in some ground-breaking decisions annulling counter-terrorism measures conflicting with the EU Charter cannot obscure the fact that this body is not specifically suited to rule on human rights issues and violations. One must hope, therefore, for the swift removal of obstacles that have hitherto prevented the EU's accession to the ECHR.

Parliamentary oversight

The lack of democratic legitimacy and control of counter-terrorism policy has been criticized.[99] It is true that in the post-Lisbon context, the European Parliament has been given a more active role in the legislative process and plays a fundamental role in strengthening fundamental rights in all the policies and actions. Now, the Commission's proposals can be examined by the relevant committees, such as the Civil Liberties, Justice and Home Affairs Committee (LIBE), or the Special Committee on Terrorism established in 2017.[100] These positive developments, however, do not seem to satisfy the necessary open and democratic debate that would require the passing of far-reaching counter-terrorism measures.

The role of the Court of Justice of the European Union

The role of the Court of Justice of the EU in guaranteeing the adequacy of the counter-terrorism legislation in respect of fundamental rights and freedoms has been outstanding.[101] Reportedly, the Court has ruled on the legality of the 16 per cent of EU counter-terrorism binding legislation.[102] A great bulk of the most recent jurisprudence is related to infringements of the right to private life, and the right to the protection of personal data of individuals.[103] In the framework of the CFSP, the EU Court of Justice has been particularly requested to rule on the legality of decisions on targeted sanctions.[104] It has notably contributed to correct the deficits of the EU restrictive measures with a view to aligning them with due process standards, with a number of ground-breaking judgements.

The increasing intervention of the Court of Justice in human rights issues is to be welcomed. However, high levels of litigation may also point to failures in providing for adequate human rights standards at the legislative stage.[105] Moreover, the Court may not be well suited to provide either the legal argumentation or the hermeneutic approach to decisions on human rights violations that is required and deserved.

Prospective accession to the ECHR

Against this background, the EU accession to the ECHR, as required by the TEU, appears to be the most natural way of introducing the human rights perspective within the EU context.[106] After three years of negotiations, an agreement was reached in 2013 but in December 2015 the Court of Justice found the final text was not compatible with EU law.[107] This new setback leaves pending the possibility of having a more stringent judicial oversight of the EU compliance with its commitments in the field. Although the Commission assures us that negotiations will continue, political and legal solutions to this deadlock seem not to be clear. In the meantime, the debate on the feasibility and desirability of the EU accession has reopened.[108]

Final remarks: the cost of non-human rights

This contribution highlights a number of concerning patterns in the EU practice that, taken together, show a worrying trend at the EU decision- and policy-making levels to sacrifice human rights principles, safeguards and protections in the name of security. More specifically, it shows a lack of systematic and accurate assessment of the human rights costs and negative impacts stemming from counter-terrorism measures. A reflection on the approach taken, together with a comprehensive evaluation of the necessity, efficacy and coherence of the whole "package" is long overdue.

This situation, along with the absence of an appropriate system of checks and balances, leads to a paradoxical outcome: measures adopted in the name of security end up curtailing rights and freedoms rather than preserving them. In the long run, this state of affairs is contributing to the erosion of the fundamental values and principles that underpin the Rule of Law.

We have to recognize that the EU is a complex and vast matrix of powers and counter powers, a work in progress. However, political difficulties should not make the EU lose sight from the values and aims it underpins. These values and aims are crystal clear in the Treaties and serve to guarantee the delicate balance on which the European project was built. Therefore, more than ever, the EU should remain true to its fundamental principles and values to stay on the right track.

Notes

1 This article was elaborated in the framework of the Visiting Professorship Programme at the Law Department of the Università degli Studi di Sassari (Academic Year 2017–2018).

2 The original human rights deficit in the Security Council's action was amended by the UN General Assembly's Resolutions A/RES/60/158 and A/RES/60/288. The latter introduces as an essential element of the UN strategy a specific pillar encompassing measures to ensure respect for human rights and the rule of law as the fundamental basis of the fight against terrorism. United Nations General Assembly, Resolution 60/158, UN Doc. A/RES/60/158, of 16 December 2005 and United Nations General Assembly, Resolution 60/288, UN Doc. A/RES/60/288, of 08 September 2006.

3 The 2018 review of the UN Global Counter-Terrorism Strategy advances important institutional and structural reforms. United Nations General Assembly, *Activities of the United Nations System in Implementing the United Nations Global Counter-Terrorism Strategy*, Report of the Secretary General, UN Doc. A/72/840, of 20 April 2018.

4 On April 24, 2019, the EU and the UN signed a Framework on Counter-Terrorism to strengthen the EU–UN partnership. Cooperation is envisaged, with the aim of contributing to the balanced implementation of the UN Global Counter-Terrorism Strategy,

> particularly in relation to the respect and protection of human rights, and the promotion of the rule of law, while respecting international humanitarian law, gender- and age-sensitive approaches to countering terrorism and the prevention and countering of violent extremism, as and when conducive to terrorism.

5 The Conclusions and Plan of Action of the Extraordinary European Council Meeting of September 21, 2001 set as main objectives: enhancing police and judicial cooperation; developing international legal instruments; putting an end to the funding of terrorism; strengthening air security; and coordinating the EU's global action.

6 Before 2001, EU action essentially focused on non-religious terrorism, mostly restricted to some specific Member States. Now, its action has clearly shifted towards a new phenomenon of terrorism that often has a cross-border dimension.

7 This approach might not completely reflect the different perceptions of Western and Southern European Member States, nor the level of concern about some of the most prominent issues on the EU agenda, such as foreign fighters and the policy on prevention of radicalization, which may differ enormously from one country to the other. Study for the LIBE Committee: European Parliament, Directorate General for Internal Policies. Policy Department. Citizen's Rights and Constitutional Affair, *The European Union's Policies on Counter-Terrorism. Relevance, Coherence and Effectiveness* (Brussels, 2017) (Hereafter LIBE Report), 15 and 70–71.

8 Ibid., 15.

9 Mai'a K Davis Cross, "Counter-Terrorism in the EU's External Relations," *Journal of European Integration* 39, no. 5 (2017): 609–24. The author argues that there is a pattern in the EU to respond to certain types of crisis with more integration.

10 Under Article 4 TEU, the EU is obliged to respect the essential State functions, including the safeguarding of national security. Also, according to Article 72 TFEU, the provisions on the Area of Freedom, Security and Justice (AFSJ) do not affect the exercise of national responsibilities regarding "the maintenance of law and order and the safeguarding of internal security."

11 Article 67(3) TFEU.

12 Article 222(1) a) TFEU.

13 European Commission, *Comprehensive Assessment of EU Security Policy* (SWD(2017) 278 final) (Brussels: European Union, 2017), 13–14.

14 Articles 43 TFEU; 75 TFEU; 83 TFEU, 88 TEU and 222 TFEU.

15 The Catalogue of the EU counter-terrorism measures adopted up to 2014 can be found in: Ben Hayes and Chris Jones, "Catalogue of EU Counter-Terrorism Measures Adopted since 11 September 2001," *Statewatch*, accessed May 8, 2019, www.statewatch.org/projects/secile/index.htm.

16 Article 51(1) of the EU Charter of Fundamental Rights establishes that the Charter addresses the institutions and bodies of the Union with due regard for the principle of subsidiarity and the Member States only when they are implementing Union law. They shall therefore respect the rights, observe the principles and promote the application thereof in accordance with their respective powers.

17 In particular, soft law instruments such as the 2002 Guidelines of the Committee of Ministers of the Council of Europe on human rights and the fight against terrorism; the 2005 Guidelines on the Protection of Victims of Terrorist Acts; and the fight against violent extremism and radicalization leading to terrorism-action plan of 2005 (legislationonline.org).

18 The scope and meaning of the rights defined by the Charter are the same as the corresponding laid down in the European Convention on Human Rights. The EU can nevertheless provide a more extensive protection.

19 Article 52 of the Charter states:

> Any limitation on the exercise of the rights and freedoms recognised by this Charter must be provided for by law and respect the essence of those rights and freedoms. Subject to the principle of proportionality, limitations may be made only if they are necessary and genuinely

meet objectives of general interest recognised by the Union or the need to protect the rights and freedoms of others.

Charter of Fundamental Rights of the European Union, OJ C 326 (Brussels: European Union, 2012).

20 Article 6(2) TEU imposes on the EU the legal obligation to accede to this convention.
21 European Commission, *Operational Guidance on Taking Account of Fundamental Rights in Commission Impact Assessments*, Commission Staff Working Paper, SEC(2011) 567 final (Brussels: European Union, 2011).
22 Council of the European Union, *EU Strategic Framework and Action Plan on Human Rights and Democracy*, 11855/12 (Luxembourg: European Union, 2012), 13. A DG of Human Rights and Democracy has been set up to support these policies.
23 The reference to human rights is nevertheless absent in some key policy declarations, such as the European Council Declaration on Combating Terrorism (March 24, 2004), adopted in the aftermath of the Madrid attacks. Another remarkable gap can be found in the 2005 Strategy.
24 For example: European Council, Council Conclusions on Counter-Terrorism (Brussels: European Union, 2015), par. 2.
25 European Commission and High Representative of the European Union for Foreign Affairs and Security Policy, Joint Communication to the European Parliament and the Council: Human Rights and Democracy at the Heart of EU External Action – Towards a More Effective Approach, COM(2011) 886 final (Brussels: European Union, December 12, 2011), 13.
26 Olivier de Schutter, "A New Direction for the Fundamental Rights Policy of the EU," Reflexive Governance in the Public Interest, Working Paper Series, REFGOV-FR-33 (2010), 3 and 8.
27 The role of the CCT was first carried out by the former Dutch minister of the interior Gijs de Vries, and from 2007 by Gilles de Kerchove.
28 European Council, Declaration on Combating Terrorism (Brussels: European Union, 2004).
29 This role was reaffirmed by the European Council held in June 2014, which established strategic guidelines in the area of AFSJ. European Council, European Council 26–27 June 2014. Conclusions (EUCO 79/14) (Brussels: European Union, 2014), par. 10.
30 For the terms of the CCT's mandate: www.consilium.europa.eu/en/policies/fight-against-terrorism/counter-terrorism-coordinator/.
31 The Strategy was proposed by the UK while holding the European Rotating Presidency in the second half of 2005, and mirrors with slight semantic changes the UK's CONTEST Strategy. Rik Coolsaet, "EU Counterterrorism Strategy: Value Added or Chimera?," *International Affairs* 86, no. 4 (2010): 860.
32 Council of the European Union, *The European Union Counterterrorism Strategy* (Brussels: European Union, 2005).
33 In 2014, the strategy was completed with guidelines for the implementation by Member States and updated to address the evolving trends, such as lone-actor terrorism, foreign fighters and the use of social media by terrorists.
34 Ben Hayes and Chris Jones, "Taking Stock of EU Counter-Terrorism Policy and Review Mechanisms: Summary of Statewatch's Findings for SECILE Project," *Statewatch* (2013): 11, accessed May 5, 2019, www.statewatch.org/news/2013/dec/SECILE-sw-summary.pdf.
35 According to Article 222(4) TFUE, the European Council "shall regularly assess the threats facing the Union in order to enable the Union and its Member States to take effective action."
36 Directive (EU) 2017/541 of the European Parliament and of the Council of 15 March 2017 on Combating Terrorism and Replacing Council Framework Decision 2002/475/JHA and Amending Council Decision 2005/671/JHA, OJ L 88 (Brussels: European Union, 2017). The Directive was complemented by Directive 2017/541 on the rights of victims of terrorism.
37 Council Framework Decision 2002/475/JHA of 13 June 2002 on combating terrorism, OJ L 164 (Brussels: European Union, 2002).
38 These offences are: public provocation to commit a terrorist offence; recruitment for terrorism; and providing (but not receiving) training for terrorism. Council Framework Decision 2008/919/JHA of 28 November 2008 Amending Framework Decision 2002/475/JHA on Combating Terrorism, OJ L 330 (Brussels: European Union, 2008), 21–23.
39 In particular, in the UNSC Resolution 2178(2014) on threats to international peace and security caused by terrorism, of 24 September 2014; the Additional Protocol of 22 October 2015 to the Council of Europe's Convention on the Prevention of Terrorism; and in the revised interpretative

Note to Recommendation 5 on the criminal offence of terrorist financing of the Financial Action Task Force 2012 Recommendation on Terrorist Financing.

40 It completes the provision of the 2002 Framework Decision on assistance to victims and their families with the requirement of establishing appropriate support systems for victims of terrorism and details the types of services and information that should be publicly available.

41 Such concerns were already raised in the drafting of the 2002 Framework Decision whereby the European Commission was criticized for "using its power to ensure the enforcement of the law but not the safeguards for individuals." Cian C. Murphy, *EU Counter-Terrorism Law. Pre-emption and the Rule of Law* (Oxford: Hart, 2012), 79.

42 The preamble also says that the EU "respects the principles recognized by Article 2 TEU, respects fundamental rights and freedoms and observes the principles recognized, in particular, by the Charter," and proclaims that it

> has to be implemented in accordance with those rights and principles taking also into account the European Convention for the Protection of Human Rights and Fundamental Freedoms, the International Covenant on Civil and Political Rights, and other human rights obligations under international law. (para. 35).

43 The definition of terrorism offences provided in Article 1(1) combines two elements: 1) Objective: drawing from a list of serious offences (i.e. attacks on a person's life, kidnapping, hostage taking, seizure of aircraft, etc.); 2) Subjective: the acts will be considered as terrorist offences only if intentionally committed with a specific terrorist aim as described.

44 As has been observed, the Directive has been shaped by UNSC mandates and, in turn, is shaping national policies in ways that have essentially created a "one-size-fits-all" solution, often with limited regard to the downstream consequences of regulation. Fionnuala Ní Aoláin, "European Counter-Terrorism Approaches: A Slow and Insidious Erosion of Fundamental Rights," *Just Security*, October 17, 2018, accessed May 5, 2019, www.justsecurity.org/61086/european-counter-terrorism-approaches-slow-insidious-erosion-fundamental-rights/.

45 Human Rights Watch, "EU Counterterrorism Directive Seriously Flawed," November 30, 2016, accessed May 8, 2019, www.hrw.org/news/2016/11/30/eu-counterterrorism-directive-seriously-flawed. The definition catches domestic political protesters and resistance groups fighting oppression in overseas jurisdiction. Murphy, *EU Counter-Terrorist Law*, 80.

46 The EU Agency of Fundamental Rights has reported that programmes that aim to prevent individuals becoming radicalized tend to target Muslims and other ethnic groups and not only interfere with their human dignity but could also be counterproductive.

47 Maria Roson, "Belgium Constitutional Court Decision on the Concept of Incitement to Terrorism," *European Digital Rights*, May 30, 2018, accessed May 8, 2019, https://edri.org/belgium-constitutional-court-decision-on-the-concept-of-incitement-to-terrorism/.

48 For example, Article 9 requires it to be ensured that "preparatory acts undertaken by a person entering that Member State with the intention to commit or contribute to the commission" of a terrorist offence as defined, which potentially may extend to any act of facilitation of such travel, are made punishable. There is no definition of such "preparatory acts." Recital 12 says that they "may include planning or conspiracy, with a view to committing or contributing to a terrorist offence."

49 Liesbeth van der Heide, "Preventing Terrorism in the Courtroom – The Criminalisation of Preparatory Acts of Terrorism in the Netherlands," *Security and Human Rights* 26 (2015): 162–92.

50 Christopher Baker-Beall, *The European Union's Fight against Terrorism: Discourse, Policies, Identity* (Manchester: Manchester University Press, 2016).

51 The imperative necessity of pursuing security justifies the abandonment of normal regulatory processes, including the checks and balances intended "to encourage the integration of democratic, transparent and human rights-compliant outcomes." Ní Aoláin, "European Counter-Terrorism Approaches;" Rosario Serra Cristóbal, "Los derechos fundamentales en la encrucijada entre seguridad y libertad," *Teoría y Realidad Constitucional* 38 (2016): 487–503.

52 Murphy, *EU Counter-Terrorist Law*, 47.

53 Ní Aoláin, "European Counter-Terrorism Approaches."

54 Ibid.

55 Such an approach contrasts with studies showing that the current scale of terrorist attacks is not unprecedented: on the contrary, it is declining. Wouter van Ballegooij and Piotr Bakowski, *The Fight against*

Terrorism, European Parliament Research Service, Study (Brussels: European Parliament, 2018), 9–10.
56 European Commission, *The European Agenda on Security*, COM(2015) 185 final (Strasbourg: European Union, 2015), 2.
57 According to the Commission, 80 per cent of European citizens share the need for a strong EU response to terrorism. European Commission, *Comprehensive Assessment of EU Security Policy*, 12.
58 José María Blanco Navarro and Jéssica Cohen Villaverde, "The Future of Counter-Terrorism in Europe. The Need to Be Lost in the Correct Direction," *European Journal of Futures Research* 2, no. 50 (2014): 4.
59 "The European Union aims to ensure that people live in an area of freedom, security and justice, without internal frontiers. Europeans need to feel confident that, wherever they move within Europe, their freedom and their security are well protected, in full compliance with the Union's values, including the rule of law and fundamental rights." European Commission, *The European Agenda on Security*, 2.
60 The British Julian King was appointed by the president of the Commission through a "letter mission," describing the tasks falling under his portfolio. The new commissioner is asked to work under the guidance of the First Vice-President of the Commission, in charge of Better Regulation, Interinstitutional Relations, the Rule of Law and the Charter of Fundamental Rights and supporting the work of the Commissioner for Migration, Home Affairs and Citizenship.
61 In the letter of assignment, the president of the Commission, Jean-Claude Junker explains that the focus of the new portfolio work should be "on concrete operational measures where the action of the EU can have an impact – and where we can show that this does not compromise our commitment to fundamental rights and values." https://ec.europa.eu/commission/commissioners/2014-2019/king_en#responsibilities.
62 European Commission, *Comprehensive Assessment of EU Security Policy*, 12.
63 The EU-funded project SECILE catalogued all the EU legislative instruments adopted in the period 2001–2013, 36 per cent of which had direct effect or required transposition by the Member States. Hayes and Jones, "Taking Stock of the EU Counter-Terrorism Policy and Review Mechanisms," 2.
64 The Cost of Non-Europe in the Fight against Terrorism, Research Paper by RAND Europe. Annexed to the Study of the European Parliament, The Fight against Terrorism, by Wouter Van Ballegooij and Piotr Bakowski, EPRS Study (Brussels: European Parliament, May 2018), 8.
65 See also LIBE Report, 73–5.
66 Ben Hayes and Chris Jones, "Report on How the EU Assesses the Impact, Legitimacy and Effectiveness of its Counterterrorism Laws," *Statewatch* (2013): 7; hereafter SECILE Report.
67 Ibid, 28.
68 According to the Commission this fact is reflected, for example "in the prominence given to preventive measures aimed at promoting common European values, fostering social inclusion, enhancing mutual understanding … compliance with fundamental rights is a key characteristic of EU security police." European Commission, *Comprehensive Assessment of EU Security Policy*, 12.
69 SECILE Report, 28. For an overview in relation to failures by the Data Retention Directive to comply with the rights to privacy and personal data protection as enshrined by the EU Charter of Fundamental Rights: Gloria González Fuster, "A Security Union in Full Respect of Fundamental Rights: But How Effectively Respectful?," in *Constitutionalising the Security Union: Effectiveness, Rule of Law and Rights in Countering Terrorism and Crime*, ed. Sergio Carrera and Valsamis Mitsilegas (Brussels: CEPS, 2017).
70 Interinstitutional Agreement between the European Parliament, the Council of the European Union and the European Commission on Better-Law Making, OJ L 123 (Brussels: European Union, 2016).
71 EU Counter terrorism policy, European Economic and Social Committee Opinion, May 2011.
72 These initiatives concerned the retention of telecommunications traffic data for law enforcement purposes the establishment of the Visa Information System, and the EU framework for critical infrastructure protection.
73 European Commission, Proposal for a Directive of the European Parliament and of the Council on Combating Terrorism and Replacing Council Framework Decision 2002/475/JHA on Combating Terrorism, COM(2015) 625 final, 2015/0281(COD) (Brussels: European Union, 2015).
74 General Secretariat of the Council, Guidelines of Methodological Steps to Be Taken to Check Fundamental Rights Compatibility at the Council's Preparatory Bodies (10140/11) (Brussels: European Union, 2011).

75 Van Ballegooij and Bakowski, *The Fight against Terrorism Study*, 20.
76 Paradoxically the current trend points to the creation of a "forum" bringing together different interested stakeholders.
77 SECILE Report, 24.
78 Ibid, 28.
79 According to the UN Special Rapporteur, since 2001, more than 140 Governments have adopted or adapted counter-terrorism laws to meet new or perceived threats. Some laws have been adopted quickly and without proper consultation. Much of that legislation contains overly broad and vague definitions of terrorism, and more recently of "extremism" or "violent extremism" and "cyber-terrorism," or terms such as "prejudicial acts," "inciting social or class hatred" and "religious hatred or enmity," which are susceptible to wide discretionary and abusive interpretations and can penalize the legitimate exercise of fundamental freedoms. United Nations General Assembly, *Report of the Secretary-General: Effects of Terrorism on the Enjoyment of Human Rights*, A/73/347, 18 August 2018, par. 13; Michael O'Flaherty, "Fundamental Rights and Human Rights Discussions and Counter-Terrorism," presentation held at the European Parliament on January 8, 2018, accessed May 8, 2019, https://fra.europa.eu/en/speech/2018/fundamental-rights-and-human-rights-discussions-and-counter-terrorism.
80 The Commission's report on the implementation of the 2002 Framework Decision found that several Member States had criminalized more types of terrorist-related behaviour than it stipulated. Sofija Voronova, "Combating Terrorism," *European Parliament Research Service, Briefing. EU Legislation in Progress* (EPRS, 2017), 3.
81 Van Ballegooij and Bakowski, *The Fight against Terrorism*, 20.
82 LIBE Report, 76.
83 In 2017 there was established, within the framework of the Council of Europe, the Committee on Counter-Terrorism (CDCT). This intergovernmental body replaces the Committee of Experts on Terrorism which had been functioning since 2003. The CDCT is in charge of overseeing and coordinating the Council of Europe's counter-terrorism action. According its mandate, it

> will take into account the human rights and rule of law standards of the Council of Europe, the relevant jurisprudence of the European Court of Human Rights, as well as the work and the best practices of Member States and other international organisations and initiatives."
> *Council of Europe*, Counter-Terrorism Strategy (2018–2022) *(CM(2018)86-addfinal) (Brussels: European Union, 2018), 3.*

84 In a resolution adopted in 2016, the European Parliament expressed

> its serious concerns about the apathy shown by Member States and EU institutions with regard to recognizing the multiple fundamental rights violations and torture which took place on European soil between 2001 and 2006, investigating them and bringing those complicit and responsible to justice.
> *Since 2006, The Civil Liberties, Justice and Home Affairs Committee (LIBE) has investigated the involvement of nearly half of EU Member States in the renditions and secret detention programme developed by the CIA.*

85 Member States opted to implement UNSC Resolution 1373(2001) through the EU though some Member States have national systems of designation. Regulations were then used to give legal effect to sanctions within the EU legal order.
86 Council of the European Union, Guidelines on Implementation and Evaluation of Restrictive Measures (Sanctions) in the Framework of the EU Common Foreign and Security Policy (6749/05, PESC 159, FIN 80) (Brussels: European Union, 2005).
87 While the decision whether to add the person to the EU's sanctions list is made by the Council, the primary responsibility for the measures, including its factual basis, resides at the State level.
88 For example: Judgment of the General Court (First Chamber), 25 November 2014, *Safa Nicu Sepahan Co.* v. *Council of the European Union*, 25 November 2014, ECLI:EU:T:2014:986, par.68ff.
89 This is a ground-breaking case since the Court has generally ruled that the annulment of unlawful restrictive measures constitutes a form of reparation for non-material damage suffered. Aleksi Pursiainen, "Targeted EU Sanctions and Fundamental Rights," SOLIDPLAN Consulting, accessed May 9, 2019, https://um.fi/documents/35732/48132/eu_targeted_sanctions_and_fundamental_rights/14ce3228-19c3-a1ca-e66f-192cad8be8de?t=1525645980751.

90 Carmen Cristina Cîrlig, "Counter-Terrorist sanctions regimes. Legal Framework and Challenges at UN and EU levels," *EPRS Briefing* (October 2016).

91 The High Representative has recently announced that a targeted assessment is ongoing of how a European Union horizontal human rights sanctions regime is to bring added value in our collective efforts to further realize human rights and prevent gross violations or abuses of human rights. Speech on behalf of HR/VP Mogherini at the plenary session of the European Parliament on a European human rights violations sanctions regime, Bruxelles, March 13, 2019. On the possible evolution of this regime see: Francesco Giumelli, "How EU Sanctions Work: A New Narrative," EU ISS Chaillot Papers 129 (EU ISS, 2013).

92 European Commission, Proposal for a Regulation on Preventing the Dissemination of Terrorist Content Online, COM(2018) 640 final (Brussels: European Union, 2018). The legislation is being considered by the responsible committee at the European Parliament and, therefore, the text may still be changed.

93 Office of the High Commissioner for Human Rights, "UN Human Rights Experts Concerned about EU's Online Counter-terrorism Proposal," OHCHR website, December 12, 2018, accessed May 8, 2019, www.ohchr.org/en/NewsEvents/Pages/DisplayNews.aspx?NewsID=24013&LangID=E; Fundamental Rights Agency, *Proposal for a Regulation on Preventing the Dissemination of Terrorist Content Online and Its Fundamental Rights*, FRA Opinion-2/2019 (Vienna: Fundamental Rights Agency, 2019).

94 Terrorist content is defined in Article 2.5 of the draft as any information: a) inciting or advocating, including by glorifying, the commission of terrorist offences, thereby causing a danger that such acts be committed; b) encouraging the contribution of terrorist offences; c) promoting the activities of a terrorist group, in particular by encouraging the participation in or support to a terrorist group within the meaning of Article 2.3 of the 2017 Directive on Terrorism. This definition goes beyond the scope of the terrorist offences set out in the 2017 Directive.

95 It is the responsibility of the service provider to establish "effective and accessible mechanisms allowing affected content providers to submit a complaint to request reinstatement of the content" (art. 10).

96 Fundamental Rights Agency, FRA Opinion, 25. There should be prior judicial authorization of restrictive measures as well as judicial review, and the principle of proportionality must be strictly respected in this endeavour.

97 The draft considers that measures shall be effective and proportionate, "taking into account the risk and level of exposure to terrorist contents, the fundamental rights of the users, and the fundamental importance of the freedom of expression and information in an open and democratic society." The revised text proposed by the Council in part has amended this lack by including under Article 1 (Subject matter and scope) the following subparagraph: "This Regulation shall not have the effect of modifying the obligation to respect fundamental rights and fundamental legal principles as enshrined in Article 6 of the Treaty on the European Union." Interinstitutional File: 2018/0331(COD), 7.12.2018.

98 Fundamental Right Agency, FRA Opinion, 11.

99 SECILE Report, 26–7.

100 The LIBE has been the one in charge of monitoring the human rights impact of EU policies, and it has commanded several reports on the impact of this measures that can be found on: www.europarl.europa.eu/committees/en/terr/home.html.

101 It has competence to examine the compatibility with fundamental rights of both, the EU legislation and measures taken by Member States in application or to comply with EU law. Many decisions in this field are "preliminary rulings" on the interpretation and substance of these laws following a request from national courts.

102 Information provided by the SECILE project. This percentage corresponds to the period 2001–2013.

103 Examples include the invalidation of the Data Retention Directive (Directive 2006/24/EC) in 2014, and the negative opinion on the proposed EU–Canada Agreement on the transfer and processing of passenger name records (PNR) delivered in 2017. Opinion 1/15 of the Court (Grand Chamber) 26 July 2017; Judgment of the Court (Grand Chamber), 8 April 2014, *Digital Rights Ireland Ltd* v. *Minister for Communications, Marine and Natural Resources and Others and Kärntner Landesregierung and Others*.

104 Despite the EU's activities under CFSP being generally beyond the competence of its review, an exception was made in relation to the legality of decisions providing for restrictive measures against natural or legal

persons (see art. 29 TEU). By 2014, there were nearly 200 relevant judgements by the General Court and the Court of First Instance, and many other cases are ongoing. Trend in appeals made by the General Court to the Court of Justice seems to have changed. Before 2015, 10 judgements out of 17 were in favour of the targeted person, while after only 1 out of 15.

105 However, procedural limitations in legal access to the Court should be taken into account.

106 Article 6.2 TEU. The annexed Protocol 8 requires that the EU's accession agreement to the ECHR must "make provision for preserving the specific characteristics of the EU and its legal system."

107 Opinion of the Court (Full Court) of 18 December 2014. Opinion pursuant to Article 218(11) TFEU, Compatibility of the draft agreement with the EU and FEU Treaties. Case Opinion 2/13.

108 Rafal Manko, "EU accession to the European Convention of Human Rights (ECHR)," *EPRS Briefing*, (2017).

Bibliography

Baker-Beall, Christopher. *The European Union's Fight against Terrorism: Discourse, Policies, Identity*. Manchester: Manchester University Press, 2016.

Blanco Navarro, José María, and Jéssica Cohen Villaverde. "The Future of Counter-Terrorism in Europe. The Need to Be Lost in the Correct Direction." *European Journal of Futures Research* 2, no. 50 (2014): 2–12.

Cîrlig, Carmen Cristina. "Counter-Terrorist Sanctions Regimes. Legal Framework and Challenges at UN and EU Levels." *EPRS Briefing* (October 2016): 1–12.

Coolsaet, Rik. "EU Counterterrorism Strategy: Value Added or Chimera?" *International Affairs* 86, no. 4 (2010): 857–73.

Council of Europe. *Counter-Terrorism Strategy (2018–2022)*. CM(2018)86-addfinal. Brussels: European Union, 2018.

Council of the European Union. Council Framework Decision 2002/475/JHA of 13 June 2002 on Combatting Terrorism. *Official Journal of the European Union* L 164. Brussels: European Union, 2002.

Council of the European Union. Council Framework Decision 2008/919/JHA of 28 November 2008 Amending Framework Decision 2002/475/JHA on Combating Terrorism. *Official Journal of the European Union* L 330. Brussels: European Union, 2008.

Council of the European Union. *The European Union Counterterrorism Strategy*. Brussels: European Union, 2005.

Council of the European Union. *EU Strategic Framework and Action Plan on Human Rights and Democracy* (11855/12). Luxembourg: European Union, 2012.

Council of the European Union. Guidelines on Implementation and Evaluation of Restrictive Measures (Sanctions) in the Framework of the EU Common Foreign and Security Policy (6749/05, PESC 159, FIN 80). Brussels: European Union, 2005.

Council of the European Union. *Revised EU Strategy for Combating Radicalisation and Recruitment to Terrorism* (9956/14). Brussels: European Union, 2014.

Cross, Mai'a K. Davis. "Counter-Terrorism in the EU's External Relations." *Journal of European Integration* 39, no. 5 (2017): 609–24.

De Schutter, Olivier. "A New Direction for the Fundamental Rights Policy of the EU." Reflexive Governance in the Public Interest, Working Paper Series, REFGOV-FR-33. 2010.

Eckes, Christina. "EU Restrictive Measures against Natural and Legal Persons: From Counterterrorist to Third Country Sanctions." *Common Market Law Review* 51, no. 3 (2014): 869–906.

"EU Counterterrorism Directive Seriously Flawed." Human Rights Watch, November 30, 2016. Accessed May 8, 2019. www.hrw.org/news/2016/11/30/eu-counterterrorism-directive-seriously-flawed.

European Commission. *Comprehensive Assessment of EU Security Policy*. Commission Staff Working Document. SWD(2017) 278 final. Brussels: European Union, July 26, 2017.

European Commission. *The European Agenda on Security*. COM(2015) 185 final. Strasbourg: European Union, 2015.

European Commission. *Operational Guidance on Taking Account of Fundamental Rights in Commission Impact Assessments*. Commission Staff Working Paper SEC(2011) 567 final. Brussels: European Union, 2011.

European Commission. Proposal for a Directive of the European Parliament and of the Council on Combating Terrorism and Replacing Council Framework Decision 2002/475/JHA on Combating Terrorism. COM(2015) 625 final, 2015/0281(COD). Brussels: European Union, 2015.

European Commission. Proposal for a Regulation on Preventing the Dissemination of Terrorist Content Online. COM(2018) 640 final. Brussels: European Union, 2018.
European Commission and High Representative of the European Union for Foreign Affairs and Security Policy. Joint Communication to the European Parliament and the Council: Human Rights and Democracy at the Heart of EU External Action – Towards a More Effective Approach. COM(2011) 886 final. Brussels: European Union, December, 12, 2011.
European Council. Council Conclusions on Counter-Terrorism. Brussels: European Union, 2015.
European Council. Declaration on Combating Terrorism. Brussels: European Union, 2004.
European Council. European Council 26–27 June 2014. Conclusions (EUCO 79/14). Brussels: European Union, 2014.
European Parliament. *The European Union's Policies on Counter-Terrorism. Relevance, Coherence and Effectiveness*. Brussels: European Union, 2017.
European Parliament and Council of the European Union. Directive (EU) 2017/541 of the European Parliament and of the Council of 15 March 2017 on Combating Terrorism and Replacing Council Framework Decision 2002/475/JHA and Amending Council Decision 2005/671/JHA, *Official Journal of the European Union* L 88. Brussels: European Union, March 3, 2017.
European Union. Charter of Fundamental Rights of the European Union. *Official Journal of the European Union*, C 326. Brussels: European Union, October 10, 2012.
European Union. Interinstitutional Agreement between the European Parliament, the Council of the European Union and the European Commission on Better-Law Making. *Official Journal of the European Union* L 123. Brussels: European Union, May 12, 2016.
Fundamental Rights Agency. *Proposal for a Regulation on Preventing the Dissemination of Terrorist Content Online and Its Fundamental Rights*. FRA Opinion-2/2019. Vienna: Fundamental Rights Agency, 2019.
General Secretariat of the Council. Guidelines of Methodological Steps to Be Taken to Check Fundamental Rights Compatibility at the Council's Preparatory Bodies. 10140/11. Brussels: European Union, 2011.
Giumelli, Francesco. "How EU Sanctions Work: a New Narrative." EU ISS Chaillot Papers 129 (EU ISS, 2013): 5–46.
González Fuster, Gloria. "A Security Union in Full Respect of Fundamental Rights: But how Effectively Respectful?" In *Constitutionalising the Security Union: Effectiveness, Rule of Law and Rights in Countering Terrorism and Crime*, edited by Sergio Carrera and Valsamis Mitsilegas, 87–92. Brussels: CEPS, 2017.
Hayes, Ben, and Chris Jones. "Catalogue of EU Counter-Terrorism Measures Adopted since 11 September 2001." *Statewatch*. Accessed May 8, 2019. www.statewatch.org/projects/secile/index.htm.
Hayes, Ben, and Chris Jones. "Report on How the EU Assesses the Impact, Legitimacy and Effectiveness of its Counterterrorism Laws." *Statewatch* (2013).
Hayes, Ben, and Chris Jones. "Taking Stock of EU Counter-Terrorism Policy and Review Mechanisms: Summary of Statewatch's Findings for SECILE Project." *Statewatch* (2013).
Manko, Rafal. "EU Accession to the European Convention of Human Rights." *EPRS Briefing* (2017).
Murphy, Cian C. *EU Counter-Terrorism Law. Pre-emption and the Rule of Law*. Oxford: Hart, 2012.
Ní Aoláin, Fionnuala. "European Counter-Terrorism Approaches: A Slow and Insidious Erosion of Fundamental Rights." *Just Security*, October 17, 2018.
Office of the High Commissioner for Human Rights. "UN Human Rights Experts Concerned about EU's Online Counter-Terrorism Proposal," OHCHR website, December 12, 2018. Accessed May 8, 2019. www.ohchr.org/en/NewsEvents/Pages/DisplayNews.aspx?NewsID=24013&LangID=E.
O'Flaherty, Michael. "Fundamental Rights and Human Rights Discussions and Counter-Terrorism." Presentation held at the European Parliament on January 8, 2018. Accessed May 8, 2019. https://fra.europa.eu/en/speech/2018/fundamental-rights-and-human-rights-discussions-and-counter-terrorism.
Pursiainen, Aleksi. "Targeted EU Sanctions and Fundamental Rights." SOLIDPLAN Consulting. Accessed May 9, 2019. https://um.fi/documents/35732/48132/eu_targeted_sanctions_and_fundamental_rights/14ce3228-19c3-a1ca-e66f-192cad8be8de?t=1525645980751.
Roson, Maria. "Belgium Constitutional Court Decision on the Concept of Incitement to Terrorism." *European Digital Rights*, May 30, 2018. Accessed May 9, 2019. https://edri.org/belgium-constitutional-court-decision-on-the-concept-of-incitement-to-terrorism/.
Serra Cristóbal, Rosario. "Los derechos fundamentales en la encrucijada entre seguridad y libertad." *Teoría y Realidad Constitucional* 38 (2016): 487–503.

United Nations General Assembly. *Activities of the United Nations System in Implementing the United Nations Global Counter-Terrorism Strategy*, Report of the Secretary-General. UN Doc. A/72/840, of 20 April 2018.
United Nations General Assembly. *Effects of Terrorism on the Enjoyment of Human Rights. Report of the Secretary General.* UN Doc. A/73/347, of 18 August 2018.
United Nations General Assembly. Resolution 60/158. UN Doc. A/RES/60/158, of 16 December 2005.
United Nations General Assembly. Resolution 60/288. UN Doc. A/RES/60/288, of 08 September 2006.
Van Ballegooij, Wouter, and Piotr Bakowski. *The Fight against Terrorism*. European Parliament Research Service Study (Brussels: European Parliament, 2018): 2–39.
Van Der Heide, Liesbeth. "Preventing Terrorism in the Courtroom – The Criminalisation of Preparatory Acts of Terrorism in the Netherlands." *Security and Human Rights* 26 (2015): 162–92.
Voronova, Sofija. "Combating Terrorism." European Parliament Research Service, Briefing. EU Legislation in Progress (EPRS, 2017): 1–12.

19

MIGRANT AND REFUGEE CHILDREN PROTECTION AGAINST TRAFFICKING AND EXPLOITATION

Assessing EU response from an international human rights law perspective

Carmen Pérez González

In memorial to Prof. Fernando M. Mariño Menéndez

> "As I walked the deck and looked round upon my fellow-passengers, thus curiously assorted from all northern Europe, I began for the first time to understand the nature of emigration. Day by day throughout the passage, and thenceforward across all the States, and on to the shores of the Pacific, this knowledge grew more clear and melancholy. Emigration, from a word of the most cheerful import, came to sound most dismally in my ear. There is nothing more agreeable to picture and nothing more pathetic to behold."
>
> *(Robert L. Stevenson,* The Amateur Emigrant*)*

Introductory remarks and conceptual considerations on the vulnerability of children in the context of international migration

The recent but sustained exodus provoked by the armed conflict in Syria has brutally shown the reality faced by those minors forced to flee from situations that put their most elemental rights at risk. In situations of internal or international displacement, minors are considered particularly vulnerable.[1] As assumed in this work, vulnerability is a condition associated with both individuals and groups that qualifies them in their relations with institutionalized power structures and it is particularly significant regarding minors on the move.[2] Minority, absence of knowledge, lack of own economic resources and social power, migratory condition, are all reasons for competitive disadvantage. Moreover, minors are in this situation not only in their relationship with power structures represented by State authorities, but also regarding organized crime groups engaged in migrant smuggling and human trafficking.

International Human Rights Law (IHRL) has assumed that because of their condition of vulnerability[3] migrants deserve reinforced protection measures.[4] Trafficking and exploitation are two of the most severe threats they face. The current work will analyse the nature and scope of EU Member States' obligations *vis a vis* this vulnerable group. These abuses are suffered particularly by those migrant children that are separated from their families, and could include their disappearance.[5] According to the figures managed by Europol,[6] 85,482 of the non-accompanied asylum seekers that entered the EU in 2015 were children. A significant proportion of those minors, 10,000 according to Europol, would have disappeared.[7] In other words, non-accompanied migrant and refugee children are likely to be victims of aggressions, violence, violations of their rights and exploitation.

The Committee on the Rights of the Child provides definitions.[8] According to its General Comment No. 6 (2005), "unaccompanied children" (also called unaccompanied minors) are children, as defined in article 1 of the Convention on the Rights of the Child (CRC),[9] who have been separated from both parents and other relatives and are not being cared for by an adult who, by law or custom, is responsible for doing so.[10] This definition would cover: (i) minors who are left unaccompanied after they have entered the territory of destination countries, (ii) those who are left unaccompanied during their journey, and (iii) those who must flee alone. Besides that, gender analysis must also be considered. If we focus on girls and female adolescents, we find a complex and multidimensional situation of vulnerability. For the purpose of this work, I will consider article 3 of the Trafficking in Persons Protocol for the definition of child trafficking.[11] Child exploitation can be understood as using the child for financial, sexual or any other purposes,[12] which may include irregular adoption.[13]

In this context, the aim of this work is twofold. First, it will examine EU law and policy normative framework on the protection of migrant and refugee children[14] against trafficking and exploitation. International obligations imposed upon the EU and its Member States by IHRL will be considered for the analysis.[15] Second, it will reflect on the weaknesses of that framework and propose adequate reforms in the light of the upcoming Global Compacts for Safe, Orderly and Regular Migration[16] and the principle of best interest of the child. In the third section, I will focus on the required assistance during the child's stay in the country of destination and on the specificities of their qualification for international protection, considering the scope of the obligation of *non-refoulement*[17] in this context. Finally, some conclusions will be drawn.

IHRL approach to EU law and policy normative framework on protection of migrant and refugee children against trafficking and exploitation

A general principle of International Law recognizes the capacity of States for dealing with migratory influxes and deciding on the requirements migrants should meet to legally stay in their territories. That principle has been recognized by the United Nations General Assembly (UNGA),[18] the International Court of Justice (ICJ),[19] and the European Court of Human Rights (ECtHR).[20] But while International Law recognizes States' "sovereign right to enact and implement migratory and border security measures,"[21] it also determines that when exercising this right, they have to "comply with their obligations under International Law, including international Human Rights Law, in order to ensure full respect for the human rights of migrants."[22] This implies that EU and national measures and policies aiming to control irregular migration should respect migrants' rights to seek international protection and not to be returned to places where they could face torture or other serious violations of their fundamental rights, including the risk of facing human trafficking.

With respect to EU migration policy, irregular migration has been conceived of as a "security challenge." Because of this, EU legislation in this field has mainly focused on adopting effective deterrence and sanction measures, leaving aside the incorporation of common rules aiming to protect those migrants who illegally try to enter or stay in the territory of Member States. This has had pernicious effects regarding the protection of their fundamental rights. Of course, it can be affirmed that other legislative elements of EU migration policy try to incorporate a different approach. The protection of certain groups of migrants, who could be considered in a particularly vulnerable situation, has driven the imposition of reinforced obligations upon States. Victims of trafficking in human beings and non-accompanied migrant children constitute two exceptional categories of irregular migrants, whose rights have been particularly addressed in EU legislation. Nevertheless, the fundamental rights dimension of its laws and policies is not at the heart of their objectives. A general environment of control, prevention and criminalization prevails in this field. Scholars and NGOs often underline the need for including a mechanism defining the way EU Member States will identify members of these groups and their needs in the framework of the EU common policies. The measures of external deterrence that the EU and its Member States have been applying in the context of FRONTEX operations to prevent third-country nationals from leaving their countries of origin are considered here to be in breach of the obligation of *non-refoulement*.

As to unaccompanied migrant children, the European Commission Action Plan on Unaccompanied Minors (2010–2014),[23] despite maintaining the central objective of helping Member States devise measures to facilitate the return of the high number of unaccompanied minors who do not require international protection, underlined that "the solution cannot be limited to return because the issue is much more complex and multidimensional and there are clear boundaries to the Member States' freedom of action when dealing with unaccompanied minors." It also verifies that EU legislation and policies do not address the situation of minors who cannot be returned, leaving the decision on granting residence permits to the national legislation. According to the European Commission, in cases where return is not possible or integration in the country of residence is considered in the best interest of the child, a legal status should be granted entitling unaccompanied minors to at least the same rights and protection as beforehand, and suitable accommodation for them should be found. In addition, the minors should be supported in their path toward successful integration in the host society.

I will outline now the content of these obligations regarding prevention, assistance and non-devolution to the country of origin. We cannot overlook the fact that an important part of the various violations of human rights suffered by migrant children is caused by non-state actors, mainly smuggling and trafficking networks,[24] but the ultimate liability of the criminals does not exclude State responsibility according to standards of due diligence.

The State obligation of protecting individuals present on its territory against human rights violations committed by other individuals has been traditionally invoked in regard to the security of aliens. Those violations were not directly attributed to the State, but it could be understood that the State is responsible for a different unlawful act: not having prevented or, if appropriate, punished those violations.[25] Contemporary IHRL imposes upon States the obligation to protect all individuals within their jurisdiction against human rights violations caused by other individuals. A due diligence principle has been gaining centrality in this regard and has been both incorporated in different international human rights treaties[26] and invoked by international human rights courts and other supervisory human rights bodies.[27] Thus, due diligence has been gradually configured as an obligation of conduct requiring "States to take reasonable measures that have real prospect of altering the outcome or mitigating the harm."[28] As formulated by international human rights bodies, due diligence should turn into effective measures, useful or able to reach the effects they seek to ensure.[29] As we will see, this is particularly important in relation to the adoption of prevention measures.

Prevention (including identification and safe access to international protection)

Slavery and forced labour, but not explicitly trafficking in human beings, are prohibited under the European Convention on Human Rights (ECHR).[30] According to its article 4, "no one shall be held in slavery of servitude" nor "shall be required to perform forced or compulsory labour." The article hinges on the principle of equal treatment between nationals and non-nationals in respect of these rights and covers various forms of abuse: slavery, servitude, forced labour and compulsory labour. Despite the absence of an express reference to trafficking, several decisions of the ECtHR[31] have progressively deduced concrete obligations in this regard.[32] Less severe forms of exploitation are not explicitly prohibited by the ECHR,[33] but they could be, at least in some cases, undeniably covered by article 3 of the Convention.

States are obliged to establish a legislative and administrative framework that is adequate to ensure practical and effective protection of the rights of victims and potential victims,[34] to take operational measures for the protection of victims, and to investigate and prosecute human trafficking and other phenomena covered by article 4 of the Convention.[35]

Applicants' vulnerability has been considered by the Court in order to qualify a particular situation as slavery.[36] In the *Siliadin* v. *France* case, the Court found that the applicant was held in servitude because, in addition to the fact that she was required to perform forced labour, she was a minor with no resources, *vulnerable* and isolated with no means of living elsewhere than the place where she worked.[37] In the *Chowdury case*, the Court considered that the fact the applicants were undocumented workers exacerbated their vulnerability.[38] The Court positively insisted on the vulnerability caused by a precarious administrative situation, exacerbated by their lack of financial means and the risk of detention or deportation.[39] Regarding the scope of the obligations imposed by article 4, the ECtHR underlined in the *Rantsev case* that

> the spectrum of safeguards set out in national legislation must be adequate to ensure the practical and effective protection of the rights of victims or potential victims of trafficking. Accordingly, in addition to criminal law measures to punish traffickers, Article 4 requires member States to put in place adequate measures regulating businesses often used as a cover for human trafficking. Furthermore, a State's immigration rules must address relevant concerns relating to encouragement, facilitation or tolerance of trafficking.[40]

Nevertheless, regarding protection against forced labour and trafficking for forced labour, some aspects need further clarification. On one hand, the ECtHR does not clearly distinguish between trafficking for forced labour and forced labour itself.[41] According to ECtHR case law, forced and compulsory labour refers to: "all work or service which is exacted from any person under the menace of any penalty and for which the said person has not offered himself voluntarily."[42] On the other hand, some scholars have denounced the way in which the broad approach to positive obligations initially imposed by the ECtHR in the *Rantsev case* has gradually been eroded, questioning the human rights–based approach to trafficking driven by IHRL.

Of course, providing migrants and refugee children (and adults) with safer legal access to protection would certainly result in the reduction of their vulnerability. This could take the shape of legal measures aimed at facilitating legal migration – job-seekers' visas, humanitarian corridors, adequate resettlement programmes, security of residence for victims of trafficking in human beings and non-accompanied minors, etc. – that would apply to individuals coming from third countries. In this regard, it must be underlined that the European Court of Justice (ECJ) has affirmed that Member States are not required, under EU law, to grant a humanitarian visa to people who wish to enter their territory with a view to applying for asylum, but they remain free to do so on the basis of their national law.[43]

Assistance

Article 19 of the CRC constitutes the starting point for our analysis. According to it,

> States Parties shall take all appropriate legislative, administrative, social and educational measures to protect the child from all forms of physical or mental violence, injury or abuse, neglect or negligent treatment, maltreatment or exploitation, including sexual abuse, while in the care of parent(s), legal guardian(s) or any other person who has the care of the child.

The second paragraph of the article adds that

> (s)uch protective measures should, as appropriate, include effective procedures for the establishment of social programmes to provide necessary support for the child and for those who have the care of the child, as well as for other forms of prevention and for identification, reporting, referral, investigation, treatment and follow-up of instances of child maltreatment described heretofore, and, as appropriate, for judicial involvement.

In 2011, the Committee on the Rights of the Child adopted its General Comment No. 13 on "The right of the child to freedom from all forms of violence,"[44] which makes clear that article 19 is applicable also to "children without a primary or proxy caregiver or another person who is entrusted with the protection and well-being of the child such as, for instance, ... children of migrating parents or unaccompanied children outside their country of origin."[45]

A positive obligation imposed upon States parties to the CRC of setting up whatever measures are within reach to protect children, including migrant children – both accompanied and non-accompanied, against any form of violence can be drawn from this statement. This should include acts of prosecution described in the Geneva Convention for the serious damages described by article 15 of Directive 2011/95.[46]

Search for durable solutions considering the best interest of the child, non-discrimination and non-refoulement

Article 3 of the CRC contains the basic guiding principle underlining the text: all rights and obligations contained therein are to be fulfilled in the best interests of the child. The principle also dominates regional frameworks regarding protection of the human rights of children.[47] Moreover, a reference must be made to the right of the child to be heard as stipulated in articles 12 of the CRC and 24 (1) of the EU Charter of Fundamental Rights.[48] Article 12 of the CRC guarantees both children's right to express their views freely in all matters affecting them and public authorities' obligation to give due weight to those views considering the child's age and maturity. The ECJ has affirmed that when the child is to be heard, article 24 of the Charter requires taking

> all measures which are appropriate to the arrangement of such a hearing, having regard to the child's best interests and the circumstances of each individual case, in order to

ensure the effectiveness of those provisions, and to offer to the child a genuine and effective opportunity to express his or her views.[49]

A final procedural aspect that should be mentioned is the one related to the length of the proceedings involving children. The ECtHR has determined, regarding article 6 of the ECHR, that "the reasonableness of the length of proceedings is to be determined with reference to the criteria laid down in the Court's case-law, in particular the complexity of the case" and that when a child is involved, authorities should "act with exceptional diligence in ensuring progress of the proceedings."[50]

Family reunion

International instruments aiming to promote and protect children's rights tend to identify family reunion of those minors who are separated from their families with their best interest.[51] The Committee on the Rights of the Child has affirmed that "following a rights-based approach, the search for a durable solution commences with analysing the possibility of family reunification."[52] Nevertheless, this solution would not be correct in every case. It will be inadvisable when the minor could face the risk of mistreatment, abuse or neglect within his/her family.[53] Articles 9 and 10 of the CRC must be considered when it comes to taking a decision regarding family reunion in the territory of the country of destination. According to article 10 (1), "applications by a child or his or her parents to enter or leave a State party for the purpose of family reunification shall be dealt with by States parties in a positive, humane and expeditious manner." Besides that, States parties must ensure that the submission of such a request shall entail no adverse consequences for the applicants and for the members of their family.

Family reunion is also a primary consideration within EU law. Thus, the Dublin III Regulation[54] requests Member States to give primary consideration to respect for family life and unaccompanied minors' best interests when applying the regulation.[55] Also, according to article 8 (1) (2), when an unaccompanied child applies for asylum in one Member State, he/she shall have his/her application examined in the Member State where a parent, responsible adult, sibling, adult aunt, uncle, or grandparent is legally present, provided this is in his/her 'best interest.' Finally, article 17 (1) and (2) allows Member States to assume responsibility for examining an application and requesting a transfer to bring together any family relations, based on humanitarian grounds. Family tracing as a key element of the principle of ensuring family unity was also set up as a priority by the European Commission Action Plan on Unaccompanied Minors.[56]

Tutelage by the country of origin

A second possibility can't be dismissed. Returning the minor to his/her country of origin following "advance secure and concrete arrangements of care and custodial responsibilities upon" it has been considered by the Committee on the Rights of the Child[57] if certain conditions are met.[58]

However, the principle of *non-refoulement* should also be considered. For this reason, when the child seeks international protection, his/her return to the country of origin shall be not an option if the sending State becomes aware of a risk that it would result in the breach of the minor's human rights.

Resettlement/relocation in a different country

The possibility of resettling the minor to a third country should be considered as a durable solution only as a last resort measure. Following the Committee on the Rights of the Child's recommendations in this regard,

> the decision to resettle an unaccompanied or separated child must be based on an updated, comprehensive and thorough best-interests assessment, taking into account, in particular, ongoing international and other protection needs. Resettlement is particularly called for if such is the only means to effectively and sustainably protect a child against *refoulement* or against persecution or other serious human rights violations in the country of stay. Resettlement is also in the best interests of the unaccompanied or separated child if it serves family reunification in the resettlement country.[59]

In the EU framework, the Communication from the Commission to the European Parliament and the Council on "The protection of children in migration"[60] affirms that

> unaccompanied or separated children and families may be eligible for urgent resettlement through Member States' national resettlement programmes or under the ongoing European resettlement schemes established by the Conclusions on resettlement of 20 July 2015 and the EU-Turkey Statement of 18 March 2016.[61]

As is well known, in July 2015 the Representatives of the Governments of the Member States met within the Council and adopted their Conclusions on resettling through multilateral and national schemes 20,000 persons in clear need of international protection. Following these Conclusions, a temporary emergency relocation scheme was established in different Council Decisions.[62] Although Member States committed to relocate up to 160,000 people from Italy and Greece (and if relevant from other Member States) by September 2017 and to consider the best interests of the child as a primary consideration, the relocation rate is clearly unsatisfactory.[63] In this sense, it is important to highlight that the Spanish Supreme Court has recently condemned the Spanish Government for its partial failure to meet its relocation target.[64]

Besides that, we cannot forget that the EU–Turkey Statement has provoked unfavourable reactions. Leaving aside the formal questions related to its legal nature, substantive doubts arise when it comes to analyse its compatibility with IHRL and the principle of *non-refoulement*.[65] Any decision on return should be adopted after a case-by-case assessment and following a procedure suitable for guaranteeing their right to protection and non-discrimination. The European Commission and States tend to assume resettlement as an appropriate durable solution, especially in cases where it means the minor will join his/her family in a third country, although article 10(1) of the CRC could be understood as urging States parties to boost reunification in their territories.[66]

Local integration: granting asylum or subsidiary protection

In general, a right to enjoy asylum has not been incorporated into national legislations. According to article 18 of the Charter of Fundamental Rights of the European Union, a

> right to asylum shall be guaranteed with due respect for the rules of the Geneva Convention of 28 July 1951 and the Protocol of 31 January 1967 relating to the status of refugees and in accordance with the Treaty establishing the European Community.

In addition, subsidiary protection could be provided given certain circumstances. In any case, primary consideration should be given to the minority status of migrant children. This question is connected to the need of defining the most favourable status for him/her.

Since the Geneva Convention does not contain a specific mention of minority when considering applicants for international protection, we must refer to the CRC, in order to determine which rights should be guaranteed to children within the State jurisdiction who are potential victims of trafficking and exploitation and apply for international protection. Article 22 of the CRC should also be considered.[67] On the other hand, we must take into account that both universal and European international treaties on anti-trafficking have been adopted.[68] The joint reading of these international instruments can define the limits imposed upon States parties when regulating this question. Besides, in the case of European States, ECtHR case law should be also considered. Both international and European human rights standards shape and should condition the response of the EU and its Member States.

International Law imposes particularly reinforced obligations of assistance and protection when the State is dealing with migrant children who potentially face a situation of trafficking or exploitation. Those obligations should define a combined statute built on the base of the *pro homine* principle. This statute should provide for the most favourable solution for those children and avoid the overlapping dimensions (they are migrants, but they are also minors) resulting in the dilution of their rights. This means that the above-mentioned faculty of State authorities for deciding on the entry, stay and exit of aliens, and on the content of the due assistance to them, is seriously reduced when the individual (alien) facing trafficking or exploitation is a minor. This hybrid or mixed statute of rights should not be just the addition of two set of rules: those applying to migrants in pursuit of international protection, on the one hand, and those applicable to minors, on the other. It should be the result of the development of a specific statute combining the most favourable elements coming from both.

As has been said, children experience many more difficulties than adults when they are in search of international protection.[69] When dealing with their applications, due protection of their rights should force States to consider, not only national or supranational rules[70] regarding proceedings for granting protection, but also IHRL obligations. The principle of non-discrimination becomes crucial in this regard.[71] This principle is enshrined in article 2 of the CRC. As is stated in the Joint General Comment No. 3 (2017) of the Committee on the protection of the Rights of All Migrants Workers and No. 22 (2017) of the Committee on the Rights of the Child on the general principles regarding the human rights of children in the context of international migration, this principle

> obliges States parties to respect and ensure the rights set forth in the Convention to all children, whether they are considered, inter alia, migrants in regular or irregular situations, asylum seekers, refugees, stateless and/or victims of trafficking, including in situations of return or deportation to the country of origin, irrespective of the child's or the parents' or legal guardians' nationality, migration status or statelessness.

These generic provisions have been set by EU law and Common European Asylum System (CEAS) provisions. Articles 18, 19 and 24 of the Charter of Fundamental Rights of the EU are also relevant in this regard. They provide for the core rules that the CEAS harmonization process has revolved around.

Legal certainty for children on the move as a means to improve security: a new global public good to be enshrined in the global compacts for safe, orderly and regular migration?

The right to leave any country, including one's own country, and the right to seek international protection are both found in numerous international instruments. Nevertheless, freedom of movement is limited, since individuals do not have the right to decide their country of residence outside of the requirements imposed by national laws on a unilateral basis, including those implementing the obligations contained in the 1951 Geneva Convention. Because of this, the international regime for human mobility is fragmented. This fragmentation turns into legal uncertainty for migrants and refugees, who too often have to "trust" in smuggling networks for doing a journey that, because of the absence of precise and clear international obligations assumed by States, they cannot legally do. This has adverse effects for people on the move, especially if they are children, since they do not travel in adequate and decent conditions, and gives rise to severe violations of human rights. Smuggled and trafficked people, refugees and asylum seekers, or non-accompanied migrant children become more vulnerable. But it also has negative consequences for States, which put up with some adverse side effects in this scenario.

The incentives States would have for agreeing on an international regime for human mobility should be explored. For doing so, a global public goods approach to the improvement and guaranteeing of legal certainty for people, especially children, on the move should be considered. Such a regime could be considered a global public good "with benefits ... that extend across countries and regions, across rich and poor population groups, and even across generations."[72]

Of course, the externalities of the establishment of the above-mentioned internationally agreed regime for human mobility should be addressed. In my view, it would turn, for example, on better managed migration flows, since States will better control the movements across borders. At the same time, it would facilitate a more efficient fight against organized crime (namely the smuggling and trafficking networks). In such case, cooperation is a rational choice. Second, I think that legal certainty for migrants resulting from such a regime is a non-excludable and non-rival good. Once in force, this international regime, which could adopt the shape of a/various multilateral treaty/ies containing precise provisions aiming to facilitate legal migration – job-seekers' visas, humanitarian corridors, adequate resettlement programmes, security of residence for victims of trafficking in human beings and non-accompanied minors, etc. – would apply to individuals coming from States non-parties in the treaty/ies. Legal certainty for migrants is also a non-rival good. Non-participant States will enjoy improvements in the fight against organized criminality. This free rider problem could be solved if we apply the treaty only among States parties (club good approach).

Available data show that, until now, the international community has failed in the objective of making migration safe for individuals. This failure has enhanced the role of mafias and criminal networks in the managing of migration flows. This work maintains that if the international legal framework offers every State's nationals the possibility of enjoying legal certainty when on the move, good benefits will facilitate the achievement of objectives typically related to national and international security. It is still too soon to affirm if the Global Compacts for Safe, Orderly and Regular Migration and for Refugees would entail a paradigm shift or are mere window dressing.[73] Although this process should involve origin, transit and destination countries, the EU must play a key role.[74] In this sense, a new conception of the "security" element of the EU Area of Freedom, Security and Justice[75] should be proposed because the tightening of the requirements for travelling to EU territory imposed on third-country nationals, and the more and more restrictive European Migration Policy are not fit for the purpose of proving security. On the contrary, a more open system offering precise legal channels of entry to migrants and refugees could better fit this goal. It would also improve the credibility of the EU's human rights policy abroad and within its territory.

Final reflections

An individual's right to migrate, to decide one's place of residency, has not yet taken shape in International Law. On the contrary, States have the right to establish migratory controls and, because of this, to define the conditions an individual must meet in order to legally migrate to their territories. Enforcing migratory law and policies is "the last bastion of sovereignty."[76] A principle of Public International Law allows States to decide on aliens' entry to, stay in and expulsion from their territories. And, as the International Law Commission (ILC) has recently confirmed, States have the right to expel an alien from their territory.[77] But this right to expel is not absolute. Contemporary International Law imposes upon States the obligation of respecting fundamental rights when adopting and enforcing return decisions in respect of irregular migrants.

In this context, human rights monitoring mechanisms have provided for a more humane and dignified approach to the legal situation of irregular migrants. In a direct or indirect way, vulnerability has been invoked by them as the legal guide for guaranteeing diverse rights to both child and adult irregular migrants. In this sense, international human rights supervisory mechanisms, both at universal and regional levels, have repeatedly affirmed that despite their sovereign right to regulate on conditions of entry and stay in their territories, States assume obligations and duties under International Law to respect, protect and fulfil the human rights of all individuals under their jurisdiction. Being considered a particularly vulnerable group, a prevailing view in international human rights protection bodies' practice is that the dignity of all migrants appears as the cornerstone for the protection of their rights. And these obligations are particularly stressed in the case of non-accompanied migrant children. In sum, it can be said that a generic obligation of protecting migrant children, both accompanied and non-accompanied, from any form of violence has been imposed upon States. This protection includes protection against trafficking and other less serious forms of exploitation, on the one hand, and against return to their countries of origin when their fundamental rights could be considered at risk once there (being this the essential element of a right to asylum).

Even though these obligations derive from international treaties, the dispositions contained therein have been interpreted by supervisory bodies. While no doubts arise regarding the binding character of ECtHR judgements *ex* article 41 (1) of the Convention, some reflections are needed in the case of the pronouncements of UN human rights treaty bodies, such as the Committee on the Rights of the Child. From a formal point of view, these bodies have not jurisdictional nature, as they have been shaped as expert Committees and do not have the competence of adopting binding decisions. This does not mean that their pronouncements lack any legal effects to be considered by States and by domestic courts.[78] It cannot be denied that they are authentic interpreters of the treaties they must monitor, so their pronouncements should be taken into account as decisive opinions. Furthermore, the concrete legal impact of those committees having competence to examine individual communications should be appreciated. This is the case of the Committee on the Rights of the Child according to article 5 of the Optional Protocol to the CRC on a communication procedure, adopted in 2012.[79] The role of domestic judiciaries becomes decisive. In the case of Spain, it must be underlined that the Supreme Court has recently stated, in a case regarding the Committee on the Elimination of Discrimination against Women, that States should comply with the Committee decisions, since they are legally binding on it.[80]

IHRL has been conceived in this work as a shield aiming to protect the most vulnerable groups and individuals against State temptation of giving priority to migration policy concerns over the defence of rights of migrant people, even if they are minors and asylum seekers.[81] Since it can be maintained that the IHRL system is, in general terms, more protective than national and EU systems when dealing with migratory issues, knowing and applying the decisions of the international human rights supervisory bodies, binding or not, can be useful, both from a theoretical and practical point of view, to support the defence of the rights of minors in seek of international protection.

Notes

1 United Nations General Assembly, Joint report of the Special Rapporteur on the Sale and Sexual Exploitation of Children, including Child Prostitution, Child Pornography and Other Child Sexual Abuse Material and the Special Rapporteur on Trafficking in Persons, especially Women and Children, section on the "Vulnerabilities of Children to Sale, Trafficking and Other Forms of Exploitation in Situations of Conflict and Humanitarian Crisis" (A/72/164), July 18, 2017, accessed October 11, 2018, http://ap.ohchr.org/documents/dpage_e.aspx?si=A/72/164. On the legal framework applicable in Spain to non-accompanied refugee children in situations of vulnerability see: Itziar Gómez Fernández and Carmen Pérez González. "El asilo en situaciones de vulnerabilidad: marco jurídico para la acogida e integración de menores refugiados," in *La crisis de las personas refugiadas y su impacto sobre la UE* (Vitoria-Gasteiz, EuroBasque-Consejo Vasco del Movimiento Europeo, 2016), 211–72.

2 As noted in the Joint General Comment No. 3 of the Committee on the Protection of the Rights of All Migrants Workers and No. 22 of the Committee on the Rights of the Child on the general principles regarding the human rights of children in the context of international migration, children on the move

> may be in a situation of double vulnerability as children and as children affected by migration who (a) are migrants themselves, either alone or with their families, (b) were born to migrant parents in countries of destination or (c) remain in their country of origin while one or both parents have migrated to another country. Additional vulnerabilities could relate to their national, ethnic or social origin; gender; sexual orientation or gender identity; religion; disability; migration or residence status; citizenship status; age; economic status; political or other opinion; or other status.

United Nations, Joint General Comment No. 3 of the Committee on the Protection of the Rights of All Migrants Workers and No. 22 of the Committee on the Rights of the Child on the General Principles Regarding the Human Rights of Children in the Context of International Migration (CMW/C/GC/3-CRC/C/GC/22), November 16, 2017, https://www.refworld.org/docid/5a1293a24.html, para. 3.

3 Vulnerability plays a foundational role in the human rights discourse, also being conceived as a source of values: Mary Neal, "Respect for Human Dignity as Substantive Basic Norm," *International Journal of Law in Context* 10 (2014): 31.

4 The Special Rapporteur on the Human Rights of Migrants has recalled the obligation of the State to ensure the protection of all children in all stages of the migration process. Report of the Special Rapporteur on the Human Rights of Migrants, A/HRC/17/33, March 21, 2011, accessed October 11, 2018, https://undocs.org/A/HRC/17/33, paras. 26–33.

5 In relation to children disappeared during migration, including those whose identities may have been changed, the Working Group on Enforced or Involuntary Disappearances has called on States to "devote their efforts to the search for and identification of such children and to the restitution of the children to their families of origin" and, to this end, to "conclude cooperation agreements with the other States involved." United Nations OHCHR, Report of the Working Group on Enforced or Involuntary Disappearances on Enforced Disappearances in the Context of Migration, A/HRC/36/39/Add.2, July 28, 2017, accessed October 11, 2018, https://documents-dds-ny.un.org/doc/UNDOC/GEN/G17/226/72/PDF/G1722672.pdf.

Cooperation has been also identified by GRETA as a key factor:

> The number of unaccompanied or separated children arriving in States Parties to the Convention has grown considerably in recent years. The lack of coordination between different national authorities, such as border officials, immigration officers, social services, law enforcement, and child protection services, as well as between the agencies of different countries, increases the risk of migrant and asylum-seeking children, particularly those who are unaccompanied, falling victim to trafficking. The identification of victims of trafficking among these children is challenging and the statistics available on identified victims do not reflect the actual scale of the phenomenon.

Group of Experts on Action against Trafficking in Human Beings, *6th General Report on GRETA's Activities Covering the Period 1 January to 31 December 2016* (Council of Europe, 2017), accessed October 11, 2018, www.coe.int/en/web/anti-human-trafficking/general-reports.

6 Europol, *Migrant Smuggling in the EU* (Brussels: Europol, 2016), accessed October 11, 2018, www.europol.europa.eu/publications-documents/migrant-smuggling-in-eu.

7 Mark Townsend, "10,000 Refugee Children Are Missing," *Guardian*, January 30, 2016, accessed October 11, 2018, www.theguardian.com/world/2016/jan/30/fears-for-missing-child-refugees.

8 United Nations, Committee on the Rights of the Child, General Comment No. 6 (2005) Treatment of Unaccompanied and Separated Children Outside Their Country of Origin, CRC/GC/2005/6, September 1, 2005, https://www.refworld.org/docid/42dd174b4.html.

9 Article 1 says "Every human being below the age of eighteen years unless under the law applicable to the child, majority is attained earlier." Convention on the Rights of the Child, September 2, 1990, accessed October 11, 2018, www.ohchr.org/en/professionalinterest/pages/crc.aspx.

10 United Nations, General Comment No. 6, paras. 7 and 8. This concept has been transplanted into European Union Law: article 2.e) of the Directive 2013/33/EU of the European Parliament and of the Council of 26 June 2013 Laying Down Standards for the Reception of Applicants for International Protection, OJ L 180, June 29, 2013.

11 Article 3 (a) and (c) of the Protocol to Prevent, Suppress and Punish Trafficking in Persons Especially Women and Children, supplementing the United Nations Convention against Transnational Organized Crime (Palermo Protocol), adopted by General Assembly Resolution 55/25 of 15 November 2000, accessed October 11, 2018, www.ohchr.org/en/professionalinterest/pages/protocoltraffickinginpersons.aspx.

12 Articles 19, 32, 34, 36 and 39 of the CRC impose upon States parties a variety of obligations aimed at protecting children against diverse forms of exploitation. UNHCR Guidelines on International Protection: The Application of Article 1A (2) of the 1951 Convention and/or 1967 Protocol Relating to the Status of Refugees to Victims of Trafficking and Persons at Risk of Being Trafficked underlines that non-accompanied minors may be also trafficked for the purposes of irregular adoption. UNHCR Guidelines on International Protection: The Application of Article 1A (2) of the 1951 Convention and/or 1967 Protocol Relating to the Status of Refugees to Victims of Trafficking and Persons at Risk of Being Trafficked, April 7, 2006, accessed October 11, 2018, www.unhcr.org/443b626b2.html.

13 Ibid., para. 19.

14 In theory, migrants and refugees deserve different legal responses. In practice, both compose contemporary mixed migratory flows.

15 Helen Stalford and Eleanor Drywood, "Using the CRC to Inform EU Law and Policy-making," in *The Human Rights of Children: From Vision to Implementation*, eds. Antonella Invernizzi and Jane Williams (Routledge, 2011), 199–218.

16 "Refugees and Migrants," accessed October 11, 2018, https://refugeesmigrants.un.org/refugees-compact, contains the updated version of the Global Compact for Safe, Orderly and Regular Migration.

17 According to Fernando M. Mariño Menéndez, "the principle of no forcible return or *non-refoulement* constitutes a norm of general International Law that doctrine and practice regard as imperative and as imposing obligations *erga omnes*." Fernando M. Mariño Menéndez, "The Prohibition of Torture in Public International Law," *Collected Courses of the Hague Academy of International Law* 391 (2018): 149.

18 Resolution A/RES/70/147 of 17 December 2015 on Protection of Migrants, accessed October 11, 2018, http://research.un.org/en/docs/ga/quick/regular/70, para. 3c.

19 International Court of Justice, Ahmadou Sadio Diallo (*Republic of Guinea* v. *Democratic Republic of the Congo*) – Judgement of 30 November 2010, accessed October 11, 2018, www.icj-cij.org/docket/files/103/16244.pdf, paras. 64 to 67.

20 European Court of Human Rights, *Chagal v UK* App no 22414/93, November 15, 1996, para. 70.
21 Resolution A/RES/70/147, para. 3c).
22 Ibid.
23 Communication from the Commission to the European Parliament and the Council on the Action Plan on Unaccompanied Minors (2010–2014), COM(2010) 213 final, May 6, 2010. A Staff Working Document reporting on the implementation of the Action Plan since 2012 was presented together with the Communication from the Commission to the European Parliament and the Council on the Protection of Children in Migration, COM(2017) 129 final (Brussels: European Union, April 12, 2017), accessed October 11, 2018, https://ec.europa.eu/home-affairs/sites/homeaffairs/files/what-we-do/policies/european-agenda-migration/20170412_communication_on_the_protection_of_children_in_migration_en.pdf.
24 A joint Europol-INTERPOL Report says that 90 per cent of the migrants coming to the EU are facilitated, mostly by members of a criminal network. Joint Europol-INTERPOL Report: Migrant Smuggling Networks, May 17, 2016, accessed October 11, 2018, www.europol.europa.eu/newsroom/news/europol-and-interpol-issue-comprehensive-review-of-migrant-smuggling-networks.
25 Riccardo Pisillo-Mazzeschi, "The Due Diligence Rules and the Nature of the International Responsibility of States," *German Yearbook of International Law* 35 (1992): 26.
26 ILO Protocol 2014 to the Forced Labour Convention, article 2.e). According to this article, the measures to be taken for the prevention of forced or compulsory labour shall include supporting due diligence by both the public and private sectors to prevent and respond to risks of forced or compulsory labour. The Protocol entered into force on November 9, 2016, accessed October 11, 2018, www.ilo.org/dyn/normlex/en/f?p=NORMLEXPUB:12100:0::NO::P12100_ILO_CODE:P029.
27 Lee Hasselbacher, "State Obligations Regarding Domestic Violence: The European Court of Human Rights, Due Diligence, and International Legal Minimums of Protection," *North-western Journal of International Human Rights* 8, no. 2 (2010): 190–215.
28 Report of the Special Rapporteur on Trafficking in Persons, Especially Women and Children (A/70/260), August 3, 2015, accessed October 11, 2018, www.un.org/en/ga/search/view_doc.asp?symbol=A/70/260, para. 17.
29 Hasselbacher, "State Obligations Regarding Domestic Violence," 207.
30 The ECtHR has affirmed that trafficking in human beings threatens human dignity: ECtHR, *Rantsev* v. *Cyprus and Russia* App no 25965/04, January 7, 2010, para. 282; ECtHR, *Chowdury and Others* v. *Greece* App no 21884/15, March 30, 2017, para. 93.
31 ECtHR, *Siliadin* v. *France* App no. 73316/01, July 26, 2005; ECtHR, *Rantsev* v. *Cyprus and Russia* App no 25965/04, January 7, 2010; ECtHR, *C.N. and V.* v. *France* App no 67724/09, October 11, 2012; ECtHR, *C.N.* v. *UK* App no 4239/08, November 13, 2012; ECtHR, *Chitos* v. *Greece* App no 51637/12, June 4, 2015; ECtHR, *L.E.* v. *Greece* App no 71545/12, January 21, 2016; ECtHR, *J. and Others* v. *Austria* App no 58216/12, January 2017, and ECtHR, *Chowdury and Others* v. *Greece* App no 21884/15, March 30, 2017.
32 Roza Pati, "State's Positive Obligations with Respect to Human Trafficking: The European Court of Human Rights Breaks New Ground in Rantsev v. Cyprus and Russia," *Boston University International Law Journal* 29 (2011): 79–142; Ryszard Piotrowicz, "States' Obligations under Human Rights Law towards Victims of Trafficking in Human Beings: Positive Developments in Positive Obligations," *International Journal of Refugee Law* 24.2 (2012): 181–201.
33 Art. 31 of the Charter of Fundamental Rights of the European Union refers to "all workers'" right to fair and just working conditions, with respect to their health, safety and *dignity* (emphasis added). According to para. 2, fair and just working conditions would include the right to limitation of maximum working hours, to daily and weekly rest periods and to an annual period of paid leave.
34 In the *Siliadin case*, the victim was a 15-year-old girl of Togolese origin who arrived in France in 1994. Her passport had been confiscated and her employers had reduced her "to the status of an object." The Court found that the French criminal law in force at the time of the crimes had not protected her sufficiently. In the *C.N.* v. *UK case*, the Court affirmed that the legislative provisions in force in the United Kingdom at the relevant time had been inadequate to afford practical and effective protection against treatment contrary to article 4.
35 ECtHR refers to States' obligation to put in place not only effective criminal investigations, but also labour inspections. As has been said,

> the vulnerability of migrants might also require from the national authorities to take a much more proactive approach by not only acting when the matter has come to their attention, but also establishing "useful detection and reporting mechanisms [which] are fundamental to

the effective implementation of the relevant criminal laws". This implies that labour inspectors have a crucial role since they can detect abusive labour practices.
Vladislava Stoyanova, *Human Trafficking and Slavery Reconsidered: Conceptual Limits and State's Positive Obligations in European Law* (Cambridge: CUP, 2017), 364.

36 In any case, vulnerability plays a key role in the definition of human trafficking. Article 3 of the Palermo Protocol lists the abuse of a position of vulnerability as one of the means within the definition of trafficking in persons. In this context, the UN Office on Drugs and Crime has noted that "the existence of vulnerability is best assessed on a case-by-case basis, taking into consideration the personal, situational or circumstantial situation of the alleged victim." UN Office on Drugs and Crime. Guidance Note on "Abuse of a Position of Vulnerability" as a Means of Trafficking in Persons in Article 3 of the Protocol to Prevent, Suppress and Punish Trafficking in Persons, Especially Women and Children, supplementing the United Nations Convention against Transnational Organized Crime (New York: UN Office on Drugs and Crime, 2012), accessed October 11, 2018, www.unodc.org/documents/human-trafficking/2012/UNODC_2012_Guidance_Note_-_Abuse_of_a_Position_of_Vulnerability_E.pdf.

37 *Siliadin* v. *France*, paras. 126–27. Emphasis added.

38 *Chowdury and Others* v. *Greece*, para. 95.

39 Ibid., para. 97.

40 *Rantsev* v. *Cyprus and Russia*, para. 284.

41 Valentina Milano, "Uncovering Labour Exploitation: Lights and Shadows on the Latest European Court of Human Rights' Case Law on Human Trafficking," *Spanish Yearbook of International Law* 21 (2017): 114.

42 This definition was offered by article 2 of the ILO Convention on Forced Labour. In the *Van der Mussele* v. *Belgium case*, the Court had pointed out that this definition could provide a starting point for interpretation. ECtHR, *Van der Mussele* v. *Belgium* App. no 8919/80, November 23, 1983.

43 ECJ, *case C-638/16 PPU X and X* v. *Belgian State*, March 7, 2017. Ángel Sánchez Legido, "El Arriesgado Acceso a la Protección Internacional en la Europa Fortaleza: la Batalla por el Visado Humanitario Europeo," *Revista Derecho Comunitario Europeo* 57 (2017): 433–72. On October 10, 2018, the European Parliament's Civil Liberties Committee agreed to ask the European Commission to table, by March 31, 2019, a legislative proposal establishing a European Humanitarian Visa, giving access to European territory for the sole purpose of submitting an application for international protection. Press Releases, "Humanitarian Visas to Avoid Refugees' Deaths," European Parliament website, October 10, 2018, accessed October 11, 2018, www.europarl.europa.eu/news/en/press-room/20181008IPR15261/humanitarian-visas-to-avoid-refugees-deaths.

44 Committee on the Rights of the Child, General Comment No. 13 (2011) on The Right of the Child to Freedom from All Forms of Violence (CRC/C/GC/13), April 18, 2011, accessed October 11, 2018, https://tbinternet.ohchr.org/_layouts/treatybodyexternal/TBSearch.aspx?Lang=en&TreatyID=5&DocTypeID=11.

45 See the General Comment No. 13, para. 35.

46 Directive 2011/95/EU of the European Parliament and of the Council of 13 December 2011 on Standards for the Qualification of Third-Country Nationals or Stateless Persons as Beneficiaries of International Protection, for a Uniform Status for Refugees or for Persons Eligible for Subsidiary Protection, and for the Content of the Protection Granted, OJ L337, 9. This article refers to the death penalty or execution, torture or inhuman or degrading treatment or punishment of an individual in his/her country of origin, and a serious and individual threat to a civilian's life or person by reason of indiscriminate violence in situations of international or internal conflict.

47 What constitutes the best interest of the child should be decided on a case-by-case basis. Margrite Kalverboer et al., "The Best Interests of the Child in Cases of Migration," *The International Journal of Children's Rights* 25, no. 1 (2017): 114–39.

48 Aisling Parkes, *Children and International Human Rights Law: The Right of the Child to Be Heard* (London: Routledge, 2013).

49 ECJ, case C-491/10 PPU *Joseba Andoni Aguirre Zarraba* v. *Simone Pelz*, December 22, 2010, para. 66.

50 ECtHR, *Paulsen-Medalen and Svensson* v. *Sweden* App no 16817/90, February 19, 1998, para. 39.

51 States are obliged to not separate migrant children from their families (against their will and without judicial resolution), as a way to guarantee their rights to be cared for by their parents (art. 7.1 and 9 of the CRC). In migratory crisis contexts, families can easily face the risk of being separated, so it is especially important for States to act with due diligence in order to guarantee the above-mentioned rights.

52 General Comment No. 6, para. 79.
53 In that case, family reunion could be considered in breach of the principle of *non-refoulement*. General Comment No. 6, paras. 81 and 82.
54 Regulation No 605/2013 of the European Parliament and of the Council of 26 June 2013 Establishing the Criteria and Mechanisms for Determining the Member State Responsible for Examining an Application for International Protection Lodged in One of the Member States by a Third-Country National or a Stateless Person, OJ L180, 31.
55 See the Preamble of the Regulation, recitals 13 and 14.
56 See note 23.
57 General Comment No. 6, para. 85.
58 Ibid., paras. 84 and 88.
59 Ibid., para. 92.
60 See note 23.
61 Press Releases, "EU-Turkey Statement," March 18, 2016, accessed October 11, 2018, www.consilium.europa.eu/es/press/press-releases/2016/03/18-eu-turkey-statement/.
62 Relevant documents, including the European Commission's progress reports, are available at http://europa.eu/rapid/press-release_IP-16-3614_en.htm (accessed October 11, 2018).
63 Resettlement is conceived in this temporary protection scheme to alleviate the migratory pressure supported by two Member States, Italy and Greece. Since refugees and other individuals in need of international protection are relocated from these States, and not from origin or transit third countries, the goal of the whole system is not to provide those individuals with safe access to protection.
64 The Judgement is available at www.poderjudicial.es/cgpj/es/Poder-Judicial/Tribunal-Supremo/Noticias-Judiciales/El-Tribunal-Supremo-condena-al-Estado-por-incumplir-su-obligacion-de-tramitar-las-solicitudes-de-asilo-de-19-449-refugiados (accessed October 11, 2018). The decision is based both in the mandatory nature of Council Decisions and in the direct effect of EU Law.
65 Kim Rygiel, Feyzi Baban and Suzan Ilcan, "The Syrian Refugee Crisis: The EU-Turkey 'Deal' and Temporary Protection," *Global Social Policy* 16, no. 3 (2016): 315–20.
66 See *supra*, under "Family reunion."
67 According to Paragraph 1,

> States Parties shall take appropriate measures to ensure that a child who is seeking refugee status or who is considered a refugee in accordance with applicable international or domestic law and procedures shall, whether unaccompanied or accompanied by his or her parents or by any other person, receive appropriate protection and humanitarian assistance in the enjoyment of applicable rights set forth in the present Convention and in other international human rights or humanitarian instruments to which the said States are Parties.

Paragraph 2 refers to the State obligation to cooperate with UN and NGOs "to protect and assist such a child and to trace the parents or other members of the family of any refugee child in order to obtain information necessary for reunification with his or her family."
68 At the universal level, the most significant instrument is still the Palermo Protocol. At European level, the European Anti-Trafficking Convention was adopted under the auspices of the Council of Europe in 2005. An explicit reference is made by article 5 (3) of the EU Charter of Fundamental Rights. On April 5, 2011, the European Parliament and the Council adopted the Directive 2011/36/EU on Preventing and Combating Trafficking in Human Beings and Protecting Its Victims, and Replacing Council Framework Decision 2002/629/JHA, OJ L101, 1.
69 Jacqueline Bhabha, "Seeking Asylum Alone: Treatment of Separated and Trafficked Children in Need of Refugee Protection," *International Migration* 42, no. 1 (2004): 141–8.
70 In the case of EU Member States, the CEAS rules.
71 On the non-discrimination principle and the ECtHR: Geraldine Van Bueren, *Les droits des enfants en Europe: convergence et divergence dans la protection judiciare* (Strasbourg: Editions du Conseil de l'Europe, 2004), 44.
72 Inge Kaul et al., *Providing Global Public Goods. Managing Globalization* (New York: OUP, 2003), 3.
73 Addressing and reducing migrants' vulnerability is one of the purposes of the Global Compact for Safe, Orderly and Regular Migration.
74 The current EU migration system has been described as "a legal framework leading to limited safeguards and legal certainty for vulnerable migrants and significant adverse consequences for access to the EU by those who wish to claim international protection." Valsamis Mitsilegas, *The Criminalisation of Migration in Europe. Challenges for Human Rights and the Rule of Law* (Berlin: Springer, 2015), 74.

75 As has been said, "[p]ositing 'freedom' and 'security' suggests the freedom of insiders from the security threat posed by outsiders." Cathryn Costello, *The Human Rights of Migrants and Refugees in European Law* (Oxford: OUP, 2016), 22.
76 Catherine Dauvergne, *Making People Illegal. What Globalization Means for Migration and Law* (Cambridge: CUP, 2008), 4.
77 Article 3 of ILC Draft Articles on the Expulsion of Aliens, 2014, accessed October 11, 2018, http://legal.un.org/ilc/texts/instruments/english/draft%20articles/9_12_2014.pdf. Also, the Committee on Migrant Workers has accepted "the sovereign power of States parties to control their borders and to regulate the entry and stay of migrants workers and members of their families." Committee on Migrant Workers, General Comment No. 2 (2013) on the Rights of Migrant Workers in an Irregular Situation and Members of Their Families, accessed October 11, 2018, www.ohchr.org/EN/HRBodies/CMW/Pages/CMWIndex.aspx, para. 13.
78 Machico Kanetake, "UN Human Rights Treaty Monitoring Bodies before Domestic Courts," *International and Comparative Law Quarterly* 67 (2018): 201–32; Jasper Krommendijk, "The Domestic Effectiveness of International Human Rights Monitoring in Established Democracies. The Case of the UN Human Rights Treaty Bodies," *The Review of International Organizations* 10, no. 4 (2015): 489–512.
79 Available at https://tbinternet.ohchr.org/_layouts/treatybodyexternal/Download.aspx?symbolno=A/RES/66/138&Lang=en, accessed October 11, 2018.
80 The judgement is available at www.womenslinkworldwide.org/files/3045/sentencia-angela-tribunal-supremo.pdf, accessed October 11, 2018.
81 The following statement of the ECtHR is eloquent enough:

> The Court has already had occasion to note that the States which form the external borders of the European Union are currently experiencing considerable difficulties in coping with the increasing influx of migrants and asylum-seekers. It does not underestimate the burden and pressure this situation places on the States concerned, which are all the greater in the present context of economic crisis (...) However, having regard to the absolute character of the rights secured by Article 3, that cannot absolve a State of its obligations under that provision.
>
> ECtHR: *Hirsi Jamaa and others v. Italy* (application 277765/09), February 23, 2012, para. 122. For an interesting comment on this decision: Violeta Moreno-Lax, "Hirsi Jamaa and Others v Italy or the Strasbourg Court versus Extraterritorial Migration Control?," *Human Rights Law Review* 12.3 (2012): 574–98.

References

Bhabha, Jacqueline. "Seeking Asylum Alone: Treatment of Separated and Trafficked Children in Need of Refugee Protection." *International Migration* 42, no. 1 (2004): 141–8.

Costello, Cathryn. *The Human Rights of Migrants and Refugees in European Law*. Oxford: OUP, 2016.

Dauvergne, Catherine. *Making People Illegal. What Globalization Means for Migration and Law*. Cambridge: CUP, 2008.

Gómez Fernández, Itziar, and María Carmen Pérez González. "El asilo en situaciones de especial vulnerabilidad: Marco jurídico para la acogida en integración de menores refugiados." In *La crisis de las personas refugiadas y su impacto sobre la UE*, 211–71. Vitoria-Gasteiz, EuroBasque-Consejo Vasco del Movimiento Europeo, 2016.

Hasselbacher, Lee. "State Obligations Regarding Domestic Violence: The European Court of Human Rights, Due Diligence, And International Legal Minimums of Protection." *North-western Journal of International Human Rights* 8, no. 2 (2010): 190–215.

Kalverboer, Margrite, et al. "The Best Interests of the Child in Cases of Migration." *The International Journal of Children's Rights* 25, no. 1 (2017): 114–39.

Kanetake, Machico. "UN Human Rights Treaty Monitoring Bodies before Domestic Courts." *International and Comparative Law Quarterly* 67 (2018): 201–32.

Kaul, Inge, Pedro Conceiçao, Katell Le Goulven and Ronald U. Mendoza. *Providing Global Public Goods. Managing Globalization*. New York: OUP, 2003.

Krommendijk, Jasper. "The Domestic Effectiveness of International Human Rights Monitoring in Established Democracies: The Case of the UN Human Rights Treaty Bodies." *The Review of International Organizations* 10, no. 4 (2015): 489–512.

Mariño Menéndez, Fernando M. "The Prohibition of Torture in Public International Law." *Collected Courses of the Hague Academy of International Law* 391 (2018): 103–85.

Milano, Valentina. "Uncovering Labour Exploitation: Lights and Shadows on the Latest European Court of Human Rights' Case Law on Human Trafficking." *Spanish Yearbook of International Law* 21 (2017): 83–117.

Mitsilegas, Valsamis. *The Criminalisation of Migration in Europe. Challenges for Human Rights and the Rule of Law*. Berlin: Springer, 2015.

Moreno-Lax, Violeta. "Hirsi Jamaa and Others v Italy or the Strasbourg Court versus Extraterritorial Migration Control?" *Human Rights Law Review* 12 (2012): 574–98.

Neal, Mary. "Respect for Human Dignity as Substantive Basic Norm." *International Journal of Law in Context* 10 (2014): 26–46.

Parkes, Aisling. *Children and International Human Rights Law: The Right of the Child to Be Heard*. London: Routledge, 2013.

Pati, Roza. "State's Positive Obligations with Respect to Human Trafficking: The European Court of Human Rights Breaks New Ground in Rantsev v. Cyprus and Russia." *Boston University International Law Journal* 29 (2011): 79–142.

Piotrowicz, Ryszard. "States' Obligations under Human Rights Law towards Victims of Trafficking in Human Beings: Positive Developments in Positive Obligations." *International Journal of Refugee Law* 26 (2012): 181–201.

Pisillo-Mazzeschi, Riccardo. "The Due Diligence Rules and the Nature of the International Responsibility of States." *German Yearbook of International Law* 35 (1992): 9–51.

Rygiel, Kim, Feyzi Baban and Suzan Ilcan. "The Syrian Refugee Crisis: The EU-Turkey 'Deal' and Temporary Protection." *Global Social Policy* 16, no. 3 (2016): 315–20.

Sánchez Legido, Ángel. "El Arriesgado Acceso a la Protección Internacional en la Europa Fortaleza: La Batalla por el Visado Humanitario Europeo." *Revista Derecho Comunitario Europeo* 57 (2017): 433–72.

Stalford, Helen, and Eleanor Drywood. "Using the CRC to Inform EU Law and Policy-making." In *The Human Rights of Children: From Vision to Implementation*, edited by Antonella Invernizzi and Jane Williams, 199–218. Routledge, 2011.

Stoyanova, Vladislava. *Human Trafficking and Slavery Reconsidered. Conceptual Limits and State's Positive Obligations in European Law*. Cambridge: CUP, 2017.

Van Bueren, Geraldine. *Les droits des enfants en Europe: convergence et divergence dans la protection judiciare*. Strasbourg: Editions du Conseil de l'Europe, 2004.

20

MARITIME BORDER CONTROL IN THE EUROPEAN UNION

Alexander Proelss

Introduction

Maritime border control has significantly gained in importance over the past decades. In general, States undertake to control their borders so as to safeguard and, where necessary, enforce that their laws and regulations applicable to the transboundary movement of people, animals and goods are observed. These laws and regulations address a broad range of issues, the most important ones being immigration, security (including the fight against terrorism and transnational organized crime), health protection and fiscal policy.

Under public international law, every State has the power to enact specific requirements that ought to be observed whenever a person, animal or good enters or leaves its territory. This power results from the inherent competence of the State to decide freely on to whom it grants access to its territory – a competence which is, again, enshrined in the principle of territorial sovereignty. There is thus no general right of a person to enter the territory of a foreign State, and the State is generally free to end the stay of a person with foreign nationality on its territory. At the same time, a State is free to take the sovereign decision to become party to international treaties which subject its regulatory freedom in relation to border control to certain legal limitations (e.g. in relation to the protection of refugees). Such limitations also derive from the rules and principles of customary international law. It is furthermore possible that States that are members of an international organization decide to transfer parts of their respective powers to the international organization which will then exercise, or coordinate respectively, the task of border control and security for all of its Member States. As will be demonstrated in the following, this is what has happened, at least partially, within the European Union (EU).

The task of border control is not limited to the territorial borders of a State. Rather, it is well established under the international law of the sea that coastal States are entitled to exercise sovereignty over certain parts of the sea, which thus form part of their territories. As can be demonstrated by reference to Article 2 (1) of the 1982 United Nations Convention on the Law of the Sea (LOSC),[1] this is the case in respect of the internal waters, the territorial sea and the archipelagic waters. As a matter of principle, the domestic legal system of the coastal State also applies in these maritime zones. The outer limits of the territorial sea, which may extend up to 12 nautical miles measured from the baselines drawn by the coastal State, thus establish the maritime border of the State. It follows from this that the concept of border control also has a maritime component.

This chapter analyzes the legal regime of maritime border control in the EU. Following a brief analysis of the development of the EU border regime, the scope of the Union competences in the field of external border control and the most important legislative measures adopted by the EU in relation to this field will be explored. The final section is dedicated to specific challenges, namely the issue of compatibility of the European border measures with the requirements arising from public international law as well as primary EU law.

Development and core of EU border regime

According to Article 77 (1) lit. a and b of the Treaty on the Functioning of the European Union (TFEU),[2] the EU has, on the one hand, the duty to "develop a policy with a view to [...] ensuring the absence of any controls on persons, whatever their nationality, when crossing internal borders." At the same time, it must, as far as the external borders are concerned, safeguard that checks on persons and efficient monitoring of the crossing of these borders are carried out. EU law thus distinguishes between the crossing of internal borders and that of external borders.

The absence of controls on persons at the internal borders was regarded by the European Commission as a crucial mechanism for the completion of the Single European Market as early as 1985.[3] As the then European Economic Community (EEC) did not have the competence to legislate on internal border controls, Belgium, France, Germany, Luxembourg and the Netherlands concluded what came to be known as the basic document of the Schengen Acquis: the Schengen Agreement.[4] This agreement – an international treaty outside of the scope of supranational EEC law – was later complemented by the Schengen Implementation Convention[5] which prescribed the operative rules and principles of the Schengen regime. At the core of the Schengen Acquis was (and still is) the rule that was codified in Article 2 (1) of the Schengen Implementation Agreement, according to which "[i]nternal borders may be crossed at any point without any checks on persons being carried out." At the same time, Article 6 (1) prescribed that "[c]ross-border movement at external borders shall be subject to checks by the competent authorities," and that "[c]hecks shall be carried out for the Contracting Parties territories, in accordance with uniform principles, within the scope of national powers and national law and taking account of the interests of all Contracting Parties." Taking into account that Article 1 of the Schengen Implementation Convention defined "external borders" as "the Contracting Parties land and sea borders and their airports and sea ports, provided that they are not internal borders," the Schengen Acquis thus foresaw that individual Member States remain responsible for the control of cross-border movements at their maritime borders if and to the extent to which these borders are external borders, but that the way how this control is exercised was to be based on uniform principles established under EU law.

With the entry into force of the Treaty of Amsterdam on 1 May 1999, the Schengen regime was, by way of a Protocol to that Treaty, integrated into EU law as part of the newly established Area of Freedom, Security and Justice.[6] Since that time, the two Schengen Agreements, which, as far as their legal nature was concerned, originally constituted "traditional" intergovernmental treaties governed by the rules and principles of public international law, displayed the same legal effects as secondary EU measures enacted by the European legislator. Consequently, the further development of the Schengen Acquis was made "subject to the relevant provisions of the Treaties."[7]

Under the law as its stands today, the task of establishing uniform principles in relation to external border controls is reflected in Article 77 (1) TFEU, which states in its lit. b and c that "[t]he Union shall develop a policy with a view to [...] carrying out checks on persons and efficient monitoring of the crossing of external borders [and] the gradual introduction of an integrated management system for external borders." To this aim, Article 77 (2) TFEU allocates the power to the European Parliament and the Council to enact, based on the ordinary legislative procedure in terms of Article 289 TFEU, the necessary measures under EU law.

Competences and instruments regarding EU maritime border control

Competences

The scope of legislative competences of the Union under Article 77 TFEU in relation to maritime border control cannot be addressed here in detail. Suffice to say that the EU has been allocated the power to regulate checks of persons at the external border (Article 77 (2) lit. b TFEU) and to gradually introduce an integrated control system for the external borders (Article 77 (2) lit. d TFEU), a competence that was included in what is today the TFEU by the Treaty of Lisbon. The Union powers under Article 77 (2) lit. d TFEU include the right to enact measures referring to *ex ante* control activities as well as activities carried out in the aftermath of checks of persons at the border within a broader geographical area surrounding the border, provided that these measures are conducted by the border police.[8] Furthermore, the EU may adopt measures of operative or supporting character by, e.g., establishing autonomous Union bodies.[9] In contrast, the historical background of Article 77 (2) lit. d TFEU suggests that this provision must be interpreted in such a way that the EU has not been granted the power to develop a supranational external borders regime, including rules on maritime border control that are directly applicable and enforceable.[10] The creation of a truly European Border Force, that would potentially be entitled to take coercive measures, could thus not be held to be legally viable in light of the limited Union competences.[11] Protocol No. 23 on external relations of the Member States with regard to the crossing of external borders[12] clarifies that the Member States also remain competent, in addition to the EU, to negotiate or conclude agreements with third States.[13] While this Protocol only refers to Article 77 (2) lit. b TFEU, it is submitted that the better reasons militate in favor of an interpretation according to which general border surveillance and security activities are also covered by its terms. If cooperation between individual Member States of the EU remains possible regardless of the Union competences under Article 77 (2) TFEU due to Article 73 TFEU, no reason exists why the Member States should be legally prevented from entering into arrangements with individual third States.

Measures

Based on the legislative powers described above, the EU has adopted several measures in order to pursue the objectives laid down in Article 77 (1) lit. b and c TFEU. While the more fundamental of these legislative acts apply to all external borders, regardless of whether located on land or at sea, selected instruments specifically address the issue of maritime border control.

Checks of persons at the external border

The fundamental EU law act concerning checks of persons at the external border, which has replaced the former Schengen Agreements, is the so-called Schengen Borders Code.[14] Its objective is to lay down "rules governing border control of persons crossing the external borders of the Member States of the Union" (Article 1). According to Article 5 (1) of the Code, external borders may be crossed only at border crossing points and during fixed opening hours. Article 6 prescribes entry conditions for third-State nationals. These conditions include the possession and duty to submit valid travel documents and, where applicable, a visa. According to Article 6 (1) lit. d and e of the Code, entry to the Schengen Area must be refused to persons for whom an alert has been issued in the Schengen Information System (SIS) for the purposes of refusing entry,[15] or who are considered to be a threat to public policy, internal security, public health or the international relations of any of the Member States. While it is mandatory to refuse entry into the Schengen Area if one of the conditions prescribed by Article 6 of the Code is not fulfilled (provided that none of the exceptions to this rule codified in Article 6 (5) of the Code is applicable),[16] commentators agree that the Schengen Borders Code does not establish a subjective right of entry into the Schengen Area on the basis of fulfillment of the criteria laid down in Article 6 of the Code.[17] This is in line with the situation under public international law, which leaves it to the discretion of the State the territory of which is intended to be entered by the national of a third State, whether entry is granted or not.

Annex VI of the Schengen Borders Code prescribes specific rules for the various types of border and the various means of transport used for crossing the Member States' external borders. Section 3 of this Annex is expressly dedicated to sea borders. It establishes general checking procedures on maritime traffic, which are then further specified for certain types of shipping, namely cruise ships, pleasure boats, coastal fishing vessels, ferry connections and cargo connections between EU Member States. According to Section 3.1.1., "[c]hecks on ships shall be carried out at the port of arrival or departure, or in an area set aside for that purpose, located in the immediate vicinity of the vessel or on board ship in the territorial waters as defined by the United Nations Convention on the Law of the Sea." The second sentence of this provision is only declaratory, as it re-emphasizes, in relation to the specific case of sea borders, the general competence of the Member States already enshrined in Protocol No. 23 to the TFEU to "conclude agreements according to which checks may also be carried out during crossings or, upon the ship's arrival or departure, on the territory of a third country." In order to facilitate border checks, a list of the crew members and persons on board the ship must be drawn up and submitted in advance to the responsible public authority in accordance with the requirements of Convention on Facilitation of International Maritime Traffic by an authorized person (usually the master or ship's agent).[18] As far as pleasure boats, coastal fishing vessels and cargo connections are concerned, Annex VI of the Schengen Borders Code establishes derogations from the general provisions of the Code, namely Articles 5[19] and 8, for the sake of practicality. However, these derogations are, again, subject to legal restraints with regard to ships and vessels coming from a third State, not registered in a EU port or, in the case of cargo connections, that have called at a port outside the territory of the Member States.

The second fundamental measure which was, *inter alia*, based on Article 77 (2) lit. b TFEU is Council Regulation (EC) No. 2007/2004 of 26 October 2004 establishing a European Agency for the Management of Operational Cooperation at the External Borders of the Member States of the European Union (2004 Frontex Regulation).[20] This Regulation led to the establishment of what came to be referred to as Frontex, an independent agency with the task to improve the integrated management of the external borders of the EU Member States. While the main purpose of Frontex is to contribute to the gradual introduction of an integrated control system for the external borders (which is why it will be addressed in more detail in the following section), the assistance contributed by this Agency may also cover the issue of checks of persons at the external borders.[21] In September 2016, the Frontex Regulation was replaced by the Regulation on the European Border and Coast Guard,[22] which was equally based on both Article 77 (2) lit. b and lit. d TFEU as well as on Article 79 (2) lit. c TFEU, taking into account its aim to "ensure European integrated border management at the external borders with a view to *managing the crossing of the external borders efficiently*,"[23] the last-mentioned issue thus being one of the cornerstones of the measure concerned.

Further approaches relating to checks of persons at external borders include attempts initiated by the European Commission to establish a system of "smart borders," which was intended to fill legal gaps that had been identified in relation to the existing border management.[24] After a first set of legislative measures proposed by the Commission in 2013 failed due to technical, operational and financial concerns raised by the Parliament and the Council, the Commission presented a revised proposal for a Regulation on the establishment of an Entry-Exit System to speed-up, facilitate and reinforce border check procedures for non-EU nationals traveling to the EU in 2016.[25] This proposal is part of a broader "Smart Borders Package" which aims at addressing the role of information systems in enhancing external border management, internal security and the fight against terrorism and organized crime[26] but has so far, again, not been implemented by way of adoption of the proposed legislative acts.

Gradual introduction of an integrated control system for the external borders

The gradual introduction of an integrated control system for the external borders foreseen by the TFEU becomes manifest in the establishment, and further development, of the European Agency for the Management of Operational Cooperation at the External Borders, which became to be known as Frontex, in 2004. As far as its legal status is concerned, it was designated to be an independent EU body with legal personality.[27] Article 1 (2) of the 2004 Frontex Regulation most clearly set out the purely assisting and coordinative role that the Agency was originally supposed to play. This provision emphasized that "the responsibility for the control and surveillance of external borders lies with the Member States," which is why the duties of the Agency were limited to being required to "facilitate and render more effective the application of existing and future Community measures relating to the management of external borders." These duties were to be fulfilled by "ensuring the coordination of Member States' actions in the implementation of those measures." According to Article 1 (3) of the 2004 Frontex Regulation, Frontex was also supposed to "provide the Commission and the Member States with the necessary technical support and expertise in the management of the external borders and promote solidarity between Member States." The list of tasks laid out in Article 2 (1) of the 2004 Frontex Regulation confirmed the purely coordinative and supporting functions of the Agency.[28] In particular, no coercive measures whatsoever could be taken by Frontex.

As stated above, the original Frontex Regulation was, in light of what has come to be referred to as the "refugee crisis,"[29] revised by Regulation 2016/1624, by which Frontex was developed into a "European Border and Coast Guard to ensure European integrated border management at the external borders with a view to managing the crossing of the external borders efficiently." As clarified in Recital 11 of the Regulation, the changed terminology reflects that the tasks of the Agency, which is expressly foreseen to be continued to be commonly referred to as Frontex,[30] were significantly expanded. Frontex is now responsible for the establishment of a technical and operational strategy for European integrated border management,[31] the implementation of which being designated as a "shared responsibility of the Agency and of the national authorities responsible for border management, including coast guards to the extent that they carry out maritime border surveillance operations and any other border control tasks."[32] While originally the powers of the Agency were essentially limited to the evaluation, approval and coordination of proposals for joint operations, and the launching of initiatives for joint operations by Frontex was subjected to the agreement of the Member States,[33] its tasks now include, *inter alia*, (1) the coordination and organization of joint operations, (2) the launching of rapid border interventions at the external borders of those Member States facing specific and disproportionate challenges, (3) the setting up and deployment of European Border and

Coast Guard teams, and (4) the setting up and deployment of European return intervention teams during return interventions.[34] As far as external border management is concerned, Article 14 of the 2016 Frontex Regulation allocates the power to the Agency to "take" and "carry out" "measures" which are then specified in more detail in the individual paragraphs of this provision.

Notwithstanding this, Frontex arguably has still not been transformed into a fully supranationalized body, which would be entitled to independently exercise control and enforcement powers vis-à-vis individuals – a fact that reflects not only political opposition by the Member States whose interests are represented in the Council, but also pertaining uncertainties relating to the scope of EU competence under Article 77 (2) TFEU referred to above.[35] This may be demonstrated by reference to the following selected aspects:

- Recital 6 of the 2016 Frontex Regulation emphasizes that the Member States retain primary responsibility for the management of the external borders. Frontex should only "support the application of Union measures relating to the management of the external borders by reinforcing, assessing and coordinating the actions of Member States which implement those measures."
- Notwithstanding the establishment of a shared responsibility concerning the implementation of a European integrated border management envisaged by Article 5 (1) of the 2016 Frontex Regulation, the second sentence of this provision clarifies that "Member States shall retain primary responsibility for the management of their sections of the external borders."
- Frontex does not have the power to autonomously adopt operational plans for joint operations at the external borders. Rather, these plans must be agreed upon by the executive director of the Agency *and* the host Member State, in consultation with the participating Member States.[36] European Border and Coast Guard teams may only be deployed in the context of rapid border interventions on the basis of an operational plan.[37]
- The tasks of Frontex enumerated in Article 8 of the 2016 Frontex Regulation predominantly refer to activities of a coordinating and assisting nature. In particular, while Frontex may indeed decide to take and carry out actions at the external borders, e.g. by organizing rapid border interventions[38] and deploying European Border and Coast Guard teams from the rapid reaction pool, whether or not such actions are permissible depends on the existence of operational plans. Furthermore, these actions are subject to the instructions of the host Member State, not of the Agency.[39]
- The role of the liaison officers of the Agency is limited to being required to "foster cooperation and dialogue between the Agency and the national authorities which are responsible for border management and return, including coast guards to the extent that they carry out border control tasks" (Article 12 (3) of the 2016 Frontex Regulation).
- Even in cases where the situation at the external borders requires urgent action, Frontex is not entitled to take immediate action. Rather, Article 19 (1) of the 2016 Frontex Regulation requires that the Council, on the basis of a proposal from the Commission, adopts a decision by means of an implementing act, "identifying measures to mitigate those risks to be implemented by the Agency and requiring the Member State concerned to cooperate with the Agency in the implementation of those measures."

As the Member States thus retain the primary responsibility for the management of the external borders of the Union, the proposal recently submitted by the Commission to establish a new standing corps of 10,000 operational Frontex staff in order to increase the efficiency of joint operations[40] does not seem to be a promising course of action, as long as such a step would not involve that real executive powers be allocated to the staff of the Agency. This, however, would seem to be problematic in light of the limited competences of the Union under Article 77 (2) lit. d TFEU.

As far as the specific issue of maritime border control is concerned, it should be noted that the scope of the 2016 Frontex Regulation clearly covers the carrying out of maritime border surveillance operations.[41] Thus, as a matter of principle all provisions of the Regulation also apply to maritime border control activities. Taking into account that "[n]ational authorities carrying out coast guard functions are responsible for a wide range of tasks, which may include maritime safety, security, search and rescue, border control, fisheries control, customs control, general law enforcement and environmental protection," the 2016 Frontex Regulation calls for enhanced cooperation between Frontex and other maritime actors, including the European Fisheries Control Agency and the European Maritime Safety Agency.[42] It also clarifies that the tasks and powers of Frontex ought not be read in such a way as to interfere with the obligations of the Member States under international agreements,[43] including the LOSC, the 1974 International Convention for the Safety of Life at Sea (SOLAS)[44] and the 1979 International Convention concerning Maritime Search and Rescue (SAR Convention).[45] Article 4 lit. b of the 2016 Frontex Regulation demonstrates that the carrying out of SAR operations "for persons in distress at sea launched and carried out in accordance with Regulation (EU) No 656/2014 of the European Parliament and the Council and with international law, taking place in situations which may arise during border surveillance operations at sea" is one of the components of European integrated border management.[46] This is particularly important in relation to a legal assessment of "push-back-operations," the recent "SAR crisis" in the Mediterranean etc. – issues which will be addressed in the next section. Finally, as to the content of operational plans for joint operations, Article 16 (3) lit. j of the 2016 Frontex Regulation states that such plans shall contain "specific information on the application of the relevant jurisdiction and legislation in the geographical area where the joint operation takes place, including references to national, international and Union law regarding interception, rescue at sea and disembarkation."

Based on Article 77 (2) lit. d TFEU, the Union legislator furthermore enacted Regulation (EU) No. 656/2014 Establishing Rules for the Surveillance of the External Sea Borders in the Context of Operational Cooperation coordinated by the European Agency for the Management of Operational Cooperation at the External Borders of the Members States of the European Union (External Sea Borders Regulation).[47] This legislative act, which was adopted in the aftermath of the sinking of a refugee ship which resulted in the loss of more than 300 lives off the coast of Lampedusa, succeeded a decision of the Council taken in 2010.[48] This decision had been declared invalid by the Court of Justice of the European Union (CJEU) in light of the fact that the operational measures envisaged by it went beyond the scope of "additional measures" within the meaning of the then Article 12 (5) of the Schengen Borders Code.[49] The purpose of the External Sea Borders Regulation is to efficiently monitor the crossing of external borders including through border surveillance, which, again, is conducted in order "to prevent unauthorized border crossings, to counter cross-border criminality and to apprehend or take other measures against those persons who have crossed the border in an irregular manner."[50] The Regulation provides for the possibility to intercept (i.e., to stop, board and search a vessel, its cargo and persons on board, to question persons, and, as *ultima ratio*, to seize the vessel and to apprehend persons on board) a foreign vessel where there are reasonable grounds to suspect that it may be carrying persons intending to circumvent checks at border crossing points or is engaged in the smuggling of migrants by sea.[51] The right to take such enforcement measures[52] – the exercise of which is, again, not allocated to Frontex, but rather remains within the responsibility of the Member States – is extended by Article 7 of the Regulation to the high seas, but only "subject to the authorization of the flag State, in accordance with the Protocol against the Smuggling of Migrants, and where relevant, national and international law" (Article 7 (1)). Based on a formal legal assessment, the view that the interception rights under the External Sea Borders Regulation are problematic as to their compatibility with the international law of the sea and other international treaties[53] can thus not be upheld.

Challenges

Taking into account that the competence to exercise border control and surveillance activities ought to be considered as being directly linked to the territoriality principle and, as far as the intra-EU perspective is concerned, is covered by the powers allocated to the Union by its Member States in order to contribute to the establishment of the Single European Market, the crucial challenges are related to the question not of *whether* at all the EU and its Member States are entitled to develop a system of maritime border control, but rather to that of *how* these activities are conducted. In other words, it must be safeguarded that maritime border control activities are performed in a manner compatible with the standards required under public international law[54] and, where applicable, primary EU law.

Requirements arising from the international law of the sea

As far as the perspective of public international law is concerned, any maritime border control activity, be it performed within the framework of Frontex or be it conducted by one of the Member States, must be compatible with the rules and principles of the international law of the sea. In this respect, the Member States of the EU are, according to Article 98 of the LOSC, under a duty to safeguard that all ships flying their flags render assistance to any person found at sea in danger of being lost, and proceed with all possible speed to the rescue of persons in distress. This duty is further specified by the provisions of the SAR Convention, the purpose of which it is to implement procedures and mechanisms which guarantee the effective and proactive rescue of persons in distress at sea. It is not compatible with either the LOSC or the SAR Convention to differentiate on the basis of nationality or status during a sea rescue operation.[55] However, neither the LOSC nor the SAR Convention prescribe a corresponding duty of the nearest coastal State or of the State of the next port of call to accept the disembarkation of the rescued persons.[56] While the International Maritime Organization (IMO) clarified in its 2004 Guidelines on the Treatment of Persons Rescued at Sea that "delivery to a place of safety should take into account the particular circumstances of the case,"[57] the guidelines do not mention a duty of the flag State to bring the rescued person onshore, or a corresponding duty of the coastal State to accept that the persons rescued by a ship flying a foreign flag may be disembarked on its territory. Arguably, the legally binding amendments to the SOLAS and SAR Conventions of 2004 do not result in the opposite conclusion, as they only prescribe a "responsibility to ensure" of the "government [sic!] responsible for the search and rescue region in which such assistance is rendered" – a responsibility that does not equal to a clear duty concerning disembarkation.[58]

Requirements arising from international human rights law

It is beyond serious argument that States conducting interdiction operations within their territorial seas, i.e., on their territory, are not released from their human rights obligations.[59] The question whether this also applies in the Exclusive Economic Zone (EEZ) and on the high seas is more difficult to answer and has been extensively discussed by the dispute settlement mechanisms established by the pertinent human rights treaties, in particular the International Covenant on Civil and Political Rights (ICCPR)[60] and the European Convention for the Protection of Human Rights and Fundamental Freedoms (ECHR).[61] The predominant view is that individuals are protected by the human rights codified in the ICCPR and the ECHR even if the potential violation has taken place outside the territory of the State, provided that that State exercises effective or de facto control over the territory or persons concerned.[62] In the Medvedyev case, the European Court of Human Rights (ECtHR) held that persons aboard a ship flying the flag of Cambodia were effectively within the jurisdiction of France because France "exercised full and exclusive control over the *Winner* and its crew, at least de facto, from the time of its interception."[63] It can thus be concluded that the ICCPR and ECHR will usually be applicable in the context of interdiction operations, even if conducted on the high seas. Consequently, if ships or boats of refugees are prevented from entering the territorial sea of an EU Member State, or are pushed back to the high seas, in order to prevent the persons concerned being entitled to submit an application for the granting of asylum on European territory, this practice ("push-back-operations")[64] violates, at least when the individuals are subsequently left to their own fate, the right to life and physical integrity codified in the ECHR, as well as other human rights (such as, e.g., the prohibition of collective expulsion and the right to effective legal remedy).[65]

Human rights provisions are also relevant with regard to situations where persons on board intercepted vessels are later on forced to return to their home States, or third States. According to the principle of *non-refoulement* codified in Article 3 (1) of the Convention Against Torture and Other Cruel, Inhuman or Degrading Treatment or Punishment[66] and Article 3 ECHR, a person shall not be expelled, returned or extradited to another State where there are substantial grounds for believing that he/she would be in danger of being subjected to torture. This obligation is applicable no matter whether the return of the person concerned is based on an international agreement concluded between one or more EU Member States and a third State or not.[67] It implies that prior to any decision on removing a person to another State, it must be assessed by the competent authorities of the State exercising *de jure* or de facto control over the person concerned whether a real risk exists that the person concerned is being subjected to torture or to inhuman or degrading treatment or punishment.[68] The ECtHR has expressly recognized that the principle of *non-refoulement* under Article 3 ECHR also applies to persons aboard vessels that are intercepted in areas beyond national territory.[69] In its Hirsi Jamaa judgment, the Court made the following pertinent statement:

> The Court has already had occasion to note that the States which form the external borders of the European Union are currently experiencing considerable difficulties in coping with the increasing influx of migrants and asylum seekers. It does not underestimate the burden and pressure this situation places on the States concerned, which are all the greater in the present context of economic crisis [...]. It is particularly aware of the difficulties related to the phenomenon of migration by sea, involving for States additional complications in controlling the borders in southern Europe. However, having regard to the absolute character of the rights secured by Article 3, that cannot absolve a State of its obligations under that provision.[70]

Requirements arising from the EU Charter of Fundamental Rights

In addition to international human rights standards, it is very likely that the Member States are also bound to observe the provisions of the Charter of Fundamental Rights of the European Union (CFR). According to Article 51 CFR, "[t]he provisions of this Charter are addressed to the institutions and bodies of the Union with due regard for the principle of subsidiarity and to the Member States only when they are implementing Union law." As far as its applicability towards maritime border control activities of the Member States is concerned, the decisive question is thus whether the Member States, when conducting such activities, are implementing Union law. Based on the case law of the CJEU, this would arguably presuppose that a direct nexus exists between the relevant conduct on the one hand and requirements of EU law, such as those prescribed in the Schengen Borders Code, on the other.[71] In addition, no doubt exists that Frontex is indeed a "body of the Union" in terms of Article 51 (1) CFR and as such itself bound to the fundamental rights enshrined in the Charter in respect of measures falling within the scope of its founding act, namely the 2016 Frontex Regulation.[72]

Assessment of EU measures applicable to maritime border control

In relation to international SAR standards

If the legislative measures adopted by the EU are assessed against the aforementioned standards, it is – first – noteworthy that EU law not only demands that Member States as well as the institutions of the Union ought to respect the obligations under the international law of the sea,[73] but rather prescribes specific requirements in relation to disembarkation following interception in the territorial sea, the contiguous zone, or on the high seas. As far as the high seas are concerned, the External Sea Borders Regulation stipulates that disembarkation shall take place in the host Member State, provided that this is not possible in the third State from which the vessel is assumed to have departed.[74] If and to the extent to which the External Sea Borders Regulation is applicable, EU law thus goes beyond the pertinent standards of public international law, which, as demonstrated above, do not prescribe any clear obligations concerning disembarkation.[75] Thus, if the interpretation of the SAR standards accepted under the international law of the sea submitted here is agreed with, the critique raised by one commentator that the reference made in Article 10 (1) of the External Sea Borders Regulation to specific States where disembarkation should, or ought to, take place would ignore the primary objective of SAR operations, namely to ascertain the safety of persons rescued at sea,[76] does not seem to be convincing.

With regard to interception measures, provided that no bilateral or multilateral treaty stating the opposite exists, a State is principally only entitled to stop and board ships not operating under its own flag on the high seas under very limited conditions, namely when there is reasonable suspicion that the respective ship is engaged in piracy or human trafficking, or that the ship is engaging non-authorized broadcasting signals. This implies that without the consent of the flag State, vessels operating within a Frontex mandate are not allowed to conduct border checks or other interception measures vis-à-vis persons on board of foreign ships sailing on the high seas or in the EEZ.[77] This legal situation is adequately endorsed by the External Sea Borders Regulation, which subjects in its Article 7 maritime interception measures conducted on the high seas to the authorization of the flag State of the ship that is planned to be intercepted. It has been criticized that the European legislator has refrained from making these limitations also applicable to the territorial sea. While in light of the fact that this maritime zone is subject to the territorial sovereignty of the coastal State,[78] Articles 24 (1) and 27 (1) LOSC ought to be interpreted in such a way that even foreign ships that make use of the right of innocent passage under Article 17 LOSC can lawfully be subjected to the criminal jurisdiction of the coastal State, provided that this jurisdiction is exercised in a reasonable and non-abusive manner.[79] The question whether the existence of enforcement jurisdiction of the coastal State over foreign ships also implies a right to interdict suspected ships without authorization of their flag States does not seem to be completely settled, though.

In relation to international human rights standards

As far as the issue of compatibility with international human rights standards is concerned, Article 4 of the Schengen Borders Code expressly obliges the Member States to

> act in full compliance with relevant Union law, including the Charter of Fundamental Rights of the European Union ("the Charter"), relevant international law, including the Convention Relating to the Status of Refugees done at Geneva on 28 July 1951 ("the Geneva Convention"), obligations related to access to international protection, in particular the principle of *non-refoulement*, and fundamental rights.

This duty, which furthermore stipulates that decisions under the Schengen Borders Code "shall be taken on an individual basis," transforms the international human rights standards into obligations under EU law, which thus participate, if and to the extent to which measures taken by the Member States fall within the scope of the Schengen Borders Code, in the primacy of EU law vis-à-vis the domestic legal systems of the Member States.

With specific regard to maritime border control, Article 4 (1) of the External Sea Borders Regulation recalls the principle of *non-refoulement* by stressing, in mandatory language, that persons must not be treated in a way not compatible with Article 33 Geneva Convention relating to the Status of Refugees (GRC), Article 3 ECHR and Article 3 of the UN Convention against Torture. Similar to the Schengen Borders Code, Article 4 (3) of the External Sea Borders Regulation furthermore requires that an individual assessment ought to be undertaken before intercepted or rescued persons are handed over to the authorities of a third State. Moreover, Recital 13 of the Regulation ought to be regarded as a reaction to the Hirsi Jamaa judgment of the ECtHR by stating that "[t]he possible existence of an arrangement between a Member State and a third country does not absolve Member States from their obligations under Union and international law, in particular as regards compliance with the principle of *non-refoulement*."

Whether or not the specific modalities on detection and interception laid out in Articles 5 to 8 of the External Sea Borders Regulation sufficiently consider the legal prerequisites stemming from international human rights law is not uniformly answered. Several commentators have advanced the view that the decision on whether a person faces the risk of persecution and, in the affirmative, ought not be handed over to the authorities of a third State cannot lawfully be taken on board the ship that is conducting the interception measure, but presupposes that the person concerned is granted access to the territory of the State whose authorities are competent to decide the matter.[80] While the proponents of this view admit that no general right exists to enter the territory of a foreign State, their conclusion is based on the principle that the procedure within which it is determined whether the person ought to be recognized as refugee, or as being at risk of being expelled to inhuman and cruel behavior resulting in human rights violations in the third State respectively, must be effective.[81] It should be noted, though, that the modalities on detection and interception laid out in Articles 5 to 8 of the External Sea Borders Regulation must be interpreted in conformity with Article 4 of the Regulation, which requires in its third paragraph that

> the participating units shall [...] use all means to identify the intercepted or rescued persons, assess their personal circumstances, inform them of their destination in a way that those persons understand or may reasonably be presumed to understand and give them an opportunity to express any reasons for believing that disembarkation in the proposed place would be in violation of the principle of *non-refoulement*.

Read together with the general prohibition to disembark persons in contravention of the *non-refoulement* principle laid out in Article 4 (1) of the Regulation, this ought to be understood in such a way that only in cases where it is safeguarded that the procedure for determining the status of a person is effective and performed in full compliance with international human rights standards can the decision whether to hand over the person concerned to a third State or not lawfully be taken onboard the intercepting ship. This is exactly why Article 4 (8) of the External Sea Borders Regulation requires that "[b]order guards and other staff participating in a sea operation shall be trained with regard to relevant provisions of fundamental rights, refugee law and the international legal regime of search and rescue."

In relation to European fundamental rights standards

Article 4 of the Schengen Borders Code, which requires the Member States to "act in full compliance with relevant Union law, including the Charter of Fundamental Rights of the European Union," is only declaratory, as the fundamental rights enshrined in the CFR must, according to its Article 51 (1), be observed by the Member States anytime "when they are implementing Union law." As far as Frontex itself is concerned, it is noteworthy that the 2016 Frontex Regulation contains numerous references to the CFR.[82] From an institutional perspective, the 2016 Frontex Regulation provides for (1) the appointment of a fundamental rights officer;[83] (2) the setting up of a complaints mechanism to monitor and ensure respect for fundamental rights in all the activities of the Agency;[84] and (3) the establishment of a consultative forum to assist the executive director and the management board with independent advice in fundamental rights matters.[85] Against this background, it seems fair to conclude that considerable efforts have been made in order to substantiate the duty of Frontex to adhere to the CFR arising from its Article 51 (1) by way of secondary EU law. Notwithstanding these measures, Frontex operations are frequently held by commentators to not adequately implement the obligations arising from the CFR, and that these shortcomings have become most visible at sea, namely in the course of maritime border operations.[86] However, the asserted shortcomings are perhaps more closely related to legal uncertainties concerning the issue of which actor – the EU Member States or Frontex – ought to bear the responsibility for violations of fundamental rights.

Responsibility and accountability

The most pressing challenge that is related to maritime border control in the EU is the issue of responsibility, or, from an intra-EU perspective, liability, for violations of one or more of the aforementioned legal standards, respectively. Even though European integrated border management is referred to in the 2016 Frontex Regulation as a "shared responsibility," it has been submitted in this chapter that Frontex has not been allocated the power to autonomously enact and conduct supranational measures. Based on this finding, it may seem to be self-evident that only Member States ought to accept responsibility for, say, human rights violations.

On closer examination, however, the issue turns out to be more complex. From a public international law perspective, attribution of a certain conduct to a State or international organization is governed by the rules of State responsibility in general and the 2011 Draft Articles on the Responsibility of International Organizations (DARIO)[87] in particular.[88] These articles are not by themselves legally binding, but may arguably be relied upon as indicating the state of customary international law.[89] In respect of the matter relevant here, Article 7 DARIO states that "[t]he conduct of an organ of a State or an organ or agent of an international organization that is placed at the disposal of another international organization shall be considered under international law an act of the latter organization if the organization exercises effective control over that conduct." The decisive question is thus whether the EU and/or its Member States exercise effective control over European integrated border management activities conducted within the framework of the Schengen Borders Code, the Frontex Regulation and the External Sea Borders Regulation.[90] This question cannot be answered here in detail.[91] Suffice to say that the International Law Commission (ILC) has taken the position that the standard to be applied in order to assess whether an international organization exercises effective control over a certain conduct is comparatively strict. As a matter of fact, the control ought to refer to the particular conduct, and it ought to extend to the operational level.[92] In contrast, if the States concerned retain considerable powers over their national contingents, the conduct concerned usually continues to be attributable only to the States.[93] Measured against this standard, and taking into account the coordinative and supportive role allocated to Frontex, it is submitted that it will usually not be easy to conclude that the Union exercises effective control over European integrated border management activities conducted within the framework of the Schengen Borders Code, the Frontex Regulation and the External Sea Borders Regulation.[94] That said, it must be admitted that every case is unique, and the issue of attribution will ultimately depend on the content of the operational plan in terms of Article 16 of the 2016 Frontex Regulation.[95]

As far as the perspective of EU law is concerned, it has convincingly been argued that actions for annulment, directed against individual measures taken in the context of a Frontex operation, or against an operational plan respectively, will usually not be admissible due to the lack of a subject matter that is open to challenge under Article 263 (4) TFEU.[96] A different question is whether it is possible to assert the responsibility of the Union on the basis of the 2016 Frontex Regulation, or primary EU law, due to a fundamental rights violation that has allegedly occurred in the context of a Frontex operation. While the complaints mechanism foreseen by Article 72 of the 2016 Frontex Regulation is directed against the course of action of individual border guards, not Frontex as such,[97] it has been argued that Article 60 (3) of the Regulation could be invoked as a basis for such course of action.[98] This provision, which is drafted along the lines of the more general Article 340 (2) TFEU, states that "[i]n the case of non-contractual liability, the Agency shall, in accordance with the general principles common to the laws of the Member States, make good any damage caused by its departments or by its staff in the performance of their duties." In contrast to the situation under Article 340 (2) TFEU, Article 60 (3) of the 2016 Frontex Regulation envisages direct liability of Frontex. However, whether or not the Agency can be held liable for fundamental rights violations that have occurred in the context of maritime border management activities depends on whether it can be established that Frontex has exercised effective control over the conduct in question.[99] In this respect, the legal situation is identical to that under public international law.

Conclusion

In line with the development of the broader Schengen regime, measures taken by the EU in relation to maritime border control have become more diverse and sophisticated over the years. Notwithstanding this, due to its limited legislative powers on the field concerned, the EU has not and can arguably not establish a truly supranational external border policy. While Frontex, which is supposed to play a crucial role also with regard to the control of the maritime borders, has been further developed into a "European Border and Coast Guard" following the massive increase of the number of persons attempting to enter the territories of the Member States in 2015, it is not entitled to independently exercise control and enforcement powers vis-à-vis individuals. The main legal challenges of the EU maritime border control regime continue to arise in the context of safeguarding that the measures taken on the European level are enacted and implemented in such a way that they respect the pertinent standards of international law and the CFR. These measures not only include the control of maritime borders, but extend to the fight against transnational organized crime such as human trafficking, the interception of suspected vessels and the provision of search and rescue services. This chapter submits that the EU has clearly enhanced the relevant standard of protection over the years, thereby reacting to the legitimate criticism raised vis-à-vis its policy, by amending the legal measures applicable to maritime border control – a development which has arguably sufficiently put in line these acts with the basic requirements of the international law of the sea, international human rights as well as the fundamental rights codified in the CFR. That said, the crucial issue is whether the regulations concerned are also implemented accordingly in legal practice. As recent years have demonstrated, there is still a clear need for improvements in this respect. Arguably, the protection gaps, or failures to observe the relevant standards, that have continued to exist on the level of implementation are to some extent related to the complicated division of responsibilities between Frontex on the one hand and the border patrol services of the Member States on the other. This legal issue is, again, influenced by uncertainties concerning the exact scope of the EU competences, which could be addressed by either broadening or limiting the Union powers by way of a Treaty amendment. However, it is important to note that any further extension of the competences of the EU in the field of maritime border control would necessarily have to be accompanied by the creation of effective and clear legal remedies – an issue which has already been the subject of political demands and scholarly debate in relation to the law as it stands today.

Notes

1 United Nations, *United Nations Convention on the Law of the Sea* of 10 December 1982, 1833 UNTS 3.

2 Consolidated Version of the Treaty on the Functioning of the European Union. OJ C 326, October 26, 2012, 47.

3 *Completing the Internal Market: White Paper from the Commission to the European Council (Milan, 28–29 June 1985)*, COM(85) 310 final. Brussels: European Union, June 14, 1986, paras. 47 *et seq*.

4 Agreement between the Governments of the States of the Benelux Economic Union, the Federal Republic of Germany and the French Republic on the Gradual Abolition of Checks at Their Common Borders of 14 June 1985. OJ L 239, September 22, 2000, 13.

5 Convention Implementing the Schengen Agreement of 14 June 1985 between the Governments of the States of the Benelux Economic Union, the Federal Republic of Germany and the French Republic on the Gradual Abolition of Checks at Their Common Borders of 19 June 1990. OJ L 239, September 22, 2000, 19.

6 Article 2 (1) of the Protocol to the Treaty of Amsterdam Integrating the Schengen Acquis into the Framework of the European Union, OJ C 340, November 10, 1997, 93:

> From the date of entry into force of the Treaty of Amsterdam, the Schengen acquis, including the decisions of the Executive Committee established by the Schengen agreements which have been adopted before this date, shall immediately apply to the thirteen Member States referred to in Article 1, without prejudice to the provisions of paragraph 2 of this Article. From the same date, the Council will substitute itself for the said Executive Committee.

7 Article 5 (1) of the Schengen Protocol to the Treaty of Amsterdam.

8 Daniel Thym, "Artikel 77 AEUV," in *Das Recht der Europäischen Union: Kommentar*, ed. Eberhard Grabitz, Meinhard Hilf and Martin Nettesheim (Loose-leaf-collection, C.H. Beck 2018), para. 34.

9 CJEU, Case C-217/04, Judgment of 2 May 2006, UK v. Council, ECLI:EU:C:2006:279, para. 41 *et seq*.

10 For further reasoning on this controversial matter: Thym, "Artikel 77 AEUV," para. 37; Steve Peers, *Justice and Home Affairs* (Oxford: Oxford University Press, 2011), 156–57.
11 Peers, *Justice and Home Affairs*, 221.
12 OJ C 115, 9 May 2008, 304.
13 Thym, "Artikel 77 AEUV," para. 39. He points to the example of the agreement concluded between Italy and Libya concerning cooperation in the field of maritime border control and prevention of illegal immigration in the Mediterranean.
14 Regulation (EU) 2016/399 of the European Parliament and of the Council of 9 March 2016 on a Union Code on the Rules Governing the Movement of Persons Across Borders, OJ L 77, March 23, 2016, 1. This Regulation has, in the interest of clarity, replaced Regulation (EC) 562/2006 of the European Parliament and of the Council, which had been substantially amended several times.
15 According to information provided by the European Commission (accessed March 28, 2019, http://europa.eu/rapid/press-release_IP-16-4402_en.htm), SIS currently contains around 70 million records, and was consulted 2.9 billion times in 2015. In its current form, the system was established by Regulation (EC) No 1987/2006 of the European Parliament and of the Council of 20 December 2006 on the Establishment, Operation and Use of the Second Generation Schengen Information System (SIS II), OJ L 381, December 28, 2006, 4. In June 2018, the EU institutions involved in the ordinary legislation process reached agreement on a new SIS package, but the respective measures have not yet been adopted.
16 Note that Article 6 (5) lit. c of the Schengen Borders Code leaves it to the Member State concerned to authorize a third-country national who does not fulfill one or more of the conditions laid down in para. 1 to enter its territory on humanitarian grounds, on grounds of national interest or because of international obligations. This is particularly relevant in relation to the concept of subsidiary protection granted by some States to persons that have fled from their home States due to armed violence or the danger of being subjected to torture and other human rights violations, but who do not possess the status of refugees under public international law. See, e.g., Section 4 (1) of the German Asylum Act (Federal Law Gazette 2008, Part I, 1798; last amendment: Federal Law Gazette 2018, Part I, 2250).
17 Wolfgang Weiß, "Artikel 77 AEUV," in *EUV/AEUV: Kommentar*, ed. Rudolf Streinz (München: C.H. Beck, 2018), para. 21; Matthias Rossi, "Artikel 77 AEUV," in *EUV/AEUV*, ed. Christian Calliess and Matthias Ruffert (München: C.H. Beck, 2016), para. 31; Thym, "Artikel 77 AEUV," para. 40.
18 This information, which, where applicable, also includes visa or residence permit numbers, must be provided at the latest 24 hours before arriving in the port, or, if the voyage time is less than 24 hours, at the latest at the time the ship leaves the previous port, or, if the port of call is not known or it is changed during the voyage, as soon as this information is available.
19 Derogations from Article 5 of the Borders Code are not foreseen vis-à-vis cargo connections.
20 See note 18 above.
21 See the second sentence of Article 1 (2), according to which Frontex shall administer its tasks "by ensuring the coordination of Member States actions in the implementation of those measures, thereby contributing to an efficient, high and uniform level of control on persons and surveillance of the external borders of the Member States." Note further that the EU had not yet been allocated a specific competence for border surveillance measures when the Frontex Regulation was adopted.
22 Regulation (EU) 2016/1624 of the European Parliament and of the Council of 14 September 2016 on the European Border and Coast Guard and Amending Regulation (EU) 2016/399 of the European Parliament and of the Council and Repealing Regulation (EC) No 863/2007 of the European Parliament and of the Council, Council Regulation (EC) No 2007/2004 and Council Decision 2005/267/EC, OJ L 251, September 16, 2016, 1.
23 Italics added.
24 European Commission, Communication from the Commission to the European Parliament, the Council, the European Economic and Social Committee and the Committee of the Regions: Preparing the Next Steps in Border Management in the European Union, COM(2008) 69 final (Brussels: European Union, February 13, 2008).
25 European Commission, Proposal for a Regulation of the European Parliament and of the Council Establishing an Entry/Exit System (EES) to Register Entry and Exit Data and Refusal of Entry Data of Third Country Nationals Crossing the External Borders of the Member States of the European Union and Determining the Conditions for Access to the EES for Law Enforcement Purposes and Amending Regulation (EC) No 767/2008 and Regulation (EU) No 1077/2011, COM(2016) 194 final (Brussels: European Union, 2016).

26 European Commission, Communication from the Commission to the European Parliament and the Council: Stronger and Smarter Information Systems for Borders and Security, COM(2016) 205 final (Brussels: European Union, April 6, 2016).
27 See Article 15 of the 2004 Frontex Regulation.
28 For an overview concerning the original tasks: Peers, *Justice and Home Affairs*, 217–19.
29 Recital 1 of the 2016 Frontex Regulation:

> [T]he Heads of State or Government stressed the need to tackle the dramatic situation at the external borders and to strengthen the controls at those borders, in particular through additional resources for the European Agency for the Management of Operational Cooperation at the External Borders of the Member States of the European Union, the European Asylum Support Office (EASO), and Europol, with human resources and technical contributions from Member States.

30 The legal status of Frontex has essentially remained the same. Article 56 of the 2016 Frontex Regulation.
31 Article 2 (2) of the 2016 Frontex Regulation. For an overview of the components of European integrated border management, see Article 4 of the 2016 Frontex Regulation.
32 Article 5 (1) of the 2016 Frontex Regulation.
33 Article 3 (1) of the 2004 Frontex Regulation.
34 Article 8 (1) lit. d, e, g and o of the 2016 Frontex Regulation.
35 Recital 45 of the 2016 Frontex Regulation, according to which "[t]he implementation of this Regulation does not affect the division of competence between the Union and the Member States under the Treaties." It does not require detailed analysis that the EU is not entitled to broaden its competences that have been allocated to it by the TFEU by way of enacting legislative measures.
36 Article 16 (2) of the 2016 Frontex Regulation.
37 Article 20 (5) of the 2016 Frontex Regulation.
38 Article 17 (4) of the 2016 Frontex Regulation.
39 Article 21 (1) of the 2016 Frontex Regulation.
40 https://ec.europa.eu/commission/sites/beta-political/files/soteu2018-factsheet-coast-guard_en.pdf (accessed March 28, 2019).
41 Article 5 (1) of the 2016 Frontex Regulation.
42 Recital 44, Article 8 (1) lit. t, Article 52 (1) and Article 53 of the 2016 Frontex Regulation.
43 Recital 45 of the 2016 Frontex Regulation.
44 1184 UNTS 277.
45 1405 UNTS 118.
46 Article 8 (1) lit. d to f, Article 14 (2) lit. e and Article 34 (3) of the 2016 Frontex Regulation.
47 OJ L 189, 27 June 2014, 93.
48 Council Decision 2010/252/EU of 26 April 2010 Supplementing the Schengen Borders Code as Regards the Surveillance of the Sea External Borders in the Context of Operational Cooperation Coordinated by the European Agency for the Management of Operational Cooperation at the External Borders of the Member States of the European Union, OJ L 111, May 4, 2010, 20.
49 CJEU, Case No. C-355/10, Judgment of 5 September 2012 Parliament v. Council, ECLI:EU:C:2012:516, paras. 69–85.
50 Recital 1 of the External Sea Borders Regulation.
51 Articles 6 to 8 of the External Sea Borders Regulation.
52 CJEU, Case No. C-355/10, Judgment of 5 September 2012, Parliament v. Council, ECLI:EU:C:2012:516, para. 74.
53 But see Matthias Lehnert, *Frontex und operative Maßnahmen an den europäischen Außengrenzen* (Baden-Baden: Nomos, 2014), 222–34; Anna Mrozek, "Zwischen 'Raum der Freiheit,' 'Raum der Sicherheit' und 'Raum des Rechts' – Der Mechanismus des supranationalen Grenzschutzes an den europäischen Außengrenzen," *Zeitschrift für Ausländerrecht* 10 (2014): 398; Rossi, "Artikel 77 AEUV," para. 35a.
54 For a recent in-depth assessment: Irini Papanicolopulu, *International Law and the Protection of People at Sea* (Oxford: Oxford University Press, 2018), 111–57 (in relation to the scope of the duties of States) and 159–207 (as to the content of the duties of States).
55 Section 2.1.10 of the Annex to the SAR Convention.
56 Alexander Proelss, "Rescue at Sea Revisited: What Obligations Exist Towards Refugees?," *Scandinavian Institute of Maritime Law Yearbook* (2008): 16–17; Richard Barnes, "Refugee Law at Sea," *International and Comparative Law Quarterly* 53 (2004): 49 and 67; Douglas Guilfoyle, "Article 98," in *United Nations*

Convention on the Law of the Sea: A Commentary, ed. Alexander Proelss (München, Oxford, Baden-Baden: C.H. Beck, Hart, Nomos, 2017), para. 10; Killian O'Brien, "Refugees on the High Seas: Refugee Law Solutions to a Law of the Sea Problem," *Goettingen Journal of International Law* 3 (2011): 723–25; *contra* UNHCR, Background Note on the Protection of Asylum-Seekers and Refugees Rescued at Sea, 18 March 2002, para. 12.

57 IMO Resolution MSC.167(78) of 20 May 2004, *Guidelines on the Treatment of Persons Rescued at Sea*, IMO Doc. MSC 78/26/Add.2, Annex 34, para. 6.15.

58 Guilfoyle, "Article 98," para. 10; Proelss, "Rescue at Sea," 16–21; O'Brien, "Refugees," 725; *contra* Martin Ratcovich, "The Concept of 'Place of Safety': Yet Another Self-Contained Maritime Rule or a Sustainable Solution to the Ever-Controversial Question of Where to Disembark Migrants Rescued at Sea?," *Australian Year Book of International Law* 33 (2016): 13–14.

59 Douglas Guilfoyle, "Human Rights Issues and Non-Flag State Boarding of Suspect Ships," in *Selected Contemporary Issues in the Law of the Sea*, ed. Clive Symmons (Leiden: Martinus Nijhoff, 2011), 84. See also Melanie Fink, "Salami Slicing Human Rights Accountability: How the European Border and Coast Guard Agency May Inherit Frontex' Genetic Defect," *EJIL: Talk!*, March 10, 2016, accessed March 28, 2019. www.ejiltalk.org/salami-slicing-human-rights-accountability-how-the-european-border-and-coast-guard-agency-may-inherit-frontex-genetic-defect: "external border control is inherently human rights sensitive."

60 UN General Assembly, International Covenant on Civil and Political Rights of 19 December 1966 (999 UNTS 172).

61 Council of Europe, European Convention for the Protection of Human Rights and Fundamental Freedoms of 4 November 1950 (213 UNTS 222).

62 For example: European Court of Human Rights (ECtHR), *Al-Skeini and Others* v. *UK*, Application No. 55721/07, Judgment of 7 July 2011, paras. 135–36; ECHR, *Öcalan* v. *Turkey*, Application No. 46221/99, Judgment of 12 May 2005, para. 9.

63 ECtHR, *Case of Medvedyev and Others* v. *France*, Application No. 3394/03, Judgment of 29 March 2010, para. 67 (original italics).

64 The former executive director of Frontex, Ilkka Laitinen, had to admit in 2013 that sporadic cases of push-back-operations had occurred even after the Hirsi Jamaa Judgment of 23 February 2012 had been rendered by the ECtHR; for example: www.deutschlandradio.de/frontex-gibt-menschenrechtsverletzungen-zu.331.de.html?dram:article_id=265564, accessed March 28, 2019.

65 In contrast, the *non-refoulement* principle codified in Article 33 of the 1951 Geneva Convention relating to the Status of Refugees (GRC) of 28 July 1951 (189 UNTS 137) is arguably not applicable to push-back-operations in international waters. Irrespective of the controversial question of whether this principle generally applies to measures taken in areas beyond national jurisdiction, application of Article 33 GRC requires that the life or freedom of the person concerned is threatened in the territory that he/she is being returned to *because* of his/her race, religion, nationality, his/her ethnic or social affiliation or because of his/her political belief; Guy S. Goodwin-Gill and Jane McAdam, *The Refugee in International Law* (Oxford: Oxford University Press, 2007), 277. In the case of push-back-operations, however, the threat to life is not directly related to the aforementioned criteria, but is rather a consequence of the hostile environment on the high seas.

66 UN General Assembly, Convention against Torture and Other Cruel, Inhuman or Degrading Treatment or Punishment of 10 December 1984 (1465 UNTS 112).

67 ECtHR, *Case of Hirsi Jamaa and Others* v. *Italy*, Application No. 27765/09, Judgment of 23 February 2012, para. 129:

> The Court observes that Italy cannot evade its own responsibility by relying on its obligations arising out of bilateral agreements with Libya. Even if it were to be assumed that those agreements made express provision for the return to Libya of migrants intercepted on the high seas, the Contracting States' responsibility continues even after their having entered into treaty commitments subsequent to the entry into force of the Convention or its Protocols in respect of these States.

68 Ibid, para. 133.

69 Ibid, paras. 70–82, 114.

70 Ibid, para. 122.

71 Jonathan Tomkin, "Frontex," in *EU Immigration and Asylum Law*, ed. Steve Peers *et al.*, Vol. 1 (Leiden, Boston: Martinus Nijhoff, 2012), 152. But see the broad formula invoked by the CJEU in Case No.

C-617/10, Judgment of 26 February 2013, Åkerberg Fransson, ECLI:EU:C:2013:105, para. 19: "The Court's settled case-law indeed states, in essence, that the fundamental rights guaranteed in the legal order of the European Union are applicable in all situations governed by European Union law, but not outside such situations."

72 CJEU, Case C-23/12, Judgment of 17 January 2013, Mohamad Zakaria, ECLI:EU:C:2013:24, paras. 33–41. According to the Explanations Relating to the Charter of Fundamental Rights prepared and updated by the Praesidium of the European Convention (OJ C 303, 14 December 2007, 17), the term "bodies" is "commonly used in the Treaties to refer to all authorities set up by the Treaties or by secondary legislation."

73 Recital 45 and 47 of the 2016 Frontex Regulation.

74 Article 10 (1) lit. b of the External Sea Borders Regulation.

75 Guilfoyle, "Article 98," para. 12.

76 Lehnert, *Frontex*, 268.

77 Note that according to Article 58 (1) LOSC, foreign-flagged ships enjoy freedom of navigation in the EEZ. As far as the duty to respect the exclusive jurisdiction of the flag State over its ships is concerned, para. 2 of this provision renders Articles 88 to 115 LOSC and other pertinent rules of international law applicable in the EEZ in so far as they are not incompatible with Part V LOSC.

78 Article 6 of the External Sea Borders Regulation abstains from requiring authorization of the flag State as a prerequisite for the lawfulness of interception measures undertaken in the territorial sea.

79 Alexander Proelss and Tobias Hofmann, "Law of the Sea and Transnational Organized Crime," in *International Law and Transnational Organized Crime*, ed. Pierre Hauck and Sven Peterke (Oxford: Oxford University Press, 2017), 430–1 (with further references). As to the element of reasonability: Article 6 (3) of the External Sea Borders Regulation.

80 UNHCR, Executive Committee, Provisional Annotated Agenda, UN Doc. A/AC.96/882, 1997, para. 12; Kees Wouters, *International Legal Standards for the Protection from Refoulement* (Morstel: Intersentia, 2009), 173 *et seq.*; Alice Edwards, "Human Rights, Refugees, and The Right 'To Enjoy' Asylum," *International Journal of Refugee Law* 17 (2005): 301; Goodwin-Gill and McAdam, *Refugee in International Law*, 374; James C. Hathaway, *The Rights of Refugees under International Law* (Cambridge: Cambridge University Press, 2006), 291 *et seq.*

81 Goodwin-Gill and McAdam, *Refugee in International Law*, 374–80.

82 For example: Article 16 (3) lit. d and Articles 34–36 of the Regulation.

83 The tasks and duties of the fundamental rights officer are listed in Article 71 of the 2016 Frontex Regulation.

84 Article 72 of the 2016 Frontex Regulation.

85 Article 70 of the 2016 Frontex Regulation.

86 For example: Submission of the Immigration Law Practitioners' Association to the Public Consultation by the European Ombuds on Frontex and Fundamental Rights, 2012, 2, accessed March 28, 2018, www.ombudsman.europa.eu/pdf/en/11997; Nina Perkowski, *A Normative Assessment of the Aims and Practices of The European Border Agency Frontex* (Refugee Studies Center, Working Paper Series No. 81 (2012), 4 *et seq.*

87 *Yearbook of the International Law Commission* II-2 (2011): 46–105.

88 Detailed assessments are provided by Melanie Fink, *Frontex and Human Rights: Responsibility in 'Multi-Actor Situations' under the ECHR and EU Public Liability Law* (Oxford: Oxford University Press, 2018), Chapter 3.2; Lehnert, *Frontex*, 341–90.

89 Marten Zwanenburg, *Accountability of Peace Support Operations* (Leiden: Martinus Nijhoff Publishers, 2006), 71 *et seq.*; Hathaway, *Rights of Refugees*, 24 *et seq.*

90 Note that it is not clear whether effective control necessarily implies exclusive control. The commentary to Article 7 DARIO seems to suggest that the ILC has taken the view that it is *either* the State(s) *or* the international organization that has to bear responsibility for the conduct concerned; see *Yearbook of the International Law Commission* II-2 (2011), para. 1. In contrast, most commentators militate in favor of accepting that the law of international responsibility accepts the notion of "shared effective responsibility." UN Doc. A/CN.4/541 of 2 April 2004, Second Report on Responsibility of International Organizations, by Mr. Giorgio Gaja, Special Rapporteur, para. 48; Supreme Court of the Netherlands, Case No. 12/03324, Judgment of 6 September 2013, Netherlands v. Nuhanović, para. 3.11.2; Rechtbank Den Haag, Case No. C/09/295247, Judgment of 16 July 2014, Mothers of Srebrenica v. Netherlands, ECLI:NL:RBDHA:2014:8748, para. 4.45.

91 For detailed analysis: Fink, *Frontex and Human Rights*, Chapter 3.3.3.3; Roberta Mungianu, *Frontex and Non-Refoulement: The International Responsibility of the EU* (Cambridge: Cambridge University Press,

2017), 48–88; Maïté Fernandez, "Multi-stakeholder Operations of Border Control Coordinated at the EU level and the Allocation of International Responsibilities," in *Human Rights and the Dark Side of Globalization: Transnational Law Enforcement and Migration Control*, ed. Thomas Gammeltoft-Hansen and Jens Vedsted-Hansen (London: Routledge, 2016), 238–71.

92 Commentary of the ILC to Article 7 DARIO, *Yearbook of the International Law Commission* II-2 (2011), paras. 4, 7, 8 and 10 with further references.

93 Ibid., para. 7.

94 Anna Mrozek, "Organleihe an den Außengrenzen Europas: Der (un)klare Rechtsrahmen des Einsatzes der Bundespolizei im Rahmen operativer FRONTEX-Aktionen," *Die Öffentliche Verwaltung* (2010): 892; *contra* Lehnert, *Frontex*, 391–7; Perkowski, *Normative Assessment*, 30 *et seq.*

95 Lehnert, *Frontex*, 397.

96 Ibid, 337–40.

97 Fink, "Salami Slicing Human Rights Accountability."

98 Lehnert, *Frontex*, 397–400.

99 Fink, *Frontex and Human Rights*, Chapter 4.3.7.

References

Barnes, Richard. "Refugee Law at Sea." *International and Comparative Law Quarterly* 53 (2004): 47–77.

Council of Europe. European Convention for the Protection of Human Rights and Fundamental Freedoms of 4 November 1950 (213 UNTS 222).

Council of the European Union. Council Decision 2010/252/EU of 26 April 2010 Supplementing the Schengen Borders Code as Regards the Surveillance of the Sea External Borders in the Context of Operational Cooperation Coordinated by the European Agency for the Management of Operational Cooperation at the External Borders of the Member States of the European Union. *Official Journal of the European Union* L 111, May 4, 2010.

Edwards, Alice. "Human Rights, Refugees, and The Right 'To Enjoy' Asylum." *International Journal of Refugee Law* 17 (2005): 293–330.

European Commission. Communication from the Commission to the European Parliament and the Council: Stronger and Smarter Information Systems for Borders and Security. COM(2016) 205 final. Brussels: European Union, April 6, 2016.

European Commission. Communication from the Commission to the European Parliament, the Council, the European Economic and Social Committee and the Committee of the Regions: Preparing the Next Steps in Border Management in the European Union. COM(2008) 69 final. Brussels: European Union, February 13, 2008.

European Commission. *Completing the Internal Market: White Paper from the Commission to the European Council (Milan, 28–29 June 1985).* COM(85) 310 final. Brussels: European Union, 1986.

European Commission. Proposal for a Regulation of the European Parliament and of the Council establishing an Entry/Exit System (EES) to Register Entry and Exit Data and Refusal of Entry Data of Third Country Nationals Crossing the External Borders of the Member States of the European Union and Determining the Conditions for Access to the EES for Law Enforcement Purposes and Amending Regulation (EC) No 767/2008 and Regulation (EU) No 1077/2011. COM(2016) 194 final. Brussels: European Union, 2016.

European Parliament and Council of the European Union. Regulation (EC) No. 1987/2006 of the European Parliament and of the Council of 20 December 2006 on the Establishment, Operation and Use of the Second Generation Schengen Information System (SIS II). *Official Journal of the European Union* L 381, December 28, 2006.

European Parliament and Council of the European Union. Regulation (EU) 2016/399 of the European Parliament and of the Council of 9 March 2016 on a Union Code on the Rules Governing the Movement of Persons Across Borders. *Official Journal of the European Union* L 77, March 23, 2016.

European Parliament and Council of the European Union. Regulation (EU) 2016/1624 of the European Parliament and of the Council of 14 September 2016 on the European Border and Coast Guard and Amending Regulation (EU) 2016/399 of the European Parliament and of the Council and Repealing Regulation (EC) No 863/2007 of the European Parliament and of the Council, Council Regulation (EC) No 2007/2004 and Council Decision 2005/267/EC. *Official Journal of the European Union* L 251, September 16, 2016.

European Union. Agreement between the Governments of the States of the Benelux Economic Union, the Federal Republic of Germany and the French Republic on the Gradual Abolition of Checks at Their Common Borders of 14 June 1985. *Official Journal of the European Union* L 239, September 22, 2000.
European Union. Consolidated Version of the Treaty on the Functioning of the European Union. *Official Journal of the European Union* C 326, October 26, 2012.
European Union. Convention Implementing the Schengen Agreement of 14 June 1985 between the Governments of the States of the Benelux Economic Union, the Federal Republic of Germany and the French Republic on the Gradual Abolition of Checks at Their Common Borders of 19 June 1990. *Official Journal of the European Union* L 239 of September 22, 2000.
Fernandez, Maïté. "Multi-stakeholder Operations of Border Control Coordinated at the EU level and the Allocation of International Responsibilities." In *Human Rights and the Dark Side of Globalization: Transnational Law Enforcement and Migration Control*, edited by Thomas Gammeltoft-Hansen and Jens Vedsted-Hansen, 238–71. London: Routledge, 2016.
Fink, Melanie. *Frontex and Human Rights: Responsibility in 'Multi-Actor Situations' under the ECHR and EU Public Liability Law*. Oxford: Oxford University Press, 2018.
Fink, Melanie. "Salami Slicing Human Rights Accountability: How the European Border and Coast Guard Agency May Inherit Frontex' Genetic Defect." *EJIL: Talk!*, March 10, 2016. Accessed May 8, 2019. www.ejiltalk.org/salami-slicing-human-rights-accountability-how-the-european-border-and-coast-guard-agency-may-inherit-frontex-genetic-defect.
Goodwin-Gill, Guy S., and Jane McAdam. *The Refugee in International Law*. Oxford: Oxford University Press, 2007.
Guilfoyle, Douglas. "Article 98." In *United Nations Convention on the Law of the Sea: A Commentary*, edited by Alexander Proelss, 725–30. München, Oxford, Baden-Baden: C.H. Beck, Hart, Nomos, 2017.
Guilfoyle, Douglas. "Human Rights Issues and Non-Flag State Boarding of Suspect Ships." In *Selected Contemporary Issues in the Law of the Sea*, edited by Clive Symmons, 83–104. Leiden: Martinus Nijhoff, 2011.
Hathaway, James C. *The Rights of Refugees under International Law*. Cambridge: Cambridge University Press, 2006.
Lehnert, Matthias. *Frontex und operative Maßnahmen an den europäischen Außengrenzen*. Baden-Baden: Nomos, 2014.
Mrozek, Anna. "Organleihe an den Außengrenzen Europas: Der (un)klare Rechtsrahmen des Einsatzes der Bundespolizei im Rahmen operativer FRONTEX-Aktionen." *Die Öffentliche Verwaltung* (2010): 886–93.
Mrozek, Anna. "Zwischen 'Raum der Freiheit,' 'Raum der Sicherheit' und 'Raum des Rechts' – der Mechanismus des supranationalen Grenzschutzes an den europäischen Außengrenzen." *Zeitschrift für Ausländerrecht* 10 (2014): 393–400.
Mungianu, Roberta. *Frontex and Non-Refoulement: The International Responsibility of the EU*. Cambridge: Cambridge University Press, 2017.
O'Brien, Killian. "Refugees on the High Seas: Refugee Law Solutions to a Law of the Sea Problem." *Goettingen Journal of International Law* 3 (2011): 715–32.
Papanicolopulu, Irini. *International Law and the Protection of People at Sea*. Oxford: Oxford University Press, 2018.
Peers, Steve. *EU Justice and Home Affairs Law*. Oxford: Oxford University Press, 2011.
Perkowski, Nina. *A Normative Assessment of the Aims and Practices of the European Border Agency Frontex*. Refugee Studies Center, Working Paper Series 81 (2012).
Proelss, Alexander. "Rescue at Sea Revisited: What Obligations Exist Towards Refugees?" *Scandinavian Institute of Maritime Law Yearbook* (2008): 1–39.
Proelss, Alexander, and Tobias Hofmann. "Law of the Sea and Transnational Organized Crime." In *International Law and Transnational Organized Crime*, edited by Pierre Hauck and Sven Peterke, 422–47. Oxford: Oxford University Press, 2017.
Ratcovich, Martin. "The Concept of 'Place of Safety': Yet Another Self-Contained Maritime Rule or a Sustainable Solution to the Ever-Controversial Question of Where to Disembark Migrants Rescued at Sea?" *Australian Year Book of International Law* 33 (2016): 1–52.
Rossi, Matthias. "Artikel 77 AEUV." In *EUV/AEUV*, edited by Christian Calliess and Matthias Ruffert. München: C.H. Beck, 2016.
Thym, Daniel. "Artikel 77 AEUV." In *Das Recht der Europäischen Union: Kommentar*, edited by Eberhard Grabitz, Meinhard Hilf and Martin Nettesheim. Loose-leaf-collection, C.H. Beck 2018.

Tomkin, Jonathan. "Frontex." In *EU Immigration and Asylum Law*, edited by Steve Peers, Elspeth Guild and Jonathan Tomkin, Vol. 1, 119–204. Leiden, Boston: Martinus Nijhoff, 2012.

United Nations. United Nations Convention on the Law of the Sea of 10 December 1982 (1833 UNTS 3).

United Nations General Assembly. Convention against Torture and Other Cruel, Inhuman or Degrading Treatment or Punishment of 10 December 1984 (1465 UNTS 112).

United Nations General Assembly. International Covenant on Civil and Political Rights of 19 December 1966 (999 UNTS 172).

Weiß, Wolfgang. "Artikel 77 AEUV." In *EUV/AEUV: Kommentar*, edited by Rudolf Streinz. München: C.H. Beck, 2018.

Wouters, Kees. *International Legal Standards for the Protection from Refoulement*. Morstel: Intersentia, 2009.

Zwanenburg, Marten. *Accountability of Peace Support Operations*. Leiden: Martinus Nijhoff Publishers, 2006.

21

SECURITY AND DRUGS IN THE EUROPEAN UNION

Criminal justice and drugs policy[1]

Araceli Manjón-Cabeza Olmeda

Introduction

Along with other challenges facing the European Union today, such as security, common European policy and nationalism, the issue of drugs and how to deal with them is at the forefront of discussions. The preface to the EU Drug Strategy for 2013–2020[2] establishes, among other principles, the following:

> This Drugs Strategy is based first and foremost on the fundamental principles of EU law and, in every regard, upholds the founding values of the Union: respect for human dignity, liberty, democracy, equality, solidarity, the rule of law and human rights. It aims to protect and improve the well-being of society and of the individual, to protect public health, to offer a high level of security for the general public and to take a balanced, integrated and evidence-based approach to the drugs phenomenon.

The EU's drugs policy is intended to protect public health and well-being, based on the understanding that these aims call for "a high level of security," which means the drugs issue is treated mainly from the point of view of security. This is reiterated in the 2003 European Security Strategy (ESS) "A Secure Europe in a Better World,"[3] which identified, as both an internal and external threat, organised crime dedicated to drugs trafficking and the resulting weakening of state structures, to the extent of turning some places into failed states. Organised crime as a threat to security continued to feature when this Strategy was reviewed in the 2009 Report on the implementation of the European Security Strategy "Providing Security in a Changing World."[4] It was stressed that this report does not replace the ESS, but reinforces it. It is significant that this review, although it discusses organised crime, makes no reference to drugs trafficking, focusing rather on other threats.

Naturally, European strategy on organised drugs trafficking, or on organised crime, within the framework of general security, is not absolute, but is subject on one hand to the founding values of the European Union and, on the other, to "a balanced, integrated and evidence-based approach to the drugs phenomenon." The aforementioned values, especially those of human rights, and the concept of a balanced, integrated and evidence-based approach, give us a theoretical framework that diverges from that which has informed the United Nations' approach to date.

Drugs policy and security. Key approaches: human rights, scientific evidence, health and sustainable development

International practice has been to reduce the problem of drugs to an issue of security, treating this as an absolute consideration unaffected by human rights, scientific evidence or individual and collective health needs. As a result, all measures based on international consensus have targeted the supply side, downplaying measures aimed at reducing demand. At this point it should be noted that the European strategies adopted during the heroin crisis were more effective and more humane, as they were based on tackling demand, but without criminalising the consumer, implementing policies to reduce risks and harm instead, such as needle exchanges, safe spaces for injecting, and treatment with methadone or even controlled doses of heroin. Such harm reduction policies were dismissed in the United Nations, where the goal was to achieve a "drug-free world" in which harm reduction would play no role, and this goal would be achieved through repressive measures to prevent the supply of drugs. This gave rise to the notion (untrue and unfair) that the world is divided into producer countries who are to blame for the drugs problem, and consumer countries who are victims of the former. All strategies to combat drugs must, therefore, be aimed at the producers. Although this notion became more nuanced over time, to be replaced by a concept of joint responsibility that implies the need to tackle both supply and demand, in practice very little has changed.

The main difference in the theoretical approaches of the European Union's strategy and that of the international community to drugs is that, for the EU, security is not an end in itself but rather an instrument underpinning well-being and health, and one which is always subject to the limits imposed by the principles of human rights and of the European Union. The European Union prioritises not only limiting supply, but also reducing demand, through measures to raise the age of initiation, cut consumption and prevent and reduce dependence and other risks.

For many years drugs have been treated on the American continent not just as a security issue to be dealt with by the police, as a criminal matter, but also through military actions. These include Nixon's war on drugs outside US borders, the war against the Mexican narcotics trafficker, Calderón, the military operations and incursions that took place under Plan Colombia and the Mérida Initiative, and operations carried out without any regard for national sovereignty, such as Operation Intercept in Mexico in 1969, Operation Blast Furnace in Bolivia in 1986, the invasion of Panama in 1989, codenamed Operation Just Cause, and Operation Fast and Furious in Mexico between 2009 and 2011.

The approach of the US and the United Nations over the years has tended to rule out measures aimed at reducing demand. This model has, however, been strongly challenged in recent years by many in civil society, academia, in some international organisations and in certain regional and national governments, who argue that the traditional policies to combat drugs encouraged by the United Nations fail to take into account three key aspects: human rights, scientific evidence and health. In this paper we will discuss this accusation and the effect it had at the United Nations General Assembly Special Session on Drugs (UNGASS), with a consideration of what could emerge at the 2019 Ministerial Segment of the Commission on Narcotic Drugs, where the results of UNGASS 2016 will be reviewed.

The arguments put forward by the movement calling for a paradigm shift have broadened in recent times: policy decisions concerning drugs should take into account not just the three aspects already mentioned, i.e. human rights, scientific evidence and health, but should also consider the need for sustainable development. It must be borne in mind that, following the publication of the 17 Sustainable Development Goals (SDGs),[5] grouped in five areas (social development; economic development; environmental sustainability; peaceful, just and inclusive societies;

and partnership) with 167 associated targets, voices were raised pointing out that global policy on drugs works against some of the SDGs. This seems evident, especially in parts of the world dominated by criminal organisations dedicated to drug trafficking and in the light of the war on drugs launched by some governments. This relationship between drugs policy and the SDGs has even been acknowledged by the United Nations Office on Drugs and Crime (UNODC). This does not, however, represent any real acceptance of responsibility for the policies applied and their negative effects, or an announcement of any effective change in those policies. Despite this, the 2016 World Drug Report[6] contained an extensive chapter on "The world drug problem and sustainable development" that examines "the interplay between the drug problem and the broader development context, distinguishing between the drug problem as a phenomenon (illicit drug use, production and trafficking) and the response to the drug problem."[7]

A full reading of the EU Drug Strategy for 2013–2020 reveals two key tenets:

1 The EU adheres to international law based on United Nations Conventions addressing the illicit drugs phenomenon. This means that the focus on security, in the sense of using criminal penalties to suppress the drugs cycle, has not been rejected, but it is used to address organised crime rather than petty delinquency. Consumption and possession for one's own consumption are not criminalised.
2 The EU has a more realistic, and more humane, vision of the drugs issue, above and beyond some of the tenets of the international strategy. This allows for a broader approach that tackles both supply and demand, and which builds on the three key aspects of health, scientific evidence and human rights, which the United Nations' response to date has ignored.

The problem for the European strategy lies in the difficulty of reconciling the two tenets described above with the practices demanded in the international context. A clear example of this, but not the only one, relates to reducing risks and harm.[8] As noted previously, the United Nations has for many years rejected the concept of reducing harm, as this would be unnecessary in a drug-free world. Furthermore, the international body has criticised and condemned the programmes developed by some countries.

As a consequence of the European Union's need to reconcile the two recently stated tenets and its commitments as a result of the three United Nations Conventions on drugs,[9] its current policy is a low-profile one compared with that of other countries on the American continent that have stepped outside the conventional framework in order to regulate the entire cannabis cycle. On the other hand, we must bear in mind that the current strategy is only valid until 2020 and the next strategy will not be able to ignore three key events:

1 UNGASS 2016 and its results, which we now know;
2 The 2019 Ministerial Segment of the United Nations Commission on Narcotic Drugs and the decisions it could adopt;
3 The decisions already taken by Uruguay, Canada and ten American states on regulating the entire cannabis cycle, and similar decisions that could be taken in other regions.

We must, meanwhile, highlight an extremely important issue: to date the United Nations' drugs policy has not been submitted to any assessment and it has been perpetuated and intensified despite its failures. It seems to have been forgotten that public policies are legitimised, or otherwise, by the results and not by the intentions behind them. The 2013–2020 European Strategy, on the contrary, included the concept of assessment. The operating and assessment mechanism that was designed is as follows:

1 Five objectives were set: a measurable reduction in the demand for drugs, a disruption of the illicit drugs market, coordination at EU and international level, dialogue and cooperation between the EU and third countries and international organisations, and obtaining empirically testable data to provide an evidence base for policies and action. The first two objectives are deemed to be policy areas, while the other three are cross-cutting themes.
2 These objectives formed the basis of two Action Plans drafted in 2013 and 2017. Measures selected for inclusion in the Action Plans had to be based on the following three criteria:

   a action must be evidence-based, scientifically sound and cost-effective, and aim for realistic and measurable results that can be evaluated;
   b action must be time-bound, with associated benchmarks and performance indicators;
   c action must have a clear relevance and added value for the EU.

None of this, i.e., planning based on tested data and, above all, subsequent assessment, has ever formed part of the United Nations' strategies.

Although the European Strategy is intended to comply with international law, there are clear issues of compatibility between the two programmes. We will examine the international context in more detail before returning to how this issue is handled in the European Union.

The international context based on the United Nations' Conventions

The current approach cannot be understood without re-examining the position of various European countries in the past, and how their policies responded to the paradigms developed within the United Nations through the Single Convention on Narcotic Drugs of 1961 and the Convention on Psychotropic Substances of 1971. The tenets of these two texts were hardcoded into the United Nations Convention against Illicit Traffic in Narcotic Drugs and Psychotropic Substances of 1988.

During the heroin crisis of the 1980s and 1990s, Europe developed policies focusing on reducing risks and harm, which were not limited to purely repressive approaches. This resulted in European countries moving away from the strict approach prescribed by the United Nations, seeking to strike a difficult balance between respecting the international framework established in the United Nations' treaties on drugs and developing a more realistic and effective policy which, above all, better respected basic human rights. They took the pragmatic view that if the consumption of illicit drugs could be controlled, they should try to manage its negative consequences for health and for society in general. They also took the view that these negative consequences had more to do with the prohibition itself than with the chemical composition of the substances outside the black market.

There were thus two opposing approaches to tackling the drugs issue. The enthusiasm for prohibition in the United Nations was at times euphoric: they believed that prohibition, control and repression would bring an end to the drugs problem (consumption, production and trafficking) throughout the world and would allow no dissenting voices to this notion.

The stated aim of the *Vienna Convention*[10] was to achieve a "drug-free world." This consensus, in reality, was driven by the fact that a minority of the members of the Commission on Narcotic Drugs, based in Vienna, closed down all meaningful dissent. It established a "one size fits all" policy designed to address the supply of drugs while ignoring demand, based on two instruments: the hegemonic role of the United States and the imposition of criminal penalties on all participants in the drug cycle. This approach reached its peak with the declaration of the *war on drugs*.

A time limit was put on this goal of achieving a "drug-free world." The second United Nations General Assembly Special Session on Drugs (UNGASS) was held in 1998, setting a 10-year target for the elimination of drugs throughout the world. To fulfil this goal, the world would have to be free of drugs by 2008. Clearly, this did not happen. By 2008 the trafficking and consumption of drugs had increased and new, as yet uncontrolled, drugs were constantly emerging as the supply of synthetic drugs grew unstoppably, thanks to advances in chemistry. The failure of the policies pursued to that date was undeniable on two fronts: the ideal of a "drug-free world" was further away than ever and, in addition, it had to be recognised that the strategy had produced "unintended negative consequences" that had been ignored until then. The 2008 World Drug Report had the following to say about these consequences:

> The first and most significant of these is the creation of a lucrative and violent black market. Secondly, the focus on law enforcement may have drawn away resources from health approaches to what, ultimately, is a public health problem. Thirdly, enforcement efforts in one geographic area have often meant that the problem was diverted into other areas. Fourthly, pressure on the market for one particular substance has, on occasion, inadvertently promoted the use of an alternate drug. Finally, the use of the criminal justice system against drug consumers, who often come from marginal groups, has in many instances increased their marginalisation, diminishing the capacity to offer treatment to those who need it most.[11]

This should have been enough to ensure a serious evaluation and an in-depth review of the anti-drugs strategy, but this was not the case. Just one year after this was published, it was declared that, despite these "unintended consequences," it was not appropriate to do away with the current international system based on the three drug control Conventions, arguing that "the fact of illegality alone reduces the number of potential addicts, particularly in developing countries." The way forward was to relax enforcement with measures such as focusing less on individuals and more on reducing the size of drug markets, making the incarceration of drug users exceptional and only criminalising the associated violence and corruption, and prevention through police operations and building institutional strength in producer and transit countries.[12]

Ten years later, in 2018, it is clear than none of the aforementioned policies have worked and the harm caused by prohibition remains and is growing.

But something has changed: the debate on the need for a paradigm shift in drugs policy has been legalised and institutionalised, and a number of countries and regions have defied the Conventions to establish regulated markets for the production and distribution of recreational cannabis.[13]

Stepping back to focus on the approach of some European countries, it is useful to note that not only did they apply their own policies to reduce risk and harm to address the ravages of the heroin crisis, they also tried to put their views forward in the context of the United Nations. Back in 1993, Mexico and the European bloc questioned measures focused on suppressing supply and suggested that action to tackle demand was required, both to reduce it and to alleviate the effects of consumption through non-repressive measures designed to limit harm. Mexico's position on the policies being applied at that time, many of them implemented by the US on Mexican soil, was set out in a letter to the Secretary General of the United Nations.[14] It argued for the need to tackle demand as well as supply, i.e., its North American neighbour should address the demand generated by its citizens insofar as this demand drives supply, rejecting the notion that all action should involve repressive measures against producer countries. It repudiated the idea that the world is divided into two blocs: producer countries (the perpetrators) against which action must be taken, and consumer countries (the victims), where nothing can be done. It argued that policies to eradicate drug use are ineffective, proposing instead development aide for producer countries. It warned about the strength of organised crime linked to drug trafficking, its relationship with other forms of trafficking and its capacity to corrupt and destabilise political power. This did not change anything at the time, but by the start of the twenty-first century a battle for a paradigm shift seemed to be on the cards.

United Nations General Assembly Special Session on Drugs (UNGASS 2016), the regulation of cannabis and the Brownfield Doctrine

Until 2012 it was thought that the third United Nations General Assembly Special Session on Drugs would be held in 2019. However, this was brought forward to 2016 at the request of three countries, Colombia, Mexico and Guatemala, in a Joint Declaration delivered to the Secretary General asking the Member States to assess the achievements and limits of anti-narcotics policies. This document strenuously questioned the policies sponsored by the United Nations on the basis that:

1. "*Transnational organized crime and in particular the violence it generates when carrying out their criminal activities, present a serious problem that compromises the development, security and democratic coexistence of all nations, and that the United Nations must urgently address this issue.*" The implication of this was that the response given to date by the United Nations to the issue of violent organised crime linked to narcotics trafficking had been not only ineffective but, moreover, dysfunctional and damaging to development, stability and democracy. Naturally, these damaging effects have been more intense and serious in producer and transit countries, principally in Latin America.
2. "*Despite the efforts of the international community over decades, the use of these substances continues to increase globally, generating substantial income for criminal organizations worldwide.*" Effectively, anti-narcotics policy has been a failure, never having achieved its ideal of a "drug-free world."
3. "*It is essential to implement effective measures to prevent illegal flows of arms to criminal organizations,*" which extends to "*the flow of resources from drugs users.*" This point was intended to underline the ineffectiveness of the response, highlighting, above all, the issue of the free flow of weapons and money from the US to criminal organisations in Latin American countries. It is based on the conviction that an effective response to organised crime linked to drugs calls for measures to combat not only supply, but also demand, and that such measures should not all be directed at producer countries; action to tackle demand and financing is also required. The document therefore argues for the "principle of shared and differentiated responsibility."
4. "*It is urgent to review the approach so far maintained by the international community on drugs.*" This need for a review is what academics and civil society are referring to when they talk of a "paradigm shift."[15]

The 2016 Special Session was called in response to this document, and Secretary General Ban Ki-moon promised a plural, open and inclusive debate that would consider all the options. This did not happen, however, as there were issues that were not discussed. Nobody spoke, for example, about the regulation of cannabis in Uruguay and parts of the US.[16] The final document, "Our joint commitment to effectively addressing and countering the world drug problem," meanwhile, was approved before the discussions took place, merely endorsing the work already signed off by the Commission on Narcotic Drugs.[17]

UNGASS 2016 did not question the three drug control Conventions, from 1961, 1971 and 1988, considering that they "constitute the cornerstone of the international drug control system." The debate surrounding the Conventions was replaced by a clause allowing "flexibility" in the domestic application of international commitments: the Treaties are untouchable, but their application is sufficiently flexible to allow "national solutions." This represents the triumph of the Brownfield doctrine,[18] i.e. the US position presented to UNGASS by William Brownfield, Assistant Secretary of State for the Bureau of International Narcotics and Law Enforcement Affairs. It is based on four key pillars on which national and international narcotics strategies may be built:

- Respect the integrity of the existing UN Drug Control Conventions.
- Accept flexible interpretation of those Conventions.[19]
- Tolerate different national drug policies.
- Combat and resist criminal organisations.

The above does not seem to provide a good general solution other than to legitimise US policy, within and without its borders. The flexibility allowed by the Treaties has now been exceeded by the legalisation of the entire cannabis cycle in various places. The first and last pillars serve to ensure nothing changes in the relationship between the US and Latin American countries. The second and third pillars are designed to protect Member States that have legalised the cannabis cycle and federal states that have allowed regions within them to do so. At this stage, it remains to be seen how President Trump will respond to the situation in states that have legalised recreational cannabis.[20]

Returning to the UNGASS 2016 Outcome Document, we can see some timid advances. The notion of a "drug-free world" appears to have been abandoned in favour of aiming for "a society free of drug abuse"; it recognises that drugs policy must respect human rights and the sovereignty of individual states; it accepts the role of civil society, including the populations most affected by prohibition, the scientific community and academia, in tackling the issue of drugs; it expresses concern about the accessibility of controlled substances for medical purposes; and establishes that drugs policy must respect the 2030 Agenda and its sustainable development goals. What is remarkable is that none of these, essentially basic, concepts had been openly discussed in the United Nations prior to 2016.

UNGASS also contains weaknesses: it reaffirms the importance of the Treaties, considering that they "constitute the cornerstone of the international drug control system," thereby precluding any review of them; it continues to refer to the "*world drug problem*," when in fact most of the problems are the fruit of prohibition, the exceptional criminal justice regime developed for drugs, the war on drugs and the treatment of the problem as a security issue; and it upholds the role of the United Nations' drugs bodies, without a hint of criticism for some of their highly blameworthy actions. Evidence that this exceptional criminal justice regime remains in place includes the failure of UNGASS 2016 to approve the moratoria demanded by some on the use of the death penalty, i.e., the death penalty is still considered an appropriate response for drug trafficking offences, including non-violent crimes. Furthermore, no consideration whatsoever was given to the need to assess anti-narcotics policies. It seems the only relevant indicators relate to the quantities of controlled substances seized and crops destroyed, and the number of laboratories closed down and individuals arrested, i.e. indicators of the efforts deployed against the supply side, with not one indicator addressing demand. Indicators related to supply only measure the application of repressive laws, and fail to assess the application of more rational laws that respect human rights, are concerned with public health and are based on scientific evidence. However, even with the existing indicators, we must concede that the current repressive policy, with its disastrous "unintended" consequences, is failing.

The position adopted in the Outcome Document on reducing harm is especially deplorable. The issue is not mentioned even once and, although some harm reduction strategies used successfully in Europe for a number of decades, such as needle exchanges and treatment with heroin substitutes, are referred to, these are hidden behind euphemistic terms such as "injecting equipment programmes" and "medication-assisted therapy programmes."

Council Framework Decision 2004/757/JHA of 25 October 2004 Laying Down Minimum Provisions on the Constituent Elements of Criminal Acts and Penalties in the Field of Illicit Drug Trafficking

Taking into account the general framework established by the United Nations' treaties on drugs, which we will use as a basis for comparison, we now return to the European legislative context in order to analyse Framework Decision 2004/757/JHA of 25 October 2004 establishing the "minimum standards for criminal justice" related to drugs in the EU.

EU institutions have made innumerable efforts over the years to combat drug trafficking. Just in the twenty-first century these have included the 2000–2004 and 2005–2008 Action Plans to combat drugs, the Catania Report (Proposal for a European Parliament recommendation to the Council on the European strategy on fighting drugs 2005–2012), the EU Drug Strategy for 2005–2012, the Council Recommendations of 25 April 2002 on simultaneous investigations into drug trafficking by criminal organisations and their finances and on cooperation and exchanges of information on trafficking in precursors, the creation by seven countries of the Lisbon-based Maritime Analysis and Operations Centre in October 2007, and Council Framework Decision 2004/757/JHA OF 25 October 2004 laying down minimum provisions on the constituent elements of criminal acts and penalties in the field of illicit drug trafficking (henceforth FD 2004).

An analysis of FD 2004 must begin by examining the force of Framework Decisions in the EU and be based on the fact that judicial and police cooperation on criminal matters was governed by the Third Pillar, i.e. an intergovernmental Pillar.[21] Article 29 of the Maastricht Treaty governed the "approximation, where necessary, of rules on criminal matters in the Member States, in accordance with the provisions of Article 31(e)."[22] Article 31 on common action on judicial cooperation in criminal matters stated that this shall include "progressively adopting measures establishing minimum rules relating to the constituent elements of criminal acts and to penalties in the fields of organised crime, terrorism and illicit drug trafficking." According to article 34,

> acting unanimously … the Council may … adopt framework decisions for the purpose of approximation of the laws and regulations of the Member States. Framework decisions shall be binding upon the Member States as to the result to be achieved but shall leave to the national authorities the choice of form and methods. They shall not entail direct effect.

Article 35, meanwhile, established that "the Court of Justice of the European Communities shall have jurisdiction, subject to the conditions laid down in this Article, to give preliminary rulings on the validity and interpretation of framework decisions."[23]

The 2004 Framework Decision is based on the following considerations:

- Illicit drug trafficking poses a threat to health, safety and the quality of life of citizens of the European Union, and to the legal economy, stability and security of the Member States.
- Common legislative action to tackle illicit drug trafficking has been recognised as necessary to achieve the "creation of an area of freedom, security and justice."
- By virtue of the principle of subsidiarity, European Union action should focus on the most serious types of drug offence, excluding personal consumption given the difficulties involved in harmonising legislation on this matter (article 2).
- The need to classify all conducts in the drug cycle is recognised, indicating which conducts "*when committed without right*" are punishable, meaning that uses authorised (and not just justified) by law are excluded from this classification.
- Criminal penalties also apply to the manufacture, transport or distribution of precursors.
- Punishment must be effective and proportionate, including punishments involving the deprivation of liberty. At this point it can be stated that, given the nature of the traffic, the sanctions applied in the EU, and the rest of the world, are not dissuasive.
- Penalties should take into account the quantities and the type of drugs trafficked, and whether the offence was committed within the framework of a criminal organisation. FD 2004 establishes maximum prison sentences for specific cases, stating what these should be, "of at least" X years. The way these numbers are expressed may lead to confusion, referring to a "*a maximum of at least between one and three years of imprisonment*" or "*a maximum of at least between 5 and 10 years of imprisonment*," while in other cases the term used is "*a maximum of at least 10 years of deprivation of liberty*." My understanding is that the FD is only intended to set ceilings on the length of prison sentences for each type of conduct, but does not set minimums in view of the principle of subsidiarity. The maximum values indicated are "*at least*," i.e. Member States' legislation may impose higher sentencing limits.
- Penalties may be reduced if the offender cooperates with the authorities.
- Measures must be taken to ensure the substances involved are confiscated and that legal persons can be held liable for criminal offences.
- With regard to the substances to be classified as drugs for the purpose of the offence of drugs trafficking, the 2004 version of the FD established that "drug" refers to the substances defined in the 1961 and 1971 United Nations Conventions.[24]

The original draft was revised by Directive (EU) 2017/2103 of the European Parliament and of the Council of 15 November 2017 amending Council Framework Decision 2004/757/JHA in order to include new psychoactive substances in the definition of "drug." It is intended to ensure FD 2004 is applicable not just to the narcotic drugs covered by the 1961 Convention and the psychotropic substances in the 1971 Convention, extending its scope to cover New Psychoactive Substances (NPS). These twelve NPS are listed in the Annex to the Directive. Each was already covered by other Decisions and Commission Implementing Decisions adopted between 1999 and 2017 in order to subject them to control measures and criminal sanctions. In the new version, article 1 point 1 is replaced by the following:

1) "drug" means any of the following:
   a) a substance covered by the 1961 United Nations Single Convention on Narcotic Drugs, as amended by the 1972 Protocol, or by the 1971 United Nations Convention on Psychotropic Substances;
   b) any of the substances listed in the annex.

Two new points are also added:

4) "new psychoactive substance" means a substance in pure form or in a preparation that is not covered by the 1961 United Nations Single Convention on Narcotic Drugs, as amended by the 1972 Protocol, or by the 1971 United Nations Convention on Psychotropic Substances but may pose health or social risks similar to those posed by the substances covered by those Conventions;
5) "preparation" means a mixture containing one or more new psychoactive substances.

In addition, a procedure for adding new substances to the definition of "drug" was added to the FD.

This procedure was developed by the EU as it observed the slowness of the United Nations to extend the Lists in the 1971 Convention to include the NPS that are appearing and will continue to appear, as chemistry imposes no limits on the new uncontrolled compounds that can be produced, and which may have the same effects and risks as currently controlled drugs, or greater ones, but are sought by traffickers as a means to elude existing controls.

It is clear from all of the above that the EU's response to drug trafficking is powerful, and in line with its international obligations under the United Nations Conventions, and goes beyond them with regard to controlled substances and illicit trafficking. On the other hand, the criminal justice regime in this case is exceptional and its main features include:

1 Extending the boundaries of protection to control acts prior to execution, making preparatory acts punishable in the same way as the actual crimes. This was taken to extremes in the 1988 Convention, which made conduct involving precursors an offence, this being incorporated in FD 2004 and thus in national legislation.
2 Extending the scope of persons defined as offenders, making it difficult to distinguish offences of merely aiding and abetting.
3 Very harsh penalties.
4 Introducing offences of abstract endangerment, going far beyond harm to legally protected interests.
5 The exceptional nature of the investigation instruments involved.

Security and drugs: the security-based approach

One of the Considerations of FD 2004 is that "Illicit drug trafficking poses a threat to health, safety and the quality of life of citizens of the European Union, and to the legal economy, stability and security of the Member States." Reviewing what we mean by the security of citizens and Member States leads us to question whether drugs and drug trafficking are, in themselves, a threat to that security.

We must be aware that in recent years a discourse has prevailed in various spheres and countries, based on the affirmation that certain phenomena or actions undermine security. This discourse is not founded on objective threats, but turns something that is not really a threat into one, through a forceful and compelling message. This happens to a certain extent when we talk about drugs and, specifically, illegal drugs. An atmosphere of fear has been created based on categorical statements that are not open to discussion: drugs kill, drugs take away your freedom, etc. These statements are exaggerated, mainly because they are generalisations, as they fail to distinguish between the different substances and their effects, and ignore the fact that 95 per cent of the world's drug consumers are not problematic, and that tobacco and alcohol are responsible for more deaths than all the banned drugs combined.[25] To gain legitimacy, prohibition uses messages that are simply false: the US has exploited the idea that drugs are a threat to security in its aggressive international policy towards Latin America and it continues to use that message to uphold its security-based approach towards a range of issues, including drugs, terrorism, organised crime and immigration. With regard to drugs, this strategy emerged in 1971, when Nixon announced that drugs were the country's number one enemy and declared the "war on drugs," leading to the militarisation of the struggle and the operations that took place under programmes such as Plan Colombia and the Mérida Initiative.

While recognising that there are social and health issues linked to drug consumption, drugs in themselves are not a security threat for citizens and states. The problem is that drug trafficking is one of the favourite activities of organised crime, putting a security focus on these substances. However, it is organised crime in itself that should be treated as an objective threat to security (and not just a subjective fear). Another point with regard to drugs is that the security threats linked to substance use, specifically the property crime associated with addiction and the mafias that traffic the drugs, are to a great extent a consequence of prohibition. This leads us to question what proportion of the "insecurity" is attributable to prohibition rather than the chemical composition of the substances and the consumption thereof. Furthermore, when a social problem is treated exclusively as an issue of security, the only solutions that fit are policing and repression, with recourse in some cases to military responses. We now know that imprisoning offenders and the war on drugs have not solved either the problems of dependency or of organised crime. Experience in many countries has demonstrated that consumption cannot be controlled, but it is possible, and effective, to reduce harm and risks. Furthermore, greater levels of repression do nothing to reduce the problems, in fact, they make them worse, and are in breach of human rights.

We must recognise, however, that the security-based approach to drugs and drug trafficking has had its greatest impact in Latin America. In Europe what we observe is a discourse around security, implemented in a less draconian way through an exceptional criminal justice system.

The EU's position on drugs today is low profile, compared with the approaches taken by many European countries during the heroin crisis, based on harm reduction and the non-criminalisation of users, policies that displeased the United Nations and the US. Europe is no longer the driving force it was in the international context in the 1980s and 1990s, when it held more realistic positions and implemented more effective and humane solutions. From the perspective of the results to date of our efforts to combat drugs, we can argue that the European strategy is one that is designed to maintain the *status quo*, repeating old arguments that ignore what is happening in the Americas, where calls for a paradigm shift are leading to the approval of legislation regulating the entire cannabis cycle in some countries and states. In Europe there are programmes to dispense medicinal cannabis but there is, to date, no legislation that regulates the entire cycle of any drug.

The paradigm shift on drugs that is now taking place in many parts of the world should push the EU into rethinking its general policy and its criminal drug policy.

Notes

1 This report is based on research carried out as part of R+D+i Project DER-2016-74872-R "*International Drugs Control: Problems and Solutions*" (Spanish Research Agency/ERDF, EU), for which the author is the Principal Investigator.

2 *EU Drugs Strategy for 2013–2020*, (Brussels: European Union, 2012), accessed October 29, 2018, https://eur-lex.europa.eu/legal-content/EN/TXT/?uri=uriserv:OJ.C_.2012.402.01.0001.01.ENG&toc=OJ:C:2012:402:TOC.

3 European Council, *European Security Strategy – A Secure Europe in a Better World* (Brussels: European Union, 2003), accessed October 29, 2018, www.consilium.europa.eu/en/documents-publications/publications/european-security-strategy-secure-europe-better-world/.

4 European Parliament, *Report on the Implementation of the European Security Strategy and the Common Security and Defence Policy* (2009/2198(INI)) (Brussels: European Union, 2009), accessed October 29, 2018, www.europarl.europa.eu/sides/getDoc.do?pubRef=-//EP//TEXT+REPORT+A7-2010-0026+0+DOC+XML+V0//EN.

5 General Assembly, Resolution Adopted by the General Assembly on 25 September 2015 (A/70/L.1) 70/1, Transforming Our World: the 2030 Agenda for Sustainable Development (New York: United Nations, 2015), accessed October 29, 2018, https://undocs.org/en/A/RES/70/1.

6 UNODC, *World Drug Report 2016* (New York: United Nations, 2016), accessed October 29, 2018, www.unodc.org/doc/wdr2016/WORLD_DRUG_REPORT_2016_web.pdf.

7 With regard to social development, it examines the effects of drug consumption on health and its negative impact on Goal 3, to promote health and well-being. The targets associated with this Goal include ending the AIDS epidemic by 2030, a disease of which the spread is closely linked to the use of injected drugs. It also links drug consumption with Goal 5, to achieve gender equality, given that women drug users suffer greater stigmatisation than men, and have less access to treatment programmes. The targets associated with Goal 10 include promoting social, economic and political inclusion, guaranteeing equality of opportunity and reducing inequalities of outcome. The marginalisation that affects drug users makes achieving this even harder: as indicated in the 2016 Report, drug use is linked to other risk factors leading to marginalisation, such as imprisonment, unemployment and homelessness. Access to medical drugs and supporting research to develop such drugs is another recognised aim. The World Drug Report notes that:

> this Goal is closely linked to the objective of drug control, which is to ensure access to controlled drugs for medical and research purposes while preventing diversion and abuse. In the preamble to the Single Convention on Narcotic Drugs of 1961 as amended by the 1972 Protocol, the parties to the Convention recognized that the medical use of narcotic drugs continues to be indispensable for the relief of pain and suffering and that adequate provision must be made to ensure the availability of narcotic drugs for such purposes.

Despite this, the Report goes on to note that "notwithstanding the clear intentions of the control system, 5.5 billion people, or three quarters of the world's population, have little or no access to medicines containing narcotic drugs and have inadequate access to treatment for moderate to severe pain." With regard to economic development, the report notes that the drugs problem has a negative impact on Goal 1, to reduce poverty, and Goal 8, to promote economic growth, pointing to issues such as the cost of treating people with drug problems and the application of laws against criminal activities.

8 At this point it is useful to define what we mean by reducing the risk and harm related to drug use: this refers to a policy which, based on an awareness that it is impossible to end the problematic use of drugs, abandons that goal and focuses on preventing or reducing the risks (prevention) or the harmful effects on health and society linked to such drug use. Programmes to reduce risk and harm have proved to be effective against the spread of AIDS, one of the causes of which was the sharing of needles to inject heroin.

9 The Single Convention on Narcotic Drugs of 1961 as amended by the 1972 Protocol, the Convention on Psychotropic Substances of 1971 and the United Nations Convention against Illicit Traffic in Narcotic Drugs and Psychotropic Substances of 1988.

10 This goal was expressed as: "the elimination or substantial reduction of coca leaf, opium poppy and cannabis cultivation by 2008." In the words of Kofi Annan, then Secretary General of the United Nations, "Our commitment is to make real progress towards eliminating drug crops by the year 2008. It is my hope that this session will go down in history as the time the international community found common ground to take on this task in earnest" (A/S-20/PV.1–9, General Assembly, Official Records, 20th Special Session, 10 June 1998, New York).

11 UNODC, *World Drug Report 2008*, accessed October 29, 2018, www.unodc.org/documents/wdr/WDR_2008/WDR_2008_eng_web.pdf.

12 UNODC, *World Drug Report 2009*, accessed October 29, 2018, www.unodc.org/documents/wdr/WDR_2009/WDR2009_eng_web.pdf.

13 This has occurred in Uruguay and Canada and, within the United States, in Alaska, California, Colorado, Maine, Massachusetts, Nevada, Oregon, Vermont (where marijuana has been legalised by

legislation rather than a referendum as in other states), Washington and Washington, DC (with an unusual system of permits for consumption, possession and cultivation).

14 A/C.3/48/2, October 20, 1993, accessed October 29, 2018, http://repository.un.org/bitstream/handle/11176/195099/A_C.3_48_2-ES.pdf?sequence=5&isAllowed=y.

15 See the 2009 report by the Latin American Commission on Drugs and Democracy entitled "Drugs and Democracy: Toward a Paradigm Shift." This report refers to "a failed war" and argues that "breaking the taboo and acknowledging the failure of current policies and their consequences is the inescapable prerequisite for opening up the discussion about a new paradigm leading to safer, more efficient and humane drug policies." For further information on this Commission and the content of the report: Araceli Manjón-Cabeza Olmeda, *La Solución. La legalización de las Drogas* (Barcelona: Debate, 2012), 248–53. This Latin American Commission, whose members included César Gaviria, Ernesto Cedillo, Fernando Henrique Cardoso, Paolo Coelho and Mario Vargas Llosa, went on to form the basis of the Global Commission on Drug Policy, set up in 2011, with members including Kofi Annan, Richard Branson and Ruth Dreifuss. Since that year, the Global Commission has produced extremely useful annual reports on drugs policy. The 2018 report, entitled "Regulation: The Responsible Control of Drugs," establishes that the way to control the risks posed by drugs is to control rather than ban them, noting that in a number of places this concept has now moved beyond the theoretical framework of legislation to the practical implementation thereof.

> The process of legal regulation must be cautious, incremental and evidence-based, guided at all times by the principles of protecting and promoting human rights, public health, sustainable development, and peace and security … Any regulation that is implemented must be accompanied by multidisciplinary scientific monitoring and evaluation, to assess its effectiveness and respond to any unforeseen negative impacts.

This last declaration clearly demonstrates that the Commission is proposing a model that diverges radically from that in force at present, in terms of the response (regulation not prohibition), focuses (introducing previously ignored aspects) and the need for assessment (currently non-existent). The reports of the Global Commission can be downloaded from www.globalcommissionondrugs.org/.

16 There was no discussion about cannabis, the control of the plant, its main active ingredients or synthetic cannabinoids, and no reference was made to the regulatory frameworks already in place in Uruguay and the US, reviewing them and comparing them with international law. This was in order to avoid any statement being made that would reveal the discrepancy between these internal regulations and the international Treaties on drugs, and to prevent any suggestion that the regulation of cannabis could be an appropriate or viable option, leading to the need to change the international framework governing the control of cannabis. The need to revise the three Conventions is a no-go subject in the United Nations, to the extent that accepting that some countries are acting in breach of international law is considered a lesser evil than contemplating reforming them. Two matters need to be highlighted here:

- A pre-review of cannabis just carried out by the World Health Organisation concluded with a recommendation issued on 14 December 2017 not to criminalise cannabidiol (CBD), one of the main active components of cannabis and which had not been controlled to date, but to categorise it under the pre-review stage (with tramadol and certain synthetic opioids, such as carfentanyl). The current designation of the plant, resin, extracts and THC (the primary active ingredient of cannabis) as controlled substances has, meanwhile, been earmarked for critical review. This review covers medicinal cannabis only, and could lead to a new, more realistic and scientific classification of the drug. For more on the current classification and its lack of scientific basis: David Bewley-Taylor, Tom Blickman and Martin Jelsma, *The Rise and Decline of Cannabis Prohibition* (Amsterdam/Swansea: TNI-GPDO, 2014); Sofia Aguilar, Victor Gutiérrez, Lisa Sánchez, and Marie Nougier, "Medical Cannabis Policies and Practices around the World," IDPC-MUCD, April 2018, accessed October 29, 2018, http://fileserver.idpc.net/library/Medicinal%20cannabis%20briefing_ENG_FINAL.PDF.
- In Canada, under the Cannabis Act passed in June 2018, the full cannabis cycle (production, distribution and consumption) is now regulated. The Act came into force on 17 October 2018.

17 It must be borne in mind that only 53 countries of the United Nations' Member States are represented on the Commission on Narcotic Drugs.

18 Araceli Manjón-Cabeza Olmeda, "Una evaluación de la UNGASS 2016," in *Las sendas de la regulación del cannabis en España* (Barcelona: Bellaterra, 2017), 284–97; Damond Barret, Martin Jelsma and David

Bewley-Taylor, "Fatal Attraction: Brownfield's Flexibility Doctrine and Global Drug Policy Reform," *TNI*, November, 2014, accessed October 29, 2018, www.tni.org/es/artículo/atraccion-fatal-la-doctrina-de-la-flexibilidad-de-brownfield-y-la-reforma-global-de-las?content_language=en. The latter states that "The result is a new official position on the UN drugs treaties that, despite its seductively progressive tone, serves only to sustain the status quo and may cause damage beyond drug policy."

19 The UNGASS 2016 Outcome Document affirmed that the Treaties "allow for sufficient flexibility for State parties to design and implement national drug policies according to their priorities and needs," clearly embodying the Brownfield doctrine. This declaration is, on the face of it, positive, but it leads to legal uncertainty, as it does not make clear who is the arbiter of this flexibility or what its requirements and limits are. The little flexibility that exists in the Treaties has been used in many countries, for example, to impose non-custodial sentences for the consumption of drugs, and has been exceeded in others to regulate the entire cannabis cycle. Invoking the principle of flexibility, as described above, seems to provide a useful excuse for not challenging the recent legalisation processes and having to state that some countries are violating the Treaties, but it results in legal uncertainty and once again highlights the preference to be in breach of the Treaties rather than amend them.

20 In January 2018, President Trump tried to revoke the regulatory regimes in place in the country, rescinding memoranda issued by Obama allowing US attorneys to deprioritise the prosecution of behaviours which are illegal under federal law but legalised in a number of states, except where they involve the distribution of the drug to minors, organised crime or transporting it to states subject to the federal prohibition. The purpose of revoking these memos seems to be to return to a federal legal framework allowing US attorneys to prosecute all cases of the production, distribution and consumption of marijuana. Until the policy was revoked, seven US states had legalised the entire marijuana cycle (Alaska, Oregon, Washington, Colorado, Massachusetts, Maine and Nevada), while Washington, DC had decriminalised private consumption, possession and cultivation, but not the sale of the drug, although some shops give cannabis away with purchases of other items. Since the memos were rescinded, other states have gone on to legalise cannabis (California and Vermont, the only state to do so through its state legislature rather than by referendum).

21 It must be borne in mind that only the powers included in the First Pillar were automatically subject to the European Court of Justice and to Commission oversight. The Court had no jurisdiction over the areas included in the Second Pillar and only weak jurisdiction over the Third Pillar. Nevertheless, we must not ignore the fact that the First and Third Pillars were moving closer together at that time. The intergovernmental nature of the Third Pillar began to blur in the Amsterdam Treaty, when matters previously allocated to the Third Pillar were moved to the First, and those matters which remained under the Third Pillar, police and judicial cooperation in criminal matters, began to be treated as community matters to some extent (for example, granting the Court of Justice competence to give preliminary rulings). The Judgement issued by the Grand Chamber of European Court of Justice on 16 June 2005 in Case C-105/3 (the *Pupino case*) was particularly significant. According to Vittorio Manes it represented a notable strengthening of the powers of framework decisions and formed part of an ongoing "communitization of the third pillar." "La incidencia de las 'Decisiones Marco' en la interpretación en materia penal: perfiles de Derecho sustantivo," *Revista Electrónica de Ciencia Penal y Criminología* (2007): 3. Another significant Judgement is that of case C-176/03 issued on 13 September 2005 resolving the dispute between the Commission and the Council on the protection of the environment through criminal law. A Framework Decision on the environment having been previously adopted by the Council of the European Union, the Commission proposed a Directive the content of which was almost exactly identical. It subsequently asked the Court to rule on whether measures to protect the environment through criminal law were a community competence under the First Pillar to be governed using a Directive or an intergovernmental, Third Pillar matter to be governed, therefore, by a Framework Decision. The Court ruled for the Commission, with general consequences for determining under which pillar subsequent processes to harmonise EU criminal justice should reside. Albert Escuadras Cuadras, "Vía libre al derecho penal europeo. Comentario a la Sentencia del TJCE de 13 de septiembre de 2005," *InDret*, April 2006, accessed October 29, 2018, www.indret.com/pdf/341_es.pdf; Communication from the Commission to the European Parliament and the Council "on the Implications of the Court's Judgment of 13 September 2005 (Case C-176/03 Commission v Council)," COM(2005) 583 final/2 (Brussels: European Union, November 24, 2005), accessed October 29, 2018, https://eur-lex.europa.eu/legal-content/EN/TXT/PDF/?uri=CELEX:52005DC0583&from=ES. According to the Commission, the Judgement affected a range of legal texts other than those included in FD 2004.

22 The Union's objective to provide safety within an area of freedom, security and justice shall be achieved by preventing and combating crime, in particular illicit drug trafficking (among others), through three instruments: cooperation between police forces and customs authorities, judicial cooperation and the approximation of legislation (art. 29).
23 It must be borne in mind that, when it involves ruling on a matter previously put before a court or tribunal of a Member State, this competence of the Court of Justice to give preliminary rulings on the validity and interpretation of framework decisions is subject to acceptance by those Member States, which must indicate whether the right to refer a question to the Court is to be available to all of its national courts and tribunals or is to be reserved to the courts or tribunals of last instance.
24 Article 1 of the FD states that

'drugs': shall mean any of the substances covered by the following United Nations Conventions:
a) the 1961 Single Convention on Narcotic Drugs (as amended by the 1972 Protocol);
b) the 1971 Vienna Convention on Psychotropic Substances. It shall also include the substances subject to controls under Joint Action 97/396/JHA of 16 June 1997 concerning information exchange, risk assessment and the control of new synthetic drugs.

25 A. Peacock et al., "Global statistics on alcohol, tobacco and illicit drug use: 2017 status report," *Addiction* 113, no. 10 (2018), accessed October 29, 2018, www.ncbi.nlm.nih.gov/pubmed/29749059. Based on figures from the World Health Organisation, the UNODC and Health Metrics and Evaluation, concluded that: "In 2015 alcohol use and tobacco smoking use between them cost the human population more than a quarter of a billion disability-adjusted life years, with illicit drugs costing further tens of millions."

References

Aguilar, Sofia, Victor Gutiérrez, Lisa Sánchez and Marie Nougier. "Medical Cannabis Policies and Practices around the World." *IDPC-MUCD*, April 2018. Accessed October 29, 2018. http://fileserver.idpc.net/library/Medicinal%20cannabis%20briefing_ENG_FINAL.PDF.

Barret, Damond, Martin Jelsma and David Bewley-Taylor. "Fatal Attraction: Brownfield's Flexibility Doctrine and Global Drug Policy Reform." *TNI*, November, 2014. Accessed October 29, 2018. www.tni.org/es/artículo/atraccion-fatal-la-doctrina-de-la-flexibilidad-de-brownfield-y-la-reforma-global-de-las?content_language=en.

Bewley-Taylor, David, Tom Blickman and Martin Jelsma. *The Rise and Decline of Cannabis Prohibition*. Amsterdam/Swansea: TNI-GPDO, 2014.

Commission of the European Communities. Communication from the Commission to the European Parliament and the Council on the Implications of the Court's Judgment of 13 September 2005 (Case C-176/03 Commission v Council). COM(2005) 583 final/2. Brussels: European Union, November 24, 2005. Accessed October 29, 2018. https://eur-lex.europa.eu/legal-content/EN/TXT/PDF/?uri=CELEX:52005DC0583&from=ES.

Escuadras Cuadras, Albert. "Vía libre al derecho penal europeo. Comentario a la Sentencia del TJCE de 13 de septiembre de 2005." *InDret*, April 2006. Accessed October 29, 2018. www.indret.com/pdf/341_es.pdf.

European Council. *European Security Strategy – A Secure Europe in a Better World*. Brussels: European Union, 2003. Accessed October 29, 2018. www.consilium.europa.eu/en/documents-publications/publications/european-security-strategy-secure-europe-better-world/.

European Parliament. *Report on the Implementation of the European Security Strategy and the Common Security and Defence Policy* (2009/2198(INI)). Brussels: European Union, 2009. Accessed October 29, 2018. www.europarl.europa.eu/sides/getDoc.do?pubRef=-//EP//TEXT+REPORT+A7-2010-0026+0+DOC+XML+V0//EN.

European Union. *EU Drugs Strategy for 2013–2020*. Brussels: European Union, 2012. Accessed October 29, 2018. https://eur-lex.europa.eu/legal-content/EN/TXT/?uri=uriserv:OJ.C_.2012.402.01.0001.01.ENG&toc=OJ:C:2012:402:TOC.

Manjón-Cabeza Olmeda, Araceli. *La Solución. La legalización de las Drogas*. Barcelona: Debate, 2012.

Manjón-Cabeza Olmeda, Araceli. "Una evaluación de la UNGASS 2016." In *Las sendas de la regulación del cannabis en España*, 284–97. Barcelona: Bellaterra, 2017.

Peacock, A., et al. "Global Statistics on Alcohol, Tobacco and Illicit Drug Use: 2017 Status Report." *Addiction* 113, no. 10 (2018). Accessed October 29, 2018. www.ncbi.nlm.nih.gov/pubmed/29749059.

United Nations General Assembly. Resolution Adopted by the General Assembly on 25 September 2015 (A/70/L.1) 70/1, Transforming Our World: the 2030 Agenda for Sustainable Development. New York: United Nations, 2015. Accessed October 29, 2018. https://undocs.org/en/A/RES/70/1.
UNODC. *World Drug Report 2008*. New York: United Nations, 2008. Accessed October 29, 2018. www.unodc.org/documents/wdr/WDR_2008/WDR_2008_eng_web.pdf.
UNODC. *World Drug Report 2009*. New York: United Nations, 2009. Accessed October 29, 2018. www.unodc.org/documents/wdr/WDR_2009/WDR2009_eng_web.pdf.
UNODC. *World Drug Report 2016*. New York: United Nations, 2016. Accessed October 29, 2018. www.unodc.org/doc/wdr2016/WORLD_DRUG_REPORT_2016_web.pdf.

22

THE ROLE OF EU ELECTION OBSERVATION MISSIONS IN THE PREVENTION AND RESOLUTION OF ELECTORAL CONFLICTS

Víctor Carlos Pascual Planchuelo

Introduction

Elections lead to the control of the State by a candidate or party to the detriment of other candidates. Nonetheless, such a fight to obtain power can trigger not only internal conflicts, but also international ones, particularly when these take place within fragile or less stable political regimes.

Since elections form the core on which the whole of democracy is based, any disturbance or crisis in their development could have serious repercussions.[1] Thus, holding democratic elections in compliance with international standards will generally have a positive impact on the political and institutional stability of the country. In contrast, elections that are fraudulent, defective or contrary to international standards can provoke the beginning of a conflict, worsen a latent crisis, generate an escalation in a pre-existing[2] conflict or lead to episodes of electoral violence.[3] Electoral violence can manifest itself in different ways[4] and can have varying degrees of intensity, negatively affecting any of the phases of the electoral process. This violence can be triggered before the election date or on polling day (as happened in Afghanistan in 2009), or it can unfold on a large scale immediately after polling day (for example, in Kenya in 2007–2008 or Côte d'Ivoire in 2010).

The European Union (EU), guided by the objective of maintaining peace and security, as part of its global security strategy, will also develop actions at the international level to try to prevent and resolve conflicts arising in the context of electoral processes.

The European Union security strategy and its global strategy

The concern about internal and external security was becoming an issue of great importance for the EU while its *Common Foreign and Security Policy* (CFSP) and, subsequently, its *European Security and Defence Policy* (ESDP) were being developed.

In this process, it was essential to have a clear strategic line, which was finally achieved in 2003 with the document *European Security Strategy: A Secure Europe in a Better World*, prepared by the then High Representative Javier Solana.[5] This document indicated as the main threats to European security the following phenomena: terrorism, proliferation of weapons of mass destruction, regional conflicts, disintegration of States and organized crime.[6] Moreover, to achieve the strategic objectives set out in the text, the High Representative urged States to achieve:

- more active Union by applying the various and numerous crisis management and conflict prevention instruments at its disposal (political, diplomatic, military, civil, commercial or development tools);
- more capable Union, with more resources dedicated to Defence;
- greater coherence between military, diplomatic, political and civil activities;
- greater collaboration with all the partners and neighbors of the EU.[7]

The European Security Strategy (ESS) became a milestone in the development of the EU foreign and security policy[8] and served as framework of the Union's security interests, focusing on several strategic objectives:

- to tackle the global challenges and key threats;
- to extend the security zone around Europe and stabilize the neighbourhood;
- to strengthen the international order through "effective multilateralism."[9]

Since 2003, the ESDP has been operational for both civilian and military crisis management. Thus, the EU has been able to intervene in various ways in Bosnia and Herzegovina, Macedonia, the Democratic Republic of Congo (DRC), Georgia, Sudan and other countries with ongoing conflicts.[10]

In 2008, in line with this ESS, the Union adopted the *Civilian Headline Goal* on civil crisis management,[11] in which the EU objectives were defined in relation to the civil aspects of the ESDP and a solid basis was provided for the reinforcement of the necessary capacities. Two new categories for civil crisis management were added to the traditional set of EU instruments in the field of prevention and resolution of conflicts, namely the monitoring missions[12] and the support missions to the EU Special Representative.[13] Both this Civilian Headline Goal and document 14536/03, of the Council, on the Concept for the EU monitoring missions, referred to a specific type of "monitoring missions," which were focused exclusively on security objectives created on the basis of the CFSP[14] which did not encompass the observation of elections.[15] In line with this, the Council qualified this specific type of "monitoring mission" as a:

> generic tool for conflict prevention/resolution and/or crisis management and/or peace building that consists of a mission whose primary activity is to observe, monitor and report to the sending organisation on the general political and security situation in the host country or in relation to a specific agreement. Other important potential roles may include e.g. contribution in confidence building among former disputing parties, either directly or indirectly, low level conflict resolution and de-escalation assistance, facilitating contacts between civil society and governments and/or disputants, etc.[16]

Under this conceptualization, the mission that can be considered the EU's first merited "monitoring mission" (as a new category in the context of ESDP) was the EU Observation Mission in Aceh (Indonesia), deployed in 2005, and whose main mandate was to monitor compliance with the Peace Agreements between the Jakarta Government and the Free Aceh separatist movement.[17]

The variety of EU instruments in the field of security were also reflected in the *Report on the Implementation of the European Security Strategy: Providing Security in a Changing World*, published on December 11, 2008. This report stated that:

> Drawing on a unique range of instruments, the EU already contributes to a more secure world. We have worked to build human security, by reducing poverty and inequality, promoting good governance and human rights, assisting development, and addressing the root causes of conflict and insecurity. The EU remains the biggest donor to countries in need. Long-term engagement is required for lasting stabilisation.[18]

In addition, in March 2010, the European Council approved the *Internal Security Strategy for the European Union: Towards a European Security Model*,[19] thus completing the ESS. The concept of internal security had to be understood as a wide and comprehensive concept that straddled multiple sectors which has a direct impact on the lives, safety and well-being of the citizens. In this respect, the *Internal Security Strategy* would also include the external dimension of security, pointing out the need to build relations with third countries through to the aforementioned global approach to security:

> A concept of internal security cannot exist without an external dimension, since internal security increasingly depends to a large extent on external security.... It is necessary to build relationships with other countries through a global approach to security, working closely with them and, when necessary, supporting their institutional, economic and social development.... The efforts to combat transnational crime outside the EU as well and to build up respect for the rule of law are of crucial importance.

Since then, it has become clear that social, political and economic development of the entire international community is considered relevant by the EU to guarantee its own internal security.

Under this global approach, the "monitoring missions" were already fully integrated into the set of instruments available to the EU to contribute to international and domestic security. However, we will examine next whether the Union's election observation missions have also been included within these instruments.

This global approach was maintained in the 2016 Global Strategy for the European Union's Foreign and Security Policy *Shared Vision, Common Action: A Stronger Europe*[20] that replaced the previous ESS. The new Global Strategy set out among its priorities the security of the European Union and the Member States as well as societal resilience and an integrated approach to conflicts. Regarding this integrated approach, the Global Strategy will pursue a comprehensive approach to conflicts and crises through a coherent use of all policies and tools at the EU's disposal. Accordingly, the Union is determined to act during all stages of the conflict cycle (prevention, resolution, stabilization).[21] The Global Strategy further emphasizes the importance of the "resilience" defined as "the ability of States and societies to reform, thus withstanding and recovering from internal and external crises."[22] Moreover, the EU states that "a resilient State is a secure State, and security is key for prosperity and democracy."[23] Consequently, the Union will act in favor of democracy and human rights, especially in its neighborhood, assuming that democracy and sustainable development promote resilient States and societies.[24]

EU election observation

The European Union has since the 1990s been deploying Election Observation Missions (EOMs) as a frequent action within its foreign policy. The EU election observation is not carried out among the Member States,[25] but developed in third countries, mainly motivated by the guidelines of the Community's own foreign policy as well as by the actions and agreements of cooperation for development that the Union has subscribed to with countries in Africa, Asia and Latin America.

The EOMs are clearly differentiable from other generic monitoring or electoral missions because of their individual characteristics.[26] As stated in the 2005 *Declaration of Principles for International Election Observation*, among the most relevant features and principles that govern the performance of these EOMs, the following should be highlighted: full coverage, independence, impartiality, transparency, publicity, professionalism, analysis and advice, respect for the sovereignty of the host country, including the need to receive an invitation to observe, cooperation between different observer organizations and non-validation of clearly anti-democratic electoral processes.[27]

The action of the EU in the field of election observation began in 1991 when the European Council decided to formally engage in the promotion of human rights and democracy, beginning its activities with the observation of the constitutional referendum on August 19, 1992 in Madagascar, carried out through the International Commission of Jurists, at the request of the European Commission.[28] However, what is considered the first EU election observation mission in the field was the deployment of an "ad hoc" electoral mission in the Russian Federation in 1993.[29] The EU observation activity continued with EOMs sent to the plebiscites held in South Africa (1994), Mozambique (1994), Palestine (1996), Bosnia and Herzegovina (1996) and Indonesia (1999).[30] These first actions of election observation by the EU found their legal basis, in some instances, in the Second Pillar (CFSP), and in other cases in the development cooperation policies of the First Pillar,[31] and they undertook the dual role of observing the elections and providing support and electoral assistance.

Progressively, the European institutions began developing criteria for their election observation actions which, in their early stages, suffered from a certain lack of coherence and uniformity. To resolve this, the first Community instruments that granted legal basis to the EU electoral assistance and observation activities were Council Regulations (EC) No 975/1999 and 976/1999 of 29 April 1999, which established requirements for the implementation of the Community's development cooperation actions that contributed to the overall objective of developing and consolidating democracy and rule of law, as well as respect for human rights and fundamental freedoms in third countries:

> the European Community shall provide technical and financial aid for operations aimed at:
>
> 1) Promoting and defending the human rights and fundamental freedoms proclaimed in the Universal Declaration of Human Rights and other international instruments concerning the development and consolidation of democracy and the rule of law ...;
> 2) Supporting the processes of democratisation, in particular:
>
> > ... f) Support for electoral processes, in particular by supporting independent electoral commissions, granting material, technical and legal assistance in preparing for elections, including electoral censuses, taking measures to promote the participation of specific groups, particularly women, in the electoral process, and by training observers.[32]

However, it was with the approval of the 2000 Communication from the Commission on EU Election Assistance and Observation[33] that the participation of the EU institutions and missions in the electoral processes became more coherent and systematic.[34] Through this Communication, the Commission developed a new and integral legal basis for election observation, which would increase the credibility of the EU observation missions and their political impact.[35] Since 2000, the EU has deployed more than 120 EOMs[36] in as many elections in all parts of the world.[37]

As a final milestone, in 2009, the approval of the Treaty of Lisbon substantially reinforced the activities of the Union in the area of foreign action and created the position of *High Representative of the Union for Foreign Affairs and Security Policy*, which, among other functions, has the last word on sending an EOM to a specific country.

EU election observation missions and electoral conflicts

In many occasions, EU EOMs are deployed to post-conflict situations and conflict-affected states in an effort to support the establishment of democratic institutions. The visibility of an EU EOM may act as a positive factor, as the presence of international observers may increase transparency, raise public confidence in the election process and discourage incidents of fraud, intimidation or violence. By observing every step of the election process throughout the country, an EU EOM may also be able to detect potential risks of electoral violence during the pre-election period when any perceived defects in the process may bring political tensions.[38]

The role carried out by these EOMs in the field of conflict prevention and resolution was beginning to be gradually recognized in various documents and normative instruments of the organization. Therefore, the inclusion of EU EOMs within the set of tools available for conflict prevention and resolution can be found in the 2000 Communication from the Commission "on EU Election Assistance and Observation," which states the following:

> International election observation is based on the principles of full coverage, impartiality, transparency and professionalism. Its ultimate objective is to become superfluous by entrenching democracy deep within each nation through development of national capacities. Its main goals are the legitimisation of an electoral process, where appropriate, and the enhancement of public confidence in the electoral process, to deter fraud, to strengthen respect for human rights, and to contribute to the resolution of conflicts.[39]

In the same vein, the European Parliament, in its Resolution of 8 May 2008 on EU Election Observation Missions: Objectives, Practices and Future Challenges,[40] also highlighted that:

> international election observation is aimed at strengthening the legitimacy of the electoral process, increasing public confidence in elections, deterring electoral fraud and exposing it where it occurs and analysing, reporting and making recommendations for the improvement of all aspects of the electoral process in full cooperation with the host country, the settlement of any disputes and the protection of human rights and democracy in general.

EU EOMs as mechanisms for conflict prevention and resolution even started to be expressly included in the mandates of some of these missions; thus, for some time, the mandates included among their fundamental objectives that of "contributing to the resolution of conflicts" (for instance, the mandate of the EU EOM in the presidential elections in Guinea Bissau in 2009[41] or in Ethiopia in 2010[42]). However, in other mandates[43] this objective was not included. The explanation for this may be that the outbreak of a conflict was not expected or that it was intended to avoid compromising the neutrality and impartiality of the missions, as well as to prevent them from being rejected by the authorities of the observed country if their role was considered an interference in internal affairs. It is our opinion that the elimination of such an objective from the EOM mandate may be timely in order to facilitate mandatory invitation to observe electoral processes in some States. Nevertheless, we also believe that such action may hinder the true potential of the missions aimed at preventing and resolving electoral conflicts in the observed State. Moreover, if this objective is not included in its mandate, the mission will not have the necessary legal capacity to act in the field of prevention and resolution of electoral disputes during its observation period.

We will now examine in a more specific way how EU EOMs act in the area of conflict prevention and resolution. In the present analysis, we will show how EU election observation contributes to the security of international society mainly through three channels: (1) EU election observation and use of conditionality; (2) EU election observation as an instrument for prevention of electoral conflicts; and (3) EU election observation as a mechanism for peaceful resolution of electoral conflicts.[44]

EU election observation and the use of conditionality

The EU "conditionality" means that granting benefits to third States (financial assistance, trade agreements, cooperation, political contacts or membership) is conditional upon compliance with certain elements or conditions,[45] normally, respect for human rights, democracy and rule of law.

The use of conditionality in the EU's external relations began to be systematized after the so-called *Lomé IV bis Convention*, approved in November 1995, which established respect for human rights, democracy and the rule of law as an essential element of the relations of the EU with third States.[46] On June 23, 2000, this convention was replaced by the *Cotonou Agreement* – between the African, Caribbean and Pacific Group of States and the EU – reinforcing the importance of political conditionality.[47] This Agreement has a strong political dimension, since it establishes a *regular political dialogue between the countries and develops policies for the consolidation of peace and the prevention and resolution of conflicts*. In case of breach of that clause by any country, in accordance with its Article 96,[48] the EU will first promote *political dialogue*, by opening a *consultation* phase and, only if these actions are unsuccessful, will it contemplate the imposition of negative sanctioning measures.[49]

The EU has extensively used this instrument and 18 countries have been subject to sanctions over the years:[50] Afghanistan, the Former Yugoslav Republic of Macedonia, Myanmar, Angola, Indonesia, Nigeria, Belarus, Iraq, Somalia, DRC, Liberia, Sierra Leona, Eritrea, Libya, Zimbabwe, Ethiopia, and Moldova. Given the economic importance of the EU, commercial, economic and financial sanctions constitute significant instruments of conflict prevention.[51]

To determine whether a breach of the respect for human rights, democracy and/or rule of law has occurred in the context of an electoral process, the EOMs become fundamental instruments for verification that provide valuable information from the field on the elections' development in accordance with international standards and on respect for civil and political rights set forth in international treaties.

Undoubtedly, this European conditionality is an important stimulus for the EU's partner countries – beneficiaries of financial aids, commercial privileges and cooperation funds – not to depart from the objectives of promoting and fulfilling human rights, democracy and the rule of law. Therefore, acting in this sense, these countries avoid or minimize the risk of electoral conflicts. For that reason, we affirm that the conditionality can be transcendental – in the medium and long term – for conflict prevention and resolution in the international society.[52] Accordingly, we delve in the following sections into the role that EU electoral observation can play in a more specific way in the prevention and resolution of conflicts, providing some illustrative examples.

EU election observation as an instrument for the prevention of conflicts

The Union's cornerstone in the sphere of conflict prevention revolves around the *Gothenburg Programme on the Prevention of Violent Conflict*[53] adopted by the European Council on June 16, 2001. This document identifies conflict prevention as an essential objective of the EU's external relations[54] and mainstreams the application scope of conflict prevention to all sectors of its external action.[55] As we have seen in the previous section, promotion of good governance and respect for human rights are also part of the EU Security Strategy and EU Global Strategy.

Within the framework of the Gothenburg Programme, the EU includes election observation as one of its conflict prevention mechanisms:

> the Commission ... is invited to implement its recommendations on more targeted action in support of democracy, and the particular attention paid to support to electoral processes, including electoral observers, administration of justice, improving police services and human rights training for the whole security sector, as means of contributing to conflict prevention.

Although, as we have pointed out in the previous section, the role of electoral observation in matters of conflict prevention was already established in the Communication from the Commission "on EU Election Assistance and Observation," it was also included in the Communication from the Commission "on Conflict Prevention," which states:

> The list of EU instruments directly or indirectly relevant to the prevention of conflict is long: development co-operation and external assistance, economic co-operation and trade policy instruments, humanitarian aid, social and environmental policies, diplomatic instruments such as political dialogue and mediation, as well as economic or other sanctions, and ultimately the new instruments of ESDP (including information gathering for anticipating potential conflicts situations and monitoring international agreements). Through these, the EU is already heavily engaged in conflict prevention...
>
> Support for democracy, the rule of law and civil society. Countries with conflict potential are usually those where the democratic process is the least advanced and where external support, for obvious reasons, is the most difficult to implement. In such conditions, EC support should aim, through targeted actions, at opening the way to a more favourable democratic environment.
>
> The Commission is particularly active in the field of democratic transition and elections, through voter education projects, for example, and training courses for electoral observers. South Africa in 1994 and West Bank/Gaza Strip in 1996 are very good examples where Commission support, both in terms of election observation and assistance proved a successful contribution to mitigate the conflict.

The Communication highlighted the importance of political dialogue in conflict prevention and resolution, a task in which it was recognized that election observation had played a fundamental role.[56] In this way, Communication 211/2001 made it clear that the EU election observation could be an important activity for the prevention of conflicts in the electoral field.

In line with the above, the paper prepared by the UN Institute for Disarmament Research "The European Union and Conflict Prevention"[57] remarked:

> Election observation is a significant component of the EU's policy of promoting human rights and democratization throughout the world, and thus, part of its overall conflict prevention strategy. This is an area where the Commission has asserted leadership.

On the other hand, in 2009 the EU mediation and dialogue activities in electoral processes acquired greater consistency with the approval of the *EU Concept on Mediation and Dialogue.*[58] EU mediation and dialogue will become part of the Union's comprehensive approach to conflict prevention and peace building. The document also establishes preventive mediation resources in relation to electoral processes and provides an overview of key aspects related to mediation and dialogue as part of electoral support in the context of electoral conflicts.[59] Although this Concept remarks that various EU actors (Secretary General/High Representative for Common Foreign and Security Policy (CFSP), Presidency, European Commission, EU Special Representatives (EUSRs), European Security and Defence Policy (ESDP) missions and European Commission Delegations) can be and have been involved in EU mediation activities (for example, those leading to the 2001 Ohrid Framework Agreement or the 2005 Aceh Peace Agreement), nothing similar was mentioned regarding EOMs in this field. Nevertheless, the EU EOMs work closely with the mentioned actors in the field of mediation and dialogue when electoral conflicts emerge.

As a follow-up to this document, in 2012, the European External Action Service published the Factsheet on "Mediation and Dialogue in electoral processes to prevent and mitigate electoral related violence," which reiterated the usefulness of mediation and dialogue in order to prevent or contribute to the resolution of conflicts that may arise in any of the phases or stages of the electoral process. This Factsheet pointed out that the EU electoral support comes in two forms (electoral assistance and observation missions[60]). The document also affirmed that "beyond the usually more technical electoral assistance, the EU has in fact a wide range of roles it can potentially play in relation to mediation and dialogue in electoral processes" and added that "[i]t is usually also not the task of the Electoral Observation Missions to engage in such activities," giving more importance to electoral assistance in mediation and dialogue actions, and leaving election observation activities in second place. We can understand from this expression that the very use of the adverb "usually" means that it is expressly recognized that, although dialogue and mediation are not core activities of the EU EOMs, sometimes these missions must use these resources in the context of electoral processes. We agree that this is not a main task of the EU EOMs, but, at the same time, it should be noted that occasions when such missions intervene by mediating and promoting dialogue between the parties in the electoral processes observed are neither few nor unusual, as we will outline in later paragraphs.

That is why we understand that both electoral assistance and election observation have an essential, complementary[61] and – we would say – equally valuable role in terms of dialogue and mediation regarding electoral conflict prevention and resolution. Electoral assistance is more focused on medium- and long-term technical projects, while election observation, with its presence in the field, acquires a more relevant role in the prevention and resolution of immediate conflicts in the short term.

Thus, with regards to election observation, four of the five possible modalities of EU EOM activity in the field of mediation and dialogue are frequently implemented by the EOMs (namely, mediation or facilitation of dialogue by the EU itself; promoting mediation and dialogue; leveraging mediation and dialogue; supporting mediation and dialogue). EU EOMs have acted in many cases as mediators and facilitators of dialogue between the parties (thus the EU EOM Chief Observers are very frequently engaged in dialogue between the parties to prevent conflicts and prevent the escalation of certain crises or controversies in electoral matters); similarly, they have promoted mediation and dialogue between the different actors; they have used their influence and neutral status to promote this mediating or dialogue work; and they have supported processes of dialogue and external mediation.

Finally, the approval of the *Treaty of Lisbon* would bring an important institutional advance, in terms of coherence and available tools in the field of conflict prevention, among which EOMs[62] would finally be included. Additionally, in 2015, the Directorate General for External Policies approved the document on "Developing operational tools within the EU for a comprehensive approach to prevent electoral violence"[63] that emphasizes the role of EU EOMs in conflict situations. It also considers the broad range of possible responses (political and technical) that EU institutions can implement to address both long-term structural causes of electoral violence and short-term triggers during the election period. One of these responses will be the EU EOMs, especially regarding short-term causes for electoral violence.

In short, paraphrasing Niño Pérez, all this shows that:

> electoral observation and assistance and arms controls/destruction activities can also play a very valuable role in avoiding violent conflict. A well-run election observation mission can reduce the opportunity for intimidation and conflict.[64]

This role of EOMs in the area of conflict prevention has been highlighted, among others, by Thompson, for whom, based on his Latin American experience, election observation, and in particular, international observation, continues to be an important instrument for strengthening the credibility and legitimacy of electoral processes and, as a consequence, for the prevention and resolution of conflicts in the continent.[65]

As a practical example of this preventive role – immediate and in the field – of election observation, we can mention the performance of the EU EOM in the *Nigerian 2015 general elections*, at a juncture still free of active conflict, but with serious indications that it was about to happen. The EU EOM action in the country, in a context marked by violence and insecurity, led to the celebration of an acceptable electoral process, which managed to maintain the political and institutional stability of the African country. The statements of the EU EOM Chief Observer during the pre-election phase, and before the voting day, were essential to ensure that conflict was not triggered. Among some of his statements, we can highlight the following:

> In my meetings with senior representatives they talked of honouring the Abuja Accord, for the elections to be peaceful. Violence does not change results. It is also of course critical that the elections are fair, transparent and credible, and there is electoral justice. It is up to the institutions, the political parties, and the people of Nigeria to make this happen.[66]

After election day, the Chief Observer urged candidates, political parties and citizens to have a peaceful response to the announcement of the results.[67] The risks of the outbreak of post-electoral violence led the EU to increase its presence and stay in the country longer than usual; thus, the Chief Observer visited the country in the post-electoral phase to focus attention on the complaints and claims phase, reinforcing the EU's political messaging of the need to use established arbitration mechanisms to resolve disputes instead of resorting to violence.[68]

Undoubtedly, the role of the EU EOM – duly supported by the EU Delegation and other EU institutions – was essential to avoid a conflict arising from a controversial electoral process.

EU election observation as a mechanism for the resolution of electoral conflicts

Ultimately, in line with the provisions of Article 33 of the Charter of the United Nations,[69] the EU EOMs also carry out specific actions to resolve conflicts, mainly through three means of resolving disputes of a diplomatic nature: negotiation (through political dialogue), mediation and good offices (facilitation).

Political dialogue is the most common diplomatic method associated with EU action on conflict resolution.[70] The political dialogue of the EU EOMs continues from the deployment in the country until the final phase of the post-election period and is therefore fundamental for the resolution of any of the electoral conflicts that may arise throughout the entire electoral process.[71]

In regard to the political dialogue in the electoral field, similarly to the previous section, the role of the Chief Observer of the EU EOM – who is the main responsible figure, together with the EU Delegation in the country – is essential for developing functions of dialogue and negotiation with the political agents of the country in the event of electoral conflicts during any of the stages of the electoral process. It is equally important to refer to the Factsheet "Mediation and Dialogue in electoral processes to prevent and mitigate electoral related violence,"[72] which highlighted the need to resort to mediation and dialogue in the context of electoral processes in order to contribute to the resolution of conflicts.

This political dialogue for the resolution of electoral conflicts exercised by the EU EOMs was outlined, among other instances, on the occasion of the *local, legislative and presidential elections of Haiti 2015–2016*, in which a low intensity electoral crisis or conflict had already unfolded. In the situation of political and institutional paralysis that the Caribbean country was experiencing, the EU EOM remained deployed on the island to mediate in the situation of blockade, as well as to promote dialogue between political parties and other electoral agents. This mediating and facilitating work was shown even in the press releases made by the Mission throughout the period in which the impasse was extended:

> La MOE UE considère qu'il est nécessaire que les différents acteurs du processus électoral prennent leurs responsabilités afin de mettre fin, dans les meilleurs délais, à l'actuelle impasse politique qui, malheureusement, ne fait qu'agrandir l'éloignement entre les citoyens haïtiens et leurs représentants. La Mission appelle tous les acteurs à maintenir une attitude de non-violence et de respect des normes qui encadrent le processus.[73]

Undoubtedly, the role of the EU EOM was essential to confer legitimacy to the different elections held, to denounce the deficiencies of the system, as well as to reach finally a solution to the Haitian impasse at the end of 2016. The elections of November 2016 also counted on the deployment of European election observers.[74]

In the field of electoral conflict resolution, EU EOMs also resort to mediation and good offices. However, it must be taken into account that the EU EOMs cannot carry out mediation actions in electoral conflicts, unless this is included in the deployment agreement signed with the observed State (and in the mandate of the mission itself) or unless there is prior consent of the parties.[75]

In the field of conflict resolution, the EU promotes the implementation of mediation agreements in the post-electoral phase and supports international actions of mediation.

Therefore, the role of the EU EOM chief observers can also be extended to the area of conflict resolution. It is quite frequent that the EU EOM chief observers – especially those who have gained the trust and credibility of the different parties involved – also carry out conflict resolution tasks, for example, encouraging the parties to dialogue as well as prompting the authorities to comply with international standards for elections and the recommendations of the mission.[76]

It is necessary to emphasize that the main objective of an EU EOM is to observe and evaluate the quality of an electoral process. The EU EOMs should not modify its conclusions under the pretext of avoiding or preventing possible conflicts,[77] even if, on occasion, the EU EOM's report may aggravate tensions.[78]

In this regard, the high degree of complementarity between the EU election observation missions and the mediation attempts of the Union itself should be noted. Heads of EU delegations usually initiate dialogue processes with the authorities at least two years in advance of an election to identify areas that can be addressed to prevent election-related violence and support that can be provided by the EU in this area.[79] Election observation missions gather useful data and observations on all aspects of the electoral process and, therefore, can easily identify critical points for potential conflicts. Hence, the EU EOMs – whether acting directly in the resolution of conflicts or providing the precise technical information for the agents who are going to negotiate, mediate or perform good offices in the dispute – are fundamental for the success of any attempts that the Union as a whole is making to resolve electoral conflicts.

Furthermore, in the post-election period, mediation and dialogue carried out by the EU EOMs can play a role in restoring trust and confidence in democratic structures, in strengthening local dialogue capacities and in addressing shortcomings in the electoral process by providing a forum in which election stakeholders may discuss and agree recommendations to improve future electoral processes.[80]

This role of the EU election observation in the resolution of conflicts became evident, among other cases, during the 2015 general elections held in the *United Republic Of Tanzania*, when electoral conflict emerged on the day of the elections, in the vote counting phase. The decision of the Electoral Commission of Zanzibar to suspend on October 28 – three days after the election day – the process of vote counting, based on the unsubstantiated claim that "irregularities and violations of the electoral law had been detected" caused a negative reaction from the EU EOM, as well as from the EU itself. The EU response was based on the reports of the international observers that the EU – and other organizations – had deployed on the two islands that form Zanzibar (Unguja and Pemba), who had validated the cleanliness and credibility of the electoral process and had not detected any type of irregularity that justified the annulment of the electoral process.

After the cancellation of the results by the Electoral Commission of the island, the EU EOM deployed all its mediating and good offices capacity, holding meetings with the parties involved, with the electoral authorities and with the other international organizations that were observing the process.[81] Faced with the decision of the Zanzibar Electoral Commission, the EU EOM and other international EOMs issued a joint communication[82] in which they demanded that the electoral authorities of the island continue with the recount of the votes without further delay and that they specify the polling stations in which the alleged irregularities had occurred. Such evidence was never presented. The EU EOM, supported by the EU Delegation, remained in the country, committed to resolving the crisis in Zanzibar, deploying its mediating and good offices between the parties in order to prevent an escalation of the conflict.

However, the Zanzibar authorities did not accept any other solution than the cancellation of the October elections and the holding of new elections in the country, which was rejected by the opposition – who considered themselves the winner of the elections. The elections were held again on March 20, 2016 with an opposition boycott, which gave the victory with 91.4 percent of the votes to former President Ali Mohamed Shein. The EU EOM did not observe the March 20, 2016 re-run in Zanzibar as it considered the conditions were not conducive to inclusive, genuine and credible elections.[83]

Conclusions

The deployment of an EU EOM in another country can undoubtedly contribute to institutional stability, to legitimize a government emerging from the polls following crisis situations, while at the same time it can restore constitutional order and play a key role in conflict prevention.

According to the analysis presented in this article, we can conclude that the deployment of an EOM in the field constitutes another EU instrument to contribute to internal and international peace, within the broad concept of security that the EU has managed since 2003. The EOMs are tools that contribute to the prevention of conflicts, both because of their role in the aforementioned conditionality policy and because of their dissuasive role when they are deployed in a country on the occasion of an electoral process.

The action of the EU election observation missions in the face of electoral conflicts is not limited to preventative actions (e.g., in Nigeria in 2015 or in Paraguay in 2013), but its relevant role in the peaceful resolution of internal electoral conflicts must be highlighted. For the purposes of both prevention and conflict resolution, the EOMs employ different diplomatic means to resolve disputes, from negotiation to mediation or good offices. Regarding resolution, their role becomes evident in the short term, with immediacy, during their deployment in the observed country; and this is because, being already present in the country, the EOM will become a fundamental agent for the resolution of electoral crises.

The neutrality and impartiality of the EOMs, and their technical specialization in observing the elections, make them an irreplaceable and unique electoral agent, located in a privileged position not only to observe the process but to be able to dialogue, mediate or perform good offices in case any conflict arises during an electoral process. This negotiating, mediating and facilitating work of these EU observation missions is intensified in those countries that are more fragile institutionally or in a post-conflict period. The EU election observation mission, especially if targeting countries in Africa, Latin America and Asia, develops this type of action for the prevention and peaceful resolution of electoral conflicts on a frequent basis, thanks to its singular observing role in the field (as we have demonstrated with the contribution of some specific examples).

This article has intended to highlight this, often unknown, capacity for action of the electoral observation of EU EOMs in the prevention and resolution of conflicts. We have also tried to emphasize the importance of these missions having a specific mandate that enables them to deploy their potential capacity to intervene in the prevention and resolution of electoral conflicts that may arise during their observation in the country. The inclusion or not of this purpose in the mandates of these missions, obviously, will depend on the agreement reached with the authorities of the observed country, and will be conditioned in many cases by criteria of political opportunity. However, we believe that the absence of this objective in the mandates only hides and hinders the frequent work carried out in situ by these missions in order to resolve potential electoral conflicts (as seen in Haiti and Tanzania 2015–2016, and also – among others – in Burkina Faso 2015 and Honduras 2017). In contrast, the inclusion of this purpose in their mandates would not only facilitate and enable these EOMs to carry out actions in matters of prevention and resolution of conflicts, but also reveal that these are tasks that these EOMs are usually forced to take in the field, even in spite of not having the necessary expressed mandate. Finally, and more importantly, in my opinion, it would make clear the transcendental contribution of these missions in the prevention and resolution of the conflicts that may arise in the context of the electoral processes that they observe.

Last, we cannot but emphasize that, in most cases, this task of prevention and resolution of conflicts in the context of electoral processes is carried out by the EOMs in a joint, parallel and coordinated manner with the action of other community institutions in this area, like the EU delegations in the country. In summary, it is undeniable that these missions are part of the extensive set of tools available to the EU to achieve the goals and objectives set out, first, in its European Security Strategy and subsequently in its European Global Strategy, especially in regards to the prevention and resolution of conflicts in the electoral field.

Notes

1 Paloma Biglino Campos y Luis E. Delgado, *La resolución de los conflictos electorales: un análisis comparado* (Madrid: Centro de Estudios Políticos y Constitucionales, 2010), 13–14.
2 Such was the case with the elections in Angola in 1992. Marina Ottaway, "Angola's Failed Elections," in *Post Conflict Elections, Democratization & International Assistance*, ed. Krishna Kumar (Boulder: Lynne Rienner Publishers, 1998).
3 Lisa Kammerud, *An Integrated Approach to Elections and Conflict* (Washington, DC: The International Foundation for Electoral Systems, 2012), 1.
4 Chris Fomunyoh, *Mediación de conflictos relacionados con elecciones* (Geneva: Center for Humanitarian Dialogue, 2009), 3.
5 European Union, *European Security Strategy – A Secure Europe in a Better World* (Brussels: European Union, 2003), accessed January 16, 2019, https://europa.eu/globalstrategy/en/european-security-strategy-secure-europe-better-world.
6 Susana Sanz Caballero, "Operaciones de Paz y Unión Europea," in *V Conference on National Defense Culture* (Madrid: Real Hermandad de Veteranos de las Fuerzas Armadas y de la Guardia Civil, 2008), 208.
7 Ibid., 209–10.
8 According to the High Representative: "For the first time, the EU agreed on a joint threat assessment and set clear objectives for advancing its security interests, based on our core values." Mr. Solana continued, saying:

> It is in our interest that the countries on our borders are well-governed. The European Neighbourhood Policy (ENP), launched in 2004, supports this process. In the East, all eligible countries participate except Belarus, with whom we are now taking steps in this direction.

9 Gerrard Quille, "The European Security Strategy: A Framework for EU Security Interests?" *International Peacekeeping* 11, no. 3 (2004): 422–38.
10 Georgi Kamov, *EU's Role in Conflict Resolution: The Case of Eastern Enlargement and Neighbourhood Policy Areas* (Nice: Institut Européen des Hautes Études Internationales, 2006), 22–23.
11 European Council, *Civilian Headline Goal* (Brussels: European Council, 2004), accessed January 16, 2019, https://eur-lex.europa.eu/legal-content/ES/TXT/HTML/?uri=LEGISSUM:l33239&from=ES.
12 In the 2008 *Civilian Headline Goal*, under the term "observation mission" were included those missions whose main activity was to observe, evaluate and inform the EU about the political situation and general security in the host country or in relation to a specific agreement, as well as those that could help to build trust between the parties that were previously in conflict, to help resolve and mitigate conflicts, and to facilitate contacts between the parties. Examples of these were the observation missions in the Balkans (1991) and in Aceh (2005).
13 Miguel Á. Acosta Sánchez, "La Primera Misión de Mantenimiento de la Paz de la UE: la Misión de Observación de la Unión Europea (MOUE) en los Balcanes (1991–2007)," *Revista Electrónica de Estudios Internacionales* 15 (2008), accessed January 16, 2019, www.reei.org/index.php/revista/num15.
14 María Juliá Barceló, "Las Misiones de Paz de la Unión Europea. Fundamentos Jurídicos, Origen y Desarrollo, Sistema Organizativo, Procedimiento de Creación y Seguimiento y Acuerdos Internacionales de Ejecución" (PhD diss., Universitat Oberta de Catalunya, 2012).

15 Concept for EU Monitoring Missions, doc. 14536/03 of 28 October 2003.
16 Ibid.
17 Acosta Sánchez, "La Primera Misión de Mantenimiento de la Paz de la UE," 16.
18 European Council, *Report on the Implementation of the European Security Strategy – Providing Security in a Changing World*, Doc. S407/08 (Brussels: European Union, 11 December 2008).
19 European Council, *Internal Security Strategy for the European Union: Towards a European Security Model* (Brussels: European Union, 2010), accessed January 16, 2019, www.consilium.europa.eu/media/30753/qc3010313enc.pdf.
20 European Union, *Shared Vision, Common Action: A Stronger Europe. A Global Strategy for the European Union's Foreign and Security Policy* (Brussels: European Union, 2016), accessed January 16, 2019, https://eeas.europa.eu/archives/docs/top_stories/pdf/eugs_review_web.pdf.
21 Ibid.
22 Ibid.
23 Ibid.
24 José Antonio Sanahuja, *Estrategia Global y Seguridad de la Unión Europea: narrativas securitarias, legitimidad e identidad de un actor en crisis* (Madrid: ICEI, 2018), accessed January 16, 2019, www.ucm.es/data/cont/media/www/pag-27289/WP%20011%20(1).pdf.
25 Due, mainly, to the functional and geographical distribution with the Organization for Security and Cooperation in Europe, which does observe elections in Europe (www.osce.org/odihr/elections).
26 Ayman Ayoub, "La Observación Electoral Internacional: Una Aproximación Conceptual," in *Observación Electoral Internacional: Sentido, Actores y Retos* (Valencia: CEPS Editions, 2008), 27 and 33; Víctor C. Pascual Planchuelo, "La 'observación' electoral de la OEA vs. el 'acompañamiento' de UNASUR en las recientes elecciones de Venezuela," *Revista América Latina Hoy* 75 (2017): 127–48.
27 *Declaration of Principles for International Election Observation*, New York, October 27, 2005.
28 Yves Beigbeder, *International Monitoring of Plebiscites, Referenda and National Elections: Self-determination and Transition to Democracy* (Dordrecht: Martinus Nijhoff Publishers, 1994), 255.
29 *Handbook for European Union Election Observation Missions* (Stockholm: Swedish International Development Cooperation Agency, 2005).
30 Álvaro Jarillo, *El derecho de participación política y la democracia en el ordenamiento internacional: análisis desde la perspectiva europea* (Madrid: UNED, 2006), 294.
31 European Commission, Communication from the Commission on EU Election Assistance and Observation, COM(2000) 191 final (Brussels: European Union, April 11, 2000); Fanny Castro-Rial Garrone, Álvaro Jarillo Aldeanueva and Eduardo Trillo De Martín-Pinillos, *Las misiones de observación electoral en la prevención de conflictos* (Madrid: Instituto Universitario General Gutiérrez Mellado, 2005), 52–56.
32 See art. 2 Council Regulation (EC) No 975/1999 and art. 3 Council Regulation (EC) No 976/1999.
33 European Commission, Communication from the Commission on EU Election Assistance and Observation.
34 Castro-Rial Garrone, Jarillo Aldeanueva and Trillo De Martín-Pinillos, *Las misiones de observación electoral en la prevención de conflictos*, 55.
35 Directorate General for External Policies, *EU Election Observation: Achievements, Challenges* (Brussels: European Union, 2008), 6.
36 The European External Action Service lists all the EOMs deployed by the EU at the following website: http://eeas.europa.eu/eueom/index_es.htm, accessed January 16, 2019.
37 Directorate General for External Policies, *EU Election Observation: Achievements, Challenges*, 6.
38 Directorate General for External Policies, *Developing Operational Tools within the EU for a Comprehensive Approach to Prevent Electoral Violence* (Brussels: European Union, 2015).
39 European Commission, Communication from the Commission on EU Election Assistance and Observation.
40 Available at: www.europarl.europa.eu/sides/getDoc.do?pubRef=-//EP//TEXT+TA+P6-TA-2008-0194+0+DOC+XML+V0//EN&language=EN, accessed January 16, 2019.
41 Brief information available at: http://eeas.europa.eu/archives/eueom/pdf/missions/fact_sheet_for_eu_eom_guinea_bissau_2009_en.pdf, accessed January 16, 2019.
42 Brief information available at: http://eeas.europa.eu/archives/eueom/pdf/missions/eueom-ethiopia-fact-sheet-23042010_en.pdf, accessed January 16, 2019.
43 Nepal (brief information: https://eeas.europa.eu/sites/eeas/files/eom_nepal_fact_sheet_-_final_english-nepali.pdf, accessed January 16, 2019); Honduras (brief information: https://eeas.europa.eu/

sites/eeas/files/factsheet_moeuehn17.pdf, accessed January 16, 2019); Zimbabwe (brief information: https://eeas.europa.eu/sites/eeas/files/factsheet_eueom_zimbabwe.pdf, accessed January 16, 2019).

44 European External Action Service, *Mediation and Dialogue in Electoral Processes to Prevent and Mitigate Electoral Related Violence* (Brussels: European Union, 2002).

45 Fraser Cameron, *The European Union and Conflict Prevention*, United Nations Institute for Disarmament Research, 2003, 9.

46 Amaya Úbeda De Torres, "La evolución de la condicionalidad política en el seno de la Unión Europea," *Revista de Derecho Comunitario Europeo* 32 (2009): 60.

47 Ibid.

48 Joan D. Janer Torrens, *La promoción de los derechos humanos y de los principios democráticos en las relaciones exteriores de la Unión Europea: mecanismos jurídicos* (Barcelona: Atelier, 2005), 134.

49 Mercedes Candela Soriano, "L'Union Européenne et la protection des droits de l'homme dans la coopération au développement: le rôle de la conditionnalité politique," *Revue Trimestrielle de Droit de l'Homme* 52 (2002): 891.

50 An overview of the adopted measures is available at: www.sanctionsmap.eu/#/main, accessed January 16, 2019.

51 Javier Niño Pérez, "EU Instruments for Conflict Prevention," in *EU and Conflict Prevention. Policy and Legal Aspects*, eds. V. Kronenberger and J. Wouters (The Hague: TMC Asser Press, 2004), 93–117.

52 Ibid.: "The link between conflict prevention and human rights and democracy is abundantly clear. Just as denying basic rights can fuel violent conflict, helping to guarantee those rights can prevent conflict arising in the first place."

53 Available at: www.consilium.europa.eu/media/20977/00200-r1es1.pdf, accessed January 16, 2019.

54 Susanne Gentz, *EU Influence in Conflict: Power to Mitigate or to Mediate?* (OSLO forum, Geneva: HD Centre for Humanitarian Dialogue, 2007), 54.

55 Ángel Carrascal Gutiérrez, "La mediación internacional en el Sistema de Naciones Unidas y en La Unión Europea: evolución y retos de futuro," *Revista de Mediación* 8 (2011): 31.

56 It envisages the option of political dialogue:

> The EU engages in a political dialogue of varying degrees of formality with all countries with which it has relations. A long-term dialogue on political issues including human rights and democratisation can have an early warning role by highlighting problems which could in the future lead to violent conflict as well as contributing to their early resolution.

57 UN Institute for Disarmament Research, "The European Union and Conflict Prevention," Paper Prepared for the Project "*European Action on Small Arms and Light Weapons and Explosive Remnants of War*," 2003.

58 Tanja Tamminen, "Strengthening the EU's Peace Mediation Capacities Leveraging for Peace through New Ideas and Thinking," *The Finnish Institute of International Affairs* 32 (2012): 27.

59 It reads:

> Mediation is an effective and cost-efficient instrument for conflict prevention, transformation and resolution. It is a relevant feature of crisis management at all stages of inter- and intra-state conflicts: before they escalate into armed conflict, after the outbreak of violence, and during the implementation of peace agreements. The EU is engaged in the entire spectrum of mediation, facilitation and dialogue processes.

60 European Commission, *Methodological Guide on Electoral Assistance* (Brussels: European Union, 2006), 16. It says:

> Election assistance may be defined as the technical or material support given to the electoral process. It may imply professional help to establish a legal framework for the elections. It may take the form of a general input to the National Election Commission, for example providing voting material and equipment, or helping in the registration of political parties and the registration of voters. It may also imply support to NGOs and civil society in areas such as voter and civic education or training of local observers as well as support to the media through media monitoring and training of journalists. Election observation is the political complement to election assistance. It is defined as the purposeful gathering of information regarding an electoral process, and the making of informed judgements on the conduct of such a process on the basis of the information collected, by persons who are not inherently authorised to intervene in the process.

In broad terms, election observation is part of election assistance. Technically speaking, they are different activities, but they should be considered and programmed in a complementary manner.

61 Ibid., 17. It says:

> The two activities were not considered in conflict but seen as complementary ones in the context of long-term assistance to an electoral cycle, as they are run professionally and independently, and they contribute in an equal but different manner to the democratic development of the country.

62 Ángel Carrascal Gutiérrez, "La mediación internacional en el sistema de Naciones Unidas y en la Unión Europea."

63 Directorate General for External Policies, *Developing Operational Tools*, 25–27.

64 Niño Pérez, "EU Instruments for Conflict Prevention."

65 Joseph Thompson, "The European Union's Electoral Missions from the Perspective of Current Developments in Latin American Democracy," *Idea International* (2009), 6–7.

66 "EU Election Observation Mission Following a Challenging Electoral Process," EEAS website, accessed January 16, 2019, https://eeas.europa.eu/topics/election-observation-missions-eueoms_en/23882/EU%20Election%20Observation%20Mission%20to%20Nigeria%20in%202015.

67 "Strong Electoral Competition and Commitment Demonstrated despite Systemic Problems," EEAS website, accessed January 16, 2019, eeas.europa.eu/archives/eueom/missions/2015/nigeria/pdf/30032015-nigeria-ps1_en.pdf.

68 Directorate General for External Policies, *Developing Operational Tools*, 26.

69 It says:

> The parties to any dispute, the continuance of which is likely to endanger the maintenance of international peace and security, shall, first of all, seek a solution by negotiation, enquiry, mediation, conciliation, arbitration, judicial settlement, resort to regional agencies or arrangements, or other peaceful means of their own choice.

70 Gentz, *EU Influence in Conflict: Power to Mitigate or to Mediate?*, 54–62.

71 Directorate General for External Policies, *Developing Operational Tools*, 25–27.

72 European External Action Service, *Mediation and Dialogue in Electoral Processes to Prevent and Mitigate Electoral Related Violence* (Brussels: European Union, 2012), http://ecdpm.org/wp-content/uploads/2013/11/EEAS-Mediation-Factsheet-Dialogue-Prevent-Mitigate-Electoral-Violence.pdf, accessed January 16, 2019.

73 "EU EOM condemns electoral violence and calls for respect for citizens' political rights," EEAS website, http://eeas.europa.eu/archives/eueom/missions/2015/haiti/pdf/communique_23012016.pdf, accessed January 16, 2019.

74 "Déclaration du porte-parole sur les élections en Haïti le 20 novembre 2016," EEAS website, https://eeas.europa.eu/delegations/gambia/15581/declaration-du-porte-parole-sur-les-elections-en-haiti-le-20-novembre-2016_es, accessed January 16, 2019.

75 Article 2.7 Charter of the United Nations:

> Nothing contained in the present Charter shall authorize the United Nations to intervene in matters which are essentially within the domestic jurisdiction of any state or shall require the Members to submit such matters to settlement under the present Charter; but this principle shall not prejudice the application of enforcement measures under Chapter VII.

76 Directorate General for External Policies, *Developing Operational Tools*, 25–27.

77 Antje Herrberg, *Missing a Trick? Building Bridges between EU Mediation and EU Electoral Support in Conflict-affected Countries* (Brussels: European Centre for Electoral Support, 2012).

78 In the elections held in Kenya in 2007, the critical reports of the EU EOM about the elections gave the right base to the losing candidate and his followers to challenge the official results announced due to their lack of credibility.

79 Directorate General for External Policies, *Developing Operational Tools*, 25–27.

80 Ibid.

81 The role of the EOM is confirmed in "Election Observation Missions (EUEOMs)," EEAS website, August 10, 2016, www.eueom.eu/files/pressreleases/english/06_DepartureEOM_en.pdf, accessed January 16, 2019.

82 Heads of Election Observer Missions in Tanzania, "International Observers Express Concern at the Situation in Zanzibar, and Call for Transparency in the Electoral Process," The Commonwealth

website, October 29, 2015, http://thecommonwealth.org/media/news/international-observers-express-concern-situation-zanzibar, accessed January 16, 2019.

83 Delegation of the European Union to Togo, "EU EOM Presents Its Final Report on the 2015 Elections Including Recommendations for Future Elections in Tanzania," EEAS website, June 03, 2016, https://eeas.europa.eu/delegations/togo/11789/eu-eom-presents-its-final-report-on-the-2015-elections-including-recommendations-for-future-elections-in-tanzania_en, accessed January 16, 2019.

References

Acosta Sánchez, Miguel Á. "La Primera Misión de Mantenimiento de la Paz de la UE: la Misión de Observación de la Unión Europea (MOUE) en los Balcanes (1991–2007)." *Revista Electrónica de Estudios Internacionales* 15 (2008).

Ayoub, Ayman. "La Observación Electoral Internacional: Una Aproximación Conceptual." In *Observación Electoral Internacional: Sentido, Actores y Retos*, 27–43. Valencia: CEPS Editions, 2008.

Beigbeder, Yves. *International Monitoring of Plebiscites, Referenda and National Elections: Self-determination and Transition to Democracy*. Dordrecht: Martinus Nijhoff Publishers, 1994.

Biglino Campos, Paloma, and Luis E. Delgado. *La resolución de los conflictos electorales: un análisis comparado*. Madrid: Centro de Estudios Políticos y Constitucionales, 2010.

Cameron, Fraser. *The European Union and Conflict Prevention*. United Nations Institute for Disarmament Research, 2003.

Candela Soriano, Mercedes. "L'Union Européenne et la protection des droits de l'homme dans la coopération au développement: le rôle de la conditionnalité politique." *Revue Trimestrielle de Droit de l'Homme* 52 (2002): 875–900.

Carrascal Gutiérrez, Ángel. "La mediación internacional en el sistema de Naciones Unidas y en la Unión Europea: evolución y retos de futuro." *Revista de Mediación* 8 (2011): 28–33.

Castro-Rial Garrone, Fanny, Álvaro Jarillo Aldeanueva and Eduardo Trillo de Martín-Pinillos. *Las misiones de observación electoral en la prevención de conflictos*. Madrid: Instituto Universitario General Gutiérrez Mellado, 2005.

Directorate General for External Policies. *Developing Operational Tools within the EU for a Comprehensive Approach to Prevent Electoral Violence*. Brussels: European Union, 2015.

Directorate General for External Policies. *EU Election Observation: Achievements, challenges*. Brussels: European Union, 2008.

European Commission. Communication from the Commission on Conflict Prevention. COM(2001) 211 final. Brussels: European Union, April 11, 2001.

European Commission. Communication from the Commission on EU Election Assistance and Observation. COM(2000) 191 final. Brussels: European Union, April 11, 2000.

European Commission. *Methodological Guide on Electoral Assistance*. Brussels: European Union, 2006.

European Council. *Internal Security Strategy for the European Union: Towards a European Security Model*. Brussels: European Union, 2010.

European Council. *Report on the Implementation of the European Security Strategy – Providing Security in a Changing World*. S407/08. Brussels: European Union, December 11, 2008.

European External Action Service. *European Security Strategy – A Secure Europe in a Better World*. Brussels: European Union, 2003.

European External Action Service. *Mediation and Dialogue in Electoral Processes to Prevent and Mitigate Electoral Related Violence*. Brussels: European Union, 2002.

European External Action Service. *Shared Vision, Common Action: A Stronger Europe. A Global Strategy for the European Union's Foreign and Security Policy*. Brussels: European Union, 2016.

Fomunyoh, Chris. *Mediación de conflictos relacionados con elecciones*. Geneva: Centre for Humanitarian Dialogue, 2009.

Gentz, Susanne. *EU Influence in Conflict: Power to Mitigate or to Mediate?* OSLO forum, Geneva: HD Centre for Humanitarian Dialogue, 2007.

Handbook for European Union Election Observation Missions. Stockholm: Swedish International Development Cooperation Agency, 2005.

Herrberg, Antje. *Missing a Trick? Building Bridges between EU Mediation and EU Electoral Support in Conflict-affected Countries*. Brussels: European Centre for Electoral Support, 2012.

Janer Torrens, Joan D. *La promoción de los derechos humanos y de los principios democráticos en las relaciones exteriores de la Unión Europea: mecanismos jurídicos*. Barcelona: Atelier, 2005.

Jarillo, Álvaro. *El derecho de participación política y la democracia en el ordenamiento internacional: análisis desde la perspectiva europea*. Madrid: UNED, 2006.

Juliá Barceló, María. "Las Misiones de Paz de la Unión Europea, Fundamentos Jurídicos, Origen y Desarrollo, Sistema Organizativo, Procedimiento de Creación y Seguimiento y Acuerdos Internacionales de Ejecución." PhD dissertation, Universidad Oberta de Catalunya, 2012.

Kammerud, Lisa. *An Integrated Approach to Elections and Conflict*. Washington, DC: The International Foundation for Electoral Systems, 2012.

Kamov, Georgi. *EU's Role in Conflict Resolution: The Case of Eastern Enlargement and Neighbourhood Policy Areas*. Nice: Institut Éuropéen des Hautes Études Internationales, 2006.

Niño Pérez, Javier. "EU Instruments for Conflict Prevention." In *EU and Conflict Prevention. Policy and Legal Aspects*, edited by V. Kronenberger and J. Wouters, 93–117. The Hague: TMC Asser Press, 2004.

Ottaway, Marina. "Angola's Failed Elections." In *Post Conflict Elections, Democratization & International Assistance*, edited by Krishna Kumar, 133–52. Boulder: Lynne Reiner Publishers, 1998.

Pascual Planchuelo, Víctor C. "La 'observación' electoral de la OEA vs. el 'acompañamiento' de UNASUR en las recientes elecciones de Venezuela." *Revista América Latina Hoy* 75 (2017): 127–48.

Quille, Gerrard. "The European Security Strategy: A Framework for EU Security Interests?" *International Peacekeeping* 11, no. 3 (2004): 422–38.

Sanahuja, José Antonio. *Estrategia Global y Seguridad de la Unión Europea: narrativas securitarias, legitimidad e identidad de un actor en crisis*. Madrid: ICEI, 2018.

Sanz Caballero, Susana. "Operaciones de Paz y Unión Europea." In: *V Conference on National Defense Culture*, 197–228. Madrid: Real Hermandad de Veteranos de las Fuerzas Armadas y de la Guardia Civil, 2008.

Tamminen, Tanja. "Strengthening the EU's Peace Mediation Capacities Leveraging for Peace through New Ideas and Thinking." *The Finnish Institute of International Affairs* 32 (2012): 7–16.

Thompson, José. "The European Union's Electoral Missions from the Perspective of Current Developments in Latin American Democracy." *Idea International* (2009).

Úbeda de Torres, Amaya. "La evolución de la condicionalidad política en el seno de la Unión Europea." *Revista de Derecho Comunitario Europeo* 32 (2009): 49–88.

United Nations Institute for Disarmament Research. "The European Union and Conflict Prevention." Paper Prepared for the Project "*European Action on Small Arms and Light Weapons and Explosive Remnants of War*," 2003.

23
THE EU GLOBAL STRATEGY
Security narratives, legitimacy, and identity of an actor in crisis[1]

José Antonio Sanahuja

Introduction

On the 29th of June 2016, the EU's foreign policy and security High Representative and Commission Vice President (HR/VP) Federica Mogherini released the new EU Global Strategy for Foreign and Security Policy (hereinafter EUGS).[2] However, this event had a gloomy tone due to the commotion caused by the recent Brexit referendum. After an initial lukewarm reception, the Council of the European Union only formally backed it in October of that year.[3] This document required two years of talks and a difficult pursuit of agreement between Member States and EU institutions. Once approved, it left behind the previous EU Strategy, made in 2003 under the authority of the then High Representative, Javier Solana, and its later revision in 2008.

The new EUGS responds to the usual purposes of a policy document of this kind: facing a changing global scenario, it updates the EU's vision of the world, seeks to reaffirm its status as a global actor, and redefines the objectives, tools, and strategies of its foreign and security policy. Nevertheless, the meaning and reach of the EUGS transcends that external dimension. Therefore, this chapter argues that it responds to the fear and anxiety in a more uncertain and adverse international scenario, and to the angst generated by the EU's own existential crisis, which can be understood as a crisis of all the substantive dimensions of European integration[4] or as a crisis of sovereignty, in its three dimensions of defense, borders and currency.[5] As Mogherini herself points out in the preface, and it is reaffirmed by the Strategy,[6] it is an EU whose own survival can no longer be assumed. Just days before the EUGS was released, the dramatic result of the British *Brexit* referendum opened a new breakpoint for a EU that was still recovering from the Eurozone crisis and the later failure in managing the Syrian refugee flows and the consequent migration crisis of 2015. Those can be considered as self-inflicted crises, which express deep institutional and governance problems, as well as emerging political and social cleavages within the EU.[7] For this reason, it is not surprising that when the EU speaks about the world and its security challenges, it also speaks about itself and its own existential *angst*.

Understanding the EUGS as a security or foreign policy narrative, it not only talks about a more unfavorable scenario:[8] it is also an instrument to redefine its own identity and nature as a global actor, and to reaffirm its relevance and agency regarding growingly euro skeptic Member

States and their citizens. All this, at a time of upswing of the far right and the spread of extreme nationalism and other dynamics of disintegration and renationalization. Therefore, as the Strategy argues, the threats to the European project and to the security and prosperity of its citizens come not only from abroad, but from its own troubles.

To analyze the contents and significance of the EUGS, this chapter will review the document, first from the legal/formal perspective. Nonetheless, as it will be argued, its more relevant dimension is ideational and discursive. The EUGS, therefore, should be read and decoded as a narrative discourse of security that reformulates the EU's identity and its vision of the world, with the purpose of legitimation of its identity, relevance and performance. From this perspective, the chapter will examine the evolution from the Security Strategy of 2003, also called the *Solana Document*,[9] to the new EUGS. Special attention will be paid to the 2015 "Strategic Assessment" prepared by the European External Action Service as a previous stage of diagnosis towards the EUGS. Then, the discussion will turn to the EUGS's contents, according to its double-edged external and internal dimensions. The chapter will devote special attention to some of the new proposals coming out from the EUGS as its "pragmatic turn" for the EU's external action, such as the principle and approach of "resilience" and the search for more policy coherence between the EU objectives concerning security and those of other EU policies. All this, with the aim of pointing out the conflicting relationship between the EU's stated external action principles and values. As a conclusion, the final section will affirm that the EUGS should be interpreted as a new security narrative, far away from the cosmopolitan vision of the 2003 EU Security Strategy, that tries to deliver a new securitized legitimacy for a EU which is going through a deep crisis of meaning and legitimacy in the eyes of its own citizenship.

The EUGS: narratives and "productive power"

From the material point of view, the EUGS reflects the "hybrid" nature of the EU's external action since the appearance of the Common Foreign and Security Policy (CFSP) in the Maastricht Treaty (1992) and, as a part of it, the Common Security and Defence Policy (CSDP). This hybrid nature has been maintained in the Treaty of Lisbon (2007) despite its innovations to assure more integrated and coherent external action. For this reason, the Strategy covers, on the one hand, matters of common competences, whether exclusive or shared, such as trade or development; on the other hand, it covers competences of an essentially exclusively sovereign nature, such as security and defense. As is widely known, in this sphere of activity the EU establishes an institutionalized intergovernmental framework which allows a common action if it is so decided by Member States. Given this hybrid character, the EUGS's main purpose is to assure more coherent and coordinated and therefore more effective external action, contributing to the development of both the CFSP and the CSDP. These aims concern the whole of the EU's external action, regardless of its different sectoral dimensions, as well as the activity of Member States and EU institutions.

In any case, the EUGS is not a formal instrument of the CFSP and it is not explicitly contemplated as such in the Treaties. Instead of that, it is a policy document that would express, on the one hand, the Council of the European Union's ability to adopt "general guidelines" for the CFSP (art. 22 TEU) and, on the other hand, the duties of the High Representative and Vice President of the Commission (HR/VP) in support of the Council. The holder of that role should ensure the effectiveness, unity, and coherence of foreign policy regarding other policies of the Union (art. 21.3 and 26.2 TEU), as well as its capacity of submitting proposals to the Council, and in particular, being the HR as well as the president of the Foreign Affairs Council, contributing to the formulation of the CFSP (art. 27.1 TEU). As with other decisions adopted in the framework of the CFSP, the adoption of the EUGS did not give birth to a legislative act.

Anyway, the analysis of the legal-formal nature of the EUGS does not clarify enough its role in the conformation of EU external action, its *actorness*, or the definition of both the EU's and its Member States' identities inside the international system. To understand in depth, the EUGS could be seen as a mechanism of "policy Europeanization," in which Member States transfer their foreign policy preferences – interests, identity, and values – upwards, to the EU institutions (*uploading*). Once the EUGS has been adopted with the participation of the EU own institutions, it will contribute to shape national policies and preferences in a downward logic, answering to the EU demands of coordination, coherence and unity of action (*downloading*).[10]

There are other possible interpretations of the nature of the EUGS, such as that in which the EUGS is considered as the crystallization of a new narrative or discourse with a constitutive role of the identity, power and agency of the EU.[11] Critical theory or social constructivism maintain that the narratives, as a specific kind of discourse, can have a key role in the social construction of reality, giving it some rationality and coherence, and giving meaning to the facts. Political narratives define expectations, hierarchize actors, assign roles and functions, and prescribe behaviors. Therefore, narratives become social norms setting what conduct is acceptable or punishable, with incentives and penalties expressed both in material and symbolic terms. They have an important constitutive role regarding the interests, values and identities of social and political actors, and of social and power relations. In this role, they also constitute and give meaning to the practices in foreign policy and in other policy areas, laying down frameworks of authority, and of individual and collective loyalty and solidarity of local, national and/or transnational scope. Thus, from this perspective, narratives can shape "imagined political geographies," based upon the identities of otherness, friend or foe, threat and security tension axis.

There are different contributions in the literature that have indicated how certain social facts, such as security or anarchy, are social structures defined through social interaction, communication and the language and meaning enunciated through narratives. The literature also emphasizes the important role that history and culture play in providing the substrate for this process of social construction.[12] This conceptualization of narratives is broadly consistent with the reflectivist epistemology and power ontologies offered by critical theory of international relations and social constructivism. As a teleology, narratives generate a sense of purpose to social practices and, in particular, to the political arena, with important functions of legitimation.[13] For all that, narratives are also an instrument of power, and for that matter, an arena for dispute and contestation, and they reflect both dominant social relations and political and social conflicts. All that is especially important for an actor such as the EU, in which, unlike nation states, these elements are the subject of a process of socio-political construction, whereas in the case of Member States all this is often assumed as natural consequences or given ontologies coming from sovereign nation States.

These approaches lead to a claim for more attention to the cognitive factors usually neglected in mainstream theories, recognizing their constitutive role of discourses and narratives in the construction of categories such as identity, meaning, purpose, or expectations shaping political geographies and the international political economy. This is the case with Robert Cox's concept of structure and structural power,[14] which considers these ideational and cognitive elements as a key element of hegemony, in Antonio Gramsci's definition. It is also the case with Barnett and Duvall's conceptualization of power,[15] which adapts Foucault's meaning of "productive power," defined as the socially diffuse production of subjectivity and identity. This applies in particular to those narratives that constitute the EU and its role as a global actor, both in relation to its citizens and Member States, and to other actors of the international system.

From optimism to uncertainty (2003–2015): the changing world views of the European Union

The 2003 Global Security Strategy: a cosmopolitan EU with transformative purposes

In December 2003, the then European Union's High Representative for Foreign and Security Policy and Secretary General of the Council of the European Union, Javier Solana, launched the first Security Strategy of the EU, subtitled *A Safer Europe in a Better World*.[16] This notable document, the first of its kind, was largely a reaction to the United States' invasion of Iraq, challenging the UN Security Council, which provoked a crisis of multilateralism and a remarkable transatlantic gap. Then, the EU was faced with Robert Kagan's crude metaphor picturing Europe as a weak and effeminate "Venus,"[17] unable to live up to the circumstances, against "Mars," a virile and assertive United States. The EU tried to reaffirm its rejection of the abrasive unilateralism coming from the Bush doctrine, as well as its commitment to international law and the multilateral order – with two external referents, one in the United Nations, and the other in the North Atlantic Treaty Organization (NATO). That stance, however, also had an internal reading: the Strategy tried to face the fractures between the "old" and the "new" Europe, this last encouraged by the United States and its supporters within the EU, particularly by the United Kingdom, Spain, and Poland.

In its external dimension, beyond aligning means, interests and objectives, the Strategy was configured as a "transformative" narrative of globalization defining the identity and role of the EU as a "normative" and "civilian" power, whose external action and diplomacy must be based in values and not only in interests. The formulation of this set of values was first addressed in the 2004 failed EU Constitution, which would later be codified in the Lisbon Treaty of 2007. It reflected an optimistic vision of the international order and the hegemony of liberal internationalism. It also showed a confident attitude towards the EU role, based on a particular European teleology of the governance of globalization. According to this strategy, the EU could contribute to this purpose with its own *zeitgeist*[18] of integration and cosmopolitan democracy through the pooling of sovereignty and the promotion of social cohesion and the European social "model."[19] For all this, the EU would be, in Javier Solana's words, a *force for good* that would try to legitimize itself towards its citizenship both for its values and for its actions.[20]

In terms of security, terrorism and transnational crime were recognized as "new" emerging threats, along with more traditional ones like the proliferation of weapons of mass destruction. But a multidimensional conception of security was clearly adopted, incorporating elements such as climate change, taking individuals not only States as referents. It emphasized the security–development nexus, stressing the importance of the latter. "Improving the world," as it stands in the subtitle of the Strategy, would contribute to promoting global and European security. In that endeavor the EU would be a particularly suitable actor as a "civilian power" based on its own non-military capabilities in diplomacy, trade and development aid. The use of force and military means was not excluded, and for this reason a strengthening of capacities was requested at the European level. But the document, in a strong contrast with the United States' policies at the time, excluded its unilateral application and the recourse of war, by sticking to the military and civil missions the treaty considered in the frame of CFSP, in particular those of crisis management, peace-keeping and peacebuilding.[21]

After 2003, this first Strategy was developed by carrying out sectoral and regional strategies grounded in the wider vision of the "Solana document."[22] In 2008 a revised version was adopted.[23] Although still based in the vision of the previous document, it showed a more cautious and circumspect vision of the international context. It gave more attention to subjects such as the risks of nuclear proliferation in Iran, the persistence of the Israel–Palestine conflict, and new concerns such as cyber security or energy security. Its vision of security was more restrictive and it embodied a more cautious vision of the security–development nexus – for example, in relation to State fragility. As regards the EU's capacities, it presented a positive balance of the CFSP missions, with 20 missions then on record. However, the reiteration of goals and aspirations in the realm of defense showed that little or nothing had been achieved, and that the CSDP still had "a bit of politics, a little more of security, and almost nothing of defence."[24] However, this document barely received any attention due to the pressures of the moment – the Irish referendum on the Lisbon Treaty, the war between Russia and Georgia and the financial crisis – and it didn't have real support from the new High Representative for EU foreign and security policy, Catherine Ashton, who took this new position created by the Lisbon Treaty, in 2009. Indeed, her 2012 initiative to draft a new "Global Strategy" was belated and inconclusive, and it didn't lead to any remarkable results.[25]

A transformed world: the strategic assessment of 2015

Starting in 2014, a new political cycle in EU institutions brought the designation of the Juncker Commission and the new HR/VP Federica Mogherini. It meant a quite different start in relation to the "Solana Strategy." Nathalie Tocci, coordinator of the works that gave rise to the EUGS – and also Mogherini's advisor while she was Italy's minister for foreign affairs – described it in this way: "in 2003, the liberal order seemed unchallenged – 9/11 notwithstanding, and EU soft power was at its peak. (…) In 2015 that world had gone."[26] If the "Solana Strategy" stated in 2003 that "the EU has never been so prosperous, so secure, nor so free,"[27] in 2016 the "Mogherini Strategy" claimed that "the purpose and even the existence of the EU are in question."[28] It was not only because the global scenario was radically transformed. Since 2010 the EU had jumped from one crisis to another, with deep internal disagreements in relation to key issues – Eurozone governance, relations with a defiant Russia, migration or defense, without long term vision or project, and with growing disaffection amongst its citizens and an extreme right-wing on the rise.

The new HR/VP departed from a previous mandate of the European Council from December 2013 to realize a "strategic reflection," more than a "strategy" as such. Mogherini's External European Action Service (EEAS) started a two-stage process, of diagnosis and prognosis. This gradual approach aimed to overcome the initial limitations of that mandate and the distrust from Member States – most of them being right-wing governments, reluctant to have the HR/VP commanded by a relatively inexperienced and young woman, coming from the center-left, and supposedly too "soft" in her foreign policy approach. The drafting of the EUGS in an two-year process took two stages: first, the elaboration of a "strategic review" by the EEAS and the Commission, published in May 2015, with the support of the EU Institute for Security Studies (EU–ISS), based in Paris and headed by the also Italian citizen Antonio Missiroli;[29] and a second stage aimed at drafting the Strategy itself, based in a broader range of consultations, until its presentation in June 2016.

The 2015 strategic review is a more refined and sophisticated diagnostic exercise than the cursory and confident analysis from the "Solana Strategy." It describes a changing and uncertain international scenario, as is asserted in its title, "a world more connected, contested, and complex." It has become more connected because of globalization, which transforms sovereignty, citizenship, development or security. It means citizens have more opportunities, but it also amplifies the scope for new threats such as terrorism, transnational crime, attacks on networks and other threats linked to new technologies.

It is also portrayed as a more contested and conflictive world, facing up to the appearance of ungoverned spaces and fragile states, especially in the EU's neighborhood; unsolved and protracted conflicts that increase refugee flows; and potentially disrupting demographic and social trends – such as the increasing demands of rising middle classes, which together with climate change could entail higher risks of conflict.

Finally, it is a more complex world in which power shifts and experiences deep changes in its nature, sources and patterns of diffusion. Although the United States retains the ability of projecting its power globally, the EUGS stated that its unipolar dominance is over, but that doesn't mean that in its place will arise another unipolar order: furthermore, the very notion of polarity is in question in the face of new dynamics of change and diffusion of power and an international system shifting from a world of nation states to a networked globe of state, non-state, inter-state and transnational actors. Developing countries, despite having more weight and capabilities to challenge existing multilateralism, don't constitute a homogeneous block in values and interests, and neither claim to be able nor are in fact able to build an alternative institutional architecture to govern the global system.

As it will be argued, the EUGS's pragmatic and realist turn is already advanced in the strategic assessment when defining the EU "challenges and opportunities," that are not global, but mainly located in its neighborhood in the North of Africa and the Mediterranean.[30] The review remains confident in the "transformative" capacity of the EU's accession and partnership policy regarding the Europeanization of Turkey, the Western Balkans, or Eastern Europe. However, it shows a more nuanced and prudent approach, and it is more imprecise regarding how to deal with a resurgent Russia. In the Mediterranean, the document is focused on the risks of instability and how they are affecting the internal–external link of European security. Less attention is paid to Africa, apart from the traditional EU pro-development approach for this region. Both Latin America and the United States are included in the "wider Atlantic" area, where there are opportunities to deepen NATO ties and to promote trade talks in the framework of the Transatlantic Trade and Investment Partnership (TTIP). When looking to Asia, the review recognizes its growing economic weight and also sees risks of conflict, which should be addressed through multilateral rules.

The strategic review is also a self-evaluation exercise of the EU itself, highly critical of EU fragmentation of policies, capacities, and instruments, in respect to which it identifies five main challenges:

a Lack of clear political direction in the CFSP, still mostly based on "strategic partnerships" with other powers, losing "dynamism and relevance": a CSDP with a low level of ambition and capabilities as regards the increasing "degradation" of the strategic environment; and fragmented external action, with trade and development policies in the hands of the respective director generals of the Commission with their own sectoral mandates, usually apart from or even in contradiction to the EU's foreign policy goals.

b Lack of flexibility in financial instruments as concerns other policy instruments. Again, the document complains about foreign aid programming and management requirements that prevent redirecting funds to other pressing security or foreign policy priorities.

c Scant global leverage despite the EU's significant role in trade, being the main commercial partner for more than 80 countries, and in development aid, considering that the EU is the world's largest donor when combining Member States' and EU institutions' contributions. Policy fragmentation and the relative autonomy of these policy areas regarding diplomatic action reduce or damage the EU's potential influence and its ability for being a "significant power" in the global scenario.

d Lack of coordination: the EU is capable of speaking with a single voice, as happens in trade matters, or of making its different voices speak together, as happens in climate change. But these voices are discordant or there is not a common framework in other policy areas such as energy or cyber defense. There is also a clear fragmentation and lack of coordination regarding the financial instruments deployed by both the EU institutions themselves and the Member States, as development aid shows, where the joint programming mechanisms are barely starting to operate.

e Weakness or lack of common capabilities in the field of security and defense. The already established Battle Groups[31] have never been deployed, and there are no instruments for common financing, intelligence or logistics regarding civil and military components of CFSP and CSDP operations, in a general scenario of cuts or stagnation in defense budgets of Member States, and regarding the control of external borders.

This diagnosis is also an expression of deep rooted "turf wars" and inter-bureaucratic tensions between, on one side, the EEAS and the HR/VP in charge of the direction of foreign and security policies, and, on the other side, the Commission, reluctant to lose its control over policy areas where it has extensive powers related to the EU's exclusive or shared competences, such as EU trade policy, or development aid, which is the largest item in the budget for external actions.[32] According to the EEAS's bold assessment:

> In a more connected, contested and complex world, we need a clear sense of direction. We need to agree on our priorities, our goals and the means required to achieve them. We need a common, comprehensive and consistent EU global strategy.[33]

However, this affirmation should be seen, at least in part, as an internal issue, as an assertion of the EEAS and the new HR/VP over the Council and the sectoral fiefdoms of the Commission, and against the reluctance of Member States to address the adoption of common approaches and the pooling of capacities in the fields of foreign and defense policy, which are both domains in which the EU is still based on intergovernmental logic and, therefore, Member States still retain their sovereign powers.

The 2016 Global Strategy: pragmatic turn, resilience and regional orders

Search for deliberative legitimacy: the second stage of EUGS formulation

The second stage of the elaboration of the EUGS involved an extensive consultative and deliberative process for almost ten months, focused on engaging EU institutions, academia and Member States' governments. This process contrasts with the drafting of the 2003 Strategy, developed by a small team of political advisors of the High Representative. As is highlighted by Novotná, the process has been as important as the final outcome.[34] Rather than its substantive contributions, this participatory process responded to the needs of generating ownership and deliberative legitimation of the EUGS. Initially planned were six to eight conferences, but more than 50 events finally took place: at least one in each member state, plus other regional and thematic conferences with the participation of partner countries, universities, think tanks, and international agencies.[35] Finally, in order to avoid the obstacles inherent to diplomatic negotiations, Member States were involved through national contact points, instead of submitting the draft to the Committee of Permanent Representatives and the Political and Security Committee.

Three issues were revealed as particularly difficult and divisive in the EUGS consultative process, following a similar pattern to that in EU Council decision-making: Russia, defense and migration. Regarding Russia, the limited scope of the EUGS can be explained by the need to preserve EU unity, so adopting the lowest common denominator. Regarding defense, the aim was to preserve the support for a "more Europe" approach, against the traditional Atlanticist positions and the defenders of national sovereignty in this realm. In migration, against the backdrop of the tensions generated by the Syrian refugee crisis, the disagreements were particularly harsh. On one side, some governments, and especially those from the Visegrad countries,[36] adopted positions against any sign of Europeanization in respect to this question, and, on the other side, other countries supported a common and comprehensive approach, reluctant to accept a migration policy limited to border control.[37] During the process, the *Brexit* campaign intersected with it, and the British Eurosceptics even presented the EUGS as a secret conspiracy from Brussels to create a "European Army" and further undermine British sovereignty. To avoid leaks, electioneering and the risk of the vetoes usual in diplomatic negotiations, the EEAS resorted to restricted bilateral consultations, known informally as "confessionals." Finally, the unexpected outcome of the British referendum – and the risk of a new "existential crisis" impelled an early presentation of the EUGS, using it as a message of European unity.[38]

"Principled pragmatism": interests and values in the EUGS

There are three key elements in the EUGS: first, the definition of the EU's shared interests and values towards the world; second, the five priorities of the EU's external action; and third, in the internal dimension, the strengthening of its capabilities and instruments of action.

Principled Pragmatism: The EUGS assumes that it is feasible to overcome the traditional foreign policy dilemma between interests and values by the Strategy reaffirming principles and values from the Lisbon Treaty such as democracy, human rights, a multilateral order based in rules, and a global open and fair economic system, as if it could not be otherwise. However, there is a visible turn towards pragmatism, which supposes a more cautious and circumspect evaluation about the "transformative" capacities of the EU's external action, and the central concept now is to promote societal and state "resilience" in the EU neighborhood.

> We will be guided by clear principles. These stem as much from a realistic assessment of the strategic environment as from an idealistic aspiration to advance a better world. In charting the way between the Scylla of isolationism and the Charybdis of rash interventionism, the EU will engage the world manifesting responsibility towards others and sensitivity to contingency. Principled pragmatism will guide our external action in the years ahead.[39]

The imperative to act as a Union in favor of peace and security: The EUGS recognizes that the EU is in an existential crisis in all its dimensions and its very existence cannot be taken for granted. However, it also affirms that the EU, acting together, has an unparalleled potential, with a half a billion population, high living standards, a strong political and social support, and as an aid, trade and investment partner "for almost every country in the world." Faced with an uncertain and threatening environment "a strong EU is more necessary than ever" for the sake of the peace and security of its citizenship and the world. "In hard times, a strong Union is one that thinks strategically, shares a vision and acts together."[40] Hence, the need of a truly global strategy, in both meanings of the word: in its geographical scope, and regarding the coherence of the whole of the external action and its instruments, "soft" and "hard," the internal–external dimension of its policies, and the actions as a Union and as Member States.

The search for strategic autonomy is one of the EUGS's main goals. Without undermining the transatlantic relationship and NATO, a strong and autonomous EU implies stronger capabilities and the rejection of a bandwagoning policy or a subordinate stance in relation to the United States. This strategic autonomy does not mean starting a game of balance of power: the EU is committed to sustain a rule-based multilateral order, supported by strong regional orders, such as the EU itself. As the HR/VP points out in the EUGS's foreword "it's not time for global cops or solitary warriors."[41]

Priorities of EU's external action

The EUGS clearly defines five priorities for EU external action. These are: Union security; the resiliency of Member States and also of states and societies in the neighborhood; a comprehensive approach to conflict management; the support of regional orders, which is addressed in a specific section; and the reform of global governance to respond to the challenges of the twenty-first century. Overall, these priorities indicate that, despite the alleged comprehensive and "global" scope of the EUGS, trying to deal with the whole of the foreign policy of the Union, the document is mostly governed by security concerns and a clear approach towards the neighborhood of the EU.

a The Union's own security is defined as the first of the priorities of the EUGS, covering a new range of threats affecting the territory and population of the EU. It requires "ambition" and strategic autonomy and, in particular, assuming greater responsibilities in security and defense in the frame of NATO, but as an autonomous actor, looking for more cooperation and synergies in defense expenditure. Security is conceived as an axis that integrates the internal and external dimension and, therefore, special attention is paid to cyber security, energy security, or the fight against terrorism, which means better police and intelligence cooperation to prevent radicalization, and more anti-terrorist cooperation with third countries, respectful of human rights.

b An integrated approach to conflicts. The EUGS highlights the multidimensionality of conflicts and its causes, which demands a "whole of the EU" approach, with a comprehensive approach and a coherent use of all the instruments and policies, cooperation with others, and action in all stages of the conflict: prevention, response to the crisis, and stabilization and reconstruction, avoiding its re-emergence.

c Cooperative regional orders: the EU will support "voluntary forms of regional governance" around the world. Proving that in different regions there are different configurations of power, and that the concept of "region" is variable, it will define specific objectives for each one of them.

d Global governance for the twenty-first century: in a world of emerging powers and power transition, resistance to change can mean the erosion of existing international organizations and encourage the creation of new ones that would fragment the multilateral system, to the detriment of the EU. For this reason, the EUGS commits the EU to reform the multilateral system. The EU also will act as an implementer of the 2030 Agenda and other global agreements; it will promote a rule-based and open trade system, compatible with the World Trade Organization and international norms in new areas now under-regulated, such as cyber security, biotechnology or artificial intelligence.

The resilience of states and societies in the European neighborhood (Mediterranean and Eastern Europe)

This priority sets the geographical focus of the EUGS and, at the same time, provides one of its main innovations: the concept of "resilience" is mentioned 41 times in the 60 pages of the EUGS which defines it as "the ability of states and societies to reform, thus withstanding and recovering from internal and external crises."[42] A resilient State is, according to the EUGS, a safe State as a prior condition to prosperity and democracy, and the weakness or absence of these circumstances acts in reverse. It is in this realm where the EU's action in favor of democracy and human rights in its neighborhood is placed, by assuming that democracy and sustainable development promote resilient societies. According to the Strategy, investing in resilience favors EU interests. For that purpose, accession policy must maintain a demanding conditionality to promote reforms, and the neighborhood policy must remain a vehicle for the "transformative power" of the EU in its vicinity.

The EU is not the only actor assuming resilience as a concept and objective, in the same way that the EUGS is not the first document to adopt it. The build-up of resilience is also the axis of the new European Neighbourhood policy. It also appears in the former United States National Security Strategy, released in 2015 under Obama's presidency. It is a key concept in the 2030 Sustainable Development Agenda, and with a different conceptualization it is part of the global strategy of NGOs such as Oxfam. As its pointed by Juncos, this is the expression of a "pragmatic turn" in social sciences and the approaches to global governance based in a "bottom-up" vision that emphasizes local actors, practices and institutions, rather than external actors, foreign intervention and the dominant vision of "liberal peace."[43] It allows a better understanding of the complexity and uncertainty associated with crises and their causes, and gives more space to local actors, as central actors in their own development and security. However, it also exonerates other external actors of responsibility in the problems affecting these states and societies.[44]

This turn is very noticeable when comparing two consecutive documents about resilience released by the EU. The first one is a Communication from the Commission adopted in 2012 and its subsequent Action Plan for the period 2013–2020, with a marked developmentalist approach and a focus on food security.[45] Following the EUGS, the second, a 2017 Joint Communication from the Commission and the HR/VP makes a claim for a more "strategic, multidimensional, and political approach" to resilience. Beyond the development policy, resilience must be present as an overarching goal for the whole of the EU's external action and security policies and, particularly, in the management of migrations, an issue that will be at the forefront of EU's relations with third countries. This document also asks for new and more flexible financial instruments, specifically adapted for promoting resilience in the context of crisis, because those being used in development cooperation are subordinated to their specific goals and therefore they will not adjust to this new approach.[46]

Hence, resilience is a key objective to support a more effective policy on migration: "A special focus in our work on resilience will be on origin and transit countries of migrants and refugees."[47] The EU in fact, is already implementing a new "partnership framework" in a number of these countries.[48] It is aimed to place political dialogue and all the policy instruments for external action of the EU and its Member States in an integrated and coherent framework under overarching objectives of migration control and management, with "tailor-made" approaches for each country. This includes trade, aid, and mobility and cooperation in science and technology, among others, which are conceived as "incentives" to assure the cooperation of partner countries in border control and in the control of transit flows, and specifically for agreeing and implementing readmission agreements for the forced return of migrants in irregular situations. The use of the term "incentives," carefully avoiding the word "conditionality," is significant, although the EU does not exclude suppressing European support if there is not a positive response to these "incentives."

It is important to underline that neither the 2003 Strategy nor the 2016 EUGS describe migration as a "threat" or a "risk" for EU security. Even so, it is one of the more often mentioned issues in the EUGS as a consequence of the 2015–2016 Syrian refugee crisis, as it was one of the most controversial in its elaboration. The EUGS clearly places migration under the internal–external axis of EU security and, therefore, as a CFSP matter. As it is argued by Ceccorulli and Lucarelli,[49] the EUGS encompasses in a simultaneous way a number of different narratives concerning migration: to mention the most relevant of them, they include the economic societal one, referring to the needs of the labor market and the sustainability of welfare state policies; the cosmopolitan-normative one, referring to the imperative of EU cosmopolitan principles and values and, particularly, human rights; the one referring to resilience, about the root causes of migration, with a more developmental approach; the humanitarian one, related to the protection of life and the security of migrants themselves and the fight against human trafficking, in a humanitarian context; and the securitarian one, that defines migration as a threat and defines the EU and its Member States and citizenship as the object to be secured. It emphasizes border control, the externalization of migration controls, and asks for more attention to the internal–external linkage of EU security.

Each of these narratives brings political and normative dilemmas that affect both the values and identity of the EU and the effectiveness of its policies. Although all these narratives are present in the EUGS, the approach adopted is largely securitarian. This conclusion in favor of the security nexus can be viewed in some other EU policies. For example, the European Consensus on Development adopted in 2017 in order to adapt the EU's development policy to keep to the 2030 Sustainable Development Agenda, also reflects these dilemmas:[50] in order to get the approval of the European Council of May 19, 2017, prior to its joint adoption by the EU's institutions and the Member States, some last-minute amendments were introduced in this document. They toughened the initial proposal, answering to the veto threat of the Hungarian government, who considered it to be too soft concerning migration. Specifically, the amended text reaffirmed the right of each Member State to determine the volume of admission of nationals from third states in search of employment. These amendments also linked development assistance more directly to the forced return of immigrants and to the signing of readmission agreements with third countries, as stipulated in the Association Framework with Third Countries on migration of June 2016, in the La Valetta Action Plan, and in other EU policies aimed at the externalization of migration control.[51]

The European Parliament report about the EU Development Consensus has explicitly questioned the growing trend to subordinate development cooperation to foreign policy objectives, without that meaning keeping a restrictive vision of development policy focused mainly on fighting extreme poverty or limited to the poorest countries.[52] This chamber has pointed out the risk of securitizing aid, that is, using development funds to finance migratory control and facilitate forced returns, in particular to countries that have questionable practices in human rights, known by their high rates of impunity and corruption. Supporting governments affected by these problems may contribute to achieving short-term foreign policy or security objectives in terms of migration control, forced returns, or the fight against terrorism and religious extremism. But it could also feed the root causes that explain these migration or refugee flows, and the EU action might end up playing a role opposed to the principles and aims contained in the European Development Consensus, the Agenda 2030 and the EUGS, such as sustainable development, democracy, good governance, and peaceful, inclusive and therefore resilient societies.

The shift towards resilience driven by the EUGS and other key documents of the EU external action can be seen as a signal of the EUGS "principled pragmatism." But for a EU that defines itself as a "normative actor," this shift is intrinsically problematic, in particular, because it means to place the EU at the crossroads between its stated values and interests, in particular between the universal principles of democracy and human rights, and domestic policies and local practices which question them; between the "transformative diplomacy" built into accession and neighborhood policies, and its short-term imperatives of stability.[53] Resilience, as pointed out by Biscop[54] and Wagner and Anholt,[55] pretends to establish a middle ground between the universalist idealism and cosmopolitism related to EU identity and values, and harsh realism, thus redefining the legitimizing discourse and the objectives, scope, and ambition of intervention abroad. The EU has expressly established that the concept of resilience speaks about societal transformation and not to the maintenance of the status quo, and it is expressly linked to promotion of democracy and development. However, it is a policy framework that is more ambiguous and less transformative than "democratization," which is considered here as a "source" of resilience instead of a valuable goal by itself; or than the human rights approach that assumes, for example, the European Consensus on Development. It can be argued that resilience is a concept less politically risky than the ones mentioned before, at a stage of visible erosion of the EU's normative position and of "interventionist fatigue"; that it responds to a more self-critical and circumspect view of the EU's and the West's roles in the world, in particular in respect to the limits of democratization from the outside.[56]

Regional orders beyond the neighborhood: between distance and indifference

The EUGS, as indicated, reaffirms the relevance of regionalism and regional integration – one of the EU's identifying features – and of inter-regionalism as an instrument for global governance, and it establishes differentiated objectives in each case. First, it asks for a "European security order" based on international law, in direct allusion to the Russian attack in Crimea and the war in Ukraine, recognizing that the relationship with Russia is a "key strategic challenge" that will be faced with a policy of selective engagement. To the north, specific objectives for the Arctic region are also set.

In the Mediterranean, Near East, and Africa, the EU will combine in a flexible way regional and bilateral approaches, as well as international organizations. The EU will keep its commitment to peace in the Near East and it will keep investing in peace and development in Africa, and with regard to Turkey, it will insist in its "anchoring" in democracy, being strict with the accession criteria.

The EUGS also makes a claim for "solid" relationships in the Atlantic area, based both in NATO and in trade agreements – the Transatlantic Trade and Investment Partnership (TTIP) with the United States, and Comprehensive Economic and Trade Agreement (CETA) with Canada – and to establish a "wider Atlantic space" with Latin America and the Caribbean. This is one of the fields where the EUGS was outdated even before being released, as it implicitly assumed that Hillary Clinton would be the president of the USA.

In Asia, the EUGS establishes a direct connection between European prosperity and Asian security, although the focus is primarily economic, and includes a "defensive" economic agenda towards China, in areas such as competition policy and intellectual property, as well as the search for free trade agreements with Japan, India, or ASEAN (Association of Southeast Asian Nations) countries.

The quick revision that the EUGS makes of its own geographic priorities shows that it is a strategy less "global" than the 2015 Strategic Review. It can be inferred from this that the EU, more aware of its limitations as a global actor, delegates to the United States the security challenges beyond its neighborhood, particularly in Asia. This could have some inspiration in Obama's 2012 strategy as a *pivot* towards Asia, and its foreseeable continuation with a Hillary Clinton victory in that country's elections, as the EUGS seemed to assume. But with Trump's triumph, the EUGS was born outdated and with serious shortcomings in many aspects: The United States is not the expected partner – the TTIP is discarded, its commitment to NATO is in question and, in fact, even the United States have become themselves a key factor of uncertainty and risk of conflict.

But maybe the most relevant issue to be highlighted is the lack of ambition and perspective of the EUGS to face a global process of power transition. Nothing is proposed to accommodate the rise of emerging powers, which in the EUGS have already less space than in the previous strategic review. The EUGS devotes to China merely a single paragraph and to India even less. The EUGS's silence about the geopolitical risks in the Sea of China or the Southeast Pacific is striking. Nothing is said about the growing Chinese presence in Latin America or Africa, nor the Belt and Road Initiative (BRI), the relevance of which for the EU, after Trump's victory and the abandonment of the TTIP, is even greater. The EUGS seems to hand over the management of this complex transition to the Member States' own foreign policies, either bilaterally or multilaterally, or to the United States, denying its own rationale about the imperatives of strategic autonomy, unity, and common action.

With a clear focus in the neighborhood, the EUGS confirms the peripheral position of other regions and countries. This is the case, for example, with Latin America and the Caribbean. The region is placed in a "wider Atlantic" geopolitical framework together with the United States, without any other explanation than shared values, which, according to the Strategy, would make of the Caribbean and Latin American countries "privileged partners" to address global challenges. However, with the Trump presidency it does not seem viable or advisable to place Latin America and the Caribbean in this "Atlantic Triangle," if it was at any time, and this leaves the EU lacking a clear strategy for this region, and even more urged to "strategic autonomy."

In Latin America, the EUGS admits the existence of a rich and diverse pattern of regionalism and regional integration, but without "unity of purpose." Because of this, the EU will combine regional and bilateral approaches according to each situation. It emphasizes the European economic interests in the region – Latin America concentrates more European investments than the total of Russia, China and India. However, its market share is declining and those of China and other suppliers is increasing. The achievements made by the region – absence of threats for the EU, rising middle classes and poverty reduction, and advances towards the group of upper-middle income countries, implicitly serve as an argument for the visible neglect with which this region is treated, as well as its key actors: as a significant indicator, the EUGS doesn't mention Mexico or Brazil even once.

Giving continuity to the status quo, there are no changes in EU relations with Latin America and the Caribbean, which have been characterized by inertia and the lack of a strategic horizon or narrative.[57] The EUGS merely intends to "revive" and "expand" Atlantic cooperation through the elements already known: the signing of the pending association agreements such as EU-Mercosur, and the deepening of the relations with the Community of Latin American and Caribbean States (CELAC) and other regional groups "according to their competitive advantage." The EUGS suggests innovative and advanced areas of cooperation in this region, but this faces several obstacles: if a traditional developmentalist vision of foreign aid is adopted, Latin America should be "graduated" as a destination of assistance; if the "securitized" vision of aid that permeates the EUGS is assumed, the priority is the neighborhood. Neither the EUGS nor the new

European Consensus for Development, adopted in June 2017, define the modalities and instruments underpinning these innovative forms of cooperation with the region. Paradoxically, if there are options of revitalizing this bi-regional relationship, they are out of the script traced by the EUGS, already overcome by events: Trump's electoral triumph, that drives the United States away from that supposed "community of values," could contribute to reactivating relationships between the EU and Latin America and the Caribbean, as international actors still committed to multilateralism and an open and rule-based international system.

A stronger and united EU: the internal dimension of the EUGS

Credibility, capabilities, shared vision and unity are the terms that summarize the EUGS's approach towards itself as a provider of security. In times of strong nationalist pressures and EU existential crisis, the main message of the EUGS is the enduring relevance of the Union and of common action. More specifically, the Strategy explicitly advocates for a "more integrated" action, between the external and internal dimensions of security. The latter is related to the area of freedom, security and justice, out of the decisions and scope of both CFSP and CSDP. It has also an institutional dimension: it advocates for placing the HR/VP and the EEAS "at the centre," in order to ensure greater coordination and coherence in external action and a *whole-of-EU* approach, in the face of the fiefdoms of the European Commission, reluctant to subordinate its own mandates in fields such as trade or development.

According to the EUGS, in order to be reliable as a global actor the EU's "symbolic power" is not enough. Increasing defense expenditure and improving common planning is also needed, in order to equip itself with more and better military means – land, air and naval forces, including those capable of strategic projection – improving intelligence and surveillance capabilities with independent access to satellites; meeting commitments in defense R+D, and promoting an independent and sustainable defense industry.

In terms of response capacity, the EUGS demands changes in the three "Ds" of external action: diplomacy, defense and development. In diplomacy, with a more coordinated action and a strengthening of the political leadership of the HR/VP and the EEAS; in defense, together with the priorities mentioned before, the EU should improve its ability for the deployment and interoperability of battle groups, and the civilian capabilities for CFSP/CSDP missions. Regarding development policy, the EUGS demands more flexible financial instruments in order to mobilize resources to face immediate needs of crisis management, stabilization and migratory control, without being subjected to the rigid programming requirements and technical criteria of development aid.

From the perspective of defense issues, a specific security and defense sub-strategy was presented in November 2016.[58] However, this is the field in which *Brexit* could be most hurtful for the EU: without the British contribution in terms of industrial, defensive and intelligence capabilities, the EUGS's aim of "strategic autonomy" will be more difficult, and the European security architecture will became even more complex.[59] On the contrary, *Brexit* has been a true catalyst for defense cooperation and since 2016 it can be seen that there has been a strong incentive for a "more Europe" approach in defense formerly hindered by the United Kingdom and its commitment to the United States.[60] And post-*Brexit* cooperation in defense does not exclude the UK's participation. In fact, defense cooperation has been mainly based on a British–French axis, and now the main question is the possibility of finding it in the German–French axis, that traditionally has been promoting economic and social integration. This will depend on the assumption of a more active role in this matter by Germany, overcoming the political and ideological obstacles that still dominate in its society. Since 2016, defense cooperation has had a new impetus driving decisions such as the adoption of the Permanent Structured Cooperation (PESCO), reinforced planning and command capabilities and new financial instruments in the realm of defense, that seem to show that this axis has started to act quickly and with a clear sense of unity and a new "level of ambition" in the areas identified by the EUGS: the protection of the EU and its citizenship, response to crisis and external conflicts, and the strengthening of capabilities, with a more specific agenda.[61]

Concluding remarks: the EUGS and the provision of security as a new legitimizing narrative for the EU

The EUGS can be understood as a pragmatic turn in EU's foreign and security policies: The Strategy is conditioned by geopolitical imperatives and receives the influence of actors whose vision is defined in terms of the conventional *realpolitik*. With the EUGS, the EU's universalist and transformative discourse on human rights and democracy promotion, usually associated with the neighborhood policy, is significantly weakened.[62] Anyway, it must be kept in mind that this discourse has been sometimes characterized in the past by a missionary fervor not exempt from arrogance and paternalism, and by misinformed interventions regarding local conditions, as is shown by the wreckage of the EU's Mediterranean policy. It is still not clear if the new emphasis on resilience, as an expression of this pragmatism and of the silent abandoning of the cosmopolitan vision from the previous Strategy, will be an adequate alternative for reconciling interests and values. Indeed, this turn could involve high costs in terms of the EU's identity and its normative stance, and therefore, in its legitimacy, influence and power as a civilian actor in international relations. Invoking a "principled pragmatism" can be a clever discursive gamble on paper, but it won't prevent the unavoidable dilemmas emerging in the implementation of foreign policy. If the answers turn towards pragmatism or, let's say, short-term power calculations, the EU's symbolic capital and legitimacy – which is a core asset in the power and influence of an EU still more civilian than military – will suffer substantial damage. If Europe is more pragmatic and realist, it might be a lesser Europe, or one quite different from what, according to the Treaties, it is determined to be.

More than a policy document, referred to means and goals, the EUGS can be interpreted as an exercise of discursive power or "productive power" according to Barnett and Duvall's conceptualization.[63] In this document the EU tries to redefine its identity and legitimacy, and generate agency through a self-legitimizing identity narrative. It is indeed a sophisticated discursive device aimed to convince its citizens about the supposed EU key role in times of existential crisis, centrifugal tendencies and constrictions coming from its own institutional design. The EUGS tries to show a more convinced and convincing EU through referring to its own existence and relevance to promote governance and security to the world and to itself. At the same time, it expresses its doubts and uncertainty: in its title, the document selects the expression "a stronger Europe" rather than "a secure Europe," as the previous Strategy called it.

Departing from a detailed exegesis of the EUGS, Malksoo argues that through the Strategy, the EU rewrites its "autobiography,"[64] and tries to conjure uncertainty and make the world intelligible, but it is also making explicit its fears and concerns: the anxiety of standing united, of maintaining its status as international actor, of remaining relevant in status and recognition as an interlocutor for other powers, and of remaining true to its main *raison d'etre*: to ensure peace in Europe as a true "security community," at a time when this foundational purpose can no longer be taken for granted.

It is from these perspectives that the EUGS can be seen as a new securitarian narrative for the EU. It redefines and leaves behind the cosmopolitan narrative that characterized the Union in the past, and which permeated the 2003 Strategy.[65] More than by external threats, this shift could be explained by internal trends such as increasing citizen disaffection, social crisis and erosion of economic and social rights, growing job insecurity, uncertainty towards social and economic changes, and the fears towards terrorism or migration, incited by extreme right-wing forces trying to transform them into EU identity, social, and economic threats through a marked securitarian and xenophobic discourse. The rise of the extreme right political parties that has taken advantage of this scenario, pushed the EU institutions and leaders to try to re-launch the European project by offering citizens "a Europe that protects, empowers and defends." It is an offer of protection and defense from both the threats to security and the impact of globalization, according to the expression used by the European Commission's president and other leaders,[66] such as the French president Emmanuel Macron. As Mark Leonard pointed out, this proposal supposes leaving behind the cosmopolitan and universalist narrative of the EU, with the will to transform the world according to its values, to a EU that would assume a new exceptionalist and defensive narrative – "a Kantian fortress in a Hobbesian world"[67] – reserving for itself its social and political achievements, and giving priority to its own interests and to the protection of its citizenship facing a world increasingly hostile and reluctant to be governed and reformed by the Western powers.

Notes

1 Translation to English by Héctor Sanahuja Mesa.
2 European External Action Service, *Shared Vision, Common Action: A Stronger Europe. A Global Strategy for the European Union's Foreign and Security Policy* (Brussels: European Union, 2016).
3 Council of the European Union, Council Conclusions on the Global Strategy on the European Union's Foreign and Security Policy, 13202/16 (Brussels: European Union, 2016).
4 José A. Sanahuja, "Las cuatro crisis de la Unión Europea," in *Cambio de ciclo: crisis, resistencias y respuestas globales. Anuario CEIPAZ 2012–2013*, coord. Manuela Mesa (Madrid: CEIPAZ, 2012), 51–83.
5 Jolyon Howorth, "EU Global Strategy in a Changing World: Brussels' Approach to the Emerging Powers," *Contemporary Security Policy* 37, no. 3 (2016): 389–401.
6 European External Action Service, *Shared Vision, Common Action*, 2, 5.
7 Sanahuja, "Las cuatro crisis," 51–83; José A. Sanahuja, "La Unión Europea y la crisis de los refugiados: fallas de gobernanza, securitización y 'diplomacia de chequera,'" in *Retos inaplazables en el sistema internacional. Anuario 2015–16*, coord. Manuela Mesa (Madrid: CEIPAZ, 2016), 71–105.
8 Esther Barbé, "Introducción: cambio en el sistema internacional, adversidad para la UE," *Revista CIDOB d'Afers Internacionals* 108 (2014): 7–21.
9 European Union, *A Secure Europe in a Better World. European Security Strategy* (Brussels: European Union, 2003); Council of the European Union, *Report on the Implementation of the European Security Strategy – Providing Security in a Changing World*, S407/08 (Brussels: European Union, 2008).
10 Lorena Ruano, "The Conceptual Framework," in *The Europeanization and National Foreign Policies towards Latin America* (London: Routledge, 2013), 12–34; Laia Mestres, "La europeización de las políticas exteriores nacionales," in *La Unión Europea en las Relaciones Internacionales*, ed. Esther Barbé (Madrid: Tecnos, 2014), 161.
11 Margaret R. Somers, "The Narrative Constitution of Identity: A Relational and Network Approach," *Theory and Society* 23, no. 5 (October 1994): 605–49; José A. Sanahuja, "Narrativas del multilateralismo: 'efecto Rashomon' y cambio de poder," *Revista CIDOB d'Afers Internacionals* 101 (2013): 27–54; Caterina Carta and Jean-Frédéric Morin, *EU Foreign Policy through the Lens of Discourse Analysis: Making Sense of Diversity* (Farnham: Ashgate, 2014).
12 Alexander Wendt, "Anarchy Is What States Make of It: The Social Construction of Power Politics," *International Organization* 46, no. 2 (1992): 391–425; Peter J. Katzenstein, *The Culture of National Security. Norms and Identity in World Politics* (New York: Columbia University Press, 1996).
13 Ian Manners and Philomena Murray, "The End of a Noble Narrative? European Integration Narratives after the Nobel Peace Prize," *Journal of Common Market Studies* 54, no. 1 (2016): 185–202.
14 Robert W. Cox, "Social Forces, States and World Orders: Beyond International Relations Theory," *Millennium: Journal of International Studies* 10, no. 2 (1981): 126–55.

15 Michael Barnett and Raymond Duvall, *Power in Global Governance* (Cambridge: Cambridge University Press, 2005), 3–12.
16 European Union, *A Secure Europe*, 2003.
17 Robert Kagan, *Of Paradise and Power. America and Europe in the New World Order* (New York: Alfred A. Knopf, 2003).
18 German concept that hints at the spirit of an era.
19 José A. Sanahuja, "Narrativas del multilateralismo"; Esther Barbé, "La Estrategia Global de la Unión Europa: el camino del medio," *Revista General de Derecho Europeo* 40 (2016): 1–10.
20 Javier Solana, *Inauguration of the Academic Year 2005–2006. College of Europe. Speech by Javier Solana, EU High Representative for the Common Foreign and Security Policy* (S 342/05) (Brussels: European Union, 2005), 5.
21 Cristina Churruca, "Criticizing the European Security Strategy: the EU as a Regional Security Provider," *Revista Electrónica de Estudios Internacionales* 10 (2005): 1–20.
22 Strategies about the External Dimension of Justice and Home Affairs; Small and Light Weapons; and Homeland Security, among others.
23 Council of the European Union, *Report on the Implementation of the European Security Strategy*, 2008.
24 Félix Arteaga, "¿La estrategia Global de la UE? … déjela ahí," *Blog del Real Instituto Elcano*, June 29, 2016, accessed July 31, 2018, www.blog.rielcano.org/la-estrategia-global-de-la-ue-dejela-ahi/.
25 Ricardo Martínez de Rituerto, "La UE subcontrata la elaboración de una estrategia Global," *El País*, July 23, 2012.
26 Nathalie Tocci, "The Making of the EU Global Strategy," *Contemporary Security Policy* 37, no. 3 (2016): 464.
27 European Union, *A Secure Europe*, 1.
28 European External Action Service, *Shared Vision, Common Action*, 3.
29 European External Action Service, *The European Union in a Changing Global Environment. A More Connected, Contested and Complex World* (Brussels: European Union, 2015); Antonio Missiroli, *Towards an EU Global Strategy. Background, Process. References* (Paris: EU-ISS, 2015).
30 Susi Dennison, François Godement, Richard Gowan et al., "The Road to European Power," ECFR Policy Brief (2015).
31 Multinational land military units of a number of Member States, also open to the participation of candidate countries for accession and of countries from the neighborhood, of variable composition. Equal to one battalion plus support units (1,500 to 2,500 troops). Created in 2007 for CSDP missions, the 18 battle groups existing until 2017, although fully operational, have never been deployed.
32 Tereza Novotná, "The EU as a Global Actor: United We Stand, Divided We Fall," *Journal of Common Market Studies* 55(S1) (2017): 177–91.
33 European External Action Service, *The European Union in a Changing Global Environment*, 21.
34 Novotná, "The EU as a Global Actor," 180.
35 Tocci, "The Making of the EU Global Strategy," 467. The author of this chapter attended the EUGS regional conference on Latin America, held in Rome in January 2016, co-organized by the EEAS, the Italian Government, the Italo-Latin American Institute (IILA), and the Istituto Affari Internazionali (IAI).
36 The Visegrad Group or V4 was stablished in 1991 as an informal group of like-minded countries of Central Europe. It includes the Czech Republic, Hungary, Poland and Slovakia.
37 Tocci, "The Making of the EU Global Strategy," 468–9.
38 Ibid., 470.
39 European External Action Service, *Shared Vision, Common Action*, 2, 5.
40 European External Action Service, *Shared Vision, Common Action*, 6.
41 Ibid., 3.
42 Ibid., 23.
43 Ana E. Juncos, "Resilience as the New EU Foreign Policy Paradigm: A Pragmatist Turn?" *European Security* 16, no. 1 (2017): 2.
44 Wolfgang Wagner and Rosanne Anholt, "Resilience as the EU Global Strategy's New Leitmotif: Pragmatic, Problematic or Promising?" *Contemporary Security Policy* 37, no. 3 (2016): 414–30.
45 European Commission, *The EU Approach to Resilience – Learning from Food Security Crises*, COM(2012) 586 final (Brussels: European Union, 2012).
46 High Representative of the European Union for Foreign Affairs and Security Policy, Joint Communication to the European Parliament and the Council: A Strategic Approach to Resilience in the EU's

External Action, JOIN(2017) 21 final (Brussels: European Union, June 7, 2017); Council of the European Union, A Strategic Approach to Resilience in the EU's External Action. Council Conclusions, 14191/17 (Brussels: European Union, 2017).

47 European Union, *Shared Vision, Common Action*, 27.

48 European Commission, Communication from the Commission to the European Parliament, the Council and the European Investment Bank on Establishing a New Partnership Framework with Third Countries under the European Agenda on Migration, COM(2016) 385 final (Strasbourg: European Union, June 7, 2016).

49 Michela Ceccorulli and Sonia Lucarelli, "Migration and the EU Global Strategy: Narratives and Dilemmas," *The International Spectator* 52, no. 3 (2017): 83–102.

50 Council of the European Union, *Joint Statement on the Adoption of the New European Consensus on Development* (Brussels: European Union, 2017).

51 Justine Spike, "Hungary's Foreign Minister Vetoes EU Development Plan, because 'Immigration Is a Bad Thing,'" *Budapest Beacon*, May 10, 2017; Government of Hungary, "Hungary to Veto Pro-immigration EU Development Strategy," May 11, 2017, accessed July 31, www.kormany.hu/en/ministry-of-foreign-affairs-and-trade/news/hungary-to-veto-pro-immigration-eu-development-strategy.

52 European Parliament, *Report on the Revision of the European Consensus on Development.* Rapporteurs: Bogdan Brunon Wenta, Norbert Neuser, Development Committee, 2016/2094(INI), A8-0020/2017 (Strasbourg: European Union, 2017).

53 A word that the neighborhood policy does use, but that the EUGS carefully avoids, that is usually associated to the *realpolitik*, that justifies support for authoritarian regimes and human rights violations in exchange for security.

54 Sven Biscop, "The EU Global Strategy: Realpolitik with European Characteristics," Security Policy Brief 75 (Egmont – The Royal Institute for International Relations, 2016).

55 Wagner and Anholt, "Resilience as the EU Global Strategy's New Leitmotif," 414–30.

56 Mark Leonard, "L'Europe qui protège. Conceiving the Next European Union," ECFR Essays, August 30, 2017.

57 José A. Sanahuja, *The EU and CELAC: Reinvigorating a Strategic Partnership* (Hamburg: EU-LAC Foundation, 2015).

58 Council of the European Union, *Implementation Plan on Security and Defense*, 14392/16 (Brussels: European Union, 2016); Council of the European Union, Council Conclusions on Implementing the EU Global Strategy in the Area of Security and Defence, 14149/16 (Brussels: European Union, 2016).

59 Sven Biscop, "All or Nothing? The EU Global Strategy and Defense Policy after the Brexit," *Contemporary Security Policy* 37, no. 3 (2016): 431–45.

60 Félix Arteaga, "European Defence between the Global Strategy and Its Implementation," Real Instituto Elcano Working Paper 4 (2017), 2–17.

61 Novotná, "The EU as a Global Actor."

62 Karolina Pomorska and Gergana Noutcheva, "Europe as a Regional Actor: Waning Influence in an Unstable and Authoritarian Neighbourhood," *Journal of Common Market Studies* 55(S1) (2017): 165–76.

63 Barnett and Duvall, *Power in Global Governance.*

64 Maria Maalksö, "From the ESS to the EU Global Strategy: External Policy, Internal Purpose," *Contemporary Security Policy* 37, no. 3 (2016): 374–88.

65 Sanahuja, "Narrativas del multilateralismo," 27–54.

66 Jean Claude Juncker, *Towards a Better Europe, a Europe That Protects, Empowers and Defends. State of the Union Speech* (Strasbourg: European Union, 2016).

67 Leonard, "L'Europe," 5.

References

Arteaga, Félix. "¿La estrategia Global de la UE? … déjela ahí." *Blog del Real Instituto Elcano*, June 29, 2016. Accessed July 31, 2018. www.blog.rielcano.org/la-estrategia-global-de-la-ue-dejela-ahi/.

Arteaga, Félix. "European Defence between the Global Strategy and Its Implementation." Real Instituto Elcano Working Paper 4 (2017): 2–17.

Barbé, Esther. "La Estrategia Global de la Unión Europa: el camino del medio." *Revista General de Derecho Europeo* 40 (2016): 1–10.

Barbé, Esther. "Introducción: cambio en el sistema internacional, adversidad para la UE." *Revista CIDOB d'Afers Internacionals* 108 (2014): 7–21.

Barnett, Michael, and Raymond Duvall. *Power in Global Governance*. Cambridge: Cambridge University Press, 2005.

Biscop, Sven. "All or Nothing? The EU Global Strategy and Defense Policy after the Brexit." *Contemporary Security Policy* 37, no. 3 (2016): 431–45.

Biscop, Sven. "The EU Global Strategy: Realpolitik with European Characteristics." Security Policy Brief 75. Egmont – The Royal Institute for International Relations, 2016.

Carta, Caterina, and Jean-Frédéric Morin. *EU Foreign Policy through the Lens of Discourse Analysis: Making Sense of Diversity*. Farnham: Ashgate, 2014.

Ceccorulli, Michela, and Sonia Lucarelli. "Migration and the EU Global Strategy: Narratives and Dilemmas." *The International Spectator* 52, no. 3 (2017): 83–102.

Churruca, Cristina. "Criticizing the European Security Strategy: The EU as a Regional Security Provider." *Revista Electrónica de Estudios Internacionales* 10 (2005): 1–20.

Council of the European Union. Council Conclusions on the Global Strategy on the European Union's Foreign and Security Policy. 13202/16. Brussels: European Union, 2016.

Council of the European Union. Council Conclusions on Implementing the EU Global Strategy in the Area of Security and Defence. 14149/16. Brussels: European Union, 2016.

Council of the European Union. *Implementation Plan on Security and Defense*. 14392/16. Brussels: European Union, 2016.

Council of the European Union. *Joint Statement on the Adoption of the New European Consensus on Development*. Brussels: European Union, 2017.

Council of the European Union. *Report on the Implementation of the European Security Strategy – Providing Security in a Changing World*. S407/08. Brussels: European Union, 2008.

Council of the European Union. A Strategic Approach to Resilience in the EU's External Action. Council Conclusions. 14191/17. Brussels: European Union, 2017.

Cox, Robert, W. "Social Forces, States and World Orders: Beyond International Relations Theory." *Millennium: Journal of International Studies* 10, no. 2 (1981): 126–55.

Dennison, Susi, François Godement, Richard Gowan et al. "The Road to European power." ECFR Policy Brief (2015).

European Commission. Communication from the Commission to the European Parliament, the Council and the European Investment Bank on Establishing a new Partnership Framework with Third Countries under the European Agenda on Migration. COM(2016) 385 final. Strasbourg: European Union, June 7, 2016.

European Commission. Communication from the Commission to the European Parliament and the Council: The EU Approach to Resilience: Learning from Food Security Crises. COM(2012) 586 final. Brussels: European Union, 2012.

European External Action Service. *The European Union in a Changing Global Environment. A More Connected, Contested and Complex World*. Brussels: European Union, 2015.

European External Action Service. *Shared Vision, Common Action: A Stronger Europe. A Global Strategy for the European Union's Foreign and Security Policy*. Brussels: European Union, 2016.

European Parliament. *Report on the Revision of the European Consensus on Development*. Rapporteurs: Bogdan Brunon Wenta, Norbert Neuser, Development Committee, 2016/2094(INI), A8-0020/2017. Strasbourg: European Union, 2017.

European Union. *A Secure Europe in a Better World. European Security Strategy*. Brussels: European Union, 2003.

Government of Hungary. "Hungary to Veto Pro-immigration EU Development Strategy." May 11, 2017. Accessed May 8, 2019. www.kormany.hu/en/ministry-of-foreign-affairs-and-trade/news/hungary-to-veto-pro-immigration-eu-development-strategy.

High Representative of the European Union for Foreign Affairs and Security Policy. Joint Communication to the European Parliament and the Council: A Strategic Approach to Resilience in the EU's External Action. JOIN(2017) 21 final. Brussels: European Union, June 7, 2017.

Howorth, Jolyon. "EU Global Strategy in a Changing World: Brussels' Approach to the Emerging Powers." *Contemporary Security Policy* 37, no. 3 (2016): 389–401.

Juncker, Jean Claude. *Towards a Better Europe, a Europe That Protects, Empowers and Defends. State of the Union Speech*. Strasbourg: European Union, 2016.

Juncos, Ana E. "Resilience as the New EU Foreign Policy Paradigm: A Pragmatist Turn?" *European Security* 16, no. 1 (2017): 1–18.

Kagan, Robert. *Of Paradise and Power. America and Europe in the New World Order*. New York: Alfred A. Knopf, 2003.

Katzenstein, Peter, J. *The Culture of National Security. Norms and Identity in World Politics*. New York: Columbia University Press, 1996.

Leonard, Mark. "L'Europe qui protège. Conceiving the Next European Union." ECFR Essays, August 30, 2017.

Maalksö, Maria. "From the ESS to the EU Global Strategy: External Policy, Internal Purpose." *Contemporary Security Policy* 37, no. 3 (2016): 374–88.

Manners, Ian, and Philomena Murray. "The End of a Noble Narrative? European Integration Narratives after the Nobel Peace Prize." *Journal of Common Market Studies* 54, no. 1 (2016): 185–202.

Martínez de Rituerto, Ricardo. "La UE subcontrata la elaboración de una estrategia Global." *El País*, July 23, 2012.

Mestres, Laia. "La europeización de las políticas exteriores nacionales." In *La Unión Europea en las Relaciones Internacionales*, edited by Esther Barbé, 154–71. Madrid: Tecnos, 2014.

Missiroli, Antonio. *Towards an EU Global Strategy. Background, Process. References*. Paris: EU-ISS, 2015.

Novotná, Tereza. "The EU as a Global Actor: United We Stand, Divided We Fall." *Journal of Common Market Studies* 55(S1) (2017): 177–91.

Pomorska, Karolina, and Gergana Noutcheva. "Europe as a Regional Actor: Waning Influence in an Unstable and Authoritarian Neighbourhood." *Journal of Common Market Studies* 55(S1) (2017): 165–76.

Ruano, Lorena. "The Conceptual Framework." In *The Europeanization of National Foreign Policies towards Latin America*, 12–34. London: Routledge, 2013.

Sanahuja, José A. "Las cuatro crisis de la Unión Europea." In *Cambio de ciclo: crisis, resistencias y respuestas globales. Anuario CEIPAZ 2012–2013*, coordinated by Manuela Mesa, 51–83. Madrid: CEIPAZ, 2012.

Sanahuja, José A. *The EU and CELAC: Reinvigorating a Strategic Partnership*. Hamburg: EU-LAC Foundation, 2015.

Sanahuja, José A. "Narrativas del multilateralismo: 'efecto Rashomon' y cambio de poder." *Revista CIDOB d'Afers Internacionals* 101 (2013): 27–54.

Sanahuja, José A. "La Unión Europea y la crisis de los refugiados: fallas de gobernanza, securitización y 'diplomacia de chequera.'" In *Retos inaplazables en el sistema internacional. Anuario 2015–16*, coordinated by Manuela Mesa, 71–105. Madrid: CEIPAZ, 2016.

Solana, Javier. *Inauguration of the Academic Year 2005–2006. College of Europe. Speech by Javier Solana, EU High Representative for the Common Foreign and Security Policy* (S 342/05). Brussels: European Union, 2005.

Somers, Margaret R. "The Narrative Constitution of Identity: A Relational and Network Approach." *Theory and Society* 23, no. 5 (1994): 605–49.

Spike, Justine. "Hungary's Foreign Minister Vetoes EU Development Plan, because 'Immigration Is a Bad Thing." *Budapest Beacon*, May 10, 2017.

Tocci, Nathalie. "The Making of the EU Global Strategy." *Contemporary Security Policy* 37, no. 3 (2016): 461–72.

Wagner, Wolfgang, and Rosanne Anholt. "Resilience as the EU Global Strategy's New Leitmotif: Pragmatic, Problematic or Promising?" *Contemporary Security Policy* 37, no. 3 (2016): 414–30.

Wendt, Alexander. "Anarchy Is What States Make of It: The Social Construction of Power Politics." *International Organization* 46, no. 2 (1992): 391–425.

INDEX

www.ingramcontent.com/pod-product-compliance
Ingram Content Group UK Ltd.
Pitfield, Milton Keynes, MK11 3LW, UK
UKHW052054230926
475702UK00031B/2791
* 9 7 8 1 0 3 2 2 4 0 0 5 3 *